CW00925514

Registered Land

Law and Practice under the Land Registration Act 2002

Registered Land

Law and Practice under the Land Registration Act 2002

Charles Harpum LLD(Cantab)

Barrister and Bencher, Lincoln's Inn; Sometime Law Commissioner;
Emeritus Fellow, Downing College, Cambridge

&

Janet Bignell MA(Cantab), BCL(Oxon)

Barrister, Lincoln's Inn

JORDANS

2004

Published by
Jordan Publishing Limited
21 St Thomas Street
Bristol BS1 6JS

British Library Cataloguing-in-Publication Data

A catalogue record for this book is available from the British Library.

ISBN 0 85308 890 X

Typeset by Jordan Publishing Limited
Printed and bound by The Cromwell Press Ltd, Trowbridge, Wiltshire

DEDICATION

To our fathers
John Harpum and Richard Bignell

PREFACE

The Land Registration Act 2002, which received Royal Assent on 26 February 2002, was brought into force on 13 October 2003. By that date, the various sets of rules that were needed to support the operation of the Act were in place, a completely new set of forms for applications to the Land Registry had been devised, and the Land Registry had created the structure necessary to implement the major changes that were brought about. The introduction of such a significant change to the conveyancing process occurring so smoothly was a remarkable achievement.

It is important to see the Land Registration Act 2002 as a fresh start. The old law is a poor guide to the new, because the changes are so fundamental and because the new Act has a clear guiding philosophy, namely the creation in time of a conclusive register. It will not usually be safe to rely on earlier authority except, perhaps, in those comparatively rare cases where the wording of the new legislation is exactly the same as the old.

In *Registered Land: The New Law*, which was published in 2002, we provided an introduction to the Act, at that stage a mere framework unclothed by the detail of the rules that were to be made under it. In this new book, we have attempted to build upon the earlier work and to analyse not just the law as it emerges from the Land Registration Act 2002 and the rules made under it (principally the Land Registration Rules 2003), but also the practice of the Land Registry under the new regime. That practice is set out in more than 50 Practice Guides that have been produced by the Land Registry. These are an invaluable and necessary source of information, because the Act and the rules do not explain the whole story of how the land registration system operates.

The Land Registration Act 2002 and the rules made under it are printed by way of an appendix to the book, as are a number of the most important Forms. The law is stated as it stands as of 1 August 2004.

Charles Harpum & Janet Bignell
Falcon Chambers
September 2004

CONTENTS

Dedication   v
Preface   vii
Table of Cases   xxi
Table of Statutes   xxv
Table of Statutory Instruments and Conventions   xxxvii
Table of other materials   xlv
Table of Abbreviations   li

**Chapter 1   The background to, underlying principles and
implementation of, the Act**   1
Land registration in England and Wales   1
The genesis of the Land Registration Act 2002   2
    The three joint reports of the Law Commission and HM Land Registry   2
The Land Registration Bill in Parliament   5
Rules and Orders made under the Act   5
    Introduction   5
    Rules under the LRA 1925   6
    Rules under LRA 2002   7
    The Rules Committee   8
    General rule-making powers   8
    The Land Registration Rules 2003   9
    Other Rules and Orders   10
Interpreting the Act and the Rules made under it   11
Land Registry practice under the Act   12

PART 1   FIRST REGISTRATION   13
The main changes at a glance   13

Chapter 2   Voluntary and compulsory first registration   15
Voluntary first registration   15
    Introduction   15
    Who may apply for voluntary first registration?   15
    The estates and interests that may be voluntarily registered   16
Compulsory first registration   18
    Introduction   18
    Dispositions of unregistered land that must be completed by registration   19
    Power to add further triggers to compulsory registration   25
    The requirement of registration and its enforcement   26
    Dispositions pending registration   27
Applications for first registration   28
    Making an application   28
    Accompanying documents   30
    Examining title   32
    First registration: specific rules   33

Chapter 3   Classes of title   39
The class of title given on first registration   39
   Introduction   39
   Freehold titles   39
   Leasehold title   40
Upgrading titles   41
   The registrar's power to upgrade titles that are not absolute   41
   The effect of upgrading title   45
   Indemnity   45

Chapter 4   The effect of first registration   47
Introduction   47
Freehold title   47
   Absolute title   47
   Qualified and possessory titles   50
Leasehold title   50
   Absolute title   50
   Good leasehold title   51
   Qualified and possessory titles   51
Unregistered interests which override first registration   51
   Introduction   51
   The interests that will override first registration   52
   Limiting the scope of unregistered interests that override first registration   55

Chapter 5   Cautions against first registration   59
Introduction   59
Recording cautions against first registration   59
   Overview   59
   The cautions register   60
Lodging cautions against first registration   60
   Who may lodge a caution?   60
   The application for a caution   62
   Who is the 'cautioner' for the purposes of the legislation?   62
Withdrawing a caution against first registration   63
Altering the cautions register   63
   Alteration by the court   63
   Alteration by the registrar   64
   Indemnity   64
The effect of lodging a caution against first registration   64
Removing or challenging a caution against first registration   65
   The power to object to an application to lodge a caution against first
     registration   65
   Applying for the cancellation of a caution against first registration   66
   Duty not to lodge a caution against first registration without reasonable
     cause   67
Transitional   68

Chapter 6   First registration by the Crown   69
Voluntary first registration   69
Compulsory first registration   69
Cautions against first registration   70

PART 2   DEALINGS WITH REGISTERED LAND   71
The main changes at a glance   71

Chapter 7   Powers of disposition   73
The principles adopted   73
Owner's powers   73
Protection of disponees   75
An example   76

Chapter 8   Registered dispositions   77
Introduction   77
Registrable dispositions of a registered estate   78
    Transfers   78
    The grant of certain leases   80
    Leases of franchises and manors   81
    Express grant or reservation of a legal easement, right or privilege   81
    Express grant or reservation of a rentcharge or a legal right of entry   84
    The grant of a legal charge   85
Registrable dispositions of a registered charge   85
Applications for registration   86
    Transfers of a registered estate   87
    The grant of a lease   90
    Other registrable dispositions   91
Miscellaneous   92
    Mines and minerals   92
    Appurtenances   93
    The determination of registered estates   95

Chapter 9   Priorities   97
Introduction   97
The basic rule   97
    Registrable dispositions for valuable consideration that have been registered   98
    Inland Revenue charges   101
    The effect of notice and knowledge on priority under the LRA 2002   101
    Special cases   102

Chapter 10   Notices and restrictions   105
Introduction   105
Prospective abolition of cautions against dealings   105
Abolition of inhibitions as a separate form of entry   106
Notices   106
    The nature and effect of a notice   106
    The circumstances in which a notice may be entered in the register   109
    Applications for entry of a notice   110

The form and content of notices entered by the registrar | 121
Protecting variations to interests that have been noted | 122
Restrictions | 123
Pending land actions, writs, orders and deeds of arrangements | 143
Cautions against dealings: transitional provisions | 145

Chapter 11   Unregistered interests which override registered dispositions | 147
Introduction | 147
The unregistered interests that will override a registered disposition | 148
   Certain short leases | 149
   Interests of persons in actual occupation | 149
   The four exceptions to the general rule | 150
   Legal easements and profits | 152
   The exceptions to the general rule | 153
   Transitional provisions | 155
Ensuring that unregistered interests are registered | 155

Chapter 12   Charges | 159
Introduction | 159
The nature of registered charges and sub-charges | 159
Equitable charges | 160
The powers of a registered chargee or sub-chargee | 160
   Power to make dispositions of the charge | 160
   Powers in relation to the property charged | 161
The creation, registration and variation of registered charges | 162
   The form of a registered charge | 162
   Approved forms of charge | 163
   Application to register a charge | 165
   Application to register a restriction | 166
   The registration of company charges | 166
   Completion of an application to register | 167
   Making an application to vary the terms of a registered charge | 167
Consolidation | 169
Transfer of a registered charge | 169
The priority of competing charges | 171
   Registered charges | 171
   Alteration of priority of registered charges | 171
   Overriding statutory charges | 172
   Equitable charges | 174
Tacking and further advances | 175
   Introduction | 175
   (1) Recognition of existing practice | 175
   (2) Further advance in pursuance of an obligation | 177
   (3) Further advance with agreement of subsequent chargee | 178
   (4) The agreement of a maximum amount | 178
Realisation of a chargee's security | 179
   Introduction | 179

Local land charges 179
Surplus after sale 180
Power of joint proprietors to give receipts 181
Foreclosure 181
Discharge and release of charges 181
Introduction 181
Documentary discharge of registered charges 182
Discharges and releases of charges protected by notice 184
Registered charges: electronic notifications of discharge 186
Restrictions 187

Chapter 13 Special cases 189
Introduction 189
The Crown 189
Devolution on the death of a registered proprietor 191
Bankruptcy 192
Introduction 192
Procedure in relation to bankruptcy petitions 192
Bankruptcy order 193
Protection of purchases 194
Registration of trustee in bankruptcy 195
Companies and other corporations 196
Introduction 196
Registration 196
Administration and liquidation 198
The effect of overseas insolvency proceedings 202
Charities 202
Settlements 204

PART 3 REGISTRATION AND THE REGISTER 207
The main changes at a glance 207

Chapter 14 The register of title and indices 209
Register of title 209
Introduction 209
The form and arrangement of the register of title 209
The arrangement of individual registers 211
The property register 211
Indices 216
Introduction 216
The index 216
The index of proprietors' names 219
The day list 220

Chapter 15 Registration and its effects 221
The effect of registration 221
Registration vests the legal title 221

Where a person is registered as proprietor following a void conveyance or
transfer, does registration vest the equitable interest as well as the legal
estate?   222
The registration of dependent estates   224
Effective date of registration   225

Chapter 16   Boundaries   227
The general boundaries rule   227
The power to determine the exact line of a boundary   227
    Introduction   227
    Applications for the determination of the exact line of the boundary   228
    Determination of the exact line of the boundary without application   231
Accretion and diluvion   232

Chapter 17   Use of register to record defects in title   235

Chapter 18   Accessing information   239
Introduction   239
The open register   239
    The right of inspection   239
    Applications to inspect and copy   241
    Applications for official copies of a registered title, the cautions register or
        for a certificate of inspection of a title plan   242
    Applications for official copies of documents referred to in the register of
        title and other documents kept by the registrar   243
    Exempt information documents   243
    Application for an official copy of an exempt information document   247
    Application for removal of the designation of a document as an exempt
        information document   248
    Transitional period documents   249
    Applications in connection with court proceedings, insolvency and tax
        liability   249
Conclusiveness of filed copies   250
Historical information   252

Chapter 19   Priority protection   255
Introduction   255
Terminology   258
Official searches with priority   259
    Making an application   259
    Official search certificates   260
Priority protection   262
Official searches without priority   264
Official searches by a mortgagee for the purposes of the Family Law Act 1996 265
Outline applications   266

Chapter 20   Forms, applications, execution of documents and notices 269
Introduction   269

Forms   269
   Schedule 1 forms   269
   Schedule 3 forms   271
Applications   274
   Form and content of applications   276
   Evidence accompanying applications   277
   The time when the application is made and the priority of applications   278
   Objections to applications   280
   Completion of applications   282
   Registered charges and company charges   283
Execution of documents   283
Notices and addresses for service   285

Chapter 21   Land and charge certificates   289
The previous law   289
The abolition of land and charge certificates under the LRA 2002 and the
   LRR 2003   290

Chapter 22   Alterations to the register   293
Introduction   293
Alteration of the register of title   293
Alteration of the register pursuant to an order of the court   295
   The powers of the court   295
   The protection given to a proprietor in possession   296
Alteration of the register other than under an order of the court   299
   The powers of the registrar   299
   Alterations under network access agreements   300
   Costs in non-rectification cases   301
   Alteration of the cautions register   301
   Alteration of documents   301

Chapter 23   Indemnity   303
Introduction   303
The grounds on which indemnity is payable   303
   Introduction   303
   1. Rectification of the register   303
   2. Loss by reason of a mistake   304
   3. Mistake in an official search   304
   4. Mistake in an official copy   304
   5. Mistake in a document kept by the registrar which is not an original   304
   6. Loss or destruction of a document lodged in the registry for inspection
      or safe custody   305
   7. A mistake in the cautions register   305
   8. Failure by the registrar to perform his duty under s 50   305
The special case of mines and minerals   305
The measure of indemnity   306
When a claim for indemnity will fail or will be reduced   308
Claiming indemnity   310

The registrar's rights of recourse   311

PART 4   CONVEYANCING   313
The main changes at a glance   313

Chapter 24   Proving title   315
Proof of title under LRA 1925   315
Proof of title under the Act   316

Chapter 25   Covenants and covenants for title   319
Introduction   319
Covenants for title   319
Positive covenants   320
Indemnity covenants   321
Covenants implied in a transfer of a pre-1996 lease   321
Transfer of a registered estate subject to a rentcharge   322
Restrictive covenants   323

PART 5   ELECTRONIC CONVEYANCING   325
The main changes at a glance   325

Chapter 26   Electronic conveyancing   327
What is e-conveyancing?   327
Formal requirements   329
    Introduction   329
    The statutory requirements   330
    Dispositions within the LRA 2002, s 91   330
    The four conditions to be satisfied   331
    The effect of compliance   332
    Execution by corporations   334
    Rights of a purchaser as to execution   335

Chapter 27   The Land Registry network   337
Introduction: a typical transaction in electronic form   337
The provisions of the LRA 2002   340
    The electronic communications network   340
    Network access agreements   341
    Terms of access   342
    Termination of access   344
    Overriding nature of network access obligations   346
    Presumption of authority   346
    Management of network transactions   347
    Do-it-yourself conveyancing   348

Chapter 28   Making e-conveyancing compulsory   349
Other steps to facilitate e-conveyancing   350
    Electronic settlement   350

PART 6   ADVERSE POSSESSION 353
The main changes at a glance 353

Chapter 29   Aims and scheme of the Act 355
The aims of the scheme 355
The effect of the LRA 2002 356
The general principle: no limitation period for the recovery of a registered
estate or rentcharge 356
The application of the principle to registered estates and rentcharges 357
Mortgagors in possession 357
Mortgagees in possession 358

**Chapter 30   Application for registration by a person in adverse
possession** 359
The general position 359
The meaning of 'adverse possession' 359
An extended right to apply for registration 362
Circumstances where no valid application can be made 362
The procedure for making an application for registration 364
Notification of the application 366
The persons to be notified 366
The content of the notice 368
The treatment of the application 369
If a counter-notice is served 370
If no counter-notice is served 371
The procedure following service of a counter-notice 371
The squatter's right to make further application 375
When the right arises 375
Making a further application for registration 377
The status of the squatter's right to be registered 379

**Chapter 31   The effect of registration of a person who had been in
adverse possession** 381
The general principle 381
The effect of registration on registered charges 382
Apportionment and discharge of charges 383

Chapter 32   Possession proceedings 385
The general rule 385
Exceptions to the general rule: defences 385
Reasonable mistake as to boundary 385
When a squatter has a right to make further application for registration 385
When a judgment for possession ceases to be enforceable 386
Other defences 386

Chapter 33   Special cases 389
Rentcharges 389
Trusts 391

Adverse possession of land held in trust 391
Adverse possession by a trustee or beneficiary of land held in trust 392
Crown foreshore 392
Transitional provisions 393

PART 7   ADJUDICATION AND OFFENCES 395
The main changes at a glance 395

Chapter 34   Adjudication 397
The new approach to adjudication 397
The powers of the registrar 398
The office of adjudicator 399
The jurisdiction of the adjudicator 400
The procedure before the adjudicator 401
   General 401
   Proceedings on a reference under s 73(7) of the LRA 2002 402
Appeals from the adjudicator 404

Chapter 35   Offences 405
Introduction 405
Suppression of information 405
Improper alteration of the registers 405
Privilege against self-incrimination 406

PART 8   THE LAND REGISTRY 409
The main changes at a glance 409

Chapter 36   The Land Registry 411
The Land Registry and its staff 411
The conduct of business 411
Miscellaneous powers 412
Fee orders 413

Appendix 1   Statutory materials 415
Land Registration Act 2002 417
Land Registration Rules 2003; SI 2003/1417 499
Land Registration (Referral to the Adjudicator to HM Land
   Registry) Rules 2003 SI 2003/2114 600
Adjudicator to Her Majesty's Land Registry (Practice and
   Procedure) Rules 2003, SI 2003/2171 602
Land Registration Act 2002 (Transitional Provisions) Order 2003,
   SI 2003/1953 624
Land Registration (Proper Office) Order 2003, SI 2003/2040 636
Land Registration Fee Order 2003, SI 2003/2092 640
Land Registration (Acting Chief Land Registrar) Regulations 2003,
   SI 2003/2281 653
Land Registration (Acting Adjudicator) Regulations 2003, SI 2003/2342 654

Appendix 2 Statutory forms   655
Form ADV1   657
Form AN1   659
Form AP1   662
Form AS1   664
Form CH1   666
Form CT1   668
Form EX1   672
Form EX2   674
Form FR1   677
Form NAP   680
Form OC2   682
Form RX1   684
Form SIM   687
Form TP1   689
Form TR1   693
Form UN1   695

Index   699

TABLE OF CASES

References are to paragraph numbers.

Abbey National Building Society v Cann [1991] 1 AC 56, [1990] 2 WLR 833, [1990]
    1 All ER 1085, HL   19.18
Ashburner v Sewell [1891] 3 Ch 405, 60 LJ Ch 784, 65 LT 524   11.15
Aston Cantlow and Wilmcote with Billesley PCC v Wallbank [2003] UKHL 37, [2003]
    3 WLR 283, [2003] 3 All ER 1213, [2003] NLJR 1030, HL; [2001] EWCA Civ 713,
    [2002] Ch 51, [2001] 3 WLR 1323, [2001] 3 All ER 393, CA   4.14
Att-Gen v Horner (1884) 14 QBD 245, 49 JP 326, 54 LJQB 227; *affirmed* (1885) 11 App
    Cas 66, 50 JP 564, 55 LJQB 193, HL   2.5

Barclays Bank plc v Estates & Commercial Ltd (in liquidation) [1997] 1 WLR 415, (1997)
    74 P&CR 30, [1996] NPC 26, CA   9.7
Batt v Adams [2001] 2 EGLR 92, [2001] 32 EG 90, [2001] 21 EGCS 164, ChD   30.6
Benn v Hardinge (1992) 66 P&CR 246, [1992] NPC 129, (1992) *The Times*,
    October 13, CA   11.16
Bettison v Langton [2001] UKHL 24, [2002] 1 AC 27, [2001] 2 WLR 1605,
    [2001] 3 All ER 417, HL   8.3
Bridges v Mees [1957] Ch 475, [1957] 3 WLR 215, [1957] 2 All ER 577   2.2, 30.41
Brown & Root Technology Ltd v Sun Alliance and London Assurance Co Ltd
    [2001] Ch 733, [2000] 2 WLR 566, (1998) 75 P&CR 223, CA   26.2

Caballero v Henty (1874) LR 9 Ch App 447, 43 LJ Ch 635,
    22 WR 446, CA   11.9
Calgary and Edmonton Land Co Ltd v Dobinson [1947] Ch 102,
    [1974] 2 WLR 143, [1974] 1 All ER 484   10.41
Caroll v Maneck (1999) 79 P&CR 173, (1999) *The Times*, August 18, ChD   31.6, 31.8
Celsteel Ltd v Alton House Holdings Ltd [1985] 1 WLR 204, [1985] 2 All ER 562,
    (1985) 49 P&CR 165   4.14, 11.13
Chattey v Farndale Holdings Inc [1997] 1 EGLR 153, [1997] 06 EG 152,
    [1996] NPC 136, ChD   2.2
Chowood's Registered Land, Re [1933] Ch 574, 102 LJ Ch 289, [1933] All ER
    Rep 946   4.5, 22.3
Clark v Chief Land Registrar; Chancery v Ketteringham [1994] Ch 370, [1994]
    3 WLR 593, [1994] 4 All ER 96, CA   1.2
Clark (H) (Doncaster) Ltd v Wilkinson [1965] Ch 694, [1965] 2 WLR 751, [1965]
    1 All ER 934, CA   27.23
Clayhope Properties Ltd v Evans and Jennings [1986] 1 WLR 1223,
    [1986] 2 All ER 795, (1986) 52 P&CR 149, CA   10.104
Clowes Developments (UK) Ltd v Mulchinock [1998] 1 WLR 42,
    [1997] NPC 47, ChD   10.41
Corpus Christi College, Oxford v Gloucestershire County Council [1983] QB 360,
    [1982] 3 WLR 849, [1982] 3 All ER 995, CA   2.7
Cottage Holiday Associates Ltd v Customs and Excise Commissioners [1983] QB 735,
    [1983] 2 WLR 861, [1983] STC 278   2.3
Crabb v Arun District Council [1976] Ch 179, [1975] 3 WLR 847, [1975]
    3 All ER 865, CA   9.16, 30.39

Dean v Dean (2000) 80 P&CR 457, [2000] EGCS 76, (2000) 80 P&CR D42, CA   23.16
Duke v Robson [1973] 1 WLR 267, [1973] 1 All ER 481, (1972) 25 P&CR 21, CA   9.9

Eardley v Earl Granville (1876) 3 ChD 826, 45 LJ Ch 669, 24 WR 528   2.33
Earl of Leicester v Wells-next-the-Sea UDC [1973] Ch 110, [1972] 3 WLR 486,
    [1972] 3 All ER 77   25.13
Epps v Esso Petroleum Co Ltd [1973] 1 WLR 1071, [1973] 2 All ER 465,
    25 P&CR 402   15.4, 22.15

Ferrishurst Ltd v Wallcite Ltd [1999] Ch 355, [1999] 2 WLR 667, [1999]
    1 All ER 977, CA   4.14, 11.5
Freer v Unwins Ltd [1976] Ch 288, [1976] 2 WLR 609, [1976] 1 All ER 634   22.4, 23.4

Ghana Commercial Bank v Chandiram [1960] AC 732, [1960] 3 WLR 328, [1960]
    2 All ER 865   31.8
Gloag and Miller's Contract, Re (1883) 23 ChD 320, 52 LJ Ch 654, 48 LT 629   11.15

Hall v Heward (1886) 32 ChD 430, 55 LJ Ch 604, 34 WR 571, CA   31.8
Hayes v Nwajiaku [1994] EGCS 106, ChD   22.13

IDC Group Ltd v Clark [1992] 2 EGLR 184, (1992) 65 P&CR 179, [1992] NPC 88, CA;
    [1992] 1 EGLR 187, [1992] 08 EG 108, ChD   8.16

JA Pye (Oxford) Ltd v Graham [2002] UKHL 30, [2003] 1 AC 419, [2002] 3 WLR 221,
    [2002] 3 All ER 865, [2002] HRLR 34, HL   30.3
Jolly, Re, Gathercole v Norfolk [1900] 2 Ch 616, 69 LJ Ch 661, [1900–3] All ER
    Rep 286, CA   31.4

King v Smith [1950] 1 All ER 553, [1950] WN 177, CA   30.6
Kingsalton Ltd v Thames Water Developments Ltd [2001] EWCA Civ 20, [2001]
    1 P&CR 184, [2001] 5 EGCS 169, [2001] NPC 16, CA   22.14

Loubatières v Mornington Estates (UK) Ltd [2004] PLSCS 105   10.40, 10.87
Ludbrooke v Ludbrooke [1901] 2 KB 96, 70 LJKB 552, 84 LT 485, CA   31.6

Malory Enterprises Ltd v Cheshire Homes (UK) Ltd [2002] EWCA Civ 151,
    [2002] Ch 216, [2002] 3 WLR 1, [2002] 10 EGCS 155, CA   15.4, 15.7, 15.8, 22.4
Markfield Investments Ltd v Evans [2001] 1 WLR 1321, [2001] 2
    All ER 238, (2001) 81 P&CR 33, CA   30.8
Marsh v Earl Granville. *See* Marsh and Earl Granville, Re
Marsh and Earl Granville, Re (1883) 24 ChD 11; *sub nom* Marsh v Earl Granville
    52 LJ Ch 189, 31 WR 239   2.28
Marten v Flight Refuelling Ltd [1962] Ch 115, [1961] 2 WLR 1018, [1961]
    2 All ER 696   25.13
Mayor of Ludlow v Charlton (1840) 6 M&W 815, 10 LJ Ex 75, 4 Jur 657   20.38
Mount Carmel Investments Ltd v Peter Thurlow Ltd [1988] 1 WLR 1078, [1988]
    3 All ER 129, (1989) 57 P&CR 396, CA   31.4

Oceanic Village Ltd v United Attractions Ltd [2000] Ch 234, [2000] 2 WLR 476,
    [2000] 1 All ER 975   10.9
Odell, Re [1906] 2 Ch 47   23.3
Orakpo v Manson Investments Ltd [1977] 1 WLR 347, [1977] 1 All ER 666, (1977)
    121 SJ 256, CA   9.7

Pagebar Properties Ltd v Derby Investment Holdings Ltd [1972] 1 WLR 1500, [1973] 1
    All ER 65, 24 P&CR 316   8.16
Palk v Mortgage Services Funding plc [1993] Ch 330, [1993] 2 WLR 415, [1993]
    2 All ER 481, CA   12.84
Peggs v Lamb [1994] Ch 172, [1994] 2 WLR 1, [1994] 2 All ER 15   4.14
Phillips v Phillips (1862) 4 De GF & J 208, 31 LJ Ch 321, 135 RR 97   9.17
Powell v London and Provincial Bank [1893] 2 Ch 555, 62 LJ Ch 795,
    9 TLR 446, CA   26.16
Powell v McFarlane (1977) 38 P&CR 452   30.3
Prestige Properties Ltd v Scottish Provident Institution [2002] EWHC 330 (Ch),
    [2003] Ch 1, [2002] 3 WLR 1011, [2002] NPC 41, ChD   23.16, 23.17
Pritchard v Briggs [1980] Ch 338, [1979] 3 WLR 868, [1980] 1 All ER 294, CA   9.15
Prudential Assurance Co Ltd v Waterloo Real Estate Inc [1999] 2 EGLR 85, [1999]
    17 EG 131, [1999] EGCS 10, CA   30.46

Quigly v Chief Land Registrar [1993] 1 WLR 1435, [1993] 4 All ER 82,
    [1993] EGCS 119, CA   34.9

R v Oxfordshire County Council, ex parte Sunningwell Parish Council [2000] 1 AC 335,
    [1999] 3 WLR 160, [1999] 3 All ER 385, HL   2.41
R v Secretary of State for the Environment, ex parte Spath Holme Ltd [2001] 2 AC 349,
    [2001] 2 WLR 15, [2001] 1 All ER 195, HL   1.21
Rains v Buxton (1880) 14 ChD 537, 49 LJ Ch 473, 28 WR 954   30.9
Rose v Watson (1864) 10 HL Cas 672, 33 LJ Ch 385, 3 New Rep 673, HL   2.2
Rosenberg v Cook (1881) 8 QBD 162, 51 LJQB 170, 30 WR 344, CA   4.5

Saunders v Vautier (1845) 4 Beav 115; *aff'd* (1845) Cr & Ph 240, [1835–42]
    All ER Rep 58, 10 LJ Ch 354   15.4, 15.7
Scmlla Properties Ltd v Gesso Properies (BVI) Ltd [1995] BCC 793   6.1, 13.3, 13.6
Shonleigh Nominees Ltd v Att-Gen (at the Relation of Hamshire County Council)
    [1974] 1 WLR 305, [1974] 1 All ER 734; *sub nom* Shonleigh Nominees Ltd v
    Att-Gen 27 P&CR 407, HL   11.15
Smith v Colbourne [1914] 2 Ch 533, 84 LJ Ch 112, [1914–15]
    All ER Rep 800, CA   2.41
Smith v River Douglas Catchment Board. *See* Smith and Snipes Hall Farm Ltd v
    River Douglas Catchment Board
Smith and Snipes Hall Farm Ltd v River Douglas Catchment Board [1949]
    2 KB 500; *sub nom* Smith v River Douglas Catchment Board [1949]
    2 All ER 179, 47 LGR 627, CA   30.6
Southern Centre of Theosophy Inc v State of South Australia [1982] AC 706,
    [1982] 2 WLR 544, [1982] 1 All ER 283, PC   16.9
Speciality Shops Ltd v Yorkshire & Metropolitan Estates Ltd [2002] EWHC 2969,
    [2003] 2 P&CR 410   9.15
Spook Erection Ltd v Secretary of State for the Environment [1989] QB 300,
    [1988] 3 WLR 291, [1988] 2 All ER 667, (1989) 57 P&CR 440, CA   2.5
Squarey v Harris-Smith (1981) 42 P&CR 118, CA   2.41
Street v Mountford [1985] AC 809, [1985] 2 WLR 877, [1985] 2 All ER 289, HL   8.16

Thornton v France [1897] 2 KB 143, 66 LJQB 705, 46 WR 56, CA   31.6
Treloar v Bigge (1874) LR 9 Ex 151, 43 LJ Ex 95, 22 WR 843   14.8
Twentieth Century Banking Corporation Ltd v Wilkinson [1977] Ch 99,
    [1976] 3 WLR 489, [1976] 3 All ER 361   12.7

United Bank of Kuwait plc v Sahib [1997] Ch 107, [1996] 3 WLR 372, [1996]
   3 All ER 215, CA   12.5, 12.86

Vincent v Premo Enterprises (Voucher Sales) Ltd [1969] 2 QB 609, [1969]
   2 WLR 1256, [1969] 2 All ER 941, CA   26.10

Wyld v Silver [1963] Ch 243, [1962] 3 WLR 841, [1962] 3 All ER 309, CA   2.5

Yaxley v Gotts [2000] Ch 162, [1999] 3 WLR 1217, [2000] 1 All ER 711, CA   1.21

TABLE OF STATUTES

References are to paragraph numbers.

Access to Justice Act 1999	
s 10(7)	12.51
s 54	34.21
Access to Neighbouring Land	
Act 1992	
s 4	10.17
s 5(6)	10.17
Administration of Estates Act 1925	1.2
s 22(1)	2.10
s 24(1)	2.10
s 36(4)	8.27, 12.47
Administration of Justice Act 1977	7.4
Banking and Financial Dealings	
Act 1971	
s 1	30.26, 36.5
Charities Act 1993	13.38, 13.39, 13.40
Pt VII	13.41
s 18	10.79
s 22(3)	10.79
s 36	10.79, 13.39
s 37	1.17
(1)	13.40
(2)	10.79, 13.39
(5)	13.39
(7)	13.40
s 38	10.79, 13.39
s 39	1.17
(1)	13.40
(1A)	13.40
(1B)	13.39
(2)	10.79, 13.39
s 60	26.19
(2)	26.19
Sch 2	13.39
Coal Industry Act 1994	4.14
s 38	10.11
s 49	10.11
s 51	10.11
Commons Registration	
Act 1965	10.13, 11.14, 11.15, 11.20
s 1	8.3, 8.12, 10.10

Companies Act 1985	12.91, 26.19
Pt III	26.21
Pt XII	20.36
s 36A	12.95, 26.19
(2)	20.38, 26.19
(4)	20.38, 20.39, 26.21
(6)	26.21
s 395	2.25, 12.28
s 401	12.28
s 410	12.28
s 418	12.28
s 651	13.6
s 652	13.33
s 654	8.7, 13.3, 13.33
s 655	13.6
s 656	13.3, 13.5
s 718	12.91
Consumer Credit Act 1974	12.78
Copyhold Act 1852	
s 48	14.6
Copyhold Act 1894	
s 23	14.6
Courts and Legal Services	
Act 1990	*Pt 8*
s 71	34.10, 34.11
(3)(c)	34.10
Deeds of Arrangement Act 1914	10.102
Electronic Communications	
Act 2000	
s 7(2)	26.11
(3)	26.12
s 8	26.6
Enduring Powers of Attorney	
Act 1985	20.10
s 7(3) 20.10	
s 8(1) 20.10	
(2)(b)	20.10
Family Law Act 1996	
s 31(10)	10.17, 10.27, 19.22
(a)	10.26, 10.27
(b)	10.26
s 32	10.26, 10.27

Family Law Act 1996 – *cont*
s 33	10.27
(5)	10.27
s 56	19.22
(1), (2)	19.22
(3)	19.2, 19.22, 19.23
(4)	19.22
Sch 4	10.26
para 4(1)	10.27
(3)	10.17, 10.26
(a), (b)	10.27

Freedom of Information Act 2000
Pt II	2.15, 18.5

Friendly Societies Act 1992
Sch 6, para 2	26.19

Greater London Authority Act
1999	8.9, 10.12
Pt 4, Ch 7	2.3
s 210	2.3
s 217	2.11
s 219	2.3

Highways Act 1980
s 212	12.80

Housing Act 1985
Pt 5	2.12, 2.17, 2.18, 8.8
s 37	10.70
(5A)	10.64
s 154	2.17
s 157	10.70
(7)	10.64
s 171A	2.12, 2.18, 8.8
Sch 9A, para 2(1)	2.12, 2.18
para 4	10.64, 10.70

Housing Act 1988
s 81	10.70
(10)	10.64
s 133	10.64, 10.70

Housing Act 1996 | 13.21, 13.22, 13.23
s 13	10.70
(5)	10.64

Housing Associations
Act 1985	13.21, 13.22, 13.23
Sch 1	13.21, 13.22, 13.23

Human Rights Act 1998 | 4.6

Inheritance Tax Act 1984 | 9.13
s 237	9.12
(6)	9.12

s 238	9.12
Insolvency Act 1986	9.13, 13.15, 13.26,
	13.31, 18.35
s 89	13.28
s 91(1)	13.28
s 98(1)	13.29
s 171	8.53, 13.3
s 178	13.5
s 225	13.36
s 284	13.14
s 306	8.6, 13.16
s 315	8.53, 13.3
s 385(1)	13.17
Sch 4,	13.32
para 7	13.32

Land Charges Act 1925	1.2
Land Charges Act 1972	1.2, 2.25, 2.29,
	10.27, 10.102, 13.9
s 2(4)	2.22
s 4(6)	2.22
s 5(1)(a)	10.102
(b)	13.10
s 6(1)(a), (b)	10.102
(c)	13.13
s 7(1)	10.102
s 14(3)	2.24
Land Registry Act 2002	1.1
Land Registry Act 1862	1.1
Land Registration Act 1925	1.1, 1.2, 1.4,
	1.12, 1.16, 1.20, 1.21, 2.7, 2.29,
	3.19, 4.4, 4.12, 5.2, 7.1, 9.1, 9.15,
	9.17, 10.10, 10.15, 10.16, 10.41,
	10.53, 10.68, 10.102, 11.17, 12.60,
	12.80, 13.2, 15.3, 15.5, 15.8, 16.1,
	16.3, 17.1, 19.3, 20.42, 21.2, 21.4,
	22.2, 22.9, 22.21, 23.1, 23.11, 23.16,
	23.22, 23.24, 25.3, 34.1, 34.3, *Pt 8*
Pt 5	21.4
s 1(1), (2)	14.1
s 2(1)	2.6
(4)	2.20
s 3(xi)	2.6
(xv)	10.1
(xxxi)	9.6
s 4	2.2
s 5(b)	4.5
(c)	4.7, 15.4, 15.7
s 8(1)	2.2, 2.4
s 9(c)	15.4
s 18	8.1
(1)	7.5

Land Registration Act 1925 – *cont*

s 19(2)	9.10
s 20(1)	9.4
s 21	8.1
(1)	7.5
s 22(2)	9.10
s 23(1)	9.4
s 24(1)	25.6
(b)	25.6
(2)	25.6
s 25(1)(a)	7.3
(2)	12.9
s 27(1)	12.2
s 29	12.48
s 30	12.61
(1)	12.61
s 32	12.83
s 48(2)	10.15
s 49	12.98
s 50(1)	10.9
s 52(1)	10.5
s 53(3)	5.17
s 54	12.98, 20.44
s 55	10.3, 10.106, 20.45
(1)	10.107
s 56	10.3, 10.106
s 57	10.4, 10.80
(1)	10.4
s 58(2)	10.71
(3)	10.59
s 63	21.1
s 64	21.1
(5)–(7)	21.1
s 66	12.5
s 69(1)	15.1, 15.7
s 70	11.1
(1)	4.13, 4.16
(a)	4.14
(c)	4.14
(f)	4.5, 4.16
(g)	4.14, 11.5, 11.7
(h)	4.16, 22.6
(i)	8.22
(k)	29.5
s 73	9.12
s 74	9.13
s 75	30.1, 30.36, 33.18
(1)	30.62
s 77	3.13
(1)–(3)	3.16
(4)	3.15
(6)	3.20

s 79(1)	20.43
s 82(2)	22.4
(3)	4.5, 15.4, 22.11, 22.13, 22.14
(a)–(c)	22.11
s 83	1.5, 23.1
(1)	4.5
(a)	22.3
(4)	23.3
ss 86–90	13.42
s 86(2)	4.14, 11.6
s 97	2.31, 2.32
s 106	7.4
(9)	7.4
s 110	24.3, 24.5
(1)–(3)	24.1
(4)	18.38, 18.39
(5)	24.2, 24.5
s 112	18.2
(1)(b)	2.15, 18.4
s 113	18.6
s 115	35.1
s 116	35.1, 35.4
s 117	35.1
s 119(2)	35.7
s 123	1.5, 2.8, 6.2
(2)	2.19, 2.35
(3)(b), (c)	2.9
(4), (5)	2.20
(6)(b), (c)	2.11
s 123A	1.5, 2.8, 2.21
(8)	2.23
(10)	2.24
(10)(b)	2.21
s 126(1)	36.1
s 127	36.2
s 128(3)	35.1
s 131	36.1
s 132	36.3
s 144	1.13
(1)	1.13
(xxxi)	1.13
(3)	1.13
s 145	36.10
(3)	1.5
(3A)	1.5
Land Registration Act 1986	1.1, 3.13
Land Registration Act 1988	1.1, 18.2, 24.3
Land Registration Act 1997	1.1, 1.5, 1.9, 2.8, 2.19, 2.20, 2.21, 2.28, 2.35, 23.1, 23.16, 23.24, 23.27
s 2	23.17
Land Registration Act 2002	1.1, 1.3, 1.4, 1.9, 1.11, 1.12, 1.21, 1.22, 2.38, 2.41,

Land Registration Act 2002 – *cont*
    3.8, 4.1, 4.5, 4.12, 4.15, 5.15, 5.22,
    Pt 2, 7.1, 7.7, 8.2, 9.1, 9.7, 9.14, 9.16,
    10.17, 10.25, 10.33, 10.41, 10.53,
    10.54, 10.107, 11.3, 11.13, 11.15,
    11.16, 12.4, 12.22, 12.61, 12.79, 13.25,
    Pt 3, 14.4, 14.23, 18.1, 18.4, 18.42,
    19.3, 20.1, 20.18, 20.40, 21.1, 21.2,
    22.2, 22.10, 22.22, 23.1, 23.24, 23.27,
    Pt 4, 25.1, 25.14, 26.1, 26.2, 26.3, 26.4,
    27.2, 27.4, 27.23, 29.2 29.3, 29.5,
    30.4, 30.9, 30.12, 30.48, 30.49, 30.61,
    32.1, 35.1

Pt 2	*Pt 1*
Pt 2, Ch 2	5.1
Pt 3	*Pt 2*
Pt 4	*Pt 2*, 10.1
Pt 5	1.20, *Pt 2*, 12.1
Pt 6	*Pt 1*, 3.13, *Pt 3*
Pt 7	*Pt 1*, *Pt 2*, 13.1
Pt 8	*Pt 5*
Pt 9	2.32, *Pt 6*
Pt 10	30.42, *Pt 8*
Pt 11	1.15, *Pt 7*
Pt 12	*Pt 7*
s 1(1), (2)	14.1
s 3	2.1, 4.14, 6.1, 20.16
(1)	2.1, 2.5, 14.2
(a)	2.3
(c)	14.16
(2)	2.2, 2.5, 2.27
(3)	2.3, 2.5, 2.13
(4)	2.3
(5), (6)	2.2
(7)	2.3
s 4	2.8, 2.10, 2.20, 20.16, 26.8
(1)	2.20, 6.2
(a)	2.13
(i)	2.10, 10.74
(ii)	2.10
(b)	2.12
(c)	2.13
(d)	2.16, 11.12
(e)	2.17
(f)	2.18
(g)	2.19
(2)	2.9
(3)	2.11
(4)(a), (b)	2.11
(6)	2.10, 2.13
(7)	2.13
(a), (b)	2.10
(8)(a), (b)	2.19
s 4(9)	2.9
s 5	2.20
(1)(a), (b)	2.20
(2)–(4)	2.20
s 6	2.21, 19.8
(1)	2.21, 2.27
(2)–(4)	2.21
(5)	2.21, 2.22
(6)	2.21
s 7	2.22
(1)	2.22
(2)	6.2
(a), (b)	2.22
(3), (4)	2.22
s 8	2.23
(a), (b)	2.23
s 9	3.1
(2), (3)	3.3
(4)	3.4
(5)	3.5
s 10	3.1
(2)	3.7
(4)	3.7
(5)	3.11
(6)	3.12
s 11	9.8
(2)	4.2
(3)	4.2, 8.44, 23.11
(4)(a)	4.3, 10.13
(b)	4.4
(c)	4.5, 4.6, 9.13, 15.5
(5)	4.7, 15.5
(6), (7)	4.8
s 12	9.8
(2)	4.9
(3)	4.9, 8.44, 23.11
(4)	4.9
(a)	4.9
(b)	10.13
(c)	15.5
(d)	9.13
(5)	15.5
(6)	4.10, 11.5
(7), (8)	4.11
s 13	2.25
(a)	2.34
(b)	2.35
s 14	2.25, 4.3
(b)	34.5
s 15	20.16
(1), (2)	5.4
(3)	5.5, 33.18
(4)	5.4

Land Registration Act 2002 – *cont*

s 15(3)	4.6
s 16(1), (2)	5.13
(3)	5.14
(4)	5.13
s 17	5.8, 20.16
s 18	20.16, 20.29
(1)	5.17
(a), (b)	5.17
(2)	5.3, 5.20
(3), (4)	5.19
s 19	5.2
s 20	5.9, 22.1
(2)	5.10
(3)	5.9
s 21	5.9, 22.1
(1)	5.11
(2)	5.9
(3)	5.11
s 22	5.7
s 23	12.2, 12.5, 13.33, 14.8
(1)	12.2
(a), (b)	7.3
(2)(a), (b)	7.4, 12.3, 12.6
(3)	7.4, 12.3
s 24	13.33
(1)	7.2
s 25	12.6
(1)	7.5, 12.9
(2)	7.5
s 26	10.56
(1)–(3)	7.6, 12.6
s 27	8.1, 8.24, 9.5, 10.57, 19.7, 20.16
(1)	8.2, 7.3, 28.3
(2)	7.3
(a)	8.3
(b)	8.8, 10.13
(i)	2.13
(ii)	11.4, 11.12
(2)(b)(iii)–(v)	11.4
(c)	8.11, 10.13
(d)	8.12, 9.8, 10.13
(e)	8.17, 10.13
(f)	8.22, 20.36
(3)	8.23
(4)	8.2, 12.6, 20.20
(5)	8.4, 13.6
(a)	13.6
(c)	8.22
(6)	8.24
(7)	8.12

ss 28–30	12.59
s 28	12.48, 31.7
(1)	9.2, 9.3, 9.4, 9.6
(2)	9.2
s 29	10.5, 11.1, 11.2
(1)	8.41, 9.4, 10.45
(2)	8.41, 9.8, 10.45
(a)(ii)	11.1, 14.8
(iii)	4.16, 22.6
(b)	9.8
(3)	4.21, 9.8
(4)	9.10
s 30	10.5, 11.1, 11.2
(1)	8.41, 9.4
(2)	8.41, 9.8
(a)(ii)	11.1
(iii)	4.16
(b)	9.8
(3)	2.25, 4.21, 9.8
s 31	9.12
s 32	12.98, 27.7
(1)	2.24, 10.5
(2)	8.21, 10.5
(3)	10.5, 10.14, 25.13
s 33	2.37, 4.19, 4.21, 10.6, 10.13, 10.14, 11.20
(a)	10.7, 10.59, 10.105
(b)	2.14, 8.14, 10.8
(c)	9.8, 10.9
(d)	8.3, 8.12, 10.10
(e)	4.14, 10.11
s 34	12.98, 20.16
(1)	10.14
(2)(a), (b)	10.14
(3), (4)	10.15
s 35	20.16
(1)	10.34
(a)	10.31
(2)	10.29
(a)	10.46
(b)	10.30, 10.46
(3)	10.32, 10.48, 12.102
s 36	10.18, 10.91, 12.102, 20.16, 20.29
(1)	10.35, 10.36
(2)–(4)	10.36
s 37	10.13
(1)	4.21, 10.13, 11.22
(2)	4.21
s 38	8.10, 8.21, 8.50, 10.13
s 39	10.5
s 40	14.8, 14.10, 14.12

Land Registration Act 2002 – *cont*

s 40(1)	10.50, 10.105
(2)(a), (b)	10.51
(3)	10.51
(4)	10.50
s 41(1)	10.52
(2), (3)	10.52, 10.100
s 42	7.3
(1)	10.55, 10.65
(a)	10.56, 10.94
(b)	10.7, 10.57
(c)	10.7, 10.59
(2)	10.62, 10.82
(3)	10.63
(4)	10.7, 10.59
s 43	10.63, 20.16
(1)(a)	10.65, 10.68
(b)	10.65
(c)	10.65, 10.66, 10.103
(2)(a)	10.72
(b)	10.66
(c)	10.68
(d)	10.70
(3)(a), (b)	10.70
s 44	7.3, 10.94
(1), (2)	10.64
s 45	10.88
(1)(a)	10.89
(b)	10.89, 10.90
(2)	10.90
(3)	10.88
s 46	10.66, 10.85, 10.94,
	12.27, 13.31, 19.4
(1)	10.80
(2)	10.82
(3)	10.83, 19.4
(4)	10.83
(5)	10.84, 19.4
s 47	10.93, 20.16
s 48	9.11, 20.16
(1)	12.48
(2)(a)	12.48
(b)	12.50
s 49(1)	12.62, 12.64
(2)	12.62
(3)	12.67
(4)	12.73
(5)	12.78
(6)	12.72
s 50	12.51, 23.10

s 51	12.2
s 52	10.56
(1), (2)	12.7
s 53	12.7
s 54	12.50, 12.82, 19.21
s 55	2.39, 4.19, 8.22, 12.80
s 56	12.83
s 57	12.39
s 58(1)	15.1, 15.8
(2)	15.2, 15.8
s 59(1)–(3)	15.9
s 60	16.1, 16.2, 16.7, 16.10,
	20.16, 29.1, 30.42, 30.43
(1)	16.1, 30.42, 30.47
(2)	16.1
(3)	16.3, 30.42, 30.47
(a)	16.3, 30.47
s 61(1)	16.10
(2)	14.7, 16.11
(3)	13.9
s 62	3.13, 3.17, 20.16, 23.3, 31.1
(1), (2)	3.13, 3.17
(3)(a), (b)	3.13, 3.17
(4)	3.14, 3.17
(5)	3.14, 3.17
(6)	3.15
(7)	3.16
(b)	3.18
(d)	3.18
(8)	3.13
(9)	3.14
s 63	3.19
(1), (2)	3.19
s 64	14.7, 17.1, 17.3, 17.4, 17.5, 17.6
(1)	17.1, 17.4
(a)	8.28
(2)	17.3
(c)	17.6
s 65	22.3
s 66	18.9, 18.40
(1)	18.3, 18.6, 18.9, 18.10
(a)	18.3
(b)	2.15, 10.24, 18.3
(c), (d)	18.3
(2)(a)	2.15, 18.5
(b)	18.5
s 67	18.6, 18.9, 20.16
(1)	18.6
(a)–(d)	18.6
(2)	18.8, 23.6
(3)(a)–(d)	18.7
s 68	14.13, 14.14, 14.16
(1)	14.14

Land Registration Act 2002 – *cont*

s 68(1) (c)	5.2
(2)	14.14
(a), (b)	14.15
s 69	36.8
(1)	18.43
(2)	18.44
(3)	36.10
(b)	18.43
s 70	19.1, 20.16
(a)–(d)	19.1
s 71	4.20, 20.5, 27.17
(a)	4.19, 10.13
(b)	11.18
s 72	10.82, 19.4, 27.7
(1)	19.4
(2)	10.82, 18.83, 19.4, 27.7
(3)	19.4
(4)	10.83, 19.4
(5)	19.4
(6)	10.82, 19.5, 19.6
(b)	19.6
(7)	10.82, 19.6
s 73	5.16, 8.50, 10.63, 10.90,
	10.107, 16.6, 17.4, 18.29,
	20.28, 20.29, 20.31, 20.42,
	23.20, 30.30, 34.4
(1)	5.8, 18.29, 20.29, 30.28, 30.36
(2)	5.8, 20.29
(3), (4)	20.29
(5)	34.4
(a), (b)	20.30
(6)	10.37, 20.30, 34.4
(7)	5.16, 10.37, 12.58, 20.30,
	22.19, 30.30, 30.36, 34.4,
	34.12, 34.16, 34.20, 34.21
(8)	20.30
s 74	15.10, 20.33
(a)	2.24
s 75(1), (2)	34.7
(3)	34.9
s 76(1)–(3)	34.8
(4)	34.9
s 77	34.17
(1)(a)	5.21
(b)	10.39, 10.87
(c)	20.32
(2)	5.21, 10.39, 10.87, 20.32
s 78	9.13
s 79(1)–(5)	6.1
s 80(1)–(5)	6.2
s 81(1), (2)	6.3
s 82	1.18, 13.4
s 82(2)	14.7
ss 83–85	13.3
s 86	13.9, 13.10, 13.15
(1)	13.14, 13.15
(2)	10.64, 13.10, 13.11,
	14.10, 14.12
(3)	13.12, 13.14
(4)	10.104, 13.13, 13.14,
	14.10, 14.12
(5), (6)	13.15
(7)	13.10
s 87	10.23
(1)	10.102, 10.103, 10.104
(a), (b)	10.14, 10.103
(2)	10.104
(3)	10.103
(4)	10.104
(5)	10.102
s 89	13.42, 20.15
s 90	4.14, 11.2
(1)	2.3
(2)	2.11
(3)(a)	8.9
(4)	2.37, 4.19, 10.12, 11.20
(5)	4.14, 11.2
s 91	26.5, 26.6, 26.7, 26.8, 26.10,
	26.11, 26.12, 26.14, 26.16,
	26.17, 26.18, 26.20, 26.22
(2)	26.8
(3)	26.9
(a)	26.10, 27.8
(b)	26.11
(c)	26.12
(d)	26.13
(4)	26.15
(b)	26.20
(5)	26.10, 26.16
(6)	26.17
(7)	26.18
(8)	26.22
(9)	26.21
(10)	26.12
(11)	26.11
s 92	36.8
(1)	27.12
s 93	1.14, 1.20, 9.3, 27.16,
	27.17, 28.2, 28.3
(1)	28.2
(2)	28.3
(3)(a), (b)	28.3
(4)	8.2, 28.3
(5)	1.14

Land Registration Act 2002 – *cont*

s 93(6)	28.2
s 94	28.5, 36.8
s 95	27.12
s 96	30.3
(1)	29.4, 29.6
(2)	29.4, 29.7
(3)	29.4
s 98(1)	1.3, 32.2
(2)	30.11, 32.4
(3)	32.3
(4)	30.55, 32.5
(5)	32.6
(6)	32.7
(7)	33.2, 33.10
s 99(1)–(3)	36.1
s 100(1)	36.2
(2)	1.15, 1.19, 36.2
(3)	1.19, 19.17, 19.28, 20.26, 36.3
(4)	2.27, 20.31, 36.2
s 101(1)–(3)	36.4
s 102	1.3, 1.15, 1.19, 36.10
(a)	36.7, 36.10
s 104	36.6
s 105	36.8
(1), (2)	36.7
s 106	28.5, 36.9
(1)	36.8
(2)	20.16, 36.8
(3)	36.9
s 107	1.3
(1), (2)	34.10
s 108	10.63
(1)	30.36
(a)	34.12
(b)	27.21, 34.12
(2)	34.14
(a)–(c)	34.13
(3)	34.13
(4)	34.14
s 109(1)–(3)	34.15
s 110(1)	*Pt 7*, 34.17
(2)	34.18
(3)	34.19
(4)	30.40
(a), (b)	34.20
s 111(1)	30.40, 34.21
(2)	27.21, 34.22
(3)	30.40, 34.23
ss 112–114	34.15
s 115	9.15
s 116(a)	9.16
(b)	9.17
s 117	4.18, 11.2
(2)(a)	4.18
s 118(1)	2.4, 2.14
(d)	8.9
(3)	1.14, 2.4, 2.14
s 119	2.7
s 120	18.38, 18.40, 23.7
(1)	18.38
(2)(a), (b)	18.38
(3), (4)	18.41
s 121	1.15, 20.36
s 122	1.1
s 123(1)	35.2
(2)(a), (b)	35.2
s 124(1)	35.4
(2)	35.5
(3)(a), (b)	35.6
(4)	35.4, 35.5
s 125(1), (2)	35.7
s 126	1.14
s 127	27.17, 36.10
(1)	1.16
(2)	1.16
(a)–(g)	1.16
ss 128–132	1.3
s 128(1), (2)	1.11, 36.10
(4)	1.14, 2.20
(d)	3.14
(5)	1.14, 27.13, 27.14, 27.18, 27.19
s 130(a), (b)	13.2
s 131	22.12
(1)–(3)	3.14, 22.12
s 132(1)	1.15, 2.1, 2.2, 8.2, 8.44, 9.5, 9.6, 12.1, 15.1, 23.11, 27.17
(3)(b)	10.5
(c)	20.29, 34.4
s 134	4.14
(1)	1.3, 1.15, 4.14
s 136	1.3
(2)	1.15, 33.17
Sch 1	4.13, 4.14, 4.17, 4.19, 4.21, 10.13, 11.2, 12.80, 24.4
para 1	2.13, 4.14, 4.19
para 2	4.6, 4.14, 10.26, 11.5
paras 3–14	4.14
para 7	4.14
para 15	11.2
para 16	4.14, 11.2
Sch 2	8.2, 12.6, 13.15, 15.1, 15.2, 15.8, 20.20, 28.3, 36.3
para 2(1), (2)	8.3
para 3	8.10

Land Registration Act 2002 – *cont*
  Sch 2, para 3(2)   10.5, 10.13
       para 4(2)   8.11, 10.13
       para 5(2)   8.11, 10.13
       para 6   8.13, 8.18
         6(2)   10.13
       para 7   8.13, 8.51, 25.13
         (2)   8.19, 8.20, 10.13
           (a)   10.13
         (3)   8.20
       para 8   8.22
       para 10   8.23
       para 11   8.23
  Sch 3   4.13, 8.26, 9.8, 11.1, 11.2,
             11.18, 11.19, 24.4
       para 1   2.13, 11.4, 18.39
       para 2   7.3, 10.26, 11.5,
           30.62, 31.7, 33.18
           (a)   11.6
           (b)   11.7
           (c)   11.8
           (d)   11.12
       para 2A(1), (2)   11.5
       paras 4–14   11.2
       para 6   8.22, 12.80
       paras 15, 16   11.2
  Sch 4   *Pt 3*, 17.6, 22.3
       para 1   22.3, 22.10, 23.3
       para 2   22.3
         (1)   22.6
           (a)   30.1, 30.14
         (2)   22.6
       para 3(1)   22.10
         (2)   22.11
         (3)   22.15
         (4)   22.11
       para 4(a)   22.7
         (b), (c)   22.6
       para 5   22.3, 22.16
         (a)   22.16, 30.1, 30.14
         (b)   8.5, 10.13, 10.28,
           10.99, 22.16, 34.5
         (c)   22.16
         (d)   10.99, 22.16
       para 6   22.17
       para 7(b)   10.28
         (c)   22.18, 23.20
         (d)   8.5, 10.28, 22.18
       para 8   22.4
       para 9(1), (2)   22.21

Sch 5   1.14, 17.2, *Pt 5*, 27.1,
           34.12
     para 1   20.16
       (1)   27.13
       (2)   27.13
         (b)   22.20
         (c)   19.1
         (d)   18.7
       (3)   27.13
       (4)   27.14
     para 2(1)   27.15
       (2)   27.16
         (a)–(c)   27.16
       (3)   27.17
       (4)   27.18
     para 3(1)–(3)   27.19
     para 4   34.12, 34.22
       (1)–(3)   27.21
     para 5(1), (2)   27.17
     para 6   27.17, 27.22
     para 7(1), (2)   27.26
     para 8   26.17, 27.24
     para 9(1)–(3)   27.25
     para 10   27.14, 36.8
     para 11(1) 1.14, 27.13, 27.14,
           27.18, 27.19
       (2) 27.13, 27.14, 27.18
           27.19
       (3)   27.14
     para 12   27.16
  Sch 6   2.32, 3.14, 22.12, *Pt 6*,
        29.4, 30.21, 33.4, 33.17,
     para 1   20.16, 30.15, 30.52
           32.4, 34.23
       (1)   30.1
       (2) 30.10, 30.16, 33.6
       (3)   30.16
         (a), (b)   30.11
       (4)   30.2
     para 2   30.59
       (1) 30.20, 30.21 30.26
           30.28
         (d) 30.21, 30.22, 30.25,
           30.53
         (e)   14.11, 30.21
       (2)   30.26
     para 3   30.26, 30.28
       (1) 20.42, 30.21, 30.28,
           30.32
       (2) 20.42, 30.26, 30.32
     para 4   30.26, 30.28, 30.34
       (b)   30.42

Land Registration Act 2002 – *cont*

Sch 6, para 5   20.42, 30.16, 30.18,
    30.28, 30.32, 30.33,
    31.7, 33.8, 4.20
    (1)   30.33, 30.35
    (2)   30.37, 34.3, 34.20
    (3)   30.41, 34.3
    (4)   1.3, 16.3, 30.42,
    32.2, 33.8, 33.17
    (b)   16.3
    (5)   1.3, 30.42, 33.17
    para 6   30.15, 30.57, 32.3, 32.5
    (1)   30.50
    (2)   30.54, 30.55
    para 7   30.54
    para 8   30.16, 30.57
    (1)(a), (b)   30.11
    (2)(a), (b)   30.11
    (3)   30.11
    (4)   30.13
    para 9(1)   31.1
    (2)   31.5
    (3), (4)   31.6
    para 10(1)   31.8
    (2)–(4)   31.9
    para 11(1)   30.3, 33.12
    (2)   30.3, 30.6
    (3)(a), (b)   30.8
    para 12   33.11
    para 13(1)   33.14
    (2), (3)   33.15
    para 14   33.2
Sch 7   *Pt 8*
    paras 1, 2   36.1
    para 3(1), (2)   36.1
    para 4   36.1
    para 7   36.1
Sch 8   *Pt 3*, 23.13, *Pt 8*, 36.1
    para 1   13.33
    (1)   23.2, 23.19
    (a)   22.3, 23.3
    (b)   23.4
    (c)   23.5
    (d)   18.8, 23.6
    (e)   18.41, 23.7
    (f)   23.8
    (g)   5.12, 23.9
    (h)   12.55, 23.10
    (2)(a)   3.20, 23.3
    (3)   23.4
    para 2   2.33, 8.44, 8.45, 23.11
    para 3(1)–(3)   23.14
    para 4(1), (2)   23.15

para 5(1)(a), (b)   23.16
    (2)   23.17
    (3)   23.18
    para 6   23.13
    (a), (b)   23.13
    para 7(1)   23.22
    (2)   23.14
    para 8   23.16
    para 9   23.13
    para 10(1)(a)   23.25
    (b)   23.26, 23.27
    (2)(a)   23.26
    (b)   23.27
    para 11(1)   23.2
Sch 9   1.3
    paras 1, 2   34.10
    para 3(1), (2)   34.11
    para 4(1), (2)   34.11
    para 5   1.15, 1.19, 34.11
    para 8   34.2
    para 9   34.10
Sch 10   1.14, 1.17, 27.1
    Pt 2   1.17
    para 1   2.24
    para 2(1), (2)   24.4
    para 3   25.3
    para 4   21.3
    para 5   1.17
    (2)   1.17
    para 6   1.17, 20.17
    (e)   22.23
    para 7   1.17
    para 8   1.14, 1.17, 11.5
Sch 11, para 2(2)   24.6
    (4)   24.6
    (9)   12.60
    para 7(2)   10.10
    para 28   1.3
    para 31(2)   25.2
Sch 12, para 2(2)   10.4
    (3), (4)   10.3
    para 5   10.3, 20.45, 21.4
    para 7   4.6
    para 9   11.17
    para 10   11.17
    (3)   2.24
    para 11   11.2, 33.18
    para 12   4.14, 11.4
    para 14(1)   5.5, 33.18
    (2)   5.5
    para 15(1)   6.3
    para 18(1), (2)   33.18
    para 20   25.6

Land Registration Act 2002 – *cont*	
Sch 12, para 20(2), (3)	14.10, 25.6
(4)	25.6
Sch 13	1.3
Land Registry Act 1862	1.1
Land Transfer Act 1875	7.3
Land Transfer Act 1897	1.1
Landlord and Tenant Act 1927	
s 19(1)	14.8
Landlord and Tenant Act 1954	
Pt II	8.53
Landlord and Tenant Act 1987	
ss 35–37	10.17
s 38	10.17
s 39(4)	10.17
Landlord and Tenant (Covenants)	
Act 1995	25.6
s 3	8.15
(1)	9.8
s 4(a)	9.8
s 11	31.3
Lands Clauses Consolidation	
Act 1845	17.1
Law of Property Act 1922	1.1
s 145	2.13
Sch 15, para 5	2.13
Land Transfer Act 1875	12.2
Law of Property Act 1922	
Sch 12	14.6
Law of Property Act 1925	1.2, 13.24, 25.3
s 1	2.2
(1)	15.1
(2)	15.1
(a)	8.12
(b)	8.17
(e)	8.17
(4)	15.1
(6)	30.11
s 27(2)	10.7, 10.57
s 36(2)	10.73
s 44	24.6
(1)	24.6, 29.2
(2)–(4)	24.6
(4A)	3.9, 3.18, 24.6
(11), (12)	24.6
s 45(2), (3)	17.3
s 52(1), (2)	20.37
s 53(1)(a)	26.17
(b)	8.36, 26.11
s 54(2)	2.14
s 56	25.13
s 62	8.12, 8.47, 8.48

s 74	12.95
(1)	12.92, 12.94
(3)	13.32, 26.19
s 75	26.22
s 77	25.7, 25.12
(1)(A)	25.8
(B)	25.9
s 78	30.6
s 87	12.2
s 94(1), (2)	12.60
(3)	12.60, 12.61
(4)	12.60
s 99(2)	12.7, 22.12
s 104(1)	12.82
(2)	12.7
s 105	12.82, 19.21
s 121(3)	17.1
s 136(1)	26.18
s 141(1)	9.8
s 142(1)	9.8
s 149(6)	2.13
s 198(1)	12.82
Sch 2, Pt VII	25.7, 25.8
Pt VIII	25.7, 25.9
para (i)	25.11
(ii)	25.10
Law of Property Act 1969	
s 23	24.6, 29.2
Law of Property (Amendment)	
Act 1924	1.1
Law of Property (Miscellaneous	
Provisions) Act 1989	
s 1(2)	26.16
(3)	26.16
(a)(i), (ii)	20.38
s 2	10.5, 12.5
(1)	26.6
Law of Property (Miscellaneous	
Provisions) Act 1994	14.10, 25.2
Pt 1	25.2
s 4	25.3
s 6	25.2
(4)	25.2
s 11	25.3
Limitation Act 1980	*Pt 1*, 3.14, 4.6, 4.14, 9.13, 11.2, 15.5, 29.5
s 5	23.16
s 15	3.14, 4.5, 29.4, 30.3, 30.8
(1)	29.2, 29.6
(4)	31.6
s 16	2.2, 29.4, 29.7
s 17	4.5, 29.4, 31.4
s 20(1)	29.6

Limitation Act 1980 – *cont*
   s 20(4)   29.6
   s 21(1)(b)   33.12
   s 24(1)   30.55, 32.5
   s 28   30.12
   s 29   30.9
   s 38(8)   33.1
   Sch 1, para 6   30.8
      Pt 1, para 8(3)(a)   33.1
      para 9   33.12
      para 15   4.6
      Pt 2, para 11   33.14
Limitation (Enemies and War
  Prisoners) Act 1945
   s 1   30.11
Limited Liability Partnerships
  Act 2000   5.3, 12.28, 13.21, 14.10, 14.12
Local Government and Housing
  Act 1989
   s 173   10.70
      (9)   10.64
Local Land Charges Act
  1975   2.39, 4.14, 4.19

Magistrates' Courts Act 1980
   s 32(2)   35.2
      (9)   35.2
Matrimonial Homes Act 1967   19.22
Matrimonial Homes Act 1983
   s 2(8)   19.22
Mental Health Act 1983   30.12

New Parishes Measure 1943   20.13
   s 16   20.13

Pastoral Measure 1983   20.14
Powers of Attorney Act 1971   20.9
   s 3   20.10
   s 5(2)   20.11
      (4)(a)   20.11
   s 7   26.19

Prescription Act 1832   2.41

Rent Act 1977   8.16
Rentcharges Act 1977
   s 2   8.17
      (3)(a)   25.12
      (c)   8.17
      (4)   8.17
   s 11(1), (2)   25.12

Settled Land Act 1925   2.10, 4.14, 11.6
      11.20, 20.15
   s 5   1.17
   s 20   10.57
   s 73(1)(xi)   20.15
   s 94(1)   10.7, 10.57
Supreme Court Act 1981
   s 116(1)   2.10

Tribunals and Inquiries
  Act 1992   34.2
   s 10   34.2
Trustee Act 1925   1.2
   s 40   2.11, 8.4
Trusts of Land and Appointment of
  Trustees Act 1996
   s 2   13.42
      (1)   20.15
      (2)   13.43
      (4)   20.15
   s 6   10.75
      (1)   10.75
   s 8   10.68, 10.75, 10.76,
      10.77, 10.78
      (1)   10.75
   s 9   20.12
      (1), (2)   20.12
   s 11   10.56
   s 14   10.53
   Sch 1, paras 1–3   30.11

TABLE OF STATUTORY INSTRUMENTS AND CONVENTIONS

References are to paragraph numbers.

Adjudicator to Her Majesty's Land
 Registry (Practice and Procedure)
 Rules 2003, SI 2003/2171   1.19, *Pt 7*
                                     34.15, 34.18
   Pt 3   34.14
   Pt 6   34.24
   rr 6, 7   34.18
   rr 8, 9   34.18
   rr 12–14   34.15
   r 47   34.15
   r 51   34.19
   r 55   34.18

Civil Procedure Rules 1998,
 SI 1998/3132
   Pt 52   34.21
   Sch 1, r 46.2(a)   30.55
Companies (Northern Ireland) Order
 1989, SI 1989/2404 (NI 18)
   Art 403   12.28
   Art 409   12.28
Companies (Unregistered Companies)
 Regulations 1985, SI 1985/680   20.38
Companies (Unregistered Companies)
 (Amendment No 2) Regulations
 1990, SI 1990/1394   20.38

Foreign Companies (Execution of
 Documents) Regulations 1994,
 SI 1994/950   20.38, 20.39

Insolvency Rules 1986,
 SI 1986/1925   13.4, 13.10

Land Registration Act 2002
 (Commencement No 1) Order
 2003, SI 2003/935   1.3
Land Registration Act 2002
 (Commencement No 2) Order
 2003, SI 2003/1028   1.3
Land Registration Act 2002
 (Commencement No 3) Order
 2003, SI 2003/1612   1.3

Land Registration Act 2002
 (Commencement No 4) Order
 2003, SI 2003/1725   1.3
   Art 2(2)   16.3, 30.48, 33.17
Land Registration Act 2002
 (Transitional Provisions) Order
 2003, SI 2003/1953   1.19
   Art 2   36.1
   Art 14   5.22
   Art 21   14.16
   Art 24   21.3
     (1)–(3)   21.4
   Art 26(1)(a), (b)   20.3
     (3)   20.3
   Sch   20.3
Land Registration Act 2002
 (Transitional Provisions) (No 2)
 Order 2003, SI 2003/2431   1.19, 4.14,
                                     11.2

Land Registration (Acting
 Adjudicator) Regulations 2003,
 SI 2003/2342   1.19, 34.11
Land Registration (Acting Chief
 Land Registrar) Regulations 2003,
 SI 2003/2281   1.19, 36.2
Land Registration (Conduct of
 Business) Regulations 2000,
 SI 2000/2212   34.3
   Schs   *Pt 8*
Land Registration (Hearing Procedures)
 Rules 2000, SI 2000/2213   34.3
Land Registration (Official Searches)
 Rules 1993, SI 1993/3276   1.13, 19.1
   r 2(1)   19.3
   r 6   19.3
   r 9   19.3
   r 10   19.3
Land Registration (Open Register)
 Rules 1991, SI 1991/122
   rr 6, 7   18.32
   Sch 2   18.3
Land Registration (Proper Office)
 Order 2003, SI 2003/2040   1.19, 14.18

Land Registration (Proper Office)
   Order 2003, *cont*   20.26, 36.3
Land Registration (Referral to the
   Adjudicator to HM Land Registry)
   Rules 2003, SI 2003/2114   20.30
Land Registration Fee Order 2003,
   SI 2003/2092   1.19, 2.25, 36.11
     Arts 2–10   36.11
     Schs 3, 4   36.11
Land Registration Rules 1925,
   SR&O 1925/1093   2.25, 7.5, 10.3,
     12.42, 14.6 14.16, 20.2, 25.4, *Pt 8*
     r 2   14.4
     r 3   14.5
     r 7A   14.22
     r 8   18.3
     r 9   14.20
       (1)(a), (b)   14.20
     r 13   22.23
     rr 17, 18   14.3
     r 19(2)   2.21
     r 20   2.26
     r 21   2.26, 18.4
     r 23   2.31
     r 24   15.10
     r 25   2.29
     r 28   2.28
     r 29   2.29
     rr 40, 41   10.45
     r 42   15.10
     r 47   2.3
     r 53   2.26
     r 54   2.26
     s 58(1)   10.70
     s 59A   10.72
       (2)   10.70
     s 60(3)   10.70
     r 73   2.24
     r 76A   25.3
       (2)–(5)   25.3
     r 77   25.3
     r 77A(2)   25.2
     r 83   15.10
     r 87   20.20
     r 100   10.70
     r 106A(1)   10.72
       (3)   10.70
     r 109(3)   25.8
     r 110   25.5
     r 123(2)   10.70
     r 124(5)   10.70
     r 139(5)   12.14

r 154   12.39
r 158   12.56
r 163(1)   7.4
r 169A(2)   10.70
r 170(5)   13.8
r 171(1)   10.70
r 195   2.33
r 196   2.33
r 199   2.40
r 213   10.59, 10.70
   (2), (3)   10.74
   (4), (5)   10.73
r 215(2)   20.44
r 232   10.70
r 236   10.70
r 236B(1)   10.95
r 237   10.53
r 238   10.68
r 252   2.34
r 257   2.34
r 276   16.3, 30.42
r 277   30.42
r 278   1.13
   (1)   16.1
   (2)   16.2
Sch 2, Form 62   10.59, 10.64
Land Registration Rules 2003,
   SI 2003/1417   1.18, 2.5, 2.30, 5.9,
     8.46, 10.2, 10.5, 10.25, 12.14,
     12.16, 12.86, 12.89, 13.4, 13.19,
     13.25, 13.38, 14.13, 16.3, 16.4,
     18.6, 19.3 20.1, 20.2, 20.16,
     21.1, 21.3, 22.2, 25.1, 30.18,
     30.31, 33.3, 36.2
   Pt 3   2.25
   Pt 4   2.25
   Pt 5   5.1, 5.22
   Pt 6   8.24
   Pt 7   10.2
   Pt 8   10.2
   Pt 10   16.2
   Pt 13   14.22, 18.5, 19.7, 19.11,
     19.25 20.27
   Pt 14   13.1
   Pt 15   20.40
   r 2   18.11
     (1), (2)   14.2
     (2)(b)   2.5
   r 3   14.3
     (1)   14.3
     (2)   14.3
     (3)   14.3

Land Registration Rules 2003,
SI 2003/1417 – *cont*
r 3(3)(a), (b) — 8.37
(4) — 14.3
(5)(a), (b) — 14.3
r 4(1) — 14.4
(2) — 5.18, 14.4
(3), (4) — 14.4
r 5 — 14.5
(a) — 8.45, 14.5
(b) — 14.6
(i) — 2.33
(c) — 14.7
r 6(1) — 14.9
(2) — 14.8
r 7 — 14.9
r 8 — 14.14
(1) — 14.10
(2) — 8.32, 14.11, 18.22
(e) — 13.11
r 9 — 14.12
(a) — 13.11
r 10 — 14.16
(1)(a) — 14.17
(b) — 14.18
(2) — 14.16
r 11 — 14.20, 20.2
(1), (2) — 14.20
(3), (4) — 14.21
r 12 — 19.6
(1) — 14.22
(3) — 14.23
(4) — 14.22
r 13 — 8.39, 10.85, 12.49, 16.11, 17.4, 19.12, 22.18,
(1) — 2.25, 20.18
(2)(a)–(c) — 20.18
r 14 — 20.18
r 15 — 19.11, 19.17, 19.27, 20.26, 20.27, 20.28
(1)–(3) — 20.26
(4) — 19.17, 20.27
r 16(1)–(4) — 20.19
r 17 — 10.34, 10.97, 20.22, 30.21, 30.59
r 18 — 20.21
r 19 — 20.31, 30.29
(1)–(6) — 20.31
(5) — 20.31
r 20 — 10.45, 20.33
r 21 — 2.19
r 22 — 2.19, 2.35
r 23 — 8.33

r 23(1) — 2.25
r 24 — 4.19, 8.33
(1), (2) — 2.26
r 25 — 2.26
r 26 — 2.26
(1), (2) — 2.26
r 27(a), (b) — 2.27
r 28 — 4.19
(1), (2) — 4.19
r 29 — 2.28
r 30 — 2.25, 2.29
r 31 — 2.31, 2.32
(3) — 2.31
r 32 — 2.33, 8.44, 8.45, 14.6
r 33 — 2.25
(1) — 2.34
(2) — 2.34, 14.7
r 34 — 2.35
r 35(1) — 2.36
(2) — 2.36
(a) — 2.37
(b) — 2.38
(c) — 2.39
(d) — 2.40
r 36 — 2.41, 8.52, 14.7
r 37 — 2.27
(1) — 3.8
(2)(a)–(c) — 3.8
(3) — 3.8
r 38 — 2.35, 19.7
(1), (2) — 2.24
r 39 — 5.3, 5.7, 5.10
r 40 — 2.36
(1) — 5.2
(2), (3) — 5.3
r 41 — 2.36
(1) — 5.3
(2) — 5.3, 20.29
(3), (4) — 5.3
(5) — 5.3, 20.29
r 42 — 5.6
r 43 — 5.8
r 44(1) — 5.18
(3) — 5.18, 6.3
(4) — 5.20
(5) — 5.18, 6.3
r 45 — 6.3
(a), (b) — 5.17
(b)(i) — 5.18
r 46 — 5.20
r 47 — 5.3, 5.20
r 48(1)–(3) — 5.10
r 49 — 5.11, 20.29

Land Registration Rules 2003,	
SI 2003/1417 – *cont*	
r 50(1), (2)	5.11
r 51	20.29
(1)	5.7
r 52	5.7, 20.29
r 53	5.19
(1)–(4)	5.13
r 54	19.24
(2)(a), (b)	19.25
(3), (4)	19.26
(6)	19.28, 19.29
(7)	19.29
(8), (9)	19.28
r 55	20.28
(1)–(6)	20.28
r 56	20.20
(1), (2)	20.20
r 57	8.26
(1)	11.19
(2)	11.19, 11.20
(4), (5)	11.19
r 58	8.29
(1)	8.31, 8.32
(2)	8.32
r 60(1)–(3)	25.6
r 61	20.9, 20.10
(1)	20.10
r 62	20.9
(1), (2)	20.11
r 63	20.9
(1), (2)	20.12
r 64	14.10
(1)–(3)	25.4
r 65	14.10
(1)–(3)	25.5
r 66	14.10, 25.6
r 67(1)–(5)	25.3
(6)	14.10, 25.3
r 68	25.3
r 69	25.7
(1)	25.8, 25.9
(2)	25.10
(3)	25.11
(4)(a)	25.8, 25.9
r 70(1), (2)	8.45
r 71(1)	8.44, 8.45
(2),(3)	8.44
r 72	8.3
(1)(a)	8.37, 8.45, 14.7
(b)	8.37
(2)–(4)	8.37
r 73	14.7
r 73(1)–(3)	8.47
r 74	14.7
(1)	8.48
(2)	8.49
(3)	8.48
r 75	8.47, 8.50, 14.7
r 76	8.52, 14.7
r 77	8.20
r 78	8.40, 8.41
r 79	8.54, 13.6
(1)–(3)	8.54
r 80	10.17
r 81	10.48, 20.22
(1)(a)	10.19
(b)	10.20
(c)(i)	10.21, 10.22
(ii)	10.23
(2)	10.19
r 82	10.26, 10.27
(1)–(3)	10.27
r 83	10.30, 10.48
r 84(1), (2)	10.44
(3)	10.45
(4)	10.49
(5)	10.46
r 85	10.48, 12.102
(1)–(3)	10.32
r 86	12.102
(1), (2)	10.35
(3)–(6)	10.36
(7)	10.36, 20.29
r 87	10.28, 10.48
(1)–(3)	10.28
r 88	10.36
(1)	10.42
(2)	10.43
(3)(a), (b)	10.43
(4), (5)	10.43
(6)	10.42
r 89	4.21, 10.13, 11.22
(1)(a), (b)	4.21
(2)	4.21
(3)(a), (b)	4.21
r 90(a)	8.11, 10.13
(b)	8.13, 8.19, 10.13
r 91(1)	10.54
(2)	10.60
(3)	10.57
r 92	10.66, 10.85
(1)	10.66, 10.70, 12.25

Land Registration Rules 2003,
SI 2003/1417 – *cont*

r 92(2)	10.66, 12.25
(b)	20.42
(3)–(6)	10.66
(7)	10.67
(b), (c)	12.24
(8)	10.66, 10.85
(9)	10.67
r 93	10.66, 10.68
(a), (b)	10.68
(d)–(k)	10.68
(s)	10.68
r 94	10.72, 10.94
(1)(a), (b)	10.73
(2)	10.74
(3)	10.75, 10.76
(4)(a), (b)	10.77
(5)	10.78
(6)	10.76, 10.77, 10.78
(7)	10.77, 10.78
(8)	10.79
r 95(1)	10.64
(2)	10.64
(a)	10.64
r 96(1), (2)	10.100
(3), (4)	10.101
(5)	10.52
r 97	10.97
(1)–(3)	10.97
r 98	10.94, 10.95, 12.107
(1)	10.96
(2)–(5)	10.95
(6)	10.94
(7)	10.96
r 99	10.98
r 100(1)	10.83
(2)	10.84
r 101	12.48, 12.56
r 102	12.49
(1)	12.49, 12.72
(2)	12.49
(3)	12.50, 12.72
r 103	12.10, 20.3
r 104	12.81
r 105(1)	12.52
(2)	12.53
(3)	12.54
(5), (6)	12.56
(7)	12.57
r 105(8)	12.58
r 106(1)	12.51, 12.55
(2)	12.55
r 107(1)	12.63
(2)	12.63
(a)–(d)	12.63
(e)	12.64
(3)	12.63
(4)	12.63
r 108(1)	12.68
(2), (3)	12.69
(4)	12.71
r 109	12.75
(1)	12.75
(2), (3)	12.76
r 110	12.39
(2)	12.39
(3)	12.41
r 111(1), (2)	12.28
r 112(1)	12.84
(2)	12.85
(3)	12.84
r 113	12.30, 12.103
(1)	12.30
(2)	12.31
(3), (4)	12.36
r 114(1)	12.87
(2)	12.88
(3), (4)	12.90
(5)	12.87
r 115	26.1
(1)	12.103
(2)	12.103
r 116	12.42
r 118(1), (2)	16.5
r 119	16.6
(1)	16.6
(c)	16.5
(2)–(8)	16.6
r 120(1), (2)	16.7
r 121	16.7
r 122	16.8
(1)–(4)	16.8
r 123(1)	16.11
(2)	14.7, 16.11
r 124(1)–(4)	3.17
(5), (6)	3.18
r 125	17.4, 17.5
(1)	14.7, 17.4
(2)–(4)	17.4
(5), (6)	17.4
r 126	22.7
(1)	22.7

Land Registration Rules 2003,
SI 2003/1417 – *cont*

r 126(2), (3)	22.8
r 127	22.6
(1), (2)	22.6
r 128	22.18
(1)–(3)	22.18
(5)	22.18
r 129	22.18
r 130	22.18, 22.23
(2)(a), (b)	22.23
r 131	18.13, 18.15, 18.32, 19.7
r 132	14.19, 18.10, 18.11, 18.12,
	18.28, 18.44, 18.45, 19.10
r 133	18.10
(2)	18.34
(3), (4)	18.10
r 134	18.11, 19.7
(1)–(6)	18.11
r 135(1)	18.12
(2)	18.12, 18.18, 18.34
(3), (4)	18.12
r 136	14.22, 18.13, 18.25, 18.27,
	18.29, 18.31, 19.11, 19.14, 19.15
(1)	18.13
(3), (4)	18.19
(5)	18.24
(6)	18.25
(7)	18.14
r 137	18.28, 18.30, 18.32
(1), (2)	18.28
(3)	18.29
(4), (5)	18.30
r 138(1)–(4)	18.31
r 139(1), (2)	18.32
r 140(1), (2)	18.34
(3)	18.36
(4)	18.37
r 143(1), (2)	18.11
r 144	18.44
(1), (2)	18.44
(3)(a), (b)	18.45
(4)	18.45
r 145(1), (2)	14.19
(3), (4)	14.19
r 146	14.16
(1)–(3)	14.19
r 147	14.22
(1)	19.8, 19.20
(2)	19.8
r 148(1)	19.11
(3)	19.11
r 149(1)	19.13
r 149(2)(b)	19.16
(3)	19.14, 19.15
r 150(1)	19.12
(3)	19.12
r 151	19.18
(1)	19.18
(4)	19.18
r 152	19.18
(1)	19.18
r 153(1), (2)	19.19
r 154	19.17
r 155(1)–(3)	19.20
r 156(1)	19.20
(3)	19.20
r 157(1)–(4)	19.16
r 158	19.23
r 159(2)	19.23
r 160	19.23
r 161	8.4
(1)–(3)	8.4
r 162	13.8, 20.22
(1)	13.8, 20.25
(2)	13.8
r 163	13.7, 20.23
(1)–(5)	8.5
r 164	8.5
r 165	14.10, 14.12
(1)	13.11
(2)	13.12
r 166	10.64, 14.10, 14.12
(1), (2)	13.14
r 167(1)	13.12, 13.14
(2)	13.10
r 168	22.18
(1)	13.17
(2), (3)	13.17
r 169	13.18
r 170	13.18
r 171(3)	13.37
r 172	8.5
(1)	10.14
(2)	10.65, 10.103
(3)	10.14, 10.103
r 173	1.18, 8.53, 8.54, 13.6
(1)	13.5, 14.7
(2)	13.5
r 174	20.13
(2)	20.13
r 175	20.14
(1)–(3)	20.14
r 176(1)	13.39
(2)	10.79, 13.39
(3)	10.68, 10.79

Land Registration Rules 2003,
  SI 2003/1417 – *cont*

r 176(4)	10.79, 13.39
r 177	13.41
r 178	13.41
(2)	10.79
r 179	13.39
r 180	13.40
r 181	13.20
(1)–(4)	13.21
r 182	2.25, 13.20
(1)–(4)	13.22
r 183	13.20
(1)–(4)	13.23
r 184(1), (2)	13.26
(3)–(5)	13.26
r 185	13.3, 13.33, 14.11
r 186	13.42, 20.15
rr 187–194	*Pt 6*
r 187	33.4
r 188	33.4
(1)	30.15, 30.56
(a)(i)	30.15, 33.16
(ii)	30.56
(b)	30.15, 30.58
(2)	30.16
(3)	30.57
r 189	30.26, 30.32, 33.4
r 190	33.4
(1)	30.32
(b)	30.32
(2)	30.27
r 191	33.4
r 192	33.4, 33.9
r 193	33.4, 33.10
r 194	20.42, 30.21, 33.4
(1)	14.11, 30.21, 30.22, 30.24
(2)	30.22
(3)	14.11, 30.24
r 195	23.13
(1)–(3)	23.13
(4)	23.14
(5)	23.13
r 197	10.97
(1)(a), (b)	20.41
(c)	20.31, 20.41
(2)	10.89, 20.41, 30.60
r 198	4.21, 5.3, 10.30, 12.55, 14.10, 14.12, 22.18
(1)	20.42
(2)	20.42
(d)	10.89
(3)	20.43

r 198(4)	8.30, 20.43
(5)	20.43
(6)	20.42, 20.44
(7)–(9)	20.43
r 199(1)	20.45
(g)	20.45
(3)–(6)	20.45
r 200(1)(a)	2.29
r 201	20.5
(1)	34.7
(2)(b)	34.7
(3)–(8)	34.7
(9)	34.7
r 202	34.8
r 203	21.4
(1)	2.26, 20.34
(2)	2.26, 10.20, 20.34
(3)	20.34
(4)	2.26, 20.34
(5)	20.34
(6)	2.26, 20.34
(7), (8)	20.34
r 204	20.35, 21.4
(1)–(6)	20.35
r 205	20.35
r 206(1)	20.2, 20.4
(2)	20.2, 20.8
(3)	20.37
(4)	20.4
r 207	20.4
r 208	20.4, 20.8
r 209	20.4, 20.8
r 210	20.7
r 211	20.7
r 212	8.39, 20.6
(1)–(3)	20.6
r 213	20.24
(1)–(5)	20.24
s 214(1)	13.27, 20.25
(2)	20.25
r 215	20.22
r 216	2.31, 5.13, 16.6, 20.19, 20.26, 30.26, 36.5
(1)	19.7, 30.26
(2)	19.7, 30.26, 36.5
(3)–(5)	36.5
r 217	10.30
(1)	2.26, 5.3, 10.109, 14.5, 14.16, 30.23, 30.26, 36.5
rr 218–223	10.106
r 218	10.107
r 219	10.107

Land Registration Rules 2003,
SI 2003/1417 – *cont*
r 220   20.45
r 221   10.107
   (2)–(5)   10.107
   (6)   10.108
r 222   10.109, 12.98
r 223   10.107, 10.110
   (2)–(4)   10.110
Sch 1   2.25, 2.26, 2.27, 20.2, 20.3,
          20.4, 20.5, 20.6, 20.8, 20.18,
                    20.25, 20.37, 26.11
Sch 2   14.19, 18.44, 18.45, 19.26,
                20.18, 20.26, 26.1, 34.7
   para 2(c)   12.103
Sch 3   20.2, 20.4, 20.8, 20.9,
                                              20.25
   Form 1   20.10
   Form 2   20.11, 20.12
   Form 3   20.12
   Form 4   20.13
   Form 5   20.14
   Form 6   20.15, 20.37
Sch 4   10.54, 10.57, 10.70,
                        12.24, 13.43, 20.42
   Form A   10.57, 10.64, 10.68,
           10.70, 10.73, 10.74, 10.105
   Form B   10.70, 10.77, 10.78
   Form C   10.70, 10.75
   Form D   10.70
   Form E   10.70, 10.79, 13.39
   Form F   10.70, 10.79
   Form G   10.70, 13.43, 20.15
   Form H   10.70, 13.43
   Form I   10.70, 13.43
   Form J   10.68, 10.70
   Form K   10.60, 10.68, 10.70
   Form L   10.68, 10.70
   Form M   10.70
   Form N   10.56, 10.68, 10.70
   Form O   10.70
   Form P   10.70, 12.24
   Form Q   10.70
   Form R   10.70
   Form S   10.70

Sch 4, Form T   10.70
   Form U   10.64, 10.70
   Form V   10.64, 10.70
   Form W   10.64, 10.70
   Form X   10.64, 10.70
   Form Y   10.64, 10.70
   Forms AA–HH   10.81
   Form AA   10.68, 10.70
   Form BB   10.68, 10.70
   Form CC   10.68, 10.70
   Form DD   10.68, 10.70
   Form EE   10.70
   Form FF   10.70
   Form GG   10.70
   Form HH   10.70
Sch 5   18.35, 18.36
Sch 6, Pts 1, 2   14.19
   Pt 3   19.14
   Pt 4   19.15
   Pt 5   19.23
Sch 7   13.42, 20.15
   paras 1–15   13.43
   para 5   20.15

Sch 8   20.15, 33.4
   para 1(1)   33.4
   para 1(2)   33.7
   para 2(a),(b)   33.7
   para 4   33.9
   para 5   33.8, 33.9
      (2), (3)   33.8
   para 6(2)(c)   33.7
   para 7   33.9
   para 8   33.7
   para 9   33.9
Sch 9   12.44, 12.47, 20.37, 20.38
   Forms A–F   20.38
Sch 11, para 2(2)   3.9
Sch 12, para 2(3), (4)   10.106
Land Registration (Referral to the
Adjudicator to HM Land Registry)
Rules 2003, SI 2003/2114   1.19, 34.4,
                                              34.12
Limited Liability Partnerships
Regulations 2001, SI 2001/1090   20.38

TABLE OF OTHER MATERIALS

References are to paragraph numbers.

Companies Registry Form 403A	12.101
Form ACD	12.16, 12.20, 20.2
Form ADV1	20.3, 20.5, 30.15, 30.17, 30.56
Form ADV2	20.3, 30.22
Form AN1	2.25, 10.19, 20.3, 20.5
Panel 11	10.21
Panel 14	10.21, 10.22
Form AP1	2.25, 5.11, 8.5, 8.33, 8.39, 8.42, 8.47, 8.49, 10.13, 10.85, 11.19, 12.22, 12.23, 12.49, 12.87, 12.88, 12.104, 13.8, 13.25, 13.31, 13.35, 16.11, 17.4, 17.6, 19.12, 20.3, 20.5, 20.6, 20.18, 20.39, 22.6, 22.18, 30.24
Panel 4	8.33, 8.47
Panel 5	8.49
Panel 6	8.39
Panel 10	11.19
Panel 11	12.22
Form AS1	8.29, 8.32, 10.67, 13.8, 20.3, 20.5
Panel 10	8.36
Form AS2	10.67, 12.42, 12.46, 12.47, 20.3, 20.5
Form AS3	8.29, 8.32, 10.67, 20.3, 20.5
Form CC	12.39, 12.40, 20.3
Form CCD	10.110, 12.98, 20.3
Form CCT	5.18, 20.3
Panel 5	5.18
Form CH1	10.67, 12.10, 12.11, 12.12, 12.13, 12.22, 20.3
Panel 7	10.67, 12.24, 12.69
Form CH2	12.35, 12.69, 12.70, 20.3, 20.5
Form CH3	12.76, 12.77, 20.3
Form CH6	12.34
Form CI (formerly Form 102)	18.11, 20.3, 20.5
Form CIT	18.10, 18.36, 18.37, 20.3
Certificates A–M	18.36
Form CN1	10.28, 12.99, 20.3
Form CS	20.3, 20.5, 20.7
Form CT1	5.6, 20.3
Form D1	2.25, 8.26, 11.19
Form DI	4.19, 20.3, 20.5
Form DB	16.5, 20.3
Panel 9	16.5
Form DL	2.26, 8.33, 8.39, 8.42, 20.3, 20.5
Form DS1	12.87, 12.89, 12.90, 12.91, 12.92, 12.93, 12.94, 12.96, 12.100, 12.103, 12.104, 20.3
Box 7	12.96
Form DS2	12.87, 12.104, 20.3

Form DS2E	12.104
Form DS3	12.88, 12.89, 12.90, 12.91, 12.92, 12.93,
	12.94, 12.96, 12.100, 12.103, 20.3
Box 2	12.88
Box 7	12.96
Form END1	12.103, 12.104
Form EX1	18.18, 20.3
Form EX1A	18.10, 18.18, 20.3
Form EX2	18.28, 18.29, 20.3
Panels 9, 10	18.28
Form EX3	18.31, 20.3
Form FR1	2.25, 4.19, 8.33, 12.22, 13.8, 20.3, 20.5
Panel 4	2.34
Panel 11	8.36
Panel 12	4.19
para 6	2.26
Form HC1	18.44, 20.3
Form ID1	2.27
Form ID2	2.27
Form L1	1.18, 8.39
Form MH1	10.27, 20.3
Form MH2	10.27, 20.3
Form MH3	19.23, 20.3
Form MH4	20.2
Form NAP	20.3, 30.27, 30.32, 30.34
Panel 5	30.31
Form OC1 (formerly Form 109)	18.11, 20.3, 20.5
Form OC2 (formerly Form 110)	18.12, 18.36, 20.3
Form OS1 (formerly Form 94A)	19.9, 19.10, 19.20, 20.3
Form OS2 (formerly Form 94B)	19.9, 19.10, 19.20, 20.3
Form OS3 (formerly Form 94C)	19.20, 20.3
Form PIC (formerly Form 111)	18.10, 18.36, 20.3
Form PN1	14.21, 18.36, 20.3
Form PRD1	20.3, 20.5, 34.7
Form PRD2	20.3, 20.5, 34.7
Form RD1	20.2
Form RX1	2.25, 10.66, 10.67, 10.85, 12.25, 12.26, 12.35, 12.107, 20.3, 20.5
Form RX2	10.100, 20.3
Form RX3	10.97, 20.3
Form RX4	10.96, 12.107, 20.3
Form SC	12.52, 12.53, 12.54, 20.3
Form SIF	14.19, 20.3
Form SIM	14.19, 20.3
Form TP1	8.29, 8.33, 10.67, 20.3, 20.5
Panel 12	8.36
Form TP2	8.29, 8.33, 10.67, 20.3, 20.5
Form TP3	8.29, 8.33, 10.67, 20.3, 20.5
Form TR1	8.29, 8.33, 10.67, 20.3, 20.5, 26.11
Box 10	25.3
Panel 11	8.36
Form TR2	8.29, 8.33, 10.67, 20.3, 20.5
Form TR3	10.67, 12.42, 12.43, 12.45, 20.3, 20.5
Form TR4	10.67, 12.42, 12.45, 20.3, 20.5

Form TR5   8.29, 8.33, 10.67, 20.3, 20.5
Form UN1   2.25, 10.30, 20.3, 20.5
Form UN2   10.32, 12.102, 20.3
Form UN3   10.43, 20.3
Form UN4   10.35, 12.102, 20.3
Form UT1   3.17, 20.3
Form WCT   5.8, 10.109, 12.98, 20.3
Form 53   12.97
Form 69   20.44

Land Registry Practice Guides
PG1 First Registrations   1.23, *Pt 1*
    para 5.3   2.25, 2.26, 2.34
    para 8.4   2.24
PG2 First Registration of Title where Deeds have been Lost or Destroyed   2.27
PG3 Cautions Against First Registration   5.1
    para 3.3   5.6
PG4 Adverse Possession of Registered Land
    para 4   30.15
    para 4.1   30.15
    para 4.2.1   30.18
    para 5.3   30.21
    para 6   30.30
    para 7   30.33
    para 10   30.24
PG6 Devolution on the Death of a Registered Proprietor
    para 2.1   8.5
    para 2.2   13.8
    para 3   8.5
PG7 Entry of Price Paid or Value Stated on the Register   8.32
PG8 Execution of Deeds   8.27, 20.37, 20.39
    para 7.1   20.38
    para 7.2   20.39
PG9 Powers of Attorney and Registered Land   20.9
    para 3.6   20.12
    para 6   20.11
    para 7   20.10
PG12 Official Searches and Outline Applications   19.7
    paras 4.1.1–4.1.4   19.16
    para 5.2   19.17
    para 5.3   19.18
    Pt 6   19.9
    para 6.3   19.10
    s 10   19.25
PG14 Charities   13.38
PG15 Overriding Interests and Their Disclosure   4.12
PG18 Franchises   2.5, 14.16
PG19 Notices, Restrictions and the Protection of Third Party Interests in the Register   10.2
    para 3.3.2   10.25, 10.45
    para 3.3.3   10.31, 10.46
    para 3.4.2   10.16
    para 3.6.2   10.15, 10.21, 10.22

PG19 Notices, Restrictions and the Protection of Third Party Interests in the Register – *cont*
    para 3.6.3   10.23
    para 3.7.3   10.30
    para 3.9.1   10.47
    para 3.9.2   10.42, 10.43
    para 4.3.2   10.70
    para 4.4.4   10.89
    para 4.6.3   10.83
    para 4.7.3   10.96
    para 4.7.4   10.99
    para 4.8.1   10.53
    para 4.8.3   10.100
    para 6.5   10.106
PG21 Using Transfer Forms for Less Straightforward Transactions
    para 1.2   8.33
    para 2   8.34
    paras 3–5   8.35
    para 68.34
PG22 Manors   8.11
PG29 Registration of Legal Charges and Deeds of Variation of Charge
    para 3   12.15
    para 4   12.22
    para 5   12.25, 12.26
    para 6   12.69
    para 7   12.75, 12.77
    para 9   12.23
    para 11   12.29
    para 12   12.35
    para 12.1   12.37
    para 12.2   12.32, 12.33, 12.34, 12.36
PG30 Approval of Mortgage Documentation
    para 3   12.17
    para 4   12.19
    para 5   12.20
    para 6   12.19
    para 7   12.18, 12.21
    para 9   12.14
    App B   12.16
PG31 Discharge of Charges
    para 3.1   12.89
    para 3.2   12.97
    para 3.3   12.91
    para 3.4   12.92
    para 3.6   12.94
    para 3.7   12.95, 12.96
    para 3.8   12.88
    para 4.2.1   12.100
    para 4.2.2   12.101
    para 4.3   12.102
    para 5   12.86
    para 6   12.105

PG31 Discharge of Charges – *cont*

    para 6.1   12.103

    para 7   12.107

    App C   12.104

    App E   12.103

PG32 Applications affecting One or More Land Registry Office   36.3

PG33 Large Scale Applications (Calculation of Fees)   36.11

PG34 Personal Insolvency   13.9

PG35 Corporate Insolvency   13.24

    para 3   13.27

    para 3.3   13.28

    para 3.4   13.29

    para 3.5   13.30

    para 4.1   13.25

    para 4.2   13.31

    para 4.3   13.31

    para 5.1   13.32

    para 6   13.3

    para 7.2   13.33

    para 7.3   13.3

    para 7.3.2   13.5

    para 7.4   13.6

    para 7.5.1   13.6

    para 8.1   13.35

PG36 Administration and Receivership   13.24

    para 4   13.25

    para 4.3   13.26

    para 4.4   13.26

PG37 Objections and Disputes   34.4

    para 2   34.3

    paras 3–6   34.12

PG38 Costs

    para 2   34.8

PG39 Rectification and Indemnity   22.2, 23.23

    para 2.1   22.6

    para 3.1   22.18

    paras 5–11   23.1

    para 5.2   23.23

    para 8.2.2   23.23

PG40 Land Registry Plans

    para 3.3.2   16.5

    para 3.3.4   16.5

    para 3.3.5   16.5

    Pt 4   14.17

    Pt 6   2.26

PG42 Upgrading the Class of Title   3.13

PG48 Implied Covenants   25.1

    para 4   25.6

    para 5   25.7

PG51 Areas Served by Land Registry Offices   36.3

PG52 Easements Claimed by Prescription and Statutory Rights of Way for Vehicles

    paras 5–7   8.49

    para 6.1   8.49

PG52 Easements Claimed by Prescription and Statutory Rights of Way for Vehicles – *cont*
    para 7.2   8.47
PG57 Exempting Documents from the General Right to
  Inspect and Copy   18.13
    para 3.1   18.18, 18.20, 18.21, 18.22, 18.23
    para 3.2   18.18
    para 5   18.27
    para 6   18.29
    para 6.1   18.28
PB1 Lost or Destroyed Certificates – Effect of the Land Registration
  Act 2002   1.23, 21.4
PB2 Land and Charge Certificates – Effect of the Land Registration
  Act 2002   21.4
    para 2   21.4
    para 3   21.5
    para 4   21.4

Standard Conditions of Sale 3rd Edition   2.41
    para 3.4   2.41
Standard Conditions of Sale 4th Edition 2003
    Condition 4.1.1   24.5
    Condition 4.1.2   24.5
    Condition 4.6.4   25.5
    Condition 8.2.4   24.6

Directions of the Chief Land Registrar 12 May 1997   18.7
Notice 1 of the Chief Land Registrar 2 October 2003   18.11, 18.12, 19.10, 19.20,
                                                                                                            19.23, 19.26
Notice 2 of the Chief Land Registrar 2 October 2003   18.11, 18.12, 19.10, 19.20
Notice 3 of the Chief Land Registrar 2 October 2003   18.10, 18.11, 18.12, 19.10,
                                                                                                            19.23, 19.26
    para 2   20.26, 26.1
Notice 4 of the Chief Land Registrar 2 October 2003   18.10, 18.11, 18.12, 19.10, 19.20,
                                                                                                            19.23, 19.26
Notice 5 of the Chief Land Registrar 2 October 2003   18.11, 18.12
Notice 6 of the Chief Land Registrar 2 October 2003   18.10, 18.11, 18.12, 19.10,
                                                                                                            19.20, 19.26

Council Regulation (EC) No 1346/2000 on Insolvency
  Proceedings 2000 OJ L 160/1   13.37
    Art 3(1)   13.37
    Art 22   13.37

European Convention for the Protection Human Rights and
  Fundamental Freedoms 1950   4.14
    Art 6.1   34.1

TABLE OF ABBREVIATIONS

AEA 1925	Administration of Estates Act 1925
APPR 2003	Adjudicator to Her Majesty's Land Registry (Practice and Procedure) Rules 2003
ATJA 1999	Access to Justice Act 1999
CLSA 1990	Courts and Legal Services Act 1990
CPR 1998	Civil Procedure Rules 1998
CRA 1965	Commons Registration Act 1965
ECA 2000	Electronic Communications Act 2000
EDID	edited information document
EID	exempt information document
FIA 2000	Freedom of Information Act 2000
GLAA 1999	Greater London Authority Act 1999
HA 1985	Housing Act 1985
IA 1986	Insolvency Act 1986
LA 1980	Limitation Act 1980
LCA 1925	Land Charges Act 1925
LCA 1972	Land Charges Act 1972
LPA 1925	Law of Property Act 1925
LPA 1969	Law of Property Act 1969
LP(MP)A 1989	Law of Property (Miscellaneous Provisions) Act 1989
LP(MP)A 1994	Law of Property (Miscellaneous Provisions) Act 1994
LRA 1925	Land Registration Act 1925
LRA 1986	Land Registration Act 1986
LRA 1988	Land Registration Act 1988
LRA 1997	Land Registration Act 1997
LRA 2002	Land Registration Act 2002
LRORR 1991	Land Registration (Open Register) Rules 1991
LROSR 1993	Land Registration (Official Searches) Rules 1993
LRFO 2003	Land Registration Fee Order 2003
LRR 1925	Land Registration Rules 1925
LRR 2003	Land Registration Rules 2003
LRRAR 2003	Land Registration (Referred to the Adjudicator to HM Land Registry) Rules 2003
MCA 1980	Magistrates' Courts Act 1980
NLIS	National Land Information Service
SCA 1981	Supreme Court Act 1981
SCS	Standard Conditions of Sale (3rd edn)
SLA 1925	Settled Land Act 1925
TA 1925	Trustee Act 1925
TLATA 1996	Trusts of Land and Appointment of Trustees Act 1996
TPO1 2003	Land Registration Act 2002 (Transitional Provisions) Order 2003
TPO2 2003	Land Registration Act 2002 (Transitional Provisions) (No 2) Order 2003

CHAPTER 1

BACKGROUND: THE LAND REGISTRATION ACT 2002, ITS UNDERLYING PRINCIPLES AND ITS IMPLEMENTATION

LAND REGISTRATION IN ENGLAND AND WALES

1.1   The Land Registration Act 2002 (LRA 2002) is the culmination of a legislative process that began with the Land Registry Act 1862.[1] The essentials of the scheme of title registration that was adopted in England and Wales were first put forward in 1844.[2] However, it was not until 1875 that that scheme was implemented by the Land Transfer Act.[3] It was that Act that founded the Land Registry and the modern system of title registration. Further significant changes were made to the law by the Land Transfer Act 1897, the Law of Property Act 1922 and the Law of Property (Amendment) Act 1924 before the law was consolidated in the Land Registration Act 1925 (LRA 1925). That Act was itself significantly amended over the years, most recently by the Land Registration Acts of 1986, 1988 and 1997.

1.2   The LRA 1925 had always been seen as the poor relation amongst the six great statutes that made up Lord Birkenhead's reforms of 1925.[4] It was the subject of judicial and academic criticism.[5] Although it was made to work comparatively well, thanks to the ingenuity and enterprise of HM Land Registry, its replacement was inevitable. The appreciation that dealings with land, like most other forms of commerce, would have to change from a paper-based system to an electronic one, provided the catalyst for that replacement.

---

[1]   The Land Registry Act 1862 remained on the statute book until its repeal on 13 October 2003, when the LRA 2002 was brought into force: see LRA 2002, s 122.

[2]   By Robert Wilson, a solicitor. See J Stuart Anderson, *Lawyers and the Making of English Land Law 1832–1940* (1992), pp 58, 63 et seq.

[3]   It differed significantly from the system of title registration introduced by the Land Registry Act 1862.

[4]   The Acts were the Trustee Act 1925 (TA 1925), Law of Property Act 1925 (LPA 1925), LRA 1925, Land Charges Act 1925 (LCA 1925) (now replaced by Land Charges Act 1972 (LCA 1972)) and Administration of Estates Act 1925 (AEA 1925).

[5]   See, eg, *Megarry & Wade's Law of Real Property* (Sweet & Maxwell, 5th edn, 1984), p 196: 'legislation of exceptionally low quality, which is in need of a thorough overhaul'; a comment cited and endorsed by Nourse LJ in *Clark v Chief Land Registrar* [1994] Ch 370, p 382.

THE GENESIS OF THE LAND REGISTRATION ACT 2002

1.3 The LRA 2002, which is the most significant change to property law since Lord Birkenhead's reforms, received Royal Assent on 26 February 2002 and was brought fully into force on 13 October 2003.[1] The Act replaced all existing legislation on land registration.[2] The reason why the new Act is so significant is that it will introduce a completely new system of conveyancing within a comparatively short time. The present paper-based system will be replaced by a wholly electronic one. The Act is also designed to change the perception of registration. It creates a system whereby it will be the fact of registration that confers title rather than merely recording a title that has already been created. This fundamental change in the nature and perception of registration of title, which is explained more fully in the following paragraphs, has important implications for the interpretation of the Act.[3]

The three joint Reports of the Law Commission and HM Land Registry

1.4 The LRA 2002 was the outcome of a joint project between HM Land Registry and the Law Commission which had begun in 1995. In the course of the project, the Registry and the Commission published three joint Reports.[4]

1.5 The first and shortest Report was intended to deal with certain pressing matters.[5] The draft Bill that was attached to that Report was enacted with minor changes as the Land Registration Act 1997 (LRA 1997).[6] The principal objective of that Act was to increase the speed at which unregistered land was brought on to the register. To achieve this goal the Act substantially increased the number of dispositions of unregistered land that triggered compulsory registration.[7] It also made it possible for the Lord Chancellor to introduce

---

[1]   There were four Commencement Orders. The first, the Land Registration Act 2002 (Commencement No 1) Order 2003, SI 2003/935, brought into force LRA 2002, ss 128–132, 134(1) and 136 on 4 April 2002 (certain supplementary and final provisions). The second, the Land Registration Act 2002 (Commencement No 2) Order 2003, SI 2003/1028, brought into force LRA 2002, s 107, Sch 9 and Sch 11, para 28 on 28 April 2003 (the provisions on the Adjudicator). The third, the Land Registration Act 2002 (Commencement No 3) Order 2003, SI 2003/1612, brought into force LRA 2002, s 102 (power to prescribe fees) on 27 June 2003. The fourth, the Land Registration Act 2002 (Commencement No 4) Order, SI 2003/1725 brought the remainder of the Act into force on 13 October 2003 with the exception of LRA 2002, s 98(1) and Sch 6, para 5(4), (5) (provisions concerning adverse possession: see paras **30.48**, **32.2**).
[2]   See Sch 13 to the LRA 2002.
[3]   See paras **1.20–1.22**.
[4]   The Law Commission had previously published two Reports on Land Registration, proposing the replacement of the LRA 1925: see (1987) Law Com No 158 and (1988) Law Com No 173. These Reports were not written jointly with HM Land Registry and neither was accepted by the Government of the day.
[5]   (1995) Law Com No 235.
[6]   Although it was introduced as a Private Peer's Bill by Lord Browne-Wilkinson, it had Government support.
[7]   See LRA 1925, ss 123, 123A, as substituted and inserted by LRA 1997.

differential fees to encourage voluntary first registration.[1] In addition to these two measures, the Act also reformed the provisions of the LRA 1925 governing indemnity.[2]

1.6 The second Report, *Land Registration for the Twenty-First Century*,[3] took the form of a very substantial consultative document. Views were sought on wide-ranging proposals to replace the existing legislation on land registration with a new and very different Act. At the core of the proposals were two themes. The first was that registered conveyancing should move from a paper-based system to an entirely electronic one. The second was that the principles of registered land should be developed according to the logic and potential of a registered system (especially an electronic registered system), even though there would in consequence be marked differences as a matter of substantive law between registered and unregistered land. One striking illustration of the second theme was the proposal that the law of adverse possession as it applied to registered land should be recast so as to reflect the fact that the basis of registered title was registration and not possession (as it is in relation to unregistered land).[4] The second Report provoked a good deal of comment and debate. However, the great majority of the proposals in it were accepted on consultation and the responses formed the basis upon which Parliamentary Counsel at the Law Commission drafted a new Land Registration Bill. There was further consultation during the course of the drafting process with the Crown in relation to the registration of Crown land,[5] with the lending industry as regards further advances,[6] and generally, on the development of electronic conveyancing.[7]

1.7 The third joint Report, *Land Registration for the Twenty-First Century: A Conveyancing Revolution*,[8] comprised the draft Land Registration Bill together with a detailed commentary on the Bill running to some 370 pages and explanatory notes.[9] According to the Report:

'The fundamental objective of the Bill is that, under the system of electronic dealing with land that it seeks to create, the register should be a complete and accurate reflection of the state of the title of the land at any given time, so that it is

---

[1] See LRA 1925, s 145(3), (3A), as substituted and inserted by LRA 1997.
[2] See LRA 1925, s 83, as substituted by LRA 1997.
[3] (1998) Law Com No 254.
[4] This distinction has long been recognised by many Commonwealth countries that have Torrens systems of title registration.
[5] See Chapter 6.
[6] See para **12.60**.
[7] See para **26.6**.
[8] (2001) Law Com No 271. It was published on 10 July 2001 – after the Bill had been introduced into Parliament.
[9] A separate set of explanatory notes was published with the Bill when it was introduced into Parliament. These notes were drafted by the Lord Chancellor's Department rather than by the Law Commission.

possible to investigate title to land on line, with the absolute minimum of additional enquiries and inspections.'[1]

In other words, the aim was for the first time to create a conclusive register, so far as it was possible. This would facilitate conveyancing by significantly reducing the enquiries that would have to be made. It would also necessarily make title more secure.

1.8   The Report accepted that the aim of a conclusive register could only be achieved by rethinking the way in which conveyancing was undertaken. At present, there is necessarily a period of time between the making of a disposition of registered land and its subsequent registration. This is because the disposition has to be submitted to HM Land Registry for registration, which inevitably takes some time. It follows that that register *cannot* at present reflect the true state of the title at any given moment. The Report acknowledged that the only way in which this goal could be achieved was if dispositions of registered land were simultaneously registered. To make that possible, not only would there have to be an electronic conveyancing system, but also the process of registration would have to be initiated by practitioners rather than by the Registry.[2] The Report also accepted that the other obvious consequence of the fundamental objective was the elimination of overriding interests – unregistered interests that bind a registered proprietor on first registration or on the making of a registered disposition – so far as this could be done.[3] The Bill reflected these aspirations. The Bill also contained provisions to implement a new system of adverse possession for registered land along the lines proposed in the second Report.

1.9   Although this third and final Report recommended certain extensions to compulsory first registration (that are reflected in the Act), it did not propose any mechanisms to compel the registration of the remaining unregistered land in England and Wales. This was so even though the Law Commission and HM Land Registry considered that all such remaining land *should* be registered as quickly as possible. The Report did, however, recommend that, 5 years after the Bill was brought into force, consideration should be given as to how all the remaining unregistered land might be brought on to the register.[4] There were three reasons for the delay. The first was that the effects of the changes made by the LRA 1997 and the Bill itself to compel or encourage first registration should be given an opportunity to work. Secondly, it was not easy to devise mechanisms for bringing the remaining titles on to the register that were proportionate to the intended

---

[1]   (2001) Law Com No 271, para 1.5.
[2]   Ibid, para 1.7.
[3]   Ibid, para 1.8.
[4]   Ibid, paras 2.9–2.13.

goal.[1] Thirdly, the changes that the Bill would bring about were such as to stretch the resources of both the Land Registry and the legal profession for the next few years.[2]

THE LAND REGISTRATION BILL IN PARLIAMENT

1.10   The Land Registration Bill was introduced into the House of Lords on 21 June 2001, the day after the Queen's Speech following the General Election.[3] It had its Second Reading on 3 July 2001.[4] In terms of the Bill's policy, there were no significant changes to it during its passage through Parliament.[5] The only successful amendments were Government amendments, although a number of these were prompted by points raised in debate by the Opposition parties. Those parties broadly welcomed the Bill and the debates were, in general, on points of detail, not principle.[6]

RULES AND ORDERS MADE UNDER THE ACT

Introduction

1.11   The main reason for the substantial delay between the passing of the Act on 26 February 2002 and its coming into force on 13 October 2003, was the need to make the extensive body of rules under it that are necessary to support its operation.[7] All rules, regulations and orders under the Act are

---

1   The underlying problem is the cost of deducing title to such land to enable it to be registered. Even if there were no fee for registration, those conveyancing costs would have to be incurred.

2   When the Bill was in Committee in the House of Commons, there was a lively debate, triggered by Mr Adrian Saunders MP (Liberal Democrat) about the need to compel the registration of all land in England and Wales.

3   In that Speech, Her Majesty stated that 'Legislation will be introduced to reform the system of land registration to promote greater electronic conveyancing'. The proposals for the reform of land registration were in the Labour Party manifesto for the Election ('We will develop a modern basis for land registration to make conveyancing faster and cheaper') and were, accordingly, part of the Government's programme for the 2001–2 Session of Parliament.

4   *Hansard* (HL), vol 626, col 726. The timetable (with references to debates where relevant) was thereafter as follows: Committee (House of Lords), 17 and 19 July 2001 (*Hansard* (HL), vol 626, cols 1384 and 1600); Report (House of Lords), 30 October 2001 (*Hansard* (HL), vol 627, col 1301); Third Reading (House of Lords), 8 November 2001 (*Hansard* (HL), vol 628, col 307); Introduction and First Reading (House of Commons), 8 November 2001; Second Reading Committee (House of Commons), 29 November 2001 (*Hansard* (HC), Session 2001–2, Standing Committee Debates, Standing Committee D), Second Reading, 3 December 2001; Committee, 11 and 13 December 2001 (*Hansard* (HC), Session 2001–2, Standing Committee Debates, Standing Committee D; Report and Third Reading, 11 February 2002 (*Hansard* (HC), vol 380, col 23); Consideration of Commons' Amendments, 26 February 2002 (*Hansard* (HL), vol 631, col 1322); Royal Assent, 26 February 2002.

5   The Opposition did force a number of divisions, but none was successful.

6   There was, however, the interesting spectacle of the Conservative Party apparently opposing the much tougher provisions on adverse possession: see *Hansard* (HL), vol 627, col 1376.

7   For rules under the Act, see (2001) Law Com No 271, Part XVII.

made by the Lord Chancellor.[1] That power is exercisable by statutory instrument.[2]

1.12 The main changes that the LRA 2002 makes in relation to rules, regulations and orders are as follows.

— Rules are generally made under specific rule-making powers rather than (as had been the case previously) under the residual rule-making power.
— Rules are subject to a higher degree of parliamentary scrutiny than were those made under LRA 1925.
— The composition of the Rules Committee has been enlarged to include persons who will represent the interests of licensed conveyancers, chartered surveyors and consumers.

Rules under the LRA 1925

1.13 Rules have been an essential feature of the workings of the land registration system under the LRA 1925. The use of rules enabled land registration to evolve because it was much easier to change them than it was to obtain amending legislation.[3] Not only were the rules made under the LRA 1925 numerous[4] but they also contained some of the fundamental concepts of the registered system, such as the general boundaries rule[5] and the system of official searches.[6] Indeed, what was in primary legislation and what was in rules sometimes appeared arbitrary. Three other features of the old law may be mentioned. The first was that land registration rules were subject to no effective parliamentary scrutiny. They were merely required to be laid.[7] Secondly, the rule-making powers were contained in one section – s 144 of the LRA 1925. They did not arise in context in the Act. Thirdly, in practice, despite the long list of rule-making powers in s 144(1), for many years almost all rules were made under the residual rule-making power found in s 144(1)(xxxi).[8]

---

[1] LRA 2002, s 128(1).
[2] Ibid, s 128(2).
[3] Within the lifetime of LRA 1925, registered conveyancing moved from a system, used by few, that had to be conducted by personal attendance at HM Land Registry, to one that was the norm and where certain applications could be lodged electronically. That transformation was accommodated by changes in the rules.
[4] The main set of rules was found in LRR 1925, but there were also others, such as LROSR 1993.
[5] See LRR 1925, r 278.
[6] See LROSR 1993.
[7] LRA 1925, s 144(3).
[8] 'For regulating any matter to be prescribed or in respect of which rules are to or may be made under this Act and any other matter or thing, whether similar or not to those above mentioned, in respect of which it may be expedient to make rules for the purpose of carrying this Act into execution.'

Rules under LRA 2002

1.14   The approach to rules under the LRA 2002 is very different. First, in general, rule-making powers are found where they arise in the Act, although certain miscellaneous and general rule-making powers are found in Sch 10 to the Act.[1] Although the LRA 2002 does contain a residual rule-making power,[2] it is just that. In the great majority of cases, rules have been made pursuant to a specific power. This means that it is possible to read the rules in conjunction with the provisions of the Act. This should make it easier to operate the new legislation. Secondly, considerable attention has been paid by the draftsman in deciding upon the allocation of material between the Act and the rules made under it. Thirdly, the degree of parliamentary scrutiny is greater, at least in theory. Following a recommendation by the Delegated Powers Scrutiny Committee of the House of Lords, the Bill was amended in its passage through Parliament so that the great majority of rules made under the Act will be subject to annulment in pursuance of a resolution of either House of Parliament.[3] Certain rules connected with e-conveyancing are subject to an even higher degree of scrutiny. Rules that are made under s 93 (by which e-conveyancing may be made compulsory for specific dispositions)[4] and the first three paragraphs of Sch 5 (network access agreements)[5] are subject to affirmative resolution procedure.[6] In other words, they will have to be laid before and approved by resolution of each House of Parliament. It should also be noted that some rules can only be made after prior consultation by the Lord Chancellor.[7]

1.15   Not all the rules, regulations and orders that can be made under the LRA 2002 are land registration rules.[8] Land registration rules are those that explain how land registration is to be conducted. Thus, for example, rules about adjudication and the forwarding to the registrar of companies of applications relating to certain registered charges are not land registration rules.[9] Orders (such as fee orders[10] and orders made in connection with the

---

[1]   See LRA 2002, s 126. For the rule-making powers under Sch 10, see paras **1.17**, **2.24**, **20.17**, **21.3**, and Chapter 24.

[2]   See LRA 2002, Sch 10, para 8.

[3]   LRA 2002, s 128(4). Whether this will lead to greater parliamentary scrutiny is questionable if the treatment of the Bill itself is anything to go by. During the course of Report and Third Reading in the House of Commons – the only stages of the Bill that were discussed on the floor of the House of Commons – the number of Members of Parliament present was in single figures.

[4]   See paras **28.2**.

[5]   See paras **27.14** et seq.

[6]   LRA 2002, s 128(5).

[7]   See, eg, ibid, ss 93(5) (power to require dispositions to be made electronically with simultaneous registration), 118(3) (power to reduce length of registrable leases), Sch 5, para 11(1) (power to make network access rules).

[8]   See ibid, s 132(1), and the definition of 'land registration rules'.

[9]   See ibid, Part 11 and s 121 respectively.

[10]   Ibid, s 102.

bringing into force of the Act[1]) and regulations (such as regulations about the carrying out of functions of the registrar or Adjudicator in any vacancy in the office[2]) are clearly not land registration rules.

The Rules Committee

1.16   Whatever may be the position in relation to parliamentary scrutiny, the LRA 2002, like the LRA 1925 before it, provides that the Lord Chancellor can only exercise his power to make land registration rules with the advice and assistance of the Rules Committee.[3] Under the LRA 2002, the composition of the Rules Committee is wider than it was under the LRA 1925.[4] Indeed, its composition was widened during the parliamentary passage of the legislation. As under the LRA 1925, the Committee is chaired by a judge of the Chancery Division of the High Court, nominated by the Lord Chancellor.[5] Again, as under the LRA 1925, it also includes the Chief Land Registrar,[6] and a person nominated by each of the General Council of the Bar and the Council of the Law Society.[7] It no longer includes a person nominated by DEFRA.[8] For the first time, there is a person nominated by each of the Council of Mortgage Lenders, the Council of Licensed Conveyancers and the Royal Institution of Chartered Surveyors,[9] together with a person with experience in, and knowledge of, consumer affairs.[10] As under the LRA 1925, the Lord Chancellor may nominate to be a member of the Rules Committee, any person who appears to him to have qualifications or experience which would be of value to the Committee in considering any matter with which it is concerned.[11] The Rules Committee has, over the years, proved itself to be a very effective and critical scrutinising body and it is to be hoped that it will continue to be so.

General rule-making powers

1.17   As has been explained above, most of the rule-making powers in the LRA 2002 are found in the context in which they arise. However, there are a number of miscellaneous and general rule-making powers that are collected in Sch 10 to the Act. The miscellaneous powers are explained in various parts of

---

[1] LRA 2002, ss 134(1), 136(2).
[2] See ibid, s 100(2), Sch 9, para 5. For those rules, see para **1.19**.
[3] Ibid, s 127(1). In relation to other rules, the Lord Chancellor will no doubt seek the views of the Rules Committee even though he is not required to do so.
[4] Ibid, s 127(2).
[5] Ibid, s 127(2)(a). It is presently Mr Justice Blackburne.
[6] Ibid, s 127(2)(b).
[7] Ibid, s 127(2)(c), (d).
[8] Formerly MAFF. This was at the request of the Department.
[9] LRA 2002, s 127(2)(e)–(g).
[10] Ibid, s 127(2)(f).
[11] Ibid, s 127(2)(g).

this book where it is appropriate. Of the four general rule-making powers contained in Part 2 of Sch 10:

— the power to make rules in relation to applications[1] is explained in Chapter 20;[2]
— the residual rule-making power[3] has been mentioned above;[4]
— there is a power to make rules about the form, content and service of notices under the Act;[5] and
— there is a power to make rules about the form of any statement required under an enactment to be included in an instrument effecting a registrable disposition or a disposition which triggers a requirement of registration.[6]

The last power is required because, by statute, some dispositions of land have to contain certain particulars. Examples of such cases include:

— certain dispositions by charities;[7] and
— a vesting deed in favour of a tenant for life under the SLA 1925.[8]

The Land Registration Rules 2003

1.18   The principal rules made under the LRA 2002 are the Land Registration Rules 2003 (LRR 2003).[9] These came into force together with the Act on 13 October 2003. The LRR 2003 make detailed provision for the conduct of registered conveyancing and extensive reference is made to them throughout this book. A draft of the LRR 2003 was put out for consultation on 27 August 2002,[10] and the rules were revised in the light of the responses. They were then referred to the Rules Committee for consideration. The Rules were made by the Lord Chancellor in the light of the advice given to him by the Rules Committee. It is almost certain that there will be revisions to the LRR 2003 within a year or so. One reason for this is that certain matters that arose out of consultation on the draft rules were unresolved at the time when the LRR 2003 had to be finalised. Two examples may be given of this. First, the proposal on consultation for a standard form of lease, using Form L1, was

---

[1]   LRA 2002, Sch 10, para 6.
[2]   See paras **20.16** et seq.
[3]   LRA 2002, Sch 10, para 8.
[4]   See para **1.14**.
[5]   LRA 2002. Sch 10, para 5. In particular, the rules may require that an address for service be supplied and for its entry in the register. They may also make provision about the time for the service of notices, the way in which service is made, and when service is regarded as having taken place: Sch 10, para 5(2). See further, paras **20.40–20.45**.
[6]   Ibid, Sch 10, para 7.
[7]   Charities Act 1993, ss 37, 39.
[8]   SLA 1925, s 5.
[9]   SI 2003/1417.
[10]   Land Registration Rules 2003 – A Land Registry Consultation.

withdrawn for further consideration because of the critical response that it received.[1] Secondly, it proved impossible to resolve certain technical difficulties over the implementation of the provisions of the LRA 2002 on the escheat of registered freeholds,[2] and the relevant rule is very much of a holding nature until those difficulties can be resolved.[3]

Other Rules and Orders

1.19   The LRR 2003 are not the only rules that have been made under the Act.

(a)   The Land Registration (Referral to the Adjudicator to HM Land Registry) Rules 2003[4] (LRRAR 2003) deal with the procedure by which disputes arising out of applications under the LRA 2002 are referred to the Adjudicator for resolution.[5]

(b)   The Adjudicator to Her Majesty's Land Registry (Practice and Procedure) Rules 2003[6] (APPR 2003) deal with the practice and procedure before the Adjudicator.[7]

(c)   Certain orders have been made under the LRA 2002.

　　(i)   There are two orders which make transitional provisions in connection with the LRA 2002, namely the Land Registration Act 2002 (Transitional Provisions) Order 2003[8] (TPO1 2003), and the Land Registration Act 2002 (Transitional Provisions) (No 2) Order 2003[9] (TPO2 2003).

　　(ii)   The Land Registration (Proper Office) Order 2003[10] designates particular offices of the Registry as the proper office for the receipt of specified descriptions of application under the LRA 2002.

---

[1]   See the Press Release from HM Land Registry of 9 January 2003. HM Land Registry promised to bring forward revised proposals in the second half of 2003.

[2]   See LRA 2002, s 82; see also paras **13.4–13.6**.

[3]   See LRR 2003, r 173; see also para **13.5**.

[4]   SI 2003/2114.

[5]   See further, paras **34.12** et seq. These rules also followed consultation: see HM Land Registry, *Land Registration (Referral to the Adjudicator to HM Land Registry) Rules: A Land Registry Consultation* (6 January 2003).

[6]   SI 2003/2171.

[7]   See further, paras **34.15** et seq. Once again, these rules followed consultation: *Adjudicator to Her Majesty's Land Registry (Practice and Procedure) Rules 2003 – A Lord Chancellor's Department Consultation Paper* (9 April 2003). Because the Adjudicator is independent of HM Land Registry and is appointed by the Lord Chancellor, the consultation was conducted by the Lord Chancellor's Department.

[8]   SI 2003/1953.

[9]   SI 2003/2431 This deals with the status of right in respect of the repair of a church chancel: see paras **4.14**(9) and **11.21**.

[10]   SI 2003/2040, made pursuant to LRA 2002, s 100(3).

(iii) The Land Registration Fee Order 2003[1] (LRFO 2003) prescribes
     Land Registry fees.

(iv) The Land Registration (Acting Chief Land Registrar) Regulations
     2003[2] which make provision for the carrying out of the functions
     of the Chief Land Registrar during any vacancy in that office.

(v)   The Land Registration (Acting Adjudicator) Regulations 2003[3]
     which make provision for the carrying out of the functions of the
     Adjudicator during any vacancy in that office.

INTERPRETING THE ACT AND THE RULES MADE UNDER IT

1.20   The LRA 2002 replaces all existing legislation on land registration. It is
not a mere re-enactment of the existing law with some up-dating. Almost
everything under the LRA 2002 is different from what had gone before.
Furthermore, the underlying conceptual basis of land registration is
completely changed by the Act. The Act brings about a shift from a system of
registration of title to one of title by registration. In other words, it will be the
fact of registration and that alone that confers title. This change will not come
about at once but will follow the introduction of electronic conveyancing.[4]
The single most important provision in the LRA 2002 from a conceptual
point of view is s 93.[5] When that section is implemented by means of rules,
not only will it be compulsory to make the contracts and dispositions specified
by means of an electronic document communicated to the registrar, but also
that contract or disposition will have to be simultaneously registered.
Although it is only when s 93 is activated that the shift from registration of
title to title by registration will be manifest, it is suggested that the thinking
behind s 93 should colour the way in which the LRA 2002 is interpreted. The
Act's proclaimed objective of producing a conclusive register[6] is not held in
suspense until s 93 is implemented. In particular, one of the essential elements
in achieving that objective by restricting the scope and effect of overriding
interests[7] is already operative. It should also be noted that the new Act was
drafted against the background of the law as it had developed under the LRA
1925, and that body of law was carefully considered. There are many instances
where the provisions of the Act were drafted in order to clarify, modify or
reverse that law.

1.21   All these factors should, in our view, influence the way in which the
new Act is interpreted. Because the new law and its underlying objectives are

---

1   SI 2003/2092, made pursuant to LRA 2002, s 102.
2   SI 2003/2281, made pursuant to LRA 2002, s 100(2).
3   SI 2003/2342, made pursuant to LRA 2002, Sch 9, para 5.
4   For electronic conveyancing, see Part 5.
5   See paras **28.2** et seq.
6   See para **1.7**.
7   See para **1.8**.

so different from the LRA 1925, authorities on the LRA 1925 are more likely to obscure than illuminate the meaning of LRA 2002 and the rules made under it. They should therefore be discarded and the Act interpreted according to its own wording and the policy that it seeks to implement. There is in fact considerable guidance on both the purpose and intendment of the Act and its specific provisions in the substantial joint Land Registry and Law Commission reports that led to the new Act.[1] It is clear that Law Commission reports can be employed as aids to the construction of the legislation that resulted from them.[2] As Clarke LJ explained in *Yaxley v Gotts*:[3]

> 'where a statute has been enacted as a result of the recommendations of the Law Commission, it is, as I see it, both appropriate and permissible for the court to consider those recommendations in order to help to identify both the mischief which the Act is designed to cure and the public policy underlying it.'

1.22   The principles of the new Act were deliberately developed by reference to what could be done under a system of title registration with little if any reference to the principles of unregistered conveyancing.[4] It follows, therefore, that concepts that are specific to unregistered conveyancing, such as the doctrine of notice, are wholly irrelevant to the interpretation of the LRA 2002. This is especially so given that, as the Law Commission and HM Land Registry explained, 'unregistered land has had its day'[5] and 'unregistered conveyancing must be given its quietus as soon as possible'.[6] A system of conveyancing that is disappearing rapidly should not influence the interpretation of the new system, which rests on very different principles.

LAND REGISTRY PRACTICE UNDER THE ACT

1.23   The Registry is issuing a series of Practice Guides on many aspects of the workings of the Act and the Rules made under it.[7] Reference is made to these Practice Guides where appropriate with the number and title of the guide, eg, 'First Registrations, PG1'. We have not attempted to replicate in detail the contents of the Practice Guides and reference should, therefore, be made to them where they are relevant. They will be particularly useful to practitioners. There are also some shorter Practice Bulletins, to which we also refer, where appropriate with its number and title, eg, 'Lost or Destroyed Certificates – Effect of the Land Registration Act 2002, PB1'.[8]

---

[1]   See paras **1.4–1.9**.
[2]   See, eg, *R v Secretary of State for the Environment, ex parte Spath Holme Ltd* [2001] 2 AC 349 at p 397, per Lord Nicholls of Birkenhead.
[3]   [2000] Ch 162 at p 182.
[4]   See (1998) Law Com No 254, para 1.6.
[5]   (2001) Law Com No 271, para 1.6.
[6]   Ibid, para 2.6.
[7]   These Practice Guides are available from the relevant Land Registry website: www.landregistry.gov.uk/legislation, following the link to 'Land Registration Act 2002'.
[8]   These may be accessed from the same website and link as the Practice Guides.

PART 1

FIRST REGISTRATION

THE MAIN CHANGES AT A GLANCE

Part 2 of the LRA 2002, which is concerned with the first registration of title, makes provision for the following matters:

— voluntary first registration;
— compulsory first registration;
— the effect of first registration; and
— cautions against first registration.[1]

In respect of each of these matters, the LRA 2002 makes significant changes to the law. Certain other matters are also explained in this chapter, namely the provisions found in Part 6 of the Act concerning the upgrading of titles and those in Part 7 which deal with voluntary and compulsory first registration of Crown land.

The main changes made by the LRA 2002 are as follows.

Voluntary registration
— The voluntary registration of *profits à prendre* in gross and franchises with their own titles is permitted for the first time.
— It is no longer possible to register a manor.

Compulsory registration
— Leases granted for more than 7 years become subject to compulsory registration.
— All leases granted to take effect in possession more than 3 months in advance are made subject to compulsory registration whatever their length.

Classes of title
— The range of persons who can apply for the upgrading of a title is extended to include persons who are entitled to be registered, chargees and persons (such as tenants) who are interested in a derivative estate.

---

[1]   See (2001) Law Com No 271, Part III; and First Registrations, PG1.

Effect of first registration

—　By way of an exception to the general rule that first registration merely reflects priorities that have already been determined according to the principles of unregistered conveyancing, the estate is held subject to interests acquired by adverse possession under the Limitation Act 1980 (LA 1980) only if the first registered proprietor has notice of them.

—　The range of unregistered interests that can override first registration is cut back and provision is made for the phasing out of the overriding status of five categories of such interests 10 years after the LRA 2002 comes into force.

Cautions against first registration

—　A cautions register is created to record the details of cautions against first registration.

—　A person may no longer lodge a caution against the first registration of his own estate where that estate is one that he could have registered.

Crown land

—　The Crown is given power to grant to itself a fee simple out of land held in demesne in order to register the title to it. In this way demesne land becomes registrable for the first time.

CHAPTER 2

VOLUNTARY AND COMPULSORY FIRST REGISTRATION

VOLUNTARY FIRST REGISTRATION

Introduction

2.1   Section 3 of the LRA 2002 sets out the circumstances in which a person may apply to the registrar[1] to be registered as the proprietor of an unregistered estate. The types of interest which may be the subject of voluntary first registration are:

(a)   an estate in land;
(b)   a rentcharge;
(c)   a franchise; and
(d)   a *profit à prendre* in gross.[2]

Who may apply for voluntary first registration?

2.2   A person may apply to be registered as first registered proprietor in two situations.[3] The first is where the applicant is the owner of an unregistered legal estate.[4] This is subject to one qualification. In the case of a mortgage by demise *or subdemise*, a legal mortgagee may not apply to be registered as the proprietor of a leasehold estate vested in him where there is a subsisting right of redemption.[5] The second situation in which a person may apply to be registered is where he is entitled to have an unregistered legal estate vested in him. This proposition is also qualified. A person may not apply to be registered if his entitlement arises under a contract to buy the land.[6] It follows that if A holds the unregistered legal estate on a bare trust for

---

[1]   That is, the Chief Land Registrar: LRA 2002, s 132(1).

[2]   LRA 2002, s 3(1).

[3]   Ibid, s 3(2).

[4]   'Legal estate' has the same meaning as in the LPA 1925: LRA 2002, s 132(1). The relevant provision of LPA 1925 is s 1, a provision that requires close attention.

[5]   LRA 2002, s 3(5). A mortgagee can therefore apply to be registered as proprietor of the legal estate previously held by the mortgagor only when the latter can no longer redeem the mortgage. This will be so where the mortgagee has: (i) obtained an order for foreclosure; or (ii) barred the rights of the mortgagor under the LA 1980, s 16 (by which no action for redemption shall be brought where the mortgagee has been in possession for 12 years).

[6]   LRA 2002, s 3(6).

B as her nominee, B may apply for first registration. However, that will not be the case where the bare trust arises out of a contract by A to sell the land to B and B has paid the whole purchase price.[1] Were it not for this exception, it would be possible for a buyer of unregistered land to apply for voluntary first registration without first obtaining a conveyance of the legal estate to himself. This could have a number of undesirable consequences.[2] These provisions are not new but replicate the effect of the equivalent sections of the LRA 1925.[3]

The estates and interests that may be voluntarily registered

Registrable estates

2.3   As previously, a fee simple absolute in possession may be registered.[4] A lease that has more than 7 years unexpired[5] at the time of application may also be voluntarily registered.[6] This is subject to two qualifications. First, a discontinuous lease of *any* duration may be registered.[7] As its name suggests, a discontinuous lease is a grant for a series of discontinuous periods of time, such as 2 weeks in any given calendar year for a total of 20 weeks.[8] Discontinuous leases are, in practice, rare, although they are sometimes used for time-share arrangements.[9] Secondly, what is called a 'PPP lease' cannot be voluntarily registered.[10] Provision is made in the GLAA 1999[11] for the grant of PPP leases as part of the proposed arrangements for the future of transport in London.[12] That Act empowers London Regional Transport, Transport for London and any of the subsidiaries of either body to enter into public–private partnership agreements for the provision, construction,

---

[1]   It is well established that, where a buyer of land pays the entire purchase price, the seller holds the legal estate on a bare trust for him: see *Rose v Watson* (1864) 33 LJ Ch 385 (HL); *Chattey v Farndale Holdings Inc* [1997] 1 EGLR 153. See also *Bridges v Mees* [1957] Ch 475.

[2]   These include: (i) the uncertain effect on priorities in relation to interests that would have been defeated had there been a conveyance of the legal estate; and (ii) the status of the contractual obligations of the parties that would otherwise have been merged in a conveyance of the legal estate. It would also provide a means of avoiding the higher Land Registry fees that apply to compulsory (as opposed to voluntary) first registration.

[3]   See LRA 1925, ss 4, 8(1).

[4]   LRA 2002, s 3(1)(a).

[5]   For the power to reduce this period, see para **2.14**.

[6]   LRA 2002, s 3(3). In computing the length of the lease for these purposes, if the tenant holds a lease in possession and another in reversion that will take effect on, or within a month of, the end of the lease in possession, they are to be treated as one continuous term, provided that they relate to the same land: LRA 2002, s 3(7). This provision is not new, but replicates the Land Registration Rules 1925 (LRR 1925), SR&O 1925/1093, r 47.

[7]   LRA 2002, s 3(4).

[8]   Which means that the period during which the lease will in fact run is 10 years.

[9]   Cf *Cottage Holiday Associates Ltd v Customs and Excise Commissioners* [1983] QB 735.

[10]   LRA 2002, s 90(1). This replicates the effect of the Greater London Authority Act 1999 (GLAA 1999), s 219. It is anticipated that any PPP leases will be for a term of 30 years.

[11]   Part 4, chapter 7, which is concerned with Public–Private Partnership Agreements.

[12]   See (2001) Law Com No 271, para 8.11.

renewal or improvement of a railway or proposed railway.[1] A PPP lease may be granted of any land comprised in any such PPP agreement and such land might include underground railway lines, stations and other installations. The reasons for excluding PPP leases from the registered system are practical and lie principally in the difficulties of mapping them.[2] It remains to be seen whether any such leases are ever granted.

2.4   The provisions of the LRA 2002 relating to leases have significantly changed the law. Under the LRA 1925, only leases with a term of more than 21 years still to run could be registered, whether the term was continuous or discontinuous.[3] The reduction in the length of leases that may be registered is connected with the changes to the circumstances in which leases are made subject to compulsory registration by the Act and the reasons for it are explained in that context.[4] There is a power for the Lord Chancellor to reduce the period still further by statutory instrument.[5]

Registrable interests

2.5   Under the LRA 2002, a number of incorporeal rights may be voluntarily registered with their own title.[6] These are:

(a)   a rentcharge that is either perpetual or for a term of years of which more than 7 years are unexpired;

(b)   a *profit à prendre* in gross which had been granted for an interest equivalent to a fee simple absolute in possession or for a term of years of which more than 7 years are unexpired; and

(c)   a franchise which had been granted for an interest equivalent to a fee simple absolute in possession or for a term of years of which more than 7 years are unexpired.[7]

2.6   Although under the LRA 1925 rentcharges were registrable with their own titles,[8] *profits à prendre* in gross and franchises were not. The Act provides that such profits and franchises may be voluntarily registered with their own

---

1   GLAA 1999, s 210.

2   See (2001) Law Com No 271, para 8.13.

3   LRA 1925, s 8(1).

4   See paras **2.13–2.15**.

5   LRA 2002, s 118(1). The power can only be exercised after prior consultation: s 118(3).

6   Ibid, s 3(1)–(3). See also LRR 2003, r 2(b).

7   For franchises, see the Land Registry Practice Guide, Franchises, PG18. A franchise is 'a royal privilege or branch of the royal prerogative subsisting in the hands of a subject, by grant from the King': *Spook Erection Ltd v Secretary of State for the Environment* [1989] QB 300, 305, Nourse LJ. Franchises are of two kinds. Some relate to specific land (such as the right to hold on a fair on the waste land of the parish of Wraysbury that was in issue in *Wyld v Silver* [1963] Ch 243). Others are not, but are more general rights, perhaps to hold a market in a given locality, as in *Attorney-General v Horner* (1884) 14 QBD 245. This distinction is of some importance under the LRR 2003: see further, paras **2.26**(a), **14.16**.

8   LRA 1925, ss 2(1), 3(xi).

titles. This gives effect to the outcome of consultation by the Law Commission and Land Registry on whether they should be so registrable.[1] Both *profits à prendre* in gross (such as fishing rights) and franchises (typically to hold a market) can be very valuable property rights. They may be (and in practice are) bought and sold. There is, therefore, every reason to make them registrable so that they can be dealt with as registered estates with the advantages that that brings. Our inquiries suggest that this power to register *profits à prendre* in gross and franchises is likely to be widely used. At present, although such rights can be noted in the register, they have to be conveyed according to the principles of unregistered conveyancing, and title therefore has to proved afresh every time that there is a dealing.

2.7   One form of incorporeal right that was registrable under the LRA 1925 ceases to be so under the Act. The Act contains no provision for the registration of a manor.[2] Indeed, it contains provisions which enable the registered proprietor of a manor to apply to the registrar to have the title to the manor removed from the register.[3] The lordship of a manor is not an incumbrance on the land in any real sense.[4] It follows that the registration of manors offers few advantages[5] and is, in practice, the cause of some difficulties.[6]

COMPULSORY FIRST REGISTRATION

Introduction

2.8   The number of dispositions of unregistered land that trigger compulsory registration of title was considerably extended by the LRA 1997.[7] The LRA 2002 broadly replicates the provisions of the LRA 1997, but adds a number of new triggers to compulsory registration.[8] These extensions proved to be amongst the most controversial provisions of the Act during its passage

---

[1]   See (1998) Law Com No 254, paras 3.17–3.19; (2001) Law Com No 271, paras 3.19–3.20.

[2]   In other words, the lordship of the manor. For manors under the LRA 2002, see Land Registry Practice Guide, Manors, PG22.

[3]   LRA 2002, s 119.

[4]   The nature of a manor and the rights that it confers are very clearly set out by Lord Denning MR in *Corpus Christi College, Oxford v Gloucestershire County Council* [1983] QB 360 at p 365.

[5]   This view is not universally shared. Lordships of the manor are regularly bought and sold. It is not unknown for certain unscrupulous persons to 'resurrect' lordships that have long been extinct and then to sell them to unsuspecting buyers. If a lordship of the manor has been registered, the title to it will have been fully investigated by HM Land Registry and will be guaranteed. For this reason, we understand that there have been a number of applications to register lordships of the manor in advance of 13 October 2003.

[6]   See (1998) Law Com No 254, para 3.20; (2001) Law Com No 271, para 3.21. There have been recent instances of lords of the manor seeking to 'enforce' their manorial rights in ways which, as a matter of law, they could not do. For an example that attracted some public attention, see Angelique Chrisafis, '"Feudal Lord" tells villagers that they must pay for land rights', *The Guardian*, 30 August 2001.

[7]   Replacing LRA 1925, s 123 and inserting a new s 123A.

[8]   LRA 2002, s 4.

through Parliament. The reasons for the extensions are explained in paras **2.14** and **2.15**.

2.9 Compulsory registration of title may be triggered either by the transfer of a legal estate in unregistered land, or by the creation or grant of a legal estate. Some of the dispositions that trigger first registration are of what the Act calls 'a qualifying estate'. Others relate to specific types of transaction. For the purpose of the provisions on compulsory first registration, 'a qualifying estate' means an unregistered legal estate which is either a freehold estate in land or a leasehold estate in land for a term which, at the time of the transfer, grant or creation, has more than 7 years to run.[1] Dispositions of mines and minerals held apart from the surface are expressly excluded from the provisions on compulsory registration,[2] as they were under the LRA 1925.[3] However, there is no longer an express exclusion (as there was under the LRA 1925) for land which is part of a manor and which is included with the sale of the manor itself.[4] A disposition of such land will therefore be subject to the provisions of the Act on compulsory registration.

Dispositions of unregistered land that must be completed by registration

Transfers of a qualifying estate

2.10 Under s 4 of the LRA 2002, the following transfers of 'a qualifying estate' are required to be registered.

(1)   A transfer for valuable or other consideration.[5] If the estate transferred has a negative value, so that the transferor pays the transferee to take the transfer, this is still to be regarded as a transfer for valuable or other consideration.[6]

(2)   A transfer by way of gift.[7] A gift expressly includes the following situations:

---

[1]   LRA 2002, s 4(2).
[2]   Ibid, s 4(9).
[3]   LRA 1925, s 123(3)(b).
[4]   Ibid, s 123(3)(c). The reason for this rather curious exception was as follows. Where both the manor (that is, the lordship of the manor) and the lands of the manor are held by the same person and have not been severed, the lands are regarded as being appurtenant to the manor. As a manor was not subject to compulsory registration, it was thought that the sale of the lands appurtenant to it should not be either: see (1998) Law Com No 254, para 3.23. There can be practical difficulties in identifying the land which is appurtenant to the lordship of the manor, as where it includes grass verges and the like.
[5]   LRA 2002, s 4(1)(a)(i).
[6]   Ibid, s 4(6). The example that is given in (2001) Law Com No 271, para 3.26, is of a lease under which the rent payable exceeds the market rental, eg because of the operation of a rent review clause or as a result of onerous repairing obligations under the lease.
[7]   Ibid, s 4(1)(a)(i).

(a)   where land is transferred by the owner to trustees in order to constitute a trust, except where that trust is a bare trust for the benefit of that owner;[1]

(b)   where a transfer of land is made to a beneficiary under a trust who is absolutely entitled to the land. It will not, however, be a gift if the beneficiary in question is the original settlor and the land is held on a bare trust for him.[2]

(3)   A transfer in pursuance of an order of the court.[3] An example would be where, on divorce, a court ordered one spouse to transfer the matrimonial home to the other by way of a property adjustment order and the title to the home had not previously been registered.

(4)   A transfer by means of an assent, including a vesting assent.[4] If, for example, executors assent to the vesting of an unregistered freehold estate in a person who is entitled to it under the deceased landowner's will, that assent triggers the requirement of compulsory registration. Similarly, where unregistered freehold land is held on the trusts of a Settled Land Act settlement, the life tenant dies and the land remains settled, the vesting assent in favour of the new tenant for life[5] will have to be completed by registration.

2.11   It will be clear from this list that not all transfers of a qualifying estate will trigger compulsory registration (or the Act would have said so). Among the transfers that will not are:

(a)   a transfer by a landowner to a nominee to hold on a bare trust for him;

(b)   a transfer by a nominee to the beneficiary for whom she holds on bare trust; and

(c)   where unregistered land is held in trust, the vesting of the legal estate in a new trustee.[6]

Furthermore, certain transfers are expressly excluded from the provisions explained in para **2.10**. First, a transfer by operation of law is not a 'transfer' for the purposes of those provisions.[7] If, for example, an unregistered freehold estate vests in the deceased owner's executors, that transfer does not

---

[1]   LRA 2002, s 4(7)(a).

[2]   Ibid, s 4(7)(b).

[3]   Ibid, s 4(1)(a)(i).

[4]   Ibid, s 4(1)(a)(ii).

[5]   When the tenant for life dies and the land remains settled, the legal estate vests in the deceased life tenant's special personal representatives who will be the trustees of the settlement: see AEA 1925, s 22(1); Supreme Court Act 1981 (SCA 1981), s 116(1). It will be they (and not the tenant for life's general personal representatives) who will execute the vesting assent in favour of the next tenant for life: AEA 1925, s 24(1).

[6]   In consequence of the express or implied vesting declaration in the deed of appointment: TA 1925, s 40.

[7]   LRA 2002, s 4(3), replicating the effect of LRA 1925, s 123(6)(b), (c).

trigger compulsory first registration. Secondly, the provisions do not apply either to the assignment of a mortgage term[1] or to the assignment or surrender of a lease to the owner of the immediate reversion where the term is to merge in the reversion.[2] Thirdly, transfers of PPP leases[3] will not be registrable.[4]

Transfers to which s 171A of the Housing Act 1985 applies

2.12 The LRA 2002 replicates the provision, formerly found in the Housing Act 1985 (HA 1985),[5] by which certain transfers of an unregistered reversionary estate are subject to the requirements of compulsory registration, even though they would not otherwise be so.[6] This will be the case where a secure tenant had a right to buy his home under Part 5 of the HA 1985, but where the tenancy ceases to be a secure tenancy because the reversion is sold to a private sector landlord. That transfer of the reversion must be registered as part of the means by which the tenant's right to buy is preserved.

Leases granted for more than 7 years

2.13 The most striking change in the requirement of compulsory registration concerns the grant of leases. Under the LRA 2002, the grant of a lease for a term of more than 7 years from the date of the grant, whether that lease is continuous or discontinuous,[7] must be registered if that grant is made for valuable or other consideration, is by way of gift or is in pursuance of an order of the court.[8] This is a significant extension from the former requirement that only leases granted for more than 21 years were compulsorily

---

[1] LRA 2002, s 4(4)(a). As mortgages by demise are seldom if ever created, mortgage terms are, in practice, rare.

[2] Ibid, s 4(4)(b).

[3] See para **2.3**. Even if PPP leases are created, the circumstances in which they will be transferable and the bodies to which they may be transferred will be very limited: GLAA 1999, s 217.

[4] LRA 2002, s 90(2).

[5] Schedule 9A, para 2(1).

[6] LRA 2002, s 4(1)(b).

[7] Few discontinuous leases granted out of unregistered land will be subject to compulsory registration because the length of the term is determined by aggregating all of the discontinuous periods. Compare the position where a discontinuous lease is granted out of registered estate: see para **8.9**.

[8] LRA 2002, s 4(1)(c). For the meaning of 'valuable or other consideration' and 'gift', see para **2.10** and LRA 2002, s 4(6), (7). An intriguing point – which we have seen in practice – is whether a lease granted for a term of 7 years or less, but which is a perpetually renewable lease and therefore takes effect as a 2000-year term under the provisions of the Law of Property Act 1922 (LPA 1922), s 145, Sch 15, para 5, is to be regarded as the grant of a term of years absolute of more than 7 years. Our view is that, as a matter of construction, it is not. It is *granted* for a term of 7 years or less, but takes effect by operation of law as a 2000-year term. A more difficult case is the grant of a lease for life, or for a term of years determinable on the death or marriage of the lessee which, under LPA 1925, s 149(6), takes effect as a 90-year term. As a matter of construction, a lease granted for life is not a lease *granted* for a term of years and there is, therefore, a case for saying that it is not subject to the requirement of compulsory registration. By contrast, where a lease is granted for a term of years determinable on the death or marriage of the lessee, there is a grant of a term of years to which LRA 2002, s 4(1)(c) may apply. Whether or not it does should in principle depend on whether the term was granted for more than 7 years, even though the lease will take effect as a 90-year term by operation of law.

registrable. The change is carried through into other provisions of the Act. Thus:

- a lessee holding under an unregistered lease which has more than 7 years to run may, if he chooses, voluntarily register the title to that lease;[1]
- the transfer of an unregistered lease with more than 7 years to run is subject to the requirement of compulsory registration;[2]
- where a proprietor of a registered estate grants a lease for more than 7 years that is a registrable disposition;[3] and
- an unregistered lease will only override first registration or a registered disposition if it is not otherwise registrable and is for a term not exceeding 7 years.[4]

These changes were amongst the most contentious aspects of the Act during its passage through Parliament and they prompted divisions in both Houses.[5] The reasons for them appear both from the Law Commission Report[6] and from the debates in Parliament.

2.14 One of the goals of the LRA 2002 is to pave the way for a system of conveyancing that is wholly electronic and therefore entirely registered. It is intended that, in time, all dispositions of land that are required to be made by deed should be effected electronically and registered.[7] If that is to happen, all leases granted for more than 3 years will, in due course, have to be brought within the compulsory registration provisions of the Act.[8] The LRA 2002 contains powers that will enable that reduction to be made by statutory instrument.[9] Furthermore, under the Act, there is a power to enter a notice in the register in respect of a lease granted for a term of more than 3 years (and not merely in respect of a lease granted for more than 7 years).[10]

2.15 The reduction in the length of registrable lease from those in excess of 21 years to those granted for more than 7 years is not only the first step towards the Act's ultimate goal. It also means that the great majority of business leases will become registrable.[11] Although at one time such leases

---

1   LRA 2002, s 3(3); para **2.3**.
2   Ibid, s 4(1)(a); para **2.10**.
3   Ibid, s 27(2)(b)(i). See para **8.8**.
4   Ibid, Sch 1, para 1 (first registration); Sch 3, para 1 (registered dispositions); paras **4.14**(1), **11.4**.
5   See *Hansard* (HL), 8 November 2001, vol 628, cols 309, 310; *Hansard* (HC), 11 December 2001, Report of Standing Committee D (proposed Conservative amendment to Cl 4).
6   See (2001) Law Com No 271, paras 2.6, 3.14–3.17. There had been prior consultation on the length of registrable leases: see (1998) Law Com No 254, paras 3.7–3.10. The outcome was, however, inconclusive.
7   See (2001) Law Com No 271, para 3.17.
8   The only leases that can be created orally without a deed are those granted for 3 years or less at the best rent which can be reasonably obtained without taking a fine: LPA 1925, s 54(2).
9   LRA 2002, s 118(1). The Lord Chancellor must consult before he exercises the power: s 118(3).
10   This follows from LRA 2002, s 33(b); para **10.8**.
11   It was stated in Parliament by Mr Michael Wills MP (the Parliamentary Secretary in the Lord

were normally granted for terms of more than 21 years, most are now granted for 10- or 15-year terms. It was a major shortcoming in the registered system that the principal form of commercial dealing with land, namely the business lease, could not be registered. It followed that such leases had to be dealt with in accordance with the principles of unregistered conveyancing. An important factor that persuaded the Government to make the reduction in the length of registrable leases is the transparency of the property market.[1] This reduction needs to be viewed against two other factors. The first is the open register, which has become the principal source of accurate information about property dealings that have to be registered. Secondly, under the LRA 1925, it was not possible to inspect leases or charges referred to in the register.[2] The LRA 2002 removes that restriction,[3] although its operation is modified by rules.[4] These rules reflect the provisions of Part II of the Freedom of Information Act 2000 (FIA 2000), which exempt certain information from disclosure under that Act. They are explained in para **18.13**. There is little doubt that the information that will become accessible will provide a fuller and more accurate picture of the leasehold market than is presently available and will be widely used by surveyors and valuers. There will also be conveyancing advantages.[5] Registration will facilitate dealings not only with business leases themselves but also with the reversions on such leases. For example, where there is a large commercial building occupied by many tenants and sub-tenants, it will in time become possible to see from the register exactly what those interests are. This is not presently possible because many of the leases will not be registered and extensive enquiries may, therefore, have to be made.

Reversionary leases

2.16   Another important change that the LRA 2002 has introduced is the requirement that all leases of whatever length that are granted out of unregistered land must be registered if they are to take effect in possession more than 3 months from the date of the grant.[6] The reason for this requirement is that such reversionary leases are otherwise very hard to discover. This change, which reflected the outcome of consultation,[7] is

---

Chancellor's Department) that 'The Land Registry can ... expect the Bill's proposals to result in between 20,000 and 30,000 new leases, plus assignments of extant unregistered leases where the unexpired residue exceeds the relevant minimum': *Hansard* (HC), 11 December 2001, Report of Standing Committee D, discussion of a proposed Conservative amendment to Cl 4.

[1]   See, eg, the comments of Mr Michael Wills MP, *Hansard* (HC), 11 December 2001, Report of Standing Committee D, discussion of a proposed Conservative amendment to Cl 4.

[2]   See LRA 1925, s 112(1)(b).

[3]   LRA 2002, s 66(1)(b). See para **18.3**.

[4]   Made under LRA 2002, s 66(2)(a).

[5]   Although these will not necessarily be enjoyed by all leaseholders who have to register their leases under the LRA 2002.

[6]   LRA 2002, s 4(1)(d).

[7]   See (1998) Law Com No 254, paras 5.91, 5.94; (2001) Law Com No 271, para 3.32.

consistent with the stated goal of the Act to make the register as conclusive as possible and thereby to eliminate additional enquiries.[1] It needs to be kept in mind, as such reversionary leases are not uncommon.

Grant of a right to buy lease

2.17   The grant of a right to buy lease under Part 5 of the HA 1985 remains subject to the requirement of compulsory registration, regardless of the length of that lease.[2]

Grant of a lease to which s 171A of the HA 1985 applies

2.18   It has been explained in para **2.12** that where land is subject to a secure tenancy and the tenant has a right to buy under Part 5 of the HA 1985, a transfer by the landlord of its interest to a private sector landlord must be completed by registration of the transferee's title (if that interest is not already registered). This is so even though the provisions on compulsory registration would not otherwise apply. The same is true where, instead of transferring its interest, the landlord grants a lease of the reversion to a private sector landlord: that lease must be registered whatever its length.[3] Once again, the LRA 2002 replicates the previous law.

Protected first legal mortgages

2.19   Certain legal mortgages of unregistered land trigger the requirement of compulsory registration of the estate that is charged. This will be the case where the owner of an unregistered legal estate, that is either a freehold or a lease with more than 7 years unexpired, creates a protected first legal mortgage.[4] To fall within these provisions, the mortgage must take effect on its creation as one that is to be protected by the deposit of documents of title relating to the mortgaged estate.[5] It must also rank in priority ahead of any other mortgages which then affect the mortgaged estate.[6] Although these provisions of the Act largely replicate the effect of their equivalent in the LRA 1925,[7] they go further in one respect. To reflect the reduction in the length of lease that is required to be registered,[8] they apply to a mortgage of a lease with more than 7 years to run.[9] There is, inevitably, a risk that where an owner of unregistered land creates a protected mortgage, he may not register the title. It is therefore provided in the LRR 2003 that a mortgagee may make an

---

[1]   See para **1.7**.
[2]   LRA 2002, s 4(1)(e), replacing in part HA 1985, s 154.
[3]   LRA 2002, s 4(1)(f), replacing HA 1985, Sch 9A, para 2(1).
[4]   LRA 2002, s 4(1)(g).
[5]   Ibid, s 4(8)(a).
[6]   Ibid, s 4(8)(b).
[7]   See LRA 1925, s 123(2) (as substituted by LRA 1997).
[8]   See para **2.13**.
[9]   Under LRA 1925, s 123(2), the requirement of registration applied only to protected mortgages of leases granted for more than 21 years.

application for first registration of the estate charged by the mortgage in the name of the mortgagor, whether or not the mortgagor consents.[1] Whether the application for first registration is made by the mortgagor or the mortgagee, the registrar must enter the mortgagee as the proprietor of the charge if he is satisfied of the mortgagee's entitlement.[2]

Power to add further triggers to compulsory registration

2.20   Under s 5 of the LRA 2002, the Lord Chancellor may by order amend s 4 of the Act so as to add to the events[3] that trigger the requirement of registration.[4] The power is exercisable by statutory instrument.[5] Before exercising the power the Lord Chancellor is under an obligation to consult on the proposed order.[6] The 'events' to which the section refers is an event relating to any of the following interests in unregistered land:

(a)   an estate in land;

(b)   a rentcharge;

(c)   a franchise; and

(d)   a *profit à prendre* in gross.[7]

This power is wider in a number of respects than its equivalent in the LRA 1925.[8] In particular, under the LRA 1925, the power could only be employed to add to the *dispositions* of, or otherwise affecting a legal estate in unregistered land that were required to be registered. Because that power was confined to 'dispositions', it was narrower than the power contained in the LRA 2002, which applies to 'events'.[9]

---

[1]   LRR 2003, r 21.

[2]   Ibid, r 22.

[3]   This word echoes the language of LRA 2002, s 4(1), which specifies the events to which the requirement of registration applies.

[4]   LRA 2002, s 5(1)(a). He may also make such consequential amendments of any provision of any Act, or having effect under any Act (such as delegated legislation) as he thinks appropriate: s 5(1)(b).

[5]   Subject to annulment in pursuance of a resolution of either House of Parliament: see LRA 2002, s 128(4).

[6]   LRA 2002, s 5(4). There was no equivalent obligation in relation to the similar power contained in LRA 1925, s 2(4), although in practice it would not have been exercised without prior consultation.

[7]   LRA 2002, s 5(2). The power cannot, however, be exercised to require the title to an estate granted to a person as mortgagee to be registered: s 5(3). There is no point in requiring a mortgagee to register its interest if the estate charged is not registered.

[8]   See s 123(4), (5) (as substituted by LRA 1997).

[9]   It is a moot point whether (for example) it would have been possible under LRA 1925, s 123(4), to provide that where there was a disposition of unregistered land of a particular description (such as the grant of a lease) the grantor could be required to register the estate out of which he had made the grant. It would plainly be possible under LRA 2002, s 5. In the passage of the Act through Parliament, there was an attempt by Lord Goodhart to extend the triggers in s 4 to include the case given in the example: see *Hansard* (HL), 17 July 2001, vol 626, col 1389. Although the Government was sympathetic, it was concerned that it would be cumbersome in practice, particularly where landowners granted short leases of small parcels of land: see the response of Baroness Scotland of Asthal (the Parliamentary Secretary): *Hansard* (HL), 17 July 2001, vol 626, col 1390.

The requirement of registration and its enforcement

2.21 The LRA 2002 does not change the nature of the requirement of registration or the sanctions for failing to comply with that requirement.[1] First, the Act sets out who must apply for registration and when.[2] Where the requirement to register arises because of the creation of a first legal mortgage,[3] the estate that has to be registered is that which is mortgaged and it is incumbent on the owner of that estate to apply for registration within 2 months of the creation of the mortgage.[4] In all other cases, the grantee or transferee must apply for the registration of the estate transferred or granted within 2 months of the grant or transfer.[5] It is open to any interested person to apply to the registrar for an extension of the 2-month period for registration. He may by order extend the period to a specified later date if he is satisfied that there is a good reason to do so.[6]

2.22 Secondly, the LRA 2002 specifies the effect of non-compliance with the requirement of registration.[7] If registration does not take place within 2 months (or such longer period as the registrar may previously have specified by order), the transfer, grant or creation becomes void in so far as it transferred, granted or created a legal estate.[8] In the case of a transfer, the title to the legal estate then reverts to the transferor who holds it on a bare trust for the transferee.[9] In all other cases, the grant or creation has effect as a contract made for valuable consideration to grant or create the legal estate concerned.[10] If the period of 2 months has elapsed since the relevant event occurred but subsequently, following an application to him, the registrar then extends the period by order,[11] the transfer, grant or creation is treated as if it had never become void.[12]

2.23 Thirdly, the Act makes provision as to what should happen if a disposition of a legal estate becomes void for non-registration so that it has to

---

[1] For the previous law, see LRA 1925, s 123A (as inserted by LRA 1997).

[2] LRA 2002, s 6.

[3] See para **2.19**.

[4] LRA 2002, s 6(1), (2), (4). Rules may make provision whereby the mortgagee can apply for the registration of the estate charged by the mortgage whether or not the mortgagor consents: s 6(6). This replicates LRA 1925, s 123A(10)(b). For the rule made under that power, see LRR 1925, r 19(2).

[5] LRA 2002, s 6(1), (3), (4). Registration need not be in the name of the grantee or transferee. It could (for example) be vested in a nominee or a person to whom the grantee or transferee had assigned his interest.

[6] Ibid, s 6(4), (5).

[7] Ibid, s 7.

[8] Ibid, s 7(1).

[9] Ibid, s 7(2)(a). The fact that the legal estate may revert in this way does not mean that the transferee of a fee simple initially had a determinable (and therefore an equitable) fee simple: see s 7(4).

[10] Ibid, s 7(2)(b). As such it is vulnerable should the grantor or the person creating the mortgage execute a subsequent disposition of the legal estate. The estate contract may not bind that subsequent disponee unless it has been registered as a Class C(iv) land charge under LCA 1972, s 2(4): see LCA 1972, s 4(6).

[11] Under LRA 2002, s 6(5); see also para **2.21**.

[12] Ibid, s 7(3).

be repeated.[1] The transferee, grantee or mortgagor is liable to the other party for all the proper costs of, or incidental to, executing afresh the transfer, grant or mortgage.[2] He is also liable to indemnify the other party in respect of any liability reasonably incurred by him because of the failure to comply with the requirement of registration.[3] In relation to these matters, the Act does no more than set out the default position. It is open to the parties to agree otherwise.[4] In the case of a protected first legal mortgage, the parties to the charge may well agree to change the default position because the mortgagee will necessarily have custody of the documents of title that are needed to secure registration of the underlying legal estate.

Dispositions pending registration

2.24 The LRA 2002 contains a rule-making power under which the provisions of the Act are applied to a dealing with unregistered land that occurs *after* a disposition has been made that triggers the requirement of compulsory registration but *before* the disposition is registered.[5] This replicates in rather clearer form a power previously found in the LRA 1925.[6] Pursuant to the rule-making power mentioned above, r 38(1) of the LRR 2003 provides that the LRA 2002 applies to the dealing as if it had taken place after the date of first registration of that estate. The registration of any such dealing that is delivered for registration with the application that triggers compulsory registration has effect from the time of the making of the application.[7] The application to register that subsequent dealing should be made using the appropriate Land Registry Form if applicable. If, for example, W sells and conveys the unregistered freehold of 'Greenhythe' to X on 1 December 2003, X then grants a 10-year lease to Y for a term commencing on 1 December 2003, and the applications for the registration of both the conveyance of the freehold and the grant of the lease are submitted on 15 December 2003, both applications will be registered with effect from 15 December 2003. The application of r 38(1) may not always be straightforward in practice for two related reasons. The first is because it has to be read in the light of other statutory provisions and the second is that the rules for determining priority

---

[1]　LRA 2002, s 8.

[2]　Ibid, s 8(a).

[3]　Ibid, s 8(b).

[4]　LRA 1925, s 123A(8) stated explicitly that this was the case. However, 'Although not expressly stated as in the earlier provision, there is nothing in the Bill which prevents that liability being placed elsewhere on agreement between the parties. Indeed, there will usually be discussions between a buyer's advisers and those acting for the lender during the conveyancing process about the post-completion submission of a single application to the Land Registry covering all aspects of the transaction': Baroness Scotland of Asthal, *Hansard* (HL), 30 October 2001, vol 627, col 1321.

[5]　LRA 2002, Sch 10, para 1.

[6]　See s 123A(10). See LRR 1925, r 73.

[7]　LRR 2003, r 38(2). Under s 74(a) of the LRA 2002, an entry made in the register in pursuance of an application for the registration of an unregistered estate has effect from the time of the making of the application: see para **15.10**.

and for protecting interests created before the registration of the triggering conveyance are not apparent. If, in the above example, X had contracted to grant Z a legal charge before granting the 10-year lease to Y, how would Z protect his estate contract?[1] The fact that the Act applies to the dealing might suggest that Z would have to apply to protect his estate contract by means of a notice. However, as is explained at para **10.5**, to register a notice, Z must have an interest which affects a *registered estate*,[2] which at this stage he does not: X's estate is still unregistered. The correct course, it is suggested, is for Z to register his estate contract as a Class C(iv) land charge under the LCA 1972. By s 14(3) of that Act,[3] any land charge created by an instrument that *also* triggers compulsory registration is *not* subject to the provisions of the LCA 1972.[4] By necessary inference, that land charge *is* subject to the provisions of the LRA 2002. However, by further inference, any land charge created by an instrument that does *not* trigger compulsory registration (such as contract to grant a legal charge) *should* be registered as a land charge, unless and until a disposition triggering compulsory registration has been registered.[5] In this twilight world between registered and unregistered land, it is not in fact possible to apply exclusively the principles of either registered or unregistered land. We have raised this issue informally with the Land Registry, but we have not been able to obtain any clear guidance. The perfectly understandable policy of the Registry is to discourage dealings with land after a disposition that triggers compulsory first registration.

APPLICATIONS FOR FIRST REGISTRATION

Making an application

2.25   Much of the detail about applications for first registration is, as might be expected, contained in rules.[6] In addition to the general provisions of the LRR 2003 about applications,[7] explained in Chapter 20, those rules contain specific provisions about applications for first registration.[8] Application is made on the new Form FR1.[9] That is not identical to the Form FR1 that was prescribed under the LRR 1925.[10] For example, the new form does not

---

[1]   We have encountered this specific problem in practice.

[2]   See LRA 2002, s 32(1).

[3]   As amended by LRA 2002, Sch 12, para 10(3).

[4]   An example would be a transfer of a freehold estate on sale which contained a right of pre-emption in favour of the transferor.

[5]   This appears to be accepted by the Registry: see First Registrations, PG1, para 8.4.

[6]   For the relevant rule-making powers, see LRA 2002, ss 13, 14. For an account of these powers, see Harpum and Bignell, *Registered Land – The New Law* (Jordans, 2002), paras 2.53–2.54.

[7]   See LRR 2003, Part 3.

[8]   See ibid, Part 4.

[9]   LRR 2003, r 23(1); Sch 1. For guidance on how to fill in Form FR1, see First Registrations, PG1, para 5.3.

[10]   For a summary of the forms: (i) that are the same as under LRR 1925; (ii) that have changed substantially from those contained in LRR 1925; and (iii) which are new, see paras **20.3–20.8**.

contain a box for details of any superior title, but there is one for 'disclosable overriding interests' to reflect the new requirements that are explained in Chapter 4.[1] It is also necessary for the new form to accommodate applications to register a rentcharge, *profit à prendre* in gross or franchise. In such a case, the address of the relevant estate is to be in the form of 'Rentcharge, franchise etc, over 2 The Grove, Anytown, Northshire NE2 9OO'. An applicant for first registration must submit the following to the Registry (in specific cases it may be necessary for additional documents to be submitted[2]):

(a) Form FR1, duly completed.

(b) The prescribed documents, as explained in para **2.26**.

(c) Form DI (if relevant) setting out any disclosable overriding interests, explained in para **4.19**.

(d) The results of land charges searches under the LCA 1972.[3] These searches should, in practice, be made against the names of all the known previous estate owners except to the extent (as will usually be the case) that earlier search certificates have been carried forward. Any such earlier certificates should be included with the application.

(e) Where the applicant claims the benefit of rights over other land, and the existence of such rights does not appear from the deeds, an application to register them must be made,[4] supported by appropriate statutory declarations.[5]

(f) Any application for a restriction in Form RX1.[6]

(g) Where the applicant is a company, and the property is subject to a charge, a certificate of registration of a company charge under s 395 of the Companies Act 1985. This should be obtained before the application is made to register the title.

(h) The appropriate registration fee prescribed under the LRFO 2003.

---

[1] See para **4.19**. It is curious that the LRR 2003 should still use the terminology of 'overriding interests' which is abandoned by the LRA 2002. See para **4.4**.

[2] For example, where a corporation or body of trustees which holds on charitable, ecclesiastical or public trusts, other than for a non-exempt charity, applies to be registered as proprietor of a registered estate or charge, the application must be accompanied by the document creating the trust or a certified copy of it: LRR 2003, r 182.

[3] Cf LRR 2003, r 30; para **2.29**.

[4] The form of application will depend upon a number of factors. If the right is claimed over registered land, the application will be on Form UN1 (for a unilateral notice: see para **10.30**) or Form AN1 (for an agreed notice, see para **10.19**), depending on whether the owner of the land affected consents to the application: cf LRA 2002, s 30(3). If the land affected is unregistered, and the applicant wants the benefit of the right recorded in the register of title, the application will presumably be on Form AP1, which is the default form of application where no other form of application is prescribed: see LRR 2003, r 13(1). The applicant might also apply for a caution against the first registration of the land affected. For cautions against first registration, see Chapter 5.

[5] LRR 2003, r 33; para **2.34**.

[6] For restrictions, see Chapter 10.

Accompanying documents

2.26 The LRR 2003 prescribe the documents that must accompany an application for first registration unless the registrar otherwise directs.[1] The documents that are required are as follows:

(a)   Sufficient details, by plan or otherwise, so that the land can be identified clearly on the Ordnance Survey map.[2] Detailed guidance on when a plan is required[3] and the nature of that plan are set out in Part 6 of the Land Registry's Practice Guide, Land Registry Plans, PG 40. There are certain special (and, in practice, important) provisions that apply to the first registration of mines and minerals[4] and of cellars, flats and tunnels.[5] On an application to register a rentcharge, *profit à prendre* in gross or franchise, the land that has to be identified is the land affected by that estate, or to which it relates.[6] In this context, it should be noted that some franchises do not create an incumbrance as such on the land to which they relate. The LRR 2003 distinguish between an 'affecting franchise', which 'relates to a defined area and is an adverse right affecting, or capable of affecting, the title to an estate or charge', and a 'relating franchise', which is any other franchise.[7] This distinction emerges clearly from the decision of the Court of Appeal in *Attorney-General v Horner*,[8] in which it was held that there could be a royal grant of a franchise to hold a market on land that was not owned by the grantee. It was also held that the franchise did not have to be limited to a specific piece of land defined by metes and bounds. Whether the application relates to an affecting or a relating franchise, the land affected has to be identified, though this may not always be easy in relation to a relating franchise.

(b)   In the case of a leasehold estate, the lease, if it is in the control of the applicant, and also a certified copy.

---

[1]   LRR 2003, r 24(1). In substance, r 24(1) is not very different from LRR 1925, rr 20, 21.

[2]   Details of what the Registry requires are given in First Registrations, PG1, para 5.3, Panel 3.

[3]   Sometimes the postal address of the property will suffice.

[4]   LRR 2003, r 25, provides that when applying for first registration of an estate in mines and minerals held apart from the surface, the applicant must provide: (a) a plan of the surface under which the mines and minerals lie; (b) any other sufficient details by plan or otherwise so that the mines and minerals can be identified clearly; and (c) full details of rights incidental to the working of the mines and minerals. This replicates in substance LRR 1925, r 53.

[5]   LRR 2003, r 26(1), provides that unless all of the land above and below the surface is included in the application for first registration, the applicant must provide a plan of the surface on, under or over which the land to be registered lies, and sufficient information to define the vertical and horizontal extents of the land. The Registry is stressing the importance of producing accurate plans in these situations. By r 26(2), r 26 does not apply where only mines and minerals are excluded from the application. LRR 2003, r 26 is similar to LRR 1925, r 54.

[6]   LRR 2003, r 24(2). Cf para **14.16**.

[7]   See LRR 2003, r 217(1).

[8]   (1884) 14 QBD 245, affirmed on appeal to the House of Lords: (1885) 11 App Cas 66. The principles emerge most clearly from the judgments in the Court of Appeal.

(c)   All deeds and documents relating to the title that are in the control of the applicant.

(d)   A list in duplicate in the prescribed Form DL[1] of all the documents delivered.

As regards the return of documents, the Registry will assume that the applicant requests the return of the documents listed in Form DL.[2] However, the Registry will only assume that the applicant requests the return of:

(i)   a statutory declaration;

(ii)   a subsisting lease;

(iii)   a subsisting charge; and

(iv)   the latest document of title (typically the conveyance to the applicant);

if the applicant supplies a certified copy of the document.[3] If certified copies of the four types of document are not supplied, the registrar may retain the originals and they may be destroyed.[4]

2.27 It sometimes happens that an applicant for first registration cannot produce a full documentary title.[5] The Land Registry has provided detailed guidance as to what it requires in such circumstances,[6] which is, in summary, as follows. The applicant's application must be supported by evidence that satisfies the registrar that he is either entitled[7] or required[8] to apply for first registration.[9] Where appropriate, he will be required to account for the absence of documentary evidence of title.[10] Unlike the previous position

---

[1]   See LRR 2003, Sch 1. Form D1 is a new Form introduced by LRR 2003.

[2]   See Form FR1, para 6; and see LRR 2003, r 203(1), (2).

[3]   LRR 2003, r 203(4).

[4]   See Form FR1, para 6, and LRR 2003, r 203(6).

[5]   This might be because, for example, the title deeds have been lost or destroyed, the land had been owned by the applicant (typically a corporation) for centuries and there never had been any deeds, or the basis of the applicant's title is his adverse possession.

[6]   First Registration of Title where Deeds have been Lost or Destroyed, PG2, to which reference should be made for full details of what is required.

[7]   Under LRA 2002, s 3(2) (voluntary first registration); see para **2.2**.

[8]   Under ibid, s 6(1) (compulsory first registration); see para **2.21**.

[9]   LRR 2003, r 27(a). The Registry is likely to require a statutory declaration either by the conveyancer who last examined the title or by some other person who would have knowledge of the title. This should exhibit the best secondary evidence obtainable as to the applicant's title and any encumbrances that affect it.

[10]   LRR 2003, r 27(b). The Registry is likely to require statutory declarations from one or more persons with the relevant knowledge, which set out the events that led to the loss or destruction of the deeds and the steps that were taken to recover them. Any such declaration should in particular explain whether the lost or destroyed deeds had been deposited with any third party as security or for safekeeping. It should also state that the deeds have indeed been lost or destroyed and have not been passed to a person entitled to them such as a purchaser or a mortgagee. All relevant correspondence should be exhibited to the declaration.

under the LRR 1925,[1] the new rule applies not only where the applicant has *no* documents of title, but also where his chain of title is incomplete. Requiring the applicant to account for the absence of documentary title is also new. Although the applicant is no longer required to produce a statutory declaration that he is either in possession or in receipt of the rents and profits of the land as he was under the LRR 1925,[2] such a declaration may in practice be needed. An applicant who cannot explain where the title deeds may be or what caused their loss may be registered with a mere possessory title. But even registration with possessory title can only be made if the applicant proves that he is in possession of the land. Normally the applicant will have to produce evidence of identity under either Form ID1 (if he is an individual) or ID2 (if it is a corporation).[3]

Examining title

2.28   In examining the title shown by the documents that accompany any application for first registration (whether for valuable consideration or not), the registrar may (and no doubt will) have regard to any earlier examination of the title by a conveyancer and also to the nature of the property.[4] This marks an extension of the practice under the LRR 1925, under which the registrar considered a conveyancer's examination of title only where there was a transfer for value.[5] There are two aspects to this. First, it has not been the practice for a donee of land to investigate the donor's title, because, as Fry J explained in *Re Marsh and Earl Granville*:[6] 'You do not look a gift horse in the mouth'. However, it seems intrinsically desirable that there should be a prior investigation of title by a conveyancer in any case where the transfer, although not for valuable consideration, will trigger compulsory first registration.[7] Secondly, it is at least theoretically possible that, on a voluntary first registration, the registrar might consider a conveyancer's examination of title from the time when the land had last been purchased. However, given that compulsory registration has extended to the whole of England and Wales since December 1990, the value of such an elderly examination of title may be limited.

2.29   In examining title on first registration, the registrar may make searches and enquiries and give notices to other people, direct that searches and

---

[1]   See LRR 1925, r 37.
[2]   Ibid, r 37.
[3]   Forms ID1 and ID2 are not prescribed forms under Sch 1 to LRR 2003, but have been promulgated by the Chief Land Registrar under LRA 2002, s 100(4).
[4]   LRR 2003, r 29.
[5]   See LRR 1925, r 28. The conveyancer would certify that he had investigated the title: LRR 1925, r 29.
[6]   (1883) 24 ChD 11 at p 15.
[7]   This only became a significant issue as a result of the extension of the triggers for compulsory first registration by the LRA 1997.

enquiries be made by the applicant, and advertise the application.[1] If, for example, an application for first registration were made and it was not apparent that a search had been made of the land charges register under the LCA 1972,[2] the registrar could order that such a search be made by the applicant. The registrar may refer to an appropriate specialist the examination of all or part of any title lodged with an application for first registration.[3]

First registration: specific rules

2.30 The LRR 2003 contains specific requirements in relation to first registration in a number of situations.

Foreshore

2.31 The foreshore is presumptively vested in the Crown or (in the relevant parts of the country) the Duchies of Lancaster and Cornwall.[4] It can only be acquired by a subject by an express grant from the Crown or Royal Duchy, or by adverse possession. The LRR 2003 contains provision, similar (but not identical) in effect to s 97 of the LRA 1925,[5] to ensure that a subject is not registered as first registered proprietor of any foreshore when he or she is not in fact the owner.[6] Subject to one exception, it is provided by r 31 of the LRR 2003, that where it appears to the registrar that any land included in an application for first registration comprises foreshore, he must serve notice of that application on the relevant manifestation of the Crown.[7] It is unnecessary for the registrar to do so where the application is made by the Crown or Royal Duchy.[8] The notice must provide a period ending at 12 noon on the twentieth business day[9] after the date of the issue of the notice in which the Crown can object to the application.

2.32 Rule 31 is more tightly drawn than was s 97 of the LRA 1925. It is expressly limited to applications for first registration. It does not apply to subsequent dealings by a person who has been registered as the proprietor of any foreshore: the Crown will have had an opportunity to object when first registration occurred. If there is any application to be registered as a proprietor of registered Crown or Duchy foreshore on the basis of adverse

---

1. LRR 2003, r 30. See LRR 1925, r 25, for the equivalent rule under the LRA 1925.
2. See para **2.25**(d).
3. LRR 2003, r 200(1)(a). The expert might be, eg, conveyancing counsel.
4. See *Halsbury's Laws of England*, vol 12(1), para 242.
5. See also LRR 1925, r 23.
6. It was felt that this was a matter for rules rather than for primary legislation: see *Land Registration for the Twenty-First Century: A Conveyancing Revolution* (2001) Law Com No 271, para 11.38.
7. The Crown Estate Commissioners in every case and, where appropriate, having regard to its geographical location, the Duchy of Lancaster, the Duchy of Cornwall or the Port of London Authority.
8. LRR 2003, r 31(3).
9. For the meaning of 'business day', see LRR 2003, r 216; para **36.5**.

possession of foreshore that has already been registered, the provisions of Part 9 of and Sch 6 to the LRA 2002 on adverse possession will ensure that the Crown or Royal Duchy is notified of that application. The Crown or Royal Duchy will then have an opportunity to object to the application, although in certain limited circumstances the squatter will be entitled to be registered even if it does.[1]

Mines and minerals

2.33 It is explained at para **23.11**, that the State guarantee of registered title does not extend to any mines and minerals comprised in the land, unless it is expressly noted in the register that the title to the registered estate contains the mines or minerals.[2] Rule 32 of the LRR 2003 accordingly provides that where, on first registration of an estate in land which comprises or includes the land beneath the surface, the registrar is satisfied that the mines and minerals are either included in or excluded from the applicant's title, he must make an appropriate note in the applicant's title.[3] In practice, it will not be common for the registrar to have the evidence to enable him to make such an affirmative or negative entry. The sort of cases where he might make such an entry would include:

(a)   A note of entitlement to mines or minerals where the previous owner had worked minerals on the land and there was no evidence that they were vested in anyone else.

(b)   A note that minerals were excluded from the applicant's title because the documents of title disclosed that the mines and minerals were severed from the land. For example, it might be apparent from the title that the land was formerly copyhold, so that the mines and minerals were reserved to the lord of the manor.[4]

The benefit of appurtenant rights

2.34 Rule 33(1) of the LRR 2003[5] provides that where, at the time of first registration, the registrar is satisfied[6] that an appurtenant right subsists as a legal estate for the benefit of the registered estate, he may enter it in the register.[7] Where an applicant claims such rights, he must provide details in the application for first registration (Panel 4 of Form FR1), and the application must be supported by appropriate statutory declarations: see First

---

[1]   See paras **30.29** et seq, **33.12–33.16**.
[2]   See LRA 2002, Sch 8, para 2.
[3]   Cf LRR 1925, rr 195 and 196. See also LRR 2003, r 5(b)(i); para **14.6**.
[4]   See the explanation by Jessel MR in *Eardley v Earl Granville* (1876) 3 ChD 826, pp 832–833.
[5]   Which is made pursuant to the rule-making power conferred by LRA 2002, s 13(a).
[6]   Whether from an examination of the title or on receipt of a written application providing details of the right and evidence of its existence. The latter will be appropriate in a case where the right does not appear from the title deeds.
[7]   Cf LRR 1925, rr 252, 257, which were similar in effect.

Registrations, PG1, para 5.3. Typically the appurtenant right will be the benefit of an easement or a *profit à prendre*. The power does not extend to recording claimed equitable rights, such as the benefit of a restrictive covenant.[1] If the registrar is not satisfied that the right subsists as a legal interest benefiting the registered estate, he may enter such details of the right claimed in the property register with such qualification as he considers appropriate.[2]

Recording burdens on first registration

Charges

2.35   There are four circumstances in which a charge may have to be entered in the register on first registration.

(a)   The first is where the owner of an unregistered legal estate creates a protected first legal mortgage that triggers the requirement of compulsory first registration. The way in which the charge will be registered[3] has already been explained at para **2.19**.

(b)   The second is where, after the making of a disposition which triggers first registration but before it has been registered, the disponee charges the land which was subject to the disposition. The manner in which this charge will be registered[4] is explained at para **2.24**.

(c)   The third is where, at the time of first registration, the land was already subject to a charge, the creation of which did not trigger the compulsory registration of the estate. The obvious example of this is where a freehold estate is voluntarily registered and the land is subject to a charge that was created before the LRA 1997 was brought into force.[5] In these circumstances, the registrar must enter the mortgagee as the proprietor of that charge if he is satisfied of that person's entitlement.[6]

(d)   The fourth is where, at the time at the time of first registration, the land was already subject to a charge, and the chargee had created a sub-charge. The registrar must enter the sub-mortgagee as the proprietor of that sub-charge if he is satisfied of that person's entitlement.[7]

---

[1]   HM Land Registry has never recorded the benefit of restrictive covenants in the register (though it may record that such benefit is claimed). Given the frequent difficulties of identifying with precision what land if any is benefited by a restrictive covenant, it is unsurprising that the Registry is not prepared to guarantee the benefit of a restrictive covenant.

[2]   LRR 2003, r 33(2).

[3]   Pursuant to LRR 2003, r 22.

[4]   Ibid, r 38.

[5]   It was the LRA 1997 that made the creation of a protected first legal mortgage a trigger to compulsory first registration: see LRA 1925, s 123(2) (as substituted by LRA 1997).

[6]   LRR 2003, r 34. Cf LRA 2002, s 13(b), which contains the rule-making power.

[7]   Ibid, r 34. For sub-charges, see para **12.3**.

Other burdens

2.36 Subject to certain exceptions, on first registration the registrar must enter a notice in the register of the burden of any interest which appears from his own examination of the title to affect the registered estate.[1] The exceptions to this rule are as follows.[2]

2.37 First, under the provisions of the LRA 2002, the burden of certain interests cannot be protected by notice at all.[3] These interests are set out in ss 33 and 90(4) of the Act (see paras **10.6–10.12**, where the reasons are given why notices cannot be entered in respect of the interests in question).

2.38 Secondly, the registrar does not have to enter a notice of a public right.[4] Public rights, such as rights of way over public highways, will normally be obvious. The Registry appears to have decided as a matter of policy that public rights are not matters that should be the subject of registration, presumably on some cost–benefit analysis. There is nothing in the LRA 2002 to lead to such a conclusion and it might be thought to run counter to the policy of the Act to create a conclusive register.[5]

2.39 Thirdly, no notice will be entered by the registrar in respect of a local land charge.[6] There is no need for him to do so because such land charges are registered in the separate local land charges register under the Local Land Charges Act 1975. It is possible in certain circumstances to register a local land charge as *a registered charge.*[7] This is explained at paras **12.80–12.81**.

2.40 Fourthly, the registrar need not enter a notice in respect of an interest which appears to him to be of a trivial or obvious character, or in respect of which the entry of a notice would be likely to cause confusion or interference.[8] There was no equivalent provision in the LRR 1925 in relation to the entry of notices on first registration as such. However, the present exception follows closely r 199 of the LRR 1925, which relieved the registrar of having to enter a notice in the same circumstances. Rights of way over public roads and rights of drainage over public sewers were always given as the examples of where the registrar would have exercised his discretion under r 199. However, those cases would now appear to fall within the third exception to the requirement to enter a notice explained in para **2.39**. The

---

[1]   LRR 2003, r 35(1). There was no precise equivalent to this rule in the LRR 1925, but cf LRR 1925, rr 40, 41.
[2]   LRR 2003, r 35(2).
[3]   Ibid, r 35(2)(a).
[4]   Ibid, r 35(2)(b). Cf para **4.19**(c).
[5]   For that policy, see para **1.7**.
[6]   LRR 2003, r 35(2)(c).
[7]   See LRA 2002, s 55.
[8]   LRR 2003, r 35(2)(d).

circumstances in which this fourth exception may be invoked therefore remain uncertain at this stage.

Rights of light and air

2.41 Agreements, which in some way preclude the acquisition of an easement by prescription or implied grant, are common, particularly in relation to rights of light and air.[1] Thus the Standard Conditions of Sale (SCS)[2] contain a provision by which, where the seller of land retains land near the property sold, the buyer will have no right to light or air or indeed any right, over the retained land.[3] Such an agreement does not constitute an incumbrance on land, but is a mere licence that prevents the acquisition of a prescriptive right.[4] For that reason, it cannot be protected by means of a notice on the register. However, r 36 of the LRR 2003 provides that, on first registration, if it appears to the registrar that an agreement prevents the acquisition of rights of light or air for the benefit of the registered estate, he may make an entry in the property register of that estate.

---

[1] An easement cannot be acquired by prescription if the user upon which it is based is permissive: see, eg, *R v Oxfordshire County Council, ex parte Sunningwell Parish Council* [2000] 1 AC 335 at pp 350–351, per Lord Hoffmann. Under the Prescription Act 1832, the various periods which will give rise to prescriptive claims under the Act apply 'unless it shall appear that the same was enjoyed by some consent or agreement expressly made or given for that purpose by deed or writing'.

[2] References in this work are to the 3rd edition. A 4th edition is expected, to take account of LRA 2002 and the rules made under it.

[3] SCS, para 3.4. Either party may require that the transfer contain appropriate express terms. For the effect of such conditions, see *Squarey v Harris-Smith* (1981) 42 P&CR 118 at pp 127–130 per Oliver LJ.

[4] See *Smith v Colbourne* [1914] 2 Ch 533, where the Court of Appeal held that the non-disclosure of such an agreement by a vendor of land to a purchaser did not equate to the non-disclosure of an incumbrance entitling the purchaser to resist an application for a decree of specific performance.

CHAPTER 3

CLASSES OF TITLE

THE CLASS OF TITLE GIVEN ON FIRST REGISTRATION

Introduction

3.1   On an application for first registration, whether that application is voluntary or one which has to be made, the applicant will be registered with a particular class of title on satisfying the requirements of the registrar. The LRA 2002 does not change the classes of title with which an applicant for first registration may be registered.[1] Nor does it alter the nature of those classes of title.

Freehold titles

3.2   An applicant who seeks to be registered as proprietor of a freehold estate may be registered with any of the following titles.

3.3   *Absolute title* will be appropriate if the registrar is of the opinion that the title is such that a willing buyer could properly be advised to accept by a competent professional adviser.[2] The registrar may register a title with absolute title even if it is open to objection, provided that he considers that the defect is not such as will cause the holding under the title to be disturbed.[3] The vast majority of freehold titles are registered with absolute title.

3.4   *Qualified title* will be appropriate if the title has only been established for a limited period or subject to certain limitations that cannot be disregarded because there is a risk that they may cause the holding under the title to be disturbed.[4] Qualified title is very rare.[5]

3.5   *Possessory title* is a residual category. It will be appropriate where the applicant for registration is either in actual possession of the land or in receipt

---

[1]   LRA 2002, ss 9 (freehold title), 10 (leasehold title).

[2]   Ibid, s 9(2).

[3]   Ibid, s 9(3).

[4]   Ibid, s 9(4).

[5]   The example given in (2001) Law Com No 271, para 3.43(2), is where it was apparent to the registrar that the transfer to the applicant for first registration had been in breach of trust.

of the rents and profits by virtue of his estate, and there is no other class of title with which it may be registered.[1] In practice, possessory title is given where the applicant's title deeds have been lost or destroyed or where he claims title by adverse possession. In either case the registrar will have no evidence as to the title.

Leasehold title

3.6   Where the applicant seeks to be registered as proprietor of a leasehold estate he may be registered with one of the following titles.

3.7   *Absolute title* will be appropriate if: (i) the title satisfies the requirements mentioned in para **3.3**; *and* (ii) the registrar approves the lessor's title to grant the lease.[2] The latter requirement will only be satisfied if the lessor's title has itself already been registered with absolute title or if the registrar has examined that title and is satisfied with it.

3.8   In two situations, where the reversion on an unregistered lease is registered, the registrar must give notice to the registered proprietor of any application for registration of the leasehold estate with absolute title before he completes the application.[3] The two situations are as follows:

(a)   Where the reversion was *not* registered when the lease was granted and an application to register the lease is made after the registration of the reversion.

(b)   Where the reversion *was* registered when the lease was granted, but where the lease was not required to be registered at the time of grant. An example would be where, prior to the LRA 2002 coming into force, a lease was granted for a term of 21 years, and after the Act came into force, the lessee applied to have the lease registered.[4]

The purpose of this provision is to ensure that the proprietor of the reversion is aware that the lease has been registered: a notice of the lease is required to be entered in the register of the title to the reversion.[5] It *only* applies where it is not apparent from the application for registration that the proprietor of the registered reversion consents to the registration and the lease is not already noted in the register of the registered reversion. [6]

3.9   The Act changed the rules as to the title which a lessor is required to

---

[1]   LRA 2002, s 9(5).
[2]   Ibid, s 10(2), (4).
[3]   LRR 2003, r 37(1).
[4]   Ibid, r 37(2)(a).
[5]   Ibid, r 37(3).
[6]   Ibid, r 37(2)(b), (c).

deduce under a contract to grant a lease that is subject to the requirement of compulsory registration.[1] A lessor is now required to deduce his title to the intending lessee unless the parties agree otherwise (a reversal of the principle that had applied previously).[2]

3.10 *Good leasehold title* will be the appropriate title if the applicant can satisfy only the first of the two conditions for an absolute leasehold title set out in para **3.7** but not the second.

3.11 *Qualified title* will be appropriate if the title to either the lease or the reversion has been established only for a limited period or subject to certain limitations that cannot be disregarded because there is a risk that they may cause the holding under the title to be disturbed.[3]

3.12 *Possessory title* will be the appropriate title in the same circumstances as it is where the title is freehold.[4]

UPGRADING TITLES

The registrar's power to upgrade titles that are not absolute

3.13 Part 6 of the LRA 2002 contains provisions which empower the registrar to upgrade a title that is not absolute in certain circumstances.[5] First, if at any time the registrar is satisfied as to the title to a relevant estate that is not registered with absolute title he may upgrade the title. In deciding whether or not he is satisfied, he must apply the same standards as he would on first registration.[6] The registrar may upgrade as follows:

(a)   from possessory or qualified freehold to absolute;[7]
(b)   from good leasehold title to an absolute title if he is satisfied as to the superior title;[8]

1   LRR 2003, Sch 11, para 2(2), introducing a new LPA 1925, s 44(4A).
2   The intention is obviously to encourage the first registration of leaseholds with absolute title wherever possible. However, it is often the case that no contract will precede the grant of a lease, so that this change will not apply. In any event, the lease may come in for registration either on an assignment or on an application for voluntary registration where there has been no triggering event.
3   LRA 2002, s 10(5).
4   Ibid, s 10(6). See para **3.5**.
5   Ibid, s 62. The provisions are similar but not identical to those that were found in LRA 1925, s 77 (as substituted by LRA 1986). There is a Land Registry Practice Guide, Upgrading the Class of Title, PG42.
6   LRA 2002, s 62(8).
7   Ibid, s 62(1). For example, if an estate had been registered with a possessory title because the documents of title had been lost (see para **3.5**), it could be upgraded to absolute if the title deeds subsequently came to light and the title was sufficiently proved. Before a qualified title could be upgraded, the registrar would have to be satisfied that the particular problem that prompted the initial registration had ceased to cast doubt on the title.
8   Ibid, s 62(2). This might happen where, eg, the title to the freehold reversion was registered.

(c)   from possessory or qualified leasehold title to good leasehold if he is satisfied as to the title to the leasehold estate;[1] and

(d)   from possessory or qualified leasehold title to absolute if he is satisfied both as to the title to the lease and as to the superior title.[2]

3.14   Secondly, the registrar may upgrade a possessory freehold title to absolute and a possessory leasehold to good leasehold provided that:

(a)   the title has been entered in the register for at least 12 years;[3] and

(b)   the proprietor is in possession of the land.[4]

The proprietor will be in possession of the land for these purposes if it is physically either in his possession or in the possession of a person who is entitled to be registered as proprietor.[5] A proprietor will also be regarded as being in possession where:

(a)   he is a landlord and the estate is in the physical possession of his tenant (or any sub-tenant to whom he had underlet);

(b)   he is a mortgagor and the estate is in the physical possession of the mortgagee (or any tenant to whom the mortgagee had leased the land under his power of leasing);

(c)   he is a licensor and the estate is in the physical possession of a licensee; and

(d)   he is a trustee and the estate is in the physical possession of a beneficiary under the trust.[6]

It is explained in Chapter 22 that this definition of proprietor in possession is also relevant in the context of rectification of the register.[7]

3.15   The powers to upgrade explained in paras **3.13** and **3.14** cannot be exercised if:

---

[1]   LRA 2002, s 62(3)(a).

[2]   Ibid, s 62(3)(b).

[3]   There is a power to change this period by order: LRA 2002, s 62(9). Such an order has to be made by statutory instrument and is subject to annulment in pursuance of a resolution of either House of Parliament: LRA 2002, s 128(4)(d). The period of 12 years is indirectly linked to the limitation period under LA 1980, s 15 (12-year limitation period in actions to recover possession of land). After 12 years, any adverse rights are likely to have been barred even if they were not at the time of first registration. Although LA 1980 does not apply to registered estates under the Act (as explained in Part 6), it does continue to apply to matters excluded from the effect of first registration, as where registration is with a possessory title.

[4]   Ibid, s 62(4), (5).

[5]   Ibid, s 131(1). Examples of persons who are entitled to be registered as proprietor include the registered proprietor's trustee in bankruptcy, his personal representatives, or a beneficiary under a bare trust for whom he holds as nominee. It will not include a squatter who is entitled to be registered under the provisions of Sch 6 to the Act: s 131(3).

[6]   Ibid, s 131(2).

[7]   See paras **22.9–22.14**.

(a)   there is outstanding any claim that is adverse to the title of the registered proprietor; and

(b)   that claim is made by virtue of an estate, right or interest whose enforceability is preserved by the existing entry about the class of title.[1]

This provision is not new[2] and its purpose is to ensure that where there is such an outstanding claim it is resolved before title can be upgraded.

3.16   The LRA 2002 makes one material change in relation to upgrading title. Under the LRA 1925, upgrading could only happen if either the registrar decided to act on his own initiative or the registered proprietor applied to have the title upgraded.[3] It was not open to anyone else to apply for such upgrading, even though other persons might have had a very good reason for wishing to do so. Obvious cases were a mortgagee or an executor who, in either case, wished to exercise his power of sale. The most that he could do was to request the registrar to exercise his powers. The category of persons who can apply is significantly widened by the Act and comprises:

(a)   the registered proprietor of the estate in question;

(b)   a person who is entitled to be registered as proprietor of that estate;

(c)   the proprietor of a registered charge affecting that estate; and

(d)   a person interested in a registered estate which derives from the estate in question (such as a tenant).[4]

3.17   An application to the registrar to upgrade a title[5] must be made in Form UT1.[6] In making such an application, the applicant must provide the registrar with the following:

(a)   To upgrade from possessory or qualified freehold title to absolute title,[7] such documents as will satisfy the registrar as to the title.[8] This requirement does not apply to an application to upgrade a possessory freehold title in the circumstances set out in para **3.14**.[9]

(b)   To upgrade from good leasehold title to an absolute title:[10]

     (i)   such documents as will satisfy the registrar as to any superior title that is *not* registered;

     (ii)   where any superior title is merely registered with possessory,

---

[1]   LRA 2002, s 62(6).
[2]   See LRA 1925, s 77(4).
[3]   Ibid, s 77(1)–(3).
[4]   LRA 2002, s 62(7).
[5]   That is, an application under ibid, s 62.
[6]   LRR 2003, r 124(1).
[7]   Under LRA 2002, s 62(1).
[8]   LRR 2003, r 124(2).
[9]   Under LRA 2002, s 62(4). See LRR 2003, r 124(2).
[10] Ibid, s 62(2).

qualified or good leasehold title, such evidence as will satisfy the registrar that that title qualifies for upgrading to absolute title;

(iii)   evidence of any consent to the grant of the lease that is required from any chargee of any superior title or any superior lessor.[1]

(c)   To upgrade from possessory or qualified leasehold title to good leasehold title,[2] such documents as will satisfy the registrar as to the title.[3] This requirement does not apply to an application to upgrade a possessory leasehold title in the circumstances set out in para **3.14**.[4]

(d)   To upgrade from possessory or qualified leasehold title to absolute title:[5]

(i)   such documents as will satisfy the registrar as to the title;[6]

(ii)   such documents as will satisfy the registrar as to any superior title that is *not* registered;

(iii)   where any superior title is merely registered with possessory, qualified or good leasehold title, such evidence as will satisfy the registrar that that title qualifies for upgrading to absolute title; and

(iv)   evidence of any consent to the grant of the lease that is required from any chargee of any superior title or any superior lessor.[7]

3.18   An application to upgrade that is made by a person who is not the registered proprietor, but who is entitled to be registered,[8] must be accompanied by evidence of that entitlement.[9] An application by a person interested in a registered estate which derives from the estate in question (such as a tenant)[10] must be accompanied by details of the interest and, where that interest is not apparent from the register, evidence to satisfy the registrar of the applicant's interest.[11]

---

[1]   LRR 2003, r 124(3).

[2]   Under LRA 2002, s 62(3)(a).

[3]   LRR 2003, r 124(2).

[4]   Under LRA 2002, s 62(5). See LRR 2003, r 124(2).

[5]   Under ibid, s 62(3)(b).

[6]   LRR 2003, r 124(2).

[7]   Ibid, r 124(4).

[8]   See LRA 2002, s 62(7)(b); para **3.16**(b).

[9]   LRR 2003, r 124(5).

[10]   See LRA 2002, s 62(7)(d); para **3.16**(d).

[11]   LRR 2003, r 124(6). It will be unusual for the applicant's interest not to be apparent from the register, but it could happen. An example would be where A, a long leaseholder holding under an unregistered lease, granted a sub-lease to B before the requirements of compulsory registration applied. A subsequently assigned her lease to C and the title was registered with good leasehold title (because the freehold was unregistered). B now wishes to assign his sub-lease to D and wishes to ensure that D obtains an absolute title (cf LPA 1925, s 44(4A); para **3.9**). B therefore applies to have C's leasehold title upgraded to absolute. B's sub-lease will not appear on the register and he will therefore have to adduce satisfactory evidence of it to the registrar.

The effect of upgrading title

3.19 The LRA 1925 did not set out the effect of upgrading a title, but left the matter implicit. By contrast, s 63 of the LRA 2002 does specify the effect of upgrading title. Where a title is upgraded to absolute, the proprietor ceases to hold the estate subject to any estate, right or interest whose enforceability was preserved by virtue of the previous entry as to the class of title.[1] The same is true where a possessor or qualified leasehold title is upgraded to good leasehold, except that the upgrading does not affect or prejudice the enforcement of any estate, right or interest which affects or is in derogation of the lessor's title to grant the lease.[2]

Indemnity

3.20 It follows from what is said in para **3.19** that upgrading a title involves an element of risk. An estate, right or interest may be defeated in the process. The LRA 2002, therefore, like the LRA 1925 before it,[3] provides for the payment of indemnity by the registrar for any person who suffers loss by reason of the change of title.[4]

---

[1]   LRA 2002, s 63(1).
[2]   Ibid, s 63(2).
[3]   LRA 1925, s 77(6).
[4]   LRA 2002, Sch 8, para 1(2)(a). For indemnity on this ground, see para **23.3**.

CHAPTER 4

THE EFFECT OF FIRST REGISTRATION

INTRODUCTION

4.1   The effect of first registration depends upon the class of title with which the estate is registered. As a general principle and, as a result of the LRA 2002, subject to an important exception,[1] first registration does not affect priorities but merely reflects priorities that have already been determined. First registration may be voluntary so that there may have been no disposition to trigger registration. In any event, even where there is some disposition, that disposition precedes registration and any issue of competing priorities will be resolved at the time of that disposition. That resolution will depend upon the principles of unregistered conveyancing that necessarily apply to that disposition. A more difficult issue, namely whether if a person is registered as first registered proprietor in circumstances where the conveyance to him that triggered first registration was in fact void, is considered in Chapter 15.[2]

FREEHOLD TITLE

Absolute title

4.2   Where a first registered proprietor of a freehold estate is registered with absolute title, the estate is vested in him together with all interests subsisting for the benefit of that estate.[3] The estate is held subject to four matters which affect the estate on the date of first registration. These require explanation.

4.3   First, it is held subject to interests which are the subject of an entry in relation to the estate.[4] The entries in question will be notices, restrictions and registered charges.[5] On an application for first registration, the registrar will, in accordance with rules,[6] make entries in the register in respect of those interests that appear from the title to affect the estate. For example, if the property is subject to an easement, he will enter a notice in respect of that

---

[1]   See para **4.5**.
[2]   See paras **15.3** et seq.
[3]   LRA 2002, s 11(2), (3).
[4]   Ibid, s 11(4)(a).
[5]   For notices and restrictions, see Chapter 10. For registered charges, see Chapter 12.
[6]   Made under LRA 2002, s 14; para **2.25**.

encumbrance on the charges register of the title. If the registered proprietor has limited powers of disposition, he will enter a restriction to reflect this fact.

4.4   Secondly, the registered estate is held subject to certain unregistered interests.[1] These interests – known under the LRA 1925 (but not under the LRA 2002) as 'overriding interests' – are explained at paras **4.12** et seq.

4.5   Thirdly, the estate is held subject to interests acquired under the LA 1980 of which the proprietor has notice.[2] This principle is new to the LRA 2002 and it marks a striking change in the law. To understand the reasons for it, it is necessary to explain the problem that it seeks to address. Under the LRA 1925, the first registered proprietor took the estate subject to rights previously acquired by any squatter under the LA 1980.[3] This was so whether or not the squatter was in actual occupation at the time when the proprietor was first registered. Furthermore, it was immaterial that the squatter's rights were undiscoverable. The following example will demonstrate how this might happen and the injustice that it could bring.

> 'A squatter was in adverse possession of unregistered land for more than 12 years. His own title[4] had therefore become indefeasible because the former owner's title had been extinguished.[5] The squatter subsequently left the land and the former owner resumed possession. Two years later, that former owner sold and conveyed the land as the apparent paper owner to a buyer, who became the first registered proprietor. If the squatter re-appeared less than 12 years after the former owner had resumed possession,[6] he would be able to recover the land from the buyer.[7] As his interest was an overriding interest that was binding on the buyer, that buyer would be unable to recover indemnity.[8] This was so even though the buyer had purchased from the apparent paper owner and could not reasonably have discovered that the land did in fact belong to an absent squatter.'

4.6   The outcome in that example is self-evidently unsatisfactory. It seriously undermines the conclusive nature of the register of title and the guarantee of title that registration brings with it. The LRA 2002 therefore addresses the problem. Under the Act, where a person is registered as first registered proprietor in circumstances where a squatter is in fact entitled to

---

[1]   LRA 2002, s 11(4)(b).

[2]   Ibid, s 11(4)(c).

[3]   LRA 1925, ss 5(b), 70(1)(f).

[4]   A squatter has an independent and distinct fee simple absolute in possession from the moment that he takes adverse possession: see *Rosenberg v Cook* (1881) 8 QBD 162 at p 165.

[5]   See LA 1980, ss 15, 17.

[6]   Obviously, if more than 12 years had elapsed since the former owner had resumed possession of the land, the squatter's rights would themselves have been barred and extinguished under LA 1980.

[7]   Even though the buyer was a proprietor who was in possession, the register could and probably would be rectified against him: see LRA 1925, s 82(3).

[8]   See *Re Chowood's Registered Land* [1933] Ch 574. The buyer would not suffer loss by reason of the rectification (as required by LRA 1925, s 83(1)), but because he had acquired the land subject to an overriding interest.

the land by reason of his prior adverse possession, the squatter's right will only bind the first registered proprietor in two circumstances. The first (which is more fully explained at paras **4.14**(2) and **4.16**(1)) is where the squatter is in actual occupation of the land at the time of first registration. Although by virtue of that actual occupation the squatter's right to the land will override first registration,[1] that right should be readily discoverable from the fact of the squatter's presence. The second case, which is relevant here, is where the first registered proprietor has notice of the squatter's interest even though he is not in actual occupation.[2] As a result, if the facts given in the example in para **4.5** were to happen, the buyer of the land would take it free of the squatter's rights on first registration. This is so even though the squatter's rights bound him in the period between the conveyance of the land to him and the moment of first registration. This is the new principle which the LRA 2002 introduces and it constitutes an exception to the general rule, explained above,[3] that first registration does not affect priorities but merely reflects the state of the title as it was on the date of first registration. A squatter who acquires title to unregistered land by adverse possession and who ceases to occupy it should therefore take steps to protect his interest by applying for first registration of title.[4] The LRA 2002 contains a transitional provision whereby any squatter who, under the LA 1980, had become entitled to the land by virtue of his adverse possession, will be protected for a period of 3 years.[5] His rights will override any first registration in that period even though he is not in actual occupation. This will give such persons a reasonable opportunity to apply for registration during that transitional period, although it does of course mean that the evil which the LRA 2002 addresses remains for that period.[6]

4.7   Fourthly, where the registered proprietor is either not entitled to the estate for his own benefit at all or is not solely entitled, he holds the estate subject to such of the interests of those beneficially entitled as he has notice

---

[1]   LRA 2002, Sch 1, para 2.

[2]   Ibid, s 11(4)(c). The Act says 'notice' and not 'knowledge' (as it does elsewhere in the Act). It follows that the first registered proprietor will be bound by squatter's rights of which he ought to have known as well as those of which he actually knows. First registration may not have been prompted by any disposition and may be voluntary, or it may have been triggered by a gift (whether *inter vivos* or testamentary). It follows that the usual enquiries and inspections that would have been made on a purchase will not have been made. What constitutes notice must, therefore, be judged according to the circumstances and not according to one yardstick.

[3]   See para **4.1**.

[4]   They will not be able to lodge a caution against first registration: see LRA 2002, s 15(3); also para **5.5**.

[5]   Ibid, Sch 12, para 7, adding para 15 to Sch 1.

[6]   The 3-year transitional period was criticised during the passage of the Act through Parliament by Lord Lester of Herne Hill: see *Hansard* (HL), 30 October 2001, vol 627, cols 1329–1332. His concern was whether the provision was compatible with the Human Rights Act 1998. However, it appears that he did not appreciate that a squatter would be protected if he were in actual occupation of the land affected: see col 1336. A 3-year transitional period would appear to be proportionate when balancing the claims of innocent purchasers in possession against absent squatters who have done nothing to protect their rights.

of.[1] This provision ensures that, for example, where the first registered proprietor holds the estate on trust, he does not take free of those trusts.[2] However, the provision is not limited to interests under a trust, but could include, for example, the rights of a person with an equity arising by proprietary estoppel.

Qualified and possessory titles

4.8   Registration of a freehold with a qualified title has the same effect as does registration with an absolute title, with one exception. It does not affect the enforcement of any estate, right or interest which appears from the register to be excepted from the effect of registration.[3] Similarly, registration with possessory title has the same effect as registration with absolute title but, again, with an exception. It does not affect the enforcement of any estate, right or interest that is adverse to, or in derogation of, the proprietor's title, which is either subsisting at the time of first registration or is capable of arising.[4] For example, if the first registered proprietor was registered with possessory freehold title but it subsequently transpired that her title was only leasehold and not freehold, registration with a possessory title would not prevent the freeholder from enforcing his rights on the termination of the lease.

LEASEHOLD TITLE

Absolute title

4.9   Where a first registered proprietor is registered with an absolute title to a leasehold estate, the effect is the same as where a person is registered as first registered proprietor of a freehold with an absolute title, with one exception.[5] The proprietor of the lease holds it subject not only to the four matters explained in paras **4.3–4.7**, but also to the implied and express covenants, obligations and liabilities incident to the leasehold estate.[6] Those burdens found in the lease that create proprietary rights, such as the landlord's right of re-entry or any restrictive covenants, are not noted on the register, but by virtue of this provision they still bind the lessee. The register will refer to the lease and it therefore constitutes part of the register. Any person who was intending to deal with the land (whether the lease, the reversion or perhaps some derivative interest) would inspect the lease and would therefore be aware of its contents.

---

[1]   LRA 2002, s 11(5).
[2]   Cf LRA 1925, s 5(c) (the equivalent provision under the previous law).
[3]   LRA 2002, s 11(6).
[4]   Ibid, s 11(7).
[5]   Ibid, s 12(2)–(4).
[6]   Ibid, s 12(4)(a).

Good leasehold title

4.10   First registration with a good leasehold title has the same effect as the first registration of a leaseholder with absolute title, except that it does not prejudice the enforcement of any estate, right or interest affecting, or in derogation of, the title of the lessor to grant the lease.[1]

Qualified and possessory titles

4.11   The first registration of a person as the proprietor of a leasehold estate with qualified or possessory title has the same effect as registration with absolute title, but subject to the same exceptions that have been explained in para **4.8** in relation to qualified and possessory freehold title.[2]

UNREGISTERED INTERESTS WHICH OVERRIDE FIRST REGISTRATION

Introduction

4.12   It has been explained above that, on first registration, the proprietor takes the estate subject to, amongst other matters, certain unregistered interests.[3] Overriding interests, as they were known under the LRA 1925, are a well-known and unsatisfactory feature of registered conveyancing. The existence of rights that affect a registered estate but do not appear on the register run counter to the objectives of a system of registered title. Such interests are necessarily incompatible with the fundamental objective of the LRA 2002, explained in Chapter 1, which is to make the register as complete and accurate a record of the title at any given time as is possible. The Act contains many provisions by which the impact of such unregistered interests can be minimised. These are explained at various places in the course of this book.[4] The Land Registry has published a Practice Guide, 'Overriding Interests and Their Disclosure'.[5]

4.13   In s 70(1) of the LRA 1925,[6] no explicit distinction was drawn between those unregistered interests that overrode first registration and those that overrode registered dispositions. However, such a distinction necessarily exists and the LRA 2002 makes this clear. It lists the unregistered interests that override first registration in Sch 1 and those that override registered dispositions in Sch 3. The lists are not the same. As has been indicated

---

1   LRA 2002, s 12(6).
2   Ibid, s 12(7), (8).
3   See para **4.4**.
4   See paras **4.15–4.21, 11.18–11.22**.
5   PG15.
6   The subsection of LRA 1925 that listed overriding interests.

above,[1] subject to one exception that is introduced by the LRA 2002,[2] first registration reflects the state of the title at the time of first registration and does not change the priority of interests that affect it. This is because first registration does not bring about any disposition of the land, whereas the registration of a registered disposition necessarily does. Thus in Sch 3, whether or not the person to whom a registered disposition has been made is bound by an unregistered interest depends, in some cases, on whether he made any enquiries about such rights or whether they met certain requirements as to their discoverability. However, such issues have no meaning in relation to first registration and there are no equivalent provisions in Sch 1. Whether or not the rights that fall within that Schedule bind the first registered proprietor will have been determined before he applies for first registration.[3]

The interests that will override first registration

4.14   Schedule 1 to the LRA 2002 (as amended) lists 15 interests that will bind the first registered proprietor even though they are not protected on the register. A sixteenth has been added by s 90 of the Act. The interests are as follows.[4]

(1)   Any lease granted for a term of 7 years or less unless it is required to be registered under the provisions explained at paras **2.16–2.18**.[5] This is the logical concomitant of the provisions on the compulsory registration of leases explained in Chapter 2.[6] Those leases that are not subject to the requirement of registration necessarily override first registration even though they are not registered.[7]

(2)   An interest belonging to a person in actual occupation, so far as relating to land of which he is in actual occupation.[8] This provision partially replicates s 70(1)(g) of the LRA 1925 and, as was the case under that Act,[9] it is not possible to protect by actual occupation an interest under a settlement under the Settled Land Act 1925 (SLA 1925). The provision is narrower in two respects than s 70(1)(g) of the LRA 1925. First, the protection conferred on an interest is limited to the land actually occupied.[10] To the extent that the interest extends

---

[1]   See para **4.1**.

[2]   See para **4.5**.

[3]   See (2001) Law Com No 271, paras 8.3–8.5.

[4]   Three of them are grouped together in para **4.14**(7).

[5]   LRA 2002, Sch 1, para 1.

[6]   See para **2.13**.

[7]   The same protection applies to leases that were granted for more than 21 years before the Act came into force: LRA 2002, Sch 12, para 12.

[8]   LRA 2002, Sch 1, para 2.

[9]   See LRA 1925, s 86(2).

[10]   Cf *Ferrishurst Ltd v Wallcite Ltd* [1999] Ch 355, which the Act reverses.

beyond that land, it is unprotected. This point is explained more fully in the context of unregistered interests which override registered dispositions, because it is only in that context that it is really material.[1] Secondly, protection is no longer given to those who are in receipt of the rents and profits of the land as well as those who are in actual occupation. This is of more significance in relation to unregistered interests that override a registered disposition and it is, once again, explained in more detail there.[2] For the reasons explained para **4.13**, Sch 1 does not include the words 'save where enquiry is made of such person[3] and the rights are not disclosed' that were found in s 70(1)(g) of the LRA 1925.

(3)   A legal easement or profit.[4] The only easements and profits that will be capable of overriding first registration are those that are legal. Equitable easements will never do so.[5] Furthermore, the provisions on disclosure explained below[6] should ensure that many such easements are in fact protected by notice on the register at first registration.

(4)   A customary right.[7] Customary rights are those that are enjoyed by all or some of the inhabitants of a particular locality, such as the ancient right of the freeman of the borough of Huntingdon to graze animals over certain land.[8]

(5)   A public right.[9] Such rights are exercisable by any person under the general law and include, for example, public rights of way.

(6)   A local land charge.[10] Local land charges operate under the quite separate regime created by the Local Land Charges Act 1975, which makes provision for their registration in local registers. Those registers are themselves being computerised by local authorities and it will become possible to access them through the National Land Information Service (NLIS).

(7)   Certain mineral rights. Three classes of mineral right override first registration. First, any interest in any coal or coal mines, the rights attached to such interests and certain other rights under the Coal Industry Act 1994 are all incapable of any form of registration under the Act[11] and override first registration as unregistered interests.[12] The extent and complexity of coal rights made it difficult to register them.

---

1   See para **11.5**.
2   Ibid.
3   That is, the person in actual occupation.
4   LRA 2002, Sch 1, para 3.
5   They could under LRA 1925, s 70(1)(a): see *Celsteel Ltd v Alton House Holdings Ltd* [1985] 1 WLR 204 at pp 219–221.
6   See para **4.19**.
7   LRA 2002, Sch 1, para 4.
8   See *Peggs v Lamb* [1994] Ch 172.
9   LRA 2002, Sch 1, para 5.
10   Ibid, para 6.
11   See ibid, s 33(c); see also para **10.11**.
12   Ibid, Sch 1, para 7.

However, the Coal Authority provides a system of coal mining searches so it is possible to discover what mining either has been or may in future be conducted on any particular land. Again, it is likely that it will become possible to conduct such searches on-line via NLIS. Secondly, for reasons connected with the practice of registration prior to the LRA 1925 in relation to mineral rights over registered land, mineral rights over land that were registered before 1898 will override first registration.[1] Thirdly, for the same reason, as regards land that was registered between 1898 and 1925, mineral rights created prior to such registration will, again, override first registration.[2]

(8)   A franchise.[3] Franchises arise out of an actual or presumed royal grant and can be valuable.[4] As explained above, it is possible for the first time under the Act to register such rights with their own titles.[5]

(9)   A right in respect of the repair of a church chancel.[6] This curious and potentially draconian form of liability[7] had overriding status under the LRA 1925.[8] It was to have retained that status under the LRA 2002. However, about a month before the Land Registration Bill was introduced into Parliament, the Court of Appeal held that a landowner's liability for chancel repairs contravened the European Convention on Human Rights.[9] The relevant clause was therefore removed from the Bill. The House of Lords reversed the decision on 26 June 2003,[10] and the provision that was originally intended was restored by means of an order making transitional provision under s 134 of the LRA 2002.[11]

(10)   A manorial right.[12] It ceased to be possible to create manorial rights after 1925. However, such rights are quite common and include the lord's sporting rights or his rights to minerals.

---

[1]   LRA 2002, Sch 1, para 8.

[2]   Ibid, Sch 1, para 9.

[3]   Ibid, Sch 1, para 10.

[4]   Amongst the commonest is the franchise to hold a market.

[5]   LRA 2002, s 3; see also para **2.6**.

[6]   Ibid, Sch 1, para 16, added by TPO2 2003. The paragraph was inserted in exercise of the power to make transitional provisions contained in LRA 2002, s 134(1). There must be at least some doubt about the *vires* of the Order.

[7]   On which, see J H Baker, 'Lay Rectors and Chancel repairs' (1984) 100 LQR 181.

[8]   See LRA 1925, s 70(1)(c).

[9]   *Aston Cantlow and Wilmcote with Billesley PCC v Wallbank* [2001] EWCA Civ 713, [2002] Ch 51 (17 May 2001).

[10]   *Aston Cantlow and Wilmcote with Billesley PCC v Wallbank* [2003] UKHL 37, [2003] 3 WLR 283. The judgments throw open a number of fundamental aspects of chancel repair liability that will no doubt lead to further litigation. There was a sharp difference of opinion between Lord Hobhouse and Lord Scott as to whether there was a limit on the extent of a landowner's liability.

[11]   See TPO2 2003.

[12]   LRA 2002, Sch 1, para 11.

(11) What is commonly called a Crown rent.[1] This is a very obscure right and arose on the grant of a freehold estate by the Crown with the reservation of a rent.

(12) A non-statutory right in respect of an embankment or river or sea wall.[2] Once again, this is an obscure form of liability. It may affect a person who owns property that fronts on to the sea or a river. It may have arisen by prescription, grant, a covenant supported by a rentcharge, custom or tenure.

(13) What is often called a corn rent.[3] This is perhaps the most arcane of the interests that can override first registration.[4] Technically, it is a liability on the owner of the land to make payments by any Act of Parliament other than one of the Tithe Acts, out of or charged upon land in commutation of tithes.

(14) PPP leases.[5] The nature of these leases and the reasons why they are outside the registered system have been explained in para **2.3**.

(15) A right acquired under LA 1980 before 13 October 2003.[6] This provision makes it clear that where a squatter had extinguished the title of the owner by adverse possession prior to first registration, his rights remain overriding. However, this class of unregistered interests will override first registration only for a period of 3 years beginning on 13 October 2003, when LRA 2002 came into force. This has been explained at para **4.6**.

Limiting the scope of unregistered interests that override first registration

4.15 It has been explained above that the existence of unregistered interests that can override first registration runs counter to the fundamental objective of the Act, which is to create a register that is as far as possible conclusive as to the state of the title at any time.[7] The LRA 2002 therefore adopts a number of strategies for eliminating such interests as far as possible.

4.16 The first strategy is to restrict the interests that can override first registration. This strategy has two aspects. The first is to remove overriding status from interests which previously had it under s 70(1) of the LRA 1925. There are two such interests:

---

1   LRA 2002, Sch 1, para 12.
2   Ibid, Sch 1, para 13.
3   Ibid, Sch 1, para 14.
4   Liability to pay corn rent still exists. The principal (but not only) beneficiaries are the Church Commissioners, who no longer collect it because it is uneconomic to do so.
5   LRA 2002, s 90(5).
6   See LRA 2002, Sch 1, para 7.
7   See para **4.12**.

(1)   Squatter's rights.[1] If a squatter has barred the rights of the first registered proprietor before first registration, subject to the transitional provisions that have been explained above,[2] his rights will only override first registration if at the date of first registration he was in actual occupation or the first registered proprietor had notice of his rights.[3]

(2)   Estates, rights and interests excluded from the effect of first registration in the case of possessory, qualified or good leasehold titles.[4] These are dealt with in a different way under the Act by way of the provisions on priorities.[5]

4.17   The second aspect of the strategy is to narrow the scope of the interests that can override first registration. The Act does this in relation to a number of the interests that fall within Sch 1 and, in particular, in relation to the three most important categories of interest, namely, leases, the interests of persons in actual occupation and easements and profits.

4.18   Secondly, the LRA 2002 makes provision for the phasing out of six of the interests 10 years after the Act is brought into force.[6] The interests are those listed in para **4.14**(8)–(13).[7] If a person enjoys the benefit of one or more of those six interests over unregistered land, he will be entitled to lodge a caution against the first registration of the land affected without charge during that 10-year period.[8] In this way he can ensure that, on the first registration of that land, his interest will be noted on the register. If he fails to lodge a caution against first registration during that 10-year period, he will not lose his right. However, there is obviously a significant risk that if the land is then registered, the interest will not be noted on the title. Solicitors and licensed conveyancers may wish to consider whether any of their clients are likely to be affected by this provision and, if they are, to draw it to their attention.

4.19   Thirdly, in consequence of s 71(a) of the LRA 2002 and r 28 of the LRR 2003 made under it, an applicant for first registration must provide information to the registrar about any interest affecting the estate which falls within Sch 1 to the LRA 2002 (subject to specified exceptions) that is within

---

[1]   See LRA 1925, s 70(1)(f).

[2]   See para **4.6**.

[3]   Ibid.

[4]   See LRA 1925, s 70(1)(h).

[5]   See LRA 2002, ss 29(2)(a)(iii), 30(2)(a)(iii); see also para **9.8**.

[6]   Ibid, s 117.

[7]   Namely, franchises, chancel repair liability, manorial rights, Crown rents, liability to repair embankments, sea and river walls, and corn rents. For the reasons why these interests (other than chancel repair liability) were selected, see (2001) Law Com No 271, paras 8.87–8.88. There was no discussion of chancel repair liability in the Law Commission's report for the reasons given at para **4.14**(9).

[8]   LRA 2002, s 117(2)(a). For cautions against first registration, see Chapter 5.

his actual knowledge and affects the estate to which the application relates. The information has to be supplied on Form DI,[1] which is submitted together with Form FR1.[2] There is no obligation to provide information about the following interests:[3]

(a)   An interest that cannot be protected by notice.[4]

(b)   An interest that is apparent from the deeds and documents of title that accompany the application for first registration,[5] and which will therefore be entered in the register. This would be the case if (for example) the deeds recited the fact that the land was subject to a right of way that had been acquired by prescription.

(c)   A public right. The Registry has, it seems, made a decision that public rights should not be recorded in the register.[6]

(d)   A local land charge. These are registered in local land charges registers,[7] and it is only in very limited cases that they should also be registered in the land register.[8]

(e)   A lease which overrides first registration under para 1 of Sch 1 to the LRA 2002[9] and has only one year or less to run.

4.20   Although there will initially be no sanction for failing to make the necessary disclosure, once electronic conveyancing has been introduced, an obligation to comply with s 71 is likely to be a term of any network access agreement.[10]

4.21   Fourthly, under s 37(1) of the LRA 2002, the registrar is given power to enter a notice on the register in respect of any interest that falls within Sch 1, unless it is an interest of a kind that cannot be protected by notice.[11] The registrar is required to give notice of any such entry to certain persons who are specified in r 89 of LRR 2003.[12] Those persons are as follows.

(a)   The registered proprietor (unless he has made the application for the entry of the notice or otherwise consents to an application for the entry of that notice).[13] It is obviously appropriate that the registered

---

1   LRR 2003, r 28(1).
2   See Panel 12 of Form FR1.
3   LRR 2003, r 28(2)
4   See LRA 2002, ss 33, 90(4); paras **10.6–10.12**.
5   See LRR 2003, r 24; para **2.26**.
6   See para **2.38**.
7   See the Local Land Charges Act 1975.
8   See LRA 2002, s 55, explained at para **12.80**.
9   See para **4.14(1)**.
10   For network access agreements, see paras **27.13** et seq, esp at para **27.7**.
11   For those interests, see LRA 2002, s 33; see also paras **10.6–10.12**.
12   LRA 2002, s 37(2).
13   LRR 2003, r 89(1)(a), (2).

proprietor should be informed of the entry of an incumbrance on his title.

(b)   Any person who appears to the registrar to be entitled to the interest protected by the notice or whom the registrar otherwise considers appropriate.[1] The registrar does not have to give notice, however, if the person applied for the entry of the notice or otherwise consented to its entry.[2] Nor need he give notice if the person's name and address for service under LRR 2003, r 198,[3] are not set out in the register in which the notice is entered.[4] The reason why the beneficiary of the interest should be notified where possible is to enable him to apply to alter the entry should he consider that it is inaccurate or out of date. It is also relevant that he should know that once his interest has been entered in the register, it can never again have overriding status even if it is subsequently deleted from the register in error.[5]

---

[1]   LRR 2003, r 89(1)(b).
[2]   Ibid, r 89(3)(a).
[3]   For LRR 2003, r 198, see para **20.42**.
[4]   LRR 2003, r 89(3)(b).
[5]   LRA 2002, ss 29(3), 30(3); para **9.8**.

CHAPTER 5

CAUTIONS AGAINST
FIRST REGISTRATION

INTRODUCTION

5.1   Cautions against first registration provide a mechanism by which a person, who has some interest in unregistered land, can ensure that he is informed of any application for the first registration of that land. He may have grounds for wishing to oppose any such application[1] or, more commonly, he wishes to ensure that, on first registration, his interest will be protected on the register. Although the LRA 2002 prospectively abolishes cautions *against dealings*,[2] it retains cautions against first registration.[3] However, it rationalises the way in which they are recorded, it extends the circumstances in which their entry may be challenged and it places a significant limitation on what may be protected by them. Part 5 of the LRR 2003 supplies the mechanism for the operation of cautions against first registration. The Land Registry has published a Practice Guide on 'Cautions Against First Registration'.[4]

RECORDING CAUTIONS AGAINST FIRST REGISTRATION

Overview

5.2   Under the LRA 1925, cautions against first registration were recorded on an index map (thereby indicating that there was a caution lodged against a particular parcel of land). The details of any such caution[5] were kept on what was called a 'caution title'. Under the LRA 2002, cautions against first registration are recorded on what the Act calls 'the index'.[6] The details of any given caution are kept on a new cautions register which the Act creates.[7]

---

[1]   Perhaps because he has some claim to the land himself.

[2]   See para **10.3**.

[3]   See LRA 2002, Part 2, Chapter 2.

[4]   PG3.

[5]   Namely, the cautioner's name and address, the name and address of the solicitor or licensed conveyancer who lodged the caution, the estate against which the caution had been registered and an extract from the statutory declaration in support of the application to show the nature of the cautioner's interest.

[6]   LRA 2002, s 68(1)(c). For the index, see para **14.14**.

[7]   Ibid, s 19. The register may be kept in electronic or paper form, or partly in one form and partly in the other: LRR 2003, r 40(1).

The cautions register

5.3   The LRR 2003 provides detailed machinery for the recording of cautions against first registration.[1] The cautions register mentioned in para **5.2** comprises the individual caution registers that are opened for each caution against first registration.[2] The registrar does in fact have power to open an individual caution register for each separate area of land affected by the caution as he designates.[3] If, therefore, a caution was lodged in respect of an extensive land holding, separate caution registers might be opened in respect of each separate area of land. Each individual caution register has its own caution title number,[4] and is in two parts.[5]

(a)   The first part is the caution property register, which contains a description of the legal estate to which the caution relates and a description of the interest claimed by the cautioner.[6] Where the caution relates to an estate in land, a rentcharge or an affecting franchise,[7] the description will refer to a caution plan.[8] That caution plan is based upon the Ordnance Survey map.[9]

(b)   The second part is the cautioner's register. This will contain the following information:[10]

    (i)   The name of the cautioner.

    (ii)   If the cautioner is a company registered under the Companies Acts or a limited liability partnership incorporated under the Limited Liability Partnerships Act 2000, its registered number.

    (iii)   An address for service in accordance with LRR 2003, r 198.[11]

    (iv)   Where a person has consented to the lodging of the caution,[12] details of that person.

LODGING CAUTIONS AGAINST FIRST REGISTRATION

Who may lodge a caution?

5.4   Under the LRA 2002, subject to one very significant exception,[13] a

---

[1]   Cf the register of title: see Chapter 14.

[2]   LRR 2002, r 40(2).

[3]   LRR 2003, r 40(3).

[4]   Ibid, r 41(1). The title number may consist of a number or a series of letters and numbers.

[5]   Ibid, r 41(2).

[6]   Ibid, r 41(3) and see r 39.

[7]   For affecting franchises (those that relate to defined area of land and are an incumbrance upon it), see LRR 2003, r 217(1); para **2.26**(a). Franchises that are not affecting franchises are called 'relating franchises': LRR 2003, r 217(1).

[8]   LRR 2003, r 41(4).

[9]   Ibid.

[10]   Ibid, r 41(5).

[11]   For LRR 2003, r 198, see para **20.42**.

[12]   See LRA 2002, s 18(2) and LRR 2003, r 47; para **5.20**.

[13]   See para **5.5**.

person may apply to the registrar[1] to lodge a caution against first registration if he claims to be either the owner of a qualifying estate or entitled to an interest affecting such a qualifying estate.[2] For these purposes, 'a qualifying estate' means:

(a)   an estate in land;
(b)   a rentcharge;
(c)   a franchise; and
(d)   a *profit à prendre* in gross,

that relates to the land to which the caution relates.[3] Thus, for example:

(i)   a tenant holding under a lease may lodge a caution against the first registration of his landlord's reversionary freehold estate;
(ii)   a person who claims the benefit of an easement or profit over a freehold estate may lodge a caution against the first registration of that estate; or
(iii)   a beneficiary under a trust of land may lodge a caution against the first registration of the freehold estate held by the trustees.

5.5   The LRA 2002 introduces a significant limitation on the power to lodge a caution against first registration. A person may not lodge a caution against the first registration of his own estate where that estate is either a freehold estate in land or a lease of which more than 7 years remains unexpired at the time when the caution is lodged.[4] The policy of this provision is that a caution against first registration should not be used as a substitute for the first registration of a title.[5] This provision will not take effect until 2 years after the Act was brought into force.[6] However, any caution lodged within that 2-year period will cease to have effect at the end of

---

1   See LRA 2002, s 15(4).
2   Ibid, s 15(1).
3   Ibid, s 15(2).
4   Ibid, s 15(3).
5   See (2001) Law Com No 271, para 3.58. In practice, it is not common for landowners to lodge cautions against the first registration of their own estates. Nonetheless, this provision provoked criticism (and indeed a division) in the House of Lords. This was because it was said that it would force charities to register their lands when presently they could protect their unregistered estates by lodging a caution against first registration: see *Hansard* (HL), 17 July 2001, vol 626, cols 1412–1417. It seems to have been thought that lodging a caution against first registration would protect such charities from applications by squatters: see the comments of Baroness Buscombe at col 1413. However, lodging a caution against first registration would only be useful in this regard if the squatter had not barred and extinguished the landowner's title. By contrast, under the provisions explained in Part 6, registration of a title *will* protect a registered proprietor against an application for registration by a squatter in most cases. In any event, the appeal to the burden placed upon charities is questionable. Given the substantial benefits conferred on charities, there is at least a case for saying that all charities should be required to register their land so that the information about those properties is publicly available.
6   LRA 2002, Sch 12, para 14(1).

it except in relation to applications for first registration made within the period.[1]

The application for a caution

5.6   Application for a caution against first registration must be made in Form CT1.[2] It must contain sufficient details, by plan or otherwise, so that the land to which the caution relates can be identified clearly on the Ordnance Survey map.[3] In practice, the applicant must supply a plan unless the postal description of the property is such that its boundaries can be identified on the Ordnance Survey map. Part of the requirements of Form CT1 are that either:

(a)   the applicant makes a statutory declaration as to the interest which he has that entitles him to make the application; or

(b)   the applicant's conveyancer certifies the applicant's interest.

The registrar will be unable to inform the owner of the unregistered land that a caution has been lodged against it. As the title is unregistered, the registrar will have no address for service. If, therefore, the cautioner wishes the landowner to be made aware of the lodging of the caution (which in certain circumstances he might, if he wishes to bring matters to a head), he should inform the owner himself that he has lodged the caution.

Who is the 'cautioner' for the purposes of the legislation?

5.7   The system of cautions against first registration could not function properly if 'the cautioner' meant only the person who lodged the caution. That person who may either die or become insolvent, so that the interest that entitled him to lodge the caution against first registration vests by operation of law in some other person. For the purposes of the provisions of the Act, the term 'cautioner' therefore includes not only the person who lodged the caution but also such other persons as rules may provide: see LRA 2002, s 22. The relevant rules provide that:

(a)   A person, who claims that the whole of the interest that entitled the cautioner to lodge the caution has vested in him by operation of law as successor to the cautioner, can apply for the cautioner's register to be altered[4] to show him as the cautioner in place of the original cautioner.[5]

(b)   'The cautioner' is, accordingly, the person for the time being shown as

[1]   LRA 2002, Sch 12, para 14(2).
[2]   LRR 2003, r 42. See Land Registry Practice Guide, Cautions Against First Registration, PG3, para 3.3, for details of what must be included in Form CT1.
[3]   LRR 2003, r 42.
[4]   See para **5.11**.
[5]   LRR 2003, r 51(1).

the cautioner in the cautioner's register, where that person is not the person who lodged the caution against first registration.[1]

WITHDRAWING A CAUTION AGAINST FIRST REGISTRATION

5.8   The cautioner, in the extended sense explained in para **5.7**, has a right to withdraw the caution on application to the registrar.[2] The cautioner (as so defined) is the only person who can object to an application to cancel a caution against first registration: s 73(2). This is an exception to the general rule that anyone may object to an application made to the registrar: s 73(1).[3] An application to withdraw a caution against first registration must be made in Form WCT.[4] If the application is made in respect of part only of the land to which the individual caution register relates, it must contain sufficient details, by plan or otherwise, so that the extent of the part in question can be clearly identified on the Ordnance Survey map.[5]

ALTERING THE CAUTIONS REGISTER

5.9   Both the court and registrar are given powers to alter the register of cautions that are analogous to those that apply to the register of title[6] for the purpose of correcting a mistake or bringing the register up to date.[7] The LRR 2003[8] amplify the provisions of LRA 2002 and provide as follows.

Alteration by the court

5.10   First, the court must make an order for the alteration of the cautions register if, in any proceedings, it decides that:

(a)   the cautioner does not own the relevant interest;[9]
(b)   the cautioner owns only part of the relevant interest;
(c)   the relevant interest did not exist either in whole or in part; or
(d)   the relevant interest has come to an end.[10]

When such an order is served on the registrar, he is under a duty to give effect

---

[1]   LRR 2003, rr 39, 52.
[2]   LRA 2002, s 17.
[3]   See para **20.29**.
[4]   LRR 2003, r 43.
[5]   Ibid. Cf para **5.6**.
[6]   For alteration of the register of title, see Chapter 22.
[7]   LRA 2002, ss 20, 21.
[8]   The relevant rules are made pursuant to LRA 2002, ss 20(3) (alteration by the court) and 21(2) (alteration by the registrar).
[9]   The 'relevant interest' is the interest claimed in the unregistered land that entitles him to lodge a caution: see LRR 2003, r 39; and see para **5.3**.
[10]   LRR 2003, r 48(1). LRR 2003, r 48(2) sets out the matters that must be contained in the court's order.

to it.[1] An order may only be served on the registrar by making an application to him to give effect to the order.[2]

Alteration by the registrar

5.11 Secondly, if any person wishes the registrar to alter the cautions register,[3] he must apply to the registrar, using Form AP1. His application must include written details of the alteration required, the grounds on which the application is made, and any supporting document.[4] The registrar is required to serve notice on the cautioner giving details of the application, unless he is satisfied that service of the notice is unnecessary (as, for example, where the cautioner applies for, or has signified his consent to, the alteration).[5] The registrar must alter the cautions register[6] if he is satisfied that:

(a)   the cautioner does not own the relevant interest;
(b)   the cautioner owns only part of the relevant interest;
(c)   the relevant interest did not exist either in whole or in part; or
(d)   the relevant interest has come to an end.[7]

Where such an alteration is made by the registrar, the registrar may pay such amount as he thinks fit in respect of any costs reasonably incurred by a person in connection with the alteration.[8]

Indemnity

5.12 Indemnity is payable in respect of loss suffered as a result of a mistake in the cautions register.[9]

THE EFFECT OF LODGING A CAUTION AGAINST FIRST REGISTRATION

5.13 The protection that a caution against first registration confers is limited. When there is an application for the first registration of the unregistered legal estate to which the caution relates, the registrar must give the cautioner[10] notice of the application and of his right to object to it.[11] The

---

[1]   LRA 2002, s 20(2).
[2]   LRR 2003, r 48(3).
[3]   That is, under LRA 2002, s 21(1).
[4]   LRR 2003, r 50(1).
[5]   Ibid, r 50(2).
[6]   Under LRA 2002, s 21(1).
[7]   LRR 2003, r 49.
[8]   LRA 2002, s 21(3).
[9]   Ibid, Sch 8, para 1(1)(g). For indemnity, see Chapter 23.
[10]   See para **5.7**.
[11]   LRA 2002, s 16(1). The Act makes provision for an agent of the applicant for first registration to give

general rule is that the cautioner will have until 12 noon on the fifteenth business day[1] after the date of the issue of the notice in which to make his objection.[2] There is a power for the registrar to extend that period up to 12 noon on the thirtieth business day after the date of the issue of the notice, if requested to do so by the cautioner.[3] The registrar will only be able to determine an application for first registration once that period has elapsed unless the cautioner indicates before that date that he does not intend to object to the application.[4]

5.14 A caution against first registration has no effect on the validity or priority of any interest that the cautioner may have in the legal estate to which the caution relates.[5] In essence, therefore, the lodging of a caution has no substantive effect. It is merely a procedural device by which a person, who has an interest in unregistered land, is alerted to an application for first registration. He may then oppose that application if he so wishes. This will often be done to ensure that his interest is duly protected on first registration in the register of the legal estate to which it relates.

REMOVING OR CHALLENGING A CAUTION AGAINST FIRST REGISTRATION

5.15 The LRA 2002 contains a number of provisions that are intended to deter the improper lodgement of cautions against first registration. These fall into three categories.

The power to object to an application to lodge a caution against first registration

5.16 First, should the owner of land[6] become aware that there has been an application to the registrar to lodge a caution against first registration, he may object to the application under the general power conferred by the Act for any person to object to an application.[7] If that objection cannot be disposed

---

notice to the cautioner and, if he does, this is to be treated as given by the registrar: s 16(4). The persons who can serve such a notice will be prescribed by rules, but none have been made so far (it was expected that the persons would be likely to include solicitors and licensed conveyancers). Similarly, the circumstances in which a notice may be served will be a matter for rules, but, once again, none have been made so far. The intention of this provision was to enable a solicitor or licensed conveyancer, who was acting for an applicant for first registration, to serve a notice on the cautioner at the same time as the application for first registration. It was thought that this would speed up the conveyancing process. It remains to be seen whether any such rules will be made.

[1] For the meaning of 'business day', see LRR 2003, r 216; para **36.5**.
[2] LRR 2003, r 53(1).
[3] Ibid, r 53(1), (2). The request must be made before 12 noon on the fifteenth business day after the date of the issue of the notice: LRR 2003, r 53(4). The registrar may seek views of the person applying for registration in considering whether or not to grant such an extension: LRR 2003, r 53(3).
[4] LRA 2002, s 16(2).
[5] Ibid, s 16(3).
[6] Or indeed any other person with a sufficient interest in the land, such as a chargee.
[7] LRA 2002, s 73; see also para **20.29**.

of by agreement, it will be referred to the Adjudicator for resolution.[1]

Applying for the cancellation of a caution against first registration

5.17   Secondly, the Act and Rules give the following persons the right to apply *at any time* to the registrar for the cancellation of the caution:[2]

(a)   the owner of the legal estate affected by the caution;[3]

(b)   the owner of a legal estate derived out of that estate, such as legal chargee or a lessee;[4] and

(c)   where the land to which the caution relates is demesne land,[5] Her Majesty, or the owner of a legal estate affecting the demesne land, such as a lessee holding under a lease from the Crown,[6] although the legal estate does not have to be one that was granted by the Crown.[7]

Under the LRA 1925, the process whereby a caution was cancelled was referred to as 'warning off', but the LRA 2002 uses the more intelligible language of cancellation.

5.18   An application for the cancellation of a caution against first registration must be in Form CCT.[8] Where the application is made in respect of part only of the land to which the individual caution register relates, it must contain sufficient details, whether by means of a plan or otherwise, so that the extent of that part can be clearly identified on the Ordnance Survey map.[9] Evidence of the applicant's entitlement to apply for cancellation[10] must accompany the application.[11]

5.19   When an application to cancel a caution is made, the registrar must

[1]   LRA 2002, s 73(7). For the Adjudicator to HM Land Registry, see Chapter 34.
[2]   Ibid, s 18(1). Under LRA 1925, s 53(3), a landowner could *only* challenge the caution once he had made an application for first registration. This meant that a landowner, who wished to sell his land and was aware that there was a caution against first registration, could do nothing to remove it before the sale.
[3]   Ibid, s 18(1)(a).
[4]   Ibid, s 18(1)(b); LRR 2003, r 45(a).
[5]   For demesne land, see para **6.1**.
[6]   LRA 2002, s 18(1)(b); LRR 2003, r 45(b).
[7]   When a freehold escheats to the Crown, encumbrances such as legal charges continue to bind the land even though the freehold estate no longer exists. A mortgagee (for example) could therefore apply for the cancellation of a caution against first registration.
[8]   LRR 2003, r 44(1). This is subject to one qualification. Where Her Majesty applies for the cancellation of a caution against first registration in relation to demesne land under LRR 2003, r 45(b)(i) (see para **5.17**), Form CCT must be used with such modifications to it as are appropriate and have been approved by the registrar: LRR 2003, r 44(5). In practice, this is likely to be a matter for agreement between the Crown Estate and the Land Registry.
[9]   LRR 2003, r 4(2). See Form CCT, Panel 5.
[10]   See para **5.17**.
[11]   LRR 2003, r 44(3). There is an exception in relation to an application by Her Majesty where the caution relates to demesne land: ibid.

inform the cautioner[1] of the application and of the fact that, if he does not exercise his right to object within the period specified by rules, the caution must be cancelled.[2] The period specified by rules is the same as applies in relation to applications for first registration: see para **5.13**.[3] The registrar has the same power to extend that period as is there explained.

5.20   There is one limitation on a person's right[4] to apply for the cancellation of the caution. Normally, if he (or a person from whom he derives title by operation of law) consented to the entry of the caution in the manner provided for by rules he will be unable to make such an application.[5] However, even in this situation, he may apply for cancellation in two situations:

(a)   where the cautioner's interest has come to an end;[6] or

(b)   where the consent to the caution was induced by fraud, mistake or undue influence, or was given under duress.[7]

On such an application, in addition to the matters set out in para **5.18**, the applicant must provide the registrar with evidence of his entitlement to apply.[8]

Duty not to lodge a caution against first registration without reasonable cause

5.21   Thirdly, a person may not exercise his right to lodge a caution without reasonable cause.[9] This is a statutory duty that is owed to any person who suffers damage in consequence of its breach.[10] Any such breach of statutory duty will therefore be actionable in tort in the usual way. This matter is explained more fully in the context of unilateral notices: see paras **10.39– 10.40**. The principles explained there apply equally to cautions against first registration. Similarly, it is considered that the High Court has an inherent jurisdiction to order the vacation of a caution against first registration, as explained in the context of unilateral notices at para **10.41**.

---

1   As to who is the cautioner for these purposes, see para **5.7**.
2   LRA 2002, s 18(3), (4).
3   See LRR 2003, r 53.
4   See para **5.17**.
5   LRA 2002, s 18(2). A person consents for these purposes if he has confirmed in writing that he consents to the lodging of the caution and that consent has been produced to the registrar: LRR 2003, r 47.
6   The obvious case would be where the cautioner was a lessee and his lease had determined.
7   See LRR 2003, r 46, made pursuant to LRA 2002, s 18(2).
8   Ibid, r 44(4).
9   LRA 2002, s 77(1)(a).
10   Ibid, s 77(2).

TRANSITIONAL

5.22 Where a caution against first registration was lodged for registration before the LRA 2002 came into force, the rules contained in Part 5 of the LRR 2003 apply to it, subject to modifications.[1] Those modifications relate to the way in which the caution is recorded.

---

[1]   TPO1 2003, art 14.

CHAPTER 6

FIRST REGISTRATION BY THE CROWN

VOLUNTARY FIRST REGISTRATION

6.1 The legislation governing land registration in England and Wales has always made provision for the registration of *estates* in land. However, the Crown holds substantial amounts of land not for any estate but in demesne – in other words, in its capacity as sovereign or paramount feudal lord. This land includes most of the foreshore around the coast of England and Wales, land that has escheated,[1] and land that the Crown has always held and has never granted away. Because the Crown has no estate in such land it could not, prior to the LRA 2002, register the title to it.[2] The Act changes this. It empowers Her Majesty to grant herself an estate in fee simple absolute in possession in demesne land.[3] However, such a grant will not be regarded as having been made unless an application is made to register it under s 3 of the Act within 2 months of the date of the grant or such longer period as the registrar may by order provide.[4]

COMPULSORY FIRST REGISTRATION

6.2 The provisions of s 4(1) of the LRA 2002 on the compulsory registration of title[5] are extended (with necessary modifications) to the grant by Her Majesty of a fee simple or a lease of more than 7 years out of demesne land.[6] These provisions do not in fact change the law as the compulsory registration requirements of the LRA 1925 applied to conveyances and grants made by Her Majesty out of demesne land.[7]

---

[1]   Escheat occurs where a freehold estate determines. A common example of escheat is where a trustee in bankruptcy or a liquidator disclaims the freehold because it is onerous property. Disclaimer determines the fee simple. The property thereupon necessarily escheats.

[2]   See *Scmlla Properties Ltd v Gesso Properties (BVI) Ltd* [1995] BCC 793 at p 798.

[3]   LRA 2002, s 79(1). It is thought that statutory authority is required for this power as Her Majesty cannot be feudal lord and at the same time hold of herself as tenant-in-chief: see (2001) Law Com No 271, para 11.9.

[4]   LRA 2002, s 79(2)–(4). The registrar can extend the 2-month period on the application of Her Majesty provided that he is satisfied that there is a good reason for doing so: s 79(4). If the registrar makes an order under s 79(4) more than 2 months after the grant, that grant will be treated as having been made notwithstanding s 79(2): s 79(5).

[5]   See paras **2.9** et seq.

[6]   LRA 2002, s 80(1)–(4). There is also a necessary modification to s 7(2) (effect of non-compliance with requirement of registration): s 80(5).

[7]   See LRA 1925, s 123.

CAUTIONS AGAINST FIRST REGISTRATION

6.3 The provisions of the LRA 2002 on cautions against first registration cannot apply to demesne land because such a caution can only be lodged against an unregistered legal *estate*. However, those provisions are extended to demesne land as if it were held by Her Majesty for an unregistered estate in fee simple absolute in possession.[1] It has been explained above, that 2 years after the Act comes into force, it will no longer be possible for an owner of either an unregistered fee simple or of a lease with more than 7 years unexpired to lodge a caution against the first registration of that estate. He is expected to register the title to it.[2] As the Crown has not hitherto been able to register land which Her Majesty holds in demesne, it was considered appropriate that the Crown should be permitted to lodge cautions against first registration in respect of such land until such time as it could register it. It was accepted that this would take some time.[3] The Act therefore permits the Crown to lodge cautions against the first registration of demesne land for a period of 10 years in the first instance and makes provision by which that period may be extended further by rules.[4]

---

[1] LRA 2002, s 81(1). There is power to make modifications by rules in the application of the provisions to demesne land: s 81(2), and this power has been exercised: see LRR 2003, r 44(3), (5) (para **5.18**) and r 45 (para **5.17**).

[2] See para **5.5**.

[3] See (2001) Law Com No 271, para 11.18.

[4] LRA 2002, Sch 12, para 15(1). Any exercise of the rule-making power is likely to be shortly before the initial 10-year period expires.

PART 2

DEALINGS WITH REGISTERED LAND

THE MAIN CHANGES AT A GLANCE

This Part is about dealings with registered land. The relevant provisions are found in four Parts of the LRA 2002. In the order in which these are considered, those Parts are as follows.

First, Part 3 of the Act is concerned with dispositions of registered land. It makes provision for the following matters:

— owner's powers;
— the protection of disponees;
— registrable dispositions;
— the effect of dispositions on priority.

Secondly, Part 4 of the LRA 2002 is concerned with notices and restrictions.

Thirdly, Part 7 of the Act sets out provisions relating to certain special cases: the Crown, pending actions and miscellaneous matters.

Finally, Part 5 is concerned with registered charges.

The main changes made by the LRA 2002 are as follows.

— Leases granted for more than 7 years become registrable dispositions.
— The registration requirements for registrable dispositions are prescribed by the LRA 2002.
— The principles of priority that apply to registered land are modified and are set out in their entirety in statutory form.
— The status of rights of pre-emption, equities arising by estoppel and mere equities is clarified: all are treated as proprietary interests from the time of their creation.
— The methods of protecting third party interests in the register are simplified and the protection given to such interests is enhanced.
— Cautions against dealings and inhibitions are prospectively abolished. Notices and restrictions become the only two forms of protection under the LRA 2002.

- A person who applies for the entry of a notice or restriction is under a duty to act reasonably in exercising that right.
- The range of overriding interests is restricted and reduced.
- The LRA 2002 enables the Crown to grant itself a fee simple of land held by it in demesne to enable it to register such land.
- The Crown is given the power to lodge cautions against the first registration of land held in demesne.
- Entries in the register in relation to land which has escheated to the Crown remain until the land is disposed of by the Crown or pursuant to a court order.
- It is no longer possible to create a legal mortgage of registered land by demise or sub-demise.
- The present practice by which a second chargee notifies a first chargee of its charge in order to ensure the priority of that second charge over any further advances by the first chargee is given statutory effect.
- It creates a new method protecting further advances, by permitting the parties to agree a maximum sum for which a charge shall stand as security which is then appropriately protected on the register. That charge then has priority over any subsequent charges until the maximum sum secured is reached.
- Where a chargee exercises its power of sale and there is a surplus after the charge is discharged, the chargee will in practice have to search the register to ascertain whether there are any other charges. This is because it will be fixed with notice of anything in the register.

A duty is imposed on the registrar to notify existing chargees of any overriding statutory charge when it is registered. Indemnity is payable for any loss suffered by reason of a failure by the registrar.

CHAPTER 7

POWERS OF DISPOSITION

THE PRINCIPLES ADOPTED

7.1   It was explained in Chapter 1 that the fundamental objective of the LRA 2002 is, in time, to create a conclusive register.[1] A necessary feature of a conclusive register is that it should reveal whether there is any possible defect in a registered proprietor's title. One possible risk to an intending buyer of land is that the transaction might be outside the powers of the registered proprietor. Those powers might be limited by statute, by the terms of a trust deed where the owners were trustees, or, in the case of a company, by its memorandum and articles. The LRA 1925 did not spell out explicitly what powers (if any) a registered proprietor was presumed to have. In particular, it was unclear whether a buyer could assume that a seller has unrestricted powers of disposition in the absence of any entry to the contrary in the register, such as a restriction or caution.[2] If there is to be a conclusive register, those dealing with the registered proprietor ought to be able to rely upon the register to tell them whether there are any limitations on the powers of a registered proprietor. If any limitation exists it should be reflected by an entry in the register. In the absence of any such entry in the register, a registered proprietor should be taken to have unlimited dispositive powers, and a person dealing with him should be able to rely upon the register and his title should be inviolable. However, where there are limitations on a registered proprietor's powers of disposition, but these are not recorded in the register, the proprietor should not escape the consequences of a disposition in contravention of those limitations.

OWNER'S POWERS

7.2   The LRA 2002 adopts this approach. It creates the concept of 'owner's powers'. A person is entitled to exercise owner's powers in relation to a registered estate or charge if he is:

—   the registered proprietor; or
—   entitled to be registered as the proprietor.[3]

---

[1]   See para **1.7**.
[2]   Cf (2001) Law Com No 271, para 4.3.
[3]   LRA 2002, s 24(1).

7.3   In relation to a registered estate, owner's powers consist of:

—   the power to make a disposition of any kind permitted by the general law in relation to an interest of that description, except a mortgage by demise or sub-demise;[1] and

—   the power to charge the estate at law with the payment of money.[2]

Three points in this provision require explanation. First, the dispositions permitted by the general law are subject to any limitations imposed by that general law, such as the requirement that, to overreach an interest under a trust of land, payment of any capital monies must be made to two trustees.[3] For example, if X holds registered land on trust for Y, and charges the land to Z, that disposition will undoubtedly create a valid charge: X can convey a legal estate to Z. However, it will not overreach Y's beneficial interest under the trust, because Z pays the mortgage monies to just one trustee, X, and not to two.[4] If Y is in actual occupation, her unregistered interest will override Z's charge.[5] Secondly, the reason why mortgages by demise or sub-demise cannot be created in relation to registered land is because they have long been obsolete.[6] Thirdly, the power to charge the estate at law with the payment of money was the only way in which registered land could be mortgaged under the Land Transfer Act 1875. It had no equivalent in unregistered land. It could be employed under the LRA 1925,[7] and continues to be available under the LRA 2002.

7.4   In relation to a registered charge, owner's powers consist of:

—   the power to make a disposition of any kind permitted by the general law in relation to an interest of that description, other than a legal sub-mortgage;[8] and

—   the power to charge at law with the payment of money indebtedness secured by the registered charge.[9]

For these purposes, a 'legal sub-mortgage' is defined as a transfer by way of mortgage, a sub-mortgage by sub-demise, or a charge by way of legal

---

1   LRA 2002, s 23(1)(a)
2   Ibid, s 23(1)(b).
3   LPA 1925, s 27(2). The LRA 2002 makes provision for the entry of restrictions in the register to ensure that there will be at least two trustees on the making of a disposition: see LRA 2002, ss 42, 44.
4   For the sake of the example, it is assumed that Y has not entered a restriction to protect her interest. Cf para **7.6**.
5   See LRA 2002, Sch 3, para 2; see also para **11.5**.
6   See para **12.2**.
7   For the previous law, see LRA 1925, s 25(1)(a), which gave the proprietor of registered land the power to charge the registered land with the payment at an appointed time of any principal sum.
8   LRA 2002, s 23(2)(a).
9   Ibid, s 23(2)(b).

mortgage.[1] The effect of the LRA 2002 therefore is to place just one restriction on the dispositive powers of a registered chargee. He can only create a sub-charge by one method, namely that of charging the indebtedness that is secured by the registered charge: an attempt to create a sub-charge in any other way will be a nullity and will not be accepted for registration by the Registry. This restriction may be more apparent than real. Although it was in theory possible to create a sub-mortgage under LRA 1925,[2] it was in practice never done.[3] A sub-charge was always employed.[4] The essence of a sub-charge is that it effects a substitution of the sub-chargee for the chargee in relation to the principal charge and it gives the sub-chargee the *exclusive* right to exercise the chargee's rights under that principal charge. The sub-chargee also has his own rights in relation to the sub-charge and may, for example, realise his security by selling the principal charge.[5]

7.5 The LRA 2002 provides that a registrable disposition of a registered estate or charge only has effect if it complies with such requirements as to form and content as rules may provide.[6] This involves a small change in the law. Under LRA 1925, although it was possible to prescribe the form and content of most registered dispositions,[7] there was an exception in relation to registered charges.[8] Furthermore, in practice, the form and content of registered leases was never prescribed, even though they could have been.

PROTECTION OF DISPONEES

7.6 As a general rule, a person's right to exercise owner's powers in relation to a registered estate or charge is to be taken to be free from any limitation affecting the validity of a disposition.[9] In accordance with the principle set out in para **7.1**, this rule will only be displaced if a limitation is reflected by an entry in the register, or if a limitation is imposed by, or under, the LRA 2002.[10] That entry in the register might be a restriction or a caution against dealings although, after 13 October 2003, the appropriate form of entry is by way of a restriction only: cautions have been prospectively abolished.[11] However, this presumption only operates to protect the disponee's title. It does not make the

---

[1] LRA 2002, s 23(3).
[2] See LRA 1925, s 106(9), as originally enacted (s 106 was replaced by AJA 1977).
[3] See Brickdale & Stewart-Wallace, *Land Registration Act, 1925* (4th edn, 1939), p 250. Such a sub-mortgage would have been created either by an outright assignment of the registered charge or, if the registered charge took effect as a mortgage by sub-demise, by a sub-mortgage by sub-demise.
[4] See LRR 1925, r 163(1); (2001) Law Com No 271, para 7.11.
[5] See *Fisher & Lightwood's The Law of Mortgage* (11th edn, 2002), para 15-3.
[6] LRA 2002, s 25(1).
[7] See LRA 1925, ss 18(1), 21(1).
[8] Ibid, s 25(2). Under the original LRR 1925 there was, however, a *voluntary* form of registered charge that could be used.
[9] LRA 2002, s 26(1).
[10] Ibid, s 26(2).
[11] See para **10.3**.

disposition lawful if the registered proprietor's powers were in fact limited, but there was no entry in the register to reflect this.[1]

AN EXAMPLE

7.7   The workings of the new principles set out in paras **7.1–7.6** can be illustrated by an example. This example demonstrates that the protection given by the LRA 2002 does not apply to the transferor who has acted in breach of his obligations. It also shows that although the transferee's title is inviolable, he may be under other forms of liability if he was knowingly implicated in the breach of duty by the transferor.[2]

7.8   A and B hold registered land on trust for C for life, thereafter for D absolutely. Under the terms of the trust, A and B may not sell the land without the prior written consent of D. There is no restriction in the register to ensure that no sale can take place without D's consent. A and B sell the land to E without obtaining D's consent. E's title cannot be challenged by D. A and B are in breach of trust and D can take proceedings against them accordingly. If D could show that E knew that A and B were acting in breach of trust by transferring the land:

–   she could not challenge E's title; but
–   she could take proceedings against him on the basis that he was liable in equity for the knowing receipt of property transferred in breach of trust.

Liability for knowing receipt is merely a personal liability to account for the loss suffered by D. It does not give rise to a proprietary claim by D against the land which E acquired.

---

[1]   LRA 2002, s 26(3).
[2]   Cf (2001) Law Com No 271, paras 4.10, 4.11.

CHAPTER 8

REGISTERED DISPOSITIONS

INTRODUCTION

8.1   Section 27 is one of the most important sections in the LRA 2002. It defines the categories of disposition of registered land that must be completed by registration. Such registrable dispositions are particularly significant as, on registration, they take effect as legal estates at law, and are given a special priority. The provisions governing registrable dispositions are similar to, but not identical with, the equivalent provisions of the LRA 1925.[1]

8.2   As indicated above, the uniting characteristic of the dispositions in question is that they are required to be registered and do not operate at law (but only in equity) until what the LRA 2002 calls 'the registration requirements' are met.[2] Those registration requirements are set out in Sch 2 to the Act.[3] The LRA 2002 deals separately with dispositions of:

— a registered estate; and
— a registered charge.

A registered estate means a legal estate the title to which is entered in the register, other than a registered charge.[4] Not all such legal estates can be registered with their own titles under the Act. However, the following estates can:[5]

— a fee simple absolute in possession;
— certain leasehold estates;[6]
— a rentcharge;
— a franchise;

---

1   See LRA 1925, ss 18 and 21.
2   LRA 2002, s 27(1). This provision will cease to apply to any given disposition as and when compulsory electronic conveyancing is introduced in relation to it: see LRA 2002, s 93(4); see also para **28.3**.
3   See ibid, s 27(4).
4   Ibid, s 132(1).
5   Cf para **2.3**. Legal estates that cannot be registered with their own titles include legal easements and those *profits à prendre* that do not exist in gross.
6   See paras **2.13–2.18**.

–   a *profit à prendre* in gross; and
–   a manor.[1]

It is necessary to explain both the dispositions that are registrable dispositions and the registration requirements for each.

REGISTRABLE DISPOSITIONS OF A REGISTERED ESTATE

Transfers

8.3   Subject to the three exceptions mentioned in paras **8.4–8.7**, a transfer of a registered estate is required to be registered.[2] For practical purposes, the only legal estates that can be transferred are those which are registered with their own titles.[3] The registration requirements for such transfers are that the transferee or his successor in title must be registered as proprietor of the registered estate.[4] Where there is a transfer of part of the registered estate, the registrar is required to make certain entries in the register.[5] These are explained at para **8.37**.

8.4   The three exceptional cases where a transfer is not required to be registered are all transfers by operation of law.[6] Except in these three cases, transfers by operation of law, which are registrable dispositions, must be registered.[7]

8.5   The first case is a transfer on the death of a sole individual proprietor. The legal title vests by operation of law in the deceased's executors or, if there are none, in the Public Trustee. Once there has been a grant of administration, the personal representatives may apply to the registrar to be registered as

---

[1]   Any manor that had not been registered with its own title before the LRA 2002 came into force on 13 October 2003 could no longer be registered: see para **2.7**.

[2]   LRA 2002, s 27(2)(a).

[3]   On rare occasions, it may be possible to sever a *profit à prendre* of common that is appurtenant so that it becomes a *profit à prendre* of common in gross: see *Bettison v Langton* [2002] 1 AC 27, and the authorities considered there. Rights of common must be registered under the Commons Registration Act 1965 (CRA 1965), s 1, and cannot be registered under LRA 2002: see LRA 2002, s 33(d); see also para **10.10**.

[4]   LRA 2002, Sch 2, para 2(1).

[5]   Ibid, Sch 2, para 2(2); LRR 2003, r 72.

[6]   See LRA 2002, s 27(5).

[7]   LRR 2003, r 161, makes provision for the registration of such transfers. An application to register such a disposition must be accompanied by evidence of the disposition to satisfy the registrar: r 161(1). Where a vesting order has been made, it must accompany the application: r 161(2). There are specific evidential requirements that must be met where there is an application to register a vesting declaration under TA 1925, s 40, that vests trust property in new or continuing trustees: r 161(3). The application must be accompanied by the deed of appointment or retirement and either a certificate from the conveyancer acting for the persons making the appointment or effecting the retirement that they are entitled to do so, or other evidence to satisfy the registrar that the persons making the appointment or effecting the retirement are entitled to do so.

proprietors,[1] although they are not bound to do so.[2] An application by a personal representative to be registered as proprietor of a registered estate or charge[3] must be accompanied by evidence of that person's right to act.[4] The registrar must record the personal representative's capacity in the register.[5] Where a joint registered proprietor dies, an application for alteration of the register by removal from the register of the name of the deceased joint proprietor must be accompanied by evidence of his death.[6] The provisions of the LRA 2002 and LRR 2003 relating to the transmission and disposition of a deceased's registered estate are summarised at para **13.8**.

8.6   The second case is a transfer on the bankruptcy of a sole individual proprietor. An insolvent's entire estate vests automatically in his trustee in bankruptcy on his appointment or, if there is no such appointment, in the Official Receiver.[7] As with personal representatives, the trustee in bankruptcy may apply to the registrar to be registered as proprietor. The effect of a registered proprietor's bankruptcy is fully considered at paras **13.9** et seq

8.7   The third case is a transfer on the dissolution of a sole corporate proprietor. On the dissolution of a company its property passes as bona vacantia to the Crown or to the Duchy of Cornwall or Lancaster.[8] Once again, it is open to the Crown or Royal Duchy to apply to the registrar to be registered as proprietor. This is more fully explained at para **13.33**.

---

1   See LRA 2002, Sch 4, paras 7(d) (application to the registrar), 5(b) (altering the register to bring it up to date). For alteration of the register, see Chapter 22.

2   Often personal representatives do not register themselves as proprietors, but sell the land in their representative capacity or assent to its vesting in the person entitled to it under the deceased's will or intestacy.

3   Whether (a) in place of a deceased sole proprietor or last surviving joint proprietor (the situation with which this paragraph is concerned); (b) jointly with another personal representative who is already registered as proprietor; or (c) in place of another personal representative who is already registered as proprietor: see LRR 2003, r 163(1). In case (b), the registrar will serve notice on the personal representative who is registered as proprietor before he registers another personal representative: see r 163(5). In case (c), the application must be accompanied by evidence of the termination of the appointment of the personal representative who is already registered: r 163(3).

4   Application is on Form AP1. The evidence required is (a) the original grant of probate or letters of administration of the deceased proprietor showing the applicant as his personal representative; or (b) a court order appointing the applicant as the deceased's personal representative; or (c) (where a conveyancer is acting for the applicant) a certificate given by the conveyancer that he holds the original or an office copy of such grant of probate, letters of administration or court order: LRR 2003, r 163(2).

5   In the form 'Joan Smith, executrix of John Smith deceased': LRR 2003, r 163(4). See Devolution on the Death of a Registered Proprietor, PG6, para 2.1.

6   LRR 2003, r 164. This is similar to the previous provision under LRR 1925, r 172. The evidence may take the form of the original death certificate, or written confirmation by a conveyancer of the fact of the death, or the original grant of probate or letters of administration, or a certificate by a conveyancer that he holds the original or an official copy of such grant or letters: see Devolution on the Death of a Registered Proprietor, PG6, para 3.

7   Insolvency Act 1986 (IA 1986), s 306.

8   Companies Act 1985, s 654.

The grant of certain leases

8.8   The grant of a lease of registered land will be a registrable disposition and must be registered if it is one of the following:[1]

–   the grant of a lease for a term of more than 7 years from the date of the grant;

–   the grant of a reversionary lease to take effect in possession after the end of the period of 3 months beginning with the date of the grant;

–   the grant of a lease under which the right to possession is discontinuous;[2]

–   the grant of a lease in pursuance of the right to buy conferred by Part 5 of the HA 1985; or

–   the grant of a lease in circumstances where s 171A of the HA 1985 applies.[3]

8.9   With one exception, the extension of leases that are registrable dispositions mirrors the changes that have been made to the rules on compulsory first registration that have been explained in Chapter 2.[4] The one exception is that *all* discontinuous leases of whatever length granted out of registered land are registrable dispositions. Although discontinuous leases of any length granted out of unregistered land are voluntarily registrable,[5] only those granted for a term of more than 7 years after the LRA 2002 comes into force will be subject to compulsory first registration. The reason why discontinuous leases granted out of registered land are always registrable dispositions is because of the difficulty of discovering them if they are not registered. There are two classes of lease of registered land that are not registrable dispositions:

–   leases granted for 7 years or less[6] except where they are required to be registered for some other reason; and

–   PPP leases of underground railways and ancillary property granted pursuant to the GLAA 1999 (if such leases are ever in fact granted).[7]

Such leases are unregistered interests that will override a registrable disposition.[8]

---

[1]   LRA 2002, s 27(2)(b).
[2]   For discontinuous leases, see para **2.3**.
[3]   For an explanation of HA 1985, s 171A, see para **2.18**.
[4]   See paras **2.13–2.18**, where the reasons for the changes are explained.
[5]   See para **2.3**.
[6]   This period may and almost certainly will be reduced in due course by statutory instrument to include leases granted for 3 years or less: LRA 2002, s 118(1)(d); see also paras **2.4**, **2.14**.
[7]   LRA 2002, s 90(3)(a). See also para **2.3**.
[8]   See paras **11.2**, **11.4**.

8.10   Where a lease is a registrable disposition, the grantee of the lease or his successor in title must be entered in the register as the proprietor of the lease, and a notice in respect of the lease must also be entered against the superior title.[1] There is in fact a general provision in the LRA 2002 by which, in relation to every registrable disposition other than a transfer of a registered estate or charge or the grant of a legal charge, the registrar must, when registering the disposition, enter a notice in the register in respect of that interest.[2]

Leases of franchises and manors

8.11   The LRA 2002 makes no provision for the registration of a *grant* of a manor or a franchise because none is required.[3] Even if the Crown can still grant a manor today (which seems unlikely), it would not be possible to register that grant under the Act.[4] If the Crown were to grant any new franchise, it could be registered, if the grantee so wished, under the new provisions for voluntary first registration.[5] The LRA 2002 does make provision for the registration of leases granted of a manor or franchise, where the title to that manor or franchise is registered. Any lease of whatever length of such a franchise or manor is a registrable disposition,[6] although such cases are likely to be very rare indeed. *All* leases are registrable because of the difficulty of discovering them if they were not. Where the lease is granted for a term of more than 7 years, the grantee or his successor in title will be registered with his own title and a notice in respect of that lease entered in the register of the manor or franchise.[7] Where the lease is granted for a term of 7 years or less, a notice must be entered in the register of the manor or franchise.[8]

Express grant or reservation of a legal easement, right or privilege

8.12   Subject to two qualifications, the express grant or reservation of a legal easement, right or privilege[9] over registered land is a registrable disposition.[10] In practice this will apply to easements and to *profits à prendre*, whether those profits are in gross or appurtenant to an estate. The two qualifications to the requirement of registration are as follows.

---

[1]   LRA 2002, Sch 2, para 3.
[2]   Ibid, s 38; see para **8.21**, **10.13**(c).
[3]   See Manors, PG22.
[4]   See para **2.7**.
[5]   See paras **2.5–2.6**.
[6]   LRA 2002, s 27(2)(c).
[7]   Ibid, Sch 2, para 4(2).
[8]   Ibid, Sch 2, para 5(2). For the application to register, see LRR 2003, r 90(a); and para **10.13**(c)(iii).
[9]   Cf LPA 1925, s 1(2)(a).
[10]   LRA 2002, s 27(2)(d).

- First, the grant of a right of common, which must be registered under the CRA 1965,[1] is not registrable under the LRA 2002.[2] This restates the present law.
- Secondly, the grant of an easement or a *profit à prendre* as a result of the operation of s 62 of the LPA 1925 is not a registrable disposition.[3] Although technically s 62 operates as an express grant (because it writes words into a conveyance),[4] in reality it is a form of implied grant. Frequently, the parties will not have appreciated at the time of the conveyance that the section has operated, and it would be unreasonable to expect them to register a grant of which they were unaware.

8.13   The registration requirements are as follows.

- First, where the disposition involves the grant or reservation of a *profit à prendre* in gross[5] for an interest equivalent to a fee simple or a term of more than 7 years, the grantee or his successor in title must be entered in the register as the proprietor of the profit. In other words, the profit will be registered with its own title. A notice of the right must also be entered in the register of the title affected by it.[6]
- Secondly, in any other case,[7] a notice of the interest must be entered in the register of the title affected by it. If the easement or profit is for the benefit of another registered estate, the proprietor of that registered estate must be registered as proprietor of that easement or profit.[8]

8.14   There is a very important point that must be stressed. *The express grant or reservation of an easement or profit is a registrable disposition however long or short the duration of the grant or reservation may be.* For example, if an easement is granted for the benefit of a lease of 5 years' duration, the lease cannot be registered with its own title,[9] but the easement must be noted in the register nonetheless. Under the LRA 2002 – unlike the previous law – an easement or profit that has been expressly granted or reserved but has not been registered can never

---

1   See CRA 1965, s 1.
2   LRA 2002, s 27(2)(d). See also s 33(d).
3   Ibid, s 27(7). For LPA 1925, s 62, see Harpum, *Megarry & Wade's Law of Real Property* (Sweet & Maxwell, 6th edn, 2000), para 18-108.
4   See Harpum, *Megarry & Wade's Law of Real Property*, op cit, n 6, para 18-113.
5   Such as shooting or fishing rights.
6   LRA 2002, Sch 2, para 6.
7   In other words, where there is the grant or reservation of an easement or of a profit that is not a profit in gross.
8   LRA 2002, Sch 2, para 7. Obviously this cannot be done where the easement or profit is for the benefit of an estate in unregistered land. Nor can it be done in respect of an easement that is granted for the benefit of a lease that was not capable of registration when it was granted. For the application to register a notice where the interest is created for the benefit of an unregistered estate, see LRR 2003, r 90(b); and para **10.13**(c)(iv).
9   Although it may be noted in the register: see LRA 2002, s 33(b); see also para **10.8**.

override a registered disposition.[1] As the length of registrable leases is likely to be reduced to those which are granted for more than 3 years once electronic conveyancing is fully operative,[2] the disparity between the registration requirements for easements and leases is likely to be short-lived.

8.15 In relation to short leases we consider that it is possible for a landlord to confer or reserve rights akin to easements by means of covenants in the lease. Such covenants would not require registration. For example, a landlord might covenant with a tenant of part of a property owned by the landlord that he will permit the tenant to have access over the common parts of the property and to use the pipes and other media for services. If the landlord were to sell the property, the purchaser would take subject to the leases affecting it and would be bound by all the covenants in the lease that were not expressed to be personal.[3] The one situation in which the use of covenants in this way will not be effective will be where the landlord disposes of the part of property over which the tenant has rights under the covenants, but retains the reversion on that part which contains the demised premises. The purchaser of land over which the tenant has covenanted rights, will not be bound by the tenant's covenants, unless the landlord makes some form of express provision in the transfer that the purchaser will give effect to them.

8.16 It has been suggested to us that the use of covenants in this way might be ineffective, because a court might treat such covenants as being in substance easements, and therefore void for non-registration against any purchaser of the reversion.[4] However, we consider this to be unlikely, because the use of covenants in this manner does not conflict with the purpose of the legislation. The reason for requiring the registration of all easements that are expressly granted or reserved is to ensure that they can be readily discovered by those acquiring land subject to such rights.[5] A purchaser will only be bound by the covenants in a lease if he acquires the reversion on the lease and not if he acquires other land that is merely subject to rights covenanted under the lease.[6] Any intending purchaser of a reversion ought to inspect the terms of the leases that affect it, and the seller is required to disclose such leases before the purchaser contracts to purchase the reversion.[7]

---

[1] See para **11.14**.

[2] See para **2.14**.

[3] See Landlord and Tenant (Covenants) Act 1995, s 3.

[4] The analogy is the attitude adopted by the courts in relation to attempts to circumvent the Rent Act 1977 by the grant of licences when the substance of the transaction was a lease: see *Street v Mountford* [1985] AC 809. The courts have not been particularly enthusiastic in extending such an approach: see in the context of licences and easements, *IDC Group Ltd v Clark* [1992] 1 EGLR 187 (Browne-Wilkinson V-C); [1992] 2 EGLR 184 (CA).

[5] See Law Com No 271, para 8.65.

[6] See para **8.15**.

[7] See *Pagebar Properties Ltd v Derby Investment Holdings Ltd* [1972] 1 WLR 1500, at pp 1503–1504.

Express grant or reservation of a rentcharge or a legal right of entry

8.17   The express grant or reservation of either:

– a rentcharge in possession issuing out of or charged on land being either perpetual or for a term of years absolute;[1] or
– a right of entry exercisable over or in respect of a legal term of years absolute,[2] or annexed for any purpose, to a legal rentcharge;[3]

is a registrable disposition.[4] The circumstances in which rentcharges can now be created are very limited.[5]

8.18   Where the disposition involves the grant or reservation of a legal rentcharge with its own title for an interest that is either:

– equivalent to an estate in fee simple; or
– for a term of years exceeding 7 years,

the grantee or his successors in title must be entered in the register as the proprietor of the interest created, and a notice in respect of the rentcharge must also be entered in the register.[6]

8.19   Where the disposition is the creation of a right of entry annexed to a legal rentcharge, a notice in respect of the interest must be entered in the register and, where that rentcharge is registered as a registered estate, the registered proprietor of the rentcharge must also be entered in the register of that rentcharge as the proprietor of the interest.[7]

8.20   On its face, the LRA 2002 requires that, where a right of entry exercisable over or in respect of a legal term of years is created:

(a) a notice of that right of entry must be entered in the register of the lease; and
(b) the proprietor of the reversionary estate must be entered in the register as the proprietor of the right of entry.[8]

In practice these requirements would be burdensome, and the LRA 2002

---

1   Cf LPA 1925, s 1(2)(b).
2   See below, para **8.20**.
3   LPA 1925, s 1(2)(e).
4   LRA 2002, s 27(2)(e).
5   See Rentcharges Act 1977, s 2. In practice, almost all new rentcharges are estate rentcharge (see ibid, s 2(3)(c), (4)).
6   LRA 2002, Sch 2, para 6.
7   Ibid, Sch 2, para 7(2). For the application to register a notice where the interest is created for the benefit of an unregistered estate, see LRR 2003, r 90(b); and para **10.13**(c)(v).
8   Ibid.

accordingly permits their modification by rules.[1] Accordingly, LRR 2003, r 77, provides that where a right of re-entry is contained in a lease, the registrar need not make any entry of the benefit of the right of entry in the registered title of the reversionary estate. As regards the burden of the right of entry, the rules are silent. However, particulars of the lease containing the right of re-entry are entered in the property register of the title to that lease.

8.21 The LRA 2002 contains a general requirement that, where a person is entered in the register as the proprietor of an interest under any of the following dispositions:

(a) the grant of a lease;
(b) the grant of a lease of a franchise or manor;
(c) the express grant or reservation of an easement or profit;
(d) the express grant or reservation of a rentcharge; or
(e) the express grant or reservation of a right of entry annexed to a legal rentcharge;[2]

the registrar must also enter a notice in the register in respect of that interest.[3]

The grant of a legal charge

8.22 The grant of a legal charge is a registrable disposition.[4] To register the charge, the chargee or his successor in title must be entered in the register as the proprietor of the charge.[5] By way of exception to this general rule, where a charge arises under statutory powers and is registrable as a local land charge, it does not have to be registered under the LRA 2002.[6] It takes effect as an unregistered interest that overrides a registered disposition.[7] However, it cannot be realised unless it is registered as a registered charge.[8] The Act does not change the law in this regard[9] and the point is explained more fully in Chapter 12.[10]

REGISTRABLE DISPOSITIONS OF A REGISTERED CHARGE

8.23 In the case of a registered charge:

---

[1] LRA 2002, Sch 2, para 7(3).
[2] Where a *lease* contains a right of re-entry, the lessor will not be entered in the register as proprietor of that interest: see para **8.20**.
[3] LRA 2002, s 38. The entry of a notice must always be made in relation to the registered estate affected by the interest concerned: s 32(2).
[4] Ibid, s 27(2)(f).
[5] Ibid, Sch 2, para 8.
[6] Ibid, s 27(5)(c).
[7] Ibid, Sch 3, para 6; see also para **11.2**.
[8] Ibid, s 55.
[9] Cf LRA 1925, s 70(1)(i).
[10] See para **12.80**.

–   a transfer of that charge; and
–   the grant of a sub-charge,

are both registrable dispositions.[1] The registration requirement for a transfer is that the transferee or his successor in title must be entered in the register as proprietor.[2] The registration requirement for a sub-charge is that the sub-chargee or his successor in title must be registered as the proprietor of the sub-charge.[3]

APPLICATIONS FOR REGISTRATION

8.24   The LRA 2002 provides that rules may make provision about applications to the registrar for the purpose of meeting registration requirements under s 27 of the Act.[4] Those rules are found in Part 6 of LRR 2003, which contains provisions about applications for registration, registrable dispositions and miscellaneous entries. The general principles applicable to applications are explained in Chapter 20. We explain here what must be done to register registrable dispositions and we also consider certain related issues.

8.25   There are certain general rules that apply to all registrable dispositions.

8.26   First, where the transferee has actual knowledge of any unregistered interest that falls within LRA 2002, Sch 3 (unregistered dispositions which override registered dispositions) and which affects the registered estate to which the application relates, he must, when applying to register any registrable disposition, disclose these to the registrar using Form DI.[5] This is more fully explained at para **11.19**.

8.27   Secondly, the disposition must, in every case, be executed correctly. A registrable disposition that is required to be registered[6] must be made by deed in all cases except where it is an assent by personal representatives.[7] The Land Registry has provided guidance as to the proper method of execution of deeds: see Execution of Deeds, PG 8 and paras **20.37–20.39**.

8.28   Thirdly, because land certificates and charge certificates have been

---

[1]   LRA 2002, s 27(3).
[2]   Ibid, Sch 2, para 10.
[3]   Ibid, Sch 2, para 11.
[4]   Ibid, s 27(6).
[5]   LRR 2003, r 57.
[6]   For the three cases where it is not, see paras **8.4–8.7**.
[7]   An assent may be executed as a deed but it does not have to be. It is sufficient if it is made in writing, signed by the personal representative, and names the person in whose favour it is given: see AEA 1925, s 36(4).

abolished,[1] it is no longer either necessary or permissible to produce such certificate in order to register a registrable disposition.[2]

Transfers of a registered estate

8.29 A transfer of a registered estate must be in one of the following forms, as appropriate:[3]

— Form TP1: Transfer of part of registered title;
— Form TP2: Transfer of part of registered title(s) under power of sale;[4]
— Form TP3: Transfer of portfolio of titles;
— Form TR1: Transfer of whole of registered title(s);
— Form TR2: Transfer of whole of registered title(s) under power of sale;[5]
— Form TR5: Transfer of portfolio of whole titles;
— Form AS1: Assent of whole of registered title(s); or
— Form AS3: Assent of part of registered title(s) by personal representative.

8.30 All the transfer forms require the insertion of details of:

(a) the property transferred;
(b) the name of the transferee for entry on the register;
(c) the transferee's intended address for service for entry on the register;[6]
(d) where relevant, the consideration for the transfer: see para **8.32**;
(e) any title guarantee that may be given;
(f) any declaration of trust: see para **8.36**; and
(g) any additional provisions.[7]

8.31 Where there is a transfer of a registered estate that is wholly or partly in consideration of the transfer of another estate, the transaction must be carried out using one of the forms listed above at para **8.29**.[8]

8.32 In relation to all the forms listed in para **8.29** except Forms AS1 and AS3, the consideration for the disposition must be stated in the receipt panel or there must be a statement in that panel that the transfer is not for money or anything that has a monetary value. This follows from the requirement in LRR 2003, r 8(2) that the price paid or valued declared must normally be entered in

---

[1] See Chapter 21.
[2] LRA 1925, s 64(1)(a).
[3] LRR 2003, r 58.
[4] That is a sale *by a chargee* under its power of sale.
[5] Ibid.
[6] See LRR 2003, r 198(4); para **20.43**.
[7] Additional provisions include rights granted or reserved, restrictive or other covenants, agreements and declarations, other agreed provisions and required or permitted statements, certificates and applications.
[8] LRR 2003, r 59(1).

the proprietorship register of the title: see para **14.11**.[1] As Forms AS1 and AS3 relate to assents, this requirement is obviously inapplicable to them. Where the transfer is made wholly or partly in consideration of a transfer of another estate, a receipt for any equality money must be given in the receipt panel,[2] and a statement in prescribed form has to be included in the additional provisions panel stating that the transfer is in consideration of another transfer or conveyance (of which details must be given) and of the sum stated as paid for equality of exchange in the receipt panel.[3]

8.33   The correct forms of transfer are as follows:[4]

(a)   Where there is a transfer of *unregistered* land that will be completed by registration, the parties *may* use Forms TR1 or TP1 to convey the land,[5] but are not required to do so.[6] All that is required is a valid conveyance.[7] The application to register must be made using Forms FR1 (First registration application) and Form DL (list of documents).[8]

(b)   Subject to (c) below, where the whole of one or more registered titles are transferred, either Form TR1 or TR2[9] must be used. It is clear from the title of the form ('Transfer of whole of registered title(s)') that it can be used to transfer more than one title. It can also be used to transfer both freehold and leasehold titles, provided that the transfer is by the same transferor to the same transferee. The application to register the transfer must be made using Form AP1, with a statement in panel 4 of that Form that the application relates to the whole of the title.

(c)   Where a registered proprietor transfers the whole of several registered titles, it may be more convenient to use Form TR5 (transfer if portfolio of whole titles). 'Portfolio' is not defined, and it is therefore a matter of convenience whether Form TR5 is used in preference to Form TR1. It is clear from the reference in the additional provisions panel of Form TR5 that the form is appropriate where the application is more complex. Once again, the application to register the transfer must be made using Form AP1.

(d)   Subject to (e) below, where the property transferred comprises either a part of one registered title or parts of each of two or more registered

---

[1]   See Entry of Price Paid or Value Stated on the Register, PG7.

[2]   LRR 2003, r 59(1).

[3]   Ibid, r 59(2).

[4]   See Using Transfer Forms for Less Straightforward Transactions, PG21, para 1.2. That also sets out the requirements for mixed transfers of registered and unregistered land.

[5]   In such case, the title number will necessarily be left blank.

[6]   TR1 is appropriate where there is a conveyance of the whole of the property in the transferor's title. TP1 is the appropriate form where the conveyance is of only part of the land comprised in the transferor's title.

[7]   If the conveyance is an assent, it does not have to be by deed: see para **8.27**.

[8]   LRR 2003, rr 23, 24; see paras **2.25–2.26**.

[9]   Where the transfer is made by a chargee pursuant to its power of sale.

titles, Form TP1 or TP2[1] should be used. The application to register the transfer should be made in Form AP1, stating in panel 4 that the application relates to a part of a title.

(e)   Where there is a transfer of a portfolio of registered titles, including parts of a number of registered titles, it may be more convenient to use Form TP3. The application to register should be made using Form AP1, stating that the application relates to a part of a title.

8.34   A single transfer form may be used for:

(a)   a transfer of a mix of freehold and leasehold titles;
(b)   a transfer of a mix of registered and unregistered titles;
(c)   the appointment of a second trustee and a sale by the two trustees;[2]
(d)   a sale and sub-sale to be completed at the same time.[3]

8.35   By contrast, separate transfer forms must be used for:

(a)   an exchange;[4]
(b)   transfers to different people;[5] and
(c)   transfers of property in different registered ownership to a common purchaser.[6]

8.36   Where there is either an application for first registration in favour of two or more joint owners, or a transfer to two or more joint proprietors, there is provision for a declaration of trust in the relevant form of application or transfer.[7] It is highly desirable that such a declaration should be made, either in the relevant form or in a separate deed of trust, because it promotes certainty and avoids the bitter and expensive disputes that often arise when there is a breakdown of the relationship between the co-owners. Where such a declaration is made in the application or transfer, the transferees as well as the transferors must execute the instrument, so that it is an effective declaration of trust.[8] The execution of documents is explained in paras **20.37–20.39**.

---

[1]   Where the transfer is made by a chargee pursuant to its power of sale.
[2]   As where there is one surviving trustee and he wishes to sell. The same transfer form can be used to vest the legal title in the trustees and to transfer the land to the purchaser: see Using Transfer Forms for Less Straightforward Transactions, PG21, para 6, where there is an explanation as to how this should be done.
[3]   For details, see Using Transfer Forms for Less Straightforward Transactions, PG21, para 2.
[4]   Ibid, para 3.
[5]   Ibid, para 4.
[6]   Ibid, paras 5.
[7]   See, eg, Form FR1, panel 11; Form AS1, panel 10, Form TR1, panel 11; and Form TP1, panel 12.
[8]   See LPA 1925, s 53(1)(b), and the execution panel on the relevant form.

8.37   Where there is a transfer or charge of part of a registered estate[1] in a registered title,[2] the registrar must either:

(a)   make an entry in the property register referring to the removal of the estate comprised in the transfer or charge;[3] or

(b)   make a new edition of the registered title out of which the transfer or charge is made, allotting a new title to that number if he considers it desirable.[4]

In either case the registrar must also make entries in the individual register relating to any rights covenants, provisions and other matters created by the transfer or charge which the registrar considers affect either:

(a)   the retained or uncharged registered estate;[5] or

(b)   the part of the registered estate that is transferred or charged.[6]

For example, if a transfer of part of a registered estate contained a restrictive covenant that was given by the transferee for the benefit of the part retained, the burden of that covenant should be noted against the title to the land transferred.

8.38   Transfers of charges are explained in paras **12.42–12.47**.

The grant of a lease

8.39   Where a registrable lease is granted out of a registered estate, the application for registration must be made on Form AP1.[7] The documents lodged with the application should be listed on Form DL, as required by panel 6 of Form AP1. Those documents must include the lease.[8] There is as yet no prescribed form of lease. However, the move to electronic conveyancing means that it is inevitable that one will be introduced. In the consultation on the draft Land Registration Rules, a draft Form L1 was put forward for consideration, but it was not well received and is being reconsidered.

---

[1]   The part could be the mines and minerals apart from the surface.

[2]   The rules set out in paras **8.36–8.37** apply in relation to a *charge* of part of a registered estate in a registered title only if the registrar decides that the part charged will be comprised in a separate registered title from the uncharged part: LRR 2003, r 72(4). Where there is a *transfer* of part, the registrar must necessarily create a new title for the part transferred: cf LRR 2003, r 3(3)(a), (b). See para **14.3**.

[3]   LRR 2003, r 72(1)(a). For example, where mineral rights are transferred, the removal of the minerals will be recorded in the register.

[4]   Ibid, r 72(3).

[5]   Ibid, r 72(1)(b).

[6]   Ibid, r 72(2).

[7]   Ibid, r 13.

[8]   Cf ibid, r 212: documents for which no form is prescribed must be in such form as the registrar directs or allows. See para **20.6**.

8.40 It is clear from LRR 2003, r 78, that it is possible to apply to register the variation of a lease or the variation of any other registered disposition of a registered estate or charge. That rule provides that an application to register the variation must be accompanied by the instrument (if any) effecting the variation and evidence to satisfy the registrar that the variation has effect at law. That means that the variation will have to be made by deed.

8.41 Some variations of leases will alter the proprietary rights of the parties, as where the terms are varied to such an extent as to amount to an implied surrender and regrant,[1] or where additional easements are granted to the tenant. Many other variations, such as the alteration of the terms of the covenants in a lease, will not affect the parties' proprietary rights. There is no indication in LRR 2003, r 78, as to whether a variation should be registered if it does not alter the proprietary rights of the parties. However, the rule does not contain any sanction for non-registration. It follows from this that the only sanctions for failing to register a variation are those that apply generally in relation to registered land, whereby unprotected interests may be defeated by a registrable disposition for valuable consideration.[2] The relevant principles are fully explained in Chapter 9.[3] However, it is only unprotected *interests* affecting a registered estate or charge that will be so defeated, that is proprietary rights. The only variations of a lease (or other disposition that has been registered) that *must* be registered if they are to bind third parties are, accordingly, those that alter the property rights of the parties. There is nothing in LRR 2003, r 78, to restrict the registration of variations to leases or other registered disposition to those which affect the parties' proprietary rights. It is obviously desirable that any variation should be registered, because the fact of variation is then apparent from the register.

Other registrable dispositions

8.42 The creation of registered charges is explained at paras **12.9** et seq. In relation to the remaining registrable dispositions, namely, the express grant or reservation of a legal easement, right of privilege, a rentcharge or a legal right of entry, the application for registration should, once again, be made on Form AP1. The documents lodged with the application, which must include the instrument creating the interest, should be listed on Form DL.[4]

---

1   As where the length of the term is varied, or the lease is extended to include additional land.
2   For the circumstances in which the priority of an interest is protected, see LRA 2002, ss 29(2), 30(2). Those circumstances include, in particular, where the interest is the subject of a notice in the register.
3   See LRA 2002, ss 29(1), 30(1); paras **9.4** et seq.
4   See also para **8.39**.

MISCELLANEOUS

8.43   It is convenient to mention here certain miscellaneous entries that may be made in the register relating to registered estates.

Mines and minerals

8.44   It is explained at para **23.11**, that although the first registration of title to land under the Act includes mines and minerals in the absence of any entry to the contrary in the register,[1] no indemnity is payable on account of any mines or minerals, or the existence of any right to work or get mines or minerals, unless it is expressly noted in the register that the title to the registered estate concerned includes the mines or minerals.[2] The provision for making such an express note on first registration under LRR 2003, r 32, has been explained at para **2.33**. A similar power exists in relation to land that is already registered and in relation to which no such note was made on first registration. Under LRR 2003, r 71(1), the registered proprietor may apply for a note to be entered in the register that the registered estate includes the mines or minerals generally or specified mines or minerals.[3]

8.45   It may happen that there is parcel of registered land in relation to which there is *no* express entry of the kind mentioned in para **8.44**, but where it is appropriate, when describing the registered estate, to do so by reference to where the mines and minerals are or may be situated.[4] The obvious example is where the registered proprietor makes a disposition of the mines and minerals apart from the surface.[5] The registrar will be obliged to make an entry in the property register of the new title under LRR 2003, r 5(a), describing the registered land.[6] The registrar may make an entry to the effect that the description is merely an entry under r 5(a) and is not an express note that the registered estate includes the mines or minerals[7] that will be guaranteed by the Land Registry for the purposes of indemnity under LRA 2002, Sch 8, para 2.[8]

---

1   See LRA 2002, ss 11(3), 12(3), 132(1) (definition of 'land' includes mines and minerals, whether or not held with the surface).

2   Ibid, Sch 8, para 2.

3   That application must be accompanied by evidence to satisfy the registrar that the mines and minerals were vested in the applicant for first registration, and that they were vested in him in the same capacity as the remainder of the estate in the land that was then sought to be registered: LRR 2003, r 71(2). The reference to capacity is, presumably, to guard against a case where, for example, A was the first registered proprietor of Blackacre, but held the mines and minerals in Blackacre on trust for B. Provided that the registrar is satisfied that the relevant mines and minerals were vested in the first registered proprietor, the registrar must enter the appropriate note: LRR 2003, r 71(3).

4   See LRR 2003, r 70(1).

5   The registrar will make an entry in the property register recording the removal of the mines and minerals under LRR 2003, r 72(1)(a); para **8.37**.

6   See para **14.5**.

7   That is, under either LRR 2003, r 32 or r 71(1).

8   Ibid, r 70(2).

Appurtenances

8.46 There are a number of rules in LRR 2003, which are concerned with the entries that may be made in relation to rights that are or are claimed to be appurtenant to a registered estate. The rules cover two situations.

8.47 The first is where a proprietor of registered land claims the benefit of an expressly granted legal easement or *profit à prendre* over unregistered land.[1] He may apply for the benefit of that easement or profit to be registered as appurtenant to his estate.[2] That application must be accompanied by the grant and by evidence of the grantor's title to the unregistered estate.[3] Application for registration is made on Form AP1.[4] Provided that the Land Registry has been supplied by the applicant with the address of the owner of the servient land, it will serve notice upon him of the application. If there is no objection to the notices served and the Registry has no reason to believe that the notice has not been received, it will register the benefit of the easement in the same way as if the burdened land had been registered. If the registrar is not satisfied that the right claimed subsists as a legal estate appurtenant to the applicant's registered estate,[5] he may nonetheless enter details of the right claimed in the property register of the applicant's title, with such qualifications as he considers appropriate.[6] There is in fact a standard form of entry that is made by the Registry in such circumstances. It is in the following terms:

> '[Date] The registered proprietor claims that the land has the benefit of a right [terms of right as claimed by applicant]. The right claimed is not included in this registration. The claim is supported by statutory declaration/s [details of date(s) and deponent(s) of the statutory declaration(s)]. NOTE: Copy statutory declaration/s filed.'[7]

If the alleged servient owner objects to the application, the usual procedures for dealing with disputed applications apply. These are explained at paras **20.29** et seq.

8.48 The second situation that is addressed by rules is where a proprietor of a registered estate claims the benefit of a legal easement or *profit à prendre*,

---

1   For these purposes, an expressly granted easement does not include an easement that arises from the operation of LPA 1925, s 62: see LRR 2003, r 73(3).
2   LRR 2003, r 73(1).
3   Ibid, r 73(2).
4   In setting out the terms of the easement or profit that the applicant seeks to register in panel 4, the wording of the express grant should be used.
5   This may be because the applicant either fails to provide adequate evidence of the title of the servient tenement or fails to provide the address of the servient owner, or the registrar has reason to believe that any notices served by the Land Registry have not been received.
6   LRR 2003, r 75.
7   See Practice Guide, Easements Claimed by Prescription and Statutory Rights of Way for Vehicles, PG52, para 7.2.

which has been acquired otherwise than by express grant – in other words it is claimed on the basis of prescription, implied grant[1] or implied reservation. The registered proprietor may apply for the easement or profit to be registered as appurtenant to his estate.[2]

8.49 The application must be accompanied by evidence to satisfy the registrar that the right subsists as a legal estate appurtenant to the applicant's registered estate.[3] In the Practice Guide, Easements Claimed by Prescription and Statutory Rights of Way for Vehicles,[4] the Land Registry has provided detailed guidance as to what it requires on such an application, for example, as to the contents of the supporting statutory declaration. Application for registration is made on Form AP1, and in panel 5 should set out the easement claimed. The Land Registry has given the following example as to what is wanted:

> 'Registration of the benefit and noting of the burden of an easement, being a right of way on foot only for the benefit of the applicant's registered title number AB123456 over the passageway leading from the rear over registered title number AB654321 to Acacia Avenue.'[5]

8.50 Notice of the application will be served on the owner of the alleged servient owner if the applicant has supplied the address of the servient owner or because the title to the servient tenement is already registered (the title number must be given by the applicant if it is). If, in such circumstances, there is no objection from the servient owner, the title of the servient owner has been proved (if unregistered) and the registrar has no reason to believe that notices served by the registrar were not received by the servient owner, he will register the easement or profit claimed as appurtenant to the applicant's registered estate. He must also note the burden on the servient owner's title if it is registered.[6] Once again, if the registrar is not satisfied that the right claimed subsists as a legal estate appurtenant to the applicant's registered estate, he may enter details of the right claimed in the property register of the applicant's title, with such qualifications as he considers appropriate.[7] The form of entry is as set out above, at para **8.47**. If there is an objection to the application, it will be dealt with in the manner laid down by the LRA 2002.[8]

---

1   Which for these purposes includes an easement or profit arising from the operation of LPA 1925, s 62: see LRR 2003, r 74(3).
2   LRR 2003, r 74(1).
3   Ibid, r 74(2).
4   PG52, paras 5–7, to which reference should be made.
5   See Practice Guide, Easements Claimed by Prescription and Statutory Rights of Way for Vehicles, PG52, para 6.1.
6   LRA 2002, s 38.
7   LRR 2003, r 75.
8   See LRA 2002, s 73; paras **20.29** et seq.

8.51 Although the owner of an *unregistered* estate who claims the benefit of an easement or profit may apply to the registrar for the entry of a notice against a servient tenement, the title to which is registered, the Land Registry will not, as a matter of practice, accept such an application from a registered proprietor. He must apply for the registration of both the benefit and burden of the easement, even though the easement does not arise from a registrable disposition.[1]

8.52 It was explained at para **2.41**, that:

(a)   it is common for parties to conveyancing transactions to enter into agreements which restrict or prevent the acquisition of an easements of light and air by prescription or implied grant; and

(b)   LRR 2003, r 36 makes provision whereby, if it appears to the registrar on an application for first registration that an agreement prevents the acquisition of rights of light or air for the benefit of the registered estate, he may make an entry in the property register of that estate.

A similar rule exists in relation to such agreements that are made with regard to land after it has been registered. LRR 2003, r 76, again provides that, if it appears to the registrar that an agreement prevents the acquisition of rights of light or air for the benefit of the registered estate, he may make an entry in the property register of that estate.

The determination of registered estates

8.53 A registered estate may come to an end in a variety of ways. For example, a lease may terminate through the effluxion of time,[2] or it may be surrendered, forfeited or disclaimed. A freehold may be determined in a number ways, as for example, where a liquidator or a trustee in bankruptcy disclaims a freehold because it is onerous.[3] In such circumstances, the freehold escheats to the Crown.[4] Escheat is considered more fully below at paras **13.3** et seq. LRR 2003, r 173 makes special provision for the escheat of a freehold estate, and enables appropriate entries to be made in the register to ensure that the fact of escheat is apparent from the register.[5]

---

[1]   It is only in relation to registrable dispositions that the benefit and burden of an easement *must* be registered under LRA 2002, Sch 2, para 7: see para **18.13**. There are reasons in practice why a registered proprietor might only want to note the burden of an easement against the servient title, as where there are a number of unresolved disputed applications relating to the title of the dominant tenement that are pending.

[2]   Subject to statutory continuation, eg, under Part II of Landlord and Tenant Act 1954, in the case of a business tenancy.

[3]   See IA 1986, ss 171, 315.

[4]   In the form of the Crown Estate.

[5]   See para **13.4**.

8.54 Under LRR 2003, r 79, an application may be made to the registrar to record in the register the determination of a registered estate. The application must be accompanied by evidence to satisfy the registrar that the estate has determined.[1] Subject to an important exception, where the registrar is satisfied that a registered estate has determined, he must close the registered title to the estate and cancel any notice in any other registered title relating to it.[2] The exception is where a registered freehold estate has determined and an entry of this fact has been made under LRR 2003, r 173. In those circumstances, the register will not be closed.[3]

---

[1]   LRR 2003, r 79(1).
[2]   Ibid, r 79(2).
[3]   Ibid, r 79(3).

CHAPTER 9

PRIORITIES

INTRODUCTION

9.1   The scheme for determining the priority of competing interests under the LRA 2002 is completely statutory. The rules that it lays down are simpler than are those that formerly applied.[1] Previously, the law governing the priority of interests in registered land was a patchwork of statute and common law. Where the LRA 1925 was silent − principally in relation to the priority of competing minor interests[2] − the judges filled the gaps as best they could by reference to the general principles of priority that apply between competing equitable interests.[3]

THE BASIC RULE

9.2   Under s 28(1) of the LRA 2002, the basic rule of priority, which is subject to two important exceptions,[4] is that the priority of an interest affecting the title to a registered estate or charge is not affected by a disposition of the estate or charge. It makes no difference for the purposes of this rule whether the interest or disposition is registered.[5] In cases falling within the general rule, the priority of any interest in registered land is simply determined by the date of its creation. The first interest in time of creation prevails and that first in time rule is unqualified. Under the previous law, the priority of competing *minor* interests was determined by the general rule applicable to equitable interests, by which *where the equities were equal*, the first in time prevailed. The law on when the equities are or are not equal is difficult to state and in some respects uncertain. It has no place under the new law. The two exceptions to the general first in time of creation rule are:

−   the special rules of priority that apply to registrable dispositions for valuable consideration that have been registered;[6] and

−   the rules of priority applicable to Inland Revenue charges.[7]

---

1   See, generally, (2001) Law Com No 271, Part V.

2   The term 'minor interest' is not used by the LRA 2002.

3   See (1998) Law Com No 254, paras 7.15–7.19.

4   See below.

5   LRA 2002, s 28(2).

6   See para **9.4**.

7   See para **9.12**.

9.3   It should be noted that, under the provisions of the LRA 2002 that deal with e-conveyancing, it will in due course become impossible to create or dispose of many estates, rights and interests in registered land except by simultaneously registering them.[1] In this way the priority of such interests will always be apparent from the register. It also means that the principal exception to the basic rule, that applies to registrable dispositions for valuable consideration that have been registered, will cease to have much importance. The basic first in time of creation rule contained in s 28(1) of the LRA 2002 will indeed be the principal rule as to the priority of competing interests.

Registrable dispositions for valuable consideration that have been registered

The special rule of priority

9.4   The first exception to the basic rule of priority in s 28(1) stated above is as follows. If a registrable disposition of a registered estate or charge is made for valuable consideration, completion of the disposition by registration has the effect of postponing to the interest under the disposition any interest affecting the estate or charge immediately before the disposition whose priority is not protected at the time of registration.[2] In having a special rule of priority for registrable dispositions made for valuable consideration, the LRA 2002 follows the LRA 1925.[3] The elements of this exception are important and require explanation.

9.5   First, there must be a registrable disposition of a registered estate or charge. It has been explained above:

– which transactions are registrable dispositions under the LRA 2002; and
– that such transactions are required to be registered.[4]

9.6   Secondly, the registrable disposition must be made for valuable consideration. For the purposes of the LRA 2002, valuable consideration does not include either marriage consideration,[5] or a nominal consideration in money.[6] If the registrable disposition is made other than for valuable consideration (as defined), the basic rule of priority in s 28(1) applies.

9.7   Thirdly, the registrable disposition is given priority over any interest:

---

1   LRA 2002, s 93; see also paras **28.2** et seq.
2   Ibid, ss 29(1) (dispositions of registered estates), 30(1) (dispositions of registered charges).
3   See LRA 1925, ss 20(1), 23(1).
4   See paras **8.1** et seq; and see LRA 2002, ss 27 and 132(1).
5   This is a change in the law: cf LRA 1925, s 3(xxxi).
6   LRA 2002, s 132(1).

— which affects the estate or charge *immediately prior to the disposition*; and
— whose priority is not protected *at the time of registration*.

There are obvious reasons why these different times have been chosen. Until the introduction of electronic conveyancing, there will continue to be a period of time between the making of a disposition and its subsequent registration – the so-called registration gap.[1] A result of the gap is that if the disponee created an interest in favour of a third party during the registration gap, he would not be able to rely on the special rule of priority to take free of it. That is obviously right in principle. There is one potential trap – as there was under the previous law[2] – to which practitioners need to be alert. In those cases where the seller is to retain an unpaid vendor's lien over the land after its transfer, it is imperative that he should register that lien against his own title immediately after making the contract of sale. The lien arises on the making of the contract[3] and if it is not protected in the register at the time of registration, the buyer will take free of it under the special rule of priority for registrable dispositions.[4]

9.8   Fourthly, a disponee *will* take subject to interests that are protected at the time of registration. The LRA 2002 explains[5] that an interest will be protected for these purposes if it is:

— a registered charge;[6]
— the subject of a notice in the register;[7]
— one which overrides a registered disposition under any of the paragraphs of Sch 3, unless that interest has been the subject of a notice in the register at any time since the coming into force of the sections conferring special priority;[8] or
— one which appears from the register to be excepted from the effect of registration (as where the disposition is of an estate which has some title other than absolute).[9]

In the case of a disposition of a leasehold estate, or of a charge relating to such an estate, the burden of any interest incident to the estate will also be

---

1   The position will change when e-conveyancing is introduced. Under the system of e-conveyancing which the LRA 2002 creates, the making of a disposition and its registration occur simultaneously. The registration gap will, therefore, disappear. See paras **9.3** and **28.3**.
2   See *Orakpo v Manson Investments Ltd* [1977] 1 WLR 347 at 360, 369.
3   See *Barclays Bank plc v Estates & Commercial Ltd (in liquidation)* [1997] 1 WLR 415 at 419–420.
4   Cf (2001) Law Com No 271, para 5.10. This point quite often arises in practice.
5   See LRA 2002, ss 29(2), 30(2).
6   For registered charges, see Chapter 12.
7   For protection by way of a notice, see paras **10.5** et seq.
8   LRA 2002, ss 29(3), 30(3). The effect of this exception is that if an unregistered interest is noted in the register and, by mistake, that notice is deleted from the register, the interest is no longer protected. Its former overriding status does not revive.
9   See ibid, ss 11, 12; see also paras **4.8** et seq.

protected.[1] This would include, for example, the burden of any restrictive covenants affecting that estate.[2] The words 'incident to' are used in other statutory provisions to refer to the burden of leasehold covenants and conditions and rights of re-entry that affect a leasehold estate or (in the case of covenants) a leasehold reversion as such: see, eg, LPA 1925, ss 141(1), 142(1) and LTCA 1995, ss 3(1), 4(a).[3] Because of the technical meaning of 'incident', the burden of an easement will *not* be 'incident to the estate', but must be expressly reserved by the lessor and, because it is a registrable disposition, registered under LRA 2002, s 27(2)(d): see para **8.12**.

9.9   Fifthly, the interrelationship of the basic rule and the special rule of priority needs to be understood. If an interest has priority over a subsequent interest under the basic rule, the person having that priority never needs to rely upon the special rule of priority applicable to registrable dispositions. The special rule enables a registered disponee to reverse priorities where there is in existence an unprotected interest that has priority to his own interest under the basic rule. This can be illustrated by an example. W, the registered proprietor of freehold land charges the property to X Bank Plc, which registers its registered charge. W then contracts to sell the land to Y, who protects her estate contract by entering a notice in the register of title of the land. Before the contract to sell can be completed, W defaults on the mortgage payments and X Bank plc exercises its power of sale and contracts to sell the land to Z. Z takes the land free of Y's estate contract, even though it has been noted in the register. Z's priority derives from X Bank plc's charge which was created before Y's estate contract and therefore had priority over it.[4] It should be noted, in this example, that only the basic rule of priority is in play. It is unnecessary to have recourse to the special rule of priority that is given to registrable dispositions.

The grant of leases that are not registrable dispositions

9.10   The LRA 2002 – like the LRA 1925 before it[5] – makes provision for the priority of those leases granted out of a registered estate that are not registrable dispositions.[6] Under the LRA 2002, where the grant of a leasehold estate in land out of a registered estate does not involve a registrable disposition, the special rule of priority applicable to a registered disposition nonetheless applies as if:

---

[1]   LRA 2002, ss 29(2)(b), 30(2)(b).
[2]   Such restrictive covenants are not capable of registration: see LRA 2002, s 33(c); see also para **10.9**.
[3]   See, eg, LPA 1925, ss 141(1), 142(1) and LTCA 1995, ss 3(1), 4(a).
[4]   Having created the charge in favour of X Bank plc, W could only contract to sell his equity of redemption. That equity of redemption is overreached by X Bank plc's sale of W's land to Z: see *Duke v Robson* [1973] 1 WLR 267.
[5]   See LRA 1925, ss 19(2), 22(2).
[6]   For leases that are registrable dispositions, see paras **8.8–8.10**.

- the grant involved such a disposition; and
- the disposition were registered at the time of the grant.[1]

The priority of competing registered charges

9.11 The LRA 2002 makes specific provision for the priority of competing registered charges.[2] This is explained in Chapter 12.[3]

Inland Revenue charges

9.12 Like the LRA 1925,[4] the LRA 2002 preserves the special rules applicable to the priority of Inland Revenue charges under the Inheritance Tax Act 1984. The effect of a disposition of a registered estate or charge on a charge for unpaid tax under s 237 of the Inheritance Tax Act 1984 is to be determined in accordance with ss 237(6) and 238 of the Inheritance Tax Act 1984, under which a purchaser in good faith for money or money's worth takes free from the charge in the absence of registration.[5]

The effect of notice and knowledge on priority under the LRA 2002

9.13 It will be apparent from the rules of priority set out above that questions of knowledge or notice are not directly relevant in determining whether or not a disponee of an interest in registered land is bound by a prior interest.[6] However, such concepts do have a minor role under the LRA 2002 in certain clearly defined circumstances. In some cases this is because there is a pre-existing statutory regime where notice determines whether a disponee is bound by some pre-existing interest. Thus, whether or not a disponee takes subject to an Inland Revenue charge depends upon notice. The LRA 2002 applies the principles laid down in the Inheritance Tax Act 1984, as has been explained.[7] Similarly, the effect of a disposition by a registered proprietor after bankruptcy depends upon the principles of good faith and notice laid down in the IA 1986.[8] In other cases the LRA 2002 employs concepts of knowledge or notice to protect a registered proprietor from unregistered interests that he could not readily discover. This is one device that the Act uses as part of its strategy to reduce the impact of unregistered interests that override first registration or a registered disposition.[9] Thus, as has been explained, a first registered proprietor will be bound by interests acquired under the Limitation

---

[1] LRA 2002, s 29(4).
[2] Ibid, s 48.
[3] See para **12.48**.
[4] See LRA 1925, s 73.
[5] LRA 2002, s 31.
[6] The LRA 2002, s 78, preserves the rule previously found in LRA 1925, s 74, that the registrar is not affected with notice of any trust.
[7] See para **9.12**.
[8] See para **13.15**.
[9] Cf para **4.12**.

Act 1980 only if he has notice of those interests.[1] Furthermore, as is explained below,[2] certain unregistered interests will override registered dispositions only if they are known or easily discoverable.

Special cases

9.14   In relation to three types of interest, the LRA 2002 clarifies or changes its status in such a way that it may or will affect its priority. The three types of interest are rights of pre-emption, an equity arising by estoppel and a mere equity.

Rights of pre-emption

9.15   The precise status of rights of pre-emption in terms of when they take their priority as proprietary rights is uncertain. In dicta in *Pritchard v Briggs*,[3] a majority of the Court of Appeal suggested that a right of pre-emption was not a proprietary right unless and until the grantor chose to sell, at which point it became an option. However, this was not an easy rule to apply[4] and there has been some elaboration of the circumstances in which a right of pre-emption might be regarded as proprietary.[5] In relation to registered land, the LRA 2002 has reversed the effect of the dicta in *Pritchard v Briggs*. Subject to the rules regarding the effect of dispositions on priority that have been explained above,[6] the LRA 2002 provides that a right of pre-emption in relation to registered land created on or after 13 October 2003 has effect from the time of creation as an interest binding successors in title.[7]

An equity arising by estoppel

9.16   Where a party, X, acts to his detriment in reliance upon an expectation created (whether by encouragement or acquiescence) by a landowner, Y, that X will acquire some right over Y's land, an equity arises in X's favour. This 'equity' arising by estoppel is a right to go to a court to seek relief. It lies in the court's discretion how best to give effect to that equity and it will give X the minimum necessary to do justice.[8] This may or may not mean that X acquires

---

[1]   LRA 2002, ss 11(4)(c), 12(4)(d); see also para **4.5**.

[2]   See paras **11.1** et seq.

[3]   [1980] Ch 338.

[4]   See (2001) Law Com No 271, para 5.26.

[5]   For an elaborate analysis as to when rights of pre-emption would and would not be regarded as proprietary interests in registered land under LRA 1925, so as that it was possible to enter a caution in relation to them, see *Speciality Shops Ltd v Yorkshire and Metropolitan Estates Ltd* [2003] 2 P&CR 410.

[6]   See paras **9.2** et seq.

[7]   LRA 2002, s 115. This makes redundant the analysis given by Park J in *Speciality Shops Ltd v Metropolitan Estates Ltd* [2003] 2 P&CR 410.

[8]   For these principles, see *Crabb v Arun District Council* [1976] Ch 179.

a proprietary right over Y's land, although commonly it will.[1] If the court does grant X a proprietary right, that interest can be protected in the register in the appropriate way. However, there is some doubt as to the status of the 'equity' which arises in X's favour before such time as the court gives effect to it. Although the point has never been finally determined, the weight of authority undoubtedly favours the view that such an equity is a proprietary right, and this was reflected in the practice of HM Land Registry prior to the LRA 2002.[2] Subject to the rules about the effect of dispositions on priority,[3] the Act places the Registry's practice on a statutory footing by declaring that in relation to registered land, an equity by estoppel has effect from the time when the equity arises as an interest capable of binding successors in title.[4] A party can, therefore, protect his equity in the period after it has arisen but before a court has made an order giving effect to it, by entering a notice in the register. Alternatively, if the claimant is in actual occupation of the land in relation to which he has claimed an equity, he will be able to protect it as an unregistered interest which will override a registered disposition.[5]

A mere equity

9.17   The law recognises that there are equitable rights, usually referred to as 'mere equities', which fall short of being equitable interests.[6] It is not easy to define such interests,[7] but they include a right to have a deed set aside on grounds of fraud or undue influence, and the right to have a document (typically a conveyance) rectified for mutual mistake.[8] As regards unregistered land, it has been held that a purchaser in good faith of an *equitable* interest (as much as a purchaser of a legal estate) takes free of a mere equity.[9] What the position might have been in registered land under the LRA 1925, where concepts of notice were normally irrelevant, was never settled, but it might have been the same as where title was unregistered. The LRA 2002 clarifies the priority of a mere equity in relation to registered land as against a later equitable interest. Subject to the rules about the effect of dispositions on priority,[10] the Act declares that in relation to registered land, a mere equity has effect from the time when the equity arises as an interest capable of binding

---

1   See, generally, Harpum, *Megarry & Wade's Law of Real Property* (Sweet & Maxwell, 6th edn, 2000), chapter 13.

2   It would allow the entry of a caution or notice in relation to such an equity.

3   See paras **9.2** et seq.

4   LRA 2002, s 116(a). Because of the discretionary nature of the relief that a court may grant in giving effect to an equity, it is conceivable that a court might give effect to an equity in a different way in relation to a successor in title than it would have done as against the person against whom the equity arose.

5   See para **11.5**.

6   See Harpum, *Megarry & Wade's Law of Real Property* (Sweet & Maxwell, 6th edn, 2000), para 5-012.

7   See (2001) Law Com No 271, para 5.33.

8   See Harpum, *Megarry & Wade's Law of Real Property* (Sweet & Maxwell, 6th edn, 2000), para 5-012.

9   *Phillips v Phillips* (1862) 4 De GF & J 208 at p 218.

10   See paras **9.2** et seq.

successors in title.[1] In consequence, as a mere equity is an interest for the purposes of the LRA 2002, it is brought within the general principles of priority contained in the Act. This means that a mere equity will not be defeated by a later equitable interest in registered land that is created for valuable consideration where the grantee was a buyer in good faith and without notice of the mere equity. Given the uncertainty as to what rights are mere equities as opposed to equitable interests, this change should avoid difficult questions for the future. It is also consistent with the approach of the LRA 2002 under which concepts of notice are generally irrelevant in determining the priority of competing interests.

---

[1]   LRA 2002, s 116(b).

CHAPTER 10

NOTICES AND RESTRICTIONS

INTRODUCTION

10.1 The LRA 1925 contained an elaborate structure for the protection of what that Act called 'minor interests'.[1] That structure comprised notices, cautions, restrictions and inhibitions. The provisions did not work well, particularly those on cautions against dealings.[2] Part 4 of the LRA 2002 has replaced that structure.[3] Cautions against dealings and inhibitions have been prospectively abolished. Notices are the appropriate method of protecting interests (other than registered charges) that are intended to endure through changes of ownership of the land affected by them, such as the burden of options, restrictive covenants and easements. Restrictions operate to prevent the registration of a disposition that does not comply with the terms of the restriction. They can be used to protect interests in land, particularly interests under trusts which are intended to be overreached on any disposition. But they are wider than that and provide a means of ensuring that bodies with limited powers keep within them. This is a matter of some importance in the light of the concept of 'owner's powers' that has been explained above.[4]

10.2 The LRR 2003 contain the necessary rules to support the new structure. The rules governing notices are in Part 7 of the LRR 2003, and those concerning restrictions are in Part 8 of the LRR 2003. The Land Registry has provided detailed guidance on the new law and practice in the Practice Guide, Notices, Restrictions and the Protection of Third Party Interests in the Register, PG19.

PROSPECTIVE ABOLITION OF CAUTIONS AGAINST DEALINGS

10.3 The proposals by the Law Commission and the Land Registry to abolish cautions were strongly supported on consultation, with virtually no

---

[1] See LRA 1925, s 3(xv).

[2] For a critique, see (1998) Law Com No 254, Part VI. The problem with cautions was that they conferred no priority, but were merely a form of machinery by which the cautioner was notified of a proposed dealing with the land. He had then to defend his interest in the hope of securing a more permanent form of protection.

[3] For detailed comment see (2001) Law Com No 271, Part VI.

[4] See para **7.2**.

opposition.[1] Under the LRA 2002 there is no power to lodge cautions against dealings.[2] Notices and restrictions now do the work of cautions. Unlike cautions, notices confer priority on the interest protected. Restrictions operate flexibly to restrict or prevent an entry in the register with regard to a registered estate or charge. In relation to cautions against dealings that were entered in the register pursuant to an application made before 13 October 2003 (when LRA 2002 came into force), the relevant sections of the LRA 1925[3] continue to have effect under the transitional provisions in the LRA 2002.[4] Rules have also been made in relation to the operation of such cautions.[5]

ABOLITION OF INHIBITIONS AS A SEPARATE FORM OF ENTRY

10.4 The LRA 2002 does not contain any separate category of entries corresponding to an inhibition: an order made by the court or registrar that inhibits the registration or entry of any dealing in relation to any registered land or charge.[6] Inhibitions were just the most extreme form of restriction on the power of the registered proprietor to make a disposition of registered land,[7] and, as such, have been subsumed within restrictions. The provisions of the LRA 2002 on restrictions apply to inhibitions or restrictions entered under the LRA 1925,[8] thereby making unnecessary any further transitional provisions.

NOTICES

The nature and effect of a notice

10.5 The LRA 2002 explains the nature and effect of a notice. A notice is an entry in the register in respect of the burden of an interest affecting a registered estate or charge.[9] There are two points about this definition. First, it is only 'an interest affecting a registered estate or charge' that may be registered.[10] If the right is merely contractual and does not create a proprietary interest (which will be the case in relation to most but not all leasehold

---

[1]   See (2001) Law Com No 271, para 6.2.
[2]   Cautions against first registration, which are a necessary form of protection and do not suffer from the same vice as cautions against dealings, are retained: see Chapter 5.
[3]   Namely, LRA 1925, ss 55, 56.
[4]   LRA 2002, Sch 12, paras 2(3) and 5.
[5]   Ibid, Sch 12, para 2(4). The power to make rules enabled the provisions in LRR 1925 in relation to cautions, which are necessary to their operation, to be replicated. See para **10.106**.
[6]   LRA 1925, s 57.
[7]   The entry of an inhibition prevented the entry of *any* dealing in the register: LRA 1925, s 57(1).
[8]   LRA 2002, Sch 12, para 2(2).
[9]   Ibid, s 32(1).
[10] By ibid, s 132(3)(b), references to an interest affecting a registered estate or charge are to an adverse right affecting the title to the estate or charge.

covenants[1]), it cannot be protected by the entry of a notice. Secondly, as is explained in the next paragraph, the burden of some proprietary rights that undoubtedly are 'interests' cannot be protected by a notice. The entry of a notice is to be made in relation to the registered estate or charge affected by the interest concerned.[2] If the interest in question is a registered estate and a registrable lease is granted out of the registered freehold, a notice will, therefore, be entered in respect of it on the title to the freehold estate.[3] As under the LRA 1925,[4] the fact that an interest is the subject of a notice does not necessarily mean that the interest is valid. It does mean that the priority of the interest, if it is valid, is protected for the purposes of the special provisions on priority contained in ss 29 and 30 of the LRA 2002.[5] If, for example, parties had entered into an agreement that was not a binding contract because it failed to comply with the formal requirements of s 2 of the Law of Property (Miscellaneous Provisions) Act 1989 (LP(MP)A 1989), the entry of a notice in respect of the contract would not validate it. The form and content of notices in the register is governed by the LRR 2003.[6]

10.6 Section 33 of the LRA 2002 lists six interests that are *not* capable of being protected by a notice. With one important exception, the Act replicates the previous law. The list of excepted interests is informative because it sheds further light on the nature and function of a notice under the Act.

10.7 First, it is not possible to enter a notice in respect of an interest under a trust of land, or a settlement under the SLA 1925.[7] Where there is a disposition of land held in trust, the disponee does not expect to take that land subject to the beneficial interests. The interests should instead be overreached. Any capital monies should therefore be paid to the trustees, of whom there should be at least two (unless the trustee is a trust corporation).[8] A restriction is both the appropriate and, under the LRA 2002, the *only* form of entry that can be made to ensure that this occurs.[9] An interest under a trust includes a charging order over an interest under a trust, which can also only be protected by the entry of a restriction.[10]

10.8 Secondly, a notice cannot be entered in respect of a lease granted for a term of 3 years or less and which is not otherwise required to be registered.[11]

---

[1] In general, and subject to exceptions, covenants and conditions in leases are not incumbrances and are not, therefore, matters for registration.
[2] LRA 2002, s 32(2).
[3] Ibid, Sch 2, para 3(2).
[4] See LRA 1925, s 52(1).
[5] LRA 2002, s 32(3). For the special provisions on priority, see paras **9.4** et seq.
[6] Ibid, s 39.
[7] Ibid, s 33(a).
[8] SLA 1925, s 94(1); LPA 1925, s 27(2).
[9] LRA 2002, s 42(1)(b).
[10] Ibid, s 42(1)(c), (4); see also para **10.59**.
[11] Ibid, s 33(b).

This provision is a notable change from the law under which leases granted for a term of 21 years or less could not be the subject of a notice unless they were otherwise required to be registered. It might have been expected that, following the reduction of the length of registrable leases from those granted for more than 21 years to those granted for a term of more than 7 years, it would not be possible to enter a notice in respect of a lease granted for 7 years or less (except in those cases where it was otherwise required to be registered). There are two reasons why a period of more than 3 (rather than 7) years was chosen.[1] First, as has been explained, it is intended that the length of registrable leases should in due course be reduced from a period of more than 7 years to a period of more than 3 years.[2] The provision on the entry of notices is an earnest of that intention. Secondly, it has been explained that, under the LRA 2002, *any* easement or profit that is expressly granted or reserved must be registered.[3] In those circumstances, where a short lease is granted and is subject to or has the benefit of an easement, the lessee may choose to enter a notice in relation to the lease as well as the easement.

10.9   Thirdly, a restrictive covenant made between a lessor and lessee, so far as relating to the demised premises, cannot be the subject of a notice in the register.[4] These covenants are not noted, as they are normally apparent from the lease. This is a more limited exception than the equivalent provision in the LRA 1925,[5] under which any restrictive covenant made between lessor and lessee could not be protected by the entry of a notice in the register, even if it related to land not comprised in the lease. The exception under the LRA 1925 was too wide because it meant that restrictive covenants between lessor and lessee that related to property other than that demised could not be noted in the register.[6]

10.10   Fourthly, an interest which is capable of being registered under the CRA 1965 cannot be noted in the register.[7] Rights of common, which are registrable under the CRA 1965, cannot be registered under the LRA 2002.[8]

10.11   Fifthly, no notice may be entered in respect of an interest in any coal or coal mine, the rights attached to any such interest and the rights of any person under ss 38, 49 or 51 of the Coal Industry Act 1994.[9] Once again, this replicates the previous law. It is in practice impossible to locate and therefore to map all rights to coal.

---

[1]   See (2001) Law Com No 271, para 6.11.
[2]   See paras **2.4**, **2.14** and **8.9**.
[3]   See para **8.14**.
[4]   LRA 2002, s 33(c).
[5]   See LRA 1925, s 50(1).
[6]   See *Oceanic Village Ltd v United Attractions Ltd* [2000] Ch 234, at pp 252–254.
[7]   LRA 2002, s 33(d).
[8]   See CRA 1965, s 1 (as amended by LRA 2002, Sch 11, para 7(2)). The same was true under LRA 1925.
[9]   LRA 2002, s 33(e).

10.12 Finally, no notice may be entered in relation to a PPP lease created under the provisions of the GLAA 1999.[1] The curious status of PPP leases and their nature has already been explained.[2]

The circumstances in which a notice may be entered in the register

10.13 The circumstances in which a notice may be entered in the register include the following:

(a) On the first registration of a freehold or leasehold estate the registrar will note against the title the burden of any interest which affects the land of which he is aware, unless the interest is one that cannot be protected by notice.[3]

(b) Where it appears to the registrar that a registered estate is subject to an unregistered interest that falls within any of the paragraphs of Sch 1 to the LRA 2002[4] and is not excluded by s 33,[5] he may enter a notice in respect of that interest.[6] In other words, if the registrar discovers an unregistered interest of a kind that overrides first registration, he has the power to note it on the register. This has already been explained.[7]

(c) Where a person is registered as proprietor of an interest under one of the registrable dispositions listed below, the registrar *must* enter a notice in the register in respect of that interest.[8] The registrable dispositions in question are:

    (i) the grant of any lease that is required to be registered;[9]

    (ii) where the registered estate is a franchise or manor, the grant of any lease of that franchise or manor;[10]

    (iii) the express grant or reservation of an easement, right or privilege for an interest equivalent to an estate in fee simple absolute in possession or a term of years absolute, other than a right of

---

[1] LRA 2002, s 90(4).

[2] See para **2.3**.

[3] LRA 2002, ss 11(4)(a), 12(4)(b).

[4] See para **4.14**.

[5] See paras **10.6** et seq.

[6] LRA 2002, s 37. LRR 2003, r 89, provides that if the registrar enters a notice of an unregistered interest under s 37(1) of the Act, he must give notice: (1) to the registered proprietor, unless the registered proprietor has applied for entry of the notice or otherwise consents to an application to enter the notice, and (2) to any other person who appears to the registrar to be entitled to the interest protected by the notice or whom the registrar otherwise considers appropriate, unless that person applied for the entry of the notice or consented to the entry of the notice, or that person's name and address for service under r 198 are not set out in the individual register in which the notice is entered. See para **4.21**.

[7] See para **4.21**. The entry will often follow disclosure of the unregistered interest pursuant to the duty imposed by LRA 2002, s 71(a): see para **4.19**.

[8] LRA 2002, s 38.

[9] Ibid, Sch 2, para 3(2); s 27(2)(b). See also para **8.10**.

[10] Ibid, Sch 2, paras 4(2), 5(2); s 27(2)(c). See also para **8.11**. An application for entry of a notice under para 5(2) of Part I of Sch 2 to the Act must be in Form AP1: LRR 2003, r 90(a).

> common which is capable of being registered under the CRA 1965;[1]
>
> (iv)   the express grant or reservation of a rentcharge in possession which is either perpetual or for a term of years absolute;[2] and
>
> (v)   the express grant or reservation of a right of entry exercisable over or in respect of a legal lease, or annexed, for any purpose, to a legal rentcharge.[3]

(d)   Where such an entry is necessary to update the register.[4] The sort of circumstances in which that might arise might be where, for example, the registrar discovers that due to a mistake, the burden of a registered disposition was not protected (as it should have been) by the entry of a notice.

(e)   On application to the registrar: this category will, in practice, be the most important. The circumstances in which a person may make such an application are explained in detail below.

Applications for the entry of a notice

Introduction

10.14 A person who claims to be entitled to the benefit of an interest affecting a registered estate or charge may, if that interest is not excluded by LRA 2002, s 33, apply to the registrar for the entry in the register of a notice in respect of the interest.[5] Subject to rules, an application under this section may be for either an agreed notice,[6] or a unilateral notice,[7] although in some cases it may have to be for an agreed notice.[8] In both cases the notice will protect the priority of the interest, if valid, as against a subsequent registered disposition.[9] For the reasons given below at paras **10.33** et seq, a unilateral notice is (and is intended to be) a weaker form of protection than an agreed notice, because it is open to challenge in a number of different ways. However, the availability of a unilateral notice means that a person can protect

---

[1]   LRA 2002, Sch 2, para 6(2); s 27(2)(d).

[2]   Ibid, Sch 2, para 7(2); s 27(2)(e). An application for entry of a notice under para 7(2)(a) of Part 1 of Sch 2 to the Act must be in Form AP1 where the interest is created for the benefit of an unregistered estate: LRR 2003, r 90(b).

[3]   Ibid, Sch 2, para 7(2); s 27(2)(e). An application for entry of a notice under para 7(2)(a) of Part 1 of Sch 2 to the Act must be in Form AP1 where the interest is created for the benefit of an unregistered estate: LRR 2003 r 90(b).

[4]   Ibid, Sch 4, para 5(b). Cf paras **22.6**, **22.16**.

[5]   Ibid, s 34(1). In relation to an application to register either a pending land action under LRA 2002, s 87(1)(a), or a writ or order affecting land under ibid, s 87(1)(b), the person who is taking any action or proceedings or who has obtained the writ or order is treated as having the benefit of an interest for the purposes of ibid, s 34(1): see LRR 2003, r 172(1), (3).

[6]   LRA 2002, s 34(2)(a).

[7]   Ibid, s 34(2)(b).

[8]   See para **10.17**. In LRR 2003, unlike LRA 2002, the term 'agreed notice' is not used. Reference is always to 'a notice (other than a unilateral notice)'.

[9]   LRA 2002, s 32(3).

the priority of the interest which he claims from the moment of the application, if there is any risk that an application for an agreed notice might be rejected by the registrar.[1]

Agreed notices

When an agreed notice may be entered in the register

10.15 Except in those cases where an agreed notice must be entered,[2] the registrar may only approve an application for an agreed notice in three circumstances.[3] These are in practice much the same as the circumstances under which a notice could have been entered under LRA 1925. They are as follows.

(a)   Where the applicant is either the registered proprietor, or a person entitled to be registered as proprietor of the registered estate or charge that is to be affected by the notice.[4]

(b)   Where either the registered proprietor or the person entitled to be registered as proprietor of the registered estate or charge that is to be affected by the notice consents to the entry of the notice.

(c)   Where the registrar is satisfied as to the validity of the applicant's claim.[5] Such a non-consensual application may be made where an applicant can demonstrate to the satisfaction of the registrar that the registered proprietor has in fact granted him an interest even if the proprietor will not agree to the entry.

10.16 It is, therefore, possible for a person claiming an interest to apply for an agreed notice even if the registered proprietor does not consent to the application.[6] However, the evidential burden which he must satisfy is much greater than it would be were he to apply for a unilateral notice.[7]

10.17 Under LRR 2003, r 80, a person who applies for a notice in the register *must* apply for the entry of an agreed notice where the application is for:

---

[1]   In any event, the applicant would be able to apply for the entry of a unilateral notice following the cancellation of his application for an agreed notice.

[2]   See para **10.17**.

[3]   LRA 2002, s 34(3), (4).

[4]   Examples of where a person is entitled to be registered as proprietor include (i) where the estate or charge has been transferred to him, but he has not yet been registered; (ii) where the registered proprietor has died and he is the deceased's personal representative; and (iii) where he is the registered proprietor's trustee in bankruptcy: see Notices, Restrictions and the Protection of Third Party Interests in the Register, PG19, para 3.6.2.

[5]   Cf LRA 1925, s 48(2).

[6]   In the same way as it was possible to obtain the entry of a notice under LRA 1925 even where the registered proprietor did not consent to the application.

[7]   See Notices, Restrictions and the Protection of Third Party Interests in the Register, PG19, para 3.4.2.

(a)   a matrimonial home rights notice;[1]

(b)   an inheritance tax notice;

(c)   a notice in respect of an access order granted under the Access to Neighbouring Land Act 1992;[2]

(d)   a notice of any variation of a lease effected by or under an order under s 38 of the Landlord and Tenant Act 1987,[3] including any variation as modified by an order under s 39(4) of that Act; and

(e)   a notice in respect of a public right or customary right.[4]

10.18 These interests could previously be protected under the LRA 1925 without the production of the proprietor's land certificate,[5] and the new rules reflect that position.[6] The intention is to remove the risk that a unilateral notice might be entered to protect such a right or interest, but might then be cancelled subsequently under LRA 2002, s 36,[7] or otherwise challenged.

Application for the entry of an agreed notice

10.19 An application for the entry in the register of an agreed notice (other than a matrimonial home rights notice[8]) or for an agreed notice[9] must be made in Form AN1.[10] It must be accompanied by the following documents or evidence.

10.20 First, the applicant must provide either:

(a)   any order or instrument giving rise to the interest claimed (if there is one);[11] or

(b)   if there is no such order or instrument, such other details of the interest claimed as satisfy the registrar as to the nature of the applicant's claim.[12]

The implications of submitting the order or instrument to the registrar are explained at para **10.24**.

---

[1]   Pursuant to FLA 1996, s 31(10) and Sch 4, para 4(3): see also, para **10.26**.

[2]   Cf Access to Neighbouring Land Act 1992, s 4. An *application* for an access order is to be regarded as a pending land action for the purposes of LRA 2002: see Access to Neighbouring Land Act 1992, s 5(6).

[3]   For the power to apply to the Leasehold Valuation Tribunal for the variation of the terms of a long lease of residential property, see Landlord and Tenant Act 1987, ss 35–37.

[4]   Customary rights are those that are enjoyed by all or some of the inhabitants of a particular locality: see para **4.14**(4).

[5]   Cf LRA 1925, s 64(5)–(7). Land certificates have been abolished: see Chapter 21.

[6]   Land Registry New Rules – A Consultation Document, chapter 5 paras 8–9.

[7]   See para **10.35**.

[8]   LRR 2003, r 81(2). For such notices, see para **10.26**.

[9]   Including an agreed notice in respect of any variation of an interest that is protected by a notice.

[10]   LRR 2003, r 81(1)(a).

[11]   A certified copy of the deed should be sent with the application if the applicant wishes to ensure that the instrument lodged is returned on completion of the application: see LRR 2003, r 203(2); para **20.34**.

[12]   LRR 2003, r 81(1)(b).

10.21 Secondly, where the applicant either is, or has the consent of, the registered proprietor of the estate or charge affected by the interest to which the application relates, he must provide that consent,[1] which may be given either in panel 14 of Form AN1 or lodged separately: see panel 11. Where there are two or more joint proprietors, they must all join in the application or consent to it.[2]

10.22 Thirdly, where the applicant either is himself entitled to be registered as proprietor of the estate or charge affected by the interest to which the application relates or has the consent of the person so entitled, he must provide that consent.[3] Once again, this may be given either in panel 14 of Form AN1 or lodged separately. Where there are two or more persons who are entitled to be registered as joint proprietors, all of them must consent to the application.[4]

10.23 Fourthly, where the applicant does not have the consent of either the registered proprietor or the person entitled to be registered as proprietor, he must provide evidence to satisfy the registrar as to the validity of his claim.[5] The nature of this evidence will vary in each case, but the relevant Practice Guide gives the following examples of the type of evidence that may satisfy the registrar,[6] namely:

(a)   in a case where the interest was created by an express grant, the original instrument signed or executed by the registered proprietor at the time of the grant;
(b)   where the interest was established in legal proceedings to which the then registered proprietor was a party, a sealed court order in those proceedings which declares the validity of the interest; and
(c)   where the interest to be protected is a pending land action,[7] the sealed claim form and notice of issue.

10.24 The manner in which an agreed notice is entered in the register is explained at para **10.45**. However, it should be noted that the details of any instrument or order from which the interest derives, will be recorded in the register. It is explained in Chapter 18 that, subject to exceptions created by the rules, any person may inspect and make copies of any document kept by the registrar which is referred to in the register of title.[8] If the person who wishes

1   LRR 2003, r 81(1)(c)(i).
2   See Notices, Restrictions and the Protection of Third Party Interests in the Register, PG 19, para 3.6.2.
3   LRR 2003, r 81(1)(c)(i).
4   See Notices, Restrictions and the Protection of Third Party Interests in the Register, PG 19, para 3.6.2.
5   LRR 2003, r 81(1)(c)(ii).
6   Notices, Restrictions and the Protection of Third Party Interests in the Register, PG 19, para 3.6.3.
7   See LRA 2002, s 87; para **10.102**.
8   LRA 2002, s 66(1)(b); see paras **18.3** et seq.

to protect an interest wishes to keep the transaction confidential, he has two options:

(a)   He may apply to have the instrument or order designated an exempt information document: this is explained at paras **18.13** et seq. If the application is successful, the instrument or order will not be open to public inspection.

(b)   Alternatively, he may apply for a unilateral notice instead. It is explained at para **10.30** that an applicant for a unilateral notice is not required to lodge with his application any instrument or order from which that interest derives.

10.25 Where an application for an agreed notice is made without the consent of either the registered proprietor of the estate or charge affected or the person entitled to be registered as proprietor, there is no requirement in either LRA 2002 or LRR 2003 that the registrar should serve notice on that proprietor before he approves the application. As a matter of practice the registrar will:

(a)   normally determine the application on the evidence provided without involving the proprietor; but

(b)   always notify the proprietor that the entry has been made when it completes the application.[1]

Agreed notices in relation to matrimonial home rights

10.26 Rule 82 of the LRR 2003 makes provision for the application for an agreed notice in relation to a matrimonial home rights under FLA 1996, s 31(10)(a), or for the renewal of such registration under s 32 and Sch 4 of that Act.[2] As under the previous law, such rights cannot be protected by the actual occupation of the spouse having the right.[3]

10.27 Rule 82 covers the following situations:

(a)   Where a spouse applies for the registration of her matrimonial home rights under FLA 1996, s 31(10)(a). In such a case, the spouse should apply for an agreed notice on Form MH1.

(b)   Where a spouse with matrimonial home rights had obtained an occupation order under FLA 1996, s 33, that order provided that the rights should continue notwithstanding the death of the other spouse

---

[1]   Notices, Restrictions and the Protection of Third Party Interests in the Register, PG 19, para 3.3.2.

[2]   See FLA 1996, Sch 4, para 4(3).

[3]   See ibid, s 31(10(b) (as substituted by LRA 2002). For the overriding effect of the unregistered rights of a person in actual occupation in other cases, see LRA 2002, Sch 1, para 2 and Sch 3, para 2, and see paras **4.14**(2) and **11.5**.

or the termination of the marriage otherwise than by death under s 33(5), and the marriage has since terminated by death or otherwise:

(i)   if the spouse's matrimonial home rights had not previously been protected by registration under either FLA 1996, s 31(10) or LCA 1972, the spouse may apply for an agreed notice to protect them[1] using Form MH1;[2]

(ii)   if the spouse's matrimonial home rights had previously been protected by registration under either FLA 1996, s 31(10) or LCA 1972, and the registrar had cancelled the registration pursuant to FLA 1996, Sch 4, para 4(1), the spouse may apply to renew the registration of the charge as an agreed notice[3] using Form MH2.[4]

In the situations falling within (b), Form MH1 or Form MH2 must be accompanied by an office copy of the section 33(5) order, or a conveyancer's certificate that he holds an office copy of the s 33(5) order.[5]

The circumstances in which the registrar may cancel an agreed notice

10.28 Unlike the position in relation to unilateral notices that is explained below,[6] LRA 2002 make no express provision for the cancellation of an agreed notice (whether consensual or non-consensual) on the application of the registered proprietor or of some person entitled to be registered as proprietor. This is because the only circumstance in which an agreed notice can be removed is where that interest has ceased, so that the notice should be removed by the registrar under his powers to keep the register up to date, which are explained in Chapter 22.[7] LRR 2003, r 87, makes provision for this situation.[8] An application for the cancellation of an agreed notice, other than a matrimonial home rights notice, must be in Form CN1 and must be accompanied by evidence to satisfy the registrar that the interest protected by the notice has determined.[9] There is no restriction in r 87 as to who may apply for such cancellation. Where such an application is made, and the registrar is satisfied that the interest protected by the notice has come to an end, he must cancel the notice or make an entry in the registrar that the protected interest

---

[1]   See FLA 1996, s 32, Sch 4, para 4(1), (3)(b).

[2]   LRR 2003, r 82(1).

[3]   See FLA 1996, s 32, Sch 4, para 4(1), (3)(a).

[4]   LRR 2003, r 82(2).

[5]   Ibid, r 82(3).

[6]   See para **10.32**.

[7]   LRA 2002, Sch 4, para 5(b); see also para **22.16**.

[8]   LRR 2003, r 87, was made pursuant to the powers conferred by LRA 2002, Sch 4, paras 7(b) and (d) (provision as to how the register is to be altered): see Land Registration Rules 2003 – A Land Registry Consultation, p 402.

[9]   LRR 2003, r 87(1).

has come to an end.[1] If the protected interest has only come to an end in part, the registrar must make an appropriate entry.[2]

Unilateral notices

The nature of a unilateral notice

10.29 A unilateral notice may be entered on application without the consent of the registered proprietor of the estate or charge affected by it. The registrar does not have to be satisfied (as he would if the application were for an agreed notice) that the applicant's claim is valid; the registrar will simply check that the interest claimed is of a kind that may be protected by a unilateral notice. A unilateral notice must indicate that it is such a notice, and identify who is the beneficiary of the notice.[3] The purpose of a unilateral notice is to allow a person claiming an interest to protect its priority on the register (to the extent that it is valid), even though he cannot obtain the concurrence of the registered proprietor.[4] Previously, a person in that position could only enter a caution, which did not protect the priority of the interest that the applicant claimed.

Application for the entry of a unilateral notice

10.30 An application for the entry in the register of a unilateral notice must be in Form UN1,[5] and details of the interest claimed must be given either in a statutory declaration or in a conveyancer's certificate.[6] It is not necessary for the applicant to lodge any other document to support his application (such as the instrument which, he says, created the interest), and the applicant will not normally wish to do so. This is because if he does, the registrar may refer to that document in the entry in the register and the document would thereby be open to public inspection.[7] To comply with the statutory requirements,[8] the application must also identify who is to be named in the entry as the beneficiary of the notice, and must provide up to three addresses for service to be entered in the register.[9] If, as will often be the case, there is a risk that an

---

[1]   LRR 2003, r 87(2).

[2]   Ibid r 87(3).

[3]   LRA 2002, s 35(2). Like cautions under the previous law, unilateral notices do not identify the interest that they protect. In this way unilateral notices can be used (as cautions were sometimes used in the past) as a means of protecting an interest without disclosing its nature, thereby protecting the confidentiality of a transaction. It was intended that this should be so: see (2001) Law Com No 271, para 6.26.

[4]   Or a person entitled to be registered.

[5]   LRR 2003, r 83.

[6]   'Conveyancer' is defined by LRR 2003, r 217, to mean a solicitor, licensed conveyancer or a Fellow of the Institute of Legal Executives.

[7]   See para **10.24**.

[8]   LRA 2002, s 35(2)(b); para **10.29**.

[9]   See LRR 2003, r 198: see para **20.42**. At least one address must be a postal address. The others may be an electronic or a DX address.

application may be made to cancel the unilateral notice (see para **10.35**), it may be prudent for one of the addresses to be that of the beneficiary's solicitor.[1]

10.31 The registered proprietor must be notified of the entry of the unilateral notice (see para **10.34**), but, in accordance with the requirements of LRA 2002, this is done after the entry has been made.[2] The registered proprietor is not given an opportunity to object to the *application* for the entry of a unilateral notice.[3]

Application for the removal of a unilateral notice

10.32 An application may be made for the removal of a unilateral notice from the register by:

(a)   the beneficiary of a unilateral notice; and
(b)   such other persons as rules may provide,[4] namely the personal representative or trustee in bankruptcy of the person shown in the register as the beneficiary of a unilateral notice.[5]

An application for the removal of a unilateral notice must be in Form UN2.[6] If the registrar is satisfied that the application is in order he must remove the notice.[7]

Safeguards against the abuse of unilateral notices

10.33 There are obvious dangers in permitting such unilateral entries. The procedure could be abused and (for example) serious damage could be inflicted on a registered proprietor who was trying to sell his property by a disgruntled person who had unsuccessfully tried to purchase the land. There are, however, safeguards against abuse, both under LRA 2002 and, it is thought, under the general law.

SAFEGUARD 1: NOTIFICATION TO THE REGISTERED PROPRIETOR

10.34 First, as mentioned above,[8] the LRA 2002 creates a procedure for notifying the registered proprietor. If the registrar enters a unilateral notice in the register in pursuance of an application, he must give notice of the entry to

---

[1]   See Notices, Restrictions and the Protection of Third Party Interests in the Register, PG 19, para 3.7.3.
[2]   See LRA 2002, s 35(1)(a); Notices, Restrictions and the Protection of Third Party Interests in the Register, PG 19, para 3.3.3.
[3]   But see below, para **10.40** for a case where the registered proprietor was able to compel an applicant to withdraw his pending application for a unilateral notice.
[4]   LRA 2002, s 35(3).
[5]   LRR 2003, r 85(2). Such person must provide evidence to satisfy the registrar as to his appointment as personal representative or trustee in bankruptcy: ibid.
[6]   Ibid, r 85(1).
[7]   Ibid, r 85(3).
[8]   See para **10.31**.

the proprietor of the registered estate or charge to which it relates, and such other persons as rules may provide.[1]

10.35 Secondly, the LRA 2002 confers on both the registered proprietor of a registered estate or charge and any person who is entitled to be registered as proprietor, the right at any time to apply to the registrar for the cancellation of a unilateral notice.[2] Such an application must be made in Form UN4[3] and must be accompanied by evidence to satisfy the registrar of either:

(a)   the applicant's entitlement to be registered as the proprietor of the estate or charge affected by the unilateral notice; or

(b)   a conveyancer's certificate that the conveyancer is satisfied that the applicant is entitled to be registered as the proprietor of the estate or charge to which the unilateral notice relates.[4]

10.36 If an application is made for the cancellation of a unilateral notice the registrar must notify the beneficiary of the notice[5] of the following matters:

(a)   the application; and

(b)   the fact he must cancel the notice if the beneficiary of the notice does not exercise his right to object to the application within the time specified.[6]

The cancellation notice will be sent to the beneficiary at the addresses for service in the register.

10.37 On an application to the registrar for cancellation of a unilateral notice, one or other of the following will occur.

---

1   LRA 2002, s 35(1). It was envisaged that rules might provide for the notification of persons such as the liquidator, where the registered proprietor was a company which was in liquidation at the relevant time. No such rules have in fact been made, but see LRR 2003, r 17, which gives the registrar a general power to give any notice if he considers it is necessary or desirable to do so: see para **20.22**.
2   LRA 2002, s 36(1).
3   LRR 2003, r 86(1).
4   Ibid, r 86(2).
5   This means not only the person shown as the beneficiary of the notice in the register, but such other persons as rules may provide: see LRA 2002, s 36(4). LRR 2003, r 86(7), provides that a person entitled to be registered as the beneficiary of a notice under LRR 2003, r 88, may object to an application under LRA 2002, s 36(1), for cancellation of that notice and the reference to the beneficiary in s 36(3) includes such a person.
6   LRA 2002, s 36(2), (3) and LRR 2003, r 86(3). The beneficiary will be required to object before 12 noon on the fifteenth business day after the date of issue of the notice or such longer period, not exceeding a period ending at 12 noon on the thirtieth business day after the issue of the notice, as the registrar may allow following a request by the beneficiary of the notice: LRR 2003, r 86(3), (4). For the date by which such a request must be made and the procedure to be followed by the registrar on its receipt from the beneficiary, see ibid, r 86(5), (6).

(a) First, if the beneficiary of the notice does not object to the application, the registrar will cancel the notice.

(b) Secondly, if the beneficiary of the notice does object to the application, the registrar is bound to refer the matter to the Adjudicator for determination unless the matter can be disposed of by agreement between the parties,[1] or the registrar is satisfied that the objection is groundless.[2]

10.38 If the matter goes to the Adjudicator, there are various conclusions which he may reach. He may (for example) determine that:

(a) the person who had entered a unilateral notice was entitled to do so, and that the unilateral notice should, therefore, be replaced by a more permanent form of protection, such as an agreed notice or a registered charge;

(b) although the beneficiary of the notice does have an interest that is entitled to be protected in the register, a unilateral notice is not the appropriate entry, but that a restriction should be entered instead; or

(c) the beneficiary of the unilateral notice had no right to enter the notice and he may therefore direct that it should be cancelled.

SAFEGUARD 3: DUTY TO ACT REASONABLY

10.39 The third form of protection against the improper entry of a unilateral notice takes the form of a financial deterrent. A person who applies for the entry of such a notice without reasonable cause will be in breach of statutory duty. As such, he will be liable in damages in tort to any person who suffers damage in consequence of that breach.[3]

10.40 The fact that the entry of a unilateral notice without reasonable cause is a breach of statutory duty means that a court may, in an appropriate case, order a person whose application for a unilateral notice is pending, to withdraw it: see *Loubatières v Mornington Estates (UK) Ltd.*[4] Presumably, the court could, on the same basis, also order the applicant to withdraw such a notice even after it had been entered in the register. This power will be particularly useful where there is some urgency about either preventing the registration of the notice at all or removing the entry, and there is insufficient time to challenge the unilateral notice before the Adjudicator. However, it can only be exercised where there has been a breach of the statutory duty, namely where a person has applied for the entry of a unilateral notice without reasonable cause. There may be cases where the initial entry of the unilateral

---

1   LRA 2002, s 73(7); see also paras **20.19** et seq.
2   Ibid, s 73(6). This might be the case if it was apparent that the beneficiary of the notice had no interest that was capable of being protected by a notice.
3   LRA 2002, ss 77(1)(b), 77(2).
4   [2004] PLSCS 105.

notice was not unreasonable, but where in the light of subsequent events, it can no longer be sustained. If the removal of such a notice becomes urgent, it may be necessary to have recourse to the High Court's inherent jurisdiction explained in para **10.41**.

SAFEGUARD 4: INHERENT JURISDICTION OF THE HIGH COURT TO VACATE

10.41 In relation to cautions lodged under LRA 1925, the High Court exercised an inherent jurisdiction to order the vacation of a caution where it could not be sustained.[1] There is nothing in LRA 2002 to abrogate the jurisdiction of the High Court to order the vacation of an entry in the register and there is no good reason why it should not continue to be exercised, not only in relation to cautions that were entered before 13 October 2003, but also as regards unilateral notices entered since the new Act came into force.[2]

Updating the identity of the beneficiary

10.42 If the interest protected by the unilateral notice is transferred or, in some other way vests in a new or additional beneficiary, it is important that the register should be amended to reflect this change.[3] It was explained above, at paras **10.35** and **10.36** that:

(a)   a unilateral notice may be cancelled if the beneficiary of the notice does not object within the prescribed period; and

(b)   notice of the application for cancellation will only be served in the person shown on the register as the beneficiary of the unilateral notice.

There is, accordingly, a danger that if the register is not amended, the beneficiary of the unilateral notice may lose its protection because he is not notified of the application for cancellation. The LRR 2003, therefore, provide that a person entitled to the benefit of an interest protected by a unilateral notice may apply to be entered in the register in place of, or in addition to, the registered beneficiary.[4]

10.43 Any application to update the identity of the beneficiary of a unilateral notice must be made in Form UN3 and accompanied by evidence to satisfy the registrar of the applicant's title to the interest protected by the unilateral notice.[5] The registrar must serve notice of the application on the registered

---

[1]   The leading case was *Calgary and Edmonton Land Co Ltd v Dobinson* [1974] Ch 102. For a comparatively recent example, see *Clowes Developments (UK) Ltd v Mulchinock* [1998] 1 WLR 42.

[2]   As the county court is a statutory creation, it seems unlikely that it has any equivalent jurisdiction.

[3]   See Notices, Restrictions and the Protection of Third Party Interests in the Register, PG 19, para 3.9.2.

[4]   LRR 2003, r 88(1). The 'registered beneficiary' is defined as the person shown in the register as the beneficiary of the notice at the time the application is made: r 88(6).

[5]   LRR 2003, r 88(2). See generally, Notices, Restrictions and the Protection of Third Party Interests in the Register, PG 19, para 3.9.2.

beneficiary before entering the applicant in the register.[1] Such notice is not, however, necessary if the registered beneficiary signs Form UN3, or otherwise consents to the application, or the applicant is the registered proprietor's personal representative and evidence of his title to act accompanies the application.[2] If the registrar is satisfied that the interest protected by the unilateral notice is vested in the applicant, the registrar must enter the applicant in place of the registered beneficiary.[3] If the registrar is satisfied that the interest protected by the unilateral notice is vested both in the applicant and the registered beneficiary, the registrar must enter the applicant in addition to the registered beneficiary.[4] In the event of dispute, the new claimant could apply for a new notice instead.[5]

The form and content of notices entered by the registrar

10.44 The LRR 2003 provide for the form and content of the entry of a notice in the register. A notice must be entered in the charges register of the registered title affected.[6] The entry must identify the registered estate or registered charge affected.[7] Where the interest protected by the notice only relates to part of the registered estate in a registered title, the entry must contain sufficient details, for example by reference to a plan, to identify the affected part clearly.[8]

10.45 In the case of an agreed notice (what the rules call 'a notice (other than a unilateral notice)'), the entry must give details of the interest protected.[9] The exact form of entry is not specified, but the Registry appears to be following the previous practice by which details of the interest are given either by description of the interest or by reference to the instrument creating the interest.[10] The following is an example of an entry of an agreed notice entry. It is based on one given in the Land Registry's Practice Guide,[11] and it shows the Registry's practice:

'(5 July 2004) Option dated 14 June 2004 in favour of Annabel Smith.
NOTE: Copy filed.'

The date in brackets is the date on which the notice is taken to be entered in

---

[1]   LRR 2003, r 88(4).
[2]   Ibid, r 88(5).
[3]   Ibid, r 88(3)(a).
[4]   Ibid, r 88(3)(b).
[5]   See Notices, Restrictions and the Protection of Third Party Interests in the Register, PG 19, para 3.9.2.
[6]   LRR 2003, r 84(1).
[7]   Ibid, r 84(2).
[8]   Ibid.
[9]   Ibid, r 84(3).
[10] LRR 1925, rr 40, 41, provided that the notice must either refer to the interest it protects directly or by reference to the instrument creating it, or by setting out extracts.
[11] Notices, Restrictions and the Protection of Third Party Interests in the Register, PG 19, para 3.3.2.

the register.[1] The priority of an interest that is the subject of a notice in the register is protected against a registered disposition for valuable consideration.[2] That date is, therefore, of importance for the purposes of priority.

10.46 The entry in the register of a unilateral notice states that it is a unilateral notice,[3] it gives brief details of the interest that is protected in the register,[4] and it gives the name and address of the beneficiary of the notice.[5] An example of a unilateral notice, again based upon one given in the Land Registry's Practice Guide,[6] might be as follows:

> '(5 July 2004) UNILATERAL NOTICE in respect of an agreement dated 14 June 2004 made between (1) Peter Jones and (2) Annabel Smith.
>
> (5 July 2004) BENEFICIARY: Annabel Smith of 84 Steep Street, Hilltown, Westshire, WS99 4ZA.'

As regards the two dates in brackets, the first is the date on which the notice is taken to be entered in the register, and the second is the date on which the present beneficiary was entered in the register. In the example given, those two dates are the same because there has been no change in the beneficiary. That will not always be the case.

Protecting variations to interests that have been noted

10.47 The variation of registrable dispositions has already been explained: see para **8.40**. If an interest protected by a notice is varied, as where the terms of a restrictive covenant are changed, there are two ways of protecting the priority of the interest as varied.[7]

10.48 First, the existing notice may be replaced with a new one. In the case of an agreed notice, this requires:

(a)   an application to cancel the existing notice pursuant to LRR 2003, r 87 (see para **10.28**); and

(b)   an application for a new notice pursuant to LRR 2003, r 81 (see para **10.19**).

In the case of a unilateral notice, there must be:

---

[1]   See LRR 2003, r 20; see also para **20.33**.
[2]   LRA 2002, s 29(1), (2); see also paras **9.4–9.9**.
[3]   As required by LRA 2002, s 35(2)(a).
[4]   LRR 2002, r 84(5).
[5]   See LRA 2002, s 35(2)(b).
[6]   Notices, Restrictions and the Protection of Third Party Interests in the Register, PG 19, para 3.3.3.
[7]   Ibid, para 3.9.1.

(a)   an application by the beneficiary of the notice for the removal of the notice pursuant to LRA 2002, s 35(3) and LRR 2003, r 85 (see para **10.32**);

(b)   an application by the beneficiary for a new notice pursuant to LRR 2003, r 83 (see para **10.30**).

10.49 Secondly, in the alternative, there may be an application for an additional notice in respect of the variation. Where the application relates to an interest that is protected by an agreed notice, any agreed notice of a variation of that interest must give details of that variation.[1]

Restrictions

Nature and effect

10.50 A restriction is an entry in the register regulating the circumstances in which a disposition of a registered estate or charge may be the subject of an entry in the register.[2] A restriction can be entered, therefore, only in respect of a disposition of a registered estate or charge in relation to which some entry in the register may be made. No restriction can be entered in relation to dealings with unregistered interests as there is no title in the register against which to enter it, and no restriction can be entered to prevent any disposition of registered land in relation to which no entry in the register is needed. The entry of a restriction is to be made in relation to the registered estate or charge to which it relates.[3]

10.51 A restriction may in particular prohibit the making of:

(a)   an entry in respect of any disposition (thereby freezing the register);[4] or

(b)   a disposition of a kind specified in the restriction (as where a registered proprietor had only limited powers of disposition).[5]

The restriction may prohibit the making of a particular entry indefinitely,[6] for the period specified in the restriction,[7] or until the occurrence of an event specified in the restriction,[8] such as the giving of notice, the obtaining of a consent, or the making of an order by the court or registrar.[9]

---

[1]   LRR 2003, r 84(4).
[2]   LRA 2002, s 40(1).
[3]   Ibid, s 40(4).
[4]   Such an entry would be appropriate where a person obtained a freezing injunction in relation to any dealings with the property.
[5]   LRA 2002, s 40(2)(a).
[6]   As where the registered proprietor's powers are limited.
[7]   As where the proprietor has contracted not to make a disposition of the property for that period.
[8]   LRA 2002, s 40(2)(b).
[9]   Ibid, s 40(3).

10.52 As a general rule, where a restriction is entered in the register, no entry in respect of a disposition to which the restriction applies may be made in the register except in accordance with the terms of the restriction.[1] This rule is subject to one qualification: on the application of a person who appears to the registrar to have a sufficient interest in the restriction,[2] the registrar has power to make an order to:

(a)   disapply a restriction in relation to a disposition specified in the order or dispositions of a kind specified in the order; or

(b)   provide that a restriction has effect subject to certain specified modifications, in relation to a disposition specified in the order or dispositions of a kind specified in the order.[3]

In such circumstances, a note of the terms of any order made by the registrar must be entered in the register.[4]

10.53 The registrar might exercise his power to dispense with or modify the requirements of a restriction in the following circumstances:

(a)   where a disposition could only be made with the consent of a named individual and he could not be traced. The registrar could dispense with the requirement of consent, thereby obviating the need for an application to the court;[5] and

(b)   where a registered estate is subject to a restriction prohibiting the registration of any transfer without the consent of a management company, that company has been dissolved, but the applicant is able to satisfy the registrar that the transaction should, nevertheless, proceed.[6] In those circumstances, the registrar may make an order permitting the transfer to be registered. In such circumstances it may not be appropriate to cancel the restriction completely as the company might subsequently be restored to the register.

This power of dispensation is not new,[7] but the LRA 2002 makes it apparent

---

1   LRA 2002, s 41(1).
2   Ibid, s 41(3).
3   Ibid, s 41(2).
4   LRR 2003, r 96(5).
5   It seems unlikely that this power could be exercised where, as in the Trusts of Land and Appointment of Trustees Act 1996 (TLATA 1996), s 14, there is specific provision for the *court* to dispense with the requirement of consent.
6   This example is given in Notices, Restrictions and the Protection of Third Party Interests in the Register, PG 19, para 4.8.1.
7   Under the LRA 1925 a restriction was always made subject to any order of the registrar, and it was possible to apply to the registrar in anticipation of an intended dealing, who might make an order or grant a certificate that the proposed dealing should be registered, whether conditionally or otherwise: see LRR 1925, r 237.

on the face of the legislation rather than secreting it in rules. The procedure for making such an application is explained below at para **10.100**.

The entry of restrictions

Introduction

10.54 Under the LRA 2002, in the circumstances specified:

(a)   the registrar *may* enter a restriction;
(b)   the registrar *must* enter a restriction;
(c)   an application *may* be made to the registrar for the entry of a restriction;
(d)   an application *must* be made to the registrar for the entry of a restriction; and
(e)   the court *may* order the registrar to enter a restriction.

As is explained more fully below, restrictions will often be in a standard form: see para **10.70**. These standard forms of restriction are set out in LRR 2003, Sch 4.[1]

When the registrar may enter a restriction

10.55 The registrar has power to enter a restriction in the register if it appears to him that it is necessary or desirable to do so for any one of three purposes.[2]

10.56 The first purpose is for preventing invalidity or unlawfulness in relation to dispositions of a registered estate or charge.[3] The following are examples of when a restriction might be entered for that purpose.[4]

(a)   Where the registered proprietor of an estate or charge is a body which has limited powers, as, for example, is the case as regards some corporations. If no restriction were entered recording the limitation, the proprietor's powers of disposition would, as regards any disponee, be taken to be free of any limitation affecting the validity of that disposition.[5]
(b)   An entry might also be made to prevent a breach of contract, such as where the registered proprietor has contracted with a third party that he will not make any disposition either at all or without the consent of the third party.[6] A right of pre-emption could, therefore, be the subject of a restriction. So too could the case where a chargor contracts with a

---

[1]   LRR 2003, r 91(1).
[2]   LRA 2002, s 42(1).
[3]   Ibid, s 42(1)(a).
[4]   See (2001) Law Com No 271, para 6.40, from which these examples are drawn.
[5]   See LRA 2002, ss 26, 52; see also, paras **7.6** and **12.7**.
[6]   See standard restriction Form N in LRR 2003, Sch 4 (disposition by registered proprietor of registered estate or proprietor of charge – consent required).

chargee that he will not further charge or otherwise dispose the registered estate without the chargee's consent.

(c)   An entry may also restrict a disposition in breach of trust. An example of this is where trustees of land are required to obtain the consent to a disposition of the beneficiaries of full age who are beneficially entitled to an interest in possession in the land.[1]

10.57 The second purpose for which the registrar may enter a restriction is for securing that interests which are capable of being overreached on a disposition of a registered estate or charge are overreached.[2] If there is a disposition by trustees of land or by a tenant for life under the SLA 1925,[3] if overreaching is to take place any capital monies that arise must be paid to:

(a)   the trustees of land (in the case of a trust of land); or

(b)   the trustees of the settlement (in the case of a settlement under the SLA 1925).

In either case there must be at least two trustees, unless the trustee is a trust corporation.[4] To ensure that overreaching does take place, the registrar may enter a restriction to make certain that the proceeds of any disposition are paid to at least two trustees or to a trust corporation. The standard form of restriction,[5] Form A, provides that:

> 'No disposition by a sole proprietor of the registered estate (except a trust corporation) under which capital money arises is to be registered[6] unless authorised by an order of the court.'

As explained below, the registrar is under a *duty* to enter a restriction in certain cases to ensure that overreaching takes place.[7]

10.58 The third purpose for which the registrar may enter a restriction is to protect a right or claim in relation to a registered estate or charge.[8] An example would be where a person claimed to be entitled under a resulting or constructive trust because he had contributed to the cost of the acquisition of the property in question. The restriction might record that no disposition of

---

[1]   Such persons should be consulted by reason of TLATA 1996, s 11.

[2]   LRA 2002, s 42(1)(b).

[3]   Or by a person having the powers of a tenant for life under SLA 1925, s 20.

[4]   See LPA 1925, s 27(2); SLA 1925, s 94(1).

[5]   See LRR 2003, Sch 4.

[6]   Where the word 'registered' appears in any of the standard forms of restriction in relation to any disposition, it means the completion of the registration of the disposition by meeting the relevant registration requirements under LRA 2002, s 27: LRR 2003, r 91(3). For the registration requirements under LRA 2002, s 27, see Chapter 8.

[7]   See para **10.64**.

[8]   LRA 2002, s 42(1)(c).

the land should be registered without the consent of the person claiming the interest.

10.59 The LRA 2002 expressly provides that a person entitled to the benefit of a charging order relating to an interest under a trust shall be treated as having a right or claim in relation to the trust property.[1] The reason for this provision is as follows. Under the LRA 1925, a charging order over a beneficial interest under a trust of land was in practice protected by the entry of a caution against dealings.[2] That has ceased to be possible under the LRA 2002, as cautions have been prospectively abolished. As it is not possible to protect such charging orders by the entry of a notice because the order relates to an interest under a trust of land,[3] it was necessary for the Act to provide for the protection of such a charging order by means of a restriction.

10.60 Under LRR 2003, the appropriate form of restriction in respect of a charging order over a beneficial interest under a trust of land is Form K:[4]

'No disposition of the [registered estate or registered charge dated [*date*]] is to be registered without a certificate signed by the applicant for registration or his conveyancer[5] that written notice of the disposition was given to [*name of person with the benefit of the charging order*] at [*address for service*], being the person with the benefit of [*an interim*] [*a final*] charging order on the beneficial interest of [*name of judgment debtor*] made by the [*name of court*] on [*date*] (*Court reference* …).'

10.61 The effect of this new form of restriction is that the party who has the benefit of the charging order over the beneficial interest will receive notice of any intended disposition. This will give him the opportunity to take such action as is necessary to protect his security, as, for example, by ensuring that after any sale, the trustees pay the appropriate part of the proceeds to him in discharge of his charging order.

10.62 Although a restriction may be entered by the registrar to protect a right or claim in relation to a registered estate or charge,[6] he may not exercise that power for the purpose of protecting the priority of an interest which is, or could be, the subject of a notice.[7] The reason for this limitation is to reinforce

---

1   LRA 2002, s 42(4).
2   The person having the benefit of such a charging order could also enter a restriction by which no disposition by a sole proprietor of the land (not being trust corporation) under which capital money arose was to be registered except under an order of the registrar or the court: see LRA 1925, s 58(3); LRR 1925, r 213; Sch 2, Form 62. However, the only effect of such a restriction was to ensure that the beneficial interest that had been charged was overreached by any disposition of the land.
3   LRA 2002, s 33(a).
4   See LRR 2003, Sch 4; and (2001) Law Com No 271, para 6.43.
5   LRR 2003, r 91(2), provides that where the word 'conveyancer' appears in the standard forms of restriction it has the same meaning as in the LRR 2003.
6   See para **10.58**.
7   LRA 2002, s 42(2).

the principle that a notice is the correct form of entry to protect the priority of an interest. By its very nature a restriction does not confer priority on a right or interest (although it may have that effect indirectly because it may prevent the registration of some disposition that would affect the priority of the right or interest in question). It should be stressed that the LRA 2002 does not prohibit the entry of both a restriction and a notice in relation to the same right or interest if there is a good reason to have both.[1] However, the situations in which it will be appropriate are unlikely to be ones where the purpose of the restriction is to protect a right or claim in relation to a registered estate or charge.

10.63 Where the registrar enters a restriction under the powers referred to above he must normally give notice of the entry to the proprietor of the registered estate or charge concerned.[2] If the registered proprietor wishes to challenge the exercise of the registrar's power, he must do so by an application for judicial review. The Adjudicator does not have jurisdiction in this case because the entry of a restriction does not arise out of any application to which the registered proprietor may object.[3] In one situation the registrar does not have to notify the registered proprietor where he exercises his power to enter a restriction, namely where the entry is made in pursuance of an application by a person under s 43 of the LRA 2002. Applications under s 43 are explained at para **10.65**.

When the registrar must enter a restriction

10.64 The registrar must enter a restriction in the following cases.

(a)   Where he enters two or more persons as the joint proprietors of a registered estate in land. In such circumstances he must enter such restrictions as the rules provide, for the purpose of securing that interests which are capable of being overreached on a disposition of the estate are overreached.[4] The LRR 2003 provide that the relevant form of restriction is Form A,[5] which is set out at para **10.57**.

(b)   In other cases where the LRA 2002 requires him to enter a restriction. An example is a bankruptcy restriction,[6] which is explained at para **13.14**.

(c)   Where any enactment requires the entry of a restriction.[7] Many statutes

---

[1]   For example, in relation to a right of pre-emption, a notice could be entered to protect the priority of the interest and a restriction could be entered to prevent any specified disposition without the consent of the grantee of the right of pre-emption.

[2]   LRA 2002, s 42(3).

[3]   See ibid, ss 73, 108; see also paras **20.29** et seq.

[4]   LRA 2002, s 44(1). This replicates the previous position.

[5]   LRR 2003, r 95(2)(a). The joint proprietorship restriction is brought forward in almost identical terms to the previous Form 62 restriction.

[6]   LRA 2002, s 86(2); LRR 2003, r 166.

[7]   Ibid, s 44(2).

require the entry of a restriction.[1] Under LRR 2003, r 95(1), such restrictions must be in the form specified in the Rules, the form required by the relevant enactment, or if there is neither, in such form as the registrar may direct having regard to the provisions of the relevant enactment.[2]

Where a person may apply for the entry of a restriction

10.65 A person may apply to the registrar to exercise his power to enter a restriction explained in paras **10.55** et seq[3] in three circumstances.

(a) The first is where he is the proprietor of the registered estate or charge to which the application relates, or a person entitled to be registered as proprietor of that estate or charge.[4]

(b) The second is where the proprietor of the registered estate or charge to which the application relates, or a person entitled to be registered as proprietor, consents to the application.[5]

(c) The third is where the applicant otherwise has a sufficient interest in the making of the entry.[6]

10.66 Rule 92 of the LRR 2003 prescribes the way in which an application for the entry of a restriction in the register must be made, though it does not apply to an application to the registrar to give effect to an order of the court made under s 46 of the Act[7] (these orders are explained at paras **10.80** et seq). By r 92(1), the application for the entry of a restriction must normally be made in Form RX1. In certain cases, the application may be made in the body of another Form: this is explained in para **10.67**. The application must be accompanied by the following information:[8]

---

[1] For example, by statute certain public corporations, charities, public sector landlords and other bodies require the consent of the Charity Commission or (as the case may be) the Secretary of State to a disposal of land.

[2] By LRR 20003, r 95(2), the following forms of restriction are specified for use under the following statutes:
(a) Section 37(5A) of the Housing Act 1985, Form U;
(b) Section 157(7) of the Housing Act 1985, Form V;
(c) Section 81(10) of the Housing Act 1988, Form X;
(d) Section 133 of the Housing Act 1988, Form X;
(e) Paragraph 4 of Schedule 9A to the Housing Act 1985, Form W;
(f) Section 173(9) of the Local Government and Housing Act 1989, Form X;
(g) Section 13(5) of the Housing Act 1996, Form Y.

[3] That is, under LRA 2002, s 42(1).

[4] Ibid, s 43(1)(a).

[5] Ibid, s 43(1)(b).

[6] Ibid, s 43(1)(c). See too LRR 2003, r 172(2); para **10.103**.

[7] LRR 2003, r 92(8).

[8] Ibid, r 92(2). Because land certificates have been abolished (see Chapter 21), the production of the registered proprietor's land certificate is no longer required in order to enter a restriction on application.

(a)   full details of the required restriction;

(b)   an address for service for any person:

    (i)   on whom notice must be served;

    (ii)   whose consent or certificate is required; or

    (iii)   who is referred to by name in a standard form of restriction;

(c)   if the application is made with the consent of the relevant registered proprietor, or a person entitled to be registered as such, and that consent is not given in Form RX1, either:

    (i)   the relevant consent;

    (ii)   a certificate given by a conveyancer that the conveyancer holds the relevant consent;[1]

(d)   if the application is made by or with the consent of a person entitled to be registered as the relevant registered proprietor, evidence to satisfy the registrar of his entitlement;[2] and

(e)   if the application is made by a person who claims that he has a sufficient interest in the making of the entry (see para **10.65**(c)), a statement which must either contain details of that interest or, if it is one of the class of interests specified in rule 93,[3] state which of them it is.[4]

10.67 It is unnecessary to make a separate application on Form RX1 in three circumstances,[5] namely where a person applies for the entry of a standard form restriction in:

(a)   the additional provisions panel in any of Forms TP1, TP2, TP3, TR1, TR2, TR3, TR4, TR5, AS1, AS2 or AS3;[6]

(b)   panel 7 in Form CH1;[7] or

(c)   in an approved charge.[8]

10.68 The Act also provides for rules to be made providing for classes of

---

[1]   LRR 2003, r 92(6). LRA 2002 s 43(2)(b) provides for rules to be made as to the form of consent for the purposes of an application when the relevant registered proprietor or a person entitled to be registered as such proprietor consents to the application.

[2]   The registrar may accept a certificate given by a conveyancer that the conveyancer is satisfied that the person making or consenting to the application is entitled to be registered as the proprietor, and that either (a) the conveyancer holds the originals of the documents that contain evidence of that person's entitlement, or (b) an application for registration of that person as proprietor is pending at the Land Registry: LRR 2003, r 92(5).

[3]   Which contains a list of persons who are to be regarded as having a sufficient interest for the purposes of LRA 2002, s 43(1)(c), above, para **10.65**(c). For LRR 2003, r 93, see below, para **10.68**.

[4]   LRR 2003, r 92(3). If requested to do so, the applicant must supply further evidence to satisfy the registrar that he has a sufficient interest: ibid, r 92(4).

[5]   Ibid, r 92(7).

[6]   For these Forms, see para **8.29**.

[7]   For Form CH1 (legal charge of a registered estate), see para **12.10**. For the entry of restrictions in panel 7, see para **12.24**.

[8]   For approved charges, see paras **12.14** et seq. For these purposes, the form of charge, including the application for the restriction, must have been first approved by the registrar: see LRR 2003, r 92(9).

persons who are to be regarded as having a sufficient interest in the making of the entry.[1] Rule 93 of the LRR 2003 lists 22 classes of persons who are regarded as having a sufficient interest to apply for a restriction and, in relation to many of these classes, prescribes the appropriate standard form of restriction for which application should be made. These include:

(a) a person who has an interest in a registered estate held under a trust of land;[2]

(b) the donee of a special power of appointment in relation to registered land affected by that power;[3]

(c) the Charity Commission in relation to registered land held upon charitable trusts;[4]

(d) the Church Commissioners, the Parsonages Board or the Diocesan Board of Finance, if applying for a restriction to give effect to any arrangement which is made under any enactment or Measure administered by or relating to the Church Commissioners, the Parsonages Board or the Diocesan Board of Finance or to protect any interest in registered land arising under any such arrangement or statute;[5]

(e) any person with the benefit of a freezing order or an undertaking given in place of a freezing order, who is applying for a restriction in Form AA or BB;[6]

(f) any person who has applied for (but not yet obtained) a freezing order and who is applying for a restriction in Form CC or DD;[7]

(g) a trustee in bankruptcy who has an interest in a beneficial interest in registered land that is held under a trust of land, and who is applying for a restriction in Form J to be entered in the register of that land;[8]

---

[1] LRA 2002, s 43(2)(c). See (2001) Law Com No 271, para 6.49.

[2] LRR 2003, r 93(a). The restriction is in Form A: see para **10.57**. LRR 2003, r 93(b) and (d) are concerned with cases where the powers of either trustees of land or personal representatives are limited by TLATA 1996, s 8.

[3] Ibid, r 93(e). A donee of a general power of appointment can always appoint to himself and falls within LRA 2002, s 43(1)(a).

[4] LRR 2003, r 93(f). Generally, the charity trustees must apply for entry of a restriction, see for example LRR 2003, r 176(3); and see para **13.39**. LRR 2003, 93(f) makes it clear that the Charity Commissioners have the power to apply for the necessary restriction if the charity trustees do not, so implementing the recommendations of Law Com 271, para 6.49.

[5] LRR 2003 r 93(g). This derives from LRR 1925 r 238.

[6] LRR 2003, r 93(h). Form AA is as follows: 'Under an order of the (*name of court*) made on (*date*) (*claim no*) no disposition by the proprietor of the registered estate is to be registered except under a further order of the Court'. Form BB is the equivalent in relation to a freezing order obtained against a registered charge. Under the LRA 1925, a freezing order would have been protected by the entry of an inhibition.

[7] LRR 2003, r 93(i). A restriction in Form CC is as follows: 'Pursuant to an application made on (*date*) to the (*name of court*) for a freezing order to be made under (*statutory provision*) no disposition by the proprietor of the registered estate is to be registered except with the consent of (*name of the person applying*) or under a further order of the Court'. Form DD is the equivalent in relation to an application for a freezing order on a charge.

[8] LRR 2003, r 93(j). Such an interest could previously be protected by the entry of a caution in the

(h)   any person with the benefit of a charging order over a beneficial interest in registered land held under a trust of land, and who is applying for a restriction in Form K to be entered in the register of the land;[1]

(i)   a receiver or a sequestrator appointed by order who applies for a restriction in Form L or N.[2]

10.69 If the applicant falls within one of the classes listed, he is entitled to apply for a restriction. However, even if he is not within one or more of the classes listed, he can still apply for a restriction provided that he has a sufficient interest.

10.70 In accordance with the power contained in the LRA 2002,[3] r 92(1) of and Sch 4 to the LRR 2003 specify standard forms of restriction.[4] This has already been mentioned (see para **10.54**). Schedule 4 lists 33 such restrictions.[5]

---

register, but must now be protected by entry of a restriction. Form J is as follows: 'No disposition of the [registered estate or registered charge dated [*date*]] is to be registered without a certificate signed by the applicant for registration or his conveyancer that written notice of the disposition was given to [*name of trustee in bankruptcy*] (the trustee in bankruptcy of [*name of bankrupt person*]) at [*address for service*]'.

[1]   LRR 2003, r 93(k). See para **10.60**.

[2]   Ibid, r 93(s). Restrictions in Forms L and N have the effect that no disposition can be made without a certificate (Form L) or the consent of a named person (Form N).

[3]   See LRA 2002, s 43(2)(d).

[4]   It should be noted that LRR 1925 contained a number of standard form restrictions: see LRR 1925, rr 58(1), 59A(2), 60(3), 100, 106A(3), 123(2), 124(5), 169A(2), 171(1), 213, 232, 236.

[5]   These are as follows:

Form A, Restriction on dispositions by sole proprietor;

Form B, Dispositions by trustees – certificate required;

Form C, Dispositions by personal representatives – certificate required;

Form D, Parsonage, church or churchyard land;

Form E, Non-exempt charity – certificate required;

Form F, Land vested in official custodian on trust for non-exempt charity – authority required;

Form G, Tenant for life as registered proprietor of settled land, where there are trustees of the settlement;

Form H, Statutory owners as trustees of the settlement and registered proprietors of settled land;

Form I, Tenant for life as registered proprietor of settled land – no trustees of the settlement;

Form J, Trustee in bankruptcy and beneficial interest – certificate required;

Form K, Charging order affecting beneficial interest – certificate required;

Form L, Disposition by registered proprietor of a registered estate or proprietor of charge – certificate required;

Form M, Disposition by registered proprietor of registered estate or proprietor of charge – certificate of registered proprietor of specified title number required;

Form N, Disposition by registered proprietor of registered estate or proprietor of charge – consent required;

Form O, Disposition by registered proprietor of registered estate or proprietor of charge – consent of registered proprietor of specified title number required;

Form P, Disposition by registered proprietor of registered estate or proprietor of charge – consent of proprietor of specified charge required;

Form Q, Disposition by registered proprietor of registered estate or proprietor of charge – consent of personal representative required;

Form R, Disposition by registered proprietor of registered estate or proprietor of charge – evidence of compliance with club rules required;

In certain situations a person is obliged to apply for a specified restriction (see paras **10.72** et seq). However, in many other cases, there is no requirement that a person must apply for a restriction, nor, subject to what is said in para **10.71** is there any obligation when applying for a restriction to use a standard form.[1] However, no good purpose is served by employing a non-standard restriction when a standard form covers the case. By using a standard form the applicant knows that it will be acceptable to the registrar, who will not, therefore, raise any objection in relation to it.

10.71 In any event, the LRA 2002 contains provisions[2] to protect the registrar from having to give effect to and police unreasonable and inconvenient restrictions. If an application is made for the entry of a restriction which is not in a form specified under the rules, the registrar may only approve the application if it appears to him that:

— the terms of the proposed application are reasonable;[3] and
— applying the proposed restriction would be straightforward and would not place an unreasonable burden on him.[4]

Where a person must apply for the entry of a restriction

10.72 Under the LRA 2002, there is a power to make rules that will *require* an application for a restriction to be made in such circumstances and by such persons as the rules may specify.[5] The relevant rule is LRR 2003, r 94 (which largely replicates the previous law[6]), and its effect is as follows.

Form S, Disposition by proprietor of charge – certificate of compliance required;
Form T, Disposition by proprietor of charge – consent required;
Form U, Section 37 of the Housing Act 1985;
Form V, Section 157 of the Housing Act 1985;
Form W, Paragraph 4 of Schedule 9A to the Housing Act 1985;
Form X, Section 81 or 133 of the Housing Act 1988 or section 173 of the Local Government and Housing Act 1989;
Form Y, Section 13 of the Housing Act 1996;
Form AA, freezing order on the registered estate;
Form BB, freezing order on charge;
Form CC, application for freezing order on the registered estate;
Form DD, application for freezing order on charge;
Form EE, restraint order or interim receiving order on the registered estate;
Form FF, restraint order or interim receiving order on charge;
Form GG, application for restraint order or interim receiving order on the registered estate;
Form HH, application for restraint order or interim restraining order on charge.

[1] However, the Land Registry advise that 'you should only apply for a restriction that is not in a standard form if none of the standard form restrictions is appropriate': see Notices, Restrictions and the Protection of Third Party Interests in the Register, PG19, para 4.3.2.
[2] As the LRA 1925 did previously: see LRA 1925, s 58(2).
[3] LRA 2002, s 43(3)(a).
[4] Ibid, s 43(3)(b).
[5] LRA 2002, s 43(2)(a).
[6] See LRR 1925, rr 59A, 106A(1).

10.73 First, a proprietor of a registered estate must apply for a restriction in Form A (see para **10.57**) in two situations.

(a)   The first is where that registered estate becomes subject to a trust of land, other than on a registrable disposition, and the proprietor or the survivor of joint proprietors will not be able to give a valid receipt for capital money.[1] An obvious example is where a sole registered proprietor declares himself a trustee of the registered estate for one or more beneficiaries.

(b)   The second is where the registered estate is held on a trust of land and, as a result of a change in the trusts, the proprietor or the survivor of joint proprietors will not be able to give a valid receipt for capital money.[2] An example would be where X and Y hold a registered estate on trust for themselves as joint tenants beneficially, but X then severs the joint tenant by, say, a written notice to Y under LPA 1925, s 36(2).

10.74 Secondly, a sole or last surviving trustee of land held on a trust of land must, when applying either to register a disposition of a registered estate in his favour or to be registered as proprietor of an unregistered estate, at the same time apply for a restriction in Form A.[3] Thus for example, X is the sole surviving trustee of land that was settled on trust by Y. Y then conveys more land to X to be held on the same trusts. Whether that transfer is of land that is already registered, or of land that is unregistered,[4] X must apply for a restriction in Form A.

10.75 Thirdly, under TLATA 1996, s 6(1), for the purposes of exercising their functions as trustees, trustees of land have, in relation to the land subject to the trust, all the powers of an absolute owner. However, by TLATA 1996, s 8(1), except in relation to charitable, ecclesiastical or public trusts, it is possible to exclude or restrict the powers conferred by s 6, if provision to that effect is made by the disposition which created the trust. Accordingly, LRR 2003, r 94(3) provides that a personal representative of a deceased person who holds a registered estate on a trust of land created by the deceased's will, or on a trust of land arising under the laws of intestacy which is subsequently varied, and whose powers have been limited by s 8 of the TLATA 1996, must apply for a restriction in Form C.[5] Form C is in the following terms:

---

[1]   LRR 2003, r 94(1)(a). This replicates the effect of LRR 1925, r 213(4).

[2]   LRR 2003, r 94(1)(b). This replicates the effect of LRR 1925, r 213(5).

[3]   LRR 2003, r 94(2). This replicates the effect of LRR 1925, r 213(2), (3). For Form A, see para **10.57**.

[4]   A transfer of unregistered land in such circumstances is treated as a gift and is, therefore, subject to the requirement of registration: see LRA 2002, s 4(1)(a)(i), (7)(c); and see para **2.10(2)**.

[5]   LRR 2003, Sch 4, Form C, is as follows: 'No disposition by [*name*], the [executor or administrator] of [*name*] deceased, other than a transfer as personal representative, is to be registered unless he makes a statutory declaration, or his conveyancer gives a certificate, that the disposition is in accordance with the terms [of the will of the deceased or the law relating to intestacy as varied by a deed dated *specify*

'No disposition by [*name*], the [executor or administrator] of [*name*] deceased, other than a transfer as personal representative, is to be registered unless he makes a statutory declaration, or his conveyancer gives a certificate, that the disposition is in accordance with the terms [of the will of the deceased or the law relating to intestacy as varied by a deed dated *specify details of deed or specify appropriate details*] or [some variation or further variation] thereof referred to in the declaration or certificate, or is necessary for the purposes of administration.'

10.76 Thus, for example, if, under X's will, his personal representatives hold a registered estate on trusts under which they are forbidden from charging the land, the trustees must apply for a restriction in that form, which will ensure compliance with the limitation contained in the will. Given the fact that TLATA 1996, s 8, does not apply to legal estates that are held on charitable, ecclesiastical or public trusts, the requirements of r 94(3) do not apply to such trusts because they are not needed.[1]

10.77 Fourthly, where a declaration of trust of a registered estate imposes limitations on the powers of the trustees under TLATA 1996, s 8, the registered proprietor must apply for a restriction in Form B,[2] which is as follows:

'No disposition [*or specify details*] by the proprietors of the registered estate is to be registered unless they make a statutory declaration, or their conveyancer gives a certificate, that the disposition [*or specify details*] is in accordance with [*specify the disposition creating the trust*] or some variation thereof referred to in the declaration or certificate.'

The same obligation to apply for a restriction in Form B applies where there is a variation in the trusts, which either imposes limitations, or changes the limitations, on the powers of the trustees under TLATA 1996, s 8.[3] The obligations set out in this paragraph apply not only where the legal estate is held by the trustees, but also where it is vested in the personal representatives of a sole or last surviving trustee.[4] For the reasons explained in para **10.76**, they do not apply to legal estates that are held on charitable, ecclesiastical or public trusts.[5]

10.78 Fifthly, an applicant for the first registration of a legal estate held on a trust of land in circumstances where the powers of the trustees are limited by TLATA 1996, s 8, must at the same time apply for a restriction in Form B.[6]

---

details of deed or specify appropriate details] or [some variation or further variation] thereof referred to in the declaration or certificate, or is necessary for the purposes of administration.'

[1] LRR 2003, r 94(6).
[2] Ibid, r 94(4)(a).
[3] Ibid, r 94(4)(b).
[4] Ibid, r 94(7).
[5] Ibid, r 94(6).
[6] Ibid, r 94(5). For Form B, see para **10.77**.

The same obligation applies where the legal estate is vested in the personal representatives of a sole or last surviving trustee.[1] Once again, this obligation does not apply to legal estates that are held on charitable, ecclesiastical or public trusts.[2]

10.79 Finally, the LRR 2003 contain rules that are intended to ensure that dispositions to or by charities comply with the provisions of the Charities Act 1993. These are considered more fully in Chapter 13. One aspect of these provisions is that, in certain circumstances, the entry of a restriction is mandatory.[3] Those circumstances are as follows:

(a)   Where there is a disposition of registered land in favour of a non-exempt charity, the application for registration must be accompanied by an application for entry of a restriction in Form E.[4]

(b)   Where a registered estate is held by, or in trust for, a corporation and the corporation becomes a non-exempt charity, the charity trustees must apply for entry of a restriction in Form E.[5]

(c)   Where a registered estate or charge is vested in the official custodian by virtue of an order under s 18 of the Charities Act 1993,[6] an application to register him as proprietor must be accompanied by an application for the entry of a restriction in Form F.[7]

Where the court may order the entry of a restriction

10.80 Under s 46(1) of the LRA 2002, the court may make an order requiring the registrar to enter a restriction in the register where it appears to the court that it is necessary or desirable to do so for the purpose of protecting a right or clause in relation to a registered estate or charge. A court is likely to exercise this power in similar circumstances to those where, under the previous law, it would have ordered the entry of an inhibition. However, the position under the LRA 2002 is more flexible. An inhibition prevented the entry in the register of *any* dealing with a particular registered estate or charge: in effect it froze the register.[8] As has been explained above, a restriction need

---

[1]   LRR 2003, r 94(7).

[2]   Ibid, r 94(6).

[3]   Ibid, r 94(8).

[4]   Ibid, r 176(2), (4); and see para **13.39**. The restriction is as follows: 'No disposition by the proprietor of the registered estate to which section 36 or section 38 of the Charities Act 1993 applies is to be registered unless the instrument contains a certificate complying with section 37(2) or section 39(2) of that Act as appropriate.'

[5]   LRR 2003, r 176(3).

[6]   As where there has been misconduct or mismanagement in the administration of a charity or it is otherwise necessary or desirable to act to protect a charity's property.

[7]   LRR 2003, r 178(2); and see para **13.41**. The restriction in Form F is as follows: 'No disposition executed by the trustees of [*charity*] in the name and on behalf of the proprietor shall be registered unless the transaction is authorised by an order of the court or of the Charity Commissioners, as required by section 22(3) of the Charities Act 1993.'

[8]   See LRA 1925, s 57.

not be so sweeping in its effect, and might, for example, preclude a particular kind of entry.[1]

10.81 As it happens, the standard forms of restriction that a court is most likely to order the registrar to enter are Forms AA–HH,[2] and all of these have the effect of freezing the register in the same way as inhibition formerly did. Thus, for example, Form AA (freezing order on the registered estate) is as follows:

'Under an order of the [*name of court*] made on [*date*] [*claim no*] no disposition by the proprietor of the registered estate is to be registered except under a further order of the Court.'

10.82 The court, like the registrar,[3] may not enter a restriction to protect the priority of an interest which is, or could be, the subject of a notice.[4] Given that in most cases where the court orders the entry of a restriction, it is likely to freeze the register (see para **10.81**), a potential issue of priority might arise. In Chapter 19 it is explained that, under the LRA 2002, priority protection can be obtained by an intending purchaser either by making a priority search or by applying for the entry of a notice in the register in relation to his estate contract to buy the land.[5] What this means is that, during the priority period,[6] any entry made in the register will be postponed to the purchaser's protected application to register the disposition in his favour.[7] There is the possibility of a conflict between the court's power to order the entry of a restriction and this priority protection. If a purchaser has, say, made a priority search, and during the period of priority the court orders the entry of a restriction under the powers explained in para **10.80**, the issue arises as to whether the purchaser's protected application to register the sale or other disposition in his favour has priority over the restriction, or vice versa.[8]

10.83 The general principle in the LRA 2002 is that the priority protection obtained by the purchaser prevails.[9] However, the court may include in an order requiring the registrar to enter a restriction, a direction that an entry

---

[1] See paras **10.50**, **10.51**.
[2] The Sch 4 forms are as follows: Forms AA (freezing order on the registered estate), BB (freezing order on charge), CC (application for freezing order on the registered estate), DD (application for freezing order on charge), EE (restraint order or interim receiving order on the registered estate), FF (restraint order or interim receiving order on charge), GG (application for restraint order or interim receiving order on the registered estate), and HH (application for restraint order or interim receiving order on charge).
[3] See LRA 2002, s 42(2); see also para **10.62**.
[4] Ibid, s 46(2).
[5] Ibid, s 72; see also para **19.4**.
[6] The commencement and duration of the priority period are a matter for rules: ibid, s 72(6), (7).
[7] Ibid, s 72(2).
[8] This problem could have arisen under the previous law when the court ordered the entry of an inhibition. There is no reported case in which the point arose.
[9] This is a necessary inference from LRA 2002, ss 46(3), 72(2), (4).

made in pursuance of the order is to have overriding priority.[1] If it does, the restriction will prevail over the purchaser's priority protection. In such circumstances, the entry made by the registrar in the register must be in such form as the registrar may determine so as to ensure that the priority of the restriction ordered by the court is apparent from the register.[2]

10.84 If such an order is made, the purchaser's position could be seriously prejudiced. The Act therefore provides that the court may make the exercise of the power to order overriding priority subject to such terms and conditions as it thinks fit.[3] In practice the court is likely to require an undertaking from the applicant that he should indemnify any person acting in good faith who has suffered loss as a result of the court's direction.[4] The situation is analogous to the grant of an interim injunction, where a similar undertaking in damages is required. As an additional safeguard, it is provided by LRR 2003 that, where the entry of a restriction with overriding priority is completed by the registrar during the priority period of an official search which was delivered before the application to enter the restriction was made, the registrar must give notice of the entry of the restriction to the applicant for the official search or, where his agent applied for the search on his behalf, to that agent.[5]

10.85 When a court orders the entry of a restriction under LRA 2002, s 46, that order will be addressed directly to the Chief Land Registrar. However, the Land Registry recommends that the applicant should apply for restriction to be entered in the register. Application must be made on Form AP1, because there is no other applicable form.[6]

Safeguards against improper applications for a restriction

10.86 The LRA 2002 contains a number of safeguards to protect a registered proprietor from the improper entry of restrictions.

10.87 The first safeguard is that a person must not exercise his right to apply for a restriction without reasonable cause.[7] Any person who enters a

---

[1] LRA 2002, s 46(3). The sort of case in which a court might exercise this power would if there was a risk that a third party might apply for an official search with priority before the restriction could be entered in the register: see Notices, Restrictions and the Protection of Third Party Interests in the Register, PG19, para 4.6.3.

[2] Ibid, s 46(4) and LRR 2003, r 100(1).

[3] Ibid, s 46(5).

[4] (2001) Law Com No 271, para 6.53.

[5] LRR 2003, r 100(2). The registrar need not serve such notice if he is satisfied that it is unnecessary: ibid.

[6] LRR 2003, r 13. Form RX1 cannot be used because the requirements of LRR 2003, r 92, including the requirement that application for a restriction must be made in Form RX1 (see para **10.66**), does not apply to an application to the registrar to give effect to an order of the court made under LRA 2002, s 46: see LRR 2002, r 92(8); and see para **10.66**.

[7] LRA 2002, s 77(1)(b). See also (in relation to notices), para **10.39**.

restriction without reasonable cause commits a breach of statutory duty and is liable to any person who suffers damage as a consequence.[1] Because an application for the entry of a restriction without reasonable cause is a breach of statutory duty, a court would have power to order a person to withdraw a pending application for a restriction.[2]

10.88 The second safeguard is to provide a procedure by which, when an application is made for a restriction that affects a registered estate or charge, the proprietor is notified of the application and may object to it.[3] Under the LRA 2002, a registered proprietor will be notified of *any* application for the entry of a restriction that relates to his estate or charge, except for the following:

(a)   an application which is made by or with the consent of the registered proprietor or a person entitled to be registered as proprietor;

(b)   an application which, by rules, is *required* to be made, as explained in paras **10.72** et seq; and

(c)   an application which reflects a limitation under either an order of the court or registrar, or an undertaking given in place of such order.[4]

10.89 Where a notifiable application has been made, the registrar must serve notice on the proprietor of the registered estate or charge to which it relates,[5] and on any other person on whom, by the terms of a restriction, notice is to be served.[6] The notice will give the relevant person 15 business days in which to object to the application.[7]

10.90 The registrar may not determine an application for a restriction which is notifiable until the end of the period for making objections, unless every person notified has either exercised his right to object to the application or has given the registrar notice that he does not intend to do so.[8] If the registered proprietor[9] objects to the application, the usual procedures for dealing with contested applications apply.[10] If, therefore, the objection cannot

---

[1]   LRA 2002, s 77(2). Neither the entry of a notice nor of a restriction guarantees the validity of the interest that it seeks to protect and the LRA 2002 does not provide any right to an indemnity from the registrar against loss suffered because of an entry that has been made.

[2]   See, in the context of unilateral notices, *Loubatières v Mornington Estates (UK) Ltd* [2004] PLSCS 105; at para **10.40**.

[3]   LRA 2002, s 45.

[4]   Ibid, s 45(3).

[5]   Ibid, s 45(1)(a).

[6]   See ibid, s 45(1)(b) and LRR 2003, r 198(2)(d).

[7]   LRR 2003, r 197(2); and see para **20.41**. See also Notices, Restrictions and the Protection of Third Party Interests in the Register, PG 19, para 4.4.4.

[8]   LRA 2002, s 45(2).

[9]   Or other person specified by rules under LRA 2002, s 45(1)(b); see also para **10.89**.

[10]   Cf paras **20.29** et seq.

be resolved by agreement, it will be referred to the Adjudicator for determination.[1]

10.91 It will be noted that the procedure applicable to notifiable restrictions is different from that which applies to unilateral notices. As has been explained, a unilateral notice will be entered in the register and the registered proprietor may then seek its cancellation.[2] The priority of the interest noted on the register is therefore protected pending any such application for its cancellation. By contrast, a notifiable restriction is not entered in the register until the registered proprietor[3] has had the opportunity to object to it. A restriction, unlike a notice, does not protect priority and there is, therefore, no reason why any objection to it should not be dealt with prior to its entry in the register rather than afterwards.

Withdrawal, cancellation and disapplication of a restriction

10.92 Once entered in the register, a restriction remains unless it is withdrawn or cancelled. However, even if remains in the register, there is a procedure by which it may be disapplied.

Withdrawal

10.93 Where a restriction has been entered on the application of a particular person, he or his estate may wish to apply for it to be withdrawn once it is, for whatever reason, spent. The LRA 2002 provides that a person may apply to the registrar for the withdrawal of a restriction if the restriction was entered in such circumstances as rules may provide, and the applicant is of such a description as rules may provide.[4]

10.94 Rule 98 of the LRR 2003 makes provision for the withdrawal of restrictions. First, it defines negatively which restrictions may be withdrawn, by setting out those that cannot.[5] It is not possible to apply to withdraw a restriction:

(a)   that was entered under LRA 2002, s 42(1)(a), and reflects some limitation on the registered proprietor's powers of disposition imposed by statute or the general law (see para **10.56**);

(b)   that was a mandatory restriction entered in the register following an application under LRR 2003, r 94 (see paras **10.72** et seq);

(c)   that the registrar is under an obligation to enter in the register pursuant to LRA 2002, s 44 (see para **10.64**);

---

[1]   LRA 2002, s 73.
[2]   Ibid, s 36; see also para **10.35**.
[3]   Or other person entitled by rules to object.
[4]   LRA 2002, s 47.
[5]   LRR 2003, r 98(6).

(d)   that reflects a limitation under an order of the court or registrar, or an undertaking given in place of such an order (see para **10.88**);

(e)   that is entered pursuant to a court order under LRA 2002, s 46 (see paras **10.80** et seq).

10.95 Secondly, r 98 makes provision as to who must either be parties to or consent to any application for the withdrawal of a restriction:

(a)   a person whose consent is required by the terms of the restriction;[1]

(b)   a person to whom notice must be given by the terms of the restriction;[2]

(c)   a person whose certificate is required by the terms of the restriction; [3] and

(d)   all persons who appear to the registrar to have an interest in the restriction.[4]

10.96 The application must be made in Form RX4: Application to withdraw a restriction,[5] and must be accompanied by any necessary consents from the relevant persons.[6] However, the registrar may accept a certificate given by a conveyancer that he holds any requisite consent.[7] Where such an application is made and is in order, the Registry will not, in practice, investigate whether the restriction continues to serve any function.[8] Where the withdrawal of the restriction relates to part only of a registered estate, Form RX4 requires that this part should be identified on a plan attached to the application.

Cancellation

10.97 A restriction may be cancelled in three circumstances. First, any person may apply for the cancellation of a restriction where it is no longer required.[9] An example would be where, under the terms of a restriction, a specified person's consent was required to any disposition of the registered estate, and that person has died. The application must be made in Form RX3: Application to cancel a restriction,[10] and it must be accompanied by evidence to satisfy the registrar that the restriction is no longer required.[11] If the restriction refers to a named person, the registrar will serve notice on him of the application for cancellation,[12] and will not cancel the restriction before that

---

1   LRR 2003, r 98(3).
2   Ibid, r 98(4).
3   Ibid, r 98(5).
4   Ibid, r 98(2). In substance, the rule brings forward LRR 1925, r 236B(1).
5   No fee is payable.
6   LRR 2003, r 98(1).
7   Ibid, r 98(7).
8   Notices, Restrictions and the Protection of Third Party Interests in the Register, PG19, para 4.7.3.
9   LRR 2003, r 97. No fee is payable.
10   Ibid, r 97(1).
11   Ibid, r 97(2).
12   Under the power conferred by LRR 2003, r 17: see para **20.22**.

person has had an opportunity to object.[1] If the registrar is satisfied that the restriction is no longer required, he must cancel the restriction.[2]

10.98 Secondly, when registering a disposition of a registered estate, the registrar must cancel a restriction entered for the purpose of protecting an interest, right or claim arising under a trust of land if he is satisfied that the registered estate is no longer subject to that trust of land.[3]

10.99 Thirdly, because the registrar has the power to alter the register by bringing it up to date and by removing superfluous entries,[4] explained at para **22.16**, he may cancel a restriction without any application if he is satisfied that it is spent or superfluous. Examples given by the Land Registry as to when the registrar might exercise this power include:[5]

(a)   where the restriction was operative for a specified period which has expired, as where there was a restriction on a disposal of land for a period of 5 years without the consent of X and the 5-year period has elapsed;

(b)   where, as is commonly the case, a restriction had been entered pursuant to a charge, perhaps limiting the chargor's powers to borrow from another lender without the chargee's consent, and the charge has been redeemed;

(c)   where the land had formerly been in co-ownership, the restriction entered to ensure overreaching, and there had then been a disposition that had overreached the interests of those co-owners;

(d)   where the restriction had been entered because of some limitation on the powers of a previous proprietor, but which was inapplicable to the present owner; and

(e)   where the Land Registry registers a transfer under a power of sale by the proprietor of a registered charge whose powers were not affected by the restriction, which applied only to the registered proprietor.

Disapplying or modifying a restriction

10.100 It was explained in para **10.52** that any person who has a sufficient interest in a restriction may apply for an order that it be disapplied or modified.[6] Any such application to the registrar must be made in Form RX2,[7] and it can be made either before or at the same time as an application to

---

[1]   For the period within which the recipient must respond, see LRR 2003, r 197: see para **20.41**.
[2]   LRR 2003, r 97(3).
[3]   Ibid, r 99.
[4]   LRA 2002, Sch 4, para 5(b), (d).
[5]   Notices, Restrictions and the Protection of Third Party Interests in the Register, PG19, para 4.7.4.
[6]   See LRA 2002, s 41(2), (3).
[7]   LRR 2003, r 96(1).

register the disposition that would otherwise be affected by the restriction.[1] The application must satisfy the following requirements:[2]

(a)   It must state whether the application is to disapply or modify the restriction.

(b)   If it is an application to modify the restriction it must give details of the modification requested.

(c)   It must explain why the applicant has a sufficient interest in the restriction to make the application.

(d)   It must give details of the disposition or the kind of dispositions that will be affected by the order.

(e)   It must state why the applicant considers that the registrar should make the order.

10.101   The applicant must, if requested, supply further evidence to satisfy the registrar that he should make the order.[3] The registrar may make such enquiries and serve such notices as he thinks fit in order to determine the application.[4]

Pending land actions, writs, orders and deeds of arrangements

10.102   As a result of the prospective abolition of cautions, the LRA 2002 has to make specific provision for certain matters which, under the LRA 1925, can only be protected by the entry of a caution. The matters, each of which is defined by reference to the provisions of the LCA 1972,[5] are:

(a)   pending land actions;[6]

(b)   writs or orders affecting land issued or made by any court for the purpose of enforcing a judgment or recognisance;[7]

(c)   an order appointing a receiver or sequestrator of land;[8] and

(d)   a deed of arrangement within the meaning of the Deeds of Arrangement Act 1914.[9]

10.103   All of these matters are to be treated as 'an interest affecting an estate or charge' for the purposes of the LRA 2002.[10] It is necessary that *some* entry

---

[1]   See Notices, Restrictions and the Protection of Third Party Interests in the Register, PG19, para 4.8.3.

[2]   LRR 2003, r 96(2).

[3]   Ibid, r 96(3).

[4]   Ibid, r 96(4).

[5]   See LRA 2002, s 87(1).

[6]   See LCA 1972, s 5(1)(a).

[7]   Ibid, s 6(1)(a).

[8]   Ibid, s 6(1)(b).

[9]   Ibid, s 7(1). Deed of Arrangement has the same meaning as in the Deeds of Arrangement Act 1914: LRA 2002, s 87(5).

[10]   LRA 2002, s 87(1). In relation to an application to register either a pending land action under LRA 2002, s 87(1)(a), or a writ or order affecting land under ibid, s 87(1)(b), the person who is taking any

be made in the register to protect them, not least because such interests cannot be protected as unregistered interests that override first registration or a registered disposition.[1]

10.104 The position adopted by the LRA 2002 is as follows.[2] As regards both pending land actions and any writs or orders affecting land for the purpose of enforcing a judgment or recognisance, subject to what is said in para **10.105**, a notice, restriction or both may be entered.[3] However, an order appointing a receiver or sequestrator of land and a deed of arrangement can only be protected by the entry of a restriction. The Act prohibits the entry of a notice.[4] The reasons for this are as follows.[5] First, an order appointing a receiver or sequestrator of land sometimes creates an interest in land and sometimes does not.[6] It may not be easy to tell in any given case. It is therefore appropriate to require one form of entry in every case. A restriction is the logical form of entry because it does not confer priority. Secondly, a deed of arrangement is analogous to a bankruptcy order in that it protects the interests of creditors in the period between an assignment by a debtor to his trustee for the benefit of his creditors and the registration of the trustee as proprietor of the property. As a restriction is used to protect a bankruptcy order,[7] it is also appropriate that it should be employed to protect deeds of arrangement.

10.105 The fact that the interests listed in para **10.102**(a) and (b) may in principle be protected by either a notice or by a restriction does not mean that an applicant can select at will whether to enter a notice or a restriction. It is necessary to consider in each case which form of protection is appropriate having regard to the provisions of the Act that govern notices and restrictions. Normally, a person who has brought proceedings relating to land and has a pending land action, or has the benefit of a writ or order affecting land, will wish to ensure that any purchaser of the land takes subject to his interest rather than, in some way or another, restricting or preventing a disposition of that land. A notice will therefore be the appropriate form of entry because the pending land action, writ or order is not a restriction on the circumstances in which an entry in the register can be made.[8] However, it will not always be possible to enter a notice. If, for example, a person brings proceedings in

---

action or proceedings or who has obtained the writ or order is treated as having the benefit of an interest for the purposes of ibid, s 43(1)(c): see LRR 2003, r 172(2), (3).

[1]   LRA 2002, s 87(3).

[2]   The LRA 2002 contains a power to modify the application of the Act in relation to the interests listed in s 87(1) by the making of rules: see s 87(4). Cf (2001) Law Com No 271, para 6.61.

[3]   This is a necessary inference from LRA 2002, s 87(2).

[4]   LRA 2002, s 87(2).

[5]   See (2001) Law Com No 271, para 6.60.

[6]   *Clayhope Properties Ltd v Evans and Jennings* [1986] 1 WLR 1223 at 1228.

[7]   LRA 2002, s 86(4); see also para **13.13**.

[8]   Cf LRA 2002, s 40(1); and see also para **10.50**.

which she claims a beneficial interest under a trust of land, she cannot protect her pending land action by the entry of a notice, because her claim relates to an interest under a trust of land.[1] She can only enter a restriction, which would be in Form A,[2] to ensure that her interest will be overreached on any disposition of the land affected by payment of the proceeds of sale to at least two trustees.

Cautions against dealings: transitional provisions

10.106 Although cautions against dealings have been prospectively abolished, it was necessary to make provision for the large number of such cautions that had been entered in the register prior to 13 October 2003.[3] The LRA 2002 preserves the nature and effect of existing cautions by providing that, notwithstanding their repeal, LRA 1925, ss 55 and 56 continue to have effect in relation to existing cautions.[4] The LRA 2002 contains powers to make rules about cautions against dealings lodged under the LRA 1925.[5] The rules made under that power – LRR 2003, rr 218–223 – make provision by which cautions against dealings continue to operate in the same way as they did under the LRA 1925 and LRR 1925.[6]

10.107 The rules make provision for what is to happen where the registrar serves notice on the cautioner either under LRA 1925, s 55(1),[7] where there has been an application to register a disposition or other dealing with the land which is not accompanied by the cautioner's consent,[8] or under LRR 2003, r 223, where there has been an application to cancel a caution (see para **10.110**).[9] At any time before the expiry of the notice period,[10] the cautioner may show cause why the registrar should not give effect to the application that resulted in the notice being served.[11] To show cause, the cautioner[12] must deliver to the registrar a written statement signed by the cautioner or his conveyancer setting out the grounds relied upon and show (presumably from that statement) that he has a fairly arguable case for the registrar not to give effect to the application that resulted in the notice being served.[13] If, after

---

[1]   See LRA 2002, s 33(a); and see also para **10.7**.
[2]   See para **10.57**.
[3]   See para **10.3**.
[4]   LRR 2003, Sch 12, para 2(3).
[5]   Ibid, Sch 12, para 2(4).
[6]   See Notices, Restrictions and the Protection of Third Party Interests in the Register, PG 19, para 6.5.
[7]   Which, in summary, requires the registrar to serve notice on the cautioner before registering any dealing or making any entry in the register, warning him that his caution will cease after the expiration of the notice period unless he shows cause.
[8]   Any consent must be in writing signed by the person giving it or his conveyancer: LRR 2003, r 219.
[9]   See LRR 2003, r 221.
[10] Which ends at 12 noon on the fifteenth business day after the date of issue of the notice or such later business day as the registrar may allow, within which to respond: see LRR 2003, r 218.
[11] LRR 2003, r 221(2).
[12] Which includes the cautioner's personal representative: see LRR 2003, r 218.
[13] Ibid, r 221(3).

reading the written statement, and after making any enquiries he thinks necessary, the registrar is satisfied that cause has been shown, he must order that the caution is to continue until withdrawn or otherwise disposed of under the LRA 2002 or the LRR 2003.[1] In those circumstances:

(a)   the registrar must give notice of his order to both the applicant and the cautioner;

(b)   the cautioner is to be treated as having objected to the application;

(c)   the applicant is to be taken to have been given notice of the objection;[2] and

(d)   the matter then proceeds in accordance with the usual procedure where there has been an objection to an application (see LRA 2002, s 73 and para **20.29**).

If the cautioner fails to show cause within the notice period, the caution will be cancelled.[3]

10.108   If, after notice has been served on the cautioner, the application that prompted the registrar to serve the notice is cancelled, withdrawn or otherwise does not proceed, the registrar must make an order that the caution will continue to have effect, unless it is cancelled.[4]

10.109   The cautioner may at any time apply for the withdrawal of his caution, using Form WCT, which must be signed by the cautioner or his conveyancer.[5]

10.110   The LRR 2003 make provision for an application for the cancellation of a caution by the registered proprietor or a person who, but for the existence of the caution, would have been entitled to be registered as the proprietor.[6] Application for the cancellation of the caution must be in Form CCD,[7] and the registrar must give the cautioner notice of the application.[8] Unless the registrar orders that the caution is to continue as explained in para **10.107**, the registrar must cancel the entry of the caution at the expiry of the notice period.[9]

---

[1]   LRR 2003, r 221(4).

[2]   Ibid, r 221(5).

[3]   LRA 1925, s 55(1).

[4]   LRR 2003, r 221(6).

[5]   Ibid, r 222. A conveyancer means a solicitor, licensed conveyancer, or a fellow of ILEX: see LRR 2003, r 217(1).

[6]   LRR 2003, r 223.

[7]   Ibid, r 223(2).

[8]   Ibid, r 223(3).

[9]   Ibid, r 223(4).

CHAPTER 11

UNREGISTERED INTERESTS WHICH OVERRIDE REGISTERED DISPOSITIONS

INTRODUCTION

11.1   It has been explained in Chapter 9 that, on a registered disposition for valuable consideration, the disponee takes his interest subject to interests that have priority to his own interest and are protected.[1] Amongst the interests that are protected are the unregistered interests listed in Sch 3 to the LRA 2002.[2] It was explained in Chapter 4 that the Act contains two lists of unregistered interests that override respectively: (1) first registration; and (2) a registered disposition, and the reasons were given as to why these lists were not the same.[3] It was also explained that to enable the LRA 2002 to achieve its objective of creating in time a conclusive register,[4] it necessarily contained provisions for limiting the impact of such unregistered interests.[5] The range of unregistered interests that will override a registered disposition is considerably narrower than the list of overriding interests that was found in s 70 of the LRA 1925. Unlike the position on first registration, an issue of priority arises where there is a registered disposition. In principle it is wrong that a purchaser for valuable consideration should be bound by an interest that is neither registered nor easily discoverable. The Law Commission and Land Registry concluded that 'interests should *only* have overriding status where protection against buyers was needed, but where it was neither reasonable to expect nor sensible to require any entry on the register'.[6] The list of overriding interests in Sch 3 reflects this intention. It should be noted that the introduction of electronic-conveyancing will of itself eliminate many unregistered interests because, under the system of e-conveyancing that the LRA 2002 creates, it will be necessary to register a disposition at the same time as it is made.[7]

---

[1]   LRA 2002, ss 29, 30; see also paras **9.4–9.9**.
[2]   Ibid, ss 29(2)(a)(ii), 30(2)(a)(ii).
[3]   See para **4.13**.
[4]   See para **1.7**.
[5]   See para **4.12**.
[6]   (2001) Law Com No 271, para 8.6.
[7]   See para **28.3**.

THE UNREGISTERED INTERESTS THAT WILL OVERRIDE A REGISTERED DISPOSITION

11.2 Schedule 3[1] lists 15 unregistered interests that will bind a registered disponee for valuable consideration. A sixteenth overriding unregistered interest is found in s 90 of the LRA 2002.[2] Thirteen of the 16 interests that override a registered disposition are the same as the interests that override first registration. These have already been explained at para **4.14** and therefore little more needs to be said about them. The 13 interests that are the same are as follows:

(a)   a customary right;[3]
(b)   a public right;[4]
(c)   a local land charge;[5]
(d)   certain mineral rights, including rights to coal and mineral rights that were granted before 1926;[6]
(e)   a franchise;[7]
(f)   a manorial right;[8]
(g)   what is usually called a 'Crown rent';[9]
(h)   a non-statutory right in respect of an embankment or river or sea wall;[10]
(i)   a right to payment in lieu of tithe;[11]
(j)   a PPP lease[12]; and
(k)   a right in respect of the repair of a church chancel.[13]

Many of these interests can no longer be created. The ones that can be are public rights, local land charges (which are, in any event, otherwise protected), franchises (at least in theory), and PPP leases (although it remains to be seen whether these will ever be granted). Furthermore, under the LRA 2002, the rights listed at (e), (f), (g), (h), (i) and (k) will lose their overriding status on

---

[1]   As amended by TPO2 2003, which inserted a new paragraph at the end of Schs 1 and 3 to a right in respect of the repair of a church chancel. The new paragraph is referred to as 16. For para 15, see LRA 2002, Sch 12, para 11 (a right acquired under the LA 1980 before 13 October 2003 is an overriding interest until 13 October 2006).
[2]   Cf the position on first registration under LRA 2002, Sch 1; see also para **4.14**(9).
[3]   LRA 2002, Sch 3, para 4.
[4]   Ibid, Sch 3, para 5.
[5]   Ibid, Sch 3, para 6.
[6]   Ibid, Sch 3, paras 7–9.
[7]   Ibid, Sch 3, para 10.
[8]   Ibid, Sch 3, para 11.
[9]   Ibid, Sch 3, para 12.
[10]   Ibid, Sch 3, para 13.
[11]   Ibid, Sch 3, para 14.
[12]   Ibid, s 90(5).
[13]   Ibid, Sch 3, para 16.

13 October 2013, 10 years after the Act came into force.[1] During this 10-year period, no fee will be charged for the entry of a notice in the register to protect the interest in question. Once the 10-year period has elapsed, if no notice has been entered in the register, the interest will not be lost, but it will be unprotected as against a registered disposition for valuable consideration.[2]

11.3   The LRA 2002 does make significant changes in relation to the three most important categories of unregistered interest that can override a registered disposition. It does so having regard to the principles set out in para **11.1**. The three categories of interest are short leases, the rights of persons in actual occupation and legal easements and *profits à prendre*.

Certain short leases

11.4   Any lease that was granted for a term not exceeding 7 years except for:

— a lease granted out of unregistered land that was required to be registered under the provisions on first registration explained at paras **2.16–2.18**, even though it was for a term of 7 years or less; or
— a lease granted out of registered land that was a registrable disposition even though it was for a term of 7 years or less.[3]

In short, if a lease is required to be registered, it cannot override a registered disposition if it is not in fact registered. Conversely, if a lease cannot be registered, it necessarily overrides a registered disposition.[4]

Interests of persons in actual occupation

The general rule

11.5   The general rule is that an unregistered interest belonging at the time of the disposition to a person in actual occupation, so far as relating to land of which he is in actual occupation, will override a registrable disposition.[5] That general rule is itself narrower than the equivalent provision under the previous law, s 70(1)(g) of the LRA 1925 as it was interpreted, in two respects.

---

[1]   LRA 2002, s 117 and TPO2 2003 in respect of the repair of a church chancel; see also para **4.18**.
[2]   See LRA 2002, ss 29, 30.
[3]   Ibid, Sch 3, para 1. For the leases that are registrable dispositions even though they are for a term of 7 years or less, see LRA 2002, s 27(2)(b)(ii)–(v); see also para **8.8**.
[4]   The same protection applies to leases that were granted for more than 21 years before the LRA 2002 came into force: LRA 2002, Sch 12, para 12.
[5]   Ibid, Sch 3, para 2. The 'interest' must, therefore, be an interest in land for the purposes of the Act because it must relate to land.

— First, it confines the protection to the land actually occupied, thereby reversing the decision of the Court of Appeal in *Ferrishurst Ltd v Wallcite Ltd*.[1] In that case it was held that a person in actual occupation of part of a registered title who had rights over the whole could, by virtue of his possession of part, protect his rights over the whole. The decision runs counter to the aim of the LRA 2002 to reduce the impact of unregistered interests that can override first registration or a registrable disposition. Its effect was to place an unreasonable burden of enquiry on a purchaser of registered land.

— Secondly, the protection that was given by s 70(1)(g) of LRA 1925 to persons who were not in actual occupation of registered land but were in receipt of the rents and profits is not replicated in the LRA 2002.[2] The position of those who, immediately before the Act comes into force, are protected because they are in receipt of rents and profits is, however, preserved by the transitional provisions of the Act.[3] If, however, such persons cease to be in receipt of the rents and profits of the land at any time thereafter, their interests are no longer protected.[4] If, for example, at the time when the LRA 2002 comes into force, there is a sub-lessee in possession, but the lease out of which that sub-lease was granted is not registered, the head lessee's interest will be protected until the sub-lease terminates. If the head lessee were then to grant a new sub-lease, the fact that he would be in receipt of the rents and profits from the new sub-lease would not protect him.

The general rule as to the protection of the interests of occupiers is, however, subject to four important exceptions.

The four exceptions to the general rule

11.6 The first exception is an interest under a settlement under the SLA 1925.[5] Such an interest must be protected by the entry of appropriate restrictions in the register. This exception involves no change in the law.[6]

11.7 The second exception is an interest of a person of whom inquiry was made before the disposition and who failed to disclose the right when he

---

[1] [1999] Ch 355. See (2001) Law Com No 271, paras 8.56–8.58.

[2] This applies not only to unregistered interests that override registered dispositions but also to unregistered interests that override first registration: LRA 2002, Sch 1, para 2. However, on first registration, the fact that there are superior unregistered interests will normally be reflected in the class of title that is given, which will typically be a good leasehold title. That of itself will protect the rights of those with a superior title: see LRA 2002, s 12(6); see also para **4.10**.

[3] LRA 2002, Sch 3, para 2A(1), inserted by Sch 12, para 8.

[4] Ibid, Sch 3, para 2A(2), inserted by Sch 12, para 8.

[5] Ibid, Sch 3, para 2(a).

[6] Cf LRA 1925, s 86(2).

could reasonably have been expected to do so.[1] This exception replicates the position under s 70(1)(g) of the LRA 1925.

11.8 The third exception is an interest:

– which belongs to a person whose occupation would not have been obvious on a reasonably careful inspection of the land at the time of the disposition; and

– of which the person to whom the disposition is made does not have actual knowledge at that time.[2]

This exception is new and is a significant limitation on this category of unregistered interest.

11.9 First, as regards the first of the two limbs, it should be noted that it is not the occupier's *interest* that has to be apparent on a careful inspection of the land, but his *occupation*. The test is *not* whether a buyer has *constructive notice* of the occupier's occupation, but whether that person's occupation was *obvious* on a reasonably careful inspection of the land at the relevant time. This concept is borrowed from the law on sale of land.[3] A seller of land is obliged to disclose to an intending buyer interests affecting the property that are latent, in other words, interests that are *not* obvious on a reasonable inspection of the land. In this context the Court of Appeal has expressly rejected the view that, because a person has constructive notice of an interest, that interest is patent.[4] As it relates to the discoverability of the occupation rather than the interest, the application of the principle is analogous rather than direct.

11.10 Secondly, to fall within the exception, the disponee will have to satisfy *both* limbs of the exception. If he does not, he will be bound by the interest of the person in occupation. Thus:

– if a person's occupation is *not* obvious under the first limb, a purchaser will still be bound by that interest if he had actual knowledge of the occupier's interest; and

– if a person's occupation *is* obvious under the first limb, a buyer will be bound by the occupier's interest even if he did not have actual knowledge of that interest because he failed to make inquiry of the occupier.

---

[1] LRA 2002, Sch 3, para 2(b).

[2] Ibid, Sch 3, para 2(c).

[3] See (2001) Law Com No 271, para 8.62.

[4] *Caballero v Henty* (1874) LR 9 Ch App 447.

11.11   The purpose of this third exception is clear: the unregistered interests of occupiers should only be binding on a buyer if those interests were either readily discoverable or already known to the buyer. The objective of the LRA 2002 is to eliminate as far as possible inquiries beyond the register.[1]

11.12   The fourth exception to the general principle is a leasehold estate granted to take effect in possession after the end of the period of 3 months beginning with the date of the grant and which has not taken effect in possession at the time of the disposition.[2] This exception necessarily follows from the requirement that a reversionary lease that takes effect in possession more than 3 months after grant has to be registered.[3] This exception will not commonly arise. For it to do so:

—   a lease of land would have to be granted to a person to take effect in possession more than 3 months after the grant;
—   that grantee would either have to be in actual occupation when the grant was made (as where he has an existing lease) or be permitted to go into occupation before the lease takes effect;
—   a registered disposition would then have to be made of the land affected by the reversionary lease before the lease takes effect in possession but after the tenant went into actual occupation.

Legal easements and profits

The general principle

11.13   The circumstances in which an unregistered easement or *profit à prendre* will override a registered disposition are substantially curtailed by the LRA 2002. The general principle is that an unregistered legal easement or *profit à prendre* will override a registered disposition. It is significant that only *legal* easements and profits can override a registered disposition. This means that an easement or profit that is expressly granted or reserved after the LRA 2002 comes into force but is not registered can *never* override a registrable disposition, as it can under the present law.[4] It follows that the only legal easements or profits that will override a registered disposition will be:

—   those in existence when the LRA 2002 came into force but which had not been registered; and

---

[1]   See paras **1.7**, **1.8**.
[2]   LRA 2002, Sch 3, para 2(d).
[3]   Ibid, ss 4(1)(d) (compulsory first registration), 27(2)(b)(ii).
[4]   The LRA 2002 therefore reverses the effect of part of the decision in *Celsteel Ltd v Alton House Holdings Ltd* [1985] 1 WLR 204 at 219–221.

–   those that arise subsequently by prescription or by implied grant or reservation.

As is explained below, there are important transitional provisions in relation to easements and profits that are overriding interests at the time when the LRA 2002 comes into force but would not be under the Act.[1]

The exceptions to the general rule

11.14   The general provision in para **11.13** is subject to very significant exceptions. An unregistered legal easement or *profit à prendre* will *not* override a registered disposition if *all* of the following requirements are met, namely:

–   it is *not* a right of common that has been registered under the CRA 1965;[2]
–   it has *not* been exercised within one year of the date of the disposition;
–   at the time of the disposition the person to whom the disposition is made does *not* have actual knowledge of it;
–   at the time of the disposition it would *not* have been obvious on a reasonably careful inspection of the land over which the easement or profit is exercisable

Stated positively, an unregistered legal easement or profit *will* override a registered disposition if:

–   it is a right of common that has been registered under the CRA 1965;[3] or
–   it is actually known to the disponee under the registered disposition; or
–   it would have been obvious on a reasonably careful inspection of the servient tenement; or
–   the person entitled to the easement on profit proves that it has been exercised within one year of the disposition.

11.15   This provision may at first sight seem puzzling, but on closer analysis, the reasons for it become clear.

–   First, if the easement or profit is a right of common that has been registered under the CRA 1965, then it is readily discoverable from a search of the commons register. It is protected on a register which any buyer should inspect.

---

[1]   See para **11.17**.
[2]   Cf para **8.12**.
[3]   Ibid.

–   Secondly, when a person sells land, he must disclose to the intending buyer prior to contract the existence of any latent defects in title, including any easements or profits. A defect in title is latent if it is not obvious on a reasonable inspection of the land affected by it.[1] There is, however, no duty to disclose latent defects in title of which the intending buyer actually knows.[2] The LRA 2002 applies these principles to the issue of whether an unregistered easement or profit should override a registered disposition. If a legal easement or profit is either known to a buyer or obvious, he is not prejudiced if he takes the land subject to it.

–   Thirdly, many landowners have legal easements over their neighbours' lands of which their neighbours may be unaware and which are not obvious. The commonest examples are rights for the passage of utilities and drainage rights. Many such rights are not protected in the register but have been used for many years. To deal with such cases and to prevent important rights being defeated, the LRA 2002 provides that legal easements and profits will override a registered disposition if they have been exercised within one year of the disposition. This is a limited pragmatic exception by which rights that may not be readily discoverable are nonetheless protected. In practice, standard forms of enquiry before contract are likely to be instituted to try to identify such rights in any event.

11.16   One important effect of these provisions should be noted. It is comparatively easy to acquire an easement or profit from 20 years' user under the doctrine of prescription by lost modern grant. However, once an easement has been acquired, it is virtually impossible to prove that it has been released by abandonment because it has not been exercised for many years.[3] Under the LRA 2002, subject to the transitional provisions explained below, a purchaser of registered land will not be bound by a long-dormant unregistered easement or profit that has not been exercised for many years and which is not obvious on a reasonably careful inspection of the land affected by it. It is clear that this result is intended.[4]

---

[1]   It has been repeatedly stated that a defect is patent and does not have to be disclosed to an intending buyer if it is obvious: see, eg, *Ashburner v Sewell* [1891] 3 Ch 405 at 408–409; approved by the House of Lords in *Shonleigh Nominees Ltd v Attorney-General (at the Relation of Hampshire County Council)* [1974] 1 WLR 305 at 311, 315, 323–324.
[2]   See, eg, *Re Gloag and Miller's Contract* (1883) 23 ChD 320 at 327.
[3]   See, eg, *Benn v Hardinge* (1992) 66 P&CR 246 (175 years' non-use of a right of way did not amount to abandonment).
[4]   See (2001) Law Com No 271, paras 8.65, 8.72.

Transitional provisions

11.17   As a result of the far-reaching nature of the changes that the LRA 2002 makes in relation to easements and profits, there are generous transitional provisions. First, any easement or profit that was an overriding interest immediately before the Act came into force on 13 October 2003, will retain that status.[1] To determine whether such easements or profits were overriding, it is necessary to apply the principles developed under LRA 1925. Obviously with the passage of time it will become increasingly difficult to prove that such a right was an overriding interest on 13 October 2003. There are, in any event, provisions which are intended to ensure that such rights are entered in the register.[2] Secondly, for a period of 3 years after the LRA 2002 came into force, *any* unregistered legal easement or profit will override a registered disposition.[3] This will in practice protect those easements or profits that come into being within that 3-year period by way of prescription or implied grant or reservation.

ENSURING THAT UNREGISTERED INTERESTS ARE REGISTERED

11.18   It has been explained, in the context of unregistered interests that override first registration, that the LRA 2002 contains provisions which are intended to ensure that unregistered interests are entered on the register.[4] One of these provisions also applies in relation to unregistered interests that override a registered disposition. Section 71(b) of the LRA 2002 made provision for rules to be made requiring a person who is applying to register a registrable disposition to provide the registrar with information about an interest affecting the estate which falls within Sch 3 and is of a description prescribed by the rules.[5]

11.19   LRR 2003, r 57(1) provides that, subject to the exceptions in r 57(2), on an application for the registration of a registrable disposition of a registered estate, the applicant must provide information to the registrar about any of the interests that fall within Sch 3 to the Act that are:

(a)   within the actual knowledge of the applicant; and

(b)   affect the estate to which registration relates.

---

[1]   LRA 2002, Sch 12, para 9.

[2]   See para **11.18**.

[3]   LRA 2002, Sch 12, para 10.

[4]   See para **4.19**.

[5]   Cf para **4.19**.

In the case of an application for the registration of a registrable disposition, the applicant should complete Form AP1[1] and should disclose the interest on Form D1. The applicant must also produce to the registrar any documentary evidence of the existence of a disclosable overriding interest that is under his control.[2] In either case, where such information is provided, the registrar may enter a notice in the Register in respect of that interest.[3]

11.20   By LRR 2003, r 57(2), the applicant is not required to provide information about an interest that falls within one of the following categories:

(a)   any interest that cannot be protected by a notice under LRA 2002, s 33 or s 90(4), that is:
  (i)   an interest under a trust of land;
  (ii)   an interest under a settlement under the Settled Land Act 1925;
  (iii)   a lease granted for a term of 3 years or less, unless it is of a kind that has to be registered;
  (iv)   a PPP lease;
  (v)   a restrictive covenant between lessor and lessee so far as relating to the demised premises; and
  (vi)   an interest capable of being registered under CRA 1965;
  (vii)   an interest in any coal or coal mine;
(b)   a local land charge;
(c)   a public right;
(d)   a lease granted for 7 years or less that was not required to be registered, which at the time of the application has one year or less to run.

11.21   There has, inevitably, been some concern as to when a person should disclose an unregistered interest. An example given is where there is a disposition of a registered estate, and the building on the neighbouring land has windows overlooking the estate which have obviously been there for a considerable period (as where the building is obviously Victorian), so that the neighbouring property has a prescriptive easement of light over the registered estate. Such an easement should be disclosed because, if the owner of the neighbouring building applied to register the easement, the owner of the registered estate would not be able to resist such registration.

11.22   In addition to the duty to disclose unregistered interests that override registered dispositions where there is a registrable disposition, the registrar has

---

[1]   Panel 10 deals with disclosable unregistered interests.
[2]   LRR 2003, r 57(4).
[3]   Ibid, r 57(5).

a general power (subject to service of notice) under LRA 2002, s 37(1) and LRR 2003, r 89 to note overriding interests that come to, or are brought to, his attention. This might include noting the burden of a legal easement, for example. This has already been explained: see para **4.21**.

CHAPTER 12

CHARGES OVER REGISTERED LAND

INTRODUCTION

12.1   Although a number of provisions of the LRA 2002 are concerned with charges over registered land, Part 5 is exclusively concerned with them. The Act, whether in Part 5 or elsewhere, makes provision for the following matters:

- —   the nature of registered charges and sub-charges;
- —   the powers enjoyed by chargees and sub-chargees;
- —   the priority of competing advances;
- —   tacking and further advances;
- —   the realisation of a chargee's security; and
- —   certain miscellaneous matters.

For the purposes of the Act, 'charge' is widely defined to include 'any mortgage, charge or lien for securing money or money's worth'.[1]

THE NATURE OF REGISTERED CHARGES AND SUB-CHARGES

12.2   Under the LRA 2002, it ceases to be possible to create a mortgage of registered land by demise or sub-demise.[2] This is merely a recognition of reality and is unlikely to have any practical effect. Even under the LRA 1925, there was a presumption that a registered charge took effect as a charge by way of legal mortgage,[3] but in any event, mortgages by demise or sub-demise have been obsolete for some considerable time. Legal charges of registered land can either be created as charges expressed to be by way of legal mortgage or by charging the estate with the payment of money, the means traditionally associated with registered land.[4] In either event, the charge has effect on registration as a charge by deed by way of legal mortgage.[5]

---

1   LRA 2002, s 132(1).
2   Ibid, s 23(1).
3   See LRA 1925, s 27(1).
4   LRA 2002, s 23. Under the Land Transfer Act 1875, the only means of creating a legal mortgage of registered land was by means of charging the registered legal estate with the payment of money. There was no transfer or fiction of transfer of the legal estate to the mortgagee. The introduction of the charge by way of legal mortgage by LPA 1925, s 87 was intended to provide a means of harmonising the registered and unregistered systems: (2001) Law Com No 271, para 7.2.
5   LRA 2002, s 51.

12.3   A mortgagee has an interest which he can charge and a sub-mortgage is simply a mortgage of a mortgage.[1] Under the LRA 2002, there is only one way that the proprietor of a registered charge can create a legal sub-charge, namely by charging with the payment of money the indebtedness secured by the registered charge.[2] All other means are precluded.[3]

12.4   In the unlikely event that the proprietor of a registered estate were to attempt to execute a mortgage by demise or sub-demise or the proprietor of a registered charge were to try to create a sub-charge in a manner prohibited by the LRA 2002, the attempt would have no effect. The application for registration would, accordingly, be rejected by the registrar. The rules governing the form and content of a registrable disposition of a registered charge are explained at paras **12.9** et seq.

EQUITABLE CHARGES

12.5   Subject to one minor change, the LRA 2002 does not alter the circumstances in which an equitable charge may be created[4] or imposed. The Act does not replicate the provision of the LRA 1925 that enabled a registered proprietor to create a lien over the registered estate by depositing his land certificate with the lender as security.[5] This is because that power had become obsolete as a result of a judicial decision.[6]

THE POWERS OF A REGISTERED CHARGEE OR SUB-CHARGEE

Power to make dispositions of the charge

12.6   Subject to the limitations on the methods of sub-charging mentioned in para **12.3**, a person who is the proprietor of a registered charge has power to make a disposition of that charge of any kind permitted by the general law.[7] The Act also confers on him the specific power to create a sub-charge.[8] It has already been explained[9] that a proprietor of a registered estate or charge is to be taken as free from any limitation affecting the validity of the disposition

---

[1]   For the nature of a sub-charge, see para **7.4**.

[2]   LRA 2002, s 23(2)(b).

[3]   Ibid, s 23(2)(a), (3). See also para **7.4**.

[4]   A registered proprietor, in exercise of his owner's powers, may create such a charge to the extent that is permitted under the general law: see LRA 2002, s 23; also para **7.3**.

[5]   LRA 1925, s 66.

[6]   See *United Bank of Kuwait plc v Sahib* [1997] Ch 107. The decision was based upon LP(MP)A 1989, s 2, and its abolition of the old doctrine of part performance upon which a mortgage by deposit of title deeds (the model for the lien by deposit of the land certificate) had rested.

[7]   LRA 2002, s 23(2)(a).

[8]   Ibid, s 23(2)(b).

[9]   See para **7.6**.

unless that limitation is reflected by an entry in the register[1] or is imposed by, or under, the LRA 2002.[2] However, this presumption only operates to protect the disponee. It does not validate an unlawful disposition where, for example, there should have been a restriction on the register to indicate that there was some limitation on the registered proprietor's powers of disposition.[3] It follows that, if, say, the chargee had no power to assign its charge but had failed to ensure that there was a restriction on the register to reflect this fact, the assignee's title to the charge would be good. However, the chargee would remain subject to whatever liabilities there might be for making such an *ultra vires* disposition.

Powers in relation to the property charged

12.7 In relation to the property charged, the proprietor of a registered charge is to be taken to have all the powers of disposition conferred by law on the owner of a legal mortgage, unless there is an entry to the contrary in the register.[4] For example, if under the terms of the charge the chargee's remedies were not exercisable for the first 2 years of the mortgage,[5] or his power of leasing[6] was wholly excluded, those limitations should be the subject of a restriction in the register. Once again, the presumption created by the Act only serves to protect the disponee. It does not affect the lawfulness of the disposition.[7] Thus if a registered chargee sold the land subject to the charge when his power of sale had not arisen or had not become exercisable, the buyer's title could not be challenged. But the chargee would be liable in damages to the chargor.[8]

12.8 The registered proprietor of a sub-charge has the same powers of disposition in relation to the property charged as does the registered chargee who has created the sub-charge.[9] This does not mean that the chargee can exercise the powers concurrently with the sub-chargee.[10] It has been explained that the essence of a sub-charge is that it brings about a substitution of the sub-chargee for the chargee in relation to the principal charge and it gives the

---

[1] For dispositions made on or after 13 October 2003, the only relevant entry is a restriction.
[2] LRA 2002, s 26(1), (2). Limitations imposed by the Act include the need to comply with any rules as to form and content (s 25) and the requirements for the registration of a registered disposition (s 27(4), Sch 2).
[3] Ibid, s 26(3).
[4] Ibid, s 52(1).
[5] Because the legal date for redemption was postponed: cf *Twentieth Century Banking Corporation Ltd v Wilkinson* [1977] Ch 99.
[6] Under LPA 1925, s 99(2).
[7] LRA 2002, s 52(2).
[8] Cf LPA 1925, s 104(2).
[9] LRA 2002, s 53.
[10] If it did, it would change the law. It is clear that no change in the law was intended: see (2001) Law Com No 271, para 7.12.

sub-chargee the *exclusive* right to exercise the chargee's rights under that principal charge.[1]

THE CREATION, REGISTRATION AND VARIATION OF REGISTERED CHARGES

12.9   There is a power under the Act to prescribe by rules the form and content of a registrable disposition of a registered estate or charge.[2] This is in contrast to the previous position under the LRA 1925 where, subject to certain limitations, a registered proprietor was free to create a charge in any form.[3] This power has been exercised to make rules which prescribe:

–   the form a charge of registered land *may* take;
–   the form that an application to register an instrument varying the terms of a registered charge *must* take; and
–   the form the transfer of a registered charge *must* take.

The form of a registered charge

12.10   Although there is at present no prescribed form for the creation of a charge of registered land, the rules do contain an optional form which may be utilised.[4] Form CH1 'Legal charge of a registered estate' requires details of the property, the lender, the borrower, the covenants for title given by the borrower and the sums secured, and allows for the insertion of any additional provisions agreed between lender and borrower as to the sums to be paid and the agreed amounts and dates of any payments.

12.11   Form CH1 can also be used to make the following applications:

–   an application by the lender for an obligation to make further advances to be entered on the register; and
–   an application by the borrower for the entry of a restriction in the charges register. If used for this purpose, details of the restriction must be set out on the Form.

12.12   Form CH1 must be executed as a deed whenever it is used.

12.13   The Land Registry has expressed the hope that lenders will choose to use Form CH1.[5] To encourage its use, the Form was modelled on a form used by several major lenders. In due course, it is likely that a compulsory form will

1   See para **7.4**.
2   LRA 2002, s 25(1).
3   LRA 1925, s 25(2).
4   LRR 2003, r 103.
5   Land Registry New Rules – A Consultation Document, chapter 7, para 13.

be prescribed as a standard form of charge is likely to be a prerequisite to electronic conveyancing.[1]

Approved forms of charge

12.14   The Land Registry has previously approved the form of mortgage used by most major lenders. Although the LRR 2003 make no provision for such approval in future,[2] it will remain the Land Registry's practice to encourage lenders to secure the approval of their forms of charge by the Commercial Arrangements Section at Land Registry Head Office. There is no fee for this service.[3]

12.15   It is advantageous for a lender to have its form of charge approved for the following reasons:

—   approved charges may contain applications for standard restrictions;
—   approved charges may contain an application to note a lender's obligation to make further advances on the register;
—   lenders will be able to state whether they require original charges to be returned or retained on completion of registration; and
—   lenders with approved forms of charge will be given computer codes which are intended to ensure that the agreed name and addresses for service of the individual lenders and appropriate restrictions and obligation entries are always entered accurately on the register.[4]

12.16   An application for approval should be made in Form ACD 'Application for approval of a standard form of charge deed and allocation of official Land Registry reference'.[5] The Form requires the applicant to give undertakings:

—   to forward a copy of the approved charge to Land Registry Head Office for filing when printed;
—   not to alter the charge which has been approved and, where elements of the final document are electronically stored, to ensure that data is held accurately and is not amended, without the prior agreement of the Registrar; and
—   not to alter the address for service of the lender as given on the Form until the Commercial Arrangements Section at Land Registry Head Office has been notified.

---

[1]   For electronic conveyancing, see Chapters 26–28.
[2]   There is no equivalent of LRR 1925, r 139(5).
[3]   Land Registry Practice Guide, Approval of Mortgage Documentation, PG30, para 9.
[4]   Land Registry Practice Guide, Registration of Legal Charges and Deeds of Variation of Charge, PG29, para 3.
[5]   This is not a form prescribed by LRR 2003. For the Form, see Land Registry Practice Guide, Approval of Mortgage Documentation, PG30, Appendix B.

12.17   The application should be accompanied by two copies of the draft charge.[1] The charge should be sent in draft before it is printed because the Land Registry will give it a reference which will have to be printed in the charge itself.[2] A separate form will be required for each charge.

12.18   To qualify for approval, a charge must contain:

— a date;
— the names and addresses of the borrowers;
— the name and address of the lender, including its company registration number, if any; and
— a description of the property being mortgaged, including its title number;
— a valid charging clause; and
— a valid execution clause with provision for attestation.[3]

The Land Registry will not approve any charge which fails to satisfy one or more of these criteria. Equally, it will not approve any charge which contains an application to register a restriction that is not in a standard form.

12.19   The Land Registry will approve forms of charge within 10 business days.[4] Each approved form of charge is given a unique reference beginning with the letters 'MD'. After the charge has been approved, one copy will be returned to the applicant with any amendments shown in red.[5]

12.20   If a lender wishes to amend a charge after it has been approved, the amended document will normally have to be lodged at Land Registry Head Office for re-approval with Form ACD. This requirement may be waived by the Land Registry if it considers the amendments are very minor.[6]

12.21   The Land Registry will also approve deeds of variation, deeds of priority and deeds of postponement in accordance with this procedure. Such deeds must contain:

— a date;
— the names and addresses of the parties;
— a description of the property including its title number;

---

[1]   This should be sent to Commercial Arrangements Section, Practice Direction, Land Registry, 32 Lincoln's Inn Fields, London WC2A 3PH.
[2]   Land Registry Practice Guide, Approval of Mortgage Documentation, PG30, para 3.
[3]   Ibid, para 7.
[4]   Ibid, para 4.
[5]   Ibid, para 6.
[6]   Ibid, para 5.

- identification of the charge or charges affected by the deed;
- a clause setting out the terms of the variation, the alteration in priority, or the postponement; and
- a clause permitting valid execution. [1]

A deed of variation must provide for execution by the borrowers. A deed of priority or postponement must provide for execution by the proprietor of any charge of equal or inferior priority prejudicially affected by the alteration in priority or postponement.

Application to register a charge

12.22   An application to register a charge should comprise Form AP1[2] and either Form CH1, or the lender's own form of charge.[3] Panel 11 of Form AP1 requests specific information in respect of any new charge. That panel must be completed unless a Land Registry 'MD' reference is printed on the charge. Even if such a reference is printed on the charge the panel must be completed if the charge has been transferred. The information required includes the lender's name and address and up to three addresses for service.[4] If the lender is a company, its company registration number must be stated. If the lender is a limited liability partnership, its registered number must be stated. If the lender is an overseas company and does not have a pre-existing arrangement with the Land Registry, the lender's country of incorporation and a copy of the company's constitutional documentation must accompany the application. A translation must be supplied if the document is not in English or Welsh.

12.23   The Land Registry Practice Guide contains a number of specific directions for the completion of Form AP1:[5]

- If the charge deed has been approved, it will be retained or returned, depending upon the arrangement made with the lender.
- If the charge deed has not been approved and both the original and a certified copy are provided, it will be assumed that the original deed is to be returned.
- If a certified copy is not supplied, the Land Registry may retain the original deed and it may be destroyed.

---

1   Land Registry Practice Guide, Approval of Mortgage Documentation, PG30, para 7.
2   Or, on first registration, Form FR1.
3   As land and charge certificates have no legal significance under the LRA 2002 they should not be lodged. Mortgage documents incorporated by reference in the charge should not be lodged: Land Registry Practice Guide, Registration of Legal Charges and Deeds of Variation of Charge, PG29, para 4.
4   One of these must be a postal address, but it does not have to be within the United Kingdom.
5   Land Registry Practice Guide, Registration of Legal Charges and Deeds of Variation of Charge, PG29, para 9.

Application to register a restriction

12.24   If an application is made to enter a standard form of restriction the application may be made in panel 7 of Form CH1[1] or in an approved form of charge[2]. A standard restriction is a restriction in a form set out in Sch 4 to the LRR 2003. Form P in Sch 4 is the relevant restriction where the consent of the proprietor of a charge is required, and it is as follows:

> 'No disposition [*or specify details*] of the registered estate [(other than a charge)] by the proprietor of the registered estate [or by the proprietor of any registered charge] is to be registered without a written consent signed by the proprietor for the time being of the charge dated [*date*] in favour of [*chargee*] referred to in the charges register [(or his conveyancer or *specify appropriate details*)] or, if appropriate, signed on such proprietor's behalf by [its secretary or conveyancer *or specify appropriate details*].'

12.25   In all other cases, an application for a restriction to be entered in the register must be made in Form RX1 'Application to enter a restriction'.[3] If an application is not made correctly it will be ignored.[4] The application must be accompanied by the prescribed information.[5]

12.26   If the Form RX1 is not lodged with the application to register the charge, an additional fee is payable for the restriction.[6]

12.27   These provisions do not apply if the application is made to give effect to an order of the court made under LRA 2002, s 46.

The registration of company charges

12.28   Specific provision is made for applications to register a charge created by a company registered under the Companies Acts, a limited liability partnership incorporated under the Limited Liability Partnerships Act 2000, or a Northern Ireland company. The applicant must produce the appropriate certificate that the charge has been registered in accordance with the appropriate statutory provision.[7] If the applicant does not produce the

---

[1]   LRR 2003, r 92(7)(b).

[2]   Ibid, r 92(7)(c).

[3]   Ibid, r 92(1).

[4]   Land Registry Practice Guide, Registration of Legal Charges and Deeds of Variation of Charge, PG29, para 5.

[5]   LRR 2003, r 92(2). See also para **10.66**.

[6]   Land Registry Practice Guide, Registration of Legal Charges and Deeds of Variation of Charge, PG29, para 5.

[7]   LRR 2003, r 111(1). The relevant certificates are as follows: (a) a certificate issued under Companies Act 1985, s 401 that the charge has been registered under s 395 of that Act; (b) in the case of a charge created by a company registered in Scotland, a certificate issued under Companies Act 1985 s 418 that the charge has been registered under s 410 of that Act; and (c) in the case of a charge created by a Northern Ireland company, a certificate issued under the Companies (NI) Order, art 409, that the charge has been registered under art 403 of that Order.

requisite certificate with the application for registration of the charge, the registrar must enter a note in the register that the charge is subject to the provisions of the Companies Act 1985, s 395 or s 410 or the Companies (NI) Order 1986, art 403, as appropriate.[1]

Completion of an application to register

12.29 On completion of an application to register a charge the Land Registry will issue an official copy of the register showing the entries that exist on the register on completion of the application and the Title Information Document.[2]

Making an application to vary the terms of a registered charge

12.30 The LRR 2003 make provision as to applications to register an instrument which varies the terms of a registered charge.[3] Any such application *must* be made:

(a)   by, or with the consent of, the proprietor of the registered charge and the proprietor of the estate charged; and

(b)   with the consent of the proprietor, or a person entitled to be registered as proprietor, of every other registered charge of equal or inferior priority that is prejudicially affected by the variation.

There is one qualification to these requirements: it is not necessary to obtain the consent of any person who has executed the instrument which makes the variation.[4]

12.31 The registrar may accept a conveyancer's certificate confirming that the conveyancer holds any necessary consents.[5]

12.32 Although the borrower must execute the deed of variation, the lender need not do so. The Land Registry will accept that the lender is bound by the terms of the variation if the deed is lodged either by the lender, or by a practitioner acting on behalf of the lender.[6]

12.33 It is the Registry's view that alterations resulting from a reduction in the interest rate or a reduction in the capital debt do not prejudicially affect a

---

[1]   LRR 2003, r 111(2).
[2]   Land Registry Practice Guide, Registration of Legal Charges and Deeds of Variation of Charge, PG29, para 11.
[3]   LRR 2003, r 113.
[4]   Ibid, r 113(1).
[5]   Ibid, r 113(2).
[6]   Land Registry Practice Guide, Registration of Legal Charges and Deeds of Variation of Charge, PG29, para 12.2.

subsequent lender. However, any alterations that increase the interest rate, increase the capital, extend the term of the earlier charge or create an obligation to make further advances, are likely to have such an adverse effect.[1] The subsequent lender's consent will, therefore, be required: see para **12.30**.

12.34   An application to register a deed of variation must be made using Form AP1: there is no specific form for such an application.[2] If the proprietor of any charge prejudicially affected has not executed the deed of variation, the proprietor's written consent, or a certificate by a conveyancer that he holds the requisite consents, must be lodged with the application. Alternatively, the proprietor of any charge that may be adversely affected may supply a letter confirming that it does not consider its charge to be adversely affected, so that it does not need to execute the deed.[3]

12.35   If an application is also to be made for a restriction or an entry to show that the lender is under an obligation to make further advances, separate applications must be made in Forms RX1 and CH2 respectively.[4]

12.36   If the registrar is satisfied that the proprietor of any registered charge of equal or inferior priority to the varied charge that is prejudicially affected by the variation is bound by it, he is obliged to make a note of the variation in the register.[5] If the registrar is not so satisfied by the evidence supplied, he will not raise a requisition, but may make an entry in the register that an instrument which is expressed to vary the terms of the registered charge has been entered into.[6] Such an entry is not guaranteed and will be in terms that:[7]

'A deed dated .... made between .... is expressed to alter the terms of the Charge dated .... referred to above.

NOTE: *Copy filed* '

12.37   The Land Registry will retain the original deed of variation unless the deed is in a form previously approved,[8] or, if not previously approved, where a certified copy of the deed has been supplied.[9]

---

[1]   Land Registry Practice Guide, Registration of Legal Charges and Deeds of Variation of Charge, PG29, para 12.2.

[2]   The use of a prescribed form (Form CH6) was proposed in Land Registry New Rules – A Consultation Document, but was not adopted following consultation.

[3]   Land Registry Practice Guide, Registration of Legal Charges and Deeds of Variation of Charge, PG29, para 12.2.

[4]   Ibid, para 12.

[5]   LRR 2003, r 113(3).

[6]   Ibid, r 113(4).

[7]   Land Registry Practice Guide, Registration of Legal Charges and Deeds of Variation of Charge, PG29, para 12.2.

[8]   See para **12.21**.

[9]   Land Registry Practice Guide, Registration of Legal Charges and Deeds of Variation of Charge, PG29, para 12.1.

CONSOLIDATION

12.38 A mortgagee has a right of consolidation.[1] This means that where a landowner has more than one charge from the same mortgagee, the mortgagee can refuse to permit the mortgagor to redeem one of the mortgages without redeeming them all.

12.39 Under the LRR 2003,[2] a chargee who has a right of consolidation in relation to a registered charge may apply to the registrar for an entry to be made in respect of that right in the individual register in which the charge is registered.[3] Application must be made on Form CC 'Entry of a note of consolidation of charges'.[4]

12.40 The matters that have to be included in Form CC are the date of the charge in which the right to consolidate is reserved and details of the charges consolidated with that charge. The applicant must also certify that the charge reserves a right of consolidation.

12.41 The registrar must make an entry in the individual register in such terms as he considers appropriate to give effect to an application under this rule.[5]

TRANSFER OF A REGISTERED CHARGE

12.42 A transfer of a registered charge must be in one of the following forms as appropriate:

- Form TR3 'Transfer of charge';
- Form TR4 'Transfer of a portfolio of charges'; or
- Form AS2 'Assent of charge'.[6]

These Forms are very similar to the forms previously in use under LRR 1925.[7]

12.43 The matters that must be included in Form TR3 'Transfer of a charge' include:

- the details of the property;
- the date of the transferor's charge;

---

1   Many lending institutions include a contractual right of consolidation in their standard mortgage terms.
2   LRR 2003, r 110, made under the rule-making power in LRA 2002, s 57.
3   This effectively brings forward the provisions of LRR 1925, r 154.
4   Ibid, r 110(2).
5   Ibid, r 110(3).
6   LRR 2003, r 116.
7   See the old Forms TR3, TR4 and AS2.

- the full name of the transferor;[1]
- the full name of the transferee for entry on the register;
- where the transferee is a company, the company's registered number;
- the transferee's intended address for service;
- where the transferee is a foreign company, the territory in which the company is incorporated;
- where the transfer is for money or money's worth, the consideration in words and figures;
- the covenants for title;
- any additional provisions, such as required or permitted statements, certificates or applications and any agreed covenants and declarations.

12.44   The transferor must execute the Form as a deed. If there is more than one transferor, all must execute the Form.[2] If the transfer contains transferee's covenants or declarations or contains an application by the transferee, for example for a restriction, it must also be executed by the transferee, or all of them if there is more than one.

12.45   Form TR4 'Transfer of a portfolio of charges' is in very similar form and is to be executed in the same way as Form TR3. In addition, the Form requires the completion of a list of all title numbers charged, brief descriptions of each property and the date of the transferor's charge or charges. If necessary, continuation sheet CS is to be attached to the Form.

12.46   The matters that must be included in Form AS2 'Assent of charge' are:

- details of the property charged;
- the date of the deceased proprietor's charge;
- the names of the deceased proprietor and of the personal representative of the deceased;
- the name of the transferee for entry on the register;
- the address of the transferee for service;
- the covenants for title; and
- any additional provisions, such as a required or permitted statement, certificate or application and any agreed covenants and declarations.

12.47   The personal representative must either sign Form AS2 in the presence of a witness[3] or execute it as a deed.[4] If there is more than one personal representative all must sign or execute it. If the assent contains transferee's covenants or declarations or contains an application by the

---

1   And, if it is a company, its registered number.
2   LRR 2003, Sch 9, contains forms of execution.
3   Cf AEA 1925, s 36(4). The requirement that there should be a witness is imposed by Form AS2.
4   LRR 2003, Sch 9, contains forms of execution.

transferee, for example for a restriction, it must also be signed by the transferee in the presence of a witness or executed as a deed by the transferee or all the transferees if there is more than one.

THE PRIORITY OF COMPETING CHARGES

Registered charges

12.48   Under the LRA 2002, the general rule is that registered charges on the same registered estate, or (in the case of sub-charges) on the same registered charge, rank in priority between themselves in the order shown in the register.[1] In other words, it is the order in which the charges are registered that determines their priority and not the date of their creation.[2] This is the same as under the LRA 1925.[3] Subject to the two exceptions explained at paras **12.49–12.58**, a registered charge that appears in the charges register before another registered charge will rank in priority to the charge below it. The two exceptions to the general rule are as follows. First, the chargees may decide between themselves on some different priority from that conferred by the order of registration.[4] Secondly, certain statutory charges have overriding priority.

Alteration of priority of registered charges

12.49   The LRR 2003 provide the machinery for an application to be made to alter the priority of registered charges as between themselves.[5] An application to alter the priority of registered charges must be made on Form AP1[6] by or with the consent of the proprietor or a person entitled to be registered as the proprietor of any registered charge whose priority is adversely affected by the alteration, although no such consent is required from a person

---

[1] LRA 2002, s 48(1). LRR 2003, r 101 (made under LRA 2002, s. 48(2)(a)) is to the same effect: subject to any entry in the individual register to the contrary, for the purpose of s 48(1) of the Act the order in which registered charges are entered in an individual register shows the order in which the registered charges rank as between themselves.

[2] In time, with the introduction of electronic conveyancing, it will in any event become impossible to create or transfer most estates, rights or interests in registered land except by simultaneously registering the disposition: see para **28.3**. In those circumstances, the basic rule of priority that the first in time of creation prevails (LRA 2002, s 28) will come to coincide with the rule of priority as to competing charges contained in LRA 2002, s 48(1).

[3] See LRA 1925, s 29.

[4] See para **12.49**.

[5] LRR 2003, r 102.

[6] No other form is prescribed, so Form AP1 must be used: see LRR 2003, r 13. A prescribed form was originally proposed for such application in *Land Registry New Rules – A Consultation Document*, Chapter 12, para 22. The aim was to help make the applicants' intentions clearer in all cases and avoid some of the requisitions to which such applications were commonly subject under the previous law. It was thought that use of a form would minimise the number of applications made without evidence of the appropriate parties' agreement. In the event, no form has been prescribed, so the applicant must take care to attend to such matters in his application.

who has executed the instrument which alters the priority of the charges.[1] The registrar may accept a conveyancer's certificate confirming that the conveyancer making the application holds any necessary consents.[2]

12.50   When an application is made in proper form, the registrar must make an entry in the register in such terms as the registrar considers appropriate to give effect to the application.[3]

Overriding statutory charges

12.51   The second exception to the general rule of priority relates to certain statutory charges that purport to take priority over any existing charges affecting the land.[4] On the assumption that such charges do indeed override prior charges – which is not settled[5] – there is no obligation on the body that has the benefit of the overriding charge to notify any prior chargees. There is an obvious danger, therefore, that a prior chargee might make a further advance, oblivious of the fact that its security has been eroded or even destroyed by the overriding statutory charge. To overcome this problem, the LRA 2002 imposes a duty on the registrar, when such an overriding charge is registered, to give notice of its creation to such persons as rules may provide.[6]

12.52   An application to register a statutory charge that takes priority over an existing registered charge should be made on Form SC 'Application for noting the overriding priority of a statutory charge, with the application'.[7] The matters that must be included in Form SC are:

—   the property;
—   the full name of the applicant;
—   details of the person with whom the registry is to deal if it is not the applicant;
—   the statute under which priority is claimed;
—   the registered charge over which the applicant's statutory charge has priority;
—   certification either that the statutory charge has already been registered in the charges register or that the statutory charge has arisen. In the latter case the relevant documents evidencing that the statutory charge has arisen must be lodged with the form.

---

[1] LRR 2003, r 102(1).
[2] Ibid, r 102(2).
[3] LRA 2002, s 48(2)(b), and LRR 2003, r 102(3). This could be important where one chargee exercises its power of sale and there is a surplus that has to be paid to the chargee next entitled: cf s 54, para **12.82**.
[4] They are not common. The best known example is the statutory charge in favour of the Legal Services Commission: see Access to Justice Act 1999 (ATJA 1999), s 10(7).
[5] See (2001) Law Com 271, para 7.41.
[6] LRA 2002, s 50. See LRR 2003, r 106(1); see also para **12.55**.
[7] LRR 2003, r 105(1).

12.53 If the applicant satisfies the registrar that the statutory charge has the priority specified in the Form SC, the registrar *must* make an entry showing that priority in the charges register of the affected registered title.[1]

12.54 If the applicant does not satisfy the registrar but the registrar considers that the applicant has an arguable case, the registrar may make an entry in the charges register of the affected registered title that the applicant *claims* the priority specified in that Form SC.[2] Because the effect of many statutory charges is uncertain,[3] it is likely that the majority of entries will take this form.

12.55 If the registrar makes an entry that the applicant claims priority in the charges register of the affected registered title, the registrar *must* give notice of the entry to the following persons:[4]

(a)   the registered proprietor of a registered charge entered in the charges register of the affected title at the time of registration of the statutory charge; and

(b)   any person entered in the charges register of the affected registered title at the time of registration of the statutory charge who appears to the registrar to be entitled to a charge protected by notice.

The registrar is not, however, obliged to give notice to a person within category (b) if that person's name and address for service under LRR 2003, r 198, are not set out in the individual register in which the notice is entered.[5] This is important because a person is entitled to be indemnified if a person suffers loss by reason of a failure by the registrar to perform his duty.[6]

12.56 The following may apply to the registrar for the entry to be removed or to be replaced by an entry reflecting the priority that they assert:[7]

(a)   the proprietor of the statutory charge which gave rise to the entry; and

(b)   the proprietor of a charge entered in the charges register of the affected registered title which, subject to the effect of the entry, would rank in priority to or have equal priority with that statutory charge under the general rule that charges rank in priority in the order shown in the register.[8]

---

[1]   LRR 2003, r 105(2).
[2]   Ibid, r 105(3).
[3]   See (2001) Law Com 271, para 7.41.
[4]   LRR 2003, r 106(1).
[5]   Ibid, r 106(2).
[6]   LRA 2002, Sch 8, para 1(1)(h); and see para **23.10**.
[7]   LRR 2003 r 105(5). The effect of these provisions is similar to those contained in LRR 1925, r 158.
[8]   Ibid, r 101; see para **12.48**.

It is provided that (b) includes the proprietor of a statutory charge entered in the charges register of the affected registered title in respect of which there is an entry claiming priority[1] over the statutory charge mentioned in (a).[2] This rather complicated provision means that where:

—   there is already a statutory charge;
—   it is recorded in the register that the applicant claims that the charge has priority over any pre-existing charge;
—   a second statutory charge is then registered on the basis that it has priority over the first statutory charge;
—   the proprietor of the first statutory charge claims that its charge ranks in priority to or has equal priority with the second statutory charge;

the proprietor of the first statutory charge may apply to have the entry in respect of the first statutory charge removed or replaced.

12.57   An application for the removal or replacement of the entry must be supported by evidence to satisfy the registrar that he should take the action sought by the applicant.[3]

12.58   On receipt of the application, the registrar must give notice of the application to any proprietors (other than the applicant) who could have made an application, before taking the action sought by the applicant.[4] Any dispute that arises as a result of the application must be referred to the Adjudicator.[5]

Equitable charges

12.59   The priority of equitable charges will depend upon the general rules of priority in the Act that have already been explained.[6] In other words, the order of creation of equitable charges will be determined by the order in which the charges are created. When electronic conveyancing has become fully operative, it will in time become impossible to create equitable charges except by simultaneously registering them.[7] In those circumstances the date of registration and the date of creation will coincide, so that the register will in practice become as conclusive as to the priority of equitable charges as it is for registered charges.

---

[1]   See para **12.54**.
[2]   LRR 2003, r 105(6).
[3]   Ibid, r 105(7).
[4]   Ibid, r 105(8).
[5]   LRA 2002, s 73(7).
[6]   Ibid, ss 28–30; see also Chapter 9.
[7]   See para **28.3**.

TACKING AND FURTHER ADVANCES

Introduction

12.60   The LRA 2002 makes very significant changes to the law on tacking and further advances. Although the rules which govern tacking and further advances in relation to charges over unregistered land are exclusively statutory,[1] those provisions did not apply to charges registered under the LRA 1925.[2] As a result, there was no equivalent statutory code applicable to tacking and further advances in relation to charges over registered land. The LRA 2002 provides for four methods of tacking.

(1)   Recognition of existing practice

12.61   The applicable law prior to the implementation of the LRA 2002 comprised the old common law rules of tacking that had been abolished in relation to unregistered land[3] with a partial statutory gloss.[4] The essential common law rule was that where a first chargee received notice of the charge of a second chargee, he could not thereafter make a further advance to the chargor that had priority over the charge of the second chargee. Because of this rule, where there was a second or subsequent charge over registered land, the new lender would notify prior lenders of his charge. This practice was widely employed by mortgage lenders in England and Wales and worked effectively. Indeed, it proved to be quicker and less cumbersome than the procedure contained in the LRA 1925 by which the registrar was obliged to give notice to any prior chargee before he registered a subsequent charge which would prejudicially affect further advances by the prior chargee.[5]

12.62   The LRA 2002 recognises that the practice of lenders is the right one and gives it statutory effect. It provides that the proprietor of a registered charge may make a further advance on the security of the charge that ranks in priority to a subsequent charge if he has not received from the subsequent chargee notice of the creation of the subsequent charge.[6]

12.63   Although the LRR 2003 do not prescribe any particular means by which the subsequent chargee should give notice of the creation of the subsequent charge, the Rules do set out when notice ought to have been received by reference to the common methods of service.[7] These provisions

---

[1]   LPA 1925, s 94(1)–(3).
[2]   Ibid, s 94(4). Nor do they apply to charges under LRA 2002: see Sch 11, para 2(9), amending LPA 1925, s 94(4).
[3]   See LPA 1925, s 94(3).
[4]   For the previous statutory provisions, see LRA 1925, s 30.
[5]   Ibid, s 30(1).
[6]   LRA 2002, s 49(1). Notice given for the purposes of this subsection is to be treated as received when, in accordance with rules, it ought to have been received: s 49(2).
[7]   LRR 2003, r 107(1), (2).

should be borne in mind by the subsequent chargee when determining which method of service to adopt:

- service by post to a postal address within the UK entered in the register as the prior chargee's address for service:[1] deemed receipt on the second working day after posting;[2]
- service by post to a postal address outside the UK entered in the register as the prior chargee's address for service:[3] deemed receipt on the seventh working day after posting;[4]
- service by leaving the notice at the postal address:[5] deemed receipt on the working day after it was left;[6]
- service by sending it to the box number at the relevant document exchange entered in the register as an additional address for service of the prior chargee:[7] deemed receipt on the second working day after it was left at the sender's document exchange;[8]
- service by electronic transmission to the electronic address entered in the register as an additional address for service of the prior chargee:[9] deemed receipt on the second working day after transmission.[10]

12.64   The rule as to the date on which a notice served in accordance with one of these methods ought to have been received are also applicable where the prior chargee has provided to the subsequent chargee a postal address, document exchange box number, fax number, e-mail or other electronic address, and has stated in writing to the subsequent chargee that notices to the prior chargee under LRA 2002, s 49(1) may be sent to that address, box number or fax number.[11]

12.65   The corollary of these provisions is that although the subsequent chargee may decide to use some other method of service, the subsequent chargee will not be able to rely on the certainty which the rules provide as to when the notice ought to have been received in accordance with one of the methods set out above.

12.66   It is important that the effect of these provisions should be considered by any chargee when selecting an address for entry on the register.

---

[1]   LRR 2003, r 107(2)(a).
[2]   Ibid, r 107(4).
[3]   Ibid, r 107(2)(a)
[4]   Ibid, r 107(4).
[5]   Ibid, r 107(2)(b).
[6]   Ibid, r 107(4).
[7]   Ibid, r 107(2)(c)
[8]   Ibid, r 107(4).
[9]   Ibid, r 107(2)(d).
[10]   Ibid, r 107(4).
[11]   Ibid, r 107(2)(e), (3).

The address chosen should be one at which the chargee can be certain that communications to that address will reach him in time. It is also important to ensure that the address provided for entry on the register is kept up to date.

(2) Further advance in pursuance of an obligation

12.67 A proprietor of a registered charge may make a further advance that has priority over a subsequent charge if:

—   that further advance was made in pursuance of an obligation and, at the time when the subsequent charge was created; and
—   that agreement was entered in the register in accordance with rules.[1]

12.68 Under the LRR 2003, the proprietor of a registered charge or a person applying to be so registered, who is under an obligation to make further advances on the security of that charge, may apply to the registrar for that obligation to be entered in the register.[2]

12.69 The application can be made in one of three ways.[3] First, it may be made in panel 7 of Form CH1.[4] Secondly, it may be made in a charge submitted for registration where the form of that charge has been approved by the registrar.[5] Thirdly, in any other case, the application must be made in Form CH2 'Application to enter an obligation to make further advances'.[6] If the Form CH2 is not lodged with the application to register the charge, an additional fee will be payable for the obligation entry.[7]

12.70 The matters that must be included in Form CH2 are:

—   details of the registered charge containing the obligation;
—   confirmation that under the provisions of the charge the lender is under an obligation to make further advances; and
—   an application to the registrar to enter a note in the register confirming that obligation.

12.71 Following receipt of an application to enter the obligation to make

1   LRA 2002, s 49(3).
2   LRR 2003, r 108(1).
3   Ibid, r 108(2), (3). An application that is not made in one of these three ways will be ignored by the Registry: Land Registry Practice Guide, Registration of Legal Charges and Deeds of Variation of Charge, PG29, para 6.
4   Panel 7 provides: 'Place "X" in the appropriate box(es). The lender is under an obligation to make further advances and applies for the obligation to be entered in the register.'
5   LRR 2003, r 108(3).
6   Ibid, r 108(2).
7   Land Registry Practice Guide, Registration of Legal Charges and Deeds of Variation of Charge, PG29, para 6.

further advances in the register, the registrar must make an entry in the register in such terms as he considers appropriate to give effect to an application under the rule.[1]

(3)   Further advance with agreement of subsequent chargee

12.72   A proprietor of a registered charge may make a further advance that has priority over a subsequent charge if the subsequent chargee agrees.[2] This replicates the previous law. Such an agreement must be recorded by the registrar on an application to him to alter the priority of the relevant registered charges.[3]

(4)   The agreement of a maximum amount

12.73   The final method of tacking further advances under the LRA 2002 is a novelty. The proprietor of a registered charge may make a further advance having priority over a subsequent charge if the parties to the prior charge had agreed a maximum amount for which the charge was security and, at the time when the subsequent charge was created, the agreement had been entered on the register in the manner specified in rules.[4]

12.74   For example, X agrees that he will lend money on the security of Y's registered estate and that the maximum sum for which the charge is to stand as security is £100,000. The agreement is recorded on the register in the prescribed manner. Y borrows £50,000 from X. He then borrows a further £20,000 from Z and creates a second charge over the registered estate as security. Y then borrows a further £50,000 from X. X is secured for the full sum of £100,000 in priority to Z's second charge.

12.75   The LRR 2003 make provision for an application to enter an agreement of this kind in the register.[5] No entry will be made without such an application. It is not sufficient that the maximum amount is stated in the charge itself, the charge has previously been approved by the registry, or the maximum sum is stated in a subsequent deed of variation.[6]

---

[1]   LRR 2003, r 108(4).
[2]   LRA 2002, s 49(6).
[3]   See LRR 2003, r 102(1), (3); see also para **12.49**.
[4]   LRA 2002, s 49(4). For the rules, see para **12.75**.
[5]   LRR 2003, r 109. An application can be made where the charge is either a registered charge or a registrable disposition, and it may be made by either the proprietor of the registered charge or a person applying to be registered as proprietor of the registrable disposition: LRR 2003, r 109(1).
[6]   Land Registry Practice Guide, Registration of Legal Charges and Deeds of Variation of Charge, PG29, para 7.

12.76 An application to note the maximum sum must be made in Form CH3 'Application to note agreed maximum amount of security'.[1] The matters to be completed in Form CH3 include the details of the registered charge containing the agreement and the maximum amount of the security. If such an application is made, the registrar must make an entry in the register in such terms as he considers appropriate to give effect to an application.[2]

12.77 If the parties subsequently wish to amend the amount of the maximum security entered on the register a further application in Form CH3 can be lodged. The register will then be amended to show the original entry and an additional entry.[3]

12.78 The LRA 2002 contains a power to make rules which, in relation to charges of a particular description, would either disapply this form of tacking or would require compliance with specified conditions.[4] This power has been included as a safeguard. It could be exercised if it transpired that this form of tacking was being employed oppressively in relation to particular types of charge.[5] It remains to be seen whether such rules will prove to be necessary. As yet, none have been made.

REALISATION OF A CHARGEE'S SECURITY

Introduction

12.79 The LRA 2002 addresses a number of matters concerned with the realisation of a chargee's security.

Local land charges

12.80 The provisions made by the Act relating to local land charges simply replicate what was the law under the LRA 1925. Local land charges are not normally registrable under the Act (because they are recorded instead in local land charges registers), and override both first registration and registered dispositions.[6] Where, however, the local land charge is of a type that create a charge over land for the payment of money, as, for example, where a street works authority incurs expenditure in executing street works,[7] the LRA 2002

---

1. LRR 2003, r 109(2).
2. Ibid, r 109(3).
3. Land Registry Practice Guide, Registration of Legal Charges and Deeds of Variation of Charge, PG29, para 7.
4. LRA 2002, s 49(5).
5. The Law Commission gave as a possible example of the sort of case where rules might be made regulated agreements secured by land mortgages under the Consumer Credit Act 1974: (2001) Law Com No 271, para 7.36.
6. See LRA 2002, Schs 1 and 3, para 6.
7. Under Highways Act 1980, s 212.

provides that a charge over registered land that is a local land charge can only be realised if the title has been registered.[1] The thinking behind that provision is as follows.[2] The proprietor of a registered charge has the powers of a legal mortgagee.[3] If any person has powers of disposition over registered land, that fact should appear from the register. That is consistent with the fundamental objective of the Act to ensure that the register is as conclusive as it can be made.[4]

12.81   The LRR 2003 provide that an application to register the title to a charge over registered land which is a local land charge must be supported by evidence of the charge.[5]

Surplus after sale

12.82   The Act makes provision for the situation where a registered chargee exercises its power of sale and there is a surplus after discharging its charge and related expenses. That surplus is held upon trust and must be paid to 'the person entitled to the mortgaged property'.[6] It was not settled under the previous law whether the chargee who held the surplus should search the register to see if there are any other chargees, or whether it was entitled to pay the surplus to the chargor if it had not received notice of any subsequent charge.[7] The LRA 2002 has clarified the position. It provides that a person – which in this context means the chargee who exercises his power of sale – is to be taken to have notice of anything in the register immediately before the disposition on sale.[8] The effect of this is that a chargee exercising its power of sale must inspect the register prior to the disposition to ascertain whether there are any subsequent charges on the register. Given that the Act seeks to bring about a conclusive register, and one to which most lenders are likely to have access, this is unlikely to be an unduly onerous requirement. It is also consistent with the principle that registration protects the right in question, in this case the interest of the subsequent chargee.[9]

---

[1] LRA 2002, s 55.
[2] See (2001) Law Com No 271, para 7.42.
[3] See para **12.7**.
[4] See para **1.7**.
[5] LRR 2003, r 104.
[6] LPA 1925, s 105.
[7] Where the title to land is *unregistered*, a mortgagee holding a surplus after sale *is* in practice obliged to search the Land Charges register to see if there is any subsequent charge that has been registered as a Class C(i) or C(iii) land charge. This is because registration of a land charge is actual notice to all persons for all purposes of both the charge and its registration: LPA 1925, s 198(1). There is no equivalent to s 198(1) in relation to registered land.
[8] LRA 2002, s 54. On sale, the interests of any subsequent chargees will be overreached: see LPA 1925, s 104(1).
[9] Even if a subsequent charge is *not* protected on the register, a chargee who has sold the estate subject to the charge will have to account for any surplus to the subsequent chargee if it has been given notice of its charge.

Power of joint proprietors to give receipts

12.83   The LRA 2002 contains a provision by which, where a charge is registered in the name of two or more proprietors, a valid receipt for the money secured by the charge may be given:

—   by the registered proprietors;
—   where one or more of those proprietors has died, by the survivor(s); and
—   by the personal representative of the last survivor of the registered proprietors.[1]

This replicates the previous law.[2]

FORECLOSURE

12.84   A chargee will seldom seek foreclosure nowadays: the remedy is all but obsolete.[3] Nevertheless, the remedy has not been abolished and the LRR 2003 therefore make provision for it. Where a chargee has obtained an order for foreclosure absolute, he may apply to be entered in the register as proprietor of the registered estate in respect of which the charge is registered. That application must normally be accompanied by the order.[4] However, the registrar has a discretion to accept a conveyancer's certificate confirming that the conveyancer holds the order for foreclosure absolute or an office copy of it.[5]

12.85   On receipt of a valid application, the registrar must:

—   cancel the registration of the charge in respect of which the order was made;
—   cancel all entries in respect of interests over which the charge has priority; and
—   enter the applicant as proprietor of the registered estate.[6]

DISCHARGE AND RELEASE OF CHARGES

Introduction

12.86   The LRR 2003 make provision for the discharge and release of charges. Registered charges may be discharged either in documentary form by

---

1   LRA 2002, s 56.
2   See the latter part of LRA 1925, s 32.
3   See *Palk v Mortgage Services Funding Plc* [1993] Ch 330 at 336.
4   LRR 2003, r 112(1).
5   Ibid, r 112(3).
6   Ibid, r 112(2).

means of a prescribed Form or in dematerialised form by means of the 'ENDS' system (Electronic Notification of Discharge). In this section the following matters are considered:

– documentary discharge of registered charges;
– the discharge and releases of charges that are protected by notice (in particular fixed equitable charges and floating charges); and
– electronic notification of discharges of registered charges.

It used to be possible to charge registered land by means of a deposit with the lender of the borrower's land or charge certificate. A notice of deposit was then entered in the register. The practice was discontinued in April 1995,[1] and such notices of deposit are now rare. The Land Registry has provided guidance as to the evidence it will accept to cancel a notice of deposit entry to which reference should be made.[2]

Documentary discharge of registered charges

12.87   A discharge of a registered charge must be in Form DS1 'Cancellation of entries relating to a registered charge'.[3] The form should be accompanied either by the general application form to change the register, Form AP1, or by Form DS2 'Application to cancel entries relating to a registered charge'.[4]

12.88   A release of part of the registered estate in a registered title from a registered charge must be in Form DS3 'Release of part of the land from a registered charge'.[5] The Form should also be used where part of the land in one registered title and the whole of the land in another registered title or titles are discharged from a registered charge.[6] Form DS3 must be accompanied by Application Form AP1 and should have a plan attached defining the property released from the charge.[7] The accompanying plan must be signed by, or on behalf of, the lender

12.89   The Land Registry will not accept any alteration to Forms DS1 or DS3 for which no provision is made in LRR 2003. Neither Form should be altered if money remains outstanding under the charge as a personal debt owed by the borrower to the lender.[8]

---

1   Following the decision of Chadwick J at first instance in *United Bank of Kuwait v Sahib* [1997] Ch 107; and see para **12.05**.
2   See Land Registry Practice Guide, Discharge of Charges, PG31, para 5.
3   LRR 2003, r 114(1).
4   Ibid, r 114(5).
5   Ibid, r 114(2).
6   Land Registry Practice Guide, Discharge of Charges, PG31, para 3.8.
7   See Form DS3, box 2.
8   Land Registry Practice Guide, Discharge of Charges, PG31, para 3.1.

12.90 Any discharge or release in Form DS1 or DS3 must be executed as a deed or authenticated in such other manner as the registrar may approve.[1] The registrar is, however, entitled to accept and act upon any other proof of satisfaction of a charge that he may regard as sufficient.[2]

12.91 Companies registered under the Companies Act 1985, or to which s 718 of the Companies Act 1985 applies, may execute either Forms DS1 or DS3 in any of the following ways:[3]

– affixing the seal in the presence of a director and secretary; or
– without the use of a company seal, by a director and secretary or two directors signing the form as a deed; or
– by some other method permitted under the company's constitution. In such case, a certified copy of the company's constitution and any other evidence of the company's power to execute the form of discharge by that method must be enclosed.[4]

12.92 Building societies may execute Forms DS1 and DS3 as a deed:[5]

– in accordance with the LPA 1925, s 74(1);
– in some other way permitted by their constitution or rules;
– by affixing the seal, which must be countersigned by a person acting under the authority of the society's board of directors; or
– by the signature, unaccompanied by the seal, of a person with that authority.

12.93 Foreign companies may execute Form DS1 or DS3 otherwise than under seal, if the deed:[6]

– is signed by a person or persons who, in accordance with the laws of the territory in which the company is incorporated, is or are acting under the authority (express or implied) of that company; and
– is expressed, in whatever form of words, to be executed by that company.

Evidence should be provided to support these facts.

12.94 Other corporate bodies such as industrial and provident institutions and companies incorporated by royal charter or statute, or other entities having corporate personality, must either execute the Form DS1 or DS3 as a

---

1   LRR 2003, r 114(3).
2   Ibid, r 114(4).
3   Land Registry Practice Guide, Discharge of Charges, PG31, para 3.3.
4   This does not apply in the case where a special arrangement has been made: see para **12.95**.
5   Land Registry Practice Guide, Discharge of Charges, PG31, para 3.4.
6   Ibid, para 3.5.

deed in accordance with the LPA 1925, s 74(1), or produce evidence to prove that they are entitled to execute it in some other way.[1]

12.95   Where a body corporate intends to execute a significant number of discharges otherwise than in accordance with s 74 of the LPA 1925 or s 36A of the Companies Act 1985, it may enter into a special arrangement with the Land Registry.[2] If, when such a request is made by the lender, the Land Registry is satisfied that the lender has the power to do as it proposes, it will make an arrangement which will make it unnecessary for evidence to be sent with every application to show that the discharge or release has been properly executed. The Land Registry will require the lender to undertake to inform it of any change in the power or in the identity of the persons able to grant discharges or releases in the lender's name.

12.96   A facility letter or a customised Form DS1 or DS3, as appropriate, may be used to set out the special arrangement. Where such arrangements were made:

–   before 1 April 1988, a copy of the facility letter must be lodged with the Form DS1 or DS3;
–   on or after 1 April 1988, the date of the facility letter should be entered in box 7 of the Form DS1 or DS3.[3]

If any confirmation is required that a facility letter exists, or that a Form DS1 or DS3 has been executed in accordance with it, the enquiry should be addressed to the lender.[4]

12.97   In the case of charges secured against unregistered land, the Land Registry will accept a receipt endorsed on the form of charge itself as proof of discharge. It will also accept discharges in Form 53 if dated before 1 October 1998.[5]

Discharges and releases of charges protected by notice

12.98   Some charges over registered land will be protected by a notice entered under either s 49 of the LRA 1925 or s 32 of the LRA 2002.[6] In the

---

[1]   Land Registry Practice Guide, Discharge of Charges, PG31, para 3.6.
[2]   Ibid, para 3.7.
[3]   Ibid.
[4]   Ibid.
[5]   Ibid, para 3.2.
[6]   The notice may have been entered pursuant to an application or by the registrar on first registration. Some charges may have been protected by means of a caution under LRA 1925, s 54. These should be withdrawn under LRR 2003, r 222 (using Form WCT: application to withdraw a caution), or cancelled under r 223 (using Form CCD: application to cancel a caution against dealings).

latter case, the notice may be either an agreed notice or a unilateral notice.[1]

12.99   An application to cancel a notice other than a unilateral notice must be made in Form CN1 'Application to cancel a notice other than a unilateral notice'. The form must be accompanied by sufficient evidence to demonstrate that the charge has been discharged. The evidence that the Registry will accept is as follows.

12.100   First, in the case of the discharge of a fixed equitable charge, the Registry will accept:

(a)   a Form DS1 or DS3;

(b)   an endorsed receipt on the instrument of charge; or

(c)   a letter addressed to the Registry confirming that the charge has been satisfied, signed by the noted chargee (or an authorised signatory of the noted chargee if it is a body corporate), and including confirmation that there has been no assignment of the benefit of the charge. If an assignment has been made, the normal conveyancing evidence of devolution of title must be lodged.[2]

The charge may be lodged if it is available, as useful evidence that the applicant is still entitled to the benefit of the charge. There is no requirement that it should be lodged.

12.101   Secondly, where a floating charge is discharged, the evidence that the Registry will accept is as follows:[3]

(a)   a copy of a declaration of satisfaction in a Companies Registry Form 403A, stamped as 'REGISTERED' by the Companies Registry;

(b)   a letter from the Registrar of Companies confirming that the charge has been satisfied;

(c)   a letter addressed to the Land Registry that is signed by either the noted chargee or its authorised signatory, confirming that:
        (i)   the charge has been satisfied;
        (ii)   there has been no assignment of the benefit of the charge;[4] or

(d)   where a subsequent transfer on sale of the land has been lodged for registration, a certificate signed by the solicitor, licensed conveyancer, or secretary of the chargor company that none of the events which would cause the charge to become fixed, occurred before the date of the transfer.

---

[1]   See LRA 2002, s 34.

[2]   Land Registry Practice Guide, Discharge of Charges, PG31, para 4.2.1.

[3]   Ibid, para 4.2.2.

[4]   If an assignment has been made, normal conveyancing evidence of devolution of title must be lodged.

12.102 If the charge that has been discharged is protected by a unilateral notice, an application to remove or cancel the notice must be:

(a)   in Form UN2 'Application to remove a unilateral notice', where it is made by the registered beneficiary of that notice;[1] or

(b)   in Form UN4 'Application for the cancellation of a unilateral notice', where the application to cancel a unilateral notice is made by the registered proprietor, the application must be made.[2]

Evidence of discharge is not required in either case.[3]

Registered charges: electronic notifications of discharge

12.103   As has been explained,[4] notification of the discharge of a registered charge may be delivered to the registrar in electronic form[5] by an electronic message in Form END1 'Electronic notification for discharge'.[6] At present, it is possible only to discharge a registered charge by electronic means[7] and not to release part of a registered estate from a registered charge,[8] although this will no doubt change in due course. Such notification is to be regarded as having the same effect as a discharge in Form DS1.[9] It must be executed in accordance with the rule as to variation of the terms of a registered charge,[10] by or on behalf of the person who has delivered it to the registrar.[11]

12.104   The procedure is as follows. The borrower repays the charge in the usual way. Instead of sending a completed Form DS1 to the lender, he sends a completed Form END1. The lender, having received the repayment and Form END1 will electronically notify the Registry of the repayment via a secure computer link. The borrower will send to the Registry a Form AP1, a Form DS2 or a Form DS2E 'Application to cancel entries relating to a registered charge'.[12]

12.105   If a lender intends to use the ENDs system to discharge their charges

---

[1]   Under LRA 2002, s 35(3) and in accordance with LRR 2003, r 85.

[2]   Under LRA 2002, s 36 and in accordance with LRR 2003, r 86.

[3]   Land Registry Practice Guide, Discharge of Charges, PG31, para 4.3.

[4]   See para **12.86**.

[5]   LRR 2003, r 115(1); and Sch 2, para 2(c).

[6]   For Form END1, see Land Registry Practice Guide, Discharge of Charges, PG31, Appendix E.

[7]   In other words, where a Form DS1 would otherwise be used.

[8]   In other words, where a Form DS3 must be used. See Land Registry Practice Guide, Discharge of Charges, PG31, para 6.1.

[9]   LRR 2003, r 115(2).

[10]   See LRR 2003, r 113; see also paras **12.30–12.37**.

[11]   Ibid, r 115(2).

[12]   The Form is set out at Appendix C to Land Registry Practice Guide, Discharge of Charges, PG31. Panel 7 states that 'The applicant applies for the cancellation of the entries of the registered charge relating to the Electronic Notification of Discharge transmitted by the Land Registry by the lender'.

when redeemed it should inform the borrower in the redemption statement or when a deeds packet is issued.[1]

12.106 It seems unlikely that the ENDs system will continue much longer. The Land Registry is presently piloting with two major mortgage lenders a new system, known as EDs, under which a charge is discharged without any formal application when an electronic message is sent by the lender to the Registry to indicate that the charge has been redeemed.[2] That message will be sent automatically once the amount on the lender's mortgage account drops to zero.

Restrictions

12.107 Any restriction which specifically relates to the charge that is to be discharged will normally be cancelled automatically. If, however, a restriction in favour of the lender was entered as a result of an application in Form RX1 and it does not specifically refer to the charge being discharged, it will be necessary to lodge a separate withdrawal of that restriction with the application to register the discharge. The application for withdrawal should be made using Form RX4 'Application to withdraw a restriction'.[3] If an application on Form RX4 is not lodged, the restriction will remain on the register.[4]

---

[1] For more detailed guidance on the use of the ENDS system, see Land Registry Practice Guide, Discharge of Charges, PG31, para 6.

[2] See the Land Registry's publicity leaflet, Electronic Discharges. The 6-month pilot began in December 2003.

[3] LRR 2003, r 98.

[4] Land Registry Practice Guide, Discharge of Charges, PG31, para 7.

CHAPTER 13

SPECIAL CASES

INTRODUCTION

13.1 Part 7 of the LRA 2002 and Part 14 of the LRR 2003 make provision for a number of special cases. Some of these matters are discussed elsewhere in this book. The special cases discussed below are:

- the Crown;
- devolution on the death of a registered proprietor;
- bankruptcy;
- companies and other corporations;
- charities;
- settlements.

This chapter considers these matters in outline only. It is concerned only with the manner in which the LRA 2002 and LRR 2003 treat these cases. More detailed treatment is to be found in the relevant Land Registry Practice Guides.

THE CROWN

13.2 In Chapter 6 it was explained how the LRA 2002 contains provisions that enable the Crown to register land that it holds in demesne as paramount feudal lord, something it could not previously do. It is thought that the Crown will take advantage of this new power. The provisions of the LRA 2002 on adverse possession[1] provide a strong incentive for it to do so. This is particularly so in relation to Crown land that is vulnerable to adverse possession such as the foreshore[2] and, in due course, those parts of the sea bed beyond the county boundaries that will become registrable under the Act.[3]

13.3 The LRA 2002 contains other provisions concerning the Crown. These only require brief mention because they are unlikely to affect most

---

[1] Explained in Part 6
[2] See para **33.13**.
[3] See LRA 2002, s 130(b). Like LRA 1925, LRA 2002 applies to land covered by internal waters that falls within the body of a county: see s 130(a). The applicability may be extended by order out to the base lines that define the territorial limits of the UK.

practitioners.[1] One issue that does arise from time to time is that of escheat.[2] Where a freehold estate terminates the land escheats, usually to the Crown,[3] and it then becomes part of the Crown's demesne land.[4] The two most common situations in which this happens are:

(a)   where a liquidator or a trustee in bankruptcy disclaims a freehold because it is onerous;[5] or

(b)   where property has passed as *bona vacantia* to the Crown in the person of the Treasury Solicitor[6] and the Treasury Solicitor disclaims.[7]

13.4   The problem that the escheat of a registered freehold creates is that, because the freehold has terminated, the title has to be removed from the register. This obviously runs counter to the objective of securing the registration of all land in England and Wales. There is also the danger that there will be nothing in the register to indicate that an estate has escheated, so that there could be some purported dealing with what appears to be a registered estate. The LRA 2002 contains a rule-making power that is intended to ensure that where registered freehold land escheats, the title can remain on the register, and the fact of escheat is recorded in the register.[8] There have been difficulties in drafting appropriate rules that dovetail satisfactorily with the Insolvency Rules 1986, and the rule contained in LRR 2003 on escheat is unlikely to be the final word on the subject.

13.5   LRR 2003, r 173(1), provides that where a registered freehold estate in land has determined, the registrar may enter a note of that fact in the property register and in the property register of any inferior affected registered title.[9]

---

[1]   See LRA 2002, ss 83 (Crown and Duchy land: representation), 84 (disapplication of certain requirements as to formalities and enrolment) and 85 (*bona vacantia*). As regards LRA 2002, s 85, the section confers a rule-making power to make provision about how the passing of a registered estate or charge as *bona vacantia* is to be dealt with for the purposes of the Act. For the one rule made pursuant to this power, see LRR 2003, r 185; below, para **13.33**.

[2]   The matter is explained in detail in (2001) Law Com No 271, paras 11.20–11.30. See also *Scmlla Properties Ltd v Gesso Properties (BVI) Ltd* [1995] BCC 793, the leading modern authority on escheat.

[3]   Technically, escheat is to the lord of whom the land was held. Land is usually held directly of the Crown, although it may be held of one of the two Royal Duchies (Cornwall or Lancaster). It is extremely unlikely that any other person would succeed in proving that he was a mesne lord, although we are aware of at least one individual who makes claims of this kind.

[4]   It is administered by the Crown Estate.

[5]   Under IA 1986, ss 171, 315. For a detailed account of disclaimer by a liquidator, see Corporate Insolvency, PG35, para 6.

[6]   Under Companies Act 1985, s 654.

[7]   Ibid, s 656. For a detailed account of disclaimer by the Crown, see Corporate Insolvency, PG35, para 7.3.

[8]   See LRA 2002, s 82.

[9]   The form of the entry is as follows: '(Date) The registered estate in this title has determined on disclaimer by [the liquidator of the registered proprietor][The Treasury Solicitor][The Solicitor for the [Affairs of the Duchy of Lancaster][Duke of Cornwall]] on…… pursuant to section [178 of the Insolvency Act 1986][656 of the Companies Act 1985]. **Note**: Copy disclaimer filed.' See Corporate Insolvency, PG35, para 7.3.2.

Where he considers that that there is doubt as to whether a registered freehold estate in land has determined,[1] the entry that he makes must be modified by a statement to that effect.[2]

13.6 It was explained at para **8.54**, that under LRR 2003, r 79, an application may be made to the registrar to record in the register the determination of a registered estate and that, where he is satisfied that the estate has determined, he must close the registered title to the estate and cancel any notice in any other registered title relating to it. That provision is qualified in relation to a freehold estate that has escheated. Where an entry is made under r 173, the registrar need not close the registered title to the estate until a freehold legal estate in land in respect of the land in which such former estate subsisted has been registered. What that means in practice is that the title to the escheated freehold may remain open until either:

(a)   the original freehold revives[3] and the original title is restored; or
(b)   the Crown grants a new freehold estate out of the demesne, which will be given a new title number, because it is a new estate.[4]

Escheat does not destroy the incumbrances that bind an estate.[5] Where a new freehold estate is granted by the Crown, the entries relating to incumbrances that bound the previous estate will be carried over to the new title unless it can be shown that they have ceased to subsist for some other reason.[6]

DEVOLUTION ON THE DEATH OF A REGISTERED PROPRIETOR

13.7 It was explained in Chapter 8 that the requirement that registrable dispositions should be registered applies to dispositions by operation of law as much as it does to other dispositions, but that this was subject to certain exceptions.[7] One of these exceptions is a transfer that takes place on the death of an individual proprietor.[8] It follows that, on the death of a registered proprietor, his estate will devolve either on his executors or, following a grant of letters of administration, on his administrators, without this fact necessarily appearing in the register. Once there has been a grant of probate or letters of

---

1   Such doubts most commonly arise where the dissolution of a foreign corporation is in issue.
2   LRR 2003, r 173(2).
3   It sometimes happens that a dissolved company is restored to the register: see Companies Act 1985, ss 651 and 655. If that occurs any escheated freehold estate will revive. This is common with management companies: see Corporate Insolvency, PG35, para 7.5.1.
4   For such re-grants, see Corporate Insolvency, PG35, para 7.4.
5   See *Scmlla Properties Ltd v Gesso Properties (BVI) Ltd* [1995] BCC 793, 806, referring to the relevant authorities.
6   As, for example, where a charge over the land can no longer be enforced because all rights under the charge are time-barred.
7   LRA 2002, s 27(5); above, paras **8.4–8.7**.
8   Ibid, s 27(5)(a).

administration, the executors or administrators may (but are not required to) apply to be registered, and the provisions of the LRR 2003, r 163, which govern such applications, have been explained at para **8.5**.

13.8   The personal representatives may, however, make a disposition of the deceased's registered estate without themselves being registered as proprietors. LRR 2003, r 162, makes provision for such applications.[1] The application must be made using the appropriate forms of application,[2] and transfer,[3] and must be accompanied by the original grant of probate or letters of administration showing him as the personal representative.[4] Where the transfer is of registered land by a personal representative of a deceased sole proprietor, or a deceased last surviving joint proprietor, the registrar is under no duty to investigate the reasons why that transfer is made.[5] Provided that the terms of any restriction in the register are complied with, the registrar must assume that the personal representative is acting correctly and within his powers. This is so whether he knows of the terms of the will or not.[6] What this rule makes clear is that, the responsibility for the proper administration of the deceased's estate in accordance with his will or under the rules governing intestacy, falls upon the personal representative and is of no concern to the registrar.

BANKRUPTCY

Introduction

13.9   Section 86 of the LRA 2002 makes detailed provision for the situation where a registered proprietor becomes insolvent.[7] The Act retains the essentials of the practice under the LRA 1925, with such modifications as were necessary because of the abolition of inhibitions.[8]

Procedure in relation to bankruptcy petitions

13.10   Where a bankruptcy petition is made, it must be registered as a pending action under the LCA 1972.[9] Under the LRA 2002, as soon as is

---

[1]   See Devolution on the Death of a Registered Proprietor, PG6, para 2.2.

[2]   Form AP1, or, if the title is unregistered, Form FR1. The appropriate form will be determined by the nature of the transaction to be registered.

[3]   Thus, for example, if there is a sale of the whole of the registered estate, the application should be on Form TR1. If the application is an assent of the whole to a beneficiary, the application should be on Form AS1, etc.

[4]   LRR 2003, r 162(1).

[5]   Ibid, r 162(2).

[6]   Ibid. LRR 2003, r 162(2) replicates the effect of LRR 1925, r 170(5).

[7]   See generally, Personal Insolvency, PG34.

[8]   Cf LRA 1925, s 61(3), which required the registrar to enter a *bankruptcy inhibition* as soon as possible after the registration of a bankruptcy order under LCA 1972.

[9]   LCA 1972, s 5(1)(b). The requirement that a land charge be entered is imposed by the Insolvency

practicable after the registration of the petition in bankruptcy, the registrar must enter a notice in respect of the pending action in the register in relation to any registered estate or charge which *appears* to him to be affected.[1]

13.11   The bankruptcy notice must be entered in:

(a)   the proprietorship register in relation to a registered estate;[2] and

(b)   the charges register in relation to a registered charge.[3]

It must be in the following form:

'BANKRUPTCY NOTICE entered under section 86(2) of the Land Registration Act 2002 in respect of a pending action, as the title of the [proprietor of the registered estate] *or* [the proprietor of the charge dated… referred to above] appears to be affected by a petition in bankruptcy against [*name of debtor*], presented in the [*name*] Court (Court Reference Number…) (Land Charges Reference Number PA…).'[4]

13.12   The registrar must give notice of the entry to the proprietor of the registered estate or registered charge to which it relates.[5] Unless this notice is cancelled by the registrar in the manner provided for in rules,[6] the notice continues in force until either a restriction is entered in the register or the trustee in bankruptcy is registered as proprietor.[7]

Bankruptcy order

13.13   A similar procedure applies when a bankruptcy order is made. Once again, the bankruptcy order should be registered under the LCA 1972.[8] As

---

Rules 1986, SI 1986/1925. Under LRA 2002, s 86(7), nothing in s 86 requires a person to whom a registrable disposition is made to make any search under LCA 1972. Registration under LCA 1972 cannot affect an estate in registered land.

[1]   LRA 2002, s 86(2). The use of the word 'appears' is deliberate. If the bankrupt has a common name, it can often be difficult to identify the land in question. LRR 2003, r 167(2) provides that where it appears to the registrar that there is doubt as to whether the debtor or bankrupt is the same person as the proprietor of the registered estate or registered charge in relation to which a bankruptcy notice or bankruptcy restriction has been entered, he must as soon as practicable take such action as he considers necessary to resolve the doubt.

[2]   A bankruptcy notice is unusual because it is entered in the proprietorship register of a registered estate: LRR 2003, r 8(e) (see para **14.10**). A notice is normally entered in the *charges* register of a registered estate because it protects an interest that adversely affects the registered estate: see LRR 2003, r 9(a) (see para **14.12**).

[3]   LRR 2003, r 165(1).

[4]   Ibid.

[5]   Ibid, r 165(2).

[6]   The registrar must cancel the notice as soon as practicable where he is satisfied that (a) the bankruptcy order has been annulled, or (b) the bankruptcy petition has been dismissed or withdrawn with the court's permission, or (c) the bankruptcy proceedings do not affect or have ceased to affect the registered estate or registered charge in relation to which the notice was entered: LRR 2003, r 167(1).

[7]   LRA 2002, s 86(3).

[8]   See LCA 1972, s 6(1)(c).

soon as practicable after that happens, the registrar must enter a restriction in relation to any registered estate or charge which appears to him to be affected by the order.[1]

13.14   The bankruptcy restriction must be entered in:

(c)   the proprietorship register in relation to a registered estate; and

(d)   the charges register in relation to a registered charge.[2]

It must be in the following form:

> 'BANKRUPTCY RESTRICTION entered under section 86(4) of the Land Registration Act 2002 in respect of a pending action, as the title of the [proprietor of the registered estate] or [the proprietor of the charge dated … referred to above] appears to be affected by a bankruptcy order made by the [name] Court (Court Reference Number …) against [name of debtor] (Land Charges Reference Number WO ….).
>
> [No disposition of the registered estate] or [No disposition of the charge] is to be registered until the trustee in bankruptcy of the property of the bankrupt is registered as proprietor of the [registered estate] or [charge].'[3]

The registrar must give notice of the entry to the proprietor of the registered estate or registered charge to which it relates.[4] Unless the restriction is cancelled by the registrar in the manner provided for in rules[5], the restriction continues in force until the trustee in bankruptcy is registered as proprietor.[6]

Protection of purchasers

13.15   Neither a petition in bankruptcy nor a bankruptcy order is an interest affecting an estate or charge for the purposes of the LRA 2002.[7] It follows that the effect of such a petition or order is outside the provisions on priority explained above.[8] As mentioned in para **9.13**, the LRA 2002 follows instead the provisions of the IA 1986 in this regard. It provides that where the

---

[1]   LRA 2002, s 86(4).

[2]   LRR 2003, r 166(1).

[3]   Ibid, r 166(1). The terms of that restriction must reflect the limitation under s 284 of the IA 1986 that a disposition by a bankrupt is void unless it is made with the consent of, or is subsequently ratified by, the court: see LRA 2002, s 86(1).

[4]   LRR 2003, r 166(2).

[5]   The registrar must cancel the restriction as soon as practicable where he is satisfied that (a) the bankruptcy order has been annulled, or (b) the bankruptcy petition has been dismissed or withdrawn with the court's permission, or (c) the bankruptcy proceedings do not affect or have ceased to affect the registered estate or registered charge in relation to which the restriction was entered: LRR 2003, r 167(1).

[6]   LRA 2002, s 86(3).

[7]   Ibid, s 86(1).

[8]   See paras **9.2** et seq.

proprietor of a registered estate or charge is adjudged bankrupt, the title of his trustee in bankruptcy is void as against a person to whom a registrable disposition of the estate or charge is made if:

(a)   the disposition is made for valuable consideration;
(b)   the person to whom the disposition is made acts in good faith; and
(c)   at the time of the disposition:
    (i)   no notice or restriction has been entered under s 86 in relation to the registered estate or charge, and
    (ii)   the person to whom the disposition is made has no notice of the bankruptcy petition or the adjudication. [1]

This provision only applies if the relevant registration requirements set out in Sch 2 to the LRA 2002 are met in relation to the disposition.[2]

Registration of trustee in bankruptcy

13.16   It was explained in para **8.6** that, as an exception to the general rule that a disposition by operation of law is a registrable disposition that must be completed by registration, any estate or charge of which the insolvent is the registered proprietor, vests automatically in his trustee in bankruptcy on his appointment or, if there is no such appointment, in the Official Receiver.[3] The trustee in bankruptcy may, however, apply to the registrar to be registered as proprietor.

13.17   A trustee in bankruptcy may apply to be registered as proprietor of a registered estate or charge in two situations, namely where:

(a)   a bankruptcy order has been made against the registered proprietor of an estate or charge; or
(b)   an insolvency administration order has been made in respect of a deceased proprietor;[4]

and in either case, the registered estate or registered charge has vested in the trustee.[5] The application is for the alteration of the register by registering the trustee as proprietor in place of the bankrupt or the deceased proprietor.[6] The

---

1   LRA 2002, s 86(5).
2   Ibid, s 86(6).
3   See ibid, s 27(5)(a); IA 1986, s 306.
4   As defined in IA 1986, s 385(1).
5   LRR 2003, r 168(1).
6   Ibid.

application must be supported by prescribed evidence that proves his title to act.[1]

13.18   Following registration, where the trustee in bankruptcy vacates his office and the Official Receiver or some other person is appointed instead as trustee of the relevant bankrupt's estate, the Official Receiver or other person may apply to be registered in place of the former trustee.[2] Where the Official Receiver or another trustee in bankruptcy is registered as proprietor, the words 'Official Receiver and trustee in bankruptcy of [name]' or 'Trustee in bankruptcy of [name]' must be added to the register, as appropriate.[3]

COMPANIES AND OTHER CORPORATIONS

Introduction

13.19   The LRR 2003 contain provisions which deal with:

(a)   the registration of companies and other corporations as proprietors of a registered estate or charge; and

(b)   corporate insolvency, including the effect of overseas insolvency proceedings.

Registration

13.20   The LRR 2003 make special provision in relation to the registration of:

(a)   companies and limited liability partnerships;[4]

(b)   trustees of, or corporations holding property on, charitable, ecclesiastical or public trusts;[5] and

(c)   other corporations,[6]

as proprietor of a registered estate or charge. In each case, the application for registration must be supported by specified evidence. Those requirements are as follows.

Companies and limited liability partnerships

13.21   In relation to an application for registration by a company registered

---

[1]   For this evidence, see LRR 2003, r 168(2), (3). In the usual case it will consist of the bankruptcy order or insolvency administration order and a certificate signed by the trustee that the registered estate or charge is comprised in the bankrupt's/deceased's estate.

[2]   LRR 2003, r 169.

[3]   Ibid, r 170.

[4]   Ibid, r 181.

[5]   Ibid, r 182.

[6]   Ibid, r 183.

in England and Wales or Scotland under the Companies Acts, the application must state the company's registered number.[1] Where the company is:

(a)   a registered social landlord,[2] the application must also contain or be accompanied by a certificate to that effect;[3] and

(b)   an unregistered housing association[4] and the application relates to grant-aided land,[5] the application must also contain or be accompanied by a certificate to that effect.[6]

Where a limited liability partnership incorporated under the Limited Liability Partnerships Act 2000 applies to be registered as proprietor of a registered estate or of a registered charge, the application must state the limited liability partnership's registered number.[7]

Charitable, ecclesiastical and public trusts

13.22   Where a corporation or body of trustees holding on charitable, ecclesiastical or public trusts applies to be registered as proprietor of a registered estate or registered charge, the application must be accompanied by the document creating the trust, unless the estate or charge is held by or in trust for a non-exempt charity.[8] If the estate or charge is held on trust for:

(a)   a registered social landlord,[9] the application must also contain or be accompanied by a certificate to that effect;[10]

(b)   an unregistered housing association[11] and the application relates to grant-aided land,[12] the application must also contain or be accompanied by a certificate to that effect.[13]

Registration of other corporations

13.23   Where a corporation aggregate, that is not within one of the categories set out in paras **13.21** and **13.22**, applies to be registered as proprietor of a registered estate or charge, the application for registration must be accompanied by evidence of the extent of its powers to hold and dispose

---

[1]   LRR 2003, r 181(1).
[2]   Within the meaning of the Housing Act 1996.
[3]   LRR 2003, r 181(2).
[4]   Within the meaning of the Housing Associations Act 1985.
[5]   As defined in ibid, Sch 1.
[6]   LRR 2003, r 181(3).
[7]   Ibid, r 181(4).
[8]   Ibid, r 182(1), (4).
[9]   Within the meaning of the Housing Act 1996.
[10]   LRR 2003, r 182(2).
[11]   Within the meaning of the Housing Associations Act 1985.
[12]   As defined in ibid, Sch 1.
[13]   LRR 2003, r 182(3).

of land, and, in the case of a registered charge, to lend money on mortgage.[1] That evidence must include the charter, statute, rules, memorandum and articles of association or other documents constituting the corporation, together with such further evidence as the registrar may require.[2] Once again, if the corporation is:

(a)   a registered social landlord,[3] the application must also contain or be accompanied by a certificate to that effect;[4]

(b)   an unregistered housing association[5] and the application relates to grant-aided land,[6] the application must also contain or be accompanied by a certificate to that effect.[7]

Administration and liquidation

13.24 In its two Practice Guides, Corporate Insolvency,[8] and Administration and Receivership,[9] the Land Registry has provided detailed guidance on the land registration aspects of dealings with registered land by, respectively, liquidators of companies registered under the Companies Acts and administrators and administrative receivers.[10] What follows is merely a summary of some of the main principles and reference should be made to the relevant Practice Guides for greater detail, particularly in relation to dispositions of property by a liquidator or an administrator, which are not considered here.

13.25 There is no automatic procedure under LRA 2002 or LRR 2003 for making entries in the register of title of a company which is either in liquidation,[11] or is the subject of an administration order.[12] Entries will only be made on the application of the company's liquidator, or administrator (using Form AP1).

13.26 First, where a company which is the proprietor of a registered estate or registered charge is the subject of an administration order under IA 1986, the registrar must, upon the application of the company's administrator, supported by the order, make an entry in the individual register of the relevant

---

[1] LRR 2003, r 183(1).
[2] Ibid, r 183(2).
[3] Within the meaning of the Housing Act 1996.
[4] LRR 2003, r 183(3).
[5] Within the meaning of the Housing Associations Act 1985.
[6] As defined in ibid, Sch 1.
[7] LRR 2003, r 183(4).
[8] PG35.
[9] PG36.
[10] Administration and Receivership, PG36, also deals with receivers appointed under LPA 1925, which are not considered here.
[11] See Corporate Insolvency, PG35, para 4.1.
[12] See Administration and Receivership, PG36, para 4.

registered title as to the making of the order and the appointment of the administrator.[1] Unless the appointment of the administrator is noted, the order appointing the administrator must be supplied on the occasion of each disposition of the company's property by the administrator.[2]

13.27   Secondly, where a company which is the proprietor of a registered estate or registered charge is in liquidation, the registrar must, upon the application of the company's liquidator, make an entry in the individual register of the relevant registered title as to the appointment of the liquidator.[3] The application must be supported by the order, appointment by the Secretary of State or resolution under which the liquidator was appointed and such other evidence as the registrar may require.[4] That 'other evidence' that the registrar will require depends upon the form of the liquidation.[5]

13.28   In the case of a members' voluntary winding up, the Registry requires:[6]

(a)   a certificate, by the secretary of the company or by the liquidator or by a conveyancer acting for the company or the liquidator, that a statutory declaration of solvency complying with the requirements of IA 1986, s 89, has been filed with the Registrar of Companies; and

(b)   a certified copy of the resolution passed by the general meeting of the company appointing the liquidators.[7]

13.29   In the case of a creditors' voluntary winding up, what the Registry requires is:[8]

(a)   a certified copy of the resolution passed at the company's general meeting resolving that the company be wound up and appointing the liquidator; and either

  (i)   a certified copy of the resolution passed at the creditors' meeting appointing the liquidator; or

  (ii)   a certificate by the liquidator appointed at the company's general meeting, or by his or her conveyancer, that a meeting of the

---

[1]   LRR 2003, r 184(1), (2). For the entry that is made in the register, see Administration and Receivership, PG36, para 4.3.

[2]   See Administration and Receivership, PG36, para 4.4.

[3]   LRR 2003, r 184(3), (4).

[4]   Ibid, r 184(5).

[5]   See Corporate Insolvency, PG35, para 3. Where copy documents, as of court orders, are sent in place of the original, they will have to be certified as true copies by the liquidator or his conveyancer: see LRR 2003, r 214(1). Copies of resolutions passed at company's meetings may be certified by the company secretary or by its conveyancer. See generally, para **20.25**.

[6]   See Corporate Insolvency, PG35, para 3.3.

[7]   Under IA 1986, s 91(1).

[8]   See Corporate Insolvency, PG35, para 3.4.

creditors was duly held in accordance with IA 1986, s 98(1), and that the creditors' meeting either confirmed the appointment of the liquidator by the company's meeting or did not pass a resolution nominating a liquidator.

13.30   In the case of liquidation by order of the court, the Registry requires in all cases a certified copy of the order of the court.[1] No further evidence is required if the Official Receiver is the liquidator. In all other cases, the Registry requires the following evidence:[2]

(a)   a certified copy of the resolution passed at the creditors' meeting appointing the liquidator;

(b)   a certified copy of the resolution passed at the contributories' meeting appointing the liquidator and a certificate by the liquidator, or by his conveyancer, that a meeting of the creditors was duly held and that the creditors' meeting either confirmed the appointment of the liquidator or did not pass a resolution nominating a liquidator; and

(c)   either:

    (i)   a certified copy of the order of the court appointing the liquidator; or

    (ii)   a certified copy of the appointment of the liquidator by the Secretary of State.

13.31   The type of liquidation will also be reflected in the entry that the registrar makes in the register.[3] The registrar will record the name of the liquidator, and the date and manner of his appointment either:

(a)   in the proprietorship register where the company is the proprietor of a registered estate;

(b)   in the charges register where the company is the proprietor of a registered charge.

Thus, for example, in the case of liquidation by order of the court, the entry might be as follows:

'(Date) By an Order of the court dated 1 April 2004 Arthur Smith of 54, Lincoln Crescent, Newtown, Stoneshire, SS44 6DJ has been appointed the liquidator of Scuppered PLC.'

A restriction will also be entered in the proprietorship register, usually in the following terms:

---

[1]   Corporate Insolvency, PG35, para 3.5.
[2]   Ibid.
[3]   For what follows, see ibid, paras 4.2, 4.3.

'(Date) RESTRICTION: No disposition by the proprietor of the registered estate other than a transfer on sale is to be registered unless made pursuant to powers granted by the Insolvency Act 1986.'[1]

In the case where the court orders the winding up of the company, the Land Registry will enter any restriction that is necessary to reflect the provisions of such order.[2]

13.32   Once appointed, a liquidator has wide powers of disposition under IA 1986, Sch 4. For that reason the Land Registry is 'unlikely to raise any question in the case of a disposition, such as a transfer on sale, which is apparently made for the purpose of realising the company's assets'.[3] Under IA 1986, Sch 4, para 7, a liquidator has power to execute all deeds and other documents in the name and on behalf of the company. He may, therefore, execute the transfer (a deed) either by signing the name of the company in the presence of at least one witness,[4] or by affixing the company seal and signing the document to attest that the seal has been affixed in his presence.

13.33   On the dissolution of a company, any property of the company that has not been disposed of by the liquidator and is not held in trust passes to the Crown, Duchy of Lancaster or Duchy of Cornwall as *bona vacantia*.[5] There is a danger that, where a company has been dissolved, there might be a purported disposition of its property unless the fact of dissolution is recorded in the register.[6] LRR 2003, r 185, accordingly provides that where a corporation shown in an individual register as the proprietor of the registered estate or of a registered charge has been dissolved, the registrar may enter a note of that fact in the proprietorship register or in the charges register, as appropriate. The Crown (or relevant Duchy) may apply to be registered as the

---

[1]   Where the company was the proprietor of a registered charge, the restriction would be in the following form: '(Date) RESTRICTION: No disposition by the proprietor of the Charge dated 8 December 2000 in favour of Scuppered PLC referred to above is to be registered other than a discharge, a transfer of charge for value or a transfer in exercise of the power of sale, unless made pursuant to the powers granted by the Insolvency Act 1986.'

[2]   Application must be on Form AP1, which must be submitted together with a certified copy of the court order. For the court's power to order the entry of a restriction, see LRA 2002, s 46; above, para **10.80**.

[3]   Corporate Insolvency, PG35, para 5.1.

[4]   LPA 1925, s 74(3).

[5]   Companies Act 1985, s 654.

[6]   This is especially the case having regard to the circumstances in which a company may be dissolved. Thus, the registrar of companies may strike off a company from the register of companies because he has reasonable cause to believe that it is not carrying on business or in operation: Companies Act 1985, s 652. If the company no longer exists it cannot exercise owner's powers under LRA 2002, ss 23, 24 (paras **7.2–7.5**). Although any disponee may be registered as proprietor and the circumstances are such that the register will not be rectified against him, the registrar is at risk of a claim for indemnity by the Crown or Royal Duchy because the registration of the disponee was a mistake and it thereby suffers loss: see LRA 2002, Sch 8, para 1.

proprietor of the land of a dissolved company. The evidence required upon such an application will depend upon how the company was dissolved.[1]

The effect of overseas insolvency proceedings

13.34   Brief mention may be made of the effect of the liquidation of a foreign corporation and of certain overseas insolvency proceedings.

13.35   First, where there has been a disposition by or on behalf of a foreign corporation that has been liquidated under the law of its company of incorporation, application should be made on Form AP1, together with evidence that establishes its liquidation and the effect of that liquidation.[2]

13.36   Secondly, where a foreign company has been carrying on business in Great Britain, it may be wound up as an unregistered company under IA 1986, s 225, even though it may already have been dissolved, or otherwise ceased to exist under the law of its country of incorporation. That winding up can be proved to the Land Registry by means of a certified copy of the court order in the usual way.

13.37   Thirdly, there is a power to apply for a note of a judgment opening insolvency proceedings under Council Regulation (EC) No 1346/2000 on Insolvency Proceedings.[3] If the registrar is satisfied that the judgment opening insolvency proceedings has been made, he may enter a note of the judgment in the register.[4]

CHARITIES

13.38   The LRR 2003 contain rules that are intended to ensure that dispositions to or by charities comply with the provisions of the Charities Act 1993.[5]

13.39   First, as regards dispositions in favour of a charity, the Charities Act 1993 requires the following instruments to contain specified statements, namely, any conveyance, transfer, lease or other instrument effecting a disposition of land to be held by or in trust for a charity, where that

---

[1]   For further details, see Corporate Insolvency, PG35, para 7.2.

[2]   See ibid, para 8.1.

[3]   LRR 2003, r 171(1). Under Art 3(1) of the Regulation, 'The courts of the Member State within the territory of which the centre of a debtor's main interests is situated shall have jurisdiction to open insolvency proceedings. In the case of a company or legal person, the place of the registered office shall be presumed to be the centre of its main interests in the absence of proof to the contrary.' The person who may apply for such a note under Art 22, is the liquidator, or 'any authority empowered to that effect in the Member State where the proceedings referred to in Article 3(1)'.

[4]   LRR 2003, r 171(3).

[5]   See the Land Registry's Practice Guide, Charities, PG14, for detailed treatment of the requirements.

disposition is either a registrable disposition or triggers the requirement of registration.[1] LRR 2003, r 179, lays down the form of the statements that must be made. It will be clear from that statement whether the charity is an exempt or a non-exempt charity.[2] Where there is a disposition in favour of a non-exempt charity, the application for registration must be accompanied by an application for entry of the appropriate restriction.[3] The appropriate restriction is a restriction in Form E of Sch 4 to the LRR 2003.[4] Where, as a result of executing a legal mortgage, unregistered land owned by a charity becomes subject to the requirement of registration, the registrar must enter a restriction in Form E when registering the title.[5]

13.40 Secondly, as regards dispositions by charities, the Charities Act 1993 requires the following instruments to contain specified statements:

(a) any conveyance, transfer, lease or other instrument effecting a disposition of land held by or in trust for a charity, where that disposition is either a registrable disposition or triggers the requirement of registration;[6]

(b) any mortgage of land held by or in trust for a charity;[7] and

(c) any such mortgage of unregistered land that triggers the requirement of registration.[8]

Thirdly, LRR 2003, r 180, lays down the form of the statements that must be made in each of the above.

13.41 Fourthly, the LRR 2003 also make provision for:

(a) the requirements that must be met where there is a registrable disposition in favour of charity trustees incorporated under Part VII of the Charities Act 1993;[9] and

(b) the registration of the official custodian as proprietor of a registered estate or charge.[10]

---

[1]   See Charities Act 1993, s 37(5).

[2]   For exempt charities, see ibid, Sch 2.

[3]   LRR 2003, r 176(2).

[4]   Ibid, r 176(4). The restriction is as follows: 'No disposition by the proprietor of the registered estate to which section 36 or section 38 of the Charities Act 1993 applies is to be registered unless the instrument contains a certificate complying with section 37(2) or section 39(2) of that Act as appropriate.'

[5]   See Charities Act 1993, s 39(1B); LRR 2003, r 176(1).

[6]   See Charities Act 1993, s 37(1), (7).

[7]   Ibid, s 39(1).

[8]   Ibid, s 39(1A).

[9]   LRR 2003, r 177.

[10]   Ibid, r 178.

SETTLEMENTS

13.42   The LRA 1925 contained detailed provisions on the treatment of settled land where the title was registered.[1] However, it ceased to be possible to create new settlements after 1996.[2] The LRA 2002 therefore leaves the application of the principles of registered land to settlements to rules.[3] Those rules are set out in Sch 7 to the LRR 2003.[4]

13.43   It is unnecessary to examine these rules in any detail because it will not often be necessary to consider them in practice. It is sufficient to note that the rules make provision for the following matters:

(a)   the registration of the life tenant or statutory owner as registered proprietor;[5]

(b)   the entry of a restriction in Form G, H or I[6] on the first registration of an unregistered legal estate which is settled land;[7]

(c)   the standard forms of restriction (G, H and I) that are applicable to settled land;[8]

(d)   the transfer of land into settlement and the form of transfer;[9]

(e)   where registered land is settled and the existing registered proprietor is the tenant for life under that settlement;[10]

(f)   where registered land is bought with capital money following a disposition of part of the settled land;[11]

(g)   the duty to apply for restrictions when registered land is settled;[12]

(h)   where the proprietor ceases to be the tenant for life in his lifetime;[13]

(i)   where the tenant for life or statutory owner become entitled to have the settled land vested in him;[14]

(j)   the registration of a statutory owner during a minority otherwise than on death;[15]

(k)   the registration of special personal representatives;[16]

---

[1]   See LRA 1925, ss 86–90.

[2]   TLATA 1996, s 2.

[3]   LRA 2002, s 89.

[4]   LRR 2003, r 186.

[5]   Ibid, Sch 7, para 1.

[6]   For these forms of restriction, see ibid, Sch 4.

[7]   Ibid, Sch 7, para 2.

[8]   Ibid, Sch 7, para 3.

[9]   Ibid, Sch 7, para 4.

[10]   Ibid, Sch 7, para 5. See para **20.15**.

[11]   Ibid, Sch 7, para 6. See para **20.15**.

[12]   Ibid, Sch 7, para 7. This provision is, presumably, intended to apply in two situations, namely, (i) where registered land had been settled prior to 1997, but where appropriate restrictions were not entered in the register, and (ii) in those very rare cases in which a new settlement can be created under TLATA 1996, s 2(2).

[13]   Ibid, Sch 7, para 8.

[14]   Ibid, Sch 7, para 9.

[15]   Ibid, Sch 7, para 10.

[16]   Ibid, Sch 7, para 11.

(l)   the transfer of land that remains settled following the death of the tenant for life;[1]

(m)   the position where a settlement arose under a will or intestacy of a person who died before 1997 because a minor became beneficially entitled to a legal estate in registered land;[2]

(n)   the discharge of registered land from beneficial interests and powers under the settlement by the trustees of the settlement;[3] and

(o)   the discharge from liability of the personal representatives of a deceased proprietor in respect of beneficial interests and powers under a settlement.[4]

---

[1]   LRR 2003, Sch 7, para 12.
[2]   Ibid, Sch 7, para 13.
[3]   Ibid, Sch 7, para 14.
[4]   Ibid, Sch 7, para 15.

PART 3

REGISTRATION AND THE REGISTER

THE MAIN CHANGES AT A GLANCE

Most of the provisions relating to registration and the register are contained in Part 6 of the LRA 2002.[1] The provisions of the Act governing the alteration of the register and the payment of indemnity are to be found respectively in Schs 4 and 8 to the Act.[2]

The main changes made by the LRA 2002 are as follows.

—   The concept of the open register in relation both to access to the register and to reliance upon the register is extended.
—   The registrar is given power to record certain defects in title on the register.
—   Although the Act contains a rule-making power to make provision for land certificates, that power has not been exercised and land certificates have, in practice, been abolished.
—   Charge certificates are abolished.
—   The concept of alteration of the register is introduced. Rectification is one specific form of alteration.
—   New provisions are made for alterations to the register of cautions.
—   A mortgagee in possession is classified as a proprietor in possession for the purposes of the provisions on rectification.

The registrar is given power to pay a party's costs in relation to any alteration of the register that does not amount to rectification.

---

1   See (2001) Law Com No 271, Part IX.
2   Ibid, Part X.

CHAPTER 14

THE REGISTER OF TITLE AND INDICES

REGISTER OF TITLE

Introduction

14.1   Section 1(1) of the LRA 2002 provides that there shall continue to be a register of title kept by the registrar.[1] The manner in which the register is kept is a matter for rules (so that the Act does not require the register to be kept in any particular form[2]). Such rules may, in particular, make provision about the information to be included in the register, the form in which such information is to be kept and its arrangement.[3] Searches of the register are considered in Chapter 18. The register of title is not the only register: as has been explained in paras **5.2–5.3**.

The form and arrangement of the register of title

14.2   The register of title may be kept in either electronic or paper form, or partly in one form and partly in the other.[4] It is the intention of HM Land Registry that, in time, the register and all the documents referred to in it, should be kept in dematerialised form. As a general rule, and subject to the qualifications explained in para **14.3**, the register of title must include an individual register for each registered estate, vested in a registered proprietor, which is:

(a)   an estate in land (in other words a freehold or leasehold estate); or

(b)   a rentcharge, a franchise, a manor, or a *profit à prendre* in gross.[5]

This takes account of the fact that both a franchise and a *profit à prendre* in gross may be registered with their own titles for the first time.[6]

14.3   Rule 3 of the LRR 2003 is permissive in character and it gives the registrar considerable flexibility as to how he registers the title to land both initially and in the light of subsequent events.[7]

---

[1]   Cf LRA 1925, s 1(1).
[2]   Ibid, s 1(2).
[3]   LRA 2002, s 1(2).
[4]   LRR 2003, r 2(1).
[5]   Ibid, r 2(2).
[6]   See LRA 2002, s 3(1); see also paras **2.5**, **2.6**.
[7]   Cf LRR 1925, rr 17, 18, which had similar effect.

(a)   He may include more than one registered estate in an individual register if the estates are of the same kind and are vested in the same proprietor.[1] He will presumably do this (as he did under LRR 1925) to save expense and to facilitate future transactions.[2]

(b)   On first registration of a registered estate, he may open an individual register for each separate area of land affected by the proprietor's registered estate as he designates.[3] He can therefore decide to register a large parcel of land under a number of different titles.[4]

(c)   He may subsequently open an individual register for part of the registered estate and retain the existing individual register for the remainder in three circumstances.[5] The first is on the application of the proprietor of the registered estate and of any registered charge over it.[6] The second is if he considers that it is desirable for keeping the register of title. The third is on the registration of a charge of part of the registered estate comprised in the registered title.

(d)   He may amalgamate two or more registered titles, or add an estate which is being registered for the first time to an existing registered title, if the registered estates are of the same kind and are vested in the same proprietor on the application of the proprietor of the registered estate and of any registered charge over it, or if he considers that it is desirable for keeping the register of title.[7] This is a common situation in practice, as where a registered proprietor purchases a parcel of land from his neighbour and wishes to incorporate the new land in his title.

(e)   Where he has exercised his power under (c) or (d) above, he must notify the proprietor of the registered estate and of any registered charge, unless they have agreed to his action (as where they have applied to him to exercise his powers).[8] He may also make a new edition of any individual register or make entries in any individual register to reflect the fact that it has either been divided or amalgamated.[9]

---

[1]   LRR 2003, r 3(1).

[2]   Cf LRR 1925, r 18.

[3]   LRR 2003, r 3(2).

[4]   Some practitioners have a propensity for seeking to register very large parcels of land under one title. This can cause considerable practical difficulties, not least because of the size of the plans. It is to be hoped that registrars will not be inhibited from exercising the power conferred by r 3(2).

[5]   LRR 2003, r 3(3).

[6]   The wording of the rule suggests that both the proprietor of the registered estate *and* the proprietor of any registered charge must join in the application.

[7]   LRR 2003, r 3(4).

[8]   Ibid, r 3(5)(a).

[9]   Ibid, r 3(5)(b).

The arrangement of individual registers

Introduction

14.4   Each individual register must have its own title number,[1] although the registrar may change that number.[2] The register must consist of:

(a)   a property register;
(b)   a proprietorship register;
(c)   where necessary, a charges register.[3]

An entry in an individual register may be made by reference to a plan or to some other document. In either case, the registrar must keep the original or a copy of the document.[4] The registrar may make a new edition of any individual register so that it contains only the subsisting entries. He may also rearrange the entries in the register.[5] Given the intention of the LRA 2002 to create a conclusive register,[6] these 'housekeeping' functions of the registrar will assume a much greater importance for the future.

The property register

14.5   Rule 5 of the LRR 2003 sets out the matters that the property register must contain. These are similar to those that were required under the LRR 1925.[7] First, there must be a description of the registered estate. In the case of each of the following registered estates, namely:

(a)   a registered estate in land (in other words, a freehold or a leasehold estate);
(b)   a rentcharge; or
(c)   an affecting franchise;[8]

that description must refer to a plan based on the Ordnance Survey map. That plan is known as 'the title plan'.[9]

14.6   The property register should also include details of the following where it is appropriate:[10]

1   LRR 2003, r 4(1). The title number may consist of a number or a series of letters and numbers.
2   Ibid, r 4(4).
3   Ibid, r 4(2). This replicates LRR 1925, r 2.
4   Ibid, r 4(3). In practice copies will, in future, be kept in dematerialised form.
5   Ibid, r 4(4).
6   See para **1.7**.
7   See LRR 1925, r 3.
8   An affecting franchise 'relates to a defined area and is an adverse right affecting, or capable of affecting, the title to an estate or charge': LRR 2003, r 217(1); see para **2.26**(a).
9   LRR 2003, rr 5(a), 217(1).
10   Ibid, r 5(b).

(a)   The fact that mines and minerals were expressly included or excluded on first registration under r 32 of LRR 2003.[1]

(b)   Easements, rights, privileges, conditions and covenants benefiting the registered estate and other similar matters. This is self-explanatory and is a very common form of entry.

(c)   All exceptions arising on the enfranchisement of land that was formerly copyhold.[2] These rights may be rights to mines and minerals that were excepted under one of the Copyhold Acts,[3] or rights saved to the lord of the manor under Sch 12 to the LPA 1922.[4]

(d)   Any other matter required to be entered in any other part of the register which the registrar considers may more conveniently be entered in the property register. For example, it sometimes happens that the register of title refers to a specific document of title for more than one reason, as where a conveyance both conferred the benefit of a restrictive covenant on the property but at the same time subjected it to the burden of similar covenants. The registrar could set out all the relevant parts of that document in the property register if he considered that to be the most convenient course.

14.7   There are a number of provisions in the LRR 2003, which require that an entry should be made in the property register, and these must also be included.[5] These entries are as follows:[6]

(a)   Where on first registration the registrar is not satisfied that a claimed appurtenant right subsists as a legal interest, but he nonetheless enters details of the right claimed with such qualifications as he considers appropriate.[7]

(b)   On first registration, the entry of an agreement that prevents the acquisition of rights of light or air for the benefit of the registered estate.[8]

(c)   Where there is a transfer or charge of part of a registered estate, an entry referring to the removal of the estate comprised in the transfer or charge.[9]

(d)   Where the proprietor of a registered estate claims the benefit of a legal easement or *profit à prendre*, whether under an express grant, by implied

[1]   See para **2.33**. This will not often be the case.
[2]   Although there was no express equivalent to this provision in LRR 1925, it was the practice of the Registry to enter a qualifying note in the property register in relation to such rights.
[3]   Namely, Copyhold Act 1852, s 48, and Copyhold Act 1894, s 23.
[4]   For a summary of those rights, see Harpum, *Megarry & Wade's Law of Real Property* (Sweet & Maxwell, 6th edn, 2000), para 2-054.
[5]   LRR 2003, r 5(c).
[6]   Ibid, r 173(1).
[7]   Ibid, r 33(2); para **2.34**.
[8]   Ibid, r 36; para **2.41**.
[9]   Ibid, r 72(1)(a); para **8.37**.

grant or by prescription,[1] but where the registrar is not satisfied that the right claimed subsists as a legal estate appurtenant to the applicant's registered estate, he may enter details of the right claimed with such qualification as he considers appropriate.[2]

(e)   Where it appears to the registrar that there is an agreement that prevents the acquisition of rights of light or air for the benefit of the registered estate, an entry of that fact.[3]

(f)   An entry in respect of an agreement about accretion or diluvion.[4]

(g)   An entry that a right to determine a registered estate is exercisable.[5]

(h)   An entry to record that a registered freehold estate has determined and has therefore escheated to the Crown.[6]

14.8   It is very common for leases to contain some limitation on the lessee's power to assign the lease, sub-let or part with the possession of the land demised by the lease. Typically, the landlord's consent will be required to such a disposition.[7] Given the concept of owner's powers,[8] it might be expected that such a provision would be protected by the entry of a restriction.[9] However, this has never been the practice of the Land Registry because it would be very difficult for the registrar to decide the legal and factual issues that can be thrown up by such provisions, such as, for example, whether the landlord has unreasonably withheld his consent so that the lessee can lawfully make the disposition in any event.[10] Under the LRR 2003, if the lease contains a provision that prohibits or restricts dispositions of the leasehold estate, the registrar must make an entry in the property register stating that all estates, rights, interests, powers and remedies arising by or by reason of a disposition made in breach of that prohibition or restriction are excepted from the effect of registration.[11] In that way, the landlord's rights will be protected.[12]

14.9   The property register of the following registered legal estates must contain sufficient particulars of that estate to enable it to be identified:

---

1   See LRR 2003, rr 73, 74.
2   Ibid, r 75; see also para **8.47**.
3   Ibid, r 76.
4   LRA 2002, s 61(2); LRR 2003, r 123(2); para **16.11**.
5   LRA 2002, s 64; LRR 2003, r 125(1); para **17.4**.
6   LRA 2002, s 82(2); LRR 2003, r 173(1); see also para **13.5**.
7   Such consent cannot be unreasonably withheld: see Landlord and Tenant Act 1927, s 19(1).
8   See LRA 2002, s 23; see also para **7.3**.
9   Cf ibid, s 40; see also para **10.50**.
10   See *Treloar v Bigge* (1874) LR 9 Ex 151.
11   LRR 2003, r 6(2).
12   Cf LRA 2002, s 29(2)(a)(ii); see also para **9.8**.

(a)	a registered leasehold estate;[1]
(b)	a rentcharge;
(c)	a franchise; and
(d)	a *profit à prendre* in gross.[2]

The proprietorship register

14.10	The proprietorship register must contain, where appropriate, the following matters:[3]

(a)	the class of title of the property;
(b)	the name of the proprietor of the registered estate;[4]
(c)	an address for service of the proprietor of the registered estate in accordance with r 198;[5]
(d)	restrictions,[6] including any bankruptcy restriction, in relation to a registered estate (but *not* in relation to a registered charge: see para **14.12**(f));[7]
(e)	a bankruptcy notice in relation to a registered estate (but *not* in relation to a registered charge: see para **14.12**(g));[8]
(f)	positive covenants by a transferor or transferee and indemnity covenants by a transferee;[9]
(g)	details of any modification of certain implied indemnity covenants on transfers of pre-1996 leases;[10]
(h)	details of any modification of the covenants implied under the LP(MP)A 1994;[11]
(i)	where the class of title is possessory, the name of the first proprietor of the registered estate;[12]
(j)	such other matters as are required to be entered in the proprietorship register by the LRR 2003: these are listed in para **14.11**.

14.11	The other matters that are required by the LRR 2003 to be entered in the proprietorship register are as follows:

---

[1]	LRR 2003, r 6(1).
[2]	Ibid, r 7.
[3]	Ibid, r 8(1).
[4]	Where the proprietor is a company registered under the Companies Acts, or a limited liability partnership incorporated under the Limited Liability Partnerships Act 2000, its registered number must also be given.
[5]	See para **20.42**.
[6]	See LRA 2002, s 40, and see Chapter 10.
[7]	See LRA 2002, s 86(4); LRR 2003, r 166; see also para **13.14**.
[8]	See LRA 2002, s 86(2); LRR 2003, r 165; see also para **13.11**.
[9]	See LRR 2003, rr 64, 65; para **25.4**.
[10]	See LRA 2002, Sch 12, paras 20(2), (3); LRR 2003, r 66; para **25.6**.
[11]	See LRR 2003, r 67(6); para **25.3**.
[12]	Where the proprietor is a company registered under the Companies Acts, or a limited liability partnership incorporated under the Limited Liability Partnerships Act 2000, its registered number must also be given.

(a) The price paid or value declared.[1] On first registration and on any subsequent change of proprietor, the registrar is required, wherever practicable, to enter the price paid or value declared in the proprietorship register. The entry remains in the register until there is a change in the proprietor, or some other change occurs in the register of title which the registrar considers would make the entry misleading. Although the entry of the price paid was for a long time contentious, it has now been established.

(b) Where a corporation which is registered as the proprietor of a registered estate or of a registered charge has been dissolved, the registrar is empowered to enter a note of that fact, either in the proprietorship register, or in the charges register, as is appropriate.[2]

(c) A person who can satisfy the registrar that he has an interest in a registered estate in land or in a registered rentcharge, that would be prejudiced if a squatter were registered as proprietor, may apply to be registered as a person who is to be notified.[3] The registrar must then enter that person's name in the proprietorship register as a person entitled to be notified.[4]

The charges register

14.12 The charges register must contain, where appropriate, the following matters:[5]

(a) details of leases, charges, and any other interests which adversely affect the registered estate, whether these were subsisting at the time of first registration of the estate or were created subsequently;

(b) any dealings with, or which affect the priority of, the interests referred to in (a), which are capable of being noted in the register;

(c) sufficient details to enable any registered charge to be identified;

(d) the name of the proprietor of any registered charge;[6]

(e) an address for service of the proprietor of any registered charge in accordance with r 198;[7]

(f) restrictions,[8] including any bankruptcy restriction, in relation to a registered charge;[9]

---

[1] LRR 2003, r 8(2).
[2] Ibid, r 185.
[3] Under LRA 2002, Sch 6, para 2(1)(e), LRR 2003, r 194(1); see also para **30.22**.
[4] LRR 2003, r 194(3).
[5] Ibid, r 9.
[6] Where the proprietor is a company registered under the Companies Acts, or a limited liability partnership incorporated under the Limited Liability Partnerships Act 2000, its registered number must also be given.
[7] See paras **20.42–20.43**.
[8] See LRA 2002, s 40.
[9] See LRA 2002, s 86(4); LRR 2003, r 166; see also para **13.14**.

(g)   a bankruptcy notice in relation to a registered charge;[1]

(h)   such other matters as are required to be entered in the charges register by the LRR 2003. There are in fact very few such other matters,[2] although the situation where a corporation, which has been dissolved, has already been mentioned: see para **14.12**(b). The registrar may note the fact of dissolution either in the proprietorship or the charges register.

INDICES

Introduction

14.13   Under the LRR 2003, there are three indices:

(a)   the index to be kept under s 68 of the LRA 2002;

(b)   the index of proprietors' names; and

(c)   the day list.

The nature of each of these is explained below.

The index

Introduction

14.14   Under the LRR 1925,[3] the registrar was required to keep an index map from which it was possible to ascertain whether any parcel of land was or was not registered, and its title number if it was. The index map was widely used and was of considerable practical importance. The importance of having a mechanism for ascertaining whether land is registered or not, is recognised in the LRA 2002. The index (as it is now called) finds its place in s 68 of the Act, and no longer merely in rules. Under that section, the registrar must keep an index for the purpose of enabling the following matters to be ascertained in relation to any parcel of land, whether registered or unregistered, in England and Wales:

–   whether any registered estate relates to the land;

–   how any such registered estate is identified for the purposes of the register;

–   whether the land is affected by any caution against first registration and, if so, what that caution is; and

–   such other matters as rules may provide.[4]

---

[1]   See LRA 2002, s 86(2); LRR 2003, r 165; see also paras **13.10–13.11**.

[2]   All the cases specifically mentioned in the rules appear to fall in the situations listed above.

[3]   See r 8.

[4]   LRA 2002, s 68(1). Rules may, in particular, make provision as to those matters set out in s 68(2).

14.15   It is provided that rules may be made as to how the index is to be kept, the information to be included in it, the form in which such information is to be kept and the arrangement of that information.[1] The effect of these rules is explained in paras **14.16–14.18**. There is also a power to make rules about official searches of the index.[2] For convenience, these rules are considered in para **14.19** rather than in Chapter 18 (Accessing Information).

The contents of the index

14.16   By r 10 of the LRR 2003, the index to be kept under s 68 of the LRA 2002 comprises two parts, namely an index map (which is similar to that kept under the LRR 1925) and a new index, called the index of verbal descriptions. The latter is much more limited than its title might suggest. It is concerned with the esoteric subject of relating franchises and manors, and is referred to elsewhere in the LRR 2003 (and in this book) as the 'index of relating franchises and manors'.[3] A 'relating franchise' is defined negatively as any franchise other than an 'affecting franchise'.[4] An 'affecting franchise' is one which 'relates to a defined area and is an adverse right affecting, or capable of affecting, the title to an estate or charge'.[5] Under the LRA 2003, franchises became registrable with their own titles for the first time.[6] It has been explained in para **2.26**(a), that some franchises do *not* create an incumbrance on the land to which they relate and these franchises – relating franchises – are differentiated in the LRR 2003 from affecting franchises that *are* an incumbrance on specific land. The lordship of a manor is a wholly incorporeal right, and like a relating franchise, is not, therefore, an incumbrance on land. It would be inappropriate to index relating franchises and manors by reference to the index map (with the implication that the estate encumbered specific parcels of land)[7] and it was necessary to create a mechanism for indexing such rights in some other way, hence the index of relating franchises and manors.[8] The information that is required by the rules to be shown in the index (that is in both the index map and the index of relating franchises and manors) must be entered by the registrar in the index as soon as practicable.[9]

14.17   The index map is held in part in electronic map format and all new registered titles are added to the electronic index map. The old paper index

---

[1]   LRA 2002, s 68(2)(a).

[2]   Ibid, s 68(2)(b).

[3]   See LRR 2003, r 146. See also the Land Registry Practice Guide, Franchises, PG18.

[4]   Ibid, r 217(1).

[5]   Ibid; see also para **2.26**(a).

[6]   LRA 2002, s 3(1)(c); see also paras **2.5**, **2.6**.

[7]   Manors were in fact so indexed under LRR 1925 and this sometimes gave rise 'to confusion and unnecessary concern': see Land Registry *Land Registration Rules 2003 – A Land Registry Consultation* (2002), p 91.

[8]   For the obligation imposed on the registrar to create the index of relating franchises and manors from the material parts of the index map, see TPO1 2003, art 21.

[9]   LRR 2003, r 10(2).

map is gradually being converted into electronic form.[1] It must be possible from the index map to ascertain in relation to any parcel of land, whether there is:

(i)   a pending application for first registration (other than of title to a relating franchise);
(ii)   a pending application for a caution against first registration (other than where the subject of the caution is a relating franchise);
(iii)   a registered estate in land;
(iv)   a registered rentcharge;
(v)   a registered *profit à prendre* in gross;
(vi)   a registered affecting franchise; or
(vii)   a caution against first registration (other than where the subject of the caution is a relating franchise).[2]

If there is such a registered estate or caution, the index map should also provide the title number.[3] The index map also includes information as to postal addresses.

14.18   The index of relating franchises and manors must contain a verbal description of the specified registered estates and cautions, together with their title numbers, arranged by administrative area.[4] The specified registered estates and cautions in question are:

(i)   pending applications for first registration of title to relating franchises;
(ii)   pending applications for cautions against first registration where the subject of the caution is a relating franchise;
(iii)   registered franchises which are relating franchises;
(iv)   registered manors; and
(v)   cautions against first registration where the subject of the caution is a relating franchise.

Searches of the index

14.19   Any person may apply for an official search of the index map or of the index of relating franchises.[5] The application must be made on Forms SIM and SIF respectively.[6] Where there is an application for an official search of the index map, the registrar may require the applicant to provide a copy of an

---

1   For more details about the index map, including its specification, see the Land Registry Practice Guide, Land Registry Plans, PG40, at Part 4.
2   LRR 2003, r 10(1)(a).
3   Ibid.
4   Ibid, r 10(1)(b). For the administrative areas, see the Land Registration (Proper Office) Order 2003.
5   Ibid, rr 145(1), 146(1).
6   Ibid, rr 145(2), 146(2). In each case, there is power under LRR 2003, r 132 and Sch 2, for the registrar to issue a notice which would allow for delivery of such applications by electronic means.

extract from the Ordnance Survey map on the largest scale published, showing the land to which the application relates.[1] A paper certificate of search will be issued in each case.[2] In the case of an index map search, the certificate will state whether there are any one or more of the matters set out in para **14.17** in relation to the land searched.[3] In the case of a search of the index of relating franchises, the certificate will state whether there are any one or more of the matters set out in para **14.18** in relation to the land searched.[4]

The index of proprietors' names

14.20   The index of proprietors' names is not new: it existed under the LRR 1925.[5] The registrar is required to keep an index of proprietors' names. This shows:

(a)   the name of the registered proprietor for each individual register;
(b)   the name of the proprietor of any registered charge; and
(c)   the title number.[6]

14.21   A search may be made of the index of proprietors' names, using Form PN1, but there are substantial restrictions on who may make such a search.[7] A person is entitled to apply for a search in respect of:

(a)   his own name; or
(b)   the name of some person in whose property he can satisfy the registrar that he is generally interested, as where he is that person's trustee in bankruptcy or personal representative.[8] A search of the index of proprietors' names is likely to be particularly helpful in the context of the death or insolvency of a registered proprietor.

When he receives such an application, the registrar must make the search and must supply the applicant with details of every entry in the index of proprietors' names which relates to the particulars given in the application.[9]

---

[1]   LRR 2003, r 145(3).
[2]   Ibid, rr 145(4), 146(3). There is power under LRR 2003, r 132 and Sch 2, for the registrar to issue a notice which would allow for delivery of such certificates by electronic means.
[3]   The form of the certificate is prescribed by LRR 2003, Sch 6, Part 1.
[4]   Ibid, Part 2.
[5]   See r 9.
[6]   LRR 2003, r 11(1). There are certain limits on the names that the index is required to show (joint and corporate proprietors registered before 1 May 1972): see r 11(2). These exceptions are carried forward from LRR 1925, r 9(1)(b). The much wider exception in LRR 1925, r 9(1)(a) (the name of any building society, local authority or government department as proprietor of a charge did not have to be entered in the index) is not replicated in LRR 2003, r 11.
[7]   Contrast searches of the Index, where *any* person may make a search: see para **14.19**.
[8]   LRR 2003, r 11(3).
[9]   Ibid, r 11(4).

The day list

14.22   The registrar is required to keep a record called the day list.[1] This shows the date and time at which every pending application under the LRA 2002 or the LRR 2003 was made, and of every application for an official search with priority.[2] Applications for information found in Part 13 of the LRR 2003[3] (which is concerned with applications to see documents and searches) are not recorded in the day list except:

(a)   an application for an official search with priority;[4] and

(b)   an application that the registrar should designate a document an exempt information document.[5]

14.23   In one circumstance, an act of the registrar is equated to an application. If he proposes to alter the register of title without having received an application, under the powers explained in Chapter 22, he must enter his proposal in the day list. It will then take effect as if it were an application made at the date and time of its entry.[6]

---

[1]   LRR 2003, r 12(1). Cf LRR 1925, r 7A, which introduced the day list in 1978 in a narrower form than is found in LRR 2003.

[2]   See LRR 2003, r 147; para **19.8**. The entry of a notice of an application for an official search with priority must remain on the day list until the priority conferred by the entry has ceased to have effect.

[3]   See Chapter 18.

[4]   LRR 2003, r 12(1).

[5]   Ibid, rr 12(4), 136; see also para **18.13**.

[6]   Ibid, r 12(3).

CHAPTER 15

REGISTRATION AND ITS EFFECTS

THE EFFECT OF REGISTRATION

Registration vests the legal title

15.1   It is a fundamental principle of registered conveyancing that it is registration that vests the legal estate in the registered proprietor.[1] In accordance with this principle, the LRA 2002 provides that if on the entry of a person in the register as the proprietor of the legal estate, the legal estate would not otherwise be vested in that person, the legal estate will be deemed to be vested in him as a result of the registration.[2] What this means is that the legal estate will vest in a person even if he is registered as proprietor on the basis of a forged transfer – which is itself a nullity.[3] It should be noted that the provision applies to 'a legal estate', and not merely to a legal estate *in land*. It will, therefore, include not just the two legal estates *in land* within LPA 1925, s 1(1),[4] but also the interests and charges that can be created at law under LPA 1925, s 1(2), including easements, rights and privileges, rentcharges, a charge by way of legal mortgage and certain rights of entry.[5]

15.2   There is one exception to this general principle and it gives effect to the registration requirements of Sch 2 to the LRA 2002 that were explained in Chapter 8. The legal estate will not vest if, following a registrable disposition, those registration requirements are not met.[6] In the Law Commission Report the example is given of the grant of a 99-year lease where the lease is registered with its own title, but where the registrar fails to enter a notice of the lease on the superior freehold title. The legal estate will not vest in the lessee as a result of the exception to the general principle.[7] The lease will operate only in equity. Without this exception, the provisions of Sch 2 would not, in practice, be registration *requirements*.

---

[1]   Cf LRA 1925, s 69(1).
[2]   LRA 2002, s 58(1). See paras **8.3** et seq for the registration requirements for registrable dispositions in Sch 2.
[3]   See (2001) Law Com No 271, para 9.4.
[4]   In other words, a fee simple absolute in possession and a term of years absolute.
[5]   See the definition of 'legal estate' in LRA 2002, s 132(1), referring to LPA 1925, s 1(4).
[6]   LRA 2002, s 58(2).
[7]   See (2001) Law Com No 271, para 9.5.

Where a person is registered as proprietor following a void conveyance or transfer, does registration vest the equitable interest as well as the legal estate?

15.3   An important issue that arose under the LRA 1925 but was not clearly or satisfactorily answered was whether the vesting of the legal estate would also carry the equitable interest in a case where the conveyance or transfer to the registered proprietor was, for some reason invalid, so that, but for the fact of registration, the legal estate would not have vested in him.[1] It is convenient to consider this question in relation to both first registration and registered dispositions.

15.4   As regards first registration, the position under the LRA 1925 was as follows:

(a)   There was some authority that, on first registration, a void conveyance would merely vest the bare legal title in the first registered proprietor, and he would therefore hold it on a bare trust for the previous owner.[2] If that analysis were correct, it would follow that the previous owner could then have required its re-transfer to him under the rule in *Saunders v Vautier*.[3] Such a result would have been unsatisfactory for at least three reasons. First, it would have run counter to the underlying principle of registered conveyancing that registration vests legal title in the registered proprietor and, if that registration was mistaken, the proper course is to seek rectification of the register. Secondly, and in consequence of this, it would have deprived a registered proprietor who was in physical possession of the land of the protection against rectification conferred by the LRA 1925.[4] Thirdly, it was not easy to reconcile with the provisions of the LRA 1925,[5] by which, where the first registered proprietor was not entitled to the land for his own benefit, he held it subject to the minor interests of the persons entitled to such interests of which he had notice.

---

[1]   See Harpum, 'Land Registration – A Law unto Itself', in J Getzler, *Modern Law of Real Property and Trusts – Essays for Edward Burn* (Butterworths, 2003).

[2]   *Epps v Esso Petroleum Co Ltd* [1973] 1 WLR 1071 at 1077. For cogent criticism of this approach, see Simon NL Palk 'First registration of title – just what does it do?' (1974) 34 Conv (NS) 236.

[3]   (1845) 4 Beav 115; affirmed (1845) Cr & Ph 240. Under this rule a beneficiary who is of full age and capacity and is absolutely entitled under a trust, may require the trustees to transfer the property to him or at his direction.

[4]   See LRA 1925, s 82(3). In such cases the previous owner has a claim for indemnity against the registrar. For alteration of the register, including rectification, see Chapter 22. For indemnity, see Chapter 23.

[5]   See LRA 1925, ss 5(c), 9(c); see also para **15.5**.

(b)   More recently, however, in *Malory Enterprises Ltd v Cheshire Homes (UK) Ltd*,[1] Arden LJ appears to have accepted that first registration did in fact vest both legal and beneficial title in the first registered proprietor.[2]

15.5   Whatever doubts there may have been under the LRA 1925, the effect of first registration under the LRA 2002 is clear. It vests both legal and beneficial title in the first registered proprietor. It has been explained that the first registered proprietor of a freehold or leasehold estate takes it subject to (amongst other things):

(a)   interests acquired under the Limitation Act 1980 of which the proprietor has notice;[3] and

(b)   the interests of persons beneficially entitled to the estate, where the proprietor is not entitled to that estate either for his own benefit or solely for his own benefit,[4] and has notice of those interests.[5]

15.6   The fact that it was thought necessary to make express provision for situations (a) and (b) in para **15.5**, necessarily implies that both legal and beneficial ownership are otherwise vested by statute in the proprietor on first registration. Were it not so, and only the bare legal title had vested in the first registered proprietor by registration, neither provision would have been needed.

15.7   As regards a registered disposition, it was held by the Court of Appeal in *Malory Enterprises Ltd v Cheshire Homes (UK) Ltd*,[6] in relation to the LRA 1925, that the registration of a proprietor under a forged disposition merely vested the bare legal estate in him. That proprietor took subject to the equitable title of the true owner. It is unnecessary to express any opinion about that interpretation of the previous legislation.[7] If it is correct, the effect was that, by virtue of the rule in *Saunders v Vautier*,[8] the former registered proprietor could have required the new registered proprietor to transfer the registered estate to him. If so, the machinery provided by the LRA 1925 for dealing with mistakes in the register by means of rectification and indemnity would have been circumvented.

15.8   The wording of the equivalent provision in the LRA 2002 is significantly different from that in the LRA 1925. Even if the decision in the

---

[1]   [2002] EWCA Civ 151, [2002] Ch 216. An appeal to the House of Lords is pending.
[2]   [2002] Ch 216 at 232. While the conclusion is welcome, we would respectfully question the reasoning that led to it.
[3]   LRA 2002, ss 11(4)(c), 12(4)(c); see also paras **4.5–4.6**, **4.9**.
[4]   Typically, where he holds the estate on trust.
[5]   LRA 2002, ss 11(5), 12(5); see also paras **4.7**, **4.9**.
[6]   [2002] Ch 216.
[7]   It turned upon the wording of LRA 1925, s 69(1), which was contrasted with that of s 5(c).
[8]   (1845) 4 Beav 115; affirmed (1845) Cr & Ph 240; see also para **15.4**.

Malory case was correct, it is suggested that the answer would be different under the new Act. As has been explained,[1] under the LRA 2002:

(a)   if on the entry of a person in the register as the proprietor of the legal estate, the legal estate would not otherwise be vested in that person, it will be deemed to be vested in him as a result of the registration;[2] and

(b)   this is subject to one exception, namely, where there has been registrable disposition and the registration requirements of Sch 2 to the Act have not been met.[3]

As has been explained, registration vests the *legal estate* in the proprietor.[4] Thus, if a charge were forged, and the chargee were registered as the registered chargee, that charge would be effective to vest the legal estate in the chargee. It makes no sense to speak of vesting the bare legal title to a registered charge or an easement. It must, therefore, be the case that, on the transfer of a legal estate *in land*, in other words, a transfer of the registered freehold or leasehold estate, both the legal *and* beneficial title in that estate will vest in the disponee, even if the transfer is a nullity.

THE REGISTRATION OF DEPENDENT ESTATES

15.9   The LRA 2002 makes provision as to how, what it describes as 'dependent estates', are to be entered on the register. The first case is where one legal estate – a freehold or leasehold – has the benefit of a legal estate, typically an easement or *profit à prendre* appurtenant, over some other land. The registration of a person as the proprietor of that dependent estate must be made in relation to the registered estate.[5] Thus, for example, where X is registered as proprietor of a freehold estate, 'Greenhythe', the register will also record the fact that he has the benefit of a legal easement over a neighbouring property, 'Redhills'. Secondly, the entry of a person in the register as the proprietor of a charge on a registered estate must be made in relation to the registered estate subject to the charge.[6] For example, the charges register of 'Greenhythe' will record that Y Bank plc is the registered proprietor of a charge over 'Greenhythe'. Thirdly, if Y Bank plc, the registered chargee of 'Greenhythe', has created a sub-charge in favour of Z plc, the entry of Z plc as proprietor of the sub-charge will be made in relation to Y Bank plc's registered charge.[7]

---

[1]   See paras **15.1**, **15.2**.
[2]   LRA 2002, s 58(1).
[3]   Ibid, s 58(2). For those registration requirements, see Chapter 8.
[4]   See para **15.1**.
[5]   LRA 2002, s 59(1).
[6]   Ibid, s 59(2).
[7]   Ibid, s 59(3).

EFFECTIVE DATE OF REGISTRATION

15.10   An entry made in the register in pursuance of an application for registration of an unregistered legal estate, or an application for registration in relation to a disposition required to be completed by registration, has effect from the time of the making of the application.[1] That was the position previously under the LRR 1925.[2]

---

[1]   LRA 2002, s 74.
[2]   See LRR 1925, rr 24, 42 and 83 (as amended or substituted).

CHAPTER 16

BOUNDARIES

THE GENERAL BOUNDARIES RULE

16.1   The LRA 2002 preserves what is known as the general boundaries rule.[1] It provides that the boundary of a registered estate shown for the purposes of the register is a general boundary, unless it is shown as having been determined under s 60 of the Act.[2] As a general boundary, the line that is shown on the registered plan does not determine the exact line of the boundary.[3] It follows, therefore, that unless fixed,[4] boundaries are not guaranteed by the Registry.

THE POWER TO DETERMINE THE EXACT LINE OF A BOUNDARY

Introduction

16.2   The power to fix boundaries under s 60 is not new,[5] but it has seldom been used. Apparently, this has been due to the expense involved and also to the risk that it may precipitate a boundary dispute.[6] This is because it is necessary to involve the adjoining landowners in the process of fixing the boundary. It might have been anticipated that, under the LRA 2002, the rules would be in a form that would encourage greater use of the power to fix boundaries,[7] particularly when new estates are set out and also in those cases where the legal boundary does not coincide with the physical boundaries. Modern mapping techniques are likely to make the process easier[8] and there is also an incentive in the LRA 2002 to do so. It is our view that the rules on

---

[1]   Despite its importance, the general boundaries rule was not found in LRA 1925 but in the rules made under it: see LRR 1925, r 278(1).

[2]   LRA 2002, s 60(1).

[3]   Ibid, s 60(2). This maintains the previous approach as set out in the LRR 1925, r 278(1).

[4]   See paras **16.2** et seq.

[5]   See LRR 1925, r 278(2).

[6]   (2001) Law Com No 271, para 9.10.

[7]   'We hope that this procedure [that is the procedure explained at paras **16.5**, **16.6**] will result in more people applying for the determination of their boundaries': Land Registry: *Land Registration Rules 2003 – A Land Registry Consultation* (2002), p 75.

[8]   We have been told by a number of surveyors that determining an exact boundary is nothing like as difficult or expensive as the Land Registry appears to suggest.

boundaries that have now been made pursuant to s 60[1] would, however, benefit from some reconsideration, and that as they stand, they are not likely to encourage applications for determined boundaries.

16.3   As is explained in Chapter 30, although it is in general much more difficult for a squatter to acquire title to registered land under the Act than it was under the LRA 1925, there are situations where he may still do so. Perhaps the most important of these is where a person adversely possesses adjacent land and for 10 years of his adverse possession reasonably believes that he owns it.[2] However, this exception will not apply if the boundary between the two properties has been fixed and is not a general boundary.[3] There is a power under the LRA 2002, now exercised, to make rules enabling or requiring the exact line of the boundary to be determined.[4] In particular, rules may make provision as to the circumstances in which the exact line of a boundary may or must be determined.[5] One case where it might have been thought that rules would require a boundary to be fixed is where a squatter brings himself within the exception mentioned above. To ensure that he cannot acquire any further land by adverse possession under this exception, he should be required to have the new boundary fixed. This was intended by the Law Commission and the Land Registry,[6] and in the consultation on the draft land registration rules, the Registry proposed a rule which would have that effect.[7] Although the proposed rule was overwhelmingly supported,[8] it was not included in the LRR 2003. However, as the relevant provisions of the LRA 2002 relating to adverse possession do not come into force until 13 October 2004,[9] the rule will presumably be brought in at that date.

16.4   Under LRR 2003, a boundary may be determined either on application or by the registrar without any application. These two methods are explained below. Information given by the Land Registry suggests that the registrar will not exercise his power to determine a boundary on his own volition very often.

Applications for the determination of the exact line of the boundary

16.5   First, the rules make provision for the determination of the exact line

---

[1]   They are found in LRR 2003, Part 10.

[2]   LRA 2002, Sch 6, para 5(4); see also para **30.42**.

[3]   Ibid, Sch 6, para 5(4)(b). It should be noted that this exception applies only to a boundary that has been determined under LRA 2002 and LRR 2003. It does *not* apply where the boundary was fixed prior to 13 October 2003 under LRR 1925, r 276, which was the equivalent procedure prior to 13 October 2003.

[4]   Ibid, s 60(3).

[5]   Ibid, s 60(3)(a).

[6]   See (2001) Law Com No 271, para 9.13.

[7]   *Land Registration Rules 2003 – A Land Registry Consultation* (2002), pp 76–77; draft rule 120.

[8]   Report on responses to *Land Registration Rules 2003 – A Land Registry Consultation*, p 69, para 8.7.

[9]   See the Land Registration Act 2002 (Commencement No 4) Order 2003, SI 2003/1725, art 2(2).

of the boundary on application. Only a proprietor of a registered estate may apply to the registrar for the exact line of the boundary of that estate to be determined.[1] A proprietor of a registered charge is given no equivalent right, even though the chargee might wish to have the boundary line determined to ensure the protection of its security against potential squatters.[2] Application must be made on Form DB.[3] The Land Registry state that an application must be made in relation to each adjoining landowner,[4] but this contradicts the wording of the LRR 2003.[5] Form DB must be accompanied by:

(a)   a plan, or a plan and a verbal description, identifying the exact line of the boundary claimed and showing sufficient surrounding physical features to allow the general position of the boundary to be drawn on the Ordnance Survey map;[6] and

(b)   evidence to establish the exact line of the boundary.[7]

As regards (a), the Land Registry's detailed (and very demanding) requirements as to the plan that is required are not contained in the LRR 2003, but are set out in paras 3.3.2 and 3.3.5 of Land Registry Practice Guide, Land Registry Plans, PG40, to which reference should be made.[8] As regards (b), the sort of evidence that is required is, apparently, a boundary agreement with the adjoining landowner,[9] or title documents. The judgment of a court in boundary dispute proceedings should also be acceptable evidence.[10] However, the nature of the procedure adopted on an application for the determination of a boundary is such that if such a judgment were submitted by way of evidence, the neighbour could, in effect, seek to re-litigate the issue: see para **16.6** (STEP 4). Although, in practice, any such attempt would fail on grounds of *res judicata* or abuse of process, it is unfortunate that the rules did not make express provision for this situation to avoid the potential for further strife between warring neighbours.

16.6   The procedure to be followed where there is an application for a determined boundary is as follows:

STEP 1: The registrar has first to be satisfied that:

---

[1]   LRR 2003, r 118(1).
[2]   See para **16.3**.
[3]   LRR 2003, r 118(2).
[4]   See Land Registry Practice Guide, Land Registry Plans, PG40, para 3.3.4.
[5]   See LRR 2003, r 119(1)(c); para **16.6**, STEP 1(c).
[6]   The Land Registry requires two copies of the plan.
[7]   LRR 2003, r 118(2).
[8]   The requirements are very specific and detailed.
[9]   If there is such an agreement, the adjoining landowner must sign both panel 9 of Form DB *and* the plan.
[10] Commonly in such proceedings, the judge will make a finding as to where the boundary is.

(a)   the plan or verbal description mentioned in para **16.5** identifies the exact line of the boundary claimed;

(b)   the applicant has shown an arguable case that the exact line of the boundary is in the position identified by that plan or verbal description;

(c)   he can identify all the owners of land adjoining the boundary to be determined and has an address at which each of them can be given notice.[1]

If he is not satisfied as to matters (a)–(c), he must cancel the application.[2]

STEP 2: Subject to two exceptions, the registrar must then give to the owners of the land[3] adjoining the boundary notice of the application and of the fact that, unless the recipient objects within the time specified by the notice,[4] the registrar must complete the application.[5] The registrar does not have to serve a notice in relation to:

(a)   the applicant;[6] and

(b)   where the evidence relied upon by the applicant is a written boundary agreement, the other party to that agreement.[7]

The time specified in the notice within which objections have to be made will be a period ending at 12 noon on the twentieth business day[8] after the date of issue of the notice or such longer period as the registrar may decide before he issues the notice.[9] The registrar may extend that period on an application by the recipient of the notice before it has expired.[10]

STEP 3: If there is no objection within the time specified in the notice (or as extended), the registrar must complete the application.[11]

STEP 4: If there is an objection, the matter will be dealt with in accordance with the usual procedures that apply to a disputed application to the registrar: see s 73 of the LRA 2002. These are fully explained in Chapter 20. In essence,

---

[1]   LRR 2003, r 119(1). The fact that the boundary to be determined can adjoin the land of more than one owner is a clear indication that it is *not* necessary to make a separate application for each: cf para **16.5**.
[2]   LRR 2003, r 119(7).
[3]   'Owner of the land' is defined to mean: (a) the person who could apply to be registered as proprietor if the land is unregistered; (b) the registered proprietor of any registered estate or charge if the title is registered; and (c) Her Majesty, if the land is demesne land: LRR 2003, r 119(8).
[4]   Including any extension of that time.
[5]   LRR 2003, r 119(1), (6).
[6]   Ibid, r 119(1).
[7]   Ibid, r 119(2).
[8]   For the meaning of 'business day', see LRR 2003, r 216; para **36.5**.
[9]   LRR 2003, r 119(3).
[10] Ibid, r 119(4), (5).
[11] Ibid, r 119(6).

if the dispute cannot be resolved by agreement, the registrar must refer it to the Adjudicator for resolution.

16.7 It is obviously necessary that where the exact line of a boundary has been determined, both the fact that such a determination has been made and the terms of that determination appear in the register.[1] The LRR 2003 therefore require the registrar, where he completes an application to determine the exact line of a boundary, to record the fact that there has been such determination under s 60 of the LRA 2002 in the individual register of title of, and (subject to what is said below) to add such particulars of the exact line of the boundary as he considers appropriate to the title plan of:

(a)   the applicant's registered title;
(b)   any superior or inferior registered title; and
(c)   any registered title affecting the other land adjoining the determined boundary.[2]

The registrar may make an entry in the individual registers of the titles mentioned above, referring to any other plan showing the exact line of the boundary. This may be in addition to or instead of adding the particulars to the title plans mentioned above.[3]

Determination of the exact line of the boundary without application

16.8 The registrar is given power to determine the exact line of the boundary of his own volition in certain circumstances.[4] He may do this where the following conditions are satisfied:

(a)   There is either a transfer of part of a registered estate in land or the grant of a term of years absolute which is a registrable disposition of part of a registered estate in land.
(b)   There is a common boundary between the part transferred or granted and the part retained by the grantor.
(c)   There is sufficient information in the transfer or grant to enable the registrar to determine the exact line of the common boundary.[5]

This power can only be exercised where the plans attached to the transfer or grant are sufficiently detailed and there are some suitable fixed points of

1   It should be noted that where the exact line of part of a boundary of registered land has been determined, the ends of that part are not treated as determined for the purposes of adjoining parts of the boundary in relation to which there has been no such determination: see LRR 2003, r 121. The owners of those adjoining parts can still rely upon the general boundaries rule.
2   LRR 2003, r 120(1).
3   Ibid, r 120(2).
4   Ibid, r 122.
5   Ibid, r 122(1), (4).

reference within the disponor's estate.[1] Where the registrar does determine the exact line of a boundary under this power, the same principles apply for recording that determination (set out in para **16.7**) as they do where he makes a determination on application.[2]

ACCRETION AND DILUVION

16.9   Accretion is the addition to the bank of a river or the shore of a lake or sea of soil that raises it above the water level and, in effect, creates new land out of what was previously water. Diluvion describes the reverse process, by which banks or shores are washed away by the action of water so that they disappear under water. The operation of accretion and diluvion has particular relevance given coastal erosion and accumulation, the fact that boundaries of properties along estuaries may change all the time, and also following the floods of recent years.[3] The doctrines are also of particular importance to the Crown, which in most cases owns the foreshore. The principles governing accretion and diluvion are set out in the well-known opinion of the Privy Council in *Southern Centre of Theosophy Inc v State of South Australia*.[4]

16.10   In essence, those principles are that the ownership of land follows the gradual changes in boundaries caused to land that fronts on to water, whether by the action of the water, wind or tide. A landowner may gain or lose land according to these principles. The LRA 2002 reflects these principles. Section 61(1) provides that the fact that a registered estate in land is shown in the register as having a particular boundary (whether a general boundary or a boundary determined under s 60 of the Act) does not affect the operation of accretion or diluvion.

16.11   It may be that neighbouring landowners will decide that the boundary between their respective properties should not change as a result of accretion or diluvion – the typical case would be where their properties are separated by a river.[5] Under s 61(2) of the LRA 2002, any such agreement about the operation of accretion or diluvion in relation to a registered estate in land will have effect only if registered in accordance with rules.[6] Under the LRR 2003:

(a)   There must be an application to register any such agreement.[7] As no

---

[1]   See *Land Registration Rules 2003 – A Land Registry Consultation* (2002), pp 77, 78.

[2]   LRR 2003, r 122(2), (3).

[3]   In the past few years several disputes arising from such boundary changes have been heard by the Solicitor to the Land Registry.

[4]   [1982] AC 706. See, in particular, at p 716, per Lord Wilberforce.

[5]   See (2001) Law Com No 271, para 9.15.

[6]   As a result if (for example) adjoining landowners, whose properties are separated by a stream, agree that, notwithstanding any change in the course of that stream, the boundary shall remain where it is on the date of the agreement, that agreement will have to be recorded in the register.

[7]   LRR 2003, r 123(1).

form is prescribed, the application will be on Form AP1, the default application form.[1]

(b)   The proprietor of the registered estate and of any registered charge must either make the application or (if he is not a party to the agreement) consent to it.[2]

(c)   When the agreement is registered, the registrar must make a note in the property register of the relevant title that the agreement is registered for the purposes of s 61(2) of the LRA 2002.[3]

---

[1]   See LRR 2003, r 13; see also para **20.18**.
[2]   Ibid, r 123(1).
[3]   Ibid, r 123(2).

CHAPTER 17

USE OF REGISTER TO RECORD DEFECTS IN TITLE

17.1   Under the LRA 1925, there were circumstances in which an event might occur that made a registered title liable to determination, but where it was not possible to record that fact in the register. In order to make the register as conclusive as possible,[1] s 64 of the LRA 2002 creates a new power to meet such cases. If it appears to the registrar that a right to determine a registered estate in land has become exercisable, he is given power to enter the fact in the register of title.[2] A right to determine a registered estate is as serious a defect in title as can exist. It is likely to arise out of an event which has occurred during the course of ownership of the property. The new power is particularly intended to catch those cases where there are no existing mechanisms for neutralising the defect.[3] An example would be the failure by a freeholder to pay a rentcharge, where that freehold was subject to a rentcharge that was supported by a right of re-entry.[4] Another case might be where, by the operation of a statutory provision (such as under the Land Clauses Acts[5]), land becomes subject to divestment on the occurrence of some event.[6]

17.2   At first sight, it is not obvious how this power will be made to work in practice as conveyancers are unlikely to wish to volunteer information to the Registry that will prejudicially affect their clients' titles. However, the introduction of electronic conveyancing is likely to provide a means of ensuring that such defects are disclosed and registered. A conveyancer who enters into a network access agreement is likely to be required to provide such information under the terms of that agreement.[7]

17.3   There is a power to make rules in relation to the making of entries under s 64 and, in particular, as to the circumstances in which there will be

---

[1]   Cf para **1.8**.

[2]   LRA 2002, s 64(1).

[3]   See para **17.3**.

[4]   (2001) Law Com No 271, paras 9.31 and 9.33. There are undoubtedly freeholds subject to such rights of re-entry, though they are not common. In most cases, the rent owner will rely on the more limited right of entry implied in the absence of contrary intention by LPA 1925, s 121(3).

[5]   Notably, the Lands Clauses Consolidation Act 1845.

[6]   See Harpum, *Megarry & Wade's Law of Real Property* (Sweet & Maxwell, 6th edn, 2000), para 4-042.

[7]   For network access agreements, see LRA 2002, Sch 5. See also para **27.13**.

duty to make entries, how entries may be made and as to their removal.[1] The relevant rule is explained at para **17.4**. There are circumstances where conveyancers have existing practices to identify whether an occurrence has invalidated the title,[2] and it was envisaged that such practices would continue. Section 64 of the LRA 2002 was intended to cater for those situations, such as the sale of a freehold subject to a rentcharge, for which there were no such existing safeguards.[3] Although it was expected that the rules would confine the power to such cases, this has not happened in practice.[4]

17.4   Rule 125 of the LRR 2003 provides that any entry made under s 64 of LRA 2002 is to be made in the property register of the relevant registered title.[5] The wording of s 64(1) is such that the registrar may either make such an entry on his own volition (where he becomes aware in the course of some application or other matter of the fact that a registered estate is liable to determination), or on application. Where there is an application for such an entry,[6] it must be supported by evidence to satisfy the registrar that:

(a)   the applicant has the right to determine the registered estate; and
(b)   the right is exercisable.[7]

In every case, before the registrar makes an entry under r 125, he must give notice of the application both to the proprietor of the registered estate to which the application relates and to the proprietor of any registered charge on that estate.[8] It is, presumably, open to the recipients to object to the application on the basis either that the applicant does not have the right to determine the estate or, if he does, that the right is not (or has ceased to be) exercisable. Such an objection will be dealt with in accordance with the procedures laid down in s 73 of the LRA 2002, explained in Chapter 20, by which, if the dispute cannot be resolved by agreement, the registrar must refer it to the Adjudicator for resolution.

17.5   Rule 125 contains nothing to restrict its application to cases where no

---

[1]   LRA 2002, s 64(2).
[2]   The best-known example is that of an intending assignor of a lease: see (2001) Law Com No 271, para 9.32. Provided that he produces to the intending assignee the last receipt for rent prior to the assignment, there is a rebuttable statutory presumption that all the covenants and provisions of a lease have been duly performed up until the date of the assignment: see LPA 1925, s 45(2) (and in the case of an intending sub-lessee, s 45(3)). The basis for this presumption is the doctrine of waiver. A landlord who accepts rent with knowledge of a breach of covenant is taken to waive his right to forfeit for that breach.
[3]   This is clear from (2001) Law Com No 271, paras 9.31–9.34.
[4]   See para **17.5**.
[5]   LRR 2003, r 125(1).
[6]   No Form is prescribed, so that the default Form AP1 should be used: see LRR 2003, r 13; see also para **20.18**.
[7]   LRR 2003, r 125(2).
[8]   Ibid, r 125(4).

conveyancing machinery exists for dealing with an estate that is liable to determination. There is, therefore, no reason why, for example, a landlord should not apply for an entry under s 64 of the LRA 2002 in a case where a tenant had failed to pay his rent and the lease contained the usual proviso for re-entry. This situation is a matter for concern and it provoked some adverse comment in the Report on responses to *Land Registration Rules 2003 – A Land Registry Consultation*.[1] Rule 125(3) does provide expressly for one of the principal situations for which s 64 was enacted: the registrar must make an entry under s 64 on receipt of an application which relates to a right to determine the registered estate on non-payment of a rentcharge.

17.6 As might be anticipated from the wording of s 64,[2] the rules make provision by which specified persons may apply to the registrar for the removal of an entry under the section.[3] Such an entry can only be removed if the right to determine the registered estate is not exercisable[4] and the application is supported by evidence to satisfy the registrar of this fact.[5] The persons who may apply for removal of the entry are:

(a)   the person entitled to determine the registered estate;
(b)   the proprietor of the registered estate to which the entry relates;
(c)   a person entitled to be registered as proprietor of that estate; and
(d)   any other person whom the registrar is satisfied has an interest in the removal of the entry.[6]

An example of (d) would be the proprietor of a registered charge over the estate to which the entry related.

---

1   See at p 97, paras 3–5.
2   See LRA 2002, s 64(2)(c); para **17.3**.
3   LRR 2003, r 125(5), (6). Once again, the application must be in Form AP1, there being no other prescribed form.
4   Presumably, if it transpires that the person who made the initial application for the entry had no *right* to determine the estate, an application could instead be made to alter the register under Sch 4 to the LRA 2002. See Chapter 22.
5   LRR 2003, r 125(6).
6   Ibid, r 125(5).

CHAPTER 18

ACCESSING INFORMATION

INTRODUCTION

18.1 The LRA 2002 is intended to facilitate conveyancing and to make the property market more transparent. It is therefore not surprising that it contains provisions that extend the accessibility of the titles and cautions registers and of the information referred to in them.

THE OPEN REGISTER

18.2 The LRA 1988 began the sequence of reforms that paved the way for the LRA 2002. It opened the register of title so that it was a public document.[1] It was no longer necessary to obtain the consent of a registered proprietor to investigate his title. Without an open register, it would not be possible to investigate title on line or conduct any form of electronic conveyancing.

The right of inspection

18.3 Under s 66(1) of the LRA 2002, any person may inspect and make copies of, or of any part of:

— the register of title;[2]
— any document kept by the registrar which is referred to in the register of title;[3]
— any other document kept by the registrar which relates to an application to him;[4] or
— the register of cautions against first registration.[5]

---

[1] LRA 1988, which substituted a new s 112 into LRA 1925. The LRA 1988 implemented the recommendations of the Law Commission in its Second Report on Land Registration, (1985) Law Com No 148.

[2] LRA 2002, s 66(1)(a).

[3] Ibid, s 66(1)(b).

[4] Ibid, s 66(1)(c). This is a new right. Previously, such documents could only be inspected at the discretion of the registrar unless the applicant fell within one of the categories specified in the Land Registration (Open Register) Rules 1991 (LRORR 1991), SI 1991/122, Sch 2 – an exception applicable to criminal investigations.

[5] Ibid, s 66(1)(d). The Act established for the first time a register of cautions against first registration. Formerly, cautions against first registration are recorded on the Index Map. There was previously a right to search the Index Map: LRR 1925, r 8.

18.4   The power to inspect and copy that is conferred by the LRA 2002 goes beyond that which was permitted under LRA 1925. In particular, it includes two important categories of document that could not be inspected under the LRA 1925,[1] namely leases filed at the Land Registry[2] and charges.[3] The ability to inspect leases is of considerable practical significance and the policy reasons for it have been explained in Chapter 2.[4]

18.5   LRA 2002 provides that the right to inspect the registers is subject to rules, which may provide for exceptions to be made to the right and impose conditions on its exercise, including conditions regarding the payment of fees.[5] It was anticipated that the rules would restrict access to documents of a commercially sensitive nature.[6] In this they would reflect the provisions of Part II of the FIA 2000 (which exempt certain information from disclosure under that Act).[7] The rules that have been made under this power, which are found in Part 13 of the LRR 2003, have proved to be controversial. They are explained below.

18.6   As a corollary to the power to inspect and take copies given by LRR 2002, ss 66(1), 67(1) of the LRA 2002 makes official copies[8] admissible in evidence to the same extent as the original.[9] This will be the case in relation to the following:

–   the register of title;[10]
–   any document which is referred to in the register of title and kept by the registrar;[11]

---

[1]   See LRA 1925, s 112(1)(b).
[2]   Not all leases are supplied to the Land Registry. The practice under LRA 1925 was summarised in Ruoff and Roper, *Registered Conveyancing*, at pp 21–22 as follows. When an original lessee applied for first registration he had to furnish a certified copy of his lease: LRR 1925, r 21. A lease noted as an incumbrance on first registration of the title to the reversion was seldom supplied to the Registry. When an assignee of a lease applied for the first registration of his title, he was required to supply a certified copy of the assignment but may not supply a copy of the lease itself.
[3]   In relation to domestic conveyancing, charges are not normally very informative. They do not disclose the amount borrowed and are often according to the standard terms and conditions of the borrower, which are lodged with HM Land Registry.
[4]   See para **2.15**.
[5]   LRA 2002, s 66(2)(a), (b).
[6]   There are said to be strong arguments relating to the property market in favour of wider publication. Such information could shed light on commercial property transactions, fostering a free and competitive market: see Baroness Scotland of Asthal, *Hansard* (HL), 30 October 2001, vol 627, cols 1362–1363.
[7]   See para **2.15**.
[8]   The term 'official copy' replaced the term 'office copies' used in LRA 1925, s 113.
[9]   LRA 2002, s 67.
[10]   Ibid, s 67(1)(a).
[11]   Ibid, s 67(1)(b).

– any other document kept by the registrar which is not referred to in the register of title, but which relates to an application to the registrar;[1] or
– the register of cautions against first registration.[2]

18.7 There is provision for rules to be made about the form of official copies, who may issue official copies,[3] applications for official copies[4] and the conditions to be met by applicants for official copies, including conditions requiring the payment of fees.[5]

18.8 A person who relies on an official copy in which there is a mistake is not liable for loss suffered by another by reason of the mistake.[6] A person who suffers loss by reason of a mistake in an official copy is, however, entitled to be indemnified.[7]

18.9 It is necessary to examine in some detail the rules made pursuant to ss 66 and 67 of the LRA 2002. Those rules differentiate between the following forms of application:

(a) An application by a person to inspect and copy the registers and/or documents pursuant to LRA 2002, s 66(1):[8] such personal inspections are not likely to be common as they will necessitate a visit to a Land Registry office.
(b) An application for official copies of a registered title, of the cautions register, or for a certificate of inspection of the title plan.[9]
(c) An application for official copies of documents referred to in the register of title and other documents kept by the registrar.[10]

Applications to inspect and copy

18.10 If a person wishes to inspect the registers and documents himself and make copies of them, he must apply to do so on Form PIC.[11] In other words,

---

[1] LRR 2002, s 67(1)(c).
[2] Ibid, s 67(1)(d).
[3] Under Sch 5, para 1(2)(d) of the LRA 2002, there will be power for authorised persons to issue official copies pursuant to a network access agreement. In practice, this means that solicitors and licensed conveyancers will issue such copies.
[4] The Direct Access system has already enabled such applications to be made electronically: Directions of the Chief Land Registrar, 12 May 1997 Ruoff and Roper, *Registered Conveyancing*, F-12.
[5] LRA 2002, s 67(3)(a)–(d).
[6] Ibid, s 67(2).
[7] Ibid, Sch 8, para 1(1)(d); see also para **23.6**.
[8] See para **18.10**.
[9] See para **18.11**.
[10] See para **18.12**.
[11] LRR 203, r 133(3). There is power to permit applications to be made in other forms: see LRR 2003, r 132. Under this power, applications are permitted by Land Registry Direct, by NLIS, and by oral application at a Land Registry office: see Notices 3, 4 and 6 issued by the Chief Land Registrar on 2 October 2003.

this method is only appropriate where the applicant wants to inspect and copy the relevant registers and documents himself, and *not* where he wants to receive official copies of them from the Registry. By LRR 2003, r 133, the following are excepted from the right to inspect and make copies of the registers and documents conferred by s 66(1) of LRA 2002:

(a)   Any 'exempt information document'.
(b)   Any 'edited information document' that has been replaced by a subsequent edited information document.
(c)   Any 'Form EX1A'.
(d)   Any 'Form CIT' and certain other forms and documents associated with an application to which a Form CIT has been attached.

The meaning of these terms and the function of those two forms are explained below. The rules provide that where inspection and copying under r 133 take place at an office of the Land Registry, it must be undertaken in the presence of a member of the Land Registry.[1] It should be emphasised that an application using Form PIC is only appropriate in cases where the applicant wishes himself to inspect the document and copy it. Normally, an applicant will wish to obtain an official copy of a document and should then proceed in the manner explained in para **18.12**.

Applications for official copies of a registered title, the cautions register or for a certificate of inspection of a title plan

18.11   By r 134 of the LRR 2003, a person may apply for an official copy of:

(a)   an individual register;[2]
(b)   any title plan referred to in an individual register;[3]
(c)   an individual caution register and any caution plan referred to in it;
(d)   a certificate of inspection of any title plan.[4]

Application for an official copy is made on Form OC1.[5] A separate

---

[1]   LRR 2003, r 133(4).
[2]   For individual registers, see LRR 2003, r 2; see also para **14.2**.
[3]   Where a person has applied for a certificate of inspection of title plan, on completion of the inspection the registrar must issue a certificate of inspection: LRR 2003, r 143(1). That certificate of inspection may be issued by the registrar in Form C1 or to like effect: r 143(2). This certificate may, for example, certify that the land shown on the plan sent by the applicant is contained in the specified title number.
[4]   LRR 2003, r 134(1).
[5]   Ibid, r 134(2). There is power to permit applications in other forms: see r 132. Under this power, applications are permitted by telephone, fax, Land Registry Direct, NLIS, Land Register Online and oral application at a Land Registry office: see Notices 1–6 issued by the Chief Land Registrar on 2 October 2003.

application must be made in respect of each registered title or individual caution register.[1]

Applications for official copies of documents referred to in the register of title and other documents kept by the registrar

18.12   By r 135(1) of the LRR 2003, a person may apply for an official copy of any document referred to in the register of title and kept by the registrar or of any other document kept by the registrar that relates to an application to him. This right is subject to the same exceptions as the personal right to inspect and copy that have been explained above at para **18.10**.[2] Applications must be made in Form OC2.[3]

Exempt information documents

18.13   LRR 2003, r 136, creates a procedure by which a person may apply to have a 'relevant document' designated an 'exempt information document' (EID) if he claims that the document contains 'prejudicial information'.[4] An EID means the original and copies of the document in question that the registrar has so designated.[5]

18.14   A 'relevant document' is for these purposes any one of the following:

(a)   a document referred to in the register of title;
(b)   a document that relates to an application to the registrar, the original or a copy of which is kept by the registrar;
(c)   a document that will be referred to in the register as a result of an accompanying application made at the same time as the application for an EID; or
(d)   a document that relates to the accompanying application to the registrar, the original or a copy of which will be or is for the time being kept by the registrar.[6]

18.15   Information will be 'prejudicial information' if it falls within either of two categories, namely:

1   LRR 2003, r 134(3). For the registrar's powers where an application is in respect of more than one registered title or individual register, see LRR 2003, r 134(4)–(6).
2   Ibid, r 135(2). There is a further limitation on the right to apply during the period 13 October 2003–12 October 2005 inclusive: see LRR 2003, r 135(3) and paras **18.32,18.33**.
3   LRR 2003, r 135(4). There is power to permit applications to be made in other forms: see LRR 2003, r 132. Under this power, applications are permitted by telephone, fax, Land Registry Direct, NLIS, Land Register Online and oral application at a Land Registry office: see Notices 1–6 issued by the Chief Land Registrar on 2 October 2003.
4   LRR 2003, r 136(1). See the Land Registry Practice Guide, Exempting Documents from the General Right to Inspect and Copy, PG57.
5   LRR 2003, r 131.
6   Ibid, r 136(7).

(a)   information that relates to an individual who has applied for the document to be an EID, which if disclosed to other persons (whether to the public generally or specific persons) would, or would be likely to, cause substantial unwarranted damage or substantial unwarranted distress to the applicant or another; or

(b)   information that if disclosed to other persons (whether to the public generally or specific persons) would, or would be likely to, prejudice the commercial interests of the person who has applied for the document to be an EID.[1]

18.16   It seems likely that most cases are likely to fall within (b). Cases falling within (a) are unlikely to be common but might, for example, include documents arising out of matrimonial proceedings.[2]

18.17   It will be noted that there is no restriction on the classes of documents to those relating to leases or charges. It is therefore possible to apply for a document to be an EID even though, before 13 October 2003, it would have been possible to obtain a copy of it. The power to apply for the registrar to designate a document an EID is not restricted to documents in transactions after 12 October 2003. However, this is subject to certain restrictions that are explained in paras **18.19–18.23**.

18.18   Application for an EID must be made in Form EX1 and EX1A. Form EX1 is the actual application.[3] It contains details of the document that is said to contain the prejudicial information. It must be accompanied by an edited version of that document which excludes the prejudicial information. The Registry strongly recommends that the document should be edited by leaving white space where the text would be. It suggests that the actual text to be excluded should be turned white, so that does not appear in the printed version.[4] The edited version, as and when it is accepted by the registrar, is known as an 'edited information document' (EDID). The purpose of Form EX1A is to set out why the applicant considers that the document lodged contains prejudicial information. Whereas Form EX1A is exempt from the general right of inspection and copying, Form EX1 is not.[5]

18.19   Provided that the registrar is satisfied that the applicant's claim 'is not groundless', he *must* designate the relevant document an EID.[6] The threshold for obtaining the designation of a document as an EID is therefore

---

1   LRR 2003, r 131.
2   No guidance has been provided by the Registry as to the sort of case category (a) is intended to cover.
3   For guidance as to how to fill in Form EX1, see Land Registry Practice Guide, Exempting Documents from the General Right to Inspect and Copy, PG57, para 3.2.
4   Exempting Documents from the General Right to Inspect and Copy, PG57, para 3.1.
5   See LRR 2003, r 135(2) and paras **18.10**, **18.12**.
6   Ibid, r 136(3).

remarkably low. There is, however, a significant exception to the general principle. Where the registrar considers that designating the document an exempt information document could prejudice the keeping of the register, he may cancel the application.[1] The following guidance has been provided by the Registry as to when it will consider that the register is prejudiced.

18.20   First, it advises that a document should be edited only so far as is necessary to protect the nature of the information. It will not accept applications that omit large sections of a document without apparent good reason.[2]

18.21   Secondly, the Registry advises that the applicant should not edit out information that will need to be included in an entry in the register, such as clauses containing an easement, a restrictive covenant or an option to purchase. This is because it makes entries in the register either by setting out details of the rights concerned in the register or by referring to a filed copy of the document containing the details. If it adopts the first method, the information will still appear in the register. If it adopts the second method, the application for an EID will be cancelled because it prejudices the keeping of the register. The unedited version will then be the filed copy.[3] Although the Registry does not say so explicitly, it must follow from this that an attempt to exempt the whole of (say) a lease or charge from registration as an EID will necessarily be rejected.[4]

18.22   Thirdly, although it is possible to edit out the price paid from a transfer, such editing out will have little practical effect. This is because the Registry is required to enter price paid in the Proprietorship Register whenever practicable.[5] It will do so, even if the price is edited out of the transfer.[6]

18.23   Fourthly, in a case where information from a document has been extracted and already appears in the register, such information cannot be removed by an application for an EID in relation to the document quoted. This is because to do so would prejudice the keeping of the register.[7]

---

[1]   LRR 2003, r 136(4).

[2]   Land Registry Practice Guide, Exempting Documents from the General Right to Inspect and Copy, PG57, para 3.1.

[3]   Ibid.

[4]   We are aware that there are some firms of solicitors who are trying to exempt the whole of leases.

[5]   LRR 2003, r 8(2); see also para **14.11**(a).

[6]   Land Registry Practice Guide, Exempting Documents from the General Right to Inspect and Copy, PG57, para 3.1.

[7]   Ibid. The Registry points out that the information would, in any event, be still available on a historical copy of the register, a copy of which could be obtained: see para **18.43**.

18.24   Where a document is an EID, the registrar may make an appropriate entry in the individual register of any affected registered title.[1]

18.25   The Rules make provision for the case where a document has been designated as an EID, but where there is a further application under r 136 in relation to the same document. The registrar must then prepare another EDID, which excludes both the information from the existing EDID and the additional information excluded from the EDID lodged in the further application.[2]

18.26   In practice, applications for EIDs are most likely to arise in relation to the grant of leases. In such cases, it will usually be the landlord rather than the tenant who wishes to exclude information from the lease as, for example, where the lease contains preferential terms that are not found in other leases of the same building granted by the same landlord. If this is likely to be the case, because it is the tenant rather than the landlord who must register the lease, the landlord must make specific arrangements with the tenant, whether by contract or otherwise, to ensure that the landlord's application for an EID is made at the same time as the tenant's application to register the lease. It should also be noted that while an EID enables information in a document to be removed from sight, the use of an EID cannot hide the *absence* of information in a document. For example, if a lease to the tenant does not include certain terms that are found in all other leases by the same landlord to the other tenants in the same building, those omissions will be apparent from a comparison of the lease with that of the other tenants.

18.27   An EID, once obtained, is personal to the applicant and cannot be assigned, as for example, to a purchaser. If, say, a landlord has successfully applied to have a lease designated an EID and subsequently assigns his reversion, only he will be consulted by the registrar if there is an application for an official copy of the EID under the principles explained below in para **18.28** (because it was the landlord who made the application under r 136). Similarly, only the original applicant can apply for the removal of the designation of a document as an EID under the principles explained below at para **18.31**. If, therefore, the landlord does assign his reversion, he should arrange with the assignee: (a) that he will apply for the removal of the EID; and (b) that the assignee will apply for an EID. Both applications should be made at the same time as the assignee applies to register the assignment of the reversion.[3]

---

[1]   LRR 2003, r 136(5).

[2]   Ibid, r 136(6).

[3]   Cf Land Registry Practice Guide, Exempting Documents from the General Right to Inspect and Copy, PG57, para 5.

Application for an official copy of an exempt information document

18.28   Given the low threshold for obtaining an EID,[1] it is not surprising that the LRR 2003 provide a mechanism by which a person may apply for an official copy of an EID (in other words the unamended document). There are a number of unsatisfactory aspects to these provisions. A person may apply for an official copy of an EID in Form EX2 (Application for official copy of an EID).[2] In practice the applicant will already have obtained a copy of the EDID and it will be because it is not satisfactory for his purposes that he makes the further application. In Form EX2, the applicant is required to state:

(a)   why he considers that an official copy of the EDID is not sufficient for his purposes;[3] and

(b)   either:
   (i)   why none of the information omitted from the EDID is prejudicial information; or
   (ii)   why, if the applicant accepts that some of the information omitted from the EDID is prejudicial information, he considers that the public interest in providing an official copy of the EID outweighs the public interest in not doing so.[4]

While an applicant may well be able to answer the first of those questions, he is faced with the obvious logical difficulty in answering the second that he cannot do so without seeing the EID. The Registry warns that the applicant must 'complete one or both of the alternatives' in (b) (even though they appear to be alternatives) and that it will only issue an official copy of the full copy of the EID if it agrees with what the applicant has said.[5] It should be noted that Form EX2 is itself not exempt from the general right to inspect and copy. Some care is therefore required in completing it quite apart from the difficulties outlined above.

18.29   Assuming that the applicant is able to complete Form EX2, the registrar will give notice of his application to the person who made the application for an EID under LRR 2003, r 136 unless he is satisfied that such notice is unnecessary or impracticable.[6] It might be assumed from this that, on receiving an objection from the original applicant for the EID, there would be a dispute that would be dealt with in the usual way under the provisions of

[1]   See para **18.19**.
[2]   LRR 2003, r 137(1), (2). There is power to permit applications to be made in other forms: see LRR 2003, r 132. So far as we can ascertain, this power has not yet been exercised in relation to applications under r 137.
[3]   Form EX2, panel 9.
[4]   Ibid, panel 10.
[5]   Land Registry Practice Guide, Exempting Documents from the General Right to Inspect and Copy, PG57, para 6.1.
[6]   LRR 2003, r 137(3).

LRA 2002, s 73, and that if the matter could not be resolved by agreement, the matter would be referred to the Adjudicator: see paras **20.29** et seq. That is not, however, the view of the Registry, which has stated its practice as follows:

> 'If there appears to be a case for issuing the full copy, we will normally serve notice on the person(s) who applied to designate the document and they will have the opportunity to make representations to inform the decision-making process by the registrar.' [1]

It is not thought that this view would survive a challenge in judicial review proceedings. It is provided by LRA 2002, s 73(1) that 'anyone may object to an application by the registrar'. There is therefore no obvious reason why the representations by the person who originally applied for the EID should not be regarded as an objection, so as to trigger a reference to the Adjudicator.

18.30   If the registrar decides that none of the information excluded from the EDID is prejudicial information he must provide an official copy of the EID to the applicant under r 137.[2] He must also remove the designation of the document as an EID and any entry to that effect in the register.[3] If the registrar decides that although all or some of the information excluded is prejudicial information, the public interest in providing an official copy of the EID to the applicant outweighs the public interest in not doing so, he must provide an official copy of the EID to the applicant under LRR 2003, r 137.[4]

Application for removal of the designation of a document as an exempt information document

18.31   The person who applied for a document to be designated as an EID under LRR 2003, r 136, may apply for that designation to be removed.[5] The application must be in Form EX3.[6] If the registrar is satisfied that the application is in order, he must remove the document's designation as an EID and remove any entry to that effect in the register.[7] If a document has been designated as an EID under more than one application, and not all of the applicants apply for the removal of the designation, the registrar must replace the existing EDID with a new one that excludes only that information omitted from those EIDs that have not been withdrawn.[8]

---

[1]   Land Registry Practice Guide, Exempting Documents from the General Right to Inspect and Copy, PG57, para 6.

[2]   LRR 2003, r 137(4)

[3]   Ibid, r 137(5).

[4]   Ibid, r 137(4)

[5]   Ibid, r 138(1).

[6]   Ibid, r 138(2).

[7]   Ibid r 138(3).

[8]   Ibid, r 138(4)

Transitional period documents

18.32   Transitional period documents fall into two classes. The first comprises leases and charges[1] which have been kept by the registrar since before 13 October 2003, where there was an entry referring to the lease or charge made in the register before 13 October 2003.[2] The second consists of any other document kept by the registrar which is not referred to in the register of title but which relates to an application to the registrar that was received by the registrar before 13 October 2003. Prior to 13 October 2003, such documents could be seen at the discretion of the registrar except in certain limited cases.[3] LRR 2003, r 139(1) provides that, during the period of 2 years beginning on 13 October 2003,[4] a person may only inspect and make copies of transitional period documents at the registrar's discretion (which is unlikely to be exercised in the absence of some compelling reason). There is one exception to this. If the transitional period document is an EID, a person cannot see it unless he applies under r 137 and the registrar is satisfied that he should provide an official copy.[5]

18.33   The purpose of these provisions is to provide a 2-year period within which a person may apply for any transitional period document to be designated an EID. At the end of the 2-year period, transitional period documents not so designated will be open to inspection in the same way as documents created on or after 13 October 2003.

Applications in connection with court proceedings, insolvency and tax liability

18.34   Certain persons, known as 'qualifying applicants',[6] may apply:

(a)   to inspect and make copies of documents that are excepted from the right of inspection by LRR 2003, r 133(2) (see para **18.10**);

(b)   for official copies of any documents that are excepted from the documents for which it is possible to obtain an official copy by LRR 2003, r 135(2) (see para **18.12**);

(c)   for official copies of any transitional period document during the transitional period (see paras **18.32** and **18.33**); and

(d)   for a search of the index of proprietors' names (see para **14.20**) in respect of the name of a person specified (in other words, without the usual restrictions that apply in relation to such a search: see para **14.21**).[7]

---

1   Or copy leases or charges.
2   LRR 2003, r 131.
3   For those limited cases, see LRORR 1991, r 6 (in connection with criminal proceedings, receivership under certain Acts and insolvency) and r 7 (order of a court).
4   See LRR 2003, r 131.
5   Ibid, r 139(2).
6   See ibid, r 140(1).
7   Ibid, r 140(2).

18.35   The lengthy list of qualifying applicants is found in LRR 2003, Sch 5, and includes:[1]

(a)   an Administrator appointed for the purposes of IA 1986;

(b)   a Chief Officer of Police or a police officer authorised by such a Chief Officer;

(c)   a person commissioned by the Commissioners of Customs and Excise;

(d)   a person authorised to apply by the Commissioners of Inland Revenue;

(e)   a constable;

(f)   the Director of Public Prosecutions;

(g)   the Director of the Serious Fraud Office or a member of the Serious Fraud Office authorised to apply on behalf of the Director;

(h)   a liquidator appointed for the purposes of IA 1986;

(i)   an Official Receiver for the purposes of IA 1986; and

(j)   a trustee in bankruptcy.

18.36   The application has to be made on Form PIC, OC2 or PN1 as appropriate, together with a Form CIT attached.[2] That form requires the applicant to give the appropriate certificate, specified in Sch 5 to LRR 2003 (there are 13 different certificates, numbered from A to M on Form CIT and the applicant ticks the relevant box). For example, a Chief Officer of Police gives Certificate A, certifying that he believes that a specified criminal offence has been or is reasonably suspected to have been committed and that there is reason to believe that the information required may be relevant to the investigation of the offence or to the institution of proceedings for it.

18.37   Form CIT may be used in conjunction with other applications for which no special powers of inspection are conferred.[3]

CONCLUSIVENESS OF FILED COPIES

18.38   Under s 110(4) of the LRA 1925, the register was conclusive in relation to the abstracts and excerpts from documents referred to in it. Section 120 of the LRA 2002 contains a similar but more far-reaching provision that reflects the implications of an open register – something that did not exist in 1925. The presumption created by s 120 applies where:

–   'a disposition relates to land to which a registered estate relates'; and

–   an entry in the register relating to the registered estate refers to a document kept by the registrar which is not an original.[4]

---

[1]   This is not the complete list, but merely some examples.

[2]   LRR 2003, r 140(3).

[3]   Ibid, r 140(4).

[4]   LRA 2002, s 120(1).

In those circumstances, as between the parties to the disposition, the document kept by the registrar is to be taken to be correct,[1] and to contain all the material parts of the original document.[2] Something must be said of the two elements mentioned above.

18.39 First, the rather Delphic phrase 'a disposition relates to land to which a registered estate relates', means that the section applies in relation to the parties to the following dispositions:

(a)   a registered disposition;

(b)   the grant of an interest out of registered land that is not itself capable of registration, such as a lease granted for a term of 7 years or less;[3] and

(c)   the disposition of an interest mentioned in (b), as where there is an assignment of a lease granted for a term of 7 years or less.[4]

As there is an open register, even parties to a disposition that cannot be registered may rely upon its terms. For example, a person taking a lease for 7 years might wish to search the superior freehold title to see if the land was subject to restrictive covenants. The LRA 2002 – unlike s 110(4) of the LRA 1925 – does not differentiate between registered dispositions and other dealings with registered land.

18.40 Secondly, the second element mentioned in para **18.38** is that entry in the register relates to a document kept by the registrar which is not an original.[5] The presumption in s 120 of the LRA 2002 is intended to meet the case where the register refers to an abstract, copy or extract from a document, but where the registrar no longer keeps the original. There is no need for any similar rule in a case where the registrar has retained the original, as any person may inspect and copy that document.[6]

18.41 The LRA 2002 further provides that no party to the disposition may require production of the original document,[7] and that no party to the disposition is to be affected by any provision of the original document which is not contained in the document kept by the registrar.[8] The registrar thereby precludes any further investigation in relation to such original documents. The sense of this is obvious, given that the registrar does not have the original document. A person who suffers loss by reason of a mistake in a document

---

[1]   LRA 2002, s 120(2)(a).

[2]   Ibid, s 120(2)(b).

[3]   Which takes effect as an unregistered interest that overrides a registrable disposition: LRA 2002, Sch 3, para 1.

[4]   Cf (2001) Law Com No 271, para 9.50.

[5]   As is the case with many leases: see para **18.4**.

[6]   LRA 2002, s 66. See para **18.3**.

[7]   Ibid, s 120(3).

[8]   Ibid, s 120(4).

kept by the registrar which is not an original and is referred to in the register is, however, entitled to be indemnified.[1]

HISTORICAL INFORMATION

18.42   The register of title is a record of the title to land as it stands at any given moment. It does not provide a history of the title. In contrast, in relation to unregistered conveyancing, a landowner is likely to know the history of his title back to a conveyance – his root of title – that was made at least 15 years prior to the conveyance under which he acquired title to the land. There are times when it is useful to know the history of a title. For example, if a parcel of land is apparently subject to an easement or restrictive covenant, it is important to know whether both the dominant and servient tenements were once in common ownership so as to extinguish the easement or covenant. Similarly, when a developer of an estate has sold off a plot of land, taking restrictive covenants from the purchaser for the benefit of the land which the developer retained, it is very useful to be able to see the title to the relevant parts of the estate as they were at the date when the relevant plot was sold.[2] The registrar does in fact have a computerised record of the history of many titles, although it may be incomplete. Prior to the coming into force of the LRA 2002, the registrar did sometimes provide information about the history of the title if there was a good reason to do so. Many of those who responded to the Consultative Document, *Land Registration for the Twenty-First Century*,[3] commented on the difficulties that could result from the lack of an historical record of the title.

18.43   The Law Commission and the Land Registry accepted that, where (for example) an issue or dispute had arisen which could be resolved by reference to the historical devolution of the title, it ought to be possible for a person interested to have access to such information. The LRA 2002 therefore provides that the registrar may, on application, provide information about the history of a registered title.[4] There are two important and necessary qualifications to this principle. First, there is nothing in the LRA 2002 that requires the registrar to keep an historical record of a title. It is only to the extent that he does have such a record that the power conferred by the Act is exercisable. Secondly, inquiries about the historical devolution of a title should never become a routine conveyancing inquiry – it would rather defeat the point of registered title if they did.[5]

---

[1]   LRA 2002, Sch 8, para 1(1)(c); see also para **23.7**.
[2]   For other examples, see (2001) Law Com No 271, para 9.58.
[3]   (1998) Law Com No 254.
[4]   LRA 2002, s 69(1). This power to provide historical information can be contracted out: see ibid, s 69(3)(b).
[5]   See (2001) Law Com No 271, para 9.60. It would also add materially to the cost of conveyancing, whereas one aim of the LRA 2002 is to try to reduce conveyancing costs.

18.44   The exercise of the registrar's power is subject to rules,[1] and r 144 lays down the circumstances in which historical information may be made available. A person may apply for a copy of –

(a)   the last edition for a specified day; or
(b)   every edition for a specified day;[2]

of both a current registered title and a registered title that has been closed, that is kept in electronic form.[3] The relevant date *must* be specified or the application will be rejected. Application is made in Form HC1.[4] That Form carries the warning that copies of the historical registered title may not provide a complete record of all transactions made.

18.45   Where the application is for a copy of the last edition of a registered title for a specified day, then provided that it is in order and an edition of that registered title is being kept in electronic form, the registrar must issue a paper copy of the edition of the registered title at the end of that day.[5] Similarly, and subject to the same provisos, where the application is for a copy of every edition of a registered title for a specified day, the registrar must issue a paper copy of the edition of the registered title at the end of that day and any prior edition kept in electronic form of the registered title for that same day.[6] Where only part of the edition of the registered title requested is kept by the registrar in electronic form, he must issue a paper copy of that part.[7]

---

[1]   LRA 2002, s 69(2).
[2]   A new edition of the register is frequently prepared when land is removed from a title, where a title is sub-divided, and where two or more titles are amalgamated: cf para **14.3**.
[3]   LRR 2003, r 144(1).
[4]   Ibid, r 144(2). There is power under LRR 2003, r 132 and Sch 2, for the registrar to issue a notice which would allow for delivery of such applications by other means. The power has not yet been exercised.
[5]   Ibid, r 144(3)(a). There is power under LRR 2003, r 132 and Sch 2, for the registrar to issue a notice which would allow for delivery of the results of such an application to be by other means. The power has not yet been exercised.
[6]   Ibid, r 144(3)(b). There is the same power that will allow for electronic delivery of the results of such an application.
[7]   Ibid, r 144(4). Again, in time, delivery may be in electronic form.

CHAPTER 19

OFFICIAL SEARCHES OF THE REGISTER, PRIORITY PROTECTION AND OUTLINE APPLICATIONS

INTRODUCTION

19.1 The LRA 2002 confers an express rule-making power to make provision for official searches of the register, including searches of pending applications for first registration.[1] In particular, it is provided that rules may be made[2] providing for:

—   the form of applications for searches;
—   the manner in which such applications may be made;
—   the form of official search certificates; and
—   the manner in which such certificates may be issued.[3]

19.2 Official searches of the index map and of the index of relating franchises and manors have already been explained.[4] In this chapter the following are considered:

(a)   official searches with priority;
(b)   official searches without priority; and
(c)   official searches by a mortgagee for the purposes of s 56(3) of the Family Law Act 1996 (FLA 1996).

As we explain below, official searches with priority can only be made by purchasers who are intending to enter into a registrable disposition.[5] There is a more limited form of protection for other forms of intended dealing with

---

[1]   LRA 2002, s 70. For the provision as to official searches prior to the LRA 2002, see the Land Registration (Official Searches) Rules 1993 (LROSR 1993), SI 1993/3276. The first provision for such searches was introduced in 1930. Prior to that, searches had to be conducted in person at HM Land Registry in Lincoln's Inn Fields.
[2]   LRA 2002, s 70(a)–(d).
[3]   Authorised persons may be permitted to issue official search certificates pursuant to a network access agreement: LRA 2002, Sch 5, para 1(2)(c).
[4]   See para **14.19**.
[5]   See para **19.8**.

registered land, namely by means of outline applications. These are explained at paras **19.24** et seq.

19.3   Under the LRA 1925, when an intending purchaser made an official search he received a copy of the title to land as it was on the day when the search was conducted. In order to protect the purchaser[1] from any third party rights which might supervene between the dates of search and completion, the purchaser could make an official search with priority under the LROSR 1993.[2] The official certificate of search then conferred priority on the purchaser, such that any entry which was made in that register during the 30-day[3] priority period relating to that search was postponed to a subsequent application to register the instrument effecting the purchase.[4] This principle – that an official search with priority gives the intending purchaser a period of grace within which to register his purchase, postponing subsequent applications until the end of that period of priority – is carried through into the LRA 2002 and the LRR 2003 made under it.

19.4   Section 72 of the LRA 2002 makes express provision for priority protection and extends the circumstances in which protection can be obtained.[5] Those circumstances are explained in para **19.5**. Provided that the application for registration is made within the priority period, it will be protected.[6] It follows that any entry made during that period will be postponed to the application for registration.[7] There are, however, two exceptions to this.

(1)   The first case is where the earlier entry was made in pursuance of a protected application and the priority period relating to that application ranks first in time ahead of the one relating to the application for the other entry.[8] If, for example, A has made an application for a priority search on day 1 and B then makes an application for a priority search on day 5, B's priority will not be protected against any application by A to be registered during the priority period consequent upon A's application.

(2)   The second case is where the earlier entry is one to which a direction under s 46(3) of the LRA 2002 applies, where the court has exercised its powers to order that a restriction be entered in the register with

---

[1]   Defined in LROSR 1993, r 2(1) as any person including a lessee or chargee who in good faith and for valuable consideration acquires or intends to acquire a legal estate in land.

[2]   A search without priority is also possible: LROSR 1993, rr 9, 10.

[3]   Ibid, r 2(1).

[4]   Ibid, r 6.

[5]   See (2001) Law Com No 271, paras 9.62–9.75.

[6]   LRA 2002, s 72(1).

[7]   Ibid, s 72(2). The registrar may defer dealing with an application where a period of priority protection applies: s 72(5).

[8]   Ibid, s 72(3).

overriding priority.[1] As has been explained,[2] when the court orders the entry of a restriction under s 46 of the Act, it may direct that the entry should have overriding priority. This means that the restriction will have priority over any priority protection already obtained by a person under s 72 of the Act. Such cases will be rare and the court will almost certainly require an undertaking in damages from the applicant for the restriction.[3]

19.5 The LRA 2002 makes provision for priority protection in two circumstances, although only the first of these is at present available.[4]

(a) The first situation is, as under the previous law, by making an official search with priority. This includes searches of pending applications for first registration.

(b) The second situation is new. Priority protection will be conferred by the noting on the register of a contract for the making of a registrable disposition of a registered estate or charge. The thinking behind this second case is that, when electronic conveyancing is introduced, it will become impossible to enter into a contract to make a disposition of a registered estate or charge, except by simultaneously noting the contract on the register.[5] This is in furtherance of the Act's stated aim of achieving a conclusive register.[6] At present, it is unusual for estate contracts to be noted on the register unless they are likely to remain in being for some time, as is the case with options and some conditional contracts. As a sort of quid pro quo for the requirement that such contracts should be noted where presently they are not, the entry of a notice will not only protect the purchaser against third parties, but will give him the additional benefit of priority protection for the priority period. It is thought that this second form of priority protection will be introduced as part of the development of electronic conveyancing.

19.6 The details of priority protection are a matter for rules.[7] The LRA 2002 sets out the matters for which the rules may make provision. First, it is provided that rules may make provision for the keeping of records in relation to priority periods and the inspection of such records.[8] This record is the day list,[9] which has been explained at para **14.22**. This means that it is possible to discover from a search of the register whether or not a person has the benefit

[1] LRA 2002, s 72(4).
[2] See para **10.80**.
[3] Cf LRA 2002, s 46(5).
[4] Ibid, s 72(6).
[5] See para **28.3**.
[6] See para **1.7**.
[7] LRA 2002, s 72(6).
[8] Ibid, s 72(6)(b).
[9] See LRR 2003, r 12.

of priority protection at any given time. Secondly, it is provided that rules may in particular also make provision for the following:

—   the commencement and length of a priority period: this is explained at para **19.11**;
—   the applications for registration to which such a period relates: see paras **19.8** et seq;[1]
—   the order in which competing priority periods rank: see para **19.19**; and
—   the application of the priority principle explained in para **19.3** in cases where more than one priority period relates to the same application: see para **19.18**.[2]

TERMINOLOGY

19.7   Part 13 of the LRR 2003, 'Information etc', contains the provisions on priority searches.[3] Those provisions employ certain terms, which are defined in LRR 2003, r 131, of which the following are relevant:

(a)   a 'protectable disposition' means a registrable disposition[4] of a registered estate made for valuable consideration;
(b)   a 'purchaser' means a person who has entered into or intends to enter into a protectable disposition as disponee;
(c)   the 'priority period' means the period beginning at the time when that application is entered on the day list and terminating at midnight at the end of the thirtieth business day thereafter.[5]

It is only possible to make an official search with priority if an official copy of the register has previously been obtained.[6] This is because, in making an application for an official search with priority, it is necessary to specify the 'search from date'. This is defined by r 131 as the date stated in an official

---

[1]   The protection may be for the benefit of more than one application. If an intending buyer is purchasing with the aid of a mortgage, priority protection can and should be obtained for both: cf para **19.18**.

[2]   LRA 2002, s 72(7).

[3]   See Official Searches and Outline Applications, PG12.

[4]   Including a disposition made after there has been a disposition of unregistered land that triggers compulsory registration but before that triggering disposition has been registered (see LRR 2003, r 38; and para **2.24**). For registrable dispositions, see LRA 2002, s 27; and Chapter 8.

[5]   A business day is a day on which the Registry is open to the public: see LRR 2003, r 216(1); para **36.5**. There is power to extend the opening of the Registry to include Saturdays (see LRR 2003, r 216(2)), but this has not yet been exercised.

[6]   Which in practice there will have been. The applicant will normally obtain such a copy before he agrees to enter into the transaction, typically before he exchanges contracts prior to a purchase of land. For the procedure for obtaining an official copy, see LRR 2003, r 134; para **18.11**.

copy of the individual register of the relevant title, as the date on which the entries shown on that official copy were subsisting.[1]

OFFICIAL SEARCHES WITH PRIORITY

Making an application

19.8   Under the rules, only a purchaser (as defined above) may apply for an official search with priority, and he may do so in relation to the individual register of a registered title to which the protectable disposition relates.[2] This right to make an official search with priority extends to a case where there has been a disposition of unregistered land to which the requirement of registration under LRA 2002, s 6,[3] applies. The applicant may in those circumstances apply for an official search with priority in relation to that pending application.[4] Because only a purchaser may apply for an official search with priority, other persons, such as a disponee not for value, cannot protect themselves in this way. The only way to protect such dispositions is to make an outline application. This is explained in paras **19.24** et seq.

19.9   Application for an official search with priority may be made in the following ways:[5]

(a)   Where the search is in respect of the whole of the land in a registered title or in a pending first registration application, the application is made by using Form OS1. The information required by that Form includes the search from date, a statement that the applicant intends to purchase, take a lease or take a charge of the property, the address or short description of the property and whether the search is a registered land search or a pending first registration search.

(b)   Where the search is in respect of part of the land in a registered title or in a pending first registration application, Form OS2 must be used. The information required is similar to that needed when completing Form OS1, but with one difference. An accompanying plan in duplicate will be required if there is no approved estate plan and the property is merely identified in the application by the address or short description.

19.10   Form OS1 may be used in an application lodged by post, DX, fax, Land Registry Telephone Services, Land Registry Direct, through NLIS or made orally at a Land Registry Customer Information Centre. Because of the

---

[1]   Or the equivalent, in relation to an access to the register electronically by remote terminal.
[2]   LRR 2003, r 147(1).
[3]   See paras **2.10** et seq.
[4]   LRR 2003, r 147(2).
[5]   See Official Searches and Outline Applications, PG12, Part 6, for a detailed explanation of how to apply.

requirement for a plan in many cases, Form OS2 may be used only where the application is lodged by post or fax, or through NLIS.[1]

19.11   An application for an official search with priority is to be taken as having been made on the date and at the time of the day notice of it was entered on the day list.[2] The entry on the day list of the notice of an application for a search with priority confers on the application a priority period – 30 business days[3] – for an entry in the register in respect of the protectable disposition to which the official search relates.[4] For the priority protection that is conferred, see para **19.17**.

19.12   A person who has made an application for an official search with priority of a registered title or in relation to a pending first registration application, may withdraw that official search by making an application to the registrar for that purpose.[5] As no form of application is prescribed, the application must be in Form AP1.[6] Once such an official search has been withdrawn, the priority protection conferred on it by the entry of the notice of application in the day list ceases.[7] The power to withdraw an official search with priority should be utilised whenever an intended transaction protected by such a search does not in fact proceed. Its removal will mean that other pending applications can then be completed without delay.

Official search certificates

19.13   If an application for an official search is in order, an official search certificate with priority must be issued and must give the result of the search at the date and time when the application was entered in the day list.[8]

19.14   Where the search is of an individual register of a registered title (whether in respect of all or part of that title), the certificate must include (amongst other matters) the following information:

---

[1]   See LRR 2003, r 132; and Notices and Directions by the Chief Land Registrar, Notices 1, 2, 3, 4, and 6 (October 2003: see further, Official Searches and Outline Applications, PG12, para 6.3).

[2]   LRR 2003, r 148(1). For the day list, see para **14.22**. The provisions of LRR 2003, r 15, which determine the time at which applications are to be taken to be made, do not apply to applications under Part 13 of LRR 2003 (Information, etc), except in relation to an application that the registrar designate a document an EID under r 136 (see paras **18.19** et seq). Rule 15 does not, therefore, apply to applications for an official search with priority. It *does* apply to the application to register the protectable disposition. For LRR 2003, r 15, see para **20.26**.

[3]   See para **19.7**.

[4]   LRR 2003, r 148(3).

[5]   Ibid, r 150(1).

[6]   See LRR 2003, r 13. The omission was deliberate: see Land Registration Rules 2003 – A Land Registry Consultation, p 93, para 50.

[7]   LRR 2003, r 150(3).

[8]   Ibid, r 149(1).

(a)   the date and time of the official search certificate;

(b)   details of any relevant adverse entries made in the individual register since the end of the day specified in the application as the search from date;

(c)   notice of the entry of any relevant pending application affecting the registered title entered on the day list;[1]

(d)   notice of the entry of any relevant official search the priority period of which has not expired;

(e)   the date and time at which the priority expires.[2]

19.15   Where the search is in relation to a pending application for first registration, the certificate must include (amongst other matters) the following information:

(a)   the date and time of the official search certificate;

(b)   the date and time at which the pending application for first registration was entered on the day list;

(c)   notice of the entry of any relevant pending application affecting the estate sought to be registered and entered on the day list subsequent to the date and time at which the pending application for first registration was entered on the day list;[3]

(d)   notice of the entry of any relevant official search the priority period of which has not expired affecting the pending application for first registration;

(e)   the date and time at which priority expires.[4]

19.16   Normally the certificate of search will be issued by first-class post or through the DX. Where the application is not made by post, DX or fax, the position is as follows:

(a)   Where the application is in respect of a registered title, and there have been no adverse entries in the individual register since the 'search from' date and there are no pending applications or unexpired priority searches, the official certificate of search may be given:

    (i)   by telephone, where the application is lodged by telephone;

    (ii)   by displaying it on screen, where the application is lodged through Land Registry Direct;

    (iii)   by sending the certificate through the NLIS system, where the application is lodged through NLIS; or

---

[1]   Other than an application to designate a document as an exempt information document under r 136. For such applications, see para **18.13**.
[2]   LRR 2003, r 149(3); Sch 6, Part 3.
[3]   Other than an application to designate a document as an exempt information document under r 136.
[4]   LRR 2003, r 149(3); Sch 6, Part 4.

(iv)   orally, where the application is made orally at a Land Registry Customer Information Centre.[1]

That official search, although not given in written paper form, is guaranteed by the Land Registry.[2]

(b)   Where the application is in respect of a registered title, and either there have been adverse entries in the individual register since the 'search from' date or there is some relevant entry subsisting on the day list, the official certificate of search will be sent by first-class post or through the DX. However, the registrar has a discretion (which he will in practice exercise) to inform the applicant[3] by telephone,[4] by transmission to the remote terminal,[5] or orally,[6] why he cannot at once give an official certificate of search.[7] The registrar will only give basic information. He is not required to provide the applicant with details of any relevant entry.[8] That is a matter for the written official search certificate that will be sent by first-class post or DX.

(c)   Where the application relates to a pending application for first registration and there is no relevant entry subsisting on the day list, the official certificate of search may be given in whatever is the manner explained above in (a).

(d)   Where the application relates to a pending application for first registration and there is some relevant entry subsisting on the day list, the registrar has a discretion, which he will again in practice exercise, to inform the applicant in the manner corresponding to the form of application[9] as to why he is unable to give an official search certificate there and then.[10] Once again, he need only provide basic information about the entry in question.[11] Full details will be given in the official certificate of search that is sent by first-class post or DX.

PRIORITY PROTECTION

19.17   As indicated at para **19.11**, when an application for an official search is entered on the day list, that entry confers a priority period of 30 business days. The applicant must apply for an entry in the register in respect of the relevant protectable disposition within that period if he is to enjoy the protection

---

[1]   See LRR 2003, rr 149(2)(b), 157(1), (2).
[2]   See Official Searches and Outline Applications, PG12, paras 4.1.1–4.1.4.
[3]   Whether before or after the official search has been completed.
[4]   In the case of a telephone application.
[5]   In the case of an application through Land Registry Direct or NLIS.
[6]   In the case of an oral application at a Land Registry Customer Information Centre.
[7]   See LRR 2003, r 157(1), (3).
[8]   Ibid, r 157(4).
[9]   See (b) above.
[10]   LRR 2003, r 157(2), (3).
[11]   Ibid, r 157(4).

conferred by the official search.[1] That means that the application for registration[2] or relating to a registrable estate[3] should be delivered to the proper office[4] before noon on the day on which the priority expires.[5] The LRR 2003 make provision by which, where the time at which the application is deemed to be made coincides with the expiry of the priority period (in other words, where the application is deemed to be made at midnight[6] at the end of the thirtieth business day), the application is to be taken to be within the priority period.[7]

19.18   Priority protection may be given to more than one transaction if there are two dispositions concerning the same registered land or the same registrable estate or charge, of which the second is dependent upon the first. The usual (but by no means only) case is where a purchase of land is to be financed with the aid of a legal charge. If the intending chargee obtains an official search certificate with priority, that certificate will protect not only the charge but also the disposition of the legal estate upon which that charge depends.[8] To obtain this priority, both applications for registration must be made within the priority period and must in due course be completed by registration.[9] It follows from this, that where a purchase is to be funded with the aid of a legal charge, it is only necessary for the intending chargee to obtain an official search certificate with priority in order to protect both the purchaser and the chargee.[10]

19.19   There may, at any given time, be more than one official search certificate with priority, which relates to the same registered land, or (where there is a pending application for first registration) to the same registrable estate or charge. In those circumstances, the priority accorded by the certificates is determined by the order in which the applications for official search with priority were entered on the day list, unless the applicants agree

1   For that protection, see para **19.4**.
2   Where the application relates to registered land.
3   Where there is a pending application for first registration.
4   For the 'proper office', see LRA 2002, s 100(3) and para **36.3**.
5   See LRR 2003, r 15, and para **20.26**, for the time when an application is taken to be made. An application that arrives after noon *may* be entered on the day list of the day of arrival, but the Registry cannot guarantee that this will happen: see Official Searches and Outline Applications, PG12, para 5.2. As explained at para **19.11**, although r 15 applies to the application to register the protectable disposition, it does not apply to the application for an official search with priority: see r 15(4).
6   Under LRR 2003, r 15: see para **20.26**.
7   Ibid, r 154.
8   See ibid, rr 151, 152. The rules refer to 'a *prior* registrable disposition' affecting the same registered land (where the application relates to land that is registered) or registrable estate (where the application relates to a pending application for first registration): see rr 151(1), 152(1). Strictly speaking, where there is a transfer of a legal estate which depends upon a loan from the chargee, the 'acquisition of the legal estate and the charge are not only precisely simultaneous but indissolubly bound together': see *Abbey National Building Society v Cann* [1991] 1 AC 56, at 92, per Lord Oliver of Aylmerton.
9   LRR 2003, r 151(4).
10 See Official Searches and Outline Applications, PG12, para 5.3.

otherwise.[1] Where one transaction is dependent upon another, the registrar must assume, unless the contrary is apparent, that the applicants for official search with priority have agreed that their applications have priority so as to give effect to the sequence of the documents effecting the transactions.[2] Thus, for example, where the first disposition is the grant of a long lease in exchange for a premium, to be funded by a loan secured by a legal charge, it will be presumed that the grant takes effect before the legal charge.

OFFICIAL SEARCHES WITHOUT PRIORITY

19.20   Any person may apply for an official search without priority of an individual register of a registered title.[3] The applicant need not be a 'purchaser' because there is no restriction as to who can apply, as there is in relation to an official search with priority.[4] Application should be made on Form OS3.[5] Form OS3 may be used for a search of the whole or part of a registered title.[6] It is similar in its requirements to Forms OS1 and OS2,[7] except that the applicant does not have to state why he is applying for the search. Application can be made by post, DX, fax, Land Registry Telephone Services, through NLIS or orally at a Land Registry Customer Information Centre. However, telephone and oral applications can only be made in respect of the whole of a registered estate and not merely part.[8] If the application is in order, an official search certificate without priority must be issued.[9] The information provided by the certificate will be in the same form as it is with an official search with priority of an individual register explained at para **19.14**.[10] Usually the certificate of search will be issued by first-class post or through the DX, but where the application is not made by post, DX or fax, the certificate may be issued in the appropriate manner set out at para **19.16** (save that application for an official search without priority cannot be made through Land Registry Direct).

19.21   There are a number of reasons why a person might wish to make an official search of the register without priority. For example, such a search may be made by a person who is intending to acquire a mere equitable interest in a property, such as the intending grantee of an option. A legal chargee, who has exercised his power of sale and has a surplus in his hands after discharging the

---

[1]   LRR 2003, r 153(1).
[2]   Ibid, r 153(2).
[3]   Ibid, r 155(1).
[4]   Ibid, r 147(1); see para **19.8**.
[5]   Ibid, r 155(2).
[6]   A plan in duplicate will, however, be required unless an estate plan has been approved. See Form OS3 and LRR 2003, r 155(3).
[7]   See para **19.9**.
[8]   See Notices and Directions by the Chief Land Registrar, Notices 1, 2, 4, and 6 (October 2003).
[9]   LRR 2003, r 156(1).
[10]   Ibid, r 156(3).

debt due to him from the chargor, may make an official search without priority to ensure that he pays over that surplus to the person entitled to it. As has been explained at para **12.82**, for the purposes of LPA 1925, s 105, the chargee is taken to have notice of anything in the register immediately before the disposition on sale: see LRA 2002, s 54.

OFFICIAL SEARCHES BY A MORTGAGEE FOR THE PURPOSES OF THE FAMILY LAW ACT 1996

19.22   Under s 56 of the FLA 1996, where a mortgagee of land brings proceedings to enforce its security in respect of a house which is subject to matrimonial homes rights that are protected in the register[1] at the relevant time, it must serve notice of the action on the person whose rights are so protected if he or she is not already a party to the action.[2] The 'relevant time' for these purposes is defined by s 56(3). Where the following events have occurred, namely:

(a)   an official search has been made of the register;
(b)   a certificate of search has been issued; and
(c)   the action has been commenced within the priority period;

the 'relevant time' means the date of the certificate. In any other case, it means the time when the action is commenced.[3]

19.23   The LRR 2003 make specific provision for such a 'Matrimonial Homes Rights' search: see r 158. Application must be made in Form MH3,[4] and may be made by post, DX, telephone, and through Land Registry Direct or NLIS.[5] The official certificate of search can be issued in paper form or in the form appropriate to the application: see para **19.16**(a)(i)–(iii). The form of official certificate is prescribed,[6] and it will, in particular, state whether, at the date of the official search, a matrimonial home rights notice or matrimonial home rights caution has been registered against the registered title searched and, if so, the date of registration and the name of the person in whose favour the notice or caution was registered. It will also state whether there is a pending application for the entry of a matrimonial home rights notice entered on the day list. The registrar has a discretion to inform the applicant, by any means of communication, before the official search has been completed

---

[1]   Whether by way of a notice under FLA 1996, s 31(10) or under Matrimonial Homes Act 1983, s 2(8), or by means of a caution under Matrimonial Homes Act 1967.
[2]   FLA 1996, s 56(1), (2).
[3]   Ibid, s 56(4).
[4]   Form MH3 is a very straightforward form, which requires only the obvious information necessary to identify the registered estate and contains a statement that the application is made for an official search under FLA 1996, s 56(3).
[5]   See Notices and Directions by the Chief Land Registrar, Notices 1, 3 and 4 (October 2003).
[6]   See LRR 2003, r 159(2); Sch 6, Part 5.

whether or not either a matrimonial home rights notice or matrimonial home rights caution has been entered in the register of the relevant registered title or there is a pending application for the entry of a matrimonial home rights notice entered on the day list.[1]

OUTLINE APPLICATIONS

19.24   The outline application procedure provides a mechanism by which a period of priority can be obtained for the entry in the register of some right or interest in registered land or in land which is already subject to an application for first registration for which it is not possible to make a priority search.[2]

19.25   Such an application can only be made in respect of a right, interest or matter that exists at the time when the application is made.[3] It cannot, therefore, be employed in relation to an intended transaction that has not yet been executed. The application must not be any of the following:[4]

(a)   an application that can be protected by an official search with priority;
(b)   an application for first registration;
(c)   an application for a caution against first registration or in respect of the cautions register;
(d)   an application dealing with part only of a registered title; or
(e)   an application under Part 13 of LRR 2003.[5]

Examples of applications that can properly be protected in this way include:[6]

(i)   an assent of the whole of a registered estate or of a registered charge by personal representatives;
(ii)   a transfer of the whole of a registered estate not for value;
(iii)   an application for an agreed or unilateral notice; and
(iv)   an application for a restriction.

It will be apparent that in certain situations it is not possible to make either an official search with priority or an outline application, as where there is an assent or transfer of part only of a registered estate, or an application for first registration.

---

[1]   LRR 2003, r 160.
[2]   See ibid, r 54.
[3]   Ibid, r 54(2)(b).
[4]   Ibid, r 54(2)(a).
[5]   Applications under Part 13 include applications for official copies, relating to exempt information documents, applications for historical information, and applications for official searches.
[6]   For a full list, see the table in Official Searches and Outline Applications, PG12, section 10.

19.26   There is no paper form of application.[1] The application can only be made:

(a)   orally at any Land Registry Customer Information Centre;
(b)   by telephone through Land Registry Telephone Services; or
(c)   electronically through Land Registry Direct or NLIS.[2]

The outline application must contain the following particulars:[3]

(i)   the number of the registered title or, where there is a pending application for first registration, the number allocated to that application;
(ii)   where there is only one proprietor or applicant for first registration who is an individual, his surname;
(iii)   where there is more than one proprietor or applicant for first registration, or where the proprietor is not an individual, the full name of one of the proprietors or applicants;
(iv)   the nature of the application (in other words, the nature of the right, interest or matter that is the subject of the application);
(v)   the name and address of the person or firm lodging the application;
(vi)   other particulars specified in any notice made under LRR 2003, Sch 2, such as the administrative area and postcode of the property.[4]

19.27   When such an outline application is made:

(a)   it must be allocated an official reference number;
(b)   it must be identified on the day list and marked with the date and time at which it is taken to be made;[5] and
(c)   the registrar must notify the applicant of the official reference number as soon as practicable.

19.28   The applicant must then deliver to the appropriate office,[6] before the expiry of the 'reserved period' the relevant application form duly completed in respect of the outline application. It must quote the official reference number (and the relevant forms of application contain the necessary box for this purpose) and must be accompanied by the appropriate documentation and the

---

[1]   An application can only be made during the currency of a notice under LRR 2003, Sch 2. For the relevant notices, see Notices and Directions by the Chief Land Registrar, Notices 1, 3, 4 and 6 (October 2003).
[2]   LRR 2003, r 54(3).
[3]   Ibid, r 54(4).
[4]   See Notices and Directions by the Chief Land Registrar, Notices 3 and 4.
[5]   Cf LRR 2003, r 15; below, para **20.26**.
[6]   Which means the proper office designated under an order under LRA 2002, s 100(3): see LRR 2003, r 54(8). For the proper office, see para **36.3**.

prescribed fee.[1] The 'reserved period' means the period expiring at 12 noon on the fourth business day following the day when the outline application was taken to be made.[2] This is obviously very much less than the 30 business days that an applicant for an official search with priority obtains.

19.29   If the application for registration is not made before the expiry of the reserved period, the outline application must be cancelled.[3] However, if the application is delivered subsequent to that cancellation, the registrar must accept the form as an application in its own right.[4] That application will not have the advantage of the 4 business days' priority that it would have had, if it had been delivered in time. It will, therefore, take effect subject to any application that was lodged in the interim.

---

[1]   LRR 2003, r 54(6).
[2]   Ibid, r 54(9).
[3]   Ibid, r 54(6).
[4]   Ibid, r 54(7).

CHAPTER 20

FORMS, APPLICATIONS, EXECUTION OF DOCUMENTS AND NOTICES

INTRODUCTION

20.1 In this chapter we examine four important procedural matters:

(a) the use of forms;
(b) applications to the registrar;
(c) the execution of documents; and
(d) the form, content and service of notices, and addresses for service;

under the LRA 2002 and LRR 2003.

FORMS

20.2 There are significantly more prescribed forms under the LRR 2003 than there were under the LRR 1925.[1] Those forms are found in Sch 1 and Sch 3 of the LRR 2003.[2]

Schedule 1 forms

20.3 As regards the forms in Sch 1, there are 20 forms which are broadly the same as their equivalents under LRR 1925,[3] 13 which are significantly changed,[4] and 31 new forms.[5] There was a period of grace of 3 months from 13 October 2003 when the old forms could still be used.[6] Since then they can

---

[1] There are also certain forms which can be used that are not prescribed, such as Forms MH4 (for removing a matrimonial homes right notice), ACD (for a mortgage lender to seek approval for a standard form of charge: see para **12.16**), and RD1 (to request the return of a document).

[2] See LRR 2003, rr 206(1) (Sch 1 forms) and 206(2) (Sch 3 forms). The reference at the start of Sch 1 to LRR 2003, r 11, appears to be an error, as r 11 is concerned with the index of proprietors' names.

[3] Forms AS1, AS2, AS3, CN1, CS, CT1, DL, DS1, DS2, DS3, MH1, MH2, MH3, PIC (formerly Form 111), PN1, SIM, TP1, TP2, TP3 and WCT.

[4] Forms AP1, CI (formerly, Form 102), FR1, OC1 (formerly Form 109), OC2 (formerly Form 110), OS1 (formerly Form 94A), OS2 (formerly Form 94B), OS3 (formerly Form 94C), TR1, TR2, TR3, TR4 and TR5.

[5] Forms ADV1, ADV2, AN1, CC, CCD, CCT, CH1, CH2, CH3, CIT, DB, DI, EX1, EX1A, EX2, EX3, HC1, NAP, PRD1, PRD2, RX1, RX2, RX3, RX4, SC, SIF, UN1, UN2, UN3, UN4 and UT1. The use of Form CH1 is voluntary: see LRR 2003, r 103; para **12.10**.

[6] TPO1 2003, art 26(1)(a).

only be employed where use of the relevant old form is expressly required by law or under the terms of a valid contract entered into before 13 October 2003.[1]

20.4   The general rule is that the Sch 1 forms must be used where required by, and must be prepared in accordance with, the Rules.[2] Forms issued in the Welsh language version are to be regarded as being in the scheduled form.[3] There is a power for the registrar to accept applications in a non-prescribed form if it is not possible for a person to lodge the relevant scheduled form or it is possible only at unreasonable expense.[4] The requirement to use a scheduled form is subject, where appropriate, to the provisions in the LRR 2003 relating to the making of applications and issuing results of applications other than in paper form, during the currency of a notice given under Sch 2 (which provides for the electronic delivery of applications).[5]

20.5   The scheduled forms in Sch 1 fall into several categories:

(a)   Forms of application, such as Forms ADV1 (application for registration of a person in adverse possession), AN1 (application for the entry of an agreed notice), OC1 (application for official copies), UN1 (application for the entry of a unilateral notice), RX1 (application to enter a restriction) and CH2 (application to enter an obligation to make further advances).

(b)   Forms of disposition, such as transfers of whole (Forms TR1–TR5) or part (Forms TP1–TP3), and the various forms of assent (Forms AS1–AS3).

(c)   Forms which are supplementary to other forms, namely Forms CS (continuation sheet for use with application and disposition forms), DI (to disclose unregistered interest pursuant to LRA 2002, s 71, for use with Forms AP1 or FR1), and DL (to list documents, for use with Form FR1 or any application form).

(d)   A certificate of inspection of a title plan pursuant to LRR 2003, r 143(2): Form CI.[6]

(e)   A request to the registrar that he should order the production of a document pursuant to LRR 2003, r 201: Form PRD1, and the notice issued by the registrar to the document holder in response: Form PRD2.[7]

---

1   TPO1 2003, art 26(1)(b). There are limitations on the use of such forms: see ibid, art 26(3) and Sch.
2   LRR 2003, r 206(1). There is provision for the adaptation of certain Sch 1 forms to provide for payment by direct debit: ibid, r 207.
3   Ibid, r 208.
4   Ibid, r 209, which lays down the requirements that must be met.
5   Ibid, r 206(4).
6   See para **18.11**.
7   See para **34.7**.

20.6 There are some documents for which no form is prescribed. These include the grant of a lease, the grant of an easement, or the creation of a rentcharge (in those cases where it is still permitted). In each case, the disponor must use such form as the registrar may direct or allow.[1] In practice, that means using the traditional conveyancing documents and then submitting them for registration under cover of a separate Form AP1 (application to change the register).[2] Where the document affects a registered title it must refer to the title number.[3]

20.7 It is not necessary to use the versions of the Sch 1 forms produced by the Registry. However, other versions must meet the requirements set out in LRR 2003, r 210 for any document in a Sch 1 form (matters such as the paper to be used, the wording, layout, ruling, font and point size, the use of the continuation Form CS where a panel is insufficient in size to contain the required insertions, etc). Rule 211 makes provision for the relaxation of some of the requirements of Sch 1 forms where the form used by the applicant is electronically produced.

Schedule 3 forms

20.8 Schedule 3 to LRR 2003 contains six forms. Three of them are intended for use in various situations in which a document has been executed by a donee of a power of attorney. The Sch 3 forms must be used in all matters to which they refer, or are capable of being applied or adapted, with such alterations as the registrar allows.[4] There are two exceptions to this. First, if the rules require the use of a Sch 1 form, that must be used in preference to a Sch 3 form, where that would otherwise be employed.[5] Secondly, as with Sch 1 forms, there is a power for the registrar to accept applications in a non-prescribed form if it is not possible for a person to lodge the relevant scheduled form or it is possible only at unreasonable expense.[6] Forms issued in the Welsh language version are to be regarded as being in the scheduled form.[7]

Execution by an attorney

20.9 The first three forms under Sch 3 are made pursuant to LRR 2003, rr 61–63. Those rules are concerned with the situation where a document has

---

1   LRR 2003, r 212(1).
2   For Form AP1, see para **20.18**. A document prepared under LRR 2003, r 212 (documents where no form prescribed) must not bear the number of a Sch 1 form: r 212(2).
3   LRR 2003, r 212(3).
4   Ibid, r 206(2).
5   Ibid.
6   Ibid, r 209.
7   Ibid, r 208.

been executed by an attorney.[1] Before making any entry in the register in reliance upon such a document, the registrar will wish to be satisfied either that the document was validly executed or that the party taking the benefit of any disposition made by it enjoys the statutory protection conferred by the Powers of Attorney Act 1971 should the attorney's authority have been revoked.

20.10   Form 1 of Sch 3 is a means of providing evidence to the registrar of the validity of a power of attorney.[2] By LRR 2003, r 61, an attorney who has executed a document and delivers it to the registrar, must produce to the registrar:

(a)   the instrument creating the power of attorney; or

(b)   a photocopy of that instrument that has been certified in accordance with s 3 of the Powers of Attorney Act 1971; or

(c)   in the case of an enduring power of attorney, a document that purports to be an office copy of an instrument registered under the Enduring Powers of Attorney Act 1985;[3] or

(d)   a certificate as to the execution of the power of attorney in Form 1 of LRR 2003, Sch 3, signed by a conveyancer.[4]

20.11   Form 2 of Sch 3 is concerned with the risk that a power of attorney may have been revoked. Under s 5(2) of the Powers of Attorney Act 1971, a transaction made by a donee of a power of attorney after his power of attorney has been revoked, will be treated as valid in favour of a person who had no knowledge of the revocation.[5] Where the interest of a purchaser depends on whether a transaction between the donee of a power of attorney and another person was valid by virtue of s 5(2), there is a conclusive presumption that that other person did not at the material time know of the revocation of the power if (amongst other circumstances) the transaction between that person and the donee was completed within twelve months of the date on which the power came into operation: see s 5(4)(a). Under LRR 2003, r 62(1), if any transaction between a donee of a power of attorney and the person dealing with him is not completed within 12 months of the date on which the power came into operation, the registrar can require the production of evidence to satisfy him that the power had not been revoked at the time of the transaction. By r 62(2), that evidence may consist of or include either a

---

1   See Powers of Attorney and Registered Land, PG9.

2   See ibid, para 7.

3   See Enduring Powers of Attorney Act 1985, s 7(3).

4   LRR 2003, r 61(1). There are other matters addressed in r 61. In the case of an enduring power of attorney that has been registered with the Court of Protection, the court may (amongst other things) give directions with respect to matters such as the management or disposal by the attorney of the property: see Enduring Powers of Attorney Act 1985, s 8(1), (2)(b). If there is any such order, LRR 2003, r 61(2) requires that it must be produced to the registrar.

5   Powers of Attorney Act 1971, s 5(2). See Powers of Attorney and Registered Land, PG9, para 6.

statutory declaration by the person who dealt with the attorney, or a certificate given by that person's conveyancer in Form 2 of Sch 3 to LRR 2003.

20.12 Form 3 of Sch 3 is concerned with the validity of one specific form of delegation. Under s 9(1) of TLATA 1996, trustees of land are permitted to delegate their functions as trustees which relate to the land. Such delegation can only be made by power of attorney in favour of one or more of the beneficiaries under that trust, who are entitled to an interest in possession in that land. By s 9(2), where the trustees have purported to make such a delegation, and another person in good faith deals with the donee of the power, the donee is presumed to have a been a person to whom the trustees' functions could be delegated, unless that other person has knowledge at the time of the transaction that the donee was not such a person. It is provided by LRR 2003, r 63(1), that if any document executed by an attorney to whom functions have been delegated under TLATA 1996, s 9, is delivered to the registrar, the registrar may require the production of evidence to satisfy him that the person who dealt with the attorney has the benefit of the presumption in s 9(2).[1] That evidence may consist of or include either a statutory declaration by the person who dealt with the attorney or a certificate given by that person's conveyancer either in Form 3[2] or in Form 2 if the registrar also requires evidence of non-revocation: see LRR 2003, r 63(2).

Vesting in an incumbent, etc

20.13 Under the New Parishes Measure 1943 (as amended), the Church Commissioners have power to acquire land for a number of specified purposes, such as for a church, a church yard or residence for an incumbent. By s 16 of that Measure, the land, when transferred to the Church Commissioners, vests in the incumbent for the time being of the parish in which it is situated. LRR 2003, r 174, makes provision for the registration of the incumbent on receipt of an application, the transfer to the Church Commissioners and a certificate sealed by the Church Commissioners in Form 4 of LRR 2003, Sch 3.[3] That certificate certifies that the registered estate (or charge) vests in the specified incumbent.

20.14 LRR 2003, r 175, makes provision for a case where, pursuant to some Measure, such as the Pastoral Measure 1983, registered land is transferred to the Church Commissioners, any ecclesiastical corporation (aggregate or sole) or any other person by a scheme of the Church Commissioners, an instrument taking effect on publication in the *London Gazette* made pursuant to any Act or

---

[1] See Powers of Attorney and Registered Land, PG9, para 3.6.
[2] The statutory declaration or certificate states either that the applicant or his client had no knowledge of any lack of good faith on the part of the person who dealt with the attorney, or that the applicant or his client had no knowledge that the attorney was not a person to whom the functions could be delegated under TLATA 1996, s 9.
[3] The certificate may be given either in the transfer or in a separate document: LRR 2003, r 174(2).

Measure relating to or administered by the Church Commissioners, or any transfer authorised by any such Act or Measure. On application, the registrar must register the transferee as proprietor.[1] The application for registration must be accompanied by a certificate sealed by the Church Commissioners in Form 5 of LRR 2003, Sch 3,[2] and either a copy of the *London Gazette* publishing the instrument, or the transfer (if there is one).[3] The certificate certifies that the instrument or transfer operates to vest immediately, or on publication in the *London Gazette*, or some other specified date, the registered estate (or charge) in the specified corporation or person.

Transfer when a tenant for life is already the registered proprietor

20.15   Form 6 deals with what is likely to be an exceptionally rare occurrence. Since TLATA 1996 came into force on 1 January 1997, it has not been possible to create settlements under the SLA 1925.[4] Settlements are dealt with by Sch 7 to LRR 2003.[5] Schedule 7, para 5, provides that where registered land has been settled and the existing registered proprietor is the tenant for life under the settlement, the registered proprietor must make a declaration in Form 6 of Sch 3, and must also apply for the standard form of restriction for a settlement.[6] Form 6 contains a declaration by the tenant for life that the specified land is subject to the trusts of the settlement. The way in which such land will come into settlement will be where there is a sale of part of the land comprised in the settlement and the purchase of different land.[7] The new land will then be subject to the settlement.

APPLICATIONS

20.16   The LRA 2002 contains many provisions as to when an application may be made to the registrar. The Law Commission and Land Registry listed these provisions in the final Report that accompanied the draft Bill.[8] They are as follows:

–   for first registration;[9]
–   to lodge or withdraw or cancel a caution against first registration;[10]

---

[1]   LRR 2003, r 175(1).
[2]   The certificate may be given either in the transfer or in a separate document: LRR 2003, r 175(3).
[3]   LRR 2003, r 175(2).
[4]   See TLATA 1996, s 2(1).
[5]   See LRR 2003, r 186; and LRA 2002, s 89.
[6]   See LRR 2003, Sch 4, Form G.
[7]   Cf SLA 1925, s 73(1)(xi) (power to purchase freehold land with capital money arising under the SLA 1925). If the whole of the settled land was sold, the settlement would cease, even if the proceeds were invested in the purchase of more land: see TLATA 1996, s 2(4).
[8]   See (2001) Law Com No 271, para 9.76.
[9]   LRA 2002, ss 3, 4.
[10]   Ibid, ss 15, 17, 18.

- to register a registrable disposition;[1]
- to enter, remove or cancel a notice;[2]
- to enter or withdraw a restriction;[3]
- to register the priority of registered charges;[4]
- to determine the exact line of a boundary;[5]
- to upgrade title;[6]
- to obtain an official copy;[7]
- to obtain an official search;[8]
- to enter into a network access agreement;[9]
- by a squatter to be registered as proprietor;[10] and
- for the Adjudicator to rectify or set aside a document.[11]

The LRR 2003 also contain further provisions for applications to the registrar.

20.17 In addition to any specific rule-making powers that apply in any of the situations listed in para **20.16**, there are a number of general rule-making powers in relation to applications that are found in para 6 of Sch 10 to the LRA 2002. These permit rules to be made about the following matters, a number of which have already been considered.

(a)   The first is as to the form and content of applications under the LRA 2002. As a result of this power, it will be possible to require that *all* applications should be in prescribed form. It is likely that, as electronic conveyancing is introduced, this will indeed have to be the case.[12]

(b)   The second is as to the provision of evidence in support of certain types of application. This necessarily varies according to the nature of the application.

(c)   The third is as to the time at which an application is to be taken as made. This may be considered with the fourth general power, which is as to the order in which competing applications are to be taken to rank. Rules under these powers are needed so that priority can be allocated to applications made to the Registry. The Land Registry employs a system of 'real time priority' by which the priority of any application is

---

[1]   LRA 2002, s 27.
[2]   Ibid, ss 34–36.
[3]   Ibid, ss 43, 47.
[4]   Ibid, s 48.
[5]   Ibid, s 60.
[6]   Ibid, s 62.
[7]   Ibid, s 67.
[8]   Ibid, s 70.
[9]   Ibid, Sch 5, para 1.
[10]   Ibid, Sch 6, paras 1, 6.
[11]   Ibid, s 106(2).
[12]   See (2001) Law Com No 271, para 9.78.

determined by the time at which it is entered on the day list at the Registry.

(d)   Finally, rules can (and do) make provision as to the circumstances in which an alteration by the registrar, for the purpose of correcting a mistake in the application or accompanying document, will take effect as if that alteration had been made by the applicant or other interested party or parties. This power, which enables the registrar to correct clerical errors in any application without having to obtain the applicant's consent, is explained at para **22.23**.

We examine here the relevant rules that have been made under (a)–(c) above, and certain other matters concerning applications for which rules either have or will be made.

Form and content of applications

20.18   As we have indicated at para **20.5**, LRR 2003, Sch 1, makes provision for many specific forms of application to the registrar. However, the rules do not provide forms for every possible application. Any application made under LRA 2002 or LRR 2003 for which no other application form is prescribed must be made in Form AP1,[1] which is therefore the default form of application, subject to certain exceptions.[2] In particular, Form AP1 will not be used in relation to applications that are to be delivered by electronic means.[3] As and when an appropriate notice is eventually given under Sch 2 of the LRR 2003 for the electronic delivery of applications,[4] the applicant will be required to provide such particulars as are appropriate and are required by that notice.[5]

20.19   If an application is not in order the registrar may raise such requisitions as he considers necessary. He must specify a period of not less than 20 business days within which the applicant must comply with them.[6] If the applicant fails to do so, the registrar may either cancel the application or extend the period for compliance where this appears to him to be reasonable in the circumstances.[7] Substantially defective applications may be cancelled on delivery or at any time thereafter.[8]

---

[1]   LRR 2003, r 13(1). This does not apply to an application.
[2]   Form AP1 does not have to be used where there is an application to remove from the register the name of a deceased joint proprietor: r 13(2)(a). However, in practice, it is convenient to use Form AP1, accompanied by a death certificate or a grant of probate or letters of representation. Nor does r 13(1) apply to outline applications (for which there is no form of paper application: see para **19.26**): see r 13(2)(c).
[3]   LRR 2003, r 13(2)(b).
[4]   Schedule 2 makes provision for notices publicising arrangements for the electronic delivery of applications and other matters.
[5]   LRR 2003, r 14.
[6]   Ibid, r 16(1). A business day is a day when the Land Registry is open to the public: see LRR 2003, r 216; para **36.5**.
[7]   Ibid, r 16(2).
[8]   Ibid, r 16(3). The registrar may also cancel an application if it has been paid for by a cheque that is dishonoured before the application has been completed: ibid, r 16(4).

20.20　In this context, LRR 2003, r 56, requires consideration. This rule, which is carried forward from the LRR 1925,[1] is a curious provision that, at first sight, is not easy to reconcile with the registration requirements of the LRA 2002.[2] It provides that a disposition that affects two or more registered titles may, on the written request of the applicant, be registered as to some or only one of the registered titles.[3] The applicant may later apply to have the disposition registered as to any of the other registered titles affected by it.[4] The practical function that this provision now serves is to enable the Registry to register a disposition to the extent that registration is sought, even where the application fails to apply for the registration in respect to other registered titles that are affected by that disposition. We understand that, in such circumstances, the Registry registers what it can and invites the applicant to apply for registration in relation to the other titles. This is a rule that should be redrafted so that its true function is made explicit.

20.21　It should be noted that, if an application is made, and before it is completed, the whole of the applicant's interest is transferred by operation of law, the application may be continued by the person entitled to that interest in consequence of that transfer.[5] Thus on the death or bankruptcy of an applicant, his personal representatives or his trustee in bankruptcy may continue the application.

Evidence accompanying applications

20.22　Applications must be supported by the necessary evidence, documentary or otherwise. A number of rules of LRR 2003 require specified evidence to support an application.[6] Documents may have to be produced,[7] or a certificate given by the applicant's conveyancer that he holds the original or an office or certified copy.[8] The registrar has power to require further evidence or the giving of any notice if he thinks it is necessary or desirable. He can refuse to proceed with the application, to do any act or to make any entry in the register unless and until his requirements are met.[9] Equally, the registrar

---

[1]　See LRR 1925, r 87.

[2]　See especially LRA 2002, s 27(4); Sch 2.

[3]　LRR 2003, r 56(1).

[4]　Ibid, r 56(2).

[5]　Ibid, r 18.

[6]　See, eg, LRR 2003, r 81 (application for an agreed notice).

[7]　See, eg, LRR 2003, r 162 (application to register a transfer made by a personal representative who is not registered as proprietor).

[8]　See, eg, LRR 2003, r 163 (application by a personal representative to be registered as proprietor).

[9]　LRR 2003, r 17. In practice, the registrar uses this power quite often. In particular, he may serve notice on a person in relation to some application which might affect that person. An example of this practice is given at para **30.21**, in relation to applications for registration by a person in adverse possession of registered land.

has a dispensing power and may, on request, relieve an applicant of the requirement to lodge a document.[1]

20.23   There are two specific rules about the documents that must accompany an application that are important.

20.24   First, a document lodged at the Registry which deals with part of the land in a registered title must normally have attached to it a plan which clearly identifies that land.[2] This is not necessary where that land is clearly identified by the title plan and is described in the document by reference to that plan.[3]

20.25   Secondly, where one of the rules in LRR 2003 requires that an application must be accompanied with an original document,[4] the applicant may instead lodge a certified or office copy of the document.[5] There are some significant exceptions to this, namely:

(a)   any document that is required to be lodged in relation to an application for first registration;

(b)   a scheduled form (under either Sch 1 or 3); or

(c)   a document that is a registrable disposition.[6]

Nor does it apply where the registrar considers that the circumstances are such that the original of a document should be lodged and the applicant is in a position in which he can obtain possession of the original document so that he can lodge it.

The time when the application is made and the priority of applications

20.26   LRR 2003, r 15, sets out the time when an application is taken to have been made. First, where the application is received by the Registry on a business day,[7] it is taken to be made on the earliest of the following:

(a)   the time of that business day when the notice was actually entered on the day list;

---

[1]   LRR 2003, r 215, which sets out the requirements for the exercise of this power.

[2]   Ibid, r 213(1). The disponor or applicant must sign the plan: r 213(2), (3). If a disposition complies with r 213, the application lodged in respect of it need not: r 213(5). Thus, where a registered freeholder grants a lease of more than 7 years of part of his registered estate, it is enough that the plan attached to the lease identifies the land that is let.

[3]   LRR 2003, r 213(4).

[4]   See, eg, LRR 2003, r 162(1), which requires an application to register a transfer made by a personal representative who is not already registered must be accompanied by the original grant of probate or letters of administration.

[5]   LRR 2003, r 214(1).

[6]   Ibid, r 214(2).

[7]   A business day is a day when the Registry is open to the public: see LRR 2003, r 216; para **36.5**.

(b)   where the application was received *before* 12 noon on that business day, midnight marking the end of the day it was received; or

(c)   where the application was received *after* 12 noon on that business day, midnight marking the end of the next business day.[1]

Secondly, where an application is received on a day which is not a business day, it is taken to made on the earlier of the following:

(a)   the time of a business day that notice of it is actually entered on the day list; or

(b)   midnight marking the end of the next business day after the day it was received.[2]

For these purposes, an application is received when it is delivered to:

(i)   the designated proper office;[3]

(ii)   the registrar in accordance with a written arrangement as to delivery that was made either between the registrar and the applicant or between the registrar and the applicant's conveyancer; or

(iii) to the registrar in electronic form under the provisions of any notice given under Sch 2 to LRR 2003.[4]

As regards (iii), as a result of a notice under Sch 2, a number of applications can be delivered electronically by way of Land Registry Direct. These are listed in Notice 3 of the Notices and Directions of the Chief Land Registrar, Land Registry Direct, para 2.

20.27   Rule 15 does not apply to applications under Part 13 of LRR 2003 (Information, etc), except in relation to an application to designate a document an exempt information document (see para **18.18**).[5] It does not, therefore, apply to applications such as applications for official copies, for day list information, historical information and official searches with or without priority.[6]

20.28   It may happen that, by reason of LRR 2003, r 15, two or more applications may be taken to have been made at the same time. In those circumstances, r 55 determines the order of priority in which they are to rank: see r 55(1). The principles laid down by r 55 are as follows:

---

[1]   LRR 2003, r 15(1).

[2]   Ibid, r 15(2).

[3]   See LRA 2002, s 100(3); the Land Registration (Proper Office) Order 2003 and para **36.3**.

[4]   LRR 2003, r 15(3).

[5]   Ibid, r 15(4).

[6]   Cf para **18.11**.

(i)   Where the applications are made by the same applicant, they rank in such order as he may specify.[1]

(ii)   Where the applications are not made by the same applicant, they rank in such order as the applicants may specify that they have agreed.[2]

(iii)   Where the applications are not made by the same applicant, and the applicants have not specified the agreed order of priority, the registrar must notify the applicants that their applications are regarded as having been delivered at the same time and request them to agree, within a specified time (which must be not less than 15 business days), their order of priority.[3]

(iv)   If the parties fail to indicate the order of priority of their applications within the time specified by the registrar, the registrar must propose the order of priority and serve notice on the applicants of his proposal.[4] The notice served by the registrar must draw attention to the right of any applicant who does not agree with the registrar's proposal to object to another applicant's application under the provisions of s 73 of the Act that are explained at paras **20.29** et seq.[5]

Objections to applications

20.29   Given that many of the possible applications that may be made to the registrar under the LRA 2002 or LRR 2003 could be disputed, the Act necessarily makes provision by which they may be challenged.[6] The general rule is that *anyone* may object to an application to the registrar.[7] That general right to object[8] is subject to two exceptions.

—   First, in the case of an application for the cancellation of a caution against first registration under s 18 of the LRA 2002,[9] the person who lodged the caution and the person for the time being shown as cautioner[10] in the cautioner's register may object.[11]

—   Secondly, on an application for the cancellation of a unilateral notice under s 36 of the Act,[12] the only persons who may object are the person shown in the register as the beneficiary of the notice to which

---

[1]   LRR 2003, r 55(2).
[2]   Ibid, r 55(3).
[3]   Ibid, r 55(4).
[4]   Ibid, r 55(5).
[5]   Ibid, r 55(6).
[6]   LRA 2002, s 73.
[7]   Ibid, s 73(1). The right is subject to rules: see s 73(4).
[8]   Cf ibid, s 132(3)(c).
[9]   For the cautioner's register, see LRR 2003, r 41(2), (5); para **5.3**.
[10]   For the registrar's power to change the name of the cautioner in the cautioner's register, see LRR 2003, rr 49, 51; para **5.7**.
[11]   LRA 2002, s 73(2); LRR 2003, r 52. For the right to object to the cancellation of a caution against first registration, see para **5.19**.
[12]   See para **10.35**.

the application relates and a person entitled to be registered as the beneficiary of such notice.[1]

20.30 The procedure on making an objection to an application is as follows. Unless the registrar is satisfied that the objection to the application is groundless,[2] he must give notice of the objection to the applicant.[3] In those circumstances, the registrar may not determine the application until the disposal of the objection.[4] If it is not possible to dispose of the objection by agreement, the registrar *must* refer the objection to the Adjudicator.[5] The LRRAR 2003 make provision for such references.[6] The procedure before the Adjudicator is explained in Chapter 34.[7]

20.31 LRR 2003, r 19, explains how a person may object to an application pursuant to LRA 2002, s 73. Subject to one exception, the objection must be made by delivering to the registrar at the appropriate office a written statement signed by the objector or his conveyancer.[8] The exception is where the objection is made in response to a notice given by the registrar.[9] In that case the objector may instead object in the manner and to the address stated in the notice.[10] The statement made by the objector under r 19, must state that he objects and his grounds for so doing, and must also give his full name and an address to which communications must be sent.[11] The objection must be delivered to the registrar:

(a)   in paper form at the proper office;
(b)   by e-mail to the specified electronic address for that office; or
(c)   by fax at the fax number specified for that office.[12]

20.32 It should be noted that under the LRA 2002 a person must not exercise his right to object to an application without reasonable cause.[13] If he does so, he will be in breach of statutory duty and liable accordingly to any person who suffers damage in consequence.[14]

---

1   LRA 2002, s 73(3); LRR 2003, r 86(7); see para **10.35**.
2   Ibid, s 73(6).
3   Ibid, s 73(5)(a).
4   Ibid, s 73(5)(b).
5   Ibid, s 73(7). For the Adjudicator to HM Land Registry, see para **34.10**.
6   These rules were made pursuant to LRA 2002, s 73(8). See paras **34.4**, **34.12**.
7   See para **34.15**.
8   LRR 2003, r 19(1).
9   See ibid, r 19(5).
10 Ibid, rr 19(1), (5), 197(1)(c). See para **20.41**.
11 LRR 2003, r 19(2).
12 This states the effect of LRR 2003, r 19(3), (4) and (6). The electronic addresses and fax numbers for the Land Registry offices are specified in the schedule to a direction made pursuant to LRA 2002, s 100(4), made by the Chief Land Registrar on 2 October 2003.
13 LRA 2002, s 77(1)(c).
14 Ibid, s 77(2); and see paras **10.39–10.40**.

Completion of applications

20.33   It was explained at para **15.10** that where there is either an application for first registration or an application to register a registrable disposition, registration has effect from the time of the making of the application.[1] By LRR 2003, r 20, the same rule applies to any entry in, removal of an entry from, or alteration of the register pursuant to, any other form of application.

20.34   The LRR 2003 make provision as to the retention and return of documents where an application has been completed. In that situation, the registrar may retain all or any of the documents that accompanied the application and must return all the others either to the applicant or as specified in the application.[2] When making an application, other than an application for first registration, an applicant or his conveyancer may request the return of all or any of the documents accompanying the application, and the registrar must comply with this request, provided that the applicant or his conveyancer delivers certified copies of the relevant documents with the application.[3] In the case of an application for first registration, a person who requests the return of any statutory declaration, subsisting lease, subsisting charge, or the latest document of title,[4] must deliver certified copies with his application, but need not do so in relation to any other documents whose return he requests.[5] The registrar may destroy any document that he retains if he is satisfied that he has made and retained a sufficient copy of the document or, alternatively, that further retention of the document is unnecessary.[6] There is a power to enable the registrar to dispense with the delivery of certified documents or classes of document, by giving notice to that effect.[7]

20.35   As regards all documents that were already kept by the registrar on 13 October 2003 and upon which any entry in the register was founded, LRR 2003 provided that a person who delivered any such document to the registrar may, prior to 13 October 2008, request its return, and that it must be returned.[8] After 12 October 2008, the registrar may destroy any unrequested document that he retains if he is satisfied that he has retained a sufficient copy of the document or that its further retention is unnecessary.[9] There is also a

---

[1]   LRA 2002, s 74.

[2]   LRR 2003, r 203(1).

[3]   Ibid, r 203(2), (3).

[4]   Which means the document which vested the estate that is to be registered in the applicant, or where the estate vested in the applicant by operation of law, the most recent document that vested the estate in a predecessor of the applicant: LRR 2003, r 203(8).

[5]   LRR 2003, r 203(4), (5).

[6]   Ibid, r 203(6).

[7]   Ibid, r 203(7).

[8]   Ibid, r 204(1), (2), (4). There are various ancillary provisions in r 204, relating to competing applications, the rights of registered proprietors of part, etc: see r 204(3), (5).

[9]   LRR 2003, r 204(6).

power for the registrar to release any document which he has retained upon such terms, if any, as he considers appropriate.[1]

Registered charges and company charges

20.36   Where a company creates a registered charge over its property, that charge must be registered both under the LRA 2002[2] and under the Companies Act 1985.[3] In the interests of convenience, the LRA 2002 provides that rules may be made providing for the transmission of applications from the registrar to the registrar of companies.[4] When this power is exercised it should be possible to make a combined application to the Land Registry to register the charge on the register and for that application then to be forwarded to Companies House for registration in the Companies Register.

EXECUTION OF DOCUMENTS

20.37   Many documents that are submitted for registration are dispositive in their effect. Those that transfer or create a legal estate will usually have to be executed as a deed,[5] subject to certain exceptions,[6] notably assents by personal representatives. These rules apply as much to dispositions of registered land as they do to unregistered land. This is an area of law of some technicality and the Land Registry has provided helpful guidance on the proper execution of deeds for land registration purposes: see Execution of Deeds, PG 8, to which reference should be made. The LRR 2003 prescribe certain forms of execution which are set out in Sch 9 to the rules.[7] These must be used in the execution of dispositions in the scheduled forms, which means certain of the Sch 1 forms (which, where it is relevant, always have a box headed 'Execution') and Form 6 of the Sch 3 forms, with such alterations and additions as the registrar may allow.[8]

20.38   The six forms of execution that are prescribed in Sch 9 are:

—   Form A: where the instrument is to be executed personally by an individual.[9]
—   Form B: where the instrument is to be executed by an individual directing another to sign.[10]

---

1   LRR 2003, r 205.
2   See LRA 2002, s 27(2)(f); see also para **8.22**.
3   Companies Act 1985, Part XII.
4   LRA 2002, s 121.
5   See LPA 1925, s 52(1).
6   Ibid, s 52(2).
7   See LRR 2003, r 206(3).
8   Ibid.
9   See LP(MP)A 1989, s 1(3)(a)(i).
10   See ibid, s 1(3)(a)(ii).

–   Form C: where the instrument is to be executed by a company registered under the Companies Acts, or an unregistered company, acting under its common seal.[1]

–   Form D: where the instrument is to be executed by a company registered under the Companies Acts, or an unregistered company, without using a common seal.[2]

–   Form E: where the instrument is to be executed on behalf of an overseas company without using a common seal.[3]

–   Form F: where the instrument is to be executed by a limited liability partnership incorporated under the Limited Liability Partnerships Act 2000, without using a common seal.[4]

20.39   Although these forms of execution are prescribed for the purpose of the scheduled forms, there are some significant dispositions, such as the grant of leases, for which there are no scheduled forms.[5] In such cases, the necessary deed can be executed in any way that is recognised as valid in law. For example, in relation to deeds executed by foreign corporations, there are three methods of execution that will be recognised under the Foreign Companies (Execution of Documents) Regulations 1994, namely:

(i)   execution under the corporation's common seal if it has one;

(ii)   execution in the manner permitted by the law under which the corporation is incorporated. The Land Registry will require evidence from a lawyer familiar with the relevant system of law to establish that the execution is effective under the law of the country of incorporation;[6]

(iii) execution by signature of an authorised person in accordance with s 36A(4) of the Companies Act 1985.

It is advisable in every case to follow the Land Registry's guidance as to

---

1   See Companies Act 1985, s 36A(2) and the common law (see, eg, *Mayor of Ludlow v Charlton* (1840) 6 M&W 815 at 823).

2   Companies Act 1985, s 36A(4). This provision has been extended to unregistered companies: see Companies (Unregistered Companies) Regulations 1985, SI 1985/680; Companies (Unregistered Companies) (Amendment No 2) Regulations 1990, SI 1990/1394.

3   See Companies Act 1985, s 36A(4), as modified by the Foreign Companies (Execution of Documents) Regulations 1994, SI 1994/950. In a case where an overseas company has a common seal, the Land Registry will permit the form of execution appropriate to a company registered under the Companies Acts may be used with such adaptations as may be necessary, in place of execution by a person or persons acting under the authority of the company. See Execution of Deeds, PG8, para 7.1. It should be stated that the persons in whose presence the seal was affixed are permanent officers of the company.

4   See Companies Act 1985, s 36A(4), as modified by the Limited Liability Partnership Regulations 2001, SI 2001/1090.

5   An application to register the grant of a lease will be accompanied by Form AP1, but it is the lease that has to be executed as a deed. Form AP1 is not dispositive and needs merely to be signed.

6   See Execution of Deeds, PG8, para 7.2.

execution, [1] to ensure that any application is not rejected because it has not been properly executed.

NOTICES AND ADDRESSES FOR SERVICE

20.40   There many occasions where, under the LRA 2002 or the LRR 2003, the registrar is required to or may serve a notice for some purpose, some of them of considerable importance, as in relation to applications by a person in adverse possession of registered land to be registered as proprietor (see paras **30.18** et seq). As part of the general provisions contained in Part 15 of the LRR 2003, there are a number of rules about the content and service of notices.

20.41   Every notice given by the registrar must fix the time within which the recipient is to take any action required by the notice.[2] Except where the LRR 2003 otherwise provide, the time fixed by the notice will be the period ending at 12 noon on the fifteenth business day after the date of issue of the notice.[3] The notice must state what the consequence will be of a failure to take such action as is required by the notice within the time fixed.[4] It must also state the manner in which any reply to the notice must be given and the address to which it must be sent.[5]

20.42   Certain persons must provide the registrar with an address for service to which all notices and other communications to him by the registrar may be sent.[6] The persons in question are as follows:[7]

(a)   the registered proprietor of a registered estate or registered charge;

(b)   the registered beneficiary of a unilateral notice;

(c)   a cautioner named in an individual caution register;[8]

(d)   a person whose name and address is required to be included in any of the standard restrictions set out in Sch 4 to the LRR 2003;[9]

(e)   a person whose consent or certificate is required, or upon whom notice is required to be served by the registrar or another person, under any other restriction;[10]

---

[1]   In Execution of Deeds, PG8.

[2]   LRR 2003, r 197(1)(a).

[3]   Ibid, r 197(2).

[4]   Ibid, r 197(1)(b).

[5]   Ibid, r 197(1)(c).

[6]   Ibid, r 198(1).

[7]   Ibid, r 198(2).

[8]   This is a reference to cautions against first registration and not to the old cautions against dealings created prior to 13 October 2003 under LRA 1925. See LRR 2003, r 198(6); para **20.44**.

[9]   See para **10.66**; and LRR 2003, r 92(2)(b).

[10]   Ibid.

(f)   a person entitled to be notified of an application for adverse possession under LRR 2003, r 194;[1]

(g)   a person who objects to an application under LRA 2002, s 73;

(h)   a person who has been notified of an application by a squatter to be registered pursuant to LRA 2002, Sch 6, para 3(1) and who gives the registrar notice under para 3(2) that he requires him to deal with that application in accordance with Sch 6, para 5;[2]

(i)   any person who, while dealing with the registrar in connection with registered land or a caution against first registration, is requested by the registrar to give an address for service.

20.43   The person in question *must* give the registrar an address for service which is a postal address.[3] However, it need not be in the United Kingdom,[4] as was formerly the case.[5] A person who falls within the list in para **20.42** may give the registrar one or two additional addresses for service which must be:[6]

(a)   a postal address, whether or not in the United Kingdom;

(b)   a box number at a United Kingdom document exchange;[7]

(c)   an electronic address.[8]

Provided that he does not exceed three addresses, a person may give the registrar a replacement address for service.[9]

20.44   A cautioner, who lodged a caution against dealings under LRA 1925, s 54,[10] provided the registrar with an address for service in the caution itself.[11] The LRR 2003 make provision for the cautioner to give the registrar a replacement or additional address for service, provided that he does not have more than three addresses and one of the addresses is a postal address (whether or not in the United Kingdom). The addresses must be of the kind set out in para **20.43**(a)–(c).[12]

20.45   The LRR 2003 prescribe the means by which the registrar may serve the notices which he is required to give,[13] not only under the LRA 2002 and

---

[1]   See para **30.20**.
[2]   See paras **30.31** et seq.
[3]   LRR 2003, r 198(3).
[4]   Ibid.
[5]   See LRA 1925, s 79(1).
[6]   He cannot have more than three addresses for service: LRR 2003, r 198(4).
[7]   There are restrictions on the document exchanges that can be used: see LRR 2003, r 198(7).
[8]   LRR 2003, r 198(4). An electronic address can be an e-mail address or any other form of address that has been specified by the registrar in a direction: see r 198(8), (9).
[9]   Ibid, r 198(5).
[10]   See para **10.106**.
[11]   See LRR 1925, r 215(2) and Form 69.
[12]   LRR 2003, r 198(6).
[13]   Ibid, r 199(1).

LRR 2003, but also, in relation to cautions against dealings, under LRA 1925, s 55 (as preserved by LRA 2002, Sch 12, para 5).[1] The rules also set out when service shall be taken to have taken place.[2] Expressed in tabular form these are as follows:

Method of service	*Time of service*
(a) By post,[3] to any postal address in the United Kingdom entered in the register as an address for service.	The second working day[4] after posting.
(b) By post, to any postal address outside the United Kingdom entered in the register as an address for service.	The working day after it was left.
(c) By leaving the notice at any postal address in the United Kingdom entered in the register as an address for service.	The seventh working day after posting.
(d) By directing the notice to the relevant box number at any document exchange entered in the register as an address for service.	On the second working day after it was left at the registrar's document exchange.
(e) By electronic transmission to the electronic address entered in the register as an address for service.	The working day after transmission.
(f) By fax.[5]	The second working day after transmission.

As regards methods (a)–(c), the registrar may serve any notice at any other address where the registrar believes that the addressee is likely to receive it.[6]

---

1   LRA 2003, r 220.
2   Ibid, r 199(4).
3   'Post' means pre-paid delivery by a postal service which seeks to deliver documents within the United Kingdom no later than the next working day in all or the majority of cases, and to deliver outside the United Kingdom within such a period as is reasonable in all the circumstances: LRR 2003, r 199(5).
4   For the meaning of 'working day', see LRR 2003, r 199(6): it means Mondays to Fridays, but not Christmas Day, Good Friday or a bank holiday.
5   The notice may be served by fax if the recipient has informed the registrar in writing that he is willing to accept service by fax and has provided the fax number: LRR 2003, r 199(3).
6   LRR 2003, r 199(1)(g).

CHAPTER 21

LAND AND CHARGE CERTIFICATES

THE PREVIOUS LAW

21.1   One of the most striking practical changes made by the LRA 2002 and the LRR 2003 is the abolition of land and charge certificates. Under the LRA 1925, when a registered estate was not subject to a registered charge, the proprietor was issued with a land certificate.[1] That certificate had to be produced to the registrar:

—   on an entry made in relation to a registered disposition of the estate;
—   on a registered transmission of the estate on death or insolvency; and
—   on the entry of a notice or restriction affecting that registered estate.

Where there was a registered charge affecting the estate, the land certificate was 'deposited' at the Land Registry. No such deposit was made in fact: the certificate was just not issued. In such cases, in relation to the three types of transaction where the land certificate had to be produced, the Registry required the consent of the registered proprietor or an order of the court before it would make the appropriate entry in the register. Thus, in many cases, the consent of the registered proprietor was substituted for the production of the land certificate.

21.2   It was recognised that in the system of electronic conveyancing that is to be created under the LRA 2002,[2] it was inevitable that the role of land certificates would, at very least, have to be much reduced. To require the production of a paper land certificate before an entry could be made in the register would defeat one of the objectives of an electronic paperless system of conveyancing. Furthermore, the form of the land certificate under LRA 1925 was somewhat misleading. It was a copy of the registered title as it was on the day on which the certificate was issued. However, the only true record of the title is the register as it stands at any given time.

---

[1]   LRA 1925, ss 63, 64. See generally (2001) Law Com No 271, paras 9.83–9.87.
[2]   See Chapter 26.

THE ABOLITION OF LAND AND CHARGE CERTIFICATES UNDER THE LRA 2002 AND THE LRR 2003

21.3   The LRA 2002 says very little about land certificates. The only provision in the Act relating to land certificates is in Sch 10, para 4, where it is provided that rules may make provision about:

−   when a certificate of registration of title to a legal estate may be issued;
−   the form and content of such a certificate; and
−   when such a certificate must be produced or surrendered to the registrar.

In fact, the power to make such rules has not been exercised and the LRR 2003 are silent on the subject of land certificates.[1] They are, therefore, abolished.[2] If the Act has little to say about land certificates, it has nothing whatever in it about charge certificates. In consequence, they too are abolished.[3]

21.4   As a result of these changes the Registry ceased to issue certificates on 13 October 2003 (when the LRA 2002 came into force), and all existing certificates ceased to have any legal significance.[4] This principle has been applied rigorously:

(a)   Although as a general rule, the LRA 1925 continues to have effect in relation to an entry in the register of a notice, restriction, inhibition or caution against dealings which was pending immediately before 13 October 2003,[5] that is expressly not the case in relation to the provisions of Part 5 of the LRA 1925, which dealt with land and charge certificates.[6] Applications that were pending on 13 October 2003 have been or will be completed without a land or charge certificate, even if lodged before then.[7]

(b)   The provisions of the LRR 2003 concerning the retention and return of documents when an application has been completed[8] do not apply in relation to:

---

[1]   It was envisaged initially that there would be some provision in rules, but that the land certificate would be no more than a document that certified that the registration of a registered estate had taken place and that a named person was the registered proprietor: see (2001) Law Com No 271, para 9.91.
[2]   This is recognised by TPO1 2003, art 24.
[3]   See (2001) Law Com No 271, para 9.89.
[4]   See the Land Registry Practice Bulletin, Land and Charge Certificates – Effect of the Land Registration Act 2002, PB2. Registered charges should be cautious about destroying the charge certificate. This is because it will contain the charge itself.
[5]   LRA 2002, Sch 12, para 5.
[6]   See TPO1 2003, art 24(1).
[7]   Land Registry Practice Bulletin, Land and Charge Certificates – Effect of the Land Registration Act 2002, PB2, para 2.
[8]   See LRR 2003, rr 203, 204; see also para **20.34**.

(i) any land certificate or charge certificate held by the registrar immediately before 13 October 2003;

(ii) any land certificate or charge certificate lodged in connection with any application, including any application that is pending immediately before 13 October 2003; or

(iii) any document incorporated in any land certificate or charge certificate.[1]

(c) The registrar is given authority to destroy any land certificate or charge certificate held by him or which comes into his possession, and any document incorporated in such a land certificate or charge certificate.[2] The Registry made it clear that it intended to exercise this power once the LRA 2002 was in force.[3]

(d) Since 13 October 2003, it has been unnecessary to make an application to the Registry in relation to lost or destroyed land or charge certificates.[4]

21.5 Instead of issuing a land or charge certificate, the Registry will now issue instead the following documents:

(a) An official copy of the register which shows the entries in the register at the time when an application is completed.[5]

(b) Where the application gave rise to the creation or amendment of the title plan, an official copy of the title plan.

(c) A 'Title Information Document' which explains why the official copy has been issued and how to obtain further copies in the future.[6]

---

1 TPO1 2003, art 24(2).

2 Ibid, art 24(3).

3 See Land Registry Practice Bulletin, Land and Charge Certificates – Effect of the Land Registration Act 2002, PB2, para 2.

4 Ibid, para 4. See also the Practice Bulletin, Lost or Destroyed Certificate – Effect of the Land Registration Act 2002, PB1.

5 For official copies, see para **18.11**.

6 See Land Registry Practice Bulletin, Land and Charge Certificates – Effect of the Land Registration Act 2002, PB2, para 3.

CHAPTER 22

ALTERATION OF THE REGISTER

INTRODUCTION

22.1 The register may need to be altered for one of two reasons. The first is simply as part of the process of keeping the register up to date, for example by removing spent entries. The second is to correct some error or omission in the register. The first of these grounds is unremarkable. It is self-evident that the registrar should be able to up-date the register, whether on his own initiative or by direction of the court after some determination. The second ground is, by contrast, of wider importance. If a mistake has been made in the register and some person has suffered loss in consequence, the registrar will pay an indemnity. This right to indemnity is the basis for 'the State guarantee of title' that the system of registered land embodies and it is explained in Chapter 23. The creation of the new register of cautions means that there is now an additional register which may require alteration.[1] This is explained at para **22.22**.[2]

22.2 The provisions of the LRA 1925 on rectification of the register were opaque and obscured the true nature of what actually happened in practice. What the LRA 2002 does for the most part is to codify the practice of the registrar and the courts as it had developed under the LRA 1925 and, at the same time, to make that process transparent on the face of the legislation. This aspect of the new law well illustrates why it is very unwise to rely upon the authorities on the equivalent provisions of the LRA 1925.[3] The legal principles should be gleaned from an interpretation of the LRA 2002 and the rules made under it. The Land Registry has published a Practice Guide, 'Rectification and Indemnity',[4] which contains important information that cannot be deduced from the LRA 2002 or the LRR 2003.

ALTERATION OF THE REGISTER OF TITLE

22.3 The LRA 2002[5] embodies the distinction mentioned above in para **22.1**

---

[1] See LRA 2002, ss 20, 21.
[2] For the cautions register, see para **5.3**.
[3] See para **1.21**.
[4] PG39.
[5] See LRA 2002, s 65 and Sch 4. Schedule 4 contains the provisions of the Act on alteration of the register.

between those changes to the register that are necessary to keep the register up to date and the correction of mistakes. The basic concept employed by the Act is that of *alteration* of the register and that term covers all types of alteration that may be made in the register.[1] *Rectification* is one specific form of alteration, namely one which:

(a)   involves the correction of a mistake; and
(b)   prejudicially affects the title of a registered proprietor.[2]

There are two points to note about this definition of rectification. The first is that not all cases in which the register is altered to correct a mistake will be rectification – only those which prejudicially affect the title of the registered proprietor. Secondly, there is a direct link between rectification and the right to indemnity.[3] Under the LRA 1925, there was no such link: if a person did not suffer loss as a result of rectification, he did not recover indemnity.[4] Under the LRA 2002, such a change in the register is not characterised as 'rectification', but merely as an alteration.

22.4   The LRA 2002 provides that the register may be altered to affect the priority *for the future* of interests affecting the registered estate or charge concerned.[5] In other words, alteration of the register cannot have any retrospective effect on third party rights. This provision probably does no more than restate the previous law. First, under the LRA 1925, it was expressly provided that there was a power to rectify the register even though it might affect derivative interests.[6] Secondly, although some doubt was expressed on the matter, the authorities suggested that, under the LRA 1925, rectification of the register could only have prospective effect.[7]

22.5   The register may be altered either pursuant to an order of the court or by the registrar. The circumstances in which the registrar may alter the register are necessarily wider than those of the court. It is incumbent upon him to ensure that spent entries are removed. He may do this even where:

(a)   there is no dispute between the parties; or
(b)   no application has been made to him to alter the register.

---

1   See LRA 2002, Sch 4, paras 2, 5.
2   Ibid, Sch 4, para 1.
3   Ibid, Sch 8, para 1(1)(a).
4   See LRA 1925, s 83(1)(a). Thus, where the register was rectified to give effect to an overriding interest, the proprietor could not recover indemnity: *Re Chowood's Registered Land* [1933] Ch 574.
5   LRA 2002, Sch 4, para 8.
6   LRA 1925, s 82(2).
7   See *Freer v Unwins Ltd* [1976] Ch 288 at p 296. Compare the view of Arden LJ in *Malory Enterprises Ltd v Cheshire Homes (UK) Ltd* [2002] EWCA Civ 151, [2002] Ch 216 at 236, that rectification could only be prospective (with which we would respectfully agree) with that of both Clarke and Schiemann LJJ, at p 238, who left the point open.

ALTERATION OF THE REGISTER PURSUANT TO AN ORDER OF THE COURT

The powers of the court

22.6 Under the LRA 2002, a court may make an order for alteration of the register for any one of three purposes.[1]

(a)   The first is for correcting a mistake. Where the alteration prejudicially affects the title of the registered proprietor, it will constitute rectification.

(b)   The second is to bring the register up to date. If, for example, a person established in court proceedings that she had acquired a right of way by prescription over her neighbour's land, the court could (and, in practice, should) order the register to be altered to record that easement.[2]

(c)   The third is to give effect to any estate, right or interest excepted from the effect of registration. Under the LRA 1925, where land was registered with a grade of title other than absolute, rights excepted from the effect of registration were overriding interests.[3] Under the LRA 2002 they are not. They are interests whose priority is protected, so that a purchaser of registered land takes subject to them.[4] The power to alter the register is a necessary concomitant of the way in which these rights are regulated under the Act.

Such an order has effect when served on the registrar to impose a duty on him to give effect to it.[5] The LRR 2003 make provision as to the form and service of such an order.[6] The order must:

(i)   state the title number of the title affected;
(ii)   state the alteration that is to be made; and
(iii)   direct the registrar to make the alteration.[7]

To serve the order on the registrar, an application must be made to him to give effect to the order, accompanied by the order.[8] The application must be made on the default Form AP1, there being no other Form prescribed.[9]

---

1   LRA 2002, Sch 4, para 2(1).
2   Cf (2001) Law Com No 251, para 10.10(2).
3   LRA 1925, s 70(1)(h).
4   LRA 2002, s 29(2)(a)(iii); see also para **9.8**.
5   Ibid, Sch 4, para 2(2).
6   LRR 2003, r 127, made pursuant to LRA 2002, Sch 4, para 4(b), (c).
7   Ibid, r 127(1).
8   Ibid, r 127(2).
9   See Land Registry Practice Guide, Rectification and Indemnity, PG39, para 2.1.

22.7   In any proceedings in which one or more grounds for altering the register is established, a court is in fact normally *required* to order the registrar to make the alteration, unless the case is one of rectification, where, as explained below, more restrictive rules apply.[1] This is because, under the LRR 2003,[2] the court *must* make an order for the alteration of the register, if in any proceedings, the court decides that:

(a)   there is a mistake in the register;

(b)   the register is not up to date; or

(c)   there is an estate, right or interest excepted from the effect of registration to which effect should be given.[3]

22.8   There are three limitations on this rule. First, as indicated above, it does not apply to an alteration that constitutes rectification.[4] Secondly, it only applies where a court *decides* one of those three matters in the proceedings before it. It would not be applicable if, in the proceedings, the court happened to discover that there were grounds for altering the register even though this was not an issue before the parties (as, for example, where the judge happened to notice that there was a spent entry in the register that was not relevant to the proceedings). In such a case, it would be a matter entirely for the court's discretion whether or not to order the alteration of the register.[5] Thirdly, the court is not obliged to make an order if there are exceptional circumstances that justify not doing so.[6]

The protection given to a proprietor in possession

22.9   One of the features of the land registration system under the LRA 1925 was the protection that registration of itself conferred. The LRA 1925 placed restrictions on the circumstances in which the register could be rectified against a proprietor who is in possession.[7] The relevant provision was, however, obscure and badly drafted and, despite amendments to it, its meaning was regularly litigated.[8] Some of the decisions were difficult to justify.

22.10   The LRA 2002 not only retains the principle that protection should be given to a proprietor who is in possession, but extends and clarifies the concept of who is a proprietor in possession. Although the protection is only available in relation to those alterations that amount to rectification as defined

---

[1]   See paras **22.9** et seq.

[2]   See LRR 2003, r 126, made pursuant to LRA 2002, Sch 4, para 4(a).

[3]   Ibid, r 126(1).

[4]   Ibid, r 126(3).

[5]   See (2001) Law Com No 271, para 10.12.

[6]   LRR 2003, r 126(2).

[7]   This has been described as a principle of 'qualified indefeasibility': see (1998) Law Com No 254, para 8.47.

[8]   For an analysis of the relevant law, see (1998) Law Com No 254, paras 8.23–8.31.

by the Act,[1] that does not involve any erosion of the protection. This is because any form of alteration of the register that is not rectification will not, by definition, prejudicially affect the title of that registered proprietor.[2]

22.11 Under the LRA 2002, a court may not order rectification of the register so as to affect the title of a registered proprietor[3] in relation to land in his possession without his consent unless:

(a) he has by fraud or lack of proper care caused or substantially contributed to the mistake; or

(b) it would for any other reason be unjust for the alteration not to be made.[4]

22.12 A proprietor will be a proprietor in possession of land for the purposes of this provision in three circumstances.[5] It is implicit in this that if a proprietor cannot prove that he falls within any of these circumstances, he is *not* a proprietor in possession.

(a) The first is where the land is physically in his possession.[6]

(b) The second is where the land is physically in the possession of a person who is entitled to be registered as proprietor, such as a proprietor's personal representative or trustee in bankruptcy, or a beneficiary under a bare trust.[7] A squatter who is entitled to be registered as proprietor under the provisions of Sch 6 to the LRA 2002,[8] is not, for these purposes, a person entitled to be registered.[9]

(c) The third is in certain specified relationships, where the actual or deemed[10] possession of land by another is treated as being the possession of the registered proprietor.[11]

---

1   See LRA 2002, Sch 4, para 3(1).

2   Ibid, Sch 4, para 1; see also para **22.3**.

3   For these purposes, the title includes the benefit of any appurtenant legal estates such as easements: see LRA 2002, Sch 4, para 3(4).

4   Ibid, Sch 4, para 3(2). These two exceptions replicate those in LRA 1925, s 82(3)(a) and (c). The other two exceptions found in LRA 1925, s 82(3) (giving effect to an overriding interest or to an order of the court) are no longer needed because neither involves rectification as defined by LRA 2002. Accordingly, they are not replicated: see (2001) Law Com No 271, para 10.16.

5   LRA 2002, s 131.

6   Ibid, s 131(1).

7   Ibid.

8   See Chapter 30.

9   LRA 2002, s 131(3).

10 In (2001) Law Com No 271, para 10.17, examples are given of situations where the other person may be treated as being in possession even when he is not actually in possession. These include where a tenant had sublet, or a mortgagee in possession had exercised its power of leasing under LPA 1925, s 99(2).

11 LRA 2002, s 131(2).

22.13   The specified relationships that fall within the third of these circumstances are as follows:

(a)   where a landlord is the registered proprietor and the tenant is in possession;

(b)   where a mortgagor is the registered proprietor and the mortgagee is in possession;[1]

(c)   where a licensor is registered proprietor and the licensee is in possession; and

(d)   where a trustee is registered proprietor and a beneficiary is in possession.

22.14   What needs to be stressed about these provisions is that they are intended to protect the *physical possession* of the registered proprietor, of a person lawfully in such physical possession under the registered proprietor, or of a person who is entitled to be registered as proprietor. There is no scope for any presumption, of the kind that was developed in relation to the equivalent provision of the LRA 1925,[2] by which the registered proprietor was to be *treated* as being in physical possession unless he could be shown to have been dispossessed: see *Kingsalton Ltd v Thames Water Developments Ltd*.[3] The whole point of the protection is that where (but only where) *both* registration and physical possession by or under the registered proprietor coincide, the register should not be rectified in the absence of compelling reasons.

22.15   The LRA 2002 makes provision for the converse case where a proprietor is either not in physical possession, or is in possession in circumstances where rectification can nonetheless be ordered.[4] It provides that, in any proceedings in which the court has power to make an order for the alteration of the register, it must do so, unless there are exceptional circumstances which justify its not doing so.[5] This is in fact a codification of the previous practice of the courts.[6]

---

[1]   A mortgagee in possession was *not* regarded as a proprietor in possession for the purposes of LRA 1925, s 82(3): *Hayes v Nwajiaku* [1994] EGCS 106. This is, therefore, a significant extension of the law.

[2]   LRA 1925, s 82(3).

[3]   [2001] EWCA Civ 20; [2001] 1 P&CR 184, at pp 191 (Peter Gibson LJ) and 198 (Sir Christopher Slade). We are unable to understand how this principle would apply if two persons were *both* registered as proprietors of the same land and it was not apparent which of them was in physical possession.

[4]   See para **22.11**.

[5]   LRA 2002, Sch 4, para 3(3).

[6]   See *Epps v Esso Petroleum Co Ltd* [1973] 1 WLR 1071 at 1078; (2001) Law Com No 271, para 10.18.

ALTERATION OF THE REGISTER OTHER THAN UNDER AN ORDER OF THE COURT

The powers of the registrar

22.16   Alterations to give effect to an order of the court are comparatively uncommon. Normally, it is the registrar who makes such changes. Under the LRA 2002, the registrar has power to alter the register in four circumstances, namely for the purpose of:

(a)   correcting a mistake;
(b)   bringing the register up to date;
(c)   giving effect to any estate, right or interest excepted from the effect of registration; and
(d)   removing a superfluous entry,[1] typically where that entry was spent.[2]

The first three of these circumstances[3] are the same as those in which the court may order the alteration of the register and have been explained at para **22.6**. The power to remove superfluous entries (which only the registrar may exercise)[4] and the power to bring the register up to date[5] will inevitably overlap. These powers are likely to be increasingly important with the move to electronic conveyancing. Solicitors and licensed conveyancers will be responsible for most entries that are made on the register. The registrar's functions will be increasingly to identify spent entries and to ensure that they are removed from the register.[6]

22.17   Alterations to the register by the registrar that amount to rectification are subject to the same limitations as apply to rectification by the court, and the same protection is given to a proprietor in possession, as has been explained in paras **22.11–22.13**.[7]

22.18   The LRR 2003 make provision about applications to the registrar for the alteration of the register and the procedure in relation to the exercise by the registrar of the power to alter the register, whether on application or otherwise.[8] Rule 128 applies where an application for alteration of the register has been made, or where the registrar is considering altering the register

---

1   LRA 2002, Sch 4, para 5.
2   The examples given in (2001) Law Com No 271, para 10.19, include (1) where a restriction which froze the register as a precaution ceased to be needed because the danger had passed, and (2) where a restriction on the powers of a registered proprietor had ceased to apply, as where a consent was required from a third party who had since died.
3   LRA 2002, Sch 4, para 5(a)–(c).
4   Ibid, Sch 4, para 5(d).
5   Ibid, Sch 4, para 5(b).
6   (2001) Law Com No 271, para 10.19.
7   LRA 2002, Sch 4, para 6.
8   Pursuant to LRA 2002, Sch 4, para 7(c), (d).

without an application having been made.[1] Where there is an application, it must be on Form AP1, as no other Form has been prescribed.[2] The registrar is required to give notice of the proposed alteration to certain specified persons where that estate, charge or interest would be affected by the proposed alteration, unless he is satisfied that such notice is unnecessary.[3] Those persons are:

(a)   the registered proprietor of any registered estate;

(b)   the registered proprietor of any registered charge; and

(c)   subject to one exception, any person who appears to the registrar to be entitled to an interest protected by a notice (unless that person's name and address for service under LRR 2003, r 198 are not set out in the individual register in which the notice is entered[4]).

It will be unnecessary for the registrar to serve notice where, for example, the person on whom notice would otherwise be served is the person making the application. An application must be supported by evidence to justify the alteration unless specific provision is made elsewhere in the LRR 2003.[5]

22.19   If there is an objection to an application to the registrar for the alteration of the register, the matter will be determined by the Adjudicator.[6] In making his determination, he must necessarily apply the same principles as the registrar.

Alterations under network access agreements

22.20   The framework which the LRA 2002 creates for electronic conveyancing is explained in Part 5. One of its essential features is that solicitors and licensed conveyancers will be authorised by network access agreements to make changes to the register, usually but not exclusively on the making of a disposition of registered land. That will entail the removal of entries on the register as much as the making of new ones. On a sale of land, for example, the seller's title may be subject to a charge that will be discharged on completion. That charge will therefore have to be removed from the register. The LRA 2002 provides that a person may be authorised under a network access agreement to initiate alterations to the register of title or to the

---

[1]   LRR 2003, r 128(1). The rule does not apply to alteration of the register in the specific circumstances covered by any other rule: ibid, r 128(5). For an example of another such rule, see ibid, r 130, para **22.23**.

[2]   LRR 2003, r 13; see Rectification and Indemnity, PG 39, para 3.1.

[3]   Ibid, r 128(2).

[4]   Ibid, r 128(3).

[5]   Ibid, r 129. For an example of a specific provision as to evidence on an application to alter the register, see ibid, r 168 (registration of a trustee in bankruptcy), para **13.17**.

[6]   LRA 2002, s 73(7). See para **20.30**.

cautions register.[1] Indeed, it is visualised that authorised practitioners will have a wider role in removing spent entries that they discover when conducting conveyancing transactions.[2]

Costs in non-rectification cases

22.21 Under the LRA 1925, the registrar had no discretion to pay costs in a case where the register is altered otherwise than by rectification. This was sometimes a cause of hardship, as where a person incurred costs in dealing with the registrar's inquiries concerning a spent entry. The LRA 2002 remedies this shortcoming. It gives the registrar authority to pay such amount as he thinks fit in respect of any costs or expenses reasonably incurred by a person in connection with an alteration in the register that is not rectification, provided those costs were incurred with the consent of the registrar.[3] Even if the registrar's consent was not given, the registrar may still make such a payment if:

— it appears to him that the costs or expenses had to be urgently incurred, and that it was not reasonably practicable to apply for his consent; or
— he has subsequently approved the incurring of the costs or expenses.[4]

Alteration of the cautions register

22.22 The LRA 2002 makes similar provision for alterations to the new cautions register as it does in relation to the register of title.[5] These provisions have been explained at paras **5.9–5.11**.

Alteration of documents

22.23 Not only does the registrar have power to correct mistakes in the register, but he is also given power to correct a mistake in an application or accompanying document.[6] In the circumstances prescribed by the rules, the correction will have the same effect as if made by the parties.[7] Those circumstances are as follows.

(a) First, the registrar may alter an application or accompanying document in the case of a mistake of a clerical or like nature in all circumstances.[8]
(b) Secondly, in the case of any other mistake, the registrar may alter an

---

1   LRA 2002, Sch 5, para 1(2)(b).
2   See (2001) Law Com No 271, para 10.23.
3   LRA 2002, Sch 4, para 9(1).
4   Ibid, Sch 4, para 9(2).
5   For the register of cautions, see para **5.3**.
6   LRR 2003, r 130, made pursuant to LRA 2002, Sch 10, para 6(c). See para **20.17**(d).
7   LRA 2002, Sch 10, para 6(c).
8   LRR 2003, r 130(2)(a).

application or accompanying document only if the applicant and every other interested party has requested, or consented to, the alteration.[1] The registrar will, therefore, be able to serve notice on interested parties of his intention to correct a mistake in a particular document, and then make such a correction in the absence of any objection.

A similar power was given in the LRR 1925,[2] and was widely used, for example to correct a mistake in the formal parts of a lease lodged with the Registry for registration.[3]

22.24   Because there is no change in the register, there is no power for the registrar to pay indemnity to any person in the unlikely event that he suffers loss as a result of the alteration made under this power.[4]

1   LRR 2003, r 130(2)(b).
2   LRR 1925, r 13.
3   See (2001) Law Com No 271, para 10.27.
4   For indemnity, see Chapter 23.

CHAPTER 23

INDEMNITY

INTRODUCTION

23.1 The law on the circumstances in which indemnity is payable by the registrar was substantially revised by the LRA 1997.[1] The LRA 2002 therefore makes only minor changes to the law. Although the substance of the legislation is not much altered, the form of it is recast. In particular, all the grounds on which indemnity is payable are drawn together in one provision.[2] That was not the case under the LRA 1925.

THE GROUNDS ON WHICH INDEMNITY IS PAYABLE

Introduction

23.2 The LRA 2002 lists eight circumstances in which indemnity is payable.[3] A claimant who has suffered loss in such circumstances is able to recover *any* loss, direct or consequential, that flows from that particular ground.[4] Several grounds are based upon a mistake of some kind. For these purposes, 'mistake' includes an erroneous omission as well as an erroneous inclusion.[5] There is an entitlement to indemnity if a person suffers loss by reason of any of the following.

1. Rectification of the register

23.3 Rectification of the register[6] is perhaps the commonest ground for an award of indemnity. For the purposes of the LRA 2002, a person is to be taken to have suffered loss by reason of rectification in two specific situations. The first is where a person suffers loss where the registrar exercises his power to upgrade a title under s 62 of the LRA 2002.[7] The second is where the

---

[1]   LRA 1997 substituted a new LRA 1925, s 83.
[2]   See the Land Registry Practice Guide, Rectification and Indemnity, PG39, paras 5–11.
[3]   LRA 2002, Sch 8, para 1(1).
[4]   See (2001) Law Com No 271, para 10.30.
[5]   LRA 2002, Sch 8, para 11(1).
[6]   Ibid, Sch 8, para 1(1)(a). An alteration of the register not amounting to rectification could not give rise to a claim for indemnity because it would not prejudicially affect the title of the registered proprietor: LRA 2002, Sch, 4, para 1; see also para **22.3**.
[7]   Ibid, Sch 8, para 1(2)(a). For the power to upgrade title under the LRA 2002, s 62, see para **3.13**.

register is rectified against the proprietor of a registered estate or charge claiming in good faith under a forged disposition. The proprietor is to be regarded as having suffered loss by reason of such rectification as if the disposition had not been forged. But for this provision, the proprietor would be regarded as suffering no loss because a forged disposition is a nullity.[1]

2.　Loss by reason of a mistake

23.4　Any person who suffers loss by reason of a mistake whose correction would involve rectification of the register is entitled to an indemnity.[2] This covers two situations. The first is where upon the exercise of the court's or registrar's discretion, rectification is not ordered. However, it is possible to suffer loss by reason of a mistake even if the register is altered.[3] The second case is where a person obtains rectification of the register in his favour but still suffers loss. To accommodate these two situations, the LRA 2002 provides that no indemnity is payable until a decision has been made about whether or not to alter the register.[4] The loss can then be assessed in the light of that decision.

3.　Mistake in an official search

23.5　A person who suffers loss by reason of a mistake in an official search is entitled to indemnity.[5] This is self-explanatory.

4.　Mistake in an official copy

23.6　It has been explained above[6] that, where a person relies on an official copy in which there is a mistake, he is not liable for loss suffered by another person as a result of that mistake.[7] However, the person who suffers loss in that way is entitled to be indemnified.[8]

5.　Mistake in a document kept by the registrar which is not an original

23.7　It was explained above that the register often refers to extracts from or abstracts of conveyancing documents that the registrar does not retain, or of which the registrar only keeps a copy.[9] It was also explained that the Act

---

[1]　See *Re Odell* [1906] 2 Ch 47, which was reversed by LRA 1925, s 83(4) (the precursor of the present provision).

[2]　LRA 2002, Sch 8, para 1(1)(b).

[3]　As in *Freer v Unwins Ltd* [1976] Ch 288.

[4]　LRA 2002, Sch 8, para 1(3).

[5]　Ibid, Sch 8, para 1(1)(c). For official searches, see para **18.11**.

[6]　See para **18.8**.

[7]　LRA 2002, s 67(2).

[8]　Ibid, Sch 8, para 1(1)(d).

[9]　See para **18.38**.

creates a presumption by which, where there is an entry in the register to a registered estate which refers to a document kept by the registrar which is not an original, the document kept by the registrar is to be taken as correct and to contain all the material parts of the document.[1] If, however, there is in fact a mistake in such a document, any person suffering loss in consequence is entitled to an indemnity.[2]

6. Loss or destruction of a document lodged in the registry for inspection or safe custody[3]

23.8 A person who suffers loss by reason of the loss or destruction of a document lodged in the registry for inspection or safe custody is entitled to be indemnified.[4] This provision is likely to be interpreted widely by the Land Registry so that indemnity will be payable if, for example, a document becomes unreadable because it is water damaged. For the future, documents will increasingly be held in dematerialised form, and loss and destruction will be understood accordingly.[5]

7. A mistake in the cautions register

23.9 A person who suffers loss by reason of a mistake in the cautions register is entitled to an indemnity.[6] This is a new right to indemnity that arises from the creation of the cautions register.[7]

8. Failure by the registrar to perform his duty under s 50

23.10 The new duty, imposed on the registrar by s 50 of the LRA 2002, to inform a chargee of the registration of an overriding charge, has already been explained.[8] If the registrar fails to perform that duty and, in consequence, the chargee suffers loss because (for example) it makes a further advance in circumstances where the property charged is not in fact good security because of the statutory charge, it will be entitled to indemnity.[9]

THE SPECIAL CASE OF MINES AND MINERALS

23.11 The LRA 2002 provides that no indemnity is payable on account of any mines or minerals, or the existence of any right to work or get mines or

---

1   LRA 2002, s 120.
2   Ibid, Sch 8, para 1(1)(e).
3   Ibid, Sch 8, para 1(1)(f).
4   Ibid.
5   Cf (2001) Law Com No 271, para 10.36.
6   LRA 2002, Sch 8, para 1(1)(g).
7   For the cautions register, see para **5.3**.
8   See para **12.55**.
9   LRA 2002, Sch 8, para 1(1)(h).

minerals, unless it is noted in the register that the title to the registered estate concerned includes the mines or minerals.[1] Registration of title to land under the Act includes mines and minerals, unless there is any entry to the contrary in the register.[2] However, the LRA 2002 follows the LRA 1925 by providing that the State guarantee of title does not extend to mines and minerals unless they are expressly included in the title and an appropriate entry is made in the register. The reasons for this limitation lie in the difficulty of discovering whether:

(a)   the mines and minerals have been severed from the land without this being recorded on the title; or

(b)   the land was at one time copyhold and the lord of the manor's rights to the mines and minerals were preserved when the land was enfranchised.[3]

It will only be in those rare cases where the mines and minerals are expressly included in the title that indemnity could ever be paid in relation to them.

THE MEASURE OF INDEMNITY

23.12   The purpose of indemnity is to compensate the person who has suffered loss in consequence of one or more of the eight grounds listed in paras **23.3–23.10**. The losses recoverable include those that flow directly from the particular matter (such as the value of any land that the person seeking indemnity may have lost) and also any consequential losses, such as the opportunity of an advantageous sale. It is only where the losses consist entirely of costs and expenses that there are any restrictions on them. This is explained in para **23.14**.

23.13   The LRA 2002 makes provision for the case where the claim is for the loss of an estate, interest or charge.[4] Where the register is rectified, the indemnity is the value of the estate, interest or charge immediately before rectification of the register of title, but as if there were to be no rectification.[5] By contrast, where the register is not rectified, it is the value of the estate, charge or interest at the time when the mistake which caused the loss was made.[6] The reason for the different measures is that where the register is not rectified, there is no other valuation date that can logically be taken other than the date of the mistake. In any event, it should be noted that any

---

[1]   LRA 2002, Sch 8, para 2.
[2]   See ibid, ss 11(3), 12(3), 132(1) (definition of 'land' includes mines and minerals, whether or not held with the surface).
[3]   See (2001) Law Com No 271, para 10.39.
[4]   LRA 2002, Sch 8, para 6.
[5]   Ibid, Sch 8, para 6(a).
[6]   Ibid, Sch 8, para 6(b).

consequential losses are also recoverable in addition to the sum representing the value of the estate, interest or charge.[1] Furthermore, where the value of the estate, interest or charge is valued at the date of the mistake because rectification is not ordered, there is a power to award interest on the sum from that date. There is in fact a general power to make rules as to the circumstances in which, and the periods for and rates at which, interest is payable on an indemnity under Sch 8.[2] Under the relevant rule,[3] interest is payable[4] at the rate or rates set for court judgment debts[5] for the following periods:[6]

(a) Where indemnity is awarded to a person who has suffered loss by reason of rectification, as explained in para **23.3**, the period from the date of rectification until the date on which the indemnity is paid. However, where the registrar or the court is satisfied that the person claiming indemnity has not taken reasonable steps to pursue with due diligence his claim for indemnity or, where relevant, his application for rectification, those periods may be excluded.

(b) In all the other cases listed in paras **23.4–23.10**, the period from the date the loss is suffered by reason of the relevant mistake, loss, destruction or failure until the date on which indemnity is paid.[7] This is particularly important in cases where rectification could have been ordered but was not (see para **23.4**) in the light of the limitations on the amount of indemnity in such a case that are set out in para **23.13**.

23.14   Costs and expenses incurred in relation to a matter giving rise to indemnity are recoverable by a person only if they were reasonably incurred by him with the consent of the registrar.[8] However, in three situations, costs and expenses can be recovered even if the registrar's prior consent has not been obtained, namely:

(a) where the costs or expenses incurred were incurred by the claimant urgently, and it was not reasonably practicable for him to apply for the registrar's consent in advance;[9]

---

[1]   See para **23.2**.
[2]   LRA 2002, Sch 8, para 9.
[3]   LRR 2003, r 195.
[4]   Ibid, r 195, r 195(1).
[5]   Ibid, r 195(3).
[6]   In LRR 2003, r 195, a reference to a period from a specified date until the date of payment, excludes the specified date but includes the date of payment: LRR 2003, r 195(5).
[7]   Ibid, r 195(2).
[8]   LRA 2002, Sch 8, para 3(1). Interest is payable on the amount of such costs and expenses from the date when the claimant pays them to the date of payment of indemnity in respect of them: see LRR 2003, r 195(4).
[9]   Ibid, Sch 8, para 3(2).

(b)   where the registrar subsequently approves the costs or expenses so that they are then treated as having been incurred with his consent;[1] and

(c)   where a person has applied to the court to determine whether he is entitled to an indemnity at all, or to determine the amount of any indemnity.[2] The applicant does not need the prior consent of the registrar in relation to the costs of that application.

23.15   The LRA 2002 also contains a new power in relation to costs in a case where a person incurs expenses in determining whether or not he has a claim to an indemnity. This might happen, for example, where the facts suggest that there might have been a mistake by the registrar but, on further investigation, this proves not to be the case. In such circumstances, the registrar is given a discretion to pay the claimant's costs or expenses provided that they were incurred reasonably and with the consent of the registrar.[3] Even if the registrar's prior consent was not obtained, he may still pay indemnity where:

(a)   the costs or expenses incurred were incurred by the claimant urgently, and it was not reasonably practicable for him to apply for the registrar's consent in advance; or

(b)   the registrar has subsequently approved the costs or expenses.[4]

WHEN A CLAIM FOR INDEMNITY WILL FAIL OR WILL BE REDUCED

23.16   In three situations a claim for indemnity will fail.

(a)   The first is where the claim is barred by lapse of time. A claim for indemnity is a simple contract debt and it arises when a person knows, or but for his own default might have known, of the existence of his claim.[5] It will, therefore, be barred 6 years after that date.[6]

(b)   The second situation is where the loss suffered by the claimant is wholly or partly the result of his or her own fraud.[7] The policy reasons for this rule are self-evident.

(c)   The third situation is where the loss suffered by the claimant is wholly the result of his own lack of proper care.[8]

---

[1]   LRA 2002, Sch 8, para 3(3).

[2]   Ibid, Sch 8, para 7(2).

[3]   Ibid, Sch 8, para 4(1).

[4]   Ibid, Sch 8, para 4(2).

[5]   Ibid, Sch 8, para 8.

[6]   See LA 1980, s 5.

[7]   LRA 2002, Sch 8, para 5(1)(a).

[8]   Ibid, Sch 8, para 5(1)(b).

As regards (c), there are two decisions on the equivalent provision of the LRA 1925,[1] which the LRA 2002 replicates, that provide guidance as to its meaning. First, in *Dean v Dean*,[2] the Court of Appeal held that if there were in fact several causes of the claimant's loss, the claim for indemnity would not fail on this ground. This was so, even if some or all of the other causes would not have occurred but for the claimant's conduct. Secondly, in *Prestige Properties Ltd v Scottish Provident Institution*,[3] Lightman J explained how the provisions[4] operated. The error by the Registry must have been an effective cause of loss. To establish (c), the Registry would have to show that, even though the error by the Registry was an effective cause of the loss, that loss should be regarded as wholly attributable to the claimant's lack of proper care. This might be the case where, for example, the Registry can show that proper care by the claimant could and should have prevented that error from having any such effect.[5]

23.17 If the person claiming indemnity was partly but not wholly responsible for the loss which he suffered, as a result of his own lack of proper care, any indemnity payable to him will be reduced to such extent as is fair having regard to his share in the responsibility for the loss.[6] For the registrar to invoke this defence, it is sufficient for him to establish 'the shared responsibility of the claimant's lack of care for the loss'.[7] This shared responsibility may take the form of contributory negligence in failing to prevent the occurrence of the loss, or a failure to mitigate and limit that loss.[8] 'The extent of the ordinary duty of care owed by a solicitor to his client on the conveyancing transaction in question (as opposed to the duty provided for in a particular' retainer which may extend or restrict that duty) may provide a yardstick as to the care to be expected of the claimant'.[9]

23.18 Where a claim for indemnity would be barred on grounds of fraud, or either barred or reduced because of a lack of care, it is not merely the person responsible whose claim is affected. Any person who derives title from him will be in the same position, unless the disposition to him was for valuable consideration and was registered or protected by an entry in the register.[10]

---

[1]   As amended by LRA 1997.
[2]   (2000) 80 P&CR 457.
[3]   [2002] EWHC 330 (Ch); [2003] Ch 1.
[4]   That is, what is now LRA 2002, Sch 8, para 5(1)(b).
[5]   [2003] Ch 1 at pp 15–16.
[6]   LRA 2002, Sch 8, para 5(2). This principle of contributory negligence was first introduced by LRA 1997, s 2.
[7]   *Prestige Properties Ltd v Scottish Provident Institution* [2003] Ch 1 at p 15.
[8]   Ibid, at p 15.
[9]   Ibid, at p 16.
[10]   LRA 2002, Sch 8, para 5(3).

CLAIMING INDEMNITY

23.19   Under the LRA 2002, a person is entitled to be indemnified *by the registrar*.[1] There are a number of ways in which a claim for indemnity might come to be made.

23.20   First, it might arise out of an application to the registrar for rectification of the register.[2] If there is an objection to that application that cannot be resolved by agreement, the matter will have to be referred to the Adjudicator for determination.[3] The Adjudicator will necessarily deal with any question of indemnity that is consequent upon his decision.

23.21   Secondly, as will be clear from the circumstances in which indemnity is payable,[4] there are many situations in which a claim for indemnity does not involve any possible issue of rectification. These will necessarily be dealt with by the registrar. Any challenge to his decision on an issue relating to indemnity would have to be by way of judicial review.[5]

23.22   Thirdly, as was the case under the LRA 1925, a person is entitled to apply to the court for a determination of any question as to whether he is entitled to an indemnity, or the amount of such an indemnity.[6] He does not have to apply first to the registrar.

23.23   The Land Registry's practice in any case in which indemnity is claimed is explained in the Registry's Practice Guide, Rectification and Indemnity.[7] The method of application for indemnity is not prescribed by rules as might have been anticipated. Assuming that the applicant does not apply to the court (see para **23.22**), the application for indemnity should be made by letter to the registrar and, where the claim arises from a mistake, should be accompanied by the following (if the claimant has the necessary material at that time[8]):

(a)   details of the mistake and any correction of that mistake;
(b)   what loss has been suffered;
(c)   details of the amount claimed, if possible, and how this has been calculated (see below);

---

[1]   LRA 2002, Sch 8, para 1(1).
[2]   The procedure for such applications will be a matter for rules: see LRA 2002, Sch 4, para 7(c).
[3]   LRA 2002, s 73; see also paras **20.29** et seq. For the Adjudicator, see Chapter 34.
[4]   See paras **23.3–23.10**.
[5]   See para **34.9**.
[6]   LRA 2002, Sch 8, para 7(1).
[7]   PG39: see para 5.2 (on making the application) and para 8.2.2 (on the method of determining the amount).
[8]   He may make the application before he does, but the Registry will need to have evidence of all the matters listed here before the claim can be concluded.

(d) if the loss includes any fees, bills or expenses, evidence (by invoice, etc) that these sums have been paid.

As regards (c), the Registry will ask the applicant for indemnity to suggest the figure that he considers will compensate him for the loss of his land, interest or charge. He may (and usually will) have to take the advice of a surveyor, and will usually be able to recover the costs of so doing as part of the indemnity, provided he obtains the prior consent of the registrar: see para **23.14**. The Registry may (at its own expense) employ the District Valuer in relation to a claim for indemnity, and in particular, it may ask the District Valuer:

(i) to verify the reasonableness of the claim; and

(ii) in cases where the register will not be rectified notwithstanding the mistake,[1] to provide a valuation of the estate, interest or charge as at the date when the mistake which caused the loss was made.[2]

If the applicant does not accept the District Valuer's figures, the District Valuer will usually enter into negotiations with the applicant's surveyor to try to agree a figure. That figure will have to be approved by the Registry.

THE REGISTRAR'S RIGHTS OF RECOURSE

23.24 The LRA 2002 replicates the provisions, first introduced by the LRA 1997, that give the registrar extensive rights of recourse in cases in which he has paid indemnity.[3]

23.25 First, the registrar is entitled to recover the amount paid from any person who caused or substantially contributed to the loss by fraud.[4] The registrar can make such recovery even if the recipient of the indemnity would not have been able to sue the perpetrator of the fraud had the indemnity not been paid.

23.26 Secondly, the registrar is entitled to enforce any right of action, of whatever nature and however arising, which the claimant would have been entitled to enforce had the indemnity not been paid.[5] This would apply in cases where, for example, the error in the register resulted from negligence on the part of the professional acting for the person who suffered the loss and was subsequently indemnified, and is analogous to an insurer's right of subrogation.

---

[1] See para **23.4**.

[2] See para **23.13**.

[3] It is clear from the Annual Reports of HM Land Registry, that these new rights of recourse are considerably more extensive than the equivalent rights were under the LRA 1925 as originally enacted.

[4] LRA 2002, Sch 8, para 10(1)(a).

[5] Ibid, Sch 8, para 10(1)(b), 10(2)(a).

23.27   Thirdly, where the register has been rectified, the registrar may enforce any right of action, of whatever nature and however arising, which the person in whose favour the register was rectified would have been entitled to enforce if it had not been rectified.[1]

23.28   As regards the third of those cases (para **23.27**), the Law Commission and the Land Registry in their final Report gave an example of the circumstances in which the provision might operate, and illustrates how extensive the right is. They envisaged a case where the register was rectified in favour of X because of a mistake caused by X's solicitor. As a result of the rectification, Y suffered loss for which he was indemnified by the registrar. The registrar would be entitled to recover the amount of the indemnity paid from X's solicitor. This is even though, at common law, X's solicitor might not have owed any duty of care to Y.[2]

23.29   However, although the rights of recourse are extensive, undertakings were given in Parliament both when they were first introduced under the LRA 1997 and during the passage of the Act, that they would not be invoked against solicitors and licensed conveyancers except in cases of fraud or serious cases of negligence.[3]

---

[1]   LRA 2002, Sch 8, para 10(1)(b), 10(2)(b).
[2]   See (2001) Law Com No 271, para 10.52.
[3]   See, eg, *Hansard* (HL), 8 November 2001, vol 628, col 313 (Baroness Scotland of Asthal).

PART 4

CONVEYANCING

THE MAIN CHANGES AT A GLANCE

Although the main changes that the Act makes in relation to conveyancing are in its provisions on electronic conveyancing (considered in Part 5), there are also some significant changes to other aspects of conveyancing in relation to registered land (including in relation to certain contracts that will trigger compulsory registration).

The main changes are as follows:

— The old prescriptive rules as to the proof of title which a seller of registered land has to show are replaced by a rule-making power which will enable the Lord Chancellor to make rules as to a seller's obligations in relation to his title.
— The restrictions on the title which a grantee of a lease may see are abolished where that grant is made out of a registered title and modified in relation to contracts to grant leases that trigger compulsory registration.
— Covenants for title are dealt with in a more transparent form.
— The rules deal more comprehensively with positive and indemnity covenants.

CHAPTER 24

PROVING TITLE

PROOF OF TITLE UNDER LRA 1925

24.1 Under LRA 1925,[1] on a sale or disposition of registered land, other than to a lessee or chargee, the registered proprietor was required to produce:

— copies of subsisting entries on the register and of filed plans;
— copies or abstracts of any documents noted on the register in respect of interests that would not be discharged or overridden at or prior to completion; and
— copies, abstracts and evidence in respect of estates and interests that were either appurtenant to the registered land[2] or which were excepted from the effect of registration.[3]

As regards the first two bullet points, the provisions were mandatory and could not be ousted by agreement to the contrary.[4]

24.2 There was also a provision in LRA 1925 which dealt with the situation where a seller of land was not the registered proprietor of land but could require the registered proprietor to convey at his direction. This might happen where the seller had contracted to buy the land or was the beneficiary under a bare trust. He could be required by the buyer to procure either his own registration as proprietor before transferring the registered estate to the buyer, or a disposition from the proprietor to the buyer.[5] In practice this provision, which could not be ousted by contrary intention, gave rise to serious practical difficulties.[6]

24.3 The provisions of LRA 1925 on proof of title were based upon the premise, which was applicable in 1925, that the register was not a public document and could only be searched with the consent of the registered

---

[1] LRA 1925, s 110(1), (2). For an analysis of these provisions, see (1998) Law Com No 254, paras 11.35–11.39.
[2] Such as the benefit of easements.
[3] In other words, overriding interests that affected the property.
[4] LRA 1925, s 110(3).
[5] Ibid, s 110(5).
[6] See (1998) Law Com No 254, para 11.43.

proprietor.[1] That is no longer the case. The register was made public by LRA 1988 and can be searched simply and cheaply. It is now possible to download copies of registered titles (including plans) from the internet through Land Registry Direct. The introduction of electronic conveyancing will mean that all solicitors and licensed conveyancers who are authorised to conduct such conveyancing will necessarily have on-line access to the register and will be able to call up any registered title on screen, literally at the press of a button. The provisions of LRA 1925 had become badly out of date.

PROOF OF TITLE UNDER THE ACT

24.4   The Act has replaced these provisions with a short rule-making power. This permits the Lord Chancellor to make rules about the obligations of a seller under a contract to make a disposition for valuable consideration of a registered estate or charge with respect to proof of title or perfection of title.[2] Any rules as to the perfection of title will meet the case of the seller who is not the registered proprietor but can direct the registered proprietor to make a disposition. If the Lord Chancellor does make any rules, they may be expressed to override any contrary contractual provision that the parties may have made.[3] It is implicit in this that rules might be made that are intended merely to provide guidance to parties, while leaving them free to make their own arrangements. In reality, under the present registered system, the only interests in relation to which proof of title is required from a seller (because it cannot be obtained from the Land Registry) are those that are not protected in the register, such as unregistered interests that override first registration or registered dispositions.[4]

24.5   In fact, no rules have been made under this power. Proof of title is a matter that has therefore been left to the parties to determine for themselves. The common law rule that the seller must prove both his title and his right to convey remains, and it will apply to the extent that it is not validly excluded. It might have been expected that the new edition of the Standard Conditions of Sale (SCS)[5] would have reflected this change in the law and contained conditions that recognised that it was no longer necessary for the seller to produce an official copy of the register of title. This has not happened. Condition 4.1.1 provides that, 'without cost to the buyer, the seller is to provide the buyer with proof of the title to the property and of his ability to transfer it, or to procure its transfer'. It therefore partly replicates the

---

[1]   See LRA 1925, s 110. Indeed, prior to 1930, when postal searches were introduced, the only way that the register could be searched was by attending in person at HM Land Registry in Lincoln's Inn Fields: see (2001) Law Com No 271, para 12.5.

[2]   LRA 2002, Sch 10, para 2(1). The rules would, if made, be land registration rules.

[3]   Ibid, Sch 10, para 2(2).

[4]   Under ibid, Schs 1 and 3.

[5]   4th edn, 2003.

provisions of LRA 1925, s 110, and sellers may wish to consider excluding it. The condition does, at least, stop short of reinstating the old law whereby a seller who was not yet the registered proprietor could be compelled to secure his own registration.[1] Condition 4.1.2 provides that where the property has a registered title, the proof of title is to include official copies of the register and title plan and any document referred to in the register of title and kept by the register (unless the interest or charge will be overreached or discharged on completion).

24.6 The fact of the open register has led to another change. Section 44 of the LPA 1925 makes provision for the statutory commencement of title. It provides, for example, that the period for the commencement of title which a purchaser may require, is 15 years.[2] This has no relevance to registered title where the register stands as proof of title in place of the root and chain of title required in relation to unregistered land. Section 44 also contains provisions which preclude a person who has contracted to take the grant or assignment of a lease from calling for the freehold title.[3] Where that freehold title is registered, this provision is now meaningless because the intending grantee or assignee can inspect the register of title on the open register. The Act therefore disapplies s 44 as regards registered land or a term of years to be derived out of registered land.[4] It also amends s 44 to create a new default position where the owner of unregistered land grants a lease that will trigger compulsory first registration of title. In that situation, those provisions of s 44 which restrict the title that the intending lessee can see,[5] will not apply.[6] The intending lessee will therefore be entitled to require the deduction of the superior title, so enabling him to be registered with absolute title.[7] That is, of course, the intention of the provision. However, this is only a default position, and the parties are free to provide otherwise if they so wish.[8] The Standard Conditions of Sale provide that if the term of a new lease to be granted pursuant to a contract will exceed 7 years, the seller (the grantor) is to deduce a title which will enable the buyer (the grantee) to register the lease at HM Land Registry with an absolute title.[9]

---

[1] LRA 1925, s 110(5); see also para **24.2**.
[2] Ibid, s 44(1), as amended by LPA 1969, s 23.
[3] Ibid, s 44(2).
[4] LRA 2002, Sch 11, para 2(4), inserting a new LPA 1925, s 44(12).
[5] Namely, LPA 1925, s 44(2)–(4).
[6] LRA 2002, Sch 11, para 2(2), inserting a new LPA 1925, s 44(4A).
[7] Cf SCS, c 8.2.4, which creates a similar default position in relation to the grant of a new lease for more than 21 years.
[8] LPA 1925, s 44(11).
[9] SCS, c 8.2.4.

CHAPTER 25

COVENANTS AND COVENANTS FOR TITLE

INTRODUCTION

25.1   Both LRA 2002 and LRR 2003 make provision about covenants.[1]

–   LRA 2002 contains a specific rule-making power in relation to implied covenants for title and implied covenants in conveyances subject to rents.
–   LRR 2003 contains rules in relation to positive and indemnity covenants that had hitherto been a matter of practice.

LRA 2002 does not attempt to deal with the conveyancing problems created by restrictive covenants, because these problems lie in the substantive law that governs restrictive covenants.

COVENANTS FOR TITLE

25.2   The Act does not make any substantial change to the way in which covenants for title operate in relation to registered land. The law governing covenants for title was substantially reformed by Part 1 of LP(MP)A 1994. There was therefore no reason for any fundamental reappraisal of the operation of such covenants in relation to registered land. The Act does, however, make the provisions which govern such covenants rather easier to understand. In particular, the principle that a person making a disposition of an interest in land the title to which was registered, is not liable in relation to certain of the covenants implied by LP(MP)A 1994 in respect of matters entered on the register of title of that interest,[2] is no longer a matter for rules.[3] The Act inserts a new s 6(4) into LP(MP)A 1994 to give effect to this principle.[4]

25.3   Other matters relating to the application of covenants for title to

---

1   See Land Registry Practice Guide, Implied Covenants, PG48.
2   See LP(MP)A 1994, s 6.
3   As it was: see LRR 1925, r 77A(2).
4   LRA 2002, Sch 11, para 31(2). Strictly speaking, this alteration changes the law. However, the changes are unlikely to be of any significance: see (2001) Law Com No 271, para 12.19.

registered land continue to be dealt with in rules as they were under LRA 1925.[1] Under the LRR 2003:

(a)   A registrable disposition may be expressed to be made either with full title guarantee or with limited title guarantee (or in the appropriate Welsh language form).[2]

(b)   In general, no reference may be made in the register to any implied covenant for title.[3] There is one exception to this. Where a registrable disposition of leasehold land either limits or extends the covenant implied by s 4 of the LP(MP)A 1994 (validity of lease), a reference may be made in the register.[4]

(c)   A document which effects a registrable disposition that limits or extends any covenant must include a statement in prescribed form to that effect, referring to the section in the LP(MP)A 1994 in which the relevant covenant is set out.[5]

(d)   Provision is made for those rare cases in which the old covenants for title implied under LPA 1925 and LRA 1925 can still arise where a disposition was made after LP(MP)A 1994 came into force pursuant to a contract before that date.[6]

POSITIVE COVENANTS

25.4   Under the LRR 2003, the registrar may make an appropriate entry in the proprietorship register of any positive covenant that relates to a registered estate that has been given by the present or any previous proprietor,[7] as for example, where the proprietor has covenanted to maintain a fence on the boundary with a neighbour's land. The entry in the register should, where practicable, refer to the instrument that contains the covenant,[8] and must be removed if it appears to the registrar that the covenant does not bind the current proprietor (as will generally be the case where he is not the original covenantor).[9] These rules reflect the Land Registry's existing practice, although there was no equivalent rule in the LRR 1925.

---

[1]   See LRA 2002, Sch 10, para 3.

[2]   LRR 2003, r 67(1). This replicates LRR 1925, r 76A(2).

[3]   LRR 2003, r 67(5), replicating LRR 1925, r 76A(4). It should be noted that the transfer form *will* record the fact that it was made with full or limited title guarantee: see eg Form TR1, box 10.

[4]   LRR 2003, r 67(6), replicating LRR 1925, r 76A(5).

[5]   LRR 2003, r 68. Cf LRR 1925, r 77A(3).

[6]   For these covenants, see LP(MP)A 1994, s 11. For the rules, see LRR 2003, rr 67(2)–(4). Cf LRR 1925, rr 76A, 77.

[7]   LRR 2003, r 64(1).

[8]   Ibid, r 64(2).

[9]   Ibid, r 64(3).

INDEMNITY COVENANTS

25.5 There may be circumstances where an owner transfers registered land but remains liable on covenants to which he has been subject as registered proprietor, as, for example, where he entered into covenants when he purchased the land so as to be liable to the original covenantee. He may therefore wish to take an indemnity covenant from the transferee.[1] The LRR 2003 give the registrar power to make an appropriate entry in the proprietorship register of any such indemnity covenant that has been given by the proprietor of a registered estate in respect of either:

(a) any restrictive covenant that affects the estate;[2] or
(b) a positive covenant that relates to that estate;[3]

and the entry must, where practicable, refer to the instrument that contains the indemnity covenant.[4] As with positive covenants, that entry must be removed if it appears to the registrar that the covenant does not bind the current proprietor.[5] Once again, these rules reflect the Land Registry's existing practice, which was only partially incorporated in the LRR 1925.[6]

COVENANTS IMPLIED IN A TRANSFER OF A PRE-1996 LEASE

25.6 Schedule 12, para 20 to the LRA 2002 contains indemnity covenants that will be applied on a transfer of a lease granted prior to 1996 and not, therefore, subject to the provisions of the Landlord and Tenant (Covenants) Act 1995. Those indemnity covenants replicate in more comprehensible form the covenants previously implied by LRA 1925, s 24(1)(b) and (2).[7] Where the whole of the land is comprised in the registered lease, the covenants implied on the part of the transferee are set out in para 20(2) of Sch 12. Where only part of the land is transferred, the covenants implied on the part of:

(a) the transferee, are set out in para 20(3);
(b) the transferor (if he continues to hold land subject to the lease), are set out in para 20(4).

Where a transfer of a registered leasehold estate modifies or negatives any

---

[1] Cf SCS, c 4.6.4, which requires a buyer to enter into indemnity covenants in certain circumstances.
[2] It is common for restrictive covenants to provide that a landowner's liability under the covenant ceases when he transfers the burdened land. In any event, the principle remedy for the enforcement of a restrictive covenant is an injunction. Once the original covenantor has parted with land, he will not be the appropriate defendant in proceedings for an injunction.
[3] LRR 2003, r 65(1).
[4] Ibid, r 65(2).
[5] Ibid, r 65(3).
[6] See LRR 1925, r 110, which permitted the registrar to note an indemnity covenant taken on a transfer of land subject to a charge or other incumbrance.
[7] See Land Registry Practice Guide, Implied Covenants, PG48, para 4.

covenants implied on the part of the transferee, whether in para 20(2) or (3) of Sch 12, an entry must be made in the register that the covenants have been so modified.[1] The covenants implied respectively in paras 20(3) and (4) are modified in a case in which in the transfer:

(a)   the entire rent is expressed to be borne by the part of the land transferred (the lessor not consenting);[2] and

(b)   the part transferred is expressed to be exonerated from payment of the rent (the lessor not consenting).[3]

TRANSFER OF A REGISTERED ESTATE SUBJECT TO A RENTCHARGE

25.7   LRR 2003, r 69 contains a number of provisions which modify the covenants that are implied on a transfer of a registered estate that is subject to a rentcharge.[4] As so modified, the implied covenants are as follows.[5]

25.8   First, where there is a transfer for valuable consideration of the whole of a registered estate that is subject to a rentcharge, the transferee impliedly undertakes to the transferor to perform the covenants set out in Part 7 of Sch 2 to LPA 1925.[6] Those covenants are:

(a)   to pay the rentcharge;

(b)   to observe and perform all the covenants, agreements and conditions contained in the deed or other document creating the rentcharge; and

(c)   to save harmless and keep indemnified the transferor and his successors in title in respect of any omission to pay the rentcharge or any breach of any of the covenants, agreements and conditions.

25.9   Secondly, where there is transfer for valuable consideration of part only of a registered estate subject to a rentcharge which has been, or is by the transfer apportioned without the consent of the rentcharge owner, the transferee's covenants are as set out in para **25.8**, except that of indemnity is

---

[1]   LRR 2003, r 66. Cf LRA 1925, s 24(1), which made provision for an entry in the register negativing the implication of such covenants.

[2]   LRR 2003, r 60(3).

[3]   Ibid, r 60(2). Where there is a transfer of *any* registered lease, whenever granted, and that transfer contains a legal apportionment of or an exoneration from the rent reserved by the lease, there must be a statement to that effect in prescribed form in the 'additional provisions' panel of the transfer: see LRR 2003, r 60(1).

[4]   For those covenants, see LPA 1925, s 77; Sch 2, Parts VII and VIII.

[5]   See Land Registry Practice Guide, Implied Covenants, PG48, para 5.

[6]   LPA 1925, s 77(1)(A) and Sch 2, Part VII, as modified by LRR 2003, r 69(1) (replicating LRR 1925, r 109(3)). The covenants implied by s 77(1)(A) may be modified or negatived by suitable words in the transfer: LRR 2003, r 69(4)(a).

limited to the payment of the apportioned rent. The transferor enters into similar covenants with the transferee in respect of the balance of the rent.[1]

25.10 Thirdly, where there is a transfer of part only of a registered estate for valuable consideration and that part is, without the consent of the owner of the rentcharge, expressed to be exonerated from the entire rent, the transferor's covenant implied by LPA 1925, Sch 2, Part VIII, para (ii) to pay the rentcharge extends to the entire rent.[2]

25.11 Fourthly, where there is a transfer of part only of a registered estate for valuable consideration and that part is, without the consent of the owner of the rentcharge, expressed to be subject to the entire rent, the transferee's covenant implied by LPA 1925, Sch 2, Part VIII, para (i) to pay the rentcharge extends to the entire rent.[3]

25.12 Finally, it should be noted that, where the rentcharge was created to give effect to a family charge,[4] the covenants set out in s 11(2) of the Rentcharges Act 1977 apply on a transfer of the land subject to the charge rather than those implied by s 77 of LPA 1925.[5] Those are covenants by the transferor that:

(a) he will pay the rentcharge and indemnify the transferee against all claims in respect of that rentcharge; and

(b) in the event that the rentcharge ceases to affect the land transferred, he will furnish evidence of that fact to the grantee and those deriving title under him.

RESTRICTIVE COVENANTS

25.13 The question is often asked as to why LRA 2002 does not make provision for the recording of the benefit of a restrictive covenant as well as for noting the burden of it. Comparison is made with the position in relation to the express grant and reservation of easements: where the dominant tenement is registered, its proprietor must be registered as the proprietor of the benefit of that easement.[6] The reason why restrictive covenants are treated differently arises from the legal principles that apply to them. A person may enforce a restrictive covenant if:

1 LPA 1925, s 77(1)(B) and Sch 2, Part VIII, as modified by LRR 2003, r 69(1). The covenants implied by s 77(1)(B) may be modified or negatived by suitable words in the transfer: LRR 2003, r 69(4)(a).
2 LRR 2003, r 69(2).
3 Ibid, r 69(3).
4 See Rentcharges Act 1977, s 2(3)(a) (as amended).
5 Ibid, s 11(1).
6 LRA 2003, Sch 2, para 7; see also para **8.12**.

(a)   the covenant was entered into for the benefit of the land of the covenantee;

(b)   the land benefited is sufficiently defined or ascertainable by permissible inference or evidence; and

(c)   the land is capable of being benefited by the covenant.[1]

In practice, it is the second and third requirements that effectively preclude the registration of the benefit of restrictive covenants. Such covenants are often taken for the benefit of substantial areas of land that are not precisely defined, or which may be difficult to ascertain, as where:

(a)   the covenant is expressed to be made not only with the covenantee for the benefit of her land, but also with other landowners of land that adjoins the land burdened by the restrictive covenant;[2]

(b)   the covenant is taken by a developer of an estate for the benefit of its remaining land on that estate at the date of the covenant.

Although there is a presumption that where a restrictive covenant is taken for the benefit of land, that land does benefit from the covenant, that presumption can be rebutted by contrary evidence.[3] In any event, even if the benefited land were identified in the register, this would not necessarily mean very much. The creation of a restrictive covenant is not a registrable disposition (unlike the express creation of an easement) and the validity of such covenants is not guaranteed merely because they are noted against the title of the covenantor's land.[4] In short, the reason why LRA 2002 does not address restrictive covenants is because of the substantive law governing such covenants.

25.14   It may be hoped that, in time, a proper system of land obligations, which includes both easements and positive and restrictive covenants, may be introduced, which would require the registration of both the benefit and burden of such interests. Such a system was not within the terms of reference of the Law Commission and HM Land Registry when they were preparing the new legislation.[5]

---

[1]   *Marten v Flight Refuelling Ltd* [1962] Ch 115 at 129.
[2]   Cf LPA 1925, s 56.
[3]   Cf *Earl of Leicester v Wells-next-the-Sea UDC* [1973] Ch 110 at 124–125.
[4]   See LRA 2002, s 32(3); see also para **10.5**.
[5]   It should be noted that the effect of commonhold would have to be taken into account in any scheme and that the legislation setting up the system of commonhold was not enacted until some months after LRA 2002 had received Royal Assent.

PART 5

ELECTRONIC CONVEYANCING

THE MAIN CHANGES AT A GLANCE

The most significant single feature of the LRA 2002 is that it introduces a wholly new system of electronic conveyancing (e-conveyancing). These provisions are found in Part 8 of and Sch 5 to the Act. The main elements of the new system are as follows.

—   A principal aim of e-conveyancing is to enable dispositions of registered land to be made and registered simultaneously. This can only happen if conveyancers have authority to make changes to the register.

—   E-conveyancing will be conducted through a secure electronic network. Access will be regulated by network access agreements made between the registrar and those authorised to have access to the network. Rules will prescribe the way in which e-conveyancing is to be conducted. Such rules will override any obligations that a conveyancer might otherwise owe to his client.

—   All stages of a conveyancing transaction will be conducted electronically and the Land Registry will become involved in a transaction at a much earlier stage than at present.

—   The LRA 2002 provides how electronic documents are to be made. Such documents that are made in accordance with the Act will be deemed to comply with common law and statutory requirements as to form.

—   It is likely that, in the early days of e-conveyancing, conveyancers will authenticate electronic documents on behalf of their clients, who are unlikely to have their own electronic signatures. The LRA 2002 makes provision that will ensure that conveyancers can do this.

—   It is intended that there will be a system of electronic settlement to ensure that all financial aspects of a transaction are dealt with on completion.

Although e-conveyancing has been singled out for specific comment, it must be stressed that it is merely one example of e-commerce and should be seen in that context. It is not unique and it will not develop in a vacuum. Many of the concerns that have been raised in relation to e-conveyancing apply equally to all or many other forms of e-commerce. There are likely to be common solutions. Certain forms of e-commerce have been operating very successfully for some time now, such as the electronic trading of shares on the London Stock Exchange.[1]

E-conveyancing was not introduced when the LRA 2002 came into force on 13 October 2003. It is proposed to introduce it gradually over the following 4 or 5 years. The first step towards an electronic system will be the electronic registration of registered charges. HM Land Registry was given official authority to proceed with direct electronic charges in November 2003. There is also a pilot scheme under which lenders will be able to update existing details in relation to a registered charge, such as the borrower's name and address. Electronic lodgement of notices and restrictions are also probable candidates for early introduction. These are, however, a far cry from the system of e-conveyancing that the Act seeks to create. Much of the detail as to the workings of e-conveyancing is necessarily left to rules and those rules will not be made prior to the coming into force of the Act. HM Land Registry undertook a major consultation on the form of e-conveyancing as it is to be developed and this provides an insight into the Registry's thinking.[2]

One particular concern that is frequently voiced about e-conveyancing – and indeed about all forms of e-commerce – is about the level of security that it offers and the extent to which it can provide protection from fraud. It should in fact be possible to create an electronic system of conveyancing that is *more* secure than the present paper-based one, where forgery and fraud are commonplace. HM Land Registry has a strong incentive to minimise the risk of fraud, given that it guarantees registered title and may have to pay indemnity if the register is fraudulently altered.

---

[1]   Known as CREST.

[2]   See *E-Conveyancing: A Land Registry Consultation*, May 2002 and *E-Conveyancing: A Land Registry Consultation Report*, March 2003. A second report to Ministers, outlining the procurement strategy and implementation plan is due in the spring of 2004.

CHAPTER 26

ELECTRONIC CONVEYANCING

WHAT IS E-CONVEYANCING?

26.1 At present, conveyancing is paper-based. Although it is now possible to have direct access to the register[1] in order to view its contents and to make certain applications to the Registry,[2] contracts, transfers and grants are all made using written documents. Those documents then have to be submitted to the Registry for registration. It has been explained that it is already possible for a mortgage lender to notify the Registry electronically of the discharge of a registered charge.[3] The intention of the LRA 2002 is to bring about a change whereby all dealings are conducted in dematerialised form.

26.2 It would have been possible to create an e-conveyancing system under which changes to the register were made, as now, by HM Land Registry on application, but where those applications were made electronically. However, the Act goes much further than that: the system of e-conveyancing that will be created under the powers which it confers, changes the way in which land registration is conducted. It will no longer be the Registry alone that makes changes to the register, whether on application, to give effect to a court order or on the registrar's own volition. The registrar will still make changes to the register in appropriate circumstances. However, when there are dealings with registered land, the register will be changed automatically to give effect to them as a result of electronic documents and applications created by solicitors and licensed conveyancers acting for the parties to the transaction.[4] Although such dealings will be subject to prior scrutiny by the Registry, it will no longer be the Registry that makes the change. This system is dictated by the fundamental aim of the LRA 2002 to bring about a conclusive register.[5] It is intended that, when e-conveyancing is fully functional, dealings with registered

---

1   Under the Land Registry's Direct Access Service.
2   The applications in question include applications for various official copies, to inspect and copy register entries, for an official search of the Index Map and Parcels Index, and an enquiry as to discharge of a charge by electronic means. They are listed in para 2 of Notice 3 of the Chief Land Registrar: Land Registry Direct, made pursuant to LRR 2003, Sch 2. See also Ruoff and Roper *Registered Conveyancing*, F1.006.
3   LRR 2003, r 115; and see paras **12.103–12.106**. As explained at para **12.106**, that system is itself being streamlined with the replacement of ENDs by EDs.
4   See (2001) Law Com No 271, para 2.57.
5   See para **1.7**.

land will not have any effect unless they are simultaneously registered.[1] In this way, the so-called 'registration gap' that presently exists between the making of a disposition of registered land and its registration following application to the Registry will disappear. Although it is the objective of a conclusive register that has driven the policy of the Act in this regard, the elimination of the registration gap will bring many advantages with it. In particular, it will eliminate any risk that a disposition might be made between the making of the transfer or grant and its registration.[2]

26.3   The system of e-conveyancing that the LRA 2002 creates is concerned only with dealings with registered land and with those aspects of conveyancing that involve registration. That is only one part of the conveyancing process. The Land Register will provide an intending purchaser with information about the title. However, there are many other searches that an intending purchaser of land may wish to make, such as a local authority search, an environmental search, or, in certain parts of the country, a Coal Authority search. The process for making these 'parallel' searches electronic is under way through the NLIS, which also provides a portal to access the Land Register. It is not just a conclusive Land Register that is required. If an effective e-conveyancing system is to be constructed, these other sources of data must be readily and speedily accessible on line.[3]

26.4   There are no precedents for creating an e-conveyancing system under which dealings with registered land are simultaneously registered.[4] The LRA 2002 has therefore had to proceed from first principles. The questions that arise are as follows.

(1)   What formal requirements will apply to contracts and dealings with registered land that are made in electronic form?
(2)   What mechanisms will be in place to protect the integrity of the register, given that solicitors and licensed conveyancers will be able to make changes to it?
(3)   How will e-conveyancing be made compulsory?
(4)   What other steps are needed to ensure that e-conveyancing operates as smoothly as possible?

In this chapter, the first of those questions is considered. The second is addressed in Chapter 27, and the third and fourth in Chapter 28.

---

[1]   See Chapter 28.
[2]   Cf *Brown & Root Technology Ltd v Sun Alliance and London Assurance Co Ltd* [2001] Ch 733.
[3]   There is a particular concern that local authorities are not computerising their local searches either at all or too slowly.
[4]   E-conveyancing of some kind or another has been introduced in other jurisdictions, such as Ontario.

FORMAL REQUIREMENTS

Introduction

26.5 As a consequence of a number of statutory provisions, many dealings with both land and interests in land have to comply with prescribed formal requirements of signed writing or of a deed. It was therefore necessary for the LRA 2002 to ensure that electronic documents that effected such dealings would not be invalidated by these formal requirements. Section 91 of the LRA 2002 provides a uniform system for creating electronic documents in relation to specified dispositions of estates, rights and interests in registered land. Section 91 does not apply to contracts for the sale or other disposition of an interest in land. This is because such contracts were to be dealt with in another way.

26.6 Under s 8 of the Electronic Communications Act 2000 (ECA 2000), the appropriate Minister is given power to modify by order made by statutory instrument the provisions of any enactment in such manner as he may think for the purpose of authorising or facilitating the use of electronic communications or electronic storage. In March 2001, some months prior to the introduction of the Land Registration Bill, the Lord Chancellor's Department issued for consultation a draft Order to be made under s 8.[1] Part of that draft Order was concerned with dispositions of registered land and s 91 of the LRA 2002 is an extended version of that provision.[2] The draft Order also contained a proposed new s 2A of the LP(MP)A 1989 that specified the formalities that would be required to make a contract for the sale of an interest in electronic form.[3] The new section would have applied to contracts relating to both registered and unregistered land. The LRA 2002 is limited by its scope to registered land and does not replicate the proposed s 2A, even in relation to contracts concerning registered land. It has not yet been decided whether any such Order will be required to introduce the proposed s 2A.[4] Indeed, there is some doubt as to whether such an Order is needed at all, because it has now been suggested that an electronic document can satisfy any statutory requirements of writing and signature.[5] However, it is not clear how s 2 of the LP(MP)A 1989 could apply in its present form to contracts made electronically.[6] The practice of conveyancers influenced the requirements of

---

[1] Electronic Conveyancing, a draft Order under s 8 of the ECA 2000.
[2] An Order under s 8 can only amend *statutory* requirements and not common law rules. Section 91 amends certain rules of common law as well.
[3] In place of the requirements of LP(MP)A 1989, s 2.
[4] An analysis of the responses to the draft Order was published by the Lord Chancellor's Department in December 2001: CP(R) 05/2001.
[5] See *Electronic Commerce: Formal Requirements in Commercial Transactions: Advice from the Law Commission* (December 2001), chapter 3. This Advice is not in one of the usual Law Commission series.
[6] A point acknowledged in *E-Conveyancing: A Land Registry Consultation*, para 2.3.3.

s 2[1] and, in particular, its recognition of the custom of exchanging contracts.[2] Exchange of contracts makes no sense in relation to electronic documents and the draft Order recognised this fact. In particular, it would require that all the terms which the parties had expressly agreed were incorporated in the document (whether by being set out in it or by reference to some other document), and that the contract would take effect at the date and time specified in that document.

The statutory requirements

The function of LRA 2002, s 91

26.7   The effect of s 91 of the LRA 2002 is that, if an electronic document is made in accordance with its provisions, it is to be regarded as made by signed writing and to satisfy any statutory requirements of a deed.[3] Section 91 is a remarkably concise and subtle provision. It was the subject of much comment – and misunderstanding – during the passage of the LRA 2002 through Parliament. It is *only* concerned with the formal requirements for making a disposition in electronic form.

Dispositions within LRA 2002, s 91

26.8   The section will apply to three classes of disposition.[4] The first is a disposition of a registered estate or charge. The second is something of a novelty. It is a disposition of an interest which is the subject of a notice in the register, such as an equitable charge or an option. The LRA 2002 visualises that it will become possible to transfer electronically certain interests that are only protected by a notice and are not registered with their own titles. This is a notable extension of the principles of registration. The third class of disposition is a disposition of unregistered land which triggers the requirement of registration contained in s 4 of the Act.[5] In addition to falling into one of these three categories, the disposition must be of a kind specified by rules. It is envisaged that, eventually, all possible dispositions will be specified by rules.[6] However, the need to specify in rules dispositions that can be made electronically means that e-conveyancing can be extended on a transaction-by-transaction basis over a period of time. The more difficult transactions, such as sales of part only of an existing registered title, are likely to be amongst the last to be brought within the e-conveyancing system.

---

1   See (1987) Law Com No 164, paras 4.6, 4.15.
2   See LP(MP)A 1989, s 2(1).
3   See further, para **26.14**.
4   LRA 2002, s 91(2).
5   See paras **2.10** et seq.
6   (2001) Law Com No 271, para 13.12.

The four conditions to be satisfied

26.9 It is not enough that the disposition falls within the requirements of para **26.8**. To have the effect mentioned in para **26.7**, it must meet four conditions.[1]

26.10 The first condition is that the electronic document must make provision for the time and date when it takes effect.[2] There has to be some mechanism for fixing the moment at which an electronic document takes effect. Any concept of delivery, such as applies to deeds, is inappropriate for electronic documents for at least three reasons. First, s 91 covers cases where the statutory requirements of form are for signed writing rather than a deed. Secondly, as explained below, an electronic document that complies with the requirements of the section is not in fact a deed but is merely to be regarded as one for the purposes of the section.[3] Thirdly, it is not clear how the technical concept of delivery could apply to an electronic document, because it involves words or acts by which the maker indicates that the deed binds him.[4] It follows, therefore, that some other means had to be found for fixing the moment at which an electronic document will take effect. The means adopted – the fixing of a date and time – gives the parties as much flexibility as they presently enjoy. That date and time could be inserted into the document at a late stage, just before the transaction is to be completed.

26.11 The second condition is that the document has the electronic signature of each person by whom it purports to be authenticated.[5] An electronic signature is the means by which a person authenticates an electronic document as his own.[6] There are various different forms of electronic signature presently available[7] and each has its protagonists and its detractors. With some forms of electronic signature, the recipient of the signed message can tell whether a hacker has interfered with that message. It is unlikely that any one form of electronic signature will be prescribed. What will matter will be the level of security that each offers. It will be noted that the electronic document must be signed electronically by 'every person by whom it purports to be authenticated'. Sometimes the disponees as well as the disponor may execute a document. This *should* happen when there is a disposition of registered land in favour of joint proprietors (although, in practice, it often

---

1   LRA 2002, s 91(3).

2   Ibid, s 91(3)(a).

3   Ibid, s 91(5); see also para **26.16**.

4   Cf *Vincent v Premo Enterprises (Voucher Sales) Ltd* [1969] 2 QB 609 at 619.

5   LRA 2002, s 91(3)(b).

6   For the purposes of s 91, 'electronic signature' has the meaning given to it by ECA 2000, s 7(2): see LRA 2002, s 91(10).

7   These include, for example, 'public' or 'dual' key cryptography, and iris recognition. The Land Registry's present working assumption is that some form of public key infrastructure will be employed: see *E-Conveyancing: A Land Registry Consultation*, para 8.2.2; and *E-Conveyancing: A Land Registry Consultation Report*, pp 38–42.

does not) because the transfer form sets out the trusts upon which the land is to be held by the disponees[1] and, if it is signed by them, that document will satisfy the formal requirements for an enforceable declaration of a trust respecting any land.[2]

26.12   The third condition is related to the second and it is that each electronic signature should be certified.[3] Certification is the means by which an electronic signature is itself authenticated.[4] If an electronic document is signed with Joan Smith's electronic signature, there has to be a way of ensuring that that signature really is Joan Smith's and not that of some other person who fraudulently holds herself out to be Joan Smith. What in practice will probably happen is that the certifying authority will actually *provide* Joan Smith with her electronic signature,[5] but only when it has satisfied itself of her identity. Certification is therefore likely to be an integral part of the process by which a person obtains his or her own electronic signature.[6]

26.13   The fourth condition is that such other conditions as rules may provide are met.[7] It is likely that, as e-commerce develops, it will be necessary to introduce other requirements to ensure the security or smooth working of the system. It may, for example, be necessary to require transactions to meet a specified level of security. Indeed, this may be an early requirement.[8]

The effect of compliance

26.14   Section 91 does not disapply the various statutory or common law requirements for signed writing or a deed.[9] Instead, it deems compliance with them if an electronic document is made in accordance with the requirements set out above. Indeed, s 91 contains no less than four such deeming provisions.

26.15   First, a document that is made in accordance with the requirements explained in paras **26.8–26.13** is to be regarded as in writing and signed by each individual and sealed by each corporation whose electronic signature it

---

[1]   See, eg, Form TR1 under LRR 2003, Sch 1.
[2]   See LPA 1925, s 53(1)(b).
[3]   LRA 2002, s 91(3)(c).
[4]   For the purposes of s 91, 'certification' has the meaning given to it by ECA 2000, s 7(3): see LRA 2002, s 91(10).
[5]   Perhaps in the form of a swipe card, but that is not the only possible method.
[6]   Where a person has an electronic signature, it will still be necessary to be sure that he is whom he claims to be, and that he is not impersonating the person whose electronic signature he has stolen.
[7]   LRA 2002, s 91(3)(d).
[8]   Cf para **26.11**.
[9]   Not all formal requirements are statutory. For example, some significant categories of corporation can only execute a document under the corporate seal. That is a common law and not a statutory requirement.

has.[1] The provision makes no reference to *statutory* requirements of signed or sealed writing. This is important because it will enable any corporation to have an electronic signature, even if it is one that can only execute a document under its corporate seal because it has no statutory powers of execution.

26.16 Secondly, a document that is made in accordance with the requirements of s 91 is to be regarded for the purposes of any enactment as a deed.[2] It is important to stress that the document is *not* a deed. It is merely to be regarded as a deed for the purposes set out. This means, for example, that the rule that an agent cannot execute a deed on behalf of his principal unless he is authorised to do so by a deed,[3] is inapplicable. The requirements of s 91 do in fact differ markedly from the statutory requirements for a deed. For example, an electronic document under the section does not have to state that it is a deed.[4] Nor, if it is made by an individual, does it have to be attested.[5]

26.17 Thirdly, if a document that is made in accordance with the requirements of s 91 is authenticated by a person as agent, it is to be regarded for the purposes of any enactment as authenticated by him under the written authority of his principal.[6] The purpose of this provision is to deal with a minor technical point. Under some statutory provisions, an agent can only make certain disposition on behalf of his principal if he has been authorised by that principal in writing. The most important example is the LPA 1925, s 53(1)(a), by which 'no interest in land can be created or disposed of except by writing signed by the person creating or conveying the same, or his agent thereunto lawfully authorised in writing ...'. The result of the deeming provision in s 91 is that where an agent makes a disposition in electronic form on behalf of his principal, he is deemed to comply with the formal requirement that he should have the *written* authority of his principal. As a consequence, the other party or parties to the transaction cannot require him to prove that his authority to authenticate the electronic document was given in writing. It would rather defeat the point of having e-conveyancing if they could. It should be stressed that this provision does *not* deem the agent to have authority where he has none.[7] All it does is to deem him, for the purposes of any enactment, to have authenticated the electronic document under the *written* authority of his principal.

26.18 Fourthly, if notice of an assignment is made by means of a document to which s 91 applies and is given in electronic form in accordance with the

---

[1] LRA 2002, s 91(4).

[2] Ibid, s 91(5).

[3] See, eg, *Powell v London and Provincial Bank* [1893] 2 Ch 555 at 563.

[4] Cf LP(MP)A 1989, s 1(2).

[5] Cf ibid, s 1(3).

[6] LRA 2002, s 91(6).

[7] See also LRA 2002, Sch 5, para 8, which is explained at para **27.24**, and which is concerned with an agent's lack of implied authority to contract or make a disposition on behalf of his principal.

rules, it is to be regarded for the purposes of any enactment as given in writing.[1] The reason for this provision is as follows. It has been explained in para **26.8** that it is intended that it will become possible to make electronic dispositions of certain interests that are not registered with their own titles, but are merely protected by a notice on the register. By s 136(1) of the LPA 1925, where there is an assignment of a debt or legal chose in action, it is necessary to give 'express notice in writing' to the debtor or other contracting party. The provision mentioned above is intended to meet this point. It means that if there is an electronic assignment of a debt or legal chose in action – such as an option or other estate contract – under the provisions of s 91 of the LRA 2002, notice of that assignment can be given electronically to the debtor or contracting party. Such notice will be regarded as complying with s 136(1) of the LPA 1925.

Execution by corporations

26.19   The manner in which a corporation may execute a document depends upon the type of corporation. While there are statutory provisions applicable to certain types of corporation, the common law rules on execution apply to others. First, any corporation can execute a document by affixing its common seal, whether by statute[2] or at common law. Secondly, by statute, certain corporations do not have to have a common seal.[3] Such corporations have statutory powers to execute documents in other ways by the signatures of their officers or trustees. Thirdly, all corporations may appoint an agent to execute instruments on their behalf, whether by power of attorney[4] or otherwise.

26.20   How then can a corporation execute a document under s 91 of the LRA 2002? First, the section permits every corporation to have an electronic signature (s 91(4)(b)). It will not be possible for the corporation's signature to be incorporated into or otherwise logically associated with an electronic document unless this was done at the direction of an authorised officer or trustee of that corporation.[5] Secondly, where a statute permits officers of a corporation to sign a document on its behalf, those officers will be able to sign a document electronically under s 91. Thirdly, a duly authorised agent will also be able to sign a document electronically on behalf of a corporation under s 91.

---

[1]   LRA 2002, s 91(7).

[2]   See, eg, Companies Act 1985, s 36A(2) (which applies to corporations that are companies for the purposes of the Companies Act 1985 and certain other corporations); Friendly Societies Act 1992, Sch 6, para 2 (friendly societies); Charities Act 1993, s 60(2) (incorporated charities).

[3]   See, eg, Companies Act 1985, s 36A; Friendly Societies Act 1992, Sch 6, para 2; Charities Act 1993, s 60.

[4]   See Powers of Attorney Act 1971, s 7; LPA 1925, s 74(3).

[5]   See (2001) Law Com No 271, para 13.26. In other words, the person or persons who could affix the company's seal to a document could also direct the use of the company's electronic signature.

26.21 Under s 36A(4) of the Companies Act 1985, where a document has been signed by a director and the secretary of a company, or by two directors of a company, and is expressed (in whatever form) to be executed by the company, it has the same effect as if it were executed under the common seal of the company. There is a statutory presumption in favour of a purchaser that a document is deemed to have been duly executed by a company if it purports to be signed by a director and the secretary of the company, or by two directors of the company.[1] That presumption is carried forward into e-conveyancing and will apply to a document signed electronically.[2]

Rights of a purchaser as to execution

26.22 Section 75 of the LPA 1925 provides that, although on a sale a purchaser is not entitled to require that a conveyance to him should be executed in his (or his solicitor's) presence, he is entitled to have the conveyance attested by some person appointed by him, who may be his solicitor.[3] This right does not apply to documents to which s 91 applies,[4] because attestation is inappropriate to e-conveyancing.[5]

---

1   Companies Act 1985, s 36A(6). This can be important. The presumption will protect purchasers in cases where, for example, the directors were not authorised, or were acting other than as a board of directors. In these cases, there is no protection under the provisions of Part III of the Companies Act 1985.
2   LRA 2002, s 91(9).
3   The section was passed to deal with a specific difficulty that had arisen from certain judicial decisions.
4   LRA 2002, s 91(8).
5   Cf (2001) Law Com No 271, para 13.31.

CHAPTER 27

THE LAND REGISTRY NETWORK

INTRODUCTION: A TYPICAL TRANSACTION IN ELECTRONIC FORM

27.1 The second of the four questions that have been raised at para **26.4** concerns the mechanisms that will be required to protect the integrity of the register, in a world in which solicitors and licensed conveyancers[1] will be able to make changes to it. This question necessarily underpins the whole structure of e-conveyancing. The system of e-conveyancing will be built around a secure electronic network operated by or for HM Land Registry.[2] The manner in which this network will be used in conveyancing transactions will be regulated in some detail. The framework for that regulation is found in Sch 5 to the LRA 2002. The detail will be contained in rules made under that Schedule or under general rule-making powers contained in Sch 10 to the Act.

27.2 To understand the provisions of the LRA 2002 that govern the network, it is necessary to have a picture of how HM Land Registry envisages that a typical conveyancing transaction may operate under the electronic system.[3] This will depend upon whether or not the transaction is a 'linked' transaction – in other words whether or not it is part of a chain. What will eventually be created will, no doubt, differ somewhat from the picture painted here.[4]

27.3 If the transaction is free-standing, the sequence of events as presently visualised is likely to be as follows.

27.4 First, the seller agrees in principle to sell the property to the buyer and both parties instruct conveyancers to act on their behalf. It may be that the pre-contractual information that is then supplied by the seller to the buyer will already have been prepared. This is likely to be the case, given the resurrection of the concept of a 'home information pack'.[5] The pre-contractual

---

[1] Referred to for convenience in this chapter as 'conveyancers'.

[2] Referred to for convenience in this chapter as 'the network'.

[3] The Registry put forward some ideas in *E-Conveyancing: A Land Registry Consultation*, Part 6. Predictably, these ideas received a mixed response from those who responded to the consultation.

[4] Cf *E-Conveyancing: A Land Registry Consultation Report*, which sets out the responses to the Registry's consultation on the creation of an e-conveyancing system under LRA 2002.

[5] See Part 5 of the Housing Bill.

information could be supplied electronically to the intending buyer using the network whether or not there is a requirement for such a pack. However, the provisions on the 'home information pack' contained in Part 5 of the Housing Bill only permit the information to be provided in electronic form if the potential buyer consents to receive it in that form. It is unfortunate that the potential of electronic delivery and its more widespread use were not more fully recognised in that Bill, having regard to the changes made by the LRA 2002 and the development of e-conveyancing. This is especially the case as the information that a seller will be expected to supply will include title information – which could be obtained in a more up-to-date version by the buyer if he inspected the register of title over the internet on Land Register Online.

27.5   Secondly, the draft contract will be prepared in electronic form by the seller's conveyancer. Before the draft is transmitted to the buyer's conveyancer, it will be subject to some form of automatic validation by HM Land Registry.[1] This will be some form of computerised check to ensure that, for example, the seller's name, the address and the title number of the property correspond with the details held by the Registry. In this way, common mistakes can be eliminated at the outset. It also means that the Registry can begin to build up the information about the transaction that will enable the register to be changed on completion. What will happen is that, during the course of the conveyancing process, the Registry will construct a 'notional register' – in other words, a version of the register as it will be when the transaction is completed.

27.6   Thirdly, the draft contract will be transmitted to the buyer's conveyancer for consideration. Any enquiries, such as local searches, that have not already been made by the buyer will be undertaken electronically.[2] The buyer will, in many cases, be seeking a mortgage offer. It is likely that this process itself may in future be conducted on line where the buyer has the necessary internet and e-mail facilities. The extent to which any mortgage offer will be communicated in a form that will automatically generate entries on the notional register has not yet been decided.[3]

27.7   Fourthly, the parties will proceed to the making of the contract. As has been indicated above,[4] there will be no 'exchange of contracts' in e-conveyancing. What is visualised is that there will be one electronic document which will be signed by or on behalf of each of the parties. The contract will then be 'released' by each of them and will take effect on the time and date agreed. Although individuals are likely to have their own

---

[1]   See *E-Conveyancing: A Land Registry Consultation*, para 6.2.3.
[2]   Cf para **26.3**.
[3]   See *E-Conveyancing: A Land Registry Consultation*, para 6.2.5.
[4]   See para **26.6**.

electronic signatures in due course, it is probable that initially it will be their respective conveyancers who sign electronic documents on their behalf. As is explained below, there are obstacles that would preclude conveyancers from signing conveyancing documents as agents for their clients, and the LRA 2002 contains provisions that overcome these difficulties.[1] As the contract is made, a notice will simultaneously and automatically be entered on the register. This will have two consequences:[2] first, it will protect the priority of the estate contract;[3] and secondly, it will create a priority period in the same manner as a priority search.[4] Any entry made during that priority period will be postponed to the application to register the disposition which is the subject of the estate contract.[5]

27.8 Once contracts have been made, the parties will proceed in the usual way to completion. All the draft documentation for completion will be prepared in electronic form, including not only the transfer, but also any charge that is to be executed by the buyer on completion. All of this information will be communicated electronically to the Registry so that the 'notional register' can be built up. Completion will take place at the time and date agreed by the parties.[6] Again, it is likely that, at least initially, the conveyancing documents will be signed electronically by the parties' conveyancers on their behalf.

27.9 On completion, it is intended that the following should simultaneously occur.

– The transfer and any charge take effect.
– The register is changed in accordance with the final version of the 'notional register' to record the changes that have occurred. The new owner is registered as proprietor and, if there is a charge, that too is registered. If any easements are granted or reserved or any restrictive covenants are taken, the appropriate entries will appear on the register.
– The consideration passes under the proposed electronic funds transfer system,[7] and stamp duty land tax and Land Registry fees are paid.

27.10 One of the striking features of the new system is that the transaction is concluded in all respects on completion.[8] At present, the Registry may (and often does) raise requisitions after completion when a transfer has been submitted for registration. That cannot happen under the proposed system:

[1] See paras **27.23–27.24**.
[2] LRA 2002, s 72; see also para **19.4**.
[3] Ibid, s 32; see also para **10.5**.
[4] See para **19.11**.
[5] LRA 2002, s 72(2).
[6] Ibid, s 91(3)(a); see also para **26.10**.
[7] See para **28.5**.
[8] In this one respect it resembles unregistered conveyancing.

everything must be resolved before completion. Some commercial transactions are concluded within a very short time, with contract and completion on the same day. Furthermore, deals are often concluded outside office hours. It has been accepted by HM Land Registry that, to meet this need, it will have to offer a service that is available '24 hours a day, 7 days a week, 52 weeks a year'.[1]

27.11   Where there are linked transactions, typically in a chain of domestic sales, the Registry is proposing that there should be a 'linked transaction matrix'.[2] This would enable conveyancers within the chain to know of the progress of all the other transactions in the chain, and what steps each had still to take.[3] It could also be used to synchronise the making of contracts and the subsequent completion of transactions. On consultation, about two-thirds of respondents supported the concept.[4] There was, however, little support for the suggestion that it was either necessary or desirable to have a 'chain manager'.[5] Conveyancers might be under obligations to provide information to the Registry about transactions in which they had been instructed to enable such linked transactions to be identified.[6] The Registry might, therefore, be involved in a proposed transaction at an even earlier stage than will be the case where the transaction is free-standing.

THE PROVISIONS OF THE LRA 2002

The electronic communications network

27.12   The provisions of the LRA 2002 reflect the model of e-conveyancing that is set out above. Under s 92(1), the registrar may provide, or arrange for the provision of, an electronic communications network. This network is to be used for such purposes as the registrar sees fit relating to registration or the carrying on of transactions which involve registration and are capable of being effected electronically. Those purposes are necessarily wide and, as will be apparent from what has been said in paras **27.3–27.11**, they are intended to cover the entire life of a conveyancing transaction from the stage when a property is put on the market to the completion of its sale. The network might therefore be used:

---

[1]   *E-Conveyancing: A Land Registry Consultation*, para 8.16. The proposal was strongly supported on consultation: *E-Conveyancing: A Land Registry Consultation Report*, pp 106–107.

[2]   See *E-Conveyancing: A Land Registry Consultation*, para 6.3.

[3]   To protect confidentiality, the names of the clients would not be known. Transactions would probably be recorded by reference to the name of the firm of conveyancers acting for a party and that firm's reference.

[4]   *E-Conveyancing: A Land Registry Consultation*, pp 68–72.

[5]   Ibid, pp 77–78.

[6]   See further, para **27.16**(4).

- for the provision of information by a party to a transaction that had to be completed by registration[1] either to another party or to the registrar;
- for the preparation and communication of conveyancing documents; and
- for the purpose of registering any disposition.

As a necessary adjunct to the creation of the electronic communications network and the system of e-conveyancing that it will support, there are specific rule-making powers to make provision about the communication of documents in electronic form to the registrar and for their electronic storage.[2]

Network access agreements

27.13 A person who is not a member of the Land Registry will only be able to access the network if he enters into a network access agreement made with the registrar.[3] That agreement may authorise access for one or more of the following purposes:

(a)   the communication, posting or retrieval of information;
(b)   the making of changes to the register of title[4] or to the cautions register;[5]
(c)   the issue of official search certificates;
(d)   the issue of official copies;[6] or
(e)   such other conveyancing purposes as the registrar thinks fit.[7]

There is no reason why the level of access should be the same for all professionals. For example, whereas a conveyancer might be authorised to have access for all five of the purposes listed above, an estate agent might only require access for the first of them. The second, third and fourth of the purposes listed above are functions that are presently performed by the registrar, and the fifth might include such functions. Subject to provision in rules,[8] the authority conferred by a network access agreement may include the

---

[1]   This might include a disposition of unregistered land that was subject to the requirement of compulsory registration. It remains to be seen how far e-conveyancing will come to be used in relation to first registrations. First registration is not a straightforward matter in many cases and it is likely that it will have to remain the responsibility of the Registry except perhaps in relation to the grant of certain short leases that have to be registered.
[2]   LRA 2002, s 95.
[3]   Ibid, Sch 5, para 1(1).
[4]   See para **22.3**.
[5]   See para **22.22**.
[6]   See para **18.6**.
[7]   LRA 2002, Sch 5, para 1(2).
[8]   The Lord Chancellor is required to consult before he makes such rules: LRA 2002, Sch 5, para 11(1), (2). Such rules are made by statutory instrument and are subject to affirmative resolution, the most stringent form of scrutiny that there is for statutory instruments: see LRA 2002, s 128(5).

performance of the registrar's functions.[1] Indeed, it is difficult to see how e-conveyancing as it is presently visualised could be carried out by conveyancers unless they could carry out functions that are vested in the registrar. For example, parties to a conveyancing transaction will wish to make an official search of the register and obtain official copies of documents referred to in it.

27.14   The criteria which have to be met by an applicant for a network access agreement will be laid down in rules.[2] If the applicant meets those criteria, the registrar *must* enter into a network access agreement with him.[3] In making rules as to the relevant criteria, the Lord Chancellor is required to have regard to, in particular, the need to secure:

(a)   the confidentiality of private information kept on the network;
(b)   competence in relation to the use of the network (in particular for the making of changes); and
(c)   the adequate insurance of potential liabilities in connection with the use of the network.[4]

It is not difficult to see what underlies these requirements. The Land Registry guarantees the register and the registrar must pay indemnity where loss is suffered as a result of a mistake in the register.[5] Under the system of e-conveyancing that will be established under the LRA 2002, it will be conveyancers who initiate changes to the register for the future. It is therefore important that the proper steps are taken to minimise the risk that mistakes may be made. To the same end, the Act specifically empowers the registrar to provide, or to arrange for the provision of, education and training in relation to the use of the network.[6] This will, presumably, take the form of online training packages.

Terms of access

The general principle

27.15   The LRA 2002 makes provision as to the terms upon which access to the network will be permitted. The general principle is that the terms on which access to the network is authorised will be such as the registrar thinks fit, and, in particular, may include charges for access.[7] That general principle is

---

[1]   LRA 2002, Sch 5, para 1(3).
[2]   Once again, the Lord Chancellor can only make such rules after consultation (LRA 2002, Sch 5, para 11(1), (2)) and they are then subject to affirmative resolution procedure (LRA 2002, s 128(5)).
[3]   LRA 2002, Sch 5, para 1(4).
[4]   Ibid, Sch 5, para 11(3).
[5]   See para **23.2**.
[6]   LRA 2002, Sch 5, para 10.
[7]   Ibid, Sch 5, para 2(1).

subject to a number of qualifications, which are set out in the following paragraphs.

The purposes for which the power to authorise may be exercised

27.16   The LRA 2002 specifies the purposes for which access may be authorised.

(1)   The first is for regulating the use of the network.[1] This is the principal purpose for which access will be given.

(2)   The second is for securing that the person who is granted access uses the network to carry out such 'qualifying transactions' as may be specified in, or under, the agreement.[2] A 'qualifying transaction' is a transaction that involves registration and is capable of being effected electronically.[3] In consequence of this provision, the terms of access may *require* the person authorised to conduct all of a particular type or types of transaction electronically. It would not be open to him to carry them out in paper form. The object is to ensure a speedy transition from a paper-based system of conveyancing to one that is wholly electronic. The period during which the paper-based and electronic systems exist side by side has to be kept as short as possible because of the difficulties to which it will give rise, particularly in chain transactions. It is to be noted that, in consequence of this provision, conveyancers who have network access agreements will have to conduct the specified transactions electronically before the power to make electronic conveyancing compulsory[4] is exercised.

(3)   The third is for such other purposes relating to the carrying on of qualifying transactions as rules may provide.[5] As a result of this provision, it will be possible to provide that a person authorised must use the network for purposes such as providing official search certificates and obtaining official copies.

(4)   The fourth is for enabling network transactions to be monitored.[6] The intention of this provision is that those who are authorised to use the network may have to provide the registrar (or whoever has responsibility for the matter) with information about linked transactions. This will enable chains to be managed in the way explained in para **27.11**.[7]

---

[1]   LRA 2002, Sch 5, para 2(2).
[2]   Ibid, Sch 5, para 2(2)(a).
[3]   Ibid, Sch 5, para 12.
[4]   Contained in LRA 2002, s 93; see also para **28.2**.
[5]   LRA 2002, Sch 5, para 2(2)(b).
[6]   Ibid, Sch 5, para 2(2)(c).
[7]   See further, para **27.25**.

The obligation to comply with network transaction rules

27.17   It is to be a condition of a network access agreement that the person granted access complies with the network transaction rules that are in force for the time being.[1] The network transaction rules will make provision about 'how to go about network transactions'.[2] These rules will tell conveyancers how to conduct e-conveyancing and, in particular, they may include provision about the procedure to be followed and the supply of information, including information about unregistered interests.[3] It has been explained elsewhere that, under s 71 of the LRA 2002, there is a duty imposed on a person applying for first registration or to register a registrable disposition to disclose any unregistered interest which overrides either first registration or a registrable disposition.[4] It is likely that network transaction rules will require authorised conveyancers to disclose such interests so that they can be protected on the register.[5] This will be so, even if the conveyancer's client does not want the interest disclosed.[6] It is also probable that network transaction rules will provide for the simultaneous registration of dispositions of registered land even before that is made compulsory under s 93.[7] For the purposes of the LRA 2002, network transaction rules are land registration rules.[8] As such they will be made by the Lord Chancellor with the advice and assistance of the Rules Committee.[9]

Terms of access regulated by rules

27.18   The LRA 2002 provides that rules may regulate the terms on which access to the network is authorised.[10] It is thought that such rules may prescribe terms that will be contained in all network access agreements, although these terms are likely to vary according to the level of access that is granted.[11]

Termination of access

27.19   The LRA 2002 makes provision for the termination of a network access agreement both by the person authorised and by the registrar. As regards the former, the person authorised may terminate the agreement at any

---

[1]   LRA 2002, Sch 5, para 2(3).
[2]   Ibid, Sch 5, para 5(1).
[3]   Ibid, Sch 5, para 5(2).
[4]   See paras **4.19**, **11.18**.
[5]   The policy underlying this is the fundamental principle on which the LRA 2002 rests of achieving a conclusive register: see para **1.7**.
[6]   Cf LRA 2002, Sch 5, para 6; see also para **27.22**.
[7]   For ibid, s 93, see para **28.2**.
[8]   See ibid, s 132(1).
[9]   Ibid, s 127. See paras **1.14–1.16**.
[10]   Ibid, Sch 5, para 2(4). The Lord Chancellor can only make such rules after consultation (Sch 5, para 11(1), (2)) and they are then subject to affirmative resolution procedure (s 128(5)).
[11]   See (2001) Law Com No 271, para 13.54; see also para **27.13**.

time by notice to the registrar.[1] By contrast, the circumstances in which the registrar may terminate such an agreement are much more limited. The matter will be governed by rules, which may make provision about:

—   the grounds of termination;
—   the procedure to be followed in relation to termination; and
—   the suspension of termination pending any appeal.[2]

Those rules may, in particular, authorise the registrar to terminate a network access agreement, if the person granted access:

—   fails to comply with the terms of the agreement;
—   ceases to be a person with whom the registrar would be required to enter into a network access agreement conferring the authority which the agreement confers; or
—   does not meet such conditions as those rules may provide.[3]

27.20   Termination of access by the registrar will be a very serious matter and a remedy of last resort. As all conveyancing will be e-conveyancing within a comparatively short time, termination of access will prevent a person from acting as a conveyancer. A network access agreement will normally be a contract,[4] and the registrar will, therefore, have contractual remedies that he can pursue rather than terminating access.

27.21   In any event, the LRA 2002 makes provision for appeals by a person aggrieved by a decision of the registrar:

—   not to enter into a network access agreement;[5] or
—   to terminate an existing network access agreement.[6]

The appeal will be to the Adjudicator.[7] It is the one occasion under the Act in which he may hear an appeal from a decision of the registrar.[8] An appeal to the Adjudicator is likely to be quicker, cheaper and more informal than any appeal to a court. In any event, as has been explained in para **27.19**, rules are

[1]   LRA 2002, Sch 5, para 3(1).
[2]   Ibid, Sch 5, para 3(2). The Lord Chancellor can only make such rules after consultation (Sch 5, para 11(1), (2)) and they are then subject to affirmative resolution procedure (s 128(5)).
[3]   LRA 2002, Sch 5, para 3(3).
[4]   It will not be a contract in cases where the body given authority is another emanation of the Crown. The Crown is one and indivisible and cannot contract with itself.
[5]   In other words, where the registrar takes the view that the applicant does not satisfy the criteria for entry into such an agreement: see para **27.14**.
[6]   LRA 2002, Sch 5, para 4(1).
[7]   Ibid. For the office of Adjudicator, see para **34.10**. Rules may make provision about such appeals: LRA 2002, Sch 5, para 4(3).
[8]   Ibid, s 108(1)(b). See also para **34.12**.

likely to make provision for the termination of an agreement to be suspended pending an appeal. The Adjudicator will be able to substitute his own decision for that of the registrar and give the necessary directions accordingly.[1] A further appeal lies from the Adjudicator to the High Court, but only on a point of law.[2]

Overriding nature of network access obligations

27.22   It will be apparent from what has been said above that there could be a conflict between a conveyancer's obligations to the registrar under a network access agreement and his obligations to his client. For example, a client might not want the conveyancer to disclose the fact that the land which he was purchasing was subject to an unregistered interest that overrode a registered disposition.[3] Indeed, the situation might be more extreme: the client might not wish the transaction to be conducted in electronic form at all.[4] The LRA 2002 provides that the obligation under the network access agreement prevails and discharges the other obligation to the extent that the two conflict.[5] Such cases are unlikely to be common in practice. It is plainly very important that a conveyancer should so far as possible respect his client's wishes and, in particular, observe his obligations of confidentiality to his client.[6] However, when the overriding objectives of the Act, namely to secure an effective system of e-conveyancing and to ensure that the register is as conclusive as it can be made, conflict with a client's wishes, the latter must yield to the former. Furthermore, in those circumstances, the conveyancer must be protected against any claim that could otherwise be brought against him by his client.

Presumption of authority

27.23   When e-conveyancing is first introduced, it seems likely that conveyancers will execute electronic documents on behalf of their clients. This is because it is not thought that many individuals will have their own electronic signatures at that stage.[7] However, a conveyancer has no implied authority to sign a contract on behalf of his client.[8] If, therefore, a conveyancer is to sign on behalf of his client, he must have actual authority to do so. This means that he must obtain his client's written authority. However, if no provision were

---

1   LRA 2002, Sch 5, para 4(2).
2   Ibid, s 111(2).
3   See para **27.17**.
4   In such a case, a conveyancer who had entered into a network access agreement would in practice have to decline to act.
5   LRA 2002, Sch 5, para 6.
6   It is clear that the Land Registry is well aware of this point: see *E-Conveyancing: A Land Registry Consultation*, para 6.3.
7   See paras **27.7–27.8**.
8   'A solicitor has no ostensible or apparent authority to sign a contract on behalf of a client so as to bind him when there is no contract in fact': *H Clark (Doncaster) Ltd v Wilkinson* [1965] Ch 694 at 702, per Lord Denning MR.

made in the LRA 2002, the other party's conveyancer would be entitled to see that authority before he was prepared to enter into the contract. It would rather defeat the purposes of e-conveyancing if the parties had to exchange copies of the written authority given to them by their respective clients.

27.24   The way in which this problem is to be addressed is as follows. First, it is intended to provide under network transaction rules that a conveyancer should obtain the written authority of his client to sign any electronic documents on that client's behalf.[1] The need for such authority might, for example, be explained in a conveyancer's standard client care letter. Secondly, the LRA 2002 creates a presumption of authority in certain cases where a conveyancer authenticates an electronic document on behalf of his client. It applies where a person who is authorised under a network access agreement to use the network to make either a disposition or contract, claims to do so as agent. In favour of any other party, that person will be deemed to be acting with the authority of his or her principal if the document which purports to effect the disposition or to be a contract:

—   purports to be authenticated by him or her as agent; and
—   contains a statement to the effect that he is acting under the authority of his or her principal.[2]

Concerns have been expressed that this power could enable a dishonest conveyancer to defraud his client of his property. However, a conveyancer would be acting very foolishly if he authenticated an electronic document which explicitly stated that he had his client's authority when in fact he had not obtained it. One feature of the proposed e-conveyancing system is that the Registry will be able to identify the source of any entry on the register.[3] The source of any fraud would therefore be readily apparent.

Management of network transactions

27.25   It has been explained above that it is envisaged that the electronic system should provide some means for managing linked transactions.[4] The objective is to try to facilitate chains of domestic sales, in an attempt to ensure that fewer such chains 'break'. One aspect of the strategy has already been mentioned. Under the terms of a network access agreement, a conveyancer may be obliged to provide monitoring information.[5] The LRA 2002 goes further than that. It empowers the registrar – or the person to whom he has

---

[1]   See (2001) Law Com No 271, para 13.62.
[2]   LRA 2002, Sch 5, para 8.
[3]   On this 'audit trail', see *E-Conveyancing: A Land Registry Consultation*, para 4.1.5.
[4]   See para **27.11**.
[5]   See para **27.16**(4).

delegated his 'chain management' functions[1] – to use such monitoring information[2] for the purposes of managing network transactions.[3] He is specifically authorised to disclose such information to persons authorised to use the network, and may authorise further disclosure, if he considers it necessary or desirable to do so.[4] This will mean that the registrar (or whoever is authorised to manage such transactions) can disclose to other parties in the chain the state of progress of the other transactions in the chain.[5]

Do-it-yourself conveyancing

27.26   Once there is a network, the LRA 2002 imposes a duty on the registrar to provide such assistance as he thinks appropriate for the purpose of enabling persons engaged in qualifying transactions who wish to do their own conveyancing to do so by means of the network.[6] The registrar is not allowed to provide legal advice.[7] It was suggested that such 'DIY conveyancers' would be allowed to use dedicated terminals at Land Registries to conduct e-conveyancing, where their identities could be checked and they could be given advice on the use of the electronic system.[8] However, on consultation, there was widespread feeling that access had to be much greater: it was unreasonable to expect people to go to a Land Registry.[9]

---

[1]   See LRA 2002, Sch 5, para 9(2).

[2]   See ibid, Sch 5, para 9(3).

[3]   Ibid, Sch 5, para 9(1).

[4]   Ibid.

[5]   As has been explained at para **27.11**, the names of the parties in the chain would not be disclosed. It would only be the names of the conveyancers acting and the file reference that would be made known.

[6]   LRA 2002, Sch 5, para 7(1).

[7]   Ibid, Sch 5, para 7(2).

[8]   See *E-Conveyancing: A Land Registry Consultation*, para 8.17.

[9]   *E-Conveyancing: A Land Registry Consultation Report*, pp 107–108.

CHAPTER 28

MAKING E-CONVEYANCING COMPULSORY

28.1 The third of the four issues raised in para **26.4** concerns how e-conveyancing may be made compulsory. It is inevitable that it will have to be made compulsory because many of the benefits of e-conveyancing will be lost if paper and electronic dispositions can subsist side by side for any length of time. For example, where there is a chain of sale, the chain moves at the speed of the slowest link. The potential to speed up such linked transactions by means of e-conveyancing would be defeated if paper-based links could continue.

28.2 Section 93 of the LRA 2002 contains provisions for making e-conveyancing compulsory. First, the section applies to dispositions of:

—   a registered estate or charge; or
—   an interest which is the subject of a notice in the register,

where that disposition is of a description specified in rules.[1] Because the transactions can be specified by rules, it will be possible to introduce compulsory e-conveyancing on a disposition-by-disposition basis. Indeed, that seems likely. The potential range of dispositions is substantial: it includes, quite expressly, an agreement between chargees that the respective priorities of their charges be changed.[2] It also includes dispositions of interests that are protected by the entry of a notice, such as equitable charges, or the benefit of an option or other estate contract. It has been explained above that it is not at present possible to register transfers of such interests, but it is intended that it should become so when they can be made electronically.[3]

28.3 Secondly, the section defines the nature of compulsory e-conveyancing. It embodies the essential principle in the LRA 2002 that the making of the disposition and its registration should be simultaneous. This is an important part of the strategy of making the register conclusive at any given time by

---

[1]   LRA 2002, s 93(1).
[2]   Ibid, s 93(6). See also para **12.48**.
[3]   See para **26.8**.

eliminating the 'registration gap'.[1] A disposition that is required to be made electronically, or a contract to make such a disposition will only have effect if it is made by means of a document in electronic form, is electronically communicated to the registrar, and the relevant registration requirements are met.[2] The relevant registration requirements are, in the case of registrable dispositions, those that are prescribed in Sch 2 to the LRA 2002.[3] In the case of any other disposition, or a contract to make a disposition, the registration requirements will be prescribed by rules.[4] Under s 27(1) of the Act, a disposition of a registered estate does not operate at law until the registration requirements of Sch 2 are met.[5] As an electronic disposition under s 93 will have no effect at all except on registration, s 27(1) is disapplied in relation to such dispositions.[6]

OTHER STEPS TO FACILITATE E-CONVEYANCING

28.4   The final issue raised in para **26.4** concerns the other steps that are needed to ensure that e-conveyancing operates as smoothly as possible.

Electronic settlement

28.5   The most important change that is needed concerns the system of settlement when a conveyancing transaction is completed. If dispositions are to be registered simultaneously, the necessary payments must also be made at the same time. The LRA 2002 provides that the registrar may take such steps as he thinks fit for the purpose of securing the provision of a system of electronic settlement in relation to transactions involving registration.[7] As is explained below,[8] the registrar also has power under the Act, if he considers it expedient, to form, or participate in the formation of, a company, or purchase, or invest in, a company in connection with this system of electronic settlement.[9] These provisions, which were added at a late stage in the passage of the LRA 2002 through Parliament,[10] ensure that the registrar has all the necessary powers that he might need to provide an effective system of electronic settlement. In particular, it means that there can be no doubt as to his ability to enter into a collaborative venture with a private sector partner to develop such a system. The present system of settlement is not adequate for

---

[1]   See paras **1.8**, **26.1–26.2**.

[2]   LRA 2002, s 93(2).

[3]   Ibid, s 93(3)(a). For Sch 2, see Chapter 8.

[4]   Ibid, s 93(3)(b).

[5]   See paras **8.2** et seq.

[6]   LRA 2002, s 93(4).

[7]   Ibid, s 94.

[8]   See para **36.8**.

[9]   LRA 2002, s 106.

[10]   Namely, at Report and Third Reading in the House of Commons.

an effective e-conveyancing system.[1] The Land Registry has set out what it will require of any system of electronic settlement.[2] In particular, it wants to see an integrated e-conveyancing and payments system, so that all monies can be dealt with simultaneously on completion of any transaction, including the payment of stamp duty land tax and Land Registry fees. The Registry has suggested various options as to how this might be achieved, including an electronic transfer system, a real-time settlement system (akin to CREST, which is used in relation to dealings in shares at the London Stock Exchange), or an escrow bank.

---

[1]   See the criticisms in *E-Conveyancing: A Land Registry Consultation*, paras 7.2, 7.3. This criticism was strongly endorsed on consultation: see *E-Conveyancing: A Land Registry Consultation Report*, pp 111–112.

[2]   See *E-Conveyancing: A Land Registry Consultation*, Part 7.

PART 6

ADVERSE POSSESSION

THE MAIN CHANGES AT A GLANCE

One of the most striking features of the LRA 2002 is that it disapplies the present law of adverse possession in relation to registered land. In its place it substitutes a new scheme that reflects the principles underlying registered conveyancing. Although these changes are fundamental, the relevant provisions of the Act consist of just the three sections that make up Part 9 of the Act together with Sch 6.[1] The new procedure for making and dealing with applications is set out in LRR 2003, rr 187–194.

The new system is intended to reflect the fact that, in relation to registered land, the basis of title is primarily registration rather than possession. The system is also intended to strike a fairer balance between landowner and squatter,[2] by shifting that balance in favour of the registered owner. There is little doubt that the principles of adverse possession have been abused. During the passage of the Bill, Baroness Scotland of Asthall, the Parliamentary Secretary in the Lord Chancellor's Department, made it clear that the Government's intention was to strengthen the position of registered proprietors and made no apology for doing so. She explained that, every year, the Land Registry received over 20,000 applications for registration based in whole or in part on adverse possession. In about 15,000 of those cases, the applicant was successful. Many cases were disputed and had to be resolved either by the courts or in hearings before the Solicitor to HM Land Registry. About three-quarters of the hearings before the Solicitor involved squatters, and in approximately 60 per cent of the cases, the squatter succeeded in whole or in part.[3] In practice, the new provisions are likely to provide a strong incentive to all owners of unregistered land to register their titles, and indeed, it is clear that the Government intended this to be the case.[4]

The main changes made by the LRA 2002 are as follows.

---

1   See (2001) Law Com No 271, paras 2.69–2.74 and Part XIV.
2   Ibid, para 14.4. The proposals for change were supported in principle by 60 per cent of those who responded to (1998) Law Com No 254 on the issue.
3   *Hansard* (HL), 30 October 2001, vol 627, col 1332.
4   See the comments of Baroness Scotland of Asthall: *Hansard* (HL), 30 October 2001, vol 627, col 1379.

- The Act replaces the previous 12-year limitation period with a scheme under which there is no limitation period as such. A squatter's adverse possession, however long, will not of itself bar the registered proprietor's title to a registered estate.
- A squatter will be able to apply to be registered as proprietor after 10 years' adverse possession. Whether or not he has been in adverse possession for 10 years can be challenged.
- If the application is not opposed by any of those whom the registrar is required to notify, the squatter will be registered as proprietor of the land.
- If any of those notified do oppose the application it will be refused, unless the squatter can bring himself within one of three limited exceptions.
- If the application for registration is refused, but the squatter remains in adverse possession for a further 2 years, he will be entitled to make a new application for registration, and, on this occasion, will be registered as proprietor regardless of any objection.
- The effect of the registration of a squatter.
- Where the registered proprietor commences proceedings to recover possession from a squatter, those proceedings will succeed unless the squatter can make out one of a number of limited defences.

The Act contains transitional provisions to protect the rights of squatters who have barred the rights of the registered proprietor prior to the commencement of the Act.

CHAPTER 29

AIMS AND SCHEME OF THE ACT

THE AIMS OF THE SCHEME

29.1 The new scheme recognises that, while the present law of adverse possession is both appropriate and necessary for unregistered land, it is much harder to justify in relation to registered land. The basis of title to registered land is the fact of registration not possession. However, although it is a fundamental theme of the LRA 2002 that registration should, of itself, protect the registered proprietor, this is subject to certain qualifications. Adverse possession has some limited justification even in relation to registered land.[1] In particular, it is necessary to ensure that land remains marketable where, for example, the registered proprietor has disappeared, or where he has been given the opportunity to vindicate his rights but has failed to do so. Furthermore, the register may be conclusive as to the ownership of a registered estate, but is not normally conclusive as to boundaries, because of the general boundaries rule and the fact that the power to fix boundaries is seldom exercised.[2] The protection given by the Act is not absolute, but recognises, the point made above, that adverse possession does have a limited role to play even in relation to registered land.

29.2 The new scheme could not apply to unregistered land, not only because there would not be any administrative framework within which it could operate, but also because the principles of adverse possession are essential to a system of unregistered conveyancing. Proof of title to unregistered land involves proof of a suitable root of title that is at least 15 years old and an unbroken chain of title linking that root to the landowner who is conveying the land.[3] The period prescribed by law for the root of title has always been directly linked to the limitation period applicable to possession actions.[4] It follows that, without principles of limitation and adverse possession, it would never be possible to deduce title to unregistered land. It would not be possible to be sure that any adverse claims to the land had been barred. The fact that

---

[1] See (1998) Law Com No 254, paras 10.11–10.16; (2001) Law Com No 271, para 2.72.

[2] See LRA 2002, s 60; see also Chapter 16.

[3] LPA 1925, s 44(1); LPA 1969, s 23.

[4] Presently 12 years in most cases: see LA 1980, s 15(1). For the link between the limitation period and the length of title required, see Martin Dockray, 'Why do we need adverse possession?' [1985] Conv 272.

the new scheme could not apply to unregistered land is not regarded as a reason for leaving the existing law in place for registered land, even though it could lead to anomalies.[1] One of the guiding principles of the LRA 2002 is that the rational development of registered land cannot be constrained because the principles applicable to unregistered land are different.[2] This is particularly so given the aim to eliminate unregistered land as soon as possible.[3]

29.3   The LRA 2002 makes provision to cover three situations.

(1)   Where a squatter applies to be registered as proprietor.
(2)   Where a squatter could have applied to be registered as proprietor but, before he did so, he was evicted by the registered proprietor (or person claiming under him).
(3)   Where the registered proprietor (or person claiming under him) takes proceedings to recover possession from a squatter.

The principles laid down in the Act are intended to ensure that the outcome will be the same whichever of these three situations occurs.

THE EFFECT OF THE LRA 2002

The general principle: no limitation period for the recovery of a registered estate or rentcharge

29.4   The governing principle of the new scheme is that where an estate or rentcharge is registered with its own title:

–   in relation to an action to recover land, no period of limitation under the LA 1980[4] runs against *any person other than a chargee*;[5]
–   in relation to a claim to redeem a charge against a chargee in possession, no period of limitation under the LA 1980[6] runs against *any person*.[7]

As a result, as there is no applicable period of limitation, a registered

---

[1]   As, for example, where a squatter is in adverse possession of land that includes both registered and unregistered titles.
[2]   See para **1.6**.
[3]   See (2001) Law Com No 271, paras 1.6, 2.9. Many other Commonwealth countries which have title registration systems have either abolished adverse possession in relation to registered titles, or have restricted it.
[4]   See LA 1980, s 15.
[5]   LRA 2002, s 96(1). For the reason for the exception in relation to chargees, see para **29.6**.
[6]   See LA 1980, s 16.
[7]   LRA 2002, s 96(2). See further, para **29.7**.

proprietor's title can never be extinguished under the LA 1980, s 17.[1] Ironically, this may be good news for squatters. As Lord Goodhart explained during the Second Reading Debate on the Bill in the House of Lords: 'this change will help rather than hinder squatters because unless and until squatters in a particular building serve an application for title to that building under Sch 6, the owner will not be under any pressure to remove them'.[2]

The application of the principle to registered estates and rentcharges

29.5   The limitation periods for the recovery of land are disapplied *only* in relation to registered estates in land and registered rentcharges, because the register is conclusive as to ownership of such estates and rentcharges. The limitation periods laid down in the LA 1980 will continue to apply in the following circumstances where there has been adverse possession of registered land:

— where there has been adverse possession against a leasehold estate where the lease was granted for 21 years or less prior to the coming into force of the LRA 2002, and which, consequently, took effect as an overriding interest;[3] and

— where the claim for possession is not brought by a registered proprietor but by a licensee or tenant at will or a previous squatter who is not the registered proprietor.[4]

The limitation period will also continue to apply to a right of re-entry as where:

— a lease has become liable to forfeiture for breach of a covenant or condition in the lease; or

— that right of re-entry has become exercisable in respect of a fee simple for breach of condition or on the occurrence of a specified event.

These rights are not estates in land, and the LA 1980 therefore continues to apply in relation to them.

Mortgagors in possession

29.6   The LRA 2002 does not change the law in relation to mortgagors in possession. Under the Act, where a mortgagor is in possession, the

---

[1]   LRA 2002, s 96(3).

[2]   *Hansard* (HL), 3 July 2001, vol 626, col 792.

[3]   LRA 1925, s 70(1)(k). Such a lease is not a registered estate and is generally treated in the same way as unregistered land. This type of case will disappear within 21 years of the LRA 2002 coming into force as the only leases that will take effect as overriding interests are leases for 7 years or less.

[4]   This might happen where a squatter ousted a licensee or tenant at will and the ousted occupier sought to recover possession from that squatter.

mortgagee's rights to recover possession or to foreclose remain subject to the provisions of LA 1980.[1] As a chargee's right to possession is tied directly to its rights to recover monies under the charge, the two rights should be linked. If the right to recover the money is time-barred,[2] the chargee's remedies to enforce its security should be as well.[3]

Mortgagees in possession

29.7   Under s 16 of the LA 1980, once a mortgagee has been in possession of land for 12 years, the mortgagor loses his right to redeem the mortgage and his title is extinguished, with the result that the mortgagee becomes the owner of the land. The Law Commission criticised this rule as anomalous. It over-protected mortgagees and could no longer be justified.[4] The LRA 2002 therefore disapplies s 16 of the LA 1980 in relation to an estate in land or a rentcharge registered under the LRA 2002.[5]

---

[1] LRA 2002, s 96(1). The limitation period is 12 years: LA 1980, ss 15(1), 20(4).
[2] It is subject to a 12-year limitation period: see LA 1980, s 20(1).
[3] See (2001) Law Com No 271, paras 14.12–14.14.
[4] See ibid, paras 14.15–14.18.
[5] LRA 2002, s 96(2).

CHAPTER 30

APPLICATION FOR REGISTRATION BY A PERSON IN ADVERSE POSSESSION

THE GENERAL POSITION

30.1   As a general rule,[1] a person may apply to be registered as the proprietor of a registered estate in land if he has been in adverse possession of the estate for the period of 10 years ending on the date of the application.[2] As was the case under the LRA 1925, the applicant will have to prove to the registrar that he has been in adverse possession for the relevant period.[3] It will not be presumed.[4]

30.2   It is not necessary for the estate to have been registered throughout the period of adverse possession.[5] If, for example, the squatter commenced adverse possession when the title was unregistered, and the title was voluntarily registered by the owner 6 years later, the squatter would be able to apply to be registered after 4 more years of adverse possession.

The meaning of 'adverse possession'

30.3   A person is in adverse possession of an estate in land for the purposes of the LRA 2002 if, but for s 96 of the Act, a period of limitation under s 15 of the LA 1980 would run in his favour in relation to the estate.[6] A person is also to be regarded as having been in adverse possession of an estate in land:

---

[1]   See also Chapter 33, Special Cases.

[2]   LRA 2002, Sch 6, para 1(1). For the reasons why a period of 10 rather than 12 years was chosen, see (2001) Law Com No 271, para 14.19.

[3]   For the previous law, see LRA 1925, s 75. For a detailed discussion of both the present and the previous law, see Jourdan, *Adverse Possession* (Butterworths, 2003).

[4]   If an applicant was registered under the scheme provided by the LRA 2002 and it then transpired that he had not in fact been in adverse possession for 10 years, his registration would be a mistake, and there would, therefore, be grounds for an application for rectification of the register: see LRA 2002, Sch 4, paras 2(1)(a), 5(a). See paras **22.6**, **22.16**.

[5]   LRA 2002, Sch 6, para 1(4).

[6]   Ibid, Sch 6, para 11(1). The law requires both factual possession and an intention to possess. In the recent decision of *JA Pye (Oxford) Ltd v Graham* [2003] 1 AC 419, the House of Lords affirmed the classic statement as to the requirements of intention set out in Slade J in his judgment in *Powell v McFarlane* (1977) 38 P&CR 452.

– where he is the successor in title to an estate in the land, during any period of adverse possession by a predecessor in title to that estate; or

– during any period of adverse possession by another person which comes between, and is continuous with, periods of adverse possession of his own.[1]

30.4 It is not, therefore, necessary for the applicant for registration to show that he has himself been in adverse possession for the whole of the 10-year period required under the LRA 2002. It will be sufficient for him to show that he is the successor in title to an earlier squatter from whom he acquired the land, and that, together, the two periods of adverse possession total 10 years. It will also be sufficient if the applicant demonstrates that he has been in adverse possession, has himself been dispossessed by a second squatter, and has then recovered the land from that second squatter, and that, taken together, the periods of adverse possession total 10 years.

30.5 If, however, the applicant for registration is a second squatter who has evicted a previous squatter, the second squatter will not be a successor in title of the first squatter. He will not, therefore, be able to add the first squatter's period of adverse possession to his own in order to demonstrate 10 years' adverse possession. In such circumstances, the second squatter will not be able to apply to be registered until he can show 10 years' adverse possession himself.[2]

30.6 The LRA 2002 does not define what is meant by a 'successor in title' or 'predecessor in title'.[3] However, a person cannot be either a successor or a predecessor in title of X unless that person:

(a)   holds or held the same estate as X; and

(b)   that estate passed to or from X lawfully, either by transfer or by operation of law.

A person will not be a successor or a predecessor in title of X if he holds or held some lesser or derivative estate or interest, such as where that person was a tenant or chargee and X was a freeholder. On the face of it, therefore, it will not be possible, for example, for a landlord to add a tenant's period of adverse possession to his own in order to demonstrate 10 years' adverse possession, because the tenant is not a successor in title to the landlord, or the landlord to the tenant.[4] However, the point may be somewhat academic, because a

---

[1]   LRA 2002, Sch 6, para 11(2).
[2]   See (2001) Law Com No 271, para 14.21.
[3]   See LRA 2002, Sch 6, para 11(2). The position under LPA 1925, s 78, is different as the section refers to 'persons deriving title under' persons previously in possession, which expression includes lessees: *Smith and Snipes Hall Farm Ltd v River Douglas Catchment Board* [1949] 2 KB 500.
[4]   See Jourdan, *Adverse Possession*, paras 22.24–22.25.

tenant's adverse possession is presumed to be on behalf of the landlord and therefore is that of the landlord.[1] In that way, any period of adverse possession would be attributed to the landlord.

30.7 The 10-year period of adverse possession must be continuous. If Squatter A abandoned land after several years' adverse possession of it, and, at some later date, Squatter B took adverse possession of it, Squatter B could not consolidate the two periods of adverse possession. The 10-year period would start again from the date when Squatter B took adverse possession.

30.8 The LRA 2002 qualifies the basic principle that adverse possession has the same meaning as it does for the purposes of s 15 of the LA 1980[2] in two respects. First, in determining whether a period of limitation would run under s 15 of the LA 1980, the commencement of any legal proceedings is to be disregarded.[3] Prior to the implementation of the LRA 2002, the commencement of proceedings stopped time running under the LA 1980 for the purposes of that particular action.[4] As the right of recovery is never barred by mere lapse of time under the new statutory scheme, this principle is necessarily inapplicable. Secondly, the Act disapplies a technical rule found in para 6 of Sch 1 to the LA 1980 about the adverse possession of a reversion.[5]

30.9 One consequence of the fact that the right of recovery is never barred by mere lapse of time under the LRA 2002 is that a written acknowledgement of title during the 10-year period will not cause time to run afresh as it would in the case of unregistered land.[6] In practice, however, whether a written acknowledgement of title will have any actual effect on the squatter's right to apply to be registered will depend on whether the terms of the acknowledgement demonstrate that the squatter did not have the necessary animus possidendi, and was not, therefore, in adverse possession.[7] Similarly, while the squatter's right to apply to be registered under the LRA 2002 will

---

[1] See *King v Smith* [1950] 1 All ER 553. But see the doubts expressed by Laddie J in *Batt v Adams* [2001] 2 EGLR 92, 96, when applying the presumption.

[2] See para **30.3**.

[3] LRA 2002, Sch 6, para 11(3)(a).

[4] *Markfield Investments Ltd v Evans* [2001] 1 WLR 1321.

[5] LRA 2002, Sch 6, para 11(3)(b). LA 1980 Sch 1, para 6, provides for the running of time where rent under a written lease reserving a rent of at least £10 a year is received by some person wrongfully claiming to be entitled to the land in reversion immediately expectant on the determination of the lease and no rent is subsequently received by the person rightfully so entitled. The abolition of this rule in relation to registered land is criticised in Jourdan, *Adverse Possession*, para 22.18, on the grounds that where the wrong person has been treated as landlord for a long period, the treatment of such a person as being in adverse possession of the reversion of the lease regularises the position.

[6] See Jourdan, *Adverse Possession*, para 22.20. For the effect of acknowledgment under LA 1980, see s 29 of that Act.

[7] An acknowledgement of title will not always show a lack of the necessary animus, as where a squatter admits that he is not the owner, but makes it clear that he has no intention of giving up possession.

not be affected by any deliberate concealment on his part during the 10-year period,[1] this is unlikely to have any significant practical impact.[2]

An extended right to apply for registration

30.10   Once a squatter has been in adverse possession for 10 years, the right to apply to be registered will not necessarily be lost if he is evicted. The LRA 2002 provides that a person may apply to be registered as the proprietor of a registered estate in land if he has been evicted by the registered proprietor or a person claiming under that proprietor other than pursuant to a judgment for possession. To be able to make such application he must:

–   make his application to be registered within 6 months of his eviction; and

–   have been entitled to apply to be registered under the principles explained at para **30.1** on the day before he was evicted.[3]

The rationale for this provision is that it would be wrong, in principle, for the registered proprietor to be able to defeat a squatter's right to apply to be registered by resorting to self-help.[4] Although an objection to an application for registration by the registered proprietor will normally be successful, the Act does specify certain limited circumstances in which a squatter has a right to be registered even if the registered proprietor objects to his application.[5] But for this provision, therefore, a registered proprietor could deprive a squatter of his right to be registered.

Circumstances where no valid application can be made

30.11   The LRA 2002 sets out four circumstances in which a squatter cannot make a valid application to be registered as registered proprietor despite 10 years of adverse possession.

(1)   Where the squatter is a defendant in proceedings which involve asserting a right to possession of the land.[6] The reason for this limitation is to protect the registered proprietor's right to apply for

---

[1]   See Jourdan, *Adverse Possession*, para 22.20.

[2]   The concealed fraud exception was well recognised judicially, but does not appear to have been relied upon successfully in any reported case. In *Rains v Buxton* (1880) 14 Ch D 537, the squatters and their predecessors in title had been in possession of an underground cellar for more than 60 years. The true owners argued that there had been concealed fraud such that they could not have known of the possession. Fry J rejected the argument on the grounds that the cellar door was used openly and was visible to anyone. As the door opened outwards, it was possible for any person who looked into the area to see it.

[3]   LRA 2002, Sch 6, para 1(2).

[4]   Cf para **29.3**.

[5]   See paras **30.35–30.48**. See also, in relation to possession proceedings, paras **32.2–32.3**.

[6]   LRA 2002, Sch 6, para 1(3)(a).

possession without having to fight off an application for registration at the same time.[1]

(2) Where judgment for possession of the land has been given against the squatter in the last 2 years.[2]

(3) During any period in which the existing registered proprietor is for the purposes of the Limitation (Enemies and War Prisoners) Act 1945 an enemy, or detained in enemy territory, or within 12 months of the end of any such period.[3]

(4) During any period in which the existing registered proprietor is unable because of mental disability to make decisions about issues of the kind to which such an application would give rise,[4] or unable to communicate such decisions because of mental disability or physical impairment.[5] For these purposes 'mental disability' means a disability or disorder of the mind or brain, whether permanent or temporary, which results in an impairment or disturbance of mental functioning.[6] No provision is made in relation to minors, because a legal estate in land cannot be vested in a minor.[7] If a minor were registered as proprietor, that would be a mistake, and, therefore, a ground for alteration of the register.[8] If, therefore, a squatter successfully applied to be registered as proprietor where a minor had been the registered proprietor, the mistaken registration of the minor would be a ground for seeking an alteration of the register against the squatter.

30.12 As regards the situation in para **30.11**(4), the provisions are designed to protect the registered proprietor against the possibility that an application to register may otherwise be successful because the registrar's notice of the application to the registered proprietor goes unanswered. The protection under the LRA 2002 goes beyond what was formerly given by s 28 of the LA 1980 in two respects. First, the relevant time at which a person has to be suffering from a disability is at the date that the squatter applies to be registered.[9] Secondly, the protection extends to persons suffering from a physical as well as a mental disability that prevents them from communicating their decisions. The protection will also apply even if there is a receiver appointed under the Mental Health Act 1983.

30.13 It is provided that where it appears to the registrar that either of the

---

1   Such an application could otherwise be used tactically by a squatter to harass the registered proprietor.
2   LRA 2002, Sch 6, para 1(3)(b). Cf LRA 2002, s 98(2); see also para **32.4**.
3   Ibid, Sch 6, para 8(1)(a) and (b). This provision is necessary to provide equivalent protection to that which is given by the Limitation (Enemies and War Prisoners) Act 1945, s 1.
4   Ibid, Sch 6, para 8(2)(a).
5   Ibid, Sch 6, para 8(2)(b).
6   Ibid, Sch 6, para 8(3).
7   See LPA 1925, s 1(6); TLATA 1996, Sch 1, paras 1–3.
8   See paras **22.6** and **22.16**.
9   As opposed to the date when the adverse possession commenced and the cause of action accrued.

situations described in para **30.11**(3) or (4) applies in relation to an estate in land, he may include a note to that effect in the register.[1]

30.14   In practice, the registrar is unlikely to know that a registered proprietor suffers from a physical or mental disability. As a result, it is likely that the squatter's application to be registered would be successful because the registered proprietor would be unable to oppose it. If, in consequence, the squatter is registered as proprietor, that will be a mistake. In those circumstances, the person under a disability will be entitled to apply for rectification of the register.[2] He will either recover his land or, at very least, an indemnity for his loss.

The procedure for making an application for registration

30.15   An application[3] to be registered as proprietor must be made using Form ADV1.[4] The completed form must be accompanied by a statutory declaration made by the applicant not more than one month before the date of application together with any supporting statutory declarations. These declarations must provide evidence of adverse possession of the registered estate in land or rent charge against which the application is made for a period of not less than 10 years ending on the date of the application.[5] The applicant may also submit any additional evidence which he considers necessary to support the claim.[6] Although it is not required by LRR 2003, the Registry has indicated that, where the registered proprietor of the land claimed is a company, the results of a company search should accompany the application.[7]

30.16   Where the statutory declaration is made by an applicant based on 10 years' adverse possession, LRR 2003, r 188(2), requires that the statutory declaration must also:

(a)   exhibit a plan enabling the extent of the land to be identified on the Ordnance Survey map, unless the applicant is to be registered as proprietor of a registered rent charge;

(b)   if the applicant relies upon the extended right to apply for registration as a person who has ceased to be in adverse possession because of

---

[1]   LRA 2002, Sch 6, para 8(4).

[2]   See Sch 4, paras 2(1)(a), 5(a). See also paras **22.6**, **22.16**.

[3]   That is an application under LRA 2002, Sch 6, para 1 or para 6. As to para 6, the squatter's right to make further applications see paras **30.49–30.60**. See also Land Registry Practice Guide, Adverse Possession of Registered Land, PG4, para 4.

[4]   Application for registration of a person in adverse possession under Sch 6 to the Land Registration Act 2002: LRR 2003, r 188(1).

[5]   Ibid, r 188(1)(a)(i). The rather oblique wording of this rule makes it clear that the statutory declaration might be made after adverse possession for a period of at least 9 years and 11 months, provided that 10 years can be shown on the date of application.

[6]   Ibid, LRR r 188(1)(b)

[7]   See Adverse Possession of Registered Land, PG4, para 4.1.

eviction within the period of 6 months ending with the date of the application,[1] contain the facts relied upon with any relevant exhibits;

(c)   contain confirmation that the applicant is not barred from making an application because he is a defendant in proceedings which involve asserting a right to possession, or because a judgment for possession of the land in question has been given against him in the last 2 years;[2]

(d)   where the applicant is to be registered as proprietor of a registered rent charge, contain confirmation that the proprietor of the registered rent charge has not re-entered the land out of which the rent charge issues;

(e)   contain confirmation that to the best of his knowledge the restrictions on applications explained in para **30.11**(3) and (4)[3] do not apply;

(f)   contain confirmation that to the best of the applicant's knowledge the estate or rent charge is not and has not been during any of the period of alleged adverse possession, subject to a trust (other than one where the interest of the beneficiaries is an interest in possession);

(g)   if the applicant intends to rely on one or more of the conditions set out in para 5 of Sch 6 to the Act, contain the facts supporting reliance on such conditions.[4] As is explained below, if one or more of those conditions is established, the applicant may be registered as proprietor, even if the registered proprietor objects to his application.

30.17   Whereas Form ADV1 is drafted in relatively simple terms and merely requires the applicant to indicate the provisions of the Act upon which he intends to rely, the Registry expects the accompanying statutory declaration to contain all the information required by the Act so that the application can be dealt with effectively and expeditiously.

30.18   In addition to the matters required by the LRR 2003 (see para **30.16**), the Registry has given an indication of the sort of information that the statutory declaration should contain, such as the circumstances under which adverse possession commenced with as much precision as to dates as possible, the purpose for which the land has been used, details of any enclosure of the land, information about the title of the adjoining land if the squatter owns it, confirmation that the possession was not by consent, and full details of the dispute with correspondence exhibited.[5] By providing that the statutory declaration must contain the facts to be relied upon under one or more of the conditions set out in para 5 for example, the registrar is able to set out those details in the notice which he must serve on the registered

---

[1]   Under LRA 2002, Sch 6, para 1(2), as to which see para **30.10**.

[2]   These are circumstances where no valid application can be made: LRA 2002, Sch 6, para 1(3); see para **30.11**(1) and (2).

[3]   See LRA 2002, Sch 6, para 8.

[4]   LRA 2002, Sch 6, para 5. See paras **30.37–30.48**.

[5]   See Land Registry Practice Guide, Adverse Possession of Registered Land, PG4, para 4.2.1.

proprietor.[1] As a result, the owner of the registered estate can make an informed decision as to his stance at the earliest opportunity.

NOTIFICATION OF THE APPLICATION

The persons to be notified

30.19   On receipt of an application, the Land Registry will normally arrange for one of its surveyors to inspect the land. It will then consider the surveyor's report before taking matters further.

30.20   Once the Land Registry is satisfied that a valid application has been made under the LRA 2002 and the squatter has shown an arguable case to be registered, the registrar is required by Sch 6, para 2(1) of the Act to give notice to the following:

(a)   the proprietor of the estate to which the application relates;
(b)   the proprietor of any registered charge on the estate;
(c)   where the estate is leasehold, the proprietor of any superior registered estate;
(d)   any person who is registered in accordance with rules as a person to be notified; and
(e)   such other persons as rules may provide.

30.21   In the rules made pursuant to that provision, there is just one rule, which is intended to cover situations (d) and (e).[2] By LRR 2003, r 194(1), a person who can satisfy the registrar that he has an interest in a registered estate in land or a registered rentcharge which would be prejudiced by the registration of any other person as proprietor of that estate under Sch 6 to the Act or as proprietor of a registered rentcharge under that Schedule may apply to the registrar to be registered as a person to be notified under para 2(1)(d) of Sch 6.[3] The rule as to entitlement to apply for such registration was deliberately drafted in wide terms so that there was no danger that any relevant class of persons be excluded from making an application to be notified.[4] The persons who might apply may include:

---

[1]   See para **30.20**.
[2]   It was proposed on consultation that a single rule should be made under paras 2(1)(d) and 2(1)(e): *Land Registry New Rules – A Consultation Document*, chapter 11, para 12. LRR 2003, r 194 gives effect to that recommendation.
[3]   The mere fact that a third person has an interest in the land in question, which is protected by a notice, by caution lodged before 13 October 2003, or by a restriction, does not mean that he will be prejudiced if a squatter is registered: see the relevant rules of priority, which are explained at para **31.5**.
[4]   *Land Registry New Rules – A Consultation Document*, chapter 11, paras 9–14.

(a)   an equitable chargee;[1]
(b)   the beneficiary of a trust of land;
(c)   the Charity Commission in relation to land held on charitable trusts;
(d)   the Church Commissioners in relation to benefices;
(e)   a trustee in bankruptcy in relation to land registered in the bankrupt's name;[2] and
(f)   a liquidator or an administrator of a company in relation to land registered in a company's name.[3]

The registrar may also notify any other person whom the registrar considers appropriate.[4] However, it should be noted that although such a person will be entitled to object to the application, he will not be permitted to serve a counter-notice under the procedure explained at para **30.28**, unlike those falling within Sch 6, para 2(1) to LRA 2002.[5]

30.22   What links the persons whom the registrar must notify is that they have the power to do one or more of the following:

—   to take possession proceedings against the squatter;[6]
—   to negotiate the grant of a lease or a licence to the squatter in order to regularise his occupation; or
—   to take steps to ensure that proceedings are commenced against the squatter by the person who has the immediate right to possession.

The significance of this is explained at paras **30.52** and **30.53**.

30.23   An application under LRR 2003, r 194(1), to be registered as a person entitled to be notified under Sch 6, para 2(1)(d) to the LRA 2002, must be made in Form ADV2 'Application to be registered as a person to be notified of an application for adverse possession'.[7] The form requires the applicant to

---

[1]   An equitable chargee could in certain circumstances be prejudiced if, for example, the squatter's adverse possession pre-dated the equitable charge, and the application by the squatter to register was not opposed. It might be contended that the squatter's right to be registered had priority over the equitable charge. Cf para **31.7**.

[2]   The legal estate of any land of which the bankrupt was the registered proprietor would vest by operation of law in the trustee in bankruptcy

[3]   This is not intended to be an exhaustive list. Cf Law Com No 271, para 14.33.

[4]   It is stated in Land Registry Practice Guide, Adverse Possession of Registered Land, PG4, para 5.3, that notice will normally be given to successors in title to the registered proprietor known or suspected from other available information to have become entitled to the estate affected, for example a trustee in bankruptcy or a successor local authority. The power under which the registrar gives such notice is, apparently, LRR 2003, r 17, under which (amongst other things) the registrar may, if he considers that the giving of notice is necessary or desirable, refuse to proceed with an application until such a notice has been given. See also para **20.22**.

[5]   See LRA 2002, Sch 6, para 3(1).

[6]   Both the registered proprietor and (because of his right to possession) the proprietor of a registered charge can take such possession proceedings.

[7]   LRR 2003, r 194(2).

confirm his interest in the registered estate or registered rentcharge. The nature of the applicant's interest must be set out either in a statutory declaration by the applicant or by a person authorised by him to make it, or in a certificate by a conveyancer[1] acting for the applicant. The form also requires the provision of up to three addresses for service. This is a matter of some practical importance, given that the registrar may seek to serve notice on the interested party.

30.24 If the registrar is satisfied of the applicant's interest, he must enter the name of the applicant in the proprietorship register as a person entitled to be notified under these provisions.[2] As a result, the names of those persons entitled to receive notification from the registrar should be clear on the face of the register. An application for removal of the entry made under LRR 2003, r 194(1), can be made at any time on Form AP1.[3]

30.25 Given the consequences that flow from the notice procedure, it will be of the greatest importance that:

(a)   the registered proprietor;
(b)   any registered chargee; and
(c)   any person who is registered as a person to be notified under Sch 6, para 2(1)(d);

should maintain their current address for service on the register. This is a matter that practitioners will wish to raise with their clients.

The content of the notice

30.26 The notice served by the registrar under Sch 6, para 2(1),[4] must inform the recipient of three matters:

—   the squatter's application for registration;[5]
—   that the recipient can serve a counter-notice on the registrar within 65 business days beginning on the day of issue of the notice,[6] requiring the

---

[1]   As defined in LRR 2003, r 217(1).
[2]   LRR 2003, r 194(3). See Land Registry Practice Guide, Adverse Possession of Registered Land, PG4, para 10 for the form of entry that will be made.
[3]   See Land Registry Practice Guide, Adverse Possession of Registered Land, PG4, para 10.
[4]   See para **30.20**.
[5]   LRA 2002, Sch 6, para 2(1).
[6]   LRR 2003, r 189, prescribes the period for the purposes of LRA 2002, Sch 6 para 3(2). 'Business day' is defined in LRR 2003, r 217(1) as meaning a day when the Land Registry is open to the public under r 216. LRR 2003: see para **36.15**. LRR 2003, r 216(1) provides that unless the registrar has exercised his discretion to give notice that the Land Registry is to be open to the public on a Saturday (LRR 2003, r 216(2)), the Land Registry is open to the public daily except on Saturdays, Sundays, Christmas Day, Good Friday or any other day either specified or declared by proclamation under the Banking and Financial Dealings Act 1971, s 1, or appointed by the Lord Chancellor. In practice, therefore, the recipient of the registrar's notice will have 3 months to respond to the notice.

registrar to reject the application unless the squatter can satisfy one of three conditions which will entitle him or her to be registered;[1] and

— that if such a counter-notice is not served by at least one of those persons notified of the application, the registrar must enter the applicant as the new proprietor of the registered estate.[2]

30.27 The notice must be accompanied by Form NAP 'Notice to the registrar in respect of an adverse possession application'.[3] This is the prescribed form of counter-notice.

THE TREATMENT OF THE APPLICATION

30.28 Where the registrar serves a notice of the squatter's application to be registered under LRA 2002, Sch 6, para 2(1), the recipient has three alternatives:

(a) he may consent to the application;[4]

(b) he may object to the application on the basis that the applicant does not satisfy the pre-conditions for making it (either because the applicant has not been in adverse possession for the requisite period, or because no valid application can be made: see para **30.11**); or

(c) he may both object to the application and serve a counter-notice requiring the registrar to deal with the squatter's application under Sch 6, para 5.[5]

The only persons who can serve a counter-notice are those to whom the registrar has given notice, in other words the persons listed in LRA 2002, Sch 6, para 2(1) (para **30.20**): see LRA 2002, Sch 6, para 3(1). However, under LRA 2002, *anyone* may object to an application,[6] so that even if the recipients of the notice are persons notified merely because the registrar considered it appropriate (see para **30.21**), they can object if, for example, they considered that the applicant for registration had not been in adverse possession for 10 years.

30.29 There are no prescribed forms for giving consent or objecting to an application. However, the LRR 2003 require that if a person objects to an application, he must deliver to the registrar a written statement signed by him

---

1 LRA 2002, Sch 6, para 3.
2 Ibid, Sch 6, paras 2(2), 4.
3 LRR 2003 r 190(2). For Form NAP, see further, para **18.31**.
4 This is implicit in LRA 2002, Sch 6, para 4.
5 See LRA 2002, Sch 6, para 3.
6 See s 73(1).

or his conveyancer, stating the objection and the grounds for it. That statement must also contain the objector's name and address.[1]

30.30 In accordance with the general principle under the LRA 2002,[2] unless the registrar is satisfied that the objection is groundless, the squatter's application to be registered cannot be determined until the objection is resolved.[3] In such circumstances, the registrar must give notice to the squatter. He will then ask both parties whether they wish to negotiate. If it is thought possible to settle the matter by agreement, time will be given for this purpose. If one or other side declines, or it becomes clear that no agreement will be reached, the matter will be referred to the Adjudicator.[4]

If a counter-notice is served

30.31 Although neither LRA 2002 nor LRR 2003 requires a person notified to complete and return a counter-notice to the registrar if he consents to the registration of the applicant, panel 5 of Form NAP does contain a box within which the person notified may indicate his consent. If a person consents to the registration and returns the counter-notice, the registrar will be able to register the applicant prior to the lapse of the prescribed period.

30.32 The principal function of Form NAP is, however, to enable a person who has received notice of an application for registration to require that that application should be dealt with under LRA 2002, Sch 6, para 5[5] (the effect of which is explained at paras **30.35–30.48**). To serve the necessary counter-notice,[6] he must complete Form NAP[7] within 65 business days of the day of issue of the notice.[8] The notice must be given to the registrar in the manner and at the address stated in the registrar's notice.[9] The completed Form must indicate that the person notified requires the registrar to deal with the application under LRA 2002, Sch 6, para 5, and must give details of the grounds of objection to the registration.

30.33 Once a counter-notice has been served, the registrar *must* reject the squatter's application for registration unless he can establish that he satisfies one of the three conditions set out in LRA 2002, Sch 6, para 5.[10] At this point, the Land Registry will, therefore, consider whether or not the squatter has

---

[1] LRR 2003, r 19.
[2] See para **20.30**.
[3] LRA 2002, s 73.
[4] Ibid, s 73(7). See Land Registry Practice Guide, Adverse Possession of Registered Land, PG4, para 6.
[5] Ibid, Sch 6, para 3(1).
[6] Pursuant to ibid, Sch 6, para 3(2).
[7] LRR 2003, r 190(1).
[8] LRA 2002, Sch 6, para 3(2) and LRR 2003, r 189.
[9] LRR 2003, r 190(1)(b).
[10] LRA 2002, Sch 6, para 5(1). For those conditions, see para **30.35**.

shown an arguable case for reliance on the condition. If an arguable case has been shown, the Land Registry will contact the persons who gave the counter-notice. If they dispute that the condition has been met, they can object to the application on this ground if they have not already done so in Form NAP.[1]

If no counter-notice is served

30.34   If no counter-notice is given, the applicant is entitled to be registered as the new proprietor of the estate once the time-limit has expired.[2] If the squatter's application relates to part only of a registered title, the part affected will be removed from the existing title number and the squatter will be registered as proprietor of that part.

The procedure following service of a counter-notice

30.35   If a counter-notice requiring the registrar to deal with the application under para 5 is served, the squatter is only entitled to be registered as the new proprietor of the estate if he can demonstrate that one of three express exceptional conditions is satisfied.[3] The first condition is intended to embody the equitable principles of proprietary estoppel. The second condition applies where the squatter was otherwise entitled to the land. The third condition applies where the squatter is the owner of adjacent property and has been in adverse possession of the land in question under the mistaken but reasonable belief that he is the owner of it.

30.36   The Law Commission considered that where any one of these conditions was established, the balance of fairness lay with the squatter, and he should, therefore, prevail over the registered proprietor. The first two conditions are not true 'exceptions' in that, even if the LRA 2002 were silent, a squatter could assert his claims to the land in court proceedings. The reason why they are included is procedural. If a squatter claims that he satisfies one of the three conditions, then unless the dispute can be resolved by agreement between the squatter and the registered proprietor, it will have to be referred to the Adjudicator for resolution.[4] That is likely to be cheaper, quicker and less formal than court proceedings.[5]

---

1   See Land Registry Practice Guide, Adverse Possession of Registered Land, PG4, para 7.
2   LRA 2002, Sch 6, para 4.
3   Ibid, Sch 6, para 5(1).
4   See LRA 2002, ss 73(1), (7), 108(1); see also paras **20.30, 34.12**.
5   See (2001) Law Com No 271, para 14.37. Under the previous law, where a person fell within one of the first two categories and had also been in adverse possession for 12 years, he was entitled to apply to be registered on the ground of adverse possession alone, and could do so under LRA 1925, s 75. The matter would have been determined by the Solicitor to HM Land Registry unless the registrar had exercised his discretion to refer it to the court.

The first condition: estoppel

30.37   The first condition embodies in statutory form the equitable principles of proprietary estoppel. It is applicable if:

– it would be unconscionable for the registered proprietor to seek to dispossess the applicant, and

– the circumstances are such that the applicant ought to be registered as the proprietor.[1]

30.38   In order to show that such an equity by estoppel has arisen in his favour, the applicant will have to prove that he acted to his detriment, in the belief, encouraged or acquiesced in by the registered proprietor, that he owned the land in question.[2] The circumstances will have to be such that it would be unconscionable for the proprietor to deny the applicant that ownership. Cases of this kind will be rare. Usually a person claiming an equity by estoppel such that he or she should be entitled to the land itself will not be in adverse possession, but will be on the land with the consent of the registered proprietor. However, such a situation could arise, as where a person builds a garage or other building on land which he believes to be his own but which, in fact, belongs to another, and where that other person realises the mistake, but acquiesces in it.[3]

30.39   An equity is an inchoate right. It merely gives the claimant a right to apply to the court for relief and the court has a discretion, exercisable according to equitable principles, as to how to give effect to that equity. The court will 'analyse the minimum equity to do justice' to the claimant and will grant relief accordingly.[4] The case may be such that the equity can only be satisfied by a transfer of the owner's freehold or leasehold title to the claimant. But in many other cases, some lesser relief will be appropriate. This might take the form of the grant of some less extensive right over the land, an order for the payment of monetary compensation or merely the grant of an injunction to restrain the defendant from enforcing his strict legal rights against the claimant.[5]

30.40   The Adjudicator will, similarly, have to exercise his discretion as to the relief to be granted when a squatter claims that he is entitled to be registered because an equity by estoppel has arisen in his favour.[6] The LRA 2002 expressly empowers the Adjudicator in such a case to grant the applicant

---

[1]   LRA 2002, Sch 6, para 5(2).

[2]   See Harpum, *Megarry & Wade's Law of Real Property* (Sweet & Maxwell, 6th edn, 2000), ch 13.

[3]   See (2001) Law Com No 271, para 14.42.

[4]   *Crabb v Arun District Council* [1976] Ch 179 at p 198, per Scarman LJ.

[5]   See Harpum, *Megarry & Wade's Law of Real Property* (Sweet & Maxwell, 6th edn, 2000), para 13-020; (2001) Law Com No 271, para 14.40.

[6]   LRA 2002, s 110(4).

some less extensive form of relief than that he should be registered as proprietor.[1] On any appeal from the Adjudicator's decision to the court,[2] the court has a similar power.[3]

The second condition: some other right to the land

30.41   The second condition is that the applicant is, for some other reason, entitled to be registered as the proprietor of the estate.[4] In other words, this is intended to cover the case where the squatter has a right to the land that would entitle him to be registered as proprietor irrespective of his adverse possession. Such cases may include:

— where the claimant is entitled to the land under the will or intestacy of the deceased proprietor but is on the land without the consent of the deceased's personal representatives; or
— where the claimant contracted to buy the land and paid the purchase price, but where the legal estate was never transferred to him.[5]

Such cases are likely to be rare.

The third condition: reasonable mistake as to boundary

30.42   The third condition is the most important.[6] Of the three conditions, it is the only one which entitles a squatter to be registered solely because of his adverse possession. It is, however, narrowly drawn, and to fall within it four matters have to be established:

— the land to which the application relates is adjacent to land belonging to the applicant;
— the exact line of the boundary between the two has not been determined under rules under s 60(3) of the LRA 2002;[7]
— for at least 10 years of the period of adverse possession ending on the date of the application, the applicant (or any predecessor in title)

---

1   LRA 2002, s 110(4).
2   Under ibid, s 111(1).
3   Ibid, s 111(3).
4   Ibid, Sch 6, para 5(3).
5   In this second example, the squatter-beneficiary is a beneficiary under a bare trust, and can, therefore, be in adverse possession: see (2001) Law Com No 271, para 14.43 and *Bridges v Mees* [1957] Ch 475.
6   LRA 2002, Sch 6, para 5(4).
7   LRR 2003, Part 10 sets out rules in relation to boundaries; see paras **16.5–16.7**. If the boundary has been 'determined' pursuant to LRA 2002, s 60(3), the boundary will not be a general boundary within LRA 2002, s 60(1), the register will be conclusive about the boundary, and the exception is, therefore, irrelevant. It should be noted that this exception does not apply to a boundary that was fixed prior to 13 October 2003, pursuant to LRR 1925, rr 276, 277. Such a boundary has not been determined under rules under LRA 2002, s 60, and so falls within Sch 6, para 4(b).

reasonably believed that the land to which the application relates belonged to him;[1] and
— the estate to which the application relates was registered more than one year prior to the date of the application.

30.43   The third condition reflects the fact that, as a consequence of the general boundaries rule found in s 60 of the LRA 2002, the register is not normally conclusive as to boundaries. There is, therefore, a case for permitting a squatter to acquire title within certain tightly drawn limits where he has acted in good faith and has not attempted to 'steal' his neighbour's land. This third condition is intended to meet the common situation where the boundaries as they appear on the ground and as they appear on the register do not coincide. Typically this may happen because the physical features suggest that the boundaries are in one place when in fact they are in another, or because of some mistake in the erection of the fences or walls when a new estate is laid out otherwise than in accordance with the plan.[2] Adverse possession provides a useful 'curative' method of dealing with cases of this kind.

30.44   Something must be said of the four requirements (listed in para **30.42**) that have to be met to establish the third condition.

30.45   The first requirement is factual. The applicant must own adjacent land.[3] The third condition is therefore restricted to disputes about the location of the boundary between two properties.

30.46   The second requirement is to show the necessary mental element. Adverse possession has a mental element. The squatter has to show that, for the limitation period, he had an intention to exclude the world including the true owner. One way in which he may show this intention is by proving that he believed he was the owner of the land which he claims.[4] If the squatter has been in possession of land for a period in excess of 10 years, in circumstances where the physical boundaries of the land suggest that it belongs to him, those

---

[1]   Where a squatter has been ousted by the registered proprietor or some persons claiming under him (see para **30.10**), the relevant date will not be the date of the application, but the day before the date of the applicant's eviction: see LRA 2002, Sch 6, para 5(5).

[2]   According to the Parliamentary Secretary, Lord Chancellor's Department, Baroness Scotland of Asthall, *Hansard* (HL), 17 July 2001, vol 626, cols 1622–1623, the Land Registry had found it 'very common indeed' for there to be small differences between the legal boundaries of an estate and those laid out on the ground. Problems were particularly marked in relation to new estates, where it was said to be 'rare' for properties to be exactly in the same spot marked on the original plan, the result being that a developer may build a whole estate some 3 or 4 inches in the wrong place, causing considerable potential difficulties when the new owners of individual houses naturally assume that their garden fence marks their boundary, and plan their gardens accordingly, without reference to the original plan.

[3]   There is no requirement that his title should be registered. It is, however, unclear as to whether this requirement will be fulfilled if the squatter is a tenant of the adjoining land holding under a long or short tenancy or holding as a tenant at will: see Jourdan, *Adverse Possession*, para 22-59.

[4]   See, eg, *Prudential Assurance Co Ltd v Waterloo Real Estate Inc* [1999] 2 EGLR 85.

facts are likely to raise a presumption that the squatter had the necessary intention required to establish this exception. It will then be incumbent on the registered proprietor to show that the squatter knew or ought to have known that the land did not belong to him, for example, by proving that he had told the squatter that the land was not the squatter's.[1]

30.47   The third requirement is that the boundary must be a general and not a fixed boundary. The whole justification for the third condition is the fact that the register is not normally conclusive as to boundaries. However, it is possible to fix boundaries so that the general boundaries rule does not apply.[2] Where that has been done, the third condition will not apply. Landowners who fear encroachment on their land in cases where the boundaries are not clear on the ground can, therefore, exclude any possibility that the third condition might apply.[3]

30.48   The provision that the land to which the application relates was registered more than one year prior to the date of the application is necessary as, under the LRA 2002, the third condition can be established after 10 years' adverse possession. By contrast, title to unregistered land can usually only be acquired after 12 years' adverse possession. In the absence of this fourth requirement, if an owner applied to register his title at a time when a squatter had been in adverse possession of unregistered land for more than 10 years but less than 12 years, and the requirements of the third exception were otherwise fulfilled, the squatter could apply immediately for registration as proprietor, and the owner would have no opportunity to evict him. For the same reason, the third condition was not brought into force on 13 October 2003, but one year later: see the Land Registration Act 2002 (Commencement No 4) Order, para 2(2): see para **1.3**.

THE SQUATTER'S RIGHT TO MAKE FURTHER APPLICATION

When the right arises

30.49   The new scheme is intended to produce a definite result. The LRA 2002 therefore provides for the steps that may be taken by both the squatter and the registered proprietor following the rejection of a squatter's application to be registered after service of a counter-notice and in circumstances where none of the special exceptions were fulfilled.

---

1   See (2001) Law Com No 271, para 14.52.
2   LRA 2002, s 60(1), (3); see also paras **16.2** et seq.
3   There is a power to make rules which require a boundary to be fixed in particular circumstances: see LRA 2002, s 60(3)(a). It would be possible to make rules pursuant to this power to require a successful applicant under this third condition to have the boundary with the remaining land of the registered proprietor fixed to prevent any further applications. This was anticipated by the Law Commission: see (2001) Law Com No 271, para 9.13. However, no such rules have yet been made.

30.50   Where a squatter's application to be registered is rejected, he may make a further application to be registered as the proprietor of the estate if he remains in adverse possession of the estate from the date of the application until 2 years after the date of its rejection.[1] This right reflects the rationale of adverse possession: to discourage claimants from sleeping on their rights and to bring an end to litigation.

30.51   The effect of this provision is that a proprietor of a registered estate or charge will usually have one chance to remove the squatter by taking possession proceedings against him or by agreeing to grant him a lease or licence (so that he ceases to be in adverse possession). But if he fails to take such steps within 2 years of the rejection of the squatter's action he stands to lose his land. If the registered proprietor *does* bring possession proceedings within that 2-year period, the squatter will have no defence and the registered proprietor will be able to seek summary judgment.

30.52   It was explained above at para **30.22**, that what linked those who were entitled to be notified of an application by a squatter under LRA 2002, Sch 6, para 1, to be registered as proprietor was that they were in a position to do one of the following:

(a)   take proceedings for possession against the squatter;
(b)   grant him a lease or licence (so as to legitimise his possession); or
(c)   take steps to ensure that proceedings were commenced against the squatter by the person who had the immediate right to possession.

30.53   Once the squatter's application to be registered has failed, in the light of the position set out in para **30.51**, it will be necessary to terminate the squatter's adverse possession within 2 years to ensure that he does not obtain title. Normally, the registered proprietor is likely to take the necessary steps. However, the proprietor may not have an immediate right to possession in order to be able to take possession proceedings. Such a case might arise where, for example, the registered proprietor granted an unregistered lease of the land in question, after the squatter had commenced adverse possession. However, once the squatter's application had been rejected, the registered proprietor could call upon the tenant to commence such proceedings. Indeed, unless the tenant was informed of the squatter's application by the registered proprietor, or had himself been registered as a person who was to be notified under Sch 6, para 2(1)(d), it is possible that the tenant would not otherwise know of the application in order to take steps to preserve his own position.

---

[1]   LRA 2002, Sch 6, para 6(1).

30.54   The squatter will not be able to make a new application to be registered as proprietor in three situations.[1]

—   The first is where he is a defendant in proceedings which involve asserting a right to possession of the land.
—   The second is where a judgment for possession of the land has been given against him in the last 2 years.
—   The third is where he has been evicted from the land pursuant to a judgment for possession.

Subject to these exceptions, if a squatter makes a new application, he is entitled to be entered as the new proprietor of the estate.[2]

30.55   It follows from what is said in the previous paragraph that the squatter *will* be entitled to be registered in the following situations.

—   The first is where the registered proprietor obtains a judgment for possession against the squatter in proceedings commenced within 2 years of the rejection of the latter's application to be registered, but then fails to enforce that judgment within 2 years. The LRA 2002 expressly provides that, in those circumstances, the proprietor's judgment for possession ceases to be enforceable.[3]
—   The second is where the registered proprietor of the estate or charge commences proceedings against the squatter within 2 years of the rejection of the latter's application, but they are discontinued or struck out after the 2-year period has elapsed. Provided that the squatter has remained in adverse possession throughout, he is then entitled to make a new application to be registered.[4]

In other words, it is not enough for the registered proprietor to commence proceedings within 2 years of the rejection of the squatter's application to be registered. The proprietor must both obtain judgment and then enforce it.

Making a further application for registration

30.56   A squatter who wishes to make a further application to be registered as proprietor must use Form ADV1.[5] The completed form must be accompanied by a statutory declaration made by the applicant no more than a

---

[1]   LRA 2002, Sch 6, para 6(2).
[2]   Ibid, Sch 6, para 7.
[3]   Ibid, s 98(4). In the absence of this provision, the registered proprietor of the estate or charge would have 6 years either to bring an action on the judgment for possession (LA 1980, s 24(1)), or to execute the judgment without leave of the court (Civil Procedure Rules 1998 (CPR 1998), SI 1998/3132, Sch 1, r 46.2(a)).
[4]   This follows from LRA 2002, Sch 6, para 6(2).
[5]   LRR 2003, r 188(1). For Form ADV1, see para **30.15**.

month before the application is made. That, together with any supporting statutory declarations, must provide evidence of adverse possession of the relevant registered estate in land (or rent charge) for a period of at least 2 years from the date of the rejection of the original application.[1]

30.57   By LRR 2003, r 188(3), the statutory declaration must also:

(a)   exhibit a plan enabling the extent of the land to be identified on the Ordnance Survey map, unless the application is to be registered as proprietor of a registered rent charge or the extent is the same as in the previous rejected application;

(b)   contain full details of the previous rejected application;

(c)   contain confirmation that to the best of his knowledge the restriction on applications explained at para **30.11**(3) and (4)[2] do not apply.

(d)   contain confirmation that to the best of his knowledge the estate or rentcharge is not, and has not been during any of the period of alleged adverse possession, subject to a trust (other than one where the interest of each of the beneficiaries is an interest in possession);

(e)   contain confirmation that the applicant is not precluded from making a further application for registration for the reasons set out in para **30.54**;[3] and

(f)   where the application is to be registered as proprietor of a registered rentcharge, contain confirmation that the proprietor of the registered rentcharge has not re-entered the land out of which the rentcharge issues.

30.58   The applicant may also submit any additional evidence which the applicant considers necessary to support the claim.[4]

30.59   The registrar will give notice of the squatter's application to:

(a)   the registered proprietor of the estate affected;

(b)   the registered proprietor of any registered charge on that estate;

(c)   where the estate is leasehold, the registered proprietor of any superior registered estate;

(d)   any person who has been registered as a person to be notified under para 2 of Sch 6 to the Act; and

(e)   any other person the registrar considers it appropriate to notify.[5]

---

[1]   LRR 2003, r 188 (1)(a)(ii).
[2]   That is where the proprietor is an enemy alien, prisoner of war, or subject to a disability: see LRA 2002, Sch 6, para 8.
[3]   See ibid, Sch 6, para 6.
[4]   LRR 2003, r 188(1)(b)
[5]   Ibid, r 17.

30.60   The person notified will have 15 business days to reply and may either consent to the application or object to the application.[1] If no objection is received within the specified time, the applicant will be registered as proprietor. The ground for objection will be that the squatter was not in fact in adverse possession for the 2-year period. In dealing with any such objection, the procedure explained in para **30.30**, will apply.

THE STATUS OF THE SQUATTER'S RIGHT TO BE REGISTERED

30.61   There are five situations in which a squatter may acquire an indefeasible statutory right to be registered as proprietor in place of the registered proprietor. They are:

(a)   where no counter-notice is served in response to the squatter's application to be registered;

(b)   where the squatter establishes that one of the three exceptional conditions applies;

(c)   where the squatter becomes entitled to re-apply to be registered;

(d)   where the squatter has a defence to possession proceedings;[2] or

(e)   where the squatter had barred the rights of the registered proprietor prior to the commencement of the LRA 2002.

30.62   This right to be registered is necessarily a proprietary right, because it is a statutory right to have a legal estate vested in him. As such, the squatter may assert it against the registered proprietor. It will also bind any third party to whom the registered proprietor makes a registered disposition of the land, provided that the squatter was in actual occupation of the land.[3] The Act does not give effect to the squatter's right to be registered by means of a trust, as did the previous law,[4] given the criticisms of that device.[5]

---

[1]   See LRR 2003, r 197(2).

[2]   See paras **32.2–32.6**.

[3]   The squatter's unregistered interest would, therefore, override the registered disposition under LRA 2002, Sch 3, para 2.

[4]   See LRA 1925, s 75(1).

[5]   For these criticisms, see (2001) Law Com No 271, paras 14.67, 14.70.

CHAPTER 31

THE EFFECT OF REGISTRATION OF A PERSON WHO HAD BEEN IN ADVERSE POSSESSION

THE GENERAL PRINCIPLE

31.1   Where a squatter's application is successful and a person is registered as the proprietor of an estate in land against which he had adversely possessed, the title by virtue of adverse possession which he had at the time of the application is extinguished.[1] As a result, the squatter is the successor in title to the previously registered proprietor. This means that in most cases the squatter will be registered with absolute title because the former registered owner will have been registered with absolute title. The squatter will only be registered with possessory title on the rare occasion when the former registered owner was registered with possessory title. If, however, the registered proprietor could have made an application to upgrade the possessory title to an absolute freehold prior to the date of the squatter's application to be registered, the squatter will be able to make such application immediately.[2]

31.2   Where the estate acquired is a lease, the assignment takes effect as an involuntary assignment or an assignment by operation of law. Such an assignment is not a breach of a covenant against assignment.[3]

31.3   Where the estate acquired is a lease which was granted after 1995, the

---

[1]   LRA 2002, Sch 6, para 9(1).

[2]   Ibid, s 62. See paras **3.13** et seq. During the passage of the Bill, Baroness Scotland of Asthal gave the following example of circumstances when such an application might be appropriate: 'A dies owning at her death an unregistered freehold estate; her executor cannot find the deeds and assumes that they are lost. Within a few weeks of A's death the executor applies for voluntary first registration on the basis that the deeds are lost. A possessory title is approved. Unbeknown to the executor the deeds are in the custody of a lender who has a first legal charge, created before such charges triggered first registration. As the executor has a possessory title, he is subject to the legal charge. Three years after registration, a squatter applies for registration of part of the land, based on 10 years' adverse possession. She is successful and is registered in place of the executor in respect of that land. Under the amendment, the squatter could apply for the upgrading of the possessory title to absolute freehold immediately because the title has already been registered for at least two years' *Hansard* (HL), 30 October 2001, vol 627, cols 1358–1359.

[3]   See Woodfall, *Landlord and Tenant*, para 11.166.

registration of the squatter as the new proprietor will operate as an 'excluded assignment' under s 11 of the Landlord and Tenant (Covenants) Act 1995. As a result, whatever the date of grant of the lease, the former tenant will remain liable on the covenants in the lease.

31.4 The registration of the squatter will extinguish any claims that the former registered proprietor might have had against the squatter for damages for trespass or rent. Following registration, the former registered proprietor is no longer entitled to possession, and cannot make any claim that is dependent upon such a state of affairs. This is consistent with the rule,[1] applicable where title to land is extinguished by adverse possession under s 17 of the LA 1980, that rights which that title carried must be also extinguished.[2]

31.5 Subject to the exception in relation to charges explained in para **31.6**, the registration of a squatter as the proprietor of an estate in land does not affect the priority of any interest affecting the estate.[3] The squatter will, therefore, step into the previous registered proprietor's shoes and will take the land subject to the same estates, rights and interests that bound the land previously.

THE EFFECT OF REGISTRATION ON REGISTERED CHARGES

31.6 As an exception to the general rule that registration will not affect the priority of any interest affecting the registered estate, where a squatter is registered as the proprietor of an estate, the estate will be vested in him free of any registered charge affecting the estate immediately before his registration,[4] unless the squatter has obtained title under one of the three exceptional conditions.[5] The principle behind this provision is as follows. Under the LRA 2002 the registered chargee will receive notice of the application to be registered. Because the chargee has a right to possession, it is entitled to take proceedings against the squatter to recover the land even if the registered proprietor does not. The chargee can, therefore, prevent the squatter acquiring title just as much as can the registered proprietor. If the chargee fails to take such proceedings, the squatter should, in principle, take the land free of the charge.[6] As a result, the chargee cannot assert its charge in circumstances

---

[1]   See *Re Jolly* [1900] 2 Ch 616.
[2]   *Mount Carmel Investments Ltd v Peter Thurlow Ltd* [1988] 1 WLR 1078 at 1089 per Nicholls LJ.
[3]   LRA 2002, Sch 6, para 9(2).
[4]   Ibid, Sch 6, para 9(3).
[5]   Ibid, Sch 6, para 9(4).
[6]   Under the previous law, it was probably the case that a successful squatter whose adverse possession pre-dated the registered charge was not bound by it. If, however, the charge pre-dated the adverse possession, it would be binding on a squatter who acquired title to the registered estate by adverse possession. See LA 1980, s 15(4); *Thornton v France* [1897] 2 QB 143; *Ludbrook v Ludbrook* [1901] 2 KB 96; *Carroll v Maneck* (1999) 79 P&CR 173. The point cannot be regarded as finally settled, however.

where the registered proprietor has lost his estate. The squatter can then deal with the land as he chooses.[1]

31.7 The squatter will be bound by a registered charge notwithstanding the service of a counter-notice by the registered proprietor or chargee, if the facts fall within one of the three exceptional conditions contained in Sch 6, para 5 to the LRA 2002.[2] The squatter will also be bound by any equitable charges, such as any charging order.[3] In both cases it is, however, possible that the squatter's independent right that justifies his registration as proprietor will take priority over the charge so that he will take free of it. This will often be the case if that right arose prior to the charge and (in the case of a registered charge) the squatter was in actual occupation at the time that the charge was created so that his rights overrode the disposition.[4]

APPORTIONMENT AND DISCHARGE OF CHARGES

31.8 It follows from what has been said above that there may be occasions where a squatter who is registered as proprietor will be bound by either a registered charge or an equitable charge. Sometimes the land acquired by the squatter will comprise only part – perhaps only a small part – of the property subject to the charge. Where this situation occurs under the present law, the squatter has to redeem the whole charge if he wishes to sell his land free of it.[5] In practice, he may not be able to do this and cannot therefore sell the land. As one of the aims of the LRA 2002 is to ensure that land remains in commerce, it makes provision by which a squatter who finds himself in this situation can require the chargee to apportion the amount secured by the charge. The apportionment is made at the time when the squatter seeks it and according to the respective values of the land acquired by the squatter and the remainder of the land subject to the charge.[6]

31.9 The person requiring the apportionment is entitled to a discharge of his estate from the charge on payment of the amount apportioned to the estate

1 See (2001) Law Com No 271, para 14.75. This promotes one of the aims of the LRA 2002, namely, that the land should remain in commerce whether title to the land is retained by the registered proprietor or acquired by the squatter.
2 For the three exceptional cases, see paras **30.37–30.48**.
3 Equitable chargees do not have a right to possession of the property charged, although they can obtain it in court proceedings: see Harpum, *Megarry & Wade's Law of Real Property* (Sweet & Maxwell, 6th edn, 2000), para 19-087.
4 LRA 2002, Sch 3, para 2. In the case of an equitable charge, the squatter's right to be registered would always take priority if it pre-dated the charge: see LRA 2002, s 28.
5 *Hall v Heward* (1886) 32 ChD 430; *Carroll v Manck* (1999) 79 P&CR 173. He would then be subrogated to the rights of the chargee in relation to the other land of the mortgagor: see *Ghana Commercial Bank v Chandiram* [1960] AC 732 at 745. In practice, many lenders do not insist upon their strict rights and, particularly if the squatter has only established title to a small portion of the land charge, will agree to release their charge in relation to the squatter's part.
6 LRA 2002, Sch 6, para 10(1).

together with the costs incurred by the chargee as a result of the apportionment.[1] On a discharge, the liability of the chargor to the chargee is reduced by the amount apportioned to the estate.[2] The details of the apportionment process will be prescribed in rules, [3] although to date none have been made.[4]

---

[1]   LRA 2002, Sch 6, para 10(2).

[2]   Ibid, Sch 6, para 10(3).

[3]   Ibid, Sch 6, para 10(4). Rules may, in particular, make provision about procedure, valuation, calculation of costs payable and payment by the squatter of any costs incurred by the chargor.

[4]   See *Land Registry New Rules – A Consultation Document*, paras 21–27.

CHAPTER 32

POSSESSION PROCEEDINGS

THE GENERAL RULE

32.1 The LRA 2002 ensures that the position of the squatter in possession proceedings brought by the registered proprietor or registered chargee to recover the land mirrors that of the squatter who applies for registration. Under the new scheme the rights of the proprietor are not barred by lapse of time, and the general rule is, therefore, that if the registered proprietor or registered chargee brings possession proceedings, those proceedings will succeed regardless of how long the squatter has been in possession. To this general rule there are defences that reflect the principles, explained above, as to when a squatter may be registered as proprietor, even if the existing registered proprietor objects to his application.

EXCEPTIONS TO THE GENERAL RULE: DEFENCES

Reasonable mistake as to boundary

32.2 It is a defence to an action for possession for the squatter to show that, the day before the possession proceedings were brought:

–   he would have been entitled to make an application to be registered as proprietor under para 1 of Sch 6 in accordance with the principles explained in para **30.1**; and
–   if he had made such an application, he would have established that he would have satisfied the third condition in para 5(4) of Sch 6 (reasonable mistake as to boundary),[1] explained in paras **30.42–30.48**.

When a squatter has a right to make further application for registration

32.3 A squatter will have a defence to possession proceedings if:

–   he had been in adverse possession for 10 years;
–   he had made an application for registration that had been rejected; and

---

[1]   LRA 2002, s 98(1). Like Sch 6, para 5(4), s 98(1) only comes into force on 13 October 2004 for the reasons explained at para **30.48**.

–   on the day before the proceedings were commenced he was entitled to make a further application to be registered under the provisions of para 6 of Sch 6 that have been explained at paras **30.49–30.60**.[1]

When a judgment for possession ceases to be enforceable

32.4   A theme that runs through the provisions of the LRA 2002 on adverse possession is that they are designed to achieve finality and to do so expeditiously. One aspect of this is that, if a registered proprietor obtains a judgment for possession against a squatter who would have been entitled to apply to be registered in accordance with the principles in para 1 of Sch 6,[2] that judgment ceases to be enforceable after a mere 2 years and not (as at present) after 6 years.[3]

32.5   A judgment for possession obtained against a squatter ceases to be enforceable 2 years after it was given if the following conditions are satisfied:

–   the squatter had been in adverse possession for 10 years;
–   he had made an application for registration that had been rejected; and
–   he was entitled to make a further application to be registered under the provisions of para 6 of Sch 6 that have been explained at paras **30.49–30.60**.[4]

A judgment for possession will remain enforceable after 2 years unless the squatter can satisfy each of these three conditions. In such circumstances, the normal 6-year period for enforcing the judgment without leave would apply.[5]

32.6   Where the court determines in any possession proceedings that the squatter is entitled to a defence under the LRA 2002, or that a judgment for possession has ceased to be enforceable, the court *must* order the registrar to register the squatter as the proprietor of the estate in relation to which he is entitled to make an application for registration as proprietor.[6]

Other defences

32.7   The statutory defences listed above are additional to any other defences that the squatter may have apart from the LRA 2002.[7] The squatter

---

[1]   LRA 2002, s 98(3).
[2]   See para **30.1**.
[3]   LRA 2002, s 98(2).
[4]   Ibid, s 98(4).
[5]   LA 1980, s 24(1).
[6]   LRA 2002, s 98(5).
[7]   Ibid, s 98(6).

will, therefore, be able to raise any defence available to him in the possession proceedings, such as an equity arising by proprietary estoppel or that the land was held on bare trust for him.

CHAPTER 33

SPECIAL CASES

RENTCHARGES

33.1 There are two forms of adverse possession that apply in relation to rentcharges. Under LA 1980,[1] the rights of an owner of a rentcharge are barred if:

(a)   no rent has been paid for 12 years; or
(b)   the rent has been paid to a third party for 12 years.[2]

The former situation is likely to be much more common than the latter.

33.2 The LRA 2002 does not state how its provisions are to apply to these two forms of adverse possession of a registered rentcharge. The matter is left to rules, in relation to both applications for registration[3] and actions for the recovery of rent due under a rentcharge.[4]

33.3 Because the two forms of adverse possession have different consequences, the Rules have to make different provision for them. Although in either case the applicant will apply to be registered as proprietor of the rentcharge, in the case where the application is based on non-payment of the rentcharge, the effect of a successful application will be the closure of the title to the rentcharge, rather than the registration of the applicant as registered proprietor of the rentcharge: see further, para **33.9**.

33.4 The provisions of the Act and Rules in relation to the registration of an adverse possessor as a proprietor of a registered estate[5] are applied by LRR 2003 to the registration of an adverse possessor as the proprietor of a registered rent charge, subject to modifications that flow from the nature of

---

[1]   LA 1980, s 38(8), Sch 1, Part 1, para 8(3)(a).
[2]   See Harpum, *Megarry & Wade's Law of Real Property* (Sweet & Maxwell, 6th edn, 2000), para 21-034.
[3]   LRA 2002, Sch 6, para 14.
[4]   Ibid, s 98(7).
[5]   Explained above in Chapter 30. For the relevant provisions, see LRA 2002, Sch 6 and LRR 2003, rr 188, 189, 190, 194.

rentcharges.[1] The general principle is that a person may apply to the registrar to be registered as the proprietor of a registered rentcharge if he has been in adverse possession of the registered rentcharge (in either of the two forms mentioned above) for the period of 10 years ending on the date of the application.[2]

33.5   The main differences between the principles applicable to the adverse possession of registered estates and those that apply to the adverse possession of a rentcharge are as follows.

33.6   First, there is no equivalent to the right of an evicted adverse possessor of a registered estate to apply for registration.[3]

33.7   Secondly, no valid application or further application for registration can be made in relation to a rentcharge if the person to be registered proprietor of the registered rentcharge of which that person was in adverse possession has re-entered the land out of which the registered rentcharge issues.[4] This bar to a valid application is additional to those that are equivalent to those described in paras **30.11** and **30.54**.[5]

33.8   Thirdly, there are only two grounds on which an adverse possessor of a registered rentcharge can be registered as the new proprietor if the registered proprietor requires the application to be dealt with under Sch 8, para 5 (the equivalent of Sch 6, para 5),[6] namely:

(a)   that it would be unconscionable because of an equity by estoppel for the registered proprietor to seek to assert his title to the registered rentcharge against the applicant and the circumstances are such that the applicant ought to be registered as proprietor;[7] and

(b)   that the applicant is for some other reason entitled to be registered as proprietor of the registered rentcharge.[8]

---

[1]   LRR 2003, r 191. The rule applies Sch 6 to the Act to the registration of an adverse possessor of a registered rent charge in the modified form set out in LRR 2003, Sch 8. LRR 2003, r 187 provides that where the application is to be registered as proprietor of a registered rent charge, the references in rr 188, 189, 190, 192 and 193 to LRA 2002, Sch 6, are to Sch 6 in the modified form in which is set out in LRR 2003, Sch 8. Although Sch 8 sets out the revised form of LRA 2002, Sch 6, references are given to the paragraph numbers of LRR 2003, Sch 8, to avoid confusion.

[2]   LRR 2003, Sch 8, para 1(1).

[3]   LRA 2002, Sch 6, para 1(2); see also para **30.10**.

[4]   LRR 2003, Sch 8, paras 1(2) and 6(2)(c).

[5]   Ibid, Sch 8, paras 2(a), (b) and 8.

[6]   For LRA 2002, Sch 6, para 5, see paras **30.35** et seq.

[7]   LRR 2003, Sch 8, para 5(2).

[8]   Ibid, Sch 8, para 5(3).

There is obviously no equivalent to right of an adverse possessor of a registered estate to apply to be registered on the basis of a reasonable mistake as to the boundary of his property.[1]

33.9 In the more common case of adverse possession of a rentcharge by reason of non-payment of the rentcharge, if:

(a) the application for registration is successful; and
(b) if the applicant were so registered he would not be subject to a registered charge or registered lease or other interest protected in the register;[2]

the registrar must either close the whole of the registered title of the registered rentcharge, or cancel the registered rentcharge, if the registered title to it also comprises other rentcharges.[3] In the much rarer case where a person becomes entitled to be registered as proprietor of the rentcharge because he is a third party to whom the rent has been paid for more than 10 years, the applicant will be registered as proprietor of the rentcharge.[4]

33.10   If the application for registration is successful and either:

(a) the applicant has been registered as proprietor of a rentcharge;[5] or
(b) the registered title to a rentcharge has been closed or a registered rentcharge has been cancelled, where the registered title also comprises other rentcharges;[6]

no previous registered proprietor of the rentcharge may recover any rent due under the rentcharge from the person who has been in adverse possession.[7]

TRUSTS

Adverse possession of land held in trust

33.11   A person is not to be regarded as being in adverse possession of an estate for the purposes of the LRA 2002 at any time when the estate is subject to a trust, unless the interest of each of the beneficiaries in the estate is an interest in possession.[8] Thus, for example, where land is held in trust for A for

---

[1] LRA 2002, Sch 6, para 5(4); see also para **30.42**.
[2] In other words, under the principles of priority set out in LRR 2003, Sch 8, para 9.
[3] LRR 2003, r 192.
[4] See LRR 2003, Sch 8, paras 4, 5 and 7.
[5] In other words, where a rentcharge has been paid to a third party (the applicant) for more than 10 years.
[6] In other words, where there has been non-payment of the rentcharge for more than 10 years.
[7] LRR 2003, r 193. This rule is made pursuant to LRA 2002, s 98(7), see para **33.2**.
[8] LRA 2002, Sch 6, para 12.

life, thereafter for B for life, thereafter for C absolutely, a squatter will only be able to apply to be registered under the Act if he can show that he has been in adverse possession for at least 10 years since C became entitled in possession. In this regard, the LRA 2002 follows the present law and aims to protect the interests of beneficiaries who are not yet entitled in possession.[1]

Adverse possession by a trustee or beneficiary of land held in trust

33.12   Neither a trustee nor a beneficiary is entitled to apply to be registered as proprietor on the basis of adverse possession, or to resist proceedings for possession under the provisions in the LRA 2002. Neither is an adverse possession for the purposes of the definition of adverse possession contained in the Act.[2]

CROWN FORESHORE

33.13   It was explained in Chapter 6[3] that the LRA 2002 makes provision by which the Crown can grant itself a fee simple out of land held in demesne in order to register it. Most of the foreshore is held by the Crown in demesne, and it is anticipated that much of this land will be registered to protect it from adverse possession by squatters. Such adverse possession is common, as, for example, where an owner of land adjoining the foreshore builds a jetty, slipway or pipe across the foreshore out into the sea.

33.14   Under the LA 1980, the limitation period for the recovery of the foreshore by the Crown is 60 years or, where land has ceased to be foreshore but remains in the ownership of the Crown, either 60 years from the date of accrual of the cause of action, or 30 years from the date on which the land ceased to be foreshore, whichever period expires first.[4] The extended limitation period reflects the difficulty that the Crown faces in monitoring the large areas of the foreshore that it holds. The LRA 2002 follows this approach. It provides that, where a person is in adverse possession of an estate in land, the estate belongs to the Crown or one of the Royal Duchies,[5] and the land consists of foreshore, a squatter must be in adverse possession for 60 years before he may apply to be registered as the proprietor of a registered estate.[6]

---

[1]   The policy of the LRA 2002 was criticised in Parliament by Lord Goodhart, who considered that such protection was no longer needed. If the trustees failed to oppose a squatter's application to be registered, the beneficiaries could sue the trustees for breach of trust. However, a claim for breach of trust is not a substitute for the land formerly held in trust.

[2]   This follows from the LRA 2002, Sch 6, para 11(1), and is similar in effect to LA 1980, s 21(1)(b) and Sch 1, para 9.

[3]   See para **6.1**.

[4]   LA 1980, Sch 1, Part 2, para 11.

[5]   That is, Cornwall or Lancaster.

[6]   LRA 2002, Sch 6, para 13(1).

33.15   For these purposes, land is to be treated as foreshore if it has been foreshore at any time in the previous 10 years.[1] 'Foreshore' means the shore and bed of the sea and of any tidal water, below the line of the medium high tide between the spring and neap tides.[2]

33.16   The procedure for making an application for registration set out in Chapter 30 must be followed on an application for registration by a person in adverse possession of foreshore. The applicant must, however, provide evidence of a period of adverse possession of not less than 60 years.[3]

TRANSITIONAL PROVISIONS

33.17   Pursuant to the power to bring the provisions of the LRA 2002 into force by order, and at different dates,[4] the 'boundary dispute' provisions of Sch 6, paras 5(4) and (5)[5] are to come into force on 13 October 2004, one year after the rest of Sch 6.[6] This gives registered proprietors one year's grace either to take proceedings for possession against, or regularise the position of, any squatter who might otherwise be able to take advantage of the exceptional condition in Sch 6, para 5(4) of the Act.[7]

33.18   The LRA 2002 also preserves the rights of those who are entitled to be registered prior to the coming into force of the Act. Where a registered proprietor held his estate on trust for a squatter under s 75 of the LRA 1925 immediately before the LRA 2002 came into force,[8] the squatter is entitled to be registered and that entitlement will subsist indefinitely against the registered proprietor holding on trust.[9] As that entitlement will be a proprietary right,[10] the squatter will be able to protect it against third parties as an overriding interest, provided that he is in actual occupation and none of the exceptions in LRA 2002, Sch 3, para 2, are applicable.[11] Under the transitional provisions, for a period of 3 years from 13 October 2003, this right to be registered will operate as an overriding interest regardless of occupation.[12] The squatter will also be able to rely on this right to be registered as a defence to any possession proceedings.[13]

---

[1]   LRA 2002, Sch 6, para 13(2).
[2]   Ibid, Sch 6, para 13(3).
[3]   LRR 2003, r 188(1)(a)(i).
[4]   LRA 2002, s 136(2).
[5]   See paras **30.42–30.48**.
[6]   Land Registration Act 2002 (Commencement No 4) Order 2003, art 2(2). Cf paras **1.3**, **30.48**.
[7]   See (2001) Law Com No 271, paras 14.102–14.103.
[8]   Such trusts are abolished by the repeal without replication of LRA 1925, s 75: see para **30.62**.
[9]   LRA 2002, Sch 12, para 18(1).
[10]   See paras **30.61–30.62**.
[11]   LRA 2002, Sch 3, para 2: see paras **11.5**, **11.7**, **11.8**.
[12]   Ibid, Sch 12, para 11.
[13]   Ibid, Sch 12, para 18(2).

For a period of 2 years from 13 October 2003 an adverse possessor of unregistered land claiming to be the owner of a registrable legal estate in land, is able to lodge a caution against first registration.[1] From 13 October 2005, any such caution will cease to have effect and the squatter will be expected to protect his interest by substantive registration.[2]

[1]   LRA 2002, s 15(3) and Sch 12, para 14(1).
[2]   See para **5.5**.

PART 7

ADJUDICATION AND OFFENCES

THE MAIN CHANGES AT A GLANCE

Part 11 of the LRA 2002 contains the judicial provisions applicable to adjudication.[1] The offences created by the Act are found in Part 12.[2]

The main changes made by the LRA 2002 are as follows.

– It creates a new office of Adjudicator to HM Land Registry, which is wholly independent of HM Land Registry.
– It permits a person to apply directly to the Adjudicator to rectify or set aside conveyancing documents, so saving the need for some references to court.
– It creates three new offences relating to registration, which reflect the changes that will come about with the introduction of electronic conveyancing.

The Adjudicator to HM Land Registry (Practice and Procedure) Rules 2003 govern the practice and procedure to be followed with respect to proceedings before the Adjudicator.[3] These Rules also include rules about directions made by the Adjudicator to commence proceedings in court under LRA 2002, s 110(1).

---

[1]   See (2001) Law Com No 271, Part XVI.
[2]   Ibid.
[3]   SI 2003/2171. See paras **34.15** et seq.

CHAPTER 34

ADJUDICATION

THE NEW APPROACH TO ADJUDICATION

34.1 The Adjudicator is to determine objections that are made to any application to the registrar that cannot be resolved by agreement between the parties; a function that was performed by the Solicitor to the Land Registry under the LRA 1925. As the Solicitor to the Land Registry is the senior lawyer within the Land Registry, the new office of Adjudicator has been created as a matter of principle. This is to avoid any perception of partiality in circumstances where, for example, a dispute between parties involves consideration of decisions made by Land Registry officials.[1]

34.2 The Adjudicator is under the supervision of the Council on Tribunals[2] and, as a consequence, has to comply with the requirements of the Tribunals and Inquiries Act 1992.[3]

34.3 The new procedure relates to disputes arising out of objections made on or after 13 October 2003, where there is no other objection pending that was made before that date[4]. Previously, the determinations by the Solicitor to HM Land Registry provided an inexpensive, speedy and informal means of dealing with disputes that arose out of applications to the Registry, without the need to have recourse to court proceedings. It is intended that dispute resolution by the Adjudicator should fulfil the same function. Indeed, there are provisions of the Act that are specifically intended to enable persons with claims to registered land to take advantage of the procedure before the Adjudicator, rather than compelling them to have recourse to the courts.[5]

---

[1]   See Art 6.1 of the European Convention on Human Rights, which provides that, 'In the determination of his civil rights and obligations ... everyone is entitled to a fair and public hearing within a reasonable time by an independent and impartial tribunal established by law'.

[2]   LRA 2002, Sch 9, para 8. The Solicitor to HM Land Registry is presently not under such supervision.

[3]   These requirements include the giving of reasons for the decision, if requested, under s 10 of that Act.

[4]   The matter will still be governed by the LRA 1925, the Land Registration (Hearings Procedure) Rules 2000 and the Land Registration (Conduct of Business) Regulations 2000 if the objection was made before 13 October 2003; or there is an earlier objection that was made before that date; or the objection relates to an application to warn off a caution where notice of the application was issued to the cautioner before that date: Land Registry Practice Guide, Objections and Disputes, PG 37, para 2.

[5]   See, eg, in relation to adverse possession, LRA 2002, Sch 6, para 5(2), (3); see also paras **30.37–30.41**.

THE POWERS OF THE REGISTRAR

34.4   The powers of the registrar to make determinations are defined both negatively (by conferring jurisdiction on the Adjudicator) and positively (by making express provision for certain specific functions to be carried out by the registrar). First, the general right for anyone to object to an application[1] to the registrar has already been explained.[2] The registrar must notify the applicant of any objection to an application and may not determine the application until the application has been disposed of.[3] Where the registrar is satisfied that the application is not groundless[4] and it is not possible to dispose of the objection by agreement, the registrar *must* refer the matter to the Adjudicator for resolution. He cannot deal with it himself.[5] The LRRAR 2003 govern the process by which disputed applications to the registrar will be referred to the Adjudicator[6].

34.5   Secondly, subject to the provisions relating to disputed applications, the registrar will, however, determine many matters, whether they arise on application or otherwise. Examples given by the Law Commission[7] include where the registrar:

–   examines the title of an applicant for first registration;[8] or
–   exercises his powers to alter the register so as to bring it up to date or to remove a spent entry.[9]

34.6   In any proceedings before him, the registrar is given specific powers by the Act.

34.7   First, he may require a person[10] to produce a document for the purposes of those proceedings.[11] He may only exercise this power if he receives from a person who is party to proceedings before him a request that he should require a document holder to produce a document for the purposes of those proceedings.[12] That request must be made in Form PRD1.[13] The LRR 2003 lay down a procedure for notifying the document holder,[14] and

---

1   Cf LRA 2002, s 132(3)(c).
2   Ibid, s 73; see also paras **20.29–20.32**.
3   Ibid, s 73(5).
4   See ibid, s 73(6).
5   Ibid, s 73(7).
6   SI 2003/2114. See also Land Registry Practice Guide, Objections and Disputes, PG37.
7   (2001) Law Com No 271, para 16.11.
8   Cf LRA 2002, s 14(b).
9   Ibid, Sch 4, para 5(b).
10   The 'document holder': LRR 2003, r 201(9).
11   LRA 2002, s 75(1). The power is subject to rules: s 75(2).
12   LRR 2003, r 201(1).
13   There is power under LRR 2003, r 201(2)(b) and Sch 2, as yet to be exercised, for the registrar to issue a notice which would allow for delivery of such applications by electronic means.
14   LRR 2003, r 201(3), (4).

giving him the opportunity to object to the request by delivering a written response.[1] The registrar must then determine the matter on the basis of the request and any response to it, and if he is not aware of any valid ground entitling the document holder to withhold the document may require its production, by serving a notice in Form PRD2.[2] The person requesting the document may be required to pay the reasonable costs incurred by the document holder in complying with the request.[3]

34.8   Secondly, the registrar may make orders about costs in relation to those proceedings.[4]

34.9   In each case, the registrar's requirement or order is enforceable as an order of the court,[5] and a person who is aggrieved by the registrar's requirement or order has a right to appeal to a county court which may make any order which appears appropriate.[6] With the exception of these specific matters, any other challenge to a decision of the registrar, of whatever kind, must be by way of an application for judicial review.[7]

THE OFFICE OF ADJUDICATOR

34.10   The Adjudicator is to be appointed by the Lord Chancellor.[8] To be qualified for appointment as Adjudicator, a person must have a 10-year general qualification as defined in s 71 of the Courts and Legal Services Act 1990 (CLSA 1990).[9] The LRA 2002 contains provisions about the resignation and removal from office of the Adjudicator, for his remuneration, the payment of his pension and (in special circumstances) compensation.[10] He is also disqualified from serving as a Member of Parliament or as a Member of the Northern Ireland Assembly.[11]

34.11   Under the LRA 2002, the Adjudicator may appoint such staff as he thinks fit.[12] Given the likely volume of work that will fall on the Adjudicator,

---

[1]   LRR 2003, r 201(5), (6).

[2]   Ibid, r 201(7).

[3]   Ibid, r 201(8).

[4]   LRA 2002, s 76(1). The power is subject to rules: see s 76(2), (3) and LRR 2003 r 202. The Land Registry Practice Guide, Costs, PG38, para 2, contains guidance as to the basis upon which an order for costs will be made and the procedure that will be followed.

[5]   LRA 2002, ss 75(3), 76(4).

[6]   Ibid, ss 75(4), 76(5).

[7]   Cf *Quigly v Chief Land Registrar* [1993] 1 WLR 1435 at 1438.

[8]   LRA 2002, s 107(1).

[9]   Ibid, s 107(2). Under CLSA 1990, s 71(3)(c) a person will have such a general qualification if he has a right of audience in relation to any class of proceedings in any part of the Supreme Court, or in all proceedings in county courts or magistrates' courts.

[10]   LRA 2002, Sch 9, paras 1, 2.

[11]   Ibid, Sch 9, para 9.

[12]   Ibid, Sch 9, para 3(1). The terms and conditions on which they are appointed must be approved by the Minister for the Civil Service: para 3(2).

the Act permits him to delegate any functions to those members of his staff as are authorised for that purpose.[1] However, in the case of any functions which are not of an administrative character, such as the determination of cases, an authorised member of staff must, like the Adjudicator himself, have a 10-year general qualification within the meaning of s 71 of the CLSA 1990.[2] The Land Registration (Acting Adjudicator) Regulations 2003[3] make provision about the carrying out of functions during any vacancy in the office of Adjudicator.

THE JURISDICTION OF THE ADJUDICATOR

34.12   The Adjudicator has two principal functions.

(1)   The first is to determine matters referred to him by the registrar under s 73(7) of the LRA 2002 in circumstances where an objection to an application to the registrar cannot be disposed of by agreement between the parties.[4] The registrar may either refer the whole of the disputed application to the Adjudicator or, if only one or more issues are in contention between the parties, those specific issues.[5] The LRRAR 2003[6] set out the procedure that the registrar must follow when he is obliged to refer a matter to the Adjudicator.[7]

(2)   The second is to determine appeals under para 4 of Sch 5 by a person – likely to be a solicitor or licensed conveyancer – who is aggrieved by a decision of the registrar with respect to entry into, or termination of, a network access agreement.[8]

The second of these two matters is the only case under the LRA 2002 in which there is an appeal from a decision of the registrar to the Adjudicator. In any other case, if a person is dissatisfied with a decision of the registrar, he can only challenge it by an application for judicial review.[9]

34.13   In addition to the two matters mentioned in para **34.12**, the Adjudicator also has limited jurisdiction, on application, to make any order

---

[1]   LRA 2002, Sch 9, para 4(1).
[2]   Ibid, Sch 9, para 4(2).
[3]   SI 2003/2342, made pursuant to LRA 2002, Sch 9, para 5.
[4]   LRA 2002, s 108(1)(a). See Land Registry Practice Guide, Objections and Disputes, PG37, paras 3–6, for the process the Land Registry will follow in the run up to referring an objection to the Adjudicator. For the general right to object to an application under s 73, see para **20.29**.
[5]   See (2001) Law Com No 271, para 16.6.
[6]   SI 2003/2114.
[7]   In particular, the registrar must prepare a case summary and give each party an opportunity to comment upon it before sending it to the Adjudicator. He must then send the Adjudicator a written notice of referral, together with the case summary and a copy of the documents referred to in it.
[8]   LRA 2002, s 108(1)(b). In other words, the situation will be where the registrar either refuses to enter into a network access agreement with a solicitor or licensed conveyancer (or is prepared to do so only on terms that the solicitor or licensed conveyancer considers unacceptable) or terminates an existing agreement. See further, LRA 2002, Sch 5; see also paras **27.19–27.21**.
[9]   Cf para **34.9**.

which the High Court could make for the rectification or setting aside of a document which falls into any one of three categories.

(1)   The first is an instrument which is used to make either a registrable disposition or a disposition that creates an interest which may be the subject of a notice in the register.[1] Examples of the instruments that could be rectified would therefore include a transfer or grant of a legal estate and an instrument creating a restrictive covenant.[2]

(2)   The second is a contract to make a disposition of the kind mentioned in (1).[3]

(3)   The third is an instrument that is used to make a transfer of an interest which is the subject of a notice in the register.[4] An example would be a transfer of a *profit à prendre* in gross, such as fishing or shooting rights, that was noted on the register but not registered with its own title, and where there was an error in that conveyance.[5]

34.14   This power is new. Under the present law, the registrar has no power to rectify or set aside a document.[6] On occasions, he has had to refer a matter to the High Court so that an instrument could be rectified. This is expensive for the party involved and inevitably delays the relevant application before the registrar. The new power given by the Act to the Adjudicator, although restricted in its scope,[7] overcomes these difficulties. Application for rectification by the Adjudicator is made directly to him: it is not made to the registrar.[8] The general law about the effect of an order of the High Court for the rectification or setting aside of a document applies to any order made by the Adjudicator.[9] This means, for example, that the rectification has retrospective effect, and the instrument is thereafter to be read as if it had been drafted in its rectified form.[10]

THE PROCEDURE BEFORE THE ADJUDICATOR

General

34.15   The Adjudicator may either determine matters referred to him on the papers submitted to him by the parties or may hold a hearing.[11] Hearings

---

[1]   LRA 2002, s 108(2)(a), (3).
[2]   See (2001) Law Com No 271, para 16.8.
[3]   LRA 2002, s 108(2)(b).
[4]   Ibid, s 108(2)(c).
[5]   See (2001) Law Com No 271, para 16.8.
[6]   Ibid, para 16.9.
[7]   It only applies to conveyancing documents.
[8]   This follows from LRA 2002, s 108(2). The relevant practice and procedure is contained in Part 3 of APPR 2003.
[9]   Ibid, s 108(4).
[10] See (2001) Law Com No 271, para 16.10.
[11] As with determinations by the Solicitor to HM Land Registry under the present law and practice, a hearing will not be necessary in all cases. See (2001) Law Com No 271, para 16.15.

before the Adjudicator are to be held in public, except where the Adjudicator is satisfied that exclusion of the public is just and reasonable.[1] The APPR 2003 regulate the practice and procedure to be followed and in relation to matters incidental to or consequential upon such proceedings.[2] The procedural rules as to the preparation by each party of his statement of case are demanding and the timetable for compliance with the requirements is short: see in particular, APPR 2003, rr 12–14 (statements of case) and 47 (documents). The Lord Chancellor may prescribe fees to be paid in respect of hearings before the Adjudicator and make provisions about their payment.[3] Any requirement made of a party by the Adjudicator is enforceable as an order of the court.[4]

Proceedings on a reference under s 73(7) of the LRA 2002

34.16   The LRA 2002 makes further provision in relation to proceedings before the Adjudicator on a reference under s 73(7).

34.17   First, the Adjudicator may, instead of deciding a matter himself, direct a party to the proceedings to commence proceedings within a specified time within the High Court or the county court for the purpose of obtaining the court's decision on the matter.[5] This may be appropriate where:

- the application raises a difficult legal point;
- there is a complex factual dispute between the parties;
- there are other issues between the parties before the court; or
- the court has powers which are not available to the Adjudicator, such as the power to award damages.[6]

The Adjudicator may refer the whole of the proceedings to the court or merely one or more specific issues.

34.18   Secondly, the APPR 2003 contain rules about the referral of matters to the court.[7] Where the Adjudicator intends to direct a party to commence court proceedings, the parties may make representations or objections as to:

- whether the Adjudicator should make such a direction;
- which party should be directed to commence court proceedings;

---

[1]   LRA 2002, s 109(1).
[2]   The LRA 2002 empowered the Lord Chancellor to make rules for this purpose, ss 109(2), (3), 114.
[3]   Ibid, s 113.
[4]   Ibid, s 112.
[5]   Ibid, s 110(1).
[6]   For example, under LRA 2002, s 77 (duty to act reasonably); see also para **20.32**.
[7]   Made by the Lord Chancellor under LRA 2002, s 110(2).

– the time within which court proceedings should be commenced; and
– the questions the court should determine.[1]

The APPR 2003 also make provision about the adjournment of the proceedings before the Adjudicator pending the court's decision[2], and the powers of the Adjudicator if a party fails to make the directed application to the court[3].

34.19 Thirdly, as has been explained above, the issues referred to the Adjudicator may only be in respect of certain specific issues raised on an application to the registrar and not the whole of that application.[4] APPR 2003 make provision as to what the Adjudicator may do in such a case.[5] The Rules make provision enabling the Adjudicator to determine or give directions about the determination of:

– the application to which the reference relates; or
– such other present or future application to the registrar as the rules may provide.[6]

The reason for the second of these two points is that it will enable the Adjudicator to give a ruling or general directions on a point that could be applied in other unconnected applications, whether pending or which might arise at some future date.[7]

34.20 Fourthly, one technical matter that may arise on an application under s 73(7) of the LRA 2002 has already been mentioned.[8] Where a squatter has applied to be registered as proprietor after more than 10 years' adverse possession, he may be registered as proprietor in three limited circumstances even if a counter-notice is served by the registered proprietor (or by some other person entitled to do so).[9] One of these exceptional cases is where it would be unconscionable, because of an equity arising by estoppel, for a registered proprietor to seek to dispossess the applicant.[10] If, however, on a reference in such a case where an equity by estoppel is alleged, the Adjudicator determines that it would be unconscionable for the registered proprietor to seek to dispossess the applicant, but the circumstances are not such that the

1   APPR 2003, r 6. The Rules also contain provision for notification to the Adjudicator of court proceedings following a direction to commence court proceedings: r 7.
2   Ibid, rr 8 and 9: the Adjudicator has power to adjourn the whole or part of the matter.
3   Ibid, r 55.
4   See para **34.12**.
5   Made under the power in LRA 2002, s 110(3).
6   APPR 2003, r 51.
7   See (2001) Law Com No 271, para 16.18.
8   See paras **30.37–30.40**.
9   LRA 2002, Sch 6, para 5.
10   Ibid, Sch 6, para 5(2).

applicant ought to be registered as proprietor, the Adjudicator has jurisdiction to determine how that equity should be satisfied.[1] He may for that purpose make any order that the High Court could make in the exercise of its equitable jurisdiction.[2]

APPEALS FROM THE ADJUDICATOR

34.21   If a party is aggrieved by a decision of the Adjudicator in relation to an application made under s 73(7), that party has a right of appeal to the High Court on a point of fact or law.[3]

34.22   If a party is aggrieved by a decision of the Adjudicator on an appeal under para 4 of Sch 5 to the LRA 2002, only an appeal to the High Court on a point of law is possible, as the appeal is a second appeal.[4]

34.23   The LRA 2002 makes special provision for one case where a party appeals to the High Court from a decision of the Adjudicator relating to an application by a squatter to be registered under para 1 of Sch 6 to the Act. There may be cases where the Court determines that it would be unconscionable because of an equity by estoppel for the registered proprietor to seek to dispossess the applicant.[5] If, however, it also decides that the circumstances are not such that the applicant ought to be registered as proprietor, it must then determine how best to satisfy the applicant's equity.[6]

34.24   Part 6 of APPR 2003 contains provisions in relation to appeals to the High Court from decisions by the Adjudicator and includes provisions as to the staying by the Adjudicator of the implementation of his decision pending outcome of an appeal.

---

[1]   LRA 2002, s 110(4)(a).

[2]   Ibid, s 110(4)(b).

[3]   Ibid, s 111(1). There is no appeal to the county court. The right of appeal conferred by s 111(1) is subject to any rules of court that may be made under ATJA 1999, s 54, by which any right of appeal may only be exercised with permission. Although CPR 1998, Part 52 limits second appeals, there are at present no such rules requiring leave for a first appeal.

[4]   Ibid, s 111(2).

[5]   Cf para **34.20**.

[6]   LRA 2002, s 111(3).

CHAPTER 35

OFFENCES

INTRODUCTION

35.1   Under the LRA 1925, there were three offences, although these have seldom been charged. The first related to the suppression of deeds and evidence, the second dealt with the fraudulent procurement of changes to the register, and the third with disobedience to an order of the registrar.[1] The LRA 2002 replaces the first two of these offences with three new ones. The third offence under the 1925 Act is not replicated because any requirement of the registrar or Adjudicator will be enforceable as an order of the court.[2] The three offences under the Act are as follows.

SUPPRESSION OF INFORMATION

35.2   It is an offence for a person to suppress information in the course of proceedings relating to registration if he does so with the intention either of concealing a person's right or claim or of substantiating a false claim.[3] For these purposes 'proceedings' will include both 'judicial' proceedings before the Adjudicator and any procedure relating to an application before the registrar. On conviction on indictment, a person will be liable to imprisonment for a term not exceeding 2 years or to an unlimited fine.[4] On summary conviction, a person is liable to imprisonment for a term not exceeding 6 months or to a fine not exceeding the statutory maximum, or to both.[5]

IMPROPER ALTERATION OF THE REGISTERS

35.3   The two new offences described in paras **35.5** and **35.6** relate to improper alteration of the registers. They have been enacted against the background of the introduction of e-conveyancing. When that happens, persons other than the registrar will be given authority to change the registers[6]

---

[1]   See LRA 1925, ss 115, 116, 117, 128(3).
[2]   See paras **34.9**, **34.15**. Non-compliance with an order of the registrar or Adjudicator would, therefore, be punishable as contempt.
[3]   LRA 2002, s 123(1).
[4]   Ibid, s 123(2)(a).
[5]   Ibid, s 123(2)(b). For the maximum fine that can be imposed on summary conviction, see Magistrates' Courts Act 1980 (MCA 1980), s 32(2), (9).
[6]   See para **26.2**.

and there is, therefore, an increased risk that an improper alteration might be made.

35.4   First, it is an offence if a person dishonestly induces another either:

(a)   to change the register of title or the cautions register; or

(b)   to authorise such a change.[1]

The reference to changing the register includes changing a document referred to in it.[2] The offence in (a) is very much like the former offence of fraudulently procuring a change to the register.[3] It will be committed where, for example, a person intentionally makes a false statement in an application. The offence in (b) might be committed where, after the introduction of e-conveyancing, a person dishonestly persuades the Registry to approve in advance a change to the register that he then makes.[4]

35.5   Secondly, it is an offence for a person intentionally or recklessly to make an unauthorised change in the register of title or cautions register.[5] This offence can be committed in either of two ways. The first is where the person making the change does so knowing that he is not entitled to do so, or is reckless as to that fact. The second is where a person, having authority to make specific changes to the register intentionally or recklessly makes some other unauthorised alteration.

35.6   A person guilty of an offence relating to improper alteration of the register is liable, on conviction on indictment, to imprisonment for a term not exceeding 2 years or to a fine.[6] On summary conviction, a person is liable to imprisonment for a term not exceeding 6 months or to a fine not exceeding the statutory maximum, or to both.[7]

PRIVILEGE AGAINST SELF-INCRIMINATION

35.7   In relation to the privilege against self-incrimination, the LRA 2002 replicates the position under the LRA 1925.[8] Insofar as it relates to offences under the Act, the privilege against self-incrimination does not entitle a person to refuse to answer any question or produce any document or thing in any

---

[1]   LRA 2002, s 124(1).

[2]   Ibid, s 124(4).

[3]   LRA 1925, s 116.

[4]   For the anticipated procedure in e-conveyancing, see paras **27.1–27.11**.

[5]   LRA 2002, s 124(2). Once again, the reference to a change in the register of title includes the changing of any document referred to in that register: s 124(4).

[6]   Ibid, s 124(3)(a).

[7]   Ibid, s 124(3)(b).

[8]   LRA 1925, s 119(2).

legal proceedings other than criminal proceedings.[1] No evidence obtained in such a way under the Act will be admissible in any criminal proceedings under the Act either against the person from whom it was obtained or his or her spouse.[2]

---

[1] LRA 2002, s 125(1).
[2] Ibid, s 125(2).

PART 8

THE LAND REGISTRY

THE MAIN CHANGES AT A GLANCE

This Part is concerned with the provisions of Part 10 of and Sch 7 to the LRA 2002 that concern HM Land Registry.[1] The changes that are made by these parts of the Act to the workings of the Land Registry are not likely to impinge much on practitioners. However, as has been explained,[2] there will be dramatic changes to the way in which conveyancing is conducted once e-conveyancing has been introduced. It will be the provisions governing e-conveyancing, rather than the specific provisions of the LRA 2002 on the Land Registry, that will define the radically different relationship that will exist between conveyancing practitioners and the Registry.

One other change that will affect practitioners in their dealings with the Registry has also been explained. Disputes arising out of applications to the Registry are now referred for resolution by the new independent Adjudicator to HM Land Registry.[3] The post of Solicitor to HM Land Registry disappeared when the LRA 2002 came into force.[4]

The main changes made by the LRA 2002 are as follows.

— The Registry is given express powers to publish information about land in England and Wales, to provide or arrange for the provision of consultancy or advisory services about the registration of land, and to form, acquire or invest in a company for a number of specified purposes.

— The power to determine fees is placed on a much more flexible basis and need not be fixed by reference to the value of the land registered.

---

[1]   For the provisions on indemnity found in Sch 8 to the Act, see Chapter 23.

[2]   See Chapter 26.

[3]   See para **34.12**.

[4]   The Solicitor to HM Land Registry was a registrar who was nominated by the Chief Land Registrar to deal with the matters specified in the Schedules to the Land Registration (Conduct of Business) Regulations 2000, SI 2000/2212. The matters specified were the judicial or quasi-judicial functions that were vested in the Chief Land Registrar under LRA 1925 and LRR 1925. Prior to the CLSA 1990, the Chief Land Registrar was required to be a barrister or solicitor of 10 years' standing.

CHAPTER 36

THE LAND REGISTRY

THE LAND REGISTRY AND ITS STAFF

36.1   The LRA 2002 makes provision for the continuance of the Land Registry.[1] It consists of the Chief Land Registrar as its head and the staff appointed by him.[2] The Lord Chancellor must appoint the Chief Land Registrar.[3] No member of the Land Registry is liable for any act or omission in the discharge, actual or purported, of any function relating to land registration, unless it is shown that the act or omission was in bad faith.[4] However, a person who suffers loss as a result of any erroneous act or omission by any member of the Registry will normally be able to claim indemnity from the Chief Land Registrar under the provisions of Sch 8 to the LRA 2002 that have already been explained.[5]

THE CONDUCT OF BUSINESS

36.2   The functions conferred on the Chief Land Registrar by the LRA 2002 and the LRR 2003 may be carried out by any member of the Land Registry who is authorised for the purpose by the Chief Land Registrar.[6] As under the LRA 1925,[7] the Chief Land Registrar is given power to prepare and publish such forms and directions as he considers necessary or desirable for facilitating the conduct of the business of registration under the Act.[8]

---

[1]   LRA 2002, s 99(1). For the equivalent provision under the previous law, see LRA 1925, s 126(1).

[2]   Ibid, s 99(2). The Chief Land Registrar may appoint such staff as he thinks fit: Sch 7, para 3(1). However, the terms and conditions on which they are appointed must be approved by the Minister for the Civil Service: para 3(2). Under LRA 1925, s 126(1), the appointment of the staff of the Land Registry is a matter for the Lord Chancellor rather than for the Chief Land Registrar.

[3]   LRA 2002, s 99(3). It was provided by TPO1, art 2, that the person holding the office of Chief Land Registrar immediately before commencement should continue to be the Chief Land Registrar notwithstanding that he had not been appointed under s 99(3) of the Act. The Act contains provisions about the resignation and removal from office of the Chief Land Registrar (Sch 7, para 1), for his remuneration, the payment of his pension and (in special circumstances) compensation (Sch 7, para 2). The Chief Land Registrar is, for the first time, disqualified from serving as a Member of Parliament or as a Member of the Northern Ireland Assembly (Sch 7, para 7).

[4]   LRA 2002, Sch 7, para 4. For the present provision, see LRA 1925, s 131.

[5]   See Chapter 23

[6]   LRA 2002, s 100(1). The Lord Chancellor has made regulations for the carrying out of the registrar's functions during any vacancy in that office pursuant to LRA 2002, s 100(2): see the Land Registration (Acting Chief Land Registrar) Regulations 2003.

[7]   LRA 1925, s 127.

[8]   LRA 2002, s 100(4). For the present directions, see Ruoff & Roper, *Registered Conveyancing*, App F.

36.3   The LRA 2002, unlike the LRA 1925,[1] does not make express provision for district land registries. However, it is clear that district registries will continue under the Act. Thus the Act specifically empowers the Lord Chancellor by order to designate a particular office of the Land Registry as the proper office for the receipt of applications or a specified description of application.[2] Pursuant to this power, the Land Registration (Proper Office) Order 2003,[3] designates particular offices of the Land Registry as the proper office for receipt of any application to the registrar except applications delivered to the registrar in accordance with a written arrangement, or under the provisions of any relevant notice given under Sch 2 to the Act.[4]

36.4   There is a statutory obligation on the Chief Land Registrar to make an Annual Report on the business of land registration to the Lord Chancellor[5] and to publish it in such manner as he thinks fit.[6] The Lord Chancellor must lay copies of the Annual Report before Parliament.[7]

36.5   The days upon which the Land Registry is open to the public are 'business days' for the purposes of LRR 2003.[8] Those rules provide that the Land Registry shall be open daily except on Saturdays, Sundays, Christmas Day, any bank holiday,[9] or any other day appointed by the Lord Chancellor.[10] There is provision in LRR 2003 which would permit the opening of the Land Registry to the public on Saturdays.[11]

MISCELLANEOUS POWERS

36.6   The LRA 2002 confers certain miscellaneous powers on the registrar. First, he is given express authority to publish information about land in

---

There have been directions on a number of matters, including the telephone office copy service and Direct Access.

[1]   See LRA 1925, s 132.

[2]   LRA 2002, s 100(3). There are a number of situations in which it might be appropriate to exercise this power. For example, when e-conveyancing is introduced, certain district registries might be designated for 24-hour working to ensure that transactions could be simultaneously registered at whatever time they were concluded: cf para **27.10**.

[3]   SI 2003/2040.

[4]   See also Land Registry Practice Guide, Areas Served by Land Registry Offices, PG 51, for areas served by Land Registry Offices and Land Registry Practice Guide, Applications affecting One or More Land Registry Office, PG 32, where the application affects one or more Land Registry Office.

[5]   LRA 2002, s 101(1).

[6]   Ibid, s 101(2). Thus the registrar can and does publish the report on the internet.

[7]   Ibid, s 101(3).

[8]   LRR 2002, r 217(1).

[9]   Declared by proclamation under Banking and Financial Dealings Act 1971, s 1.

[10]   LRR 2003, r 216.

[11]   If the registrar is satisfied that adequate arrangements have been made or will be in place for opening the land registry to the public on Saturdays, he may give at least 8 weeks' notice to that effect: LRR 2003, r 216(2), (4). In the event that such notice is given, the time-limit prescribed in business days in certain other specified rules will be extended: r 216(3)–(5).

England and Wales if it appears to him to be information in which there is legitimate public interest.[1]

36.7 Secondly, the LRA 2002 makes express provision for the registrar to provide or arrange for the provision of consultancy or advisory services about the registration of land, whether in England and Wales or elsewhere.[2]

36.8 Thirdly, the LRA 2002 makes provision for the registrar to form or participate in the formation of a company, or to purchase or invest in a company.[3] The registrar may do this in relation to the provision of:

– information about the history of a registered title under s 69 of the LRA 2002;[4]
– an electronic communications network under s 92 of the LRA 2002;[5]
– a system of electronic settlement under s 94 of the LRA 2002;[6]
– consultancy or advisory services under s 105 of the LRA 2002;[7] or
– education and training in relation to the use of a land registry network under Sch 5, para 10 to the LRA 2002.[8]

36.9 While such powers were probably not strictly necessary because the registrar has them by necessary implication,[9] the provision puts the matter beyond doubt and is intended to provide reassurance to those who might be interested in joint ventures with the Land Registry.[10]

FEE ORDERS

36.10 At present, many fees payable for registration are calculated on an *ad valorem* basis as prescribed by the LRA 1925.[11] The provisions of the LRA 2002 on fees are much simpler. They provide that the Lord Chancellor, with

---

1 LRA 2002, s 104. The registrar already publishes information on property prices. As more commercial leases become registrable, it is possible that information about trends in rents and the average length of registrable leases might be made available.
2 LRA 2002, s 105(1). The terms upon which such services are provided, including payment, will be such as the registrar thinks fit: s 105(2). Charges will not be prescribed by fee order as will those that apply to fees in relation to dealings with land: s 102(a).
3 LRA 2002, s 106(1). For the definition of 'company' and 'invest', see s 106(2).
4 See para **18.42**.
5 See para **27.12**.
6 See para **28.5**.
7 See para **36.7**.
8 See para **27.14**.
9 The LRA 2002 makes it clear that s 106 is without prejudice to any powers of the registrar otherwise than by virtue of that section: s 106(3).
10 These powers were a late addition to the LRA 2002, having been introduced by way of government amendment at Third Reading in the House of Commons: see *Hansard* (HC), 11 February 2002, vol 380, col 23. They were added to give effect to recommendations contained in the Quinquennial Review of the Land Registry of June 2001, para 14.4.
11 LRA 1925, s 145.

the advice and assistance of the Rules Committee[1] and the consent of the Treasury, may by order[2] prescribe fees to be paid in respect of dealings with the Land Registry and make provision about the payment of prescribed fees.[3] The power to make such orders carries with it a power to make different provision for different cases.[4]

36.11   The LRFO 2003[5] provides for the payment of scale fees on applications for first registration, applications for registration of a lease by an original lessee, transfers of registered estates for monetary consideration and otherwise than for monetary consideration and on charges of registered estates.[6] Special provision is made with regard to large area applications,[7] large-scale applications[8] and low value applications.[9] LRFO 2003 also prescribes the applicable valuation methodology.[10] Those applications which attract a fixed fee,[11] or are the subject of an exemption[12] are also specified. General and administrative provisions relating to fees are also set out.

---

[1]   For the Rules Committee, see LRA 2002, s 127; see also para **1.6**.

[2]   The power to make orders is exercisable by statutory instrument: see LRA 2002, s 128(2).

[3]   LRA 2002, s 102. The power to prescribe fees does not apply in two cases: see s 102(a). The first is where historical information about a title is provided not by the registrar but by a person authorised by him under s 69(3). The second, which has been mentioned at para **36.7**, is where the registrar provides or arranges for the provision of consultancy or advisory services.

[4]   LRA 2002, s 128(1).

[5]   SI 2003/2092.

[6]   LRFO 2003, arts 2–5.

[7]   See Land Registry Practice Guide, Large Scale Applications (Calculation of Fees), PG 33, for detailed guidance as to the making of such applications and the fees involved.

[8]   Ibid.

[9]   LRFO 2003, art 6.

[10]   Articles 7, 8.

[11]   Article 9 and Sch 3.

[12]   Article 10 and Sch 4.

APPENDIX 1

STATUTORY MATERIALS

Land Registration Act 2002   417

Land Registration Rules 2003, SI 2003/1417   499

Land Registration (Referral to the Adjudicator to HM Land Registry)
    Rules 2003, SI 2003/2114   600

Adjudicator to Her Majesty's Land Registry (Practice and Procedure)
    Rules 2003, SI 2003/2171   602

Land Registration Act 2002 (Transitional Provisions) Order 2003,
    SI 2003/1953   624

Land Registration (Proper Office) Order 2003, SI 2003/2040   636

Land Registration Fee Order 2003, SI 2003/2092   640

Land Registration (Acting Chief Land Registrar) Regulations 2003,
    SI 2003/2281   653

Land Registration (Acting Adjudicator) Regulations 2003,
    SI 2003/2342   654

LAND REGISTRATION ACT 2002

1¹ Register of title

(1) There is to continue to be a register of title kept by the registrar.

(2) Rules may make provision about how the register is to be kept and may, in particular, make provision about –
  (a) the information to be included in the register,
  (b) the form in which information included in the register is to be kept, and
  (c) the arrangement of that information.

2² Scope of title registration

This Act makes provision about the registration of title to –
  (a) unregistered legal estates which are interests of any of the following kinds –
    (i)   an estate in land,
    (ii)   a rentcharge,
    (iii) a franchise,
    (iv)   a profit a prendre in gross, and
    (v)   any other interest or charge which subsists for the benefit of, or is a charge on, an interest the title to which is registered; and
  (b) interests capable of subsisting at law which are created by a disposition of an interest the title to which is registered.

PART 2
FIRST REGISTRATION OF TITLE

Chapter 1
First Registration

Voluntary registration

3³ When title may be registered

(1) This section applies to any unregistered legal estate which is an interest of any of the following kinds –
  (a) an estate in land,
  (b) a rentcharge,
  (c) a franchise, and
  (d) a profit a prendre in gross.

---

1   Commencement: 13 October 2003 (Land Registration Act 2002 (Commencement No 4) Order 2003, SI 2003/1725).
2   Commencement: 13 October 2003 (Land Registration Act 2002 (Commencement No 4) Order 2003, SI 2003/1725).
3   Commencement: 13 October 2003 (Land Registration Act 2002 (Commencement No 4) Order 2003, SI 2003/1725).

(2) Subject to the following provisions, a person may apply to the registrar to be registered as the proprietor of an unregistered legal estate to which this section applies if –

    (a) the estate is vested in him, or

    (b) he is entitled to require the estate to be vested in him.

(3) Subject to subsection (4), an application under subsection (2) in respect of a leasehold estate may only be made if the estate was granted for a term of which more than seven years are unexpired.

(4) In the case of an estate in land, subsection (3) does not apply if the right to possession under the lease is discontinuous.

(5) A person may not make an application under subsection (2)(a) in respect of a leasehold estate vested in him as a mortgagee where there is a subsisting right of redemption.

(6) A person may not make an application under subsection (2)(b) if his entitlement is as a person who has contracted to buy under a contract.

(7) If a person holds in the same right both –

    (a) a lease in possession, and

    (b) a lease to take effect in possession on, or within a month of, the end of the lease in possession,

then, to the extent that they relate to the same land, they are to be treated for the purposes of this section as creating one continuous term.

Compulsory registration

4[1] When title must be registered

(1) The requirement of registration applies on the occurrence of any of the following events –

    (a) the transfer of a qualifying estate –

        (i) for valuable or other consideration, by way of gift or in pursuance of an order of any court, or

        (ii) by means of an assent (including a vesting assent);

    (b) the transfer of an unregistered legal estate in land in circumstances where section 171A of the Housing Act 1985 applies (disposal by landlord which leads to a person no longer being a secure tenant);

    (c) the grant out of a qualifying estate of an estate in land –

        (i) for a term of years absolute of more than seven years from the date of the grant, and

        (ii) for valuable or other consideration, by way of gift or in pursuance of an order of any court;

    (d) the grant out of a qualifying estate of an estate in land for a term of years absolute to take effect in possession after the end of the period of three months beginning with the date of the grant;

    (e) the grant of a lease in pursuance of Part 5 of the Housing Act 1985 (the right to buy) out of an unregistered legal estate in land;

    (f) the grant of a lease out of an unregistered legal estate in land in such circumstances as are mentioned in paragraph (b);

    (g) the creation of a protected first legal mortgage of a qualifying estate.

---

[1]   Commencement: 13 October 2003 (Land Registration Act 2002 (Commencement No 4) Order 2003, SI 2003/1725).

(2) For the purposes of subsection (1), a qualifying estate is an unregistered legal estate which is –

    (a) a freehold estate in land, or

    (b) a leasehold estate in land for a term which, at the time of the transfer, grant or creation, has more than seven years to run.

(3) In subsection (1)(a), the reference to transfer does not include transfer by operation of law.

(4) Subsection (1)(a) does not apply to –

    (a) the assignment of a mortgage term, or

    (b) the assignment or surrender of a lease to the owner of the immediate reversion where the term is to merge in that reversion.

(5) Subsection (1)(c) does not apply to the grant of an estate to a person as a mortgagee.

(6) For the purposes of subsection (1)(a) and (c), if the estate transferred or granted has a negative value, it is to be regarded as transferred or granted for valuable or other consideration.

(7) In subsection (1)(a) and (c), references to transfer or grant by way of gift include transfer or grant for the purpose of –

    (a) constituting a trust under which the settlor does not retain the whole of the beneficial interest, or

    (b) uniting the bare legal title and the beneficial interest in property held under a trust under which the settlor did not, on constitution, retain the whole of the beneficial interest.

(8) For the purposes of subsection (1)(g) –

    (a) a legal mortgage is protected if it takes effect on its creation as a mortgage to be protected by the deposit of documents relating to the mortgaged estate, and

    (b) a first legal mortgage is one which, on its creation, ranks in priority ahead of any other mortgages then affecting the mortgaged estate.

(9) In this section –

    'land' does not include mines and minerals held apart from the surface;

    'vesting assent' has the same meaning as in the Settled Land Act 1925.

5[1] Power to extend section 4

(1) The Lord Chancellor may by order –

    (a) amend section 4 so as to add to the events on the occurrence of which the requirement of registration applies such relevant event as he may specify in the order, and

    (b) make such consequential amendments of any provision of, or having effect under, any Act as he thinks appropriate.

(2) For the purposes of subsection (1)(a), a relevant event is an event relating to an unregistered legal estate which is an interest of any of the following kinds –

    (a) an estate in land,

    (b) a rentcharge,

    (c) a franchise, and

    (d) a profit a prendre in gross.

---

[1]   Commencement: 13 October 2003 (Land Registration Act 2002 (Commencement No 4) Order 2003, SI 2003/1725).

(3) The power conferred by subsection (1) may not be exercised so as to require the title to an estate granted to a person as a mortgagee to be registered.

(4) Before making an order under this section the Lord Chancellor must consult such persons as he considers appropriate.

6[1] Duty to apply for registration of title

(1) If the requirement of registration applies, the responsible estate owner, or his successor in title, must, before the end of the period for registration, apply to the registrar to be registered as the proprietor of the registrable estate.

(2) If the requirement of registration applies because of section 4(1)(g) –
    (a) the registrable estate is the estate charged by the mortgage, and
    (b) the responsible estate owner is the owner of that estate.

(3) If the requirement of registration applies otherwise than because of section 4(1)(g) –
    (a) the registrable estate is the estate which is transferred or granted, and
    (b) the responsible estate owner is the transferee or grantee of that estate.

(4) The period for registration is 2 months beginning with the date on which the relevant event occurs, or such longer period as the registrar may provide under subsection (5).

(5) If on the application of any interested person the registrar is satisfied that there is good reason for doing so, he may by order provide that the period for registration ends on such later date as he may specify in the order.

(6) Rules may make provision enabling the mortgagee under any mortgage falling within section 4(1)(g) to require the estate charged by the mortgage to be registered whether or not the mortgagor consents.

7[2] Effect of non-compliance with section 6

(1) If the requirement of registration is not complied with, the transfer, grant or creation becomes void as regards the transfer, grant or creation of a legal estate.

(2) On the application of subsection (1) –
    (a) in a case falling within section 4(1)(a) or (b), the title to the legal estate reverts to the transferor who holds it on a bare trust for the transferee, and
    (b) in a case falling within section 4(1)(c) to (g), the grant or creation has effect as a contract made for valuable consideration to grant or create the legal estate concerned.

(3) If an order under section 6(5) is made in a case where subsection (1) has already applied, that application of the subsection is to be treated as not having occurred.

(4) The possibility of reverter under subsection (1) is to be disregarded for the purposes of determining whether a fee simple is a fee simple absolute.

---

[1]   Commencement: 13 October 2003 (Land Registration Act 2002 (Commencement No 4) Order 2003, SI 2003/1725).

[2]   Commencement: 13 October 2003 (Land Registration Act 2002 (Commencement No 4) Order 2003, SI 2003/1725).

8¹   Liability for making good void transfers etc

If a legal estate is retransferred, regranted or recreated because of a failure to comply with the requirement of registration, the transferee, grantee or, as the case may be, the mortgagor –

  (a) is liable to the other party for all the proper costs of and incidental to the retransfer, regrant or recreation of the legal estate, and

  (b) is liable to indemnify the other party in respect of any other liability reasonably incurred by him because of the failure to comply with the requirement of registration.

Classes of title

9²   Titles to freehold estates

(1) In the case of an application for registration under this Chapter of a freehold estate, the classes of title with which the applicant may be registered as proprietor are –

  (a) absolute title,

  (b) qualified title, and

  (c) possessory title;

and the following provisions deal with when each of the classes of title is available.

(2) A person may be registered with absolute title if the registrar is of the opinion that the person's title to the estate is such as a willing buyer could properly be advised by a competent professional adviser to accept.

(3) In applying subsection (2), the registrar may disregard the fact that a person's title appears to him to be open to objection if he is of the opinion that the defect will not cause the holding under the title to be disturbed.

(4) A person may be registered with qualified title if the registrar is of the opinion that the person's title to the estate has been established only for a limited period or subject to certain reservations which cannot be disregarded under subsection (3).

(5) A person may be registered with possessory title if the registrar is of the opinion –

  (a) that the person is in actual possession of the land, or in receipt of the rents and profits of the land, by virtue of the estate, and

  (b) that there is no other class of title with which he may be registered.

10³   Titles to leasehold estates

(1) In the case of an application for registration under this Chapter of a leasehold estate, the classes of title with which the applicant may be registered as proprietor are –

  (a) absolute title,

  (b) good leasehold title,

  (c) qualified title, and

  (d) possessory title;

and the following provisions deal with when each of the classes of title is available.

(2) A person may be registered with absolute title if –

  (a) the registrar is of the opinion that the person's title to the estate is such as a willing buyer could properly be advised by a competent professional adviser to accept, and

---

¹   Commencement: 13 October 2003 (Land Registration Act 2002 (Commencement No 4) Order 2003, SI 2003/1725).

²   Commencement: 13 October 2003 (Land Registration Act 2002 (Commencement No 4) Order 2003, SI 2003/1725).

³   Commencement: 13 October 2003 (Land Registration Act 2002 (Commencement No 4) Order 2003, SI 2003/1725).

(b) the registrar approves the lessor's title to grant the lease.

(3) A person may be registered with good leasehold title if the registrar is of the opinion that the person's title to the estate is such as a willing buyer could properly be advised by a competent professional adviser to accept.

(4) In applying subsection (2) or (3), the registrar may disregard the fact that a person's title appears to him to be open to objection if he is of the opinion that the defect will not cause the holding under the title to be disturbed.

(5) A person may be registered with qualified title if the registrar is of the opinion that the person's title to the estate, or the lessor's title to the reversion, has been established only for a limited period or subject to certain reservations which cannot be disregarded under subsection (4).

(6) A person may be registered with possessory title if the registrar is of the opinion –
   (a) that the person is in actual possession of the land, or in receipt of the rents and profits of the land, by virtue of the estate, and
   (b) that there is no other class of title with which he may be registered.

Effect of first registration

11[1]   Freehold estates

(1) This section is concerned with the registration of a person under this Chapter as the proprietor of a freehold estate.

(2) Registration with absolute title has the effect described in subsections (3) to (5).

(3) The estate is vested in the proprietor together with all interests subsisting for the benefit of the estate.

(4) The estate is vested in the proprietor subject only to the following interests affecting the estate at the time of registration –
   (a) interests which are the subject of an entry in the register in relation to the estate,
   (b) unregistered interests which fall within any of the paragraphs of Schedule 1, and
   (c) interests acquired under the Limitation Act 1980 of which the proprietor has notice.

(5) If the proprietor is not entitled to the estate for his own benefit, or not entitled solely for his own benefit, then, as between himself and the persons beneficially entitled to the estate, the estate is vested in him subject to such of their interests as he has notice of.

(6) Registration with qualified title has the same effect as registration with absolute title, except that it does not affect the enforcement of any estate, right or interest which appears from the register to be excepted from the effect of registration.

(7) Registration with possessory title has the same effect as registration with absolute title, except that it does not affect the enforcement of any estate, right or interest adverse to, or in derogation of, the proprietor's title subsisting at the time of registration or then capable of arising.

---

[1]   Commencement: 13 October 2003 (Land Registration Act 2002 (Commencement No 4) Order 2003, SI 2003/1725).

12¹   Leasehold estates

(1) This section is concerned with the registration of a person under this Chapter as the proprietor of a leasehold estate.

(2) Registration with absolute title has the effect described in subsections (3) to (5).

(3) The estate is vested in the proprietor together with all interests subsisting for the benefit of the estate.

(4) The estate is vested subject only to the following interests affecting the estate at the time of registration –
      (a) implied and express covenants, obligations and liabilities incident to the estate,
      (b) interests which are the subject of an entry in the register in relation to the estate,
      (c) unregistered interests which fall within any of the paragraphs of Schedule 1, and
      (d) interests acquired under the Limitation Act 1980 of which the proprietor has notice.

(5) If the proprietor is not entitled to the estate for his own benefit, or not entitled solely for his own benefit, then, as between himself and the persons beneficially entitled to the estate, the estate is vested in him subject to such of their interests as he has notice of.

(6) Registration with good leasehold title has the same effect as registration with absolute title, except that it does not affect the enforcement of any estate, right or interest affecting, or in derogation of, the title of the lessor to grant the lease.

(7) Registration with qualified title has the same effect as registration with absolute title except that it does not affect the enforcement of any estate, right or interest which appears from the register to be excepted from the effect of registration.

(8) Registration with possessory title has the same effect as registration with absolute title, except that it does not affect the enforcement of any estate, right or interest adverse to, or in derogation of, the proprietor's title subsisting at the time of registration or then capable of arising.

Dependent estates

13²   Appurtenant rights and charges

Rules may –
      (a) make provision for the registration of the proprietor of a registered estate as the proprietor of an unregistered legal estate which subsists for the benefit of the registered estate;
      (b) make provision for the registration of a person as the proprietor of an unregistered legal estate which is a charge on a registered estate.

---

[1]   Commencement: 13 October 2003 (Land Registration Act 2002 (Commencement No 4) Order 2003, SI 2003/1725).
[2]   Commencement: 13 October 2003 (Land Registration Act 2002 (Commencement No 4) Order 2003, SI 2003/1725).

Supplementary

14[1]   Rules about first registration

Rules may –

(a) make provision about the making of applications for registration under this Chapter;

(b) make provision about the functions of the registrar following the making of such an application, including provision about –

   (i)   the examination of title, and

   (ii)   the entries to be made in the register where such an application is approved;

(c) make provision about the effect of any entry made in the register in pursuance of such an application.

Chapter 2

Cautions Against First Registration

15[2]   Right to lodge

(1) *Subject to subsection (3)*,[3] a person may lodge a caution against the registration of title to an unregistered legal estate if he claims to be –

(a) the owner of a qualifying estate, or

(b) entitled to an interest affecting a qualifying estate.

(2) For the purposes of subsection (1), a qualifying estate is a legal estate which –

(a) relates to land to which the caution relates, and

(b) is an interest of any of the following kinds –

   (i)   an estate in land,

   (ii)   a rentcharge,

   (iii)   a franchise, and

   (iv)   a profit a prendre in gross.

(3) *No caution may be lodged under subsection (1) –*

   (a)   in the case of paragraph (a), by virtue of ownership of –

      (i)   a freehold estate in land, or

      (ii)   a leasehold estate in land granted for a term of which more than seven years are unexpired;

   (b)   in the case of paragraph (b), by virtue of entitlement to such a leasehold estate as is mentioned in paragraph (a)(ii) of this subsection.[4]

(4) The right under subsection (1) is exercisable by application to the registrar.

---

[1]   Commencement: 13 October 2003 (Land Registration Act 2002 (Commencement No 4) Order 2003, SI 2003/1725).

[2]   Commencement: 13 October 2003 (Land Registration Act 2002 (Commencement No 4) Order 2003, SI 2003/1725).

[3]   Words in italics not in force until 13 October 2005, except where Land Registration Act 2002, s 15 is applied by s 81, when as regards s 15(3)(a)(i), the words in italics are not in force until 13 October 2013 or such longer period as rules may provide: Land Registration Act 2002, s 134(2), Sch 12, paras 14, 15.

[4]   Words in italics not in force until 13 October 2005, except where Land Registration Act 2002, s 15 is applied by s 81, when as regards s 15(3)(a)(i), the words in italics are not in force until 13 October 2013 or such longer period as rules may provide: Land Registration Act 2002, s 134(2), Sch 12, paras 14, 15.

16[1]   Effect

(1) Where an application for registration under this Part relates to a legal estate which is the subject of a caution against first registration, the registrar must give the cautioner notice of the application and of his right to object to it.

(2) The registrar may not determine an application to which subsection (1) applies before the end of such period as rules may provide, unless the cautioner has exercised his right to object to the application or given the registrar notice that he does not intend to do so.

(3) Except as provided by this section, a caution against first registration has no effect and, in particular, has no effect on the validity or priority of any interest of the cautioner in the legal estate to which the caution relates.

(4) For the purposes of subsection (1), notice given by a person acting on behalf of an applicant for registration under this Part is to be treated as given by the registrar if –
   (a) the person is of a description provided by rules, and
   (b) notice is given in such circumstances as rules may provide.

17[2]   Withdrawal

The cautioner may withdraw a caution against first registration by application to the registrar.

18[3]   Cancellation

(1) A person may apply to the registrar for cancellation of a caution against first registration if he is –
   (a) the owner of the legal estate to which the caution relates, or
   (b) a person of such other description as rules may provide.

(2) Subject to rules, no application under subsection (1)(a) may be made by a person who –
   (a) consented in such manner as rules may provide to the lodging of the caution, or
   (b) derives title to the legal estate by operation of law from a person who did so.

(3) Where an application is made under subsection (1), the registrar must give the cautioner notice of the application and of the effect of subsection (4).

(4) If the cautioner does not exercise his right to object to the application before the end of such period as rules may provide, the registrar must cancel the caution.

19[4]   Cautions register

(1) The registrar must keep a register of cautions against first registration.

(2) Rules may make provision about how the cautions register is to be kept and may, in particular, make provision about –
   (a) the information to be included in the register,
   (b) the form in which information included in the register is to be kept, and
   (c) the arrangement of that information.

---

1   Commencement: 13 October 2003 (Land Registration Act 2002 (Commencement No 4) Order 2003, SI 2003/1725).
2   Commencement: 13 October 2003 (Land Registration Act 2002 (Commencement No 4) Order 2003, SI 2003/1725).
3   Commencement: 13 October 2003 (Land Registration Act 2002 (Commencement No 4) Order 2003, SI 2003/1725).
4   Commencement: 13 October 2003 (Land Registration Act 2002 (Commencement No 4) Order 2003, SI 2003/1725).

20[1]   Alteration of register by court

(1) The court may make an order for alteration of the cautions register for the purpose of –

(a) correcting a mistake, or

(b) bringing the register up to date.

(2) An order under subsection (1) has effect when served on the registrar to impose a duty on him to give effect to it.

(3) Rules may make provision about –

(a) the circumstances in which there is a duty to exercise the power under subsection (1),

(b) the form of an order under that subsection, and

(c) service of such an order.

21[2]   Alteration of register by registrar

(1) The registrar may alter the cautions register for the purpose of –

(a) correcting a mistake, or

(b) bringing the register up to date.

(2) Rules may make provision about –

(a) the circumstances in which there is a duty to exercise the power under subsection (1),

(b) how the cautions register is to be altered in exercise of that power,

(c) applications for the exercise of that power, and

(d) procedure in relation to the exercise of that power, whether on application or otherwise.

(3) Where an alteration is made under this section, the registrar may pay such amount as he thinks fit in respect of any costs reasonably incurred by a person in connection with the alteration.

22[3]   Supplementary

In this Chapter, 'the cautioner', in relation to a caution against first registration, means the person who lodged the caution, or such other person as rules may provide.

PART 3
DISPOSITIONS OF REGISTERED LAND

Powers of disposition

23[4]   Owner's powers

(1) Owner's powers in relation to a registered estate consist of –

(a) power to make a disposition of any kind permitted by the general law in relation to an interest of that description, other than a mortgage by demise or sub-demise, and

(b) power to charge the estate at law with the payment of money.

---

[1]   Commencement: 13 October 2003 (Land Registration Act 2002 (Commencement No 4) Order 2003, SI 2003/1725).

[2]   Commencement: 13 October 2003 (Land Registration Act 2002 (Commencement No 4) Order 2003, SI 2003/1725).

[3]   Commencement: 13 October 2003 (Land Registration Act 2002 (Commencement No 4) Order 2003, SI 2003/1725).

[4]   Commencement: 13 October 2003 (Land Registration Act 2002 (Commencement No 4) Order 2003, SI 2003/1725).

(2) Owner's powers in relation to a registered charge consist of –

    (a) power to make a disposition of any kind permitted by the general law in relation to an interest of that description, other than a legal sub-mortgage, and

    (b) power to charge at law with the payment of money indebtedness secured by the registered charge.

(3) In subsection (2)(a), 'legal sub-mortgage' means –

    (a) a transfer by way of mortgage,

    (b) a sub-mortgage by sub-demise, and

    (c) a charge by way of legal mortgage.

24[1]   Right to exercise owner's powers

A person is entitled to exercise owner's powers in relation to a registered estate or charge if he is –

    (a) the registered proprietor, or

    (b) entitled to be registered as the proprietor.

25[2]   Mode of exercise

(1) A registrable disposition of a registered estate or charge only has effect if it complies with such requirements as to form and content as rules may provide.

(2) Rules may apply subsection (1) to any other kind of disposition which depends for its effect on registration.

26[3]   Protection of disponees

(1) Subject to subsection (2), a person's right to exercise owner's powers in relation to a registered estate or charge is to be taken to be free from any limitation affecting the validity of a disposition.

(2) Subsection (1) does not apply to a limitation –

    (a) reflected by an entry in the register, or

    (b) imposed by, or under, this Act.

(3) This section has effect only for the purpose of preventing the title of a disponee being questioned (and so does not affect the lawfulness of a disposition).

Registrable dispositions

27[4]   Dispositions required to be registered

(1) If a disposition of a registered estate or registered charge is required to be completed by registration, it does not operate at law until the relevant registration requirements are met.

(2) In the case of a registered estate, the following are the dispositions which are required to be completed by registration –

---

[1]   Commencement: 13 October 2003 (Land Registration Act 2002 (Commencement No 4) Order 2003, SI 2003/1725).

[2]   Commencement: 13 October 2003 (Land Registration Act 2002 (Commencement No 4) Order 2003, SI 2003/1725).

[3]   Commencement: 13 October 2003 (Land Registration Act 2002 (Commencement No 4) Order 2003, SI 2003/1725).

[4]   Commencement: 13 October 2003 (Land Registration Act 2002 (Commencement No 4) Order 2003, SI 2003/1725).

(a) a transfer,

(b) where the registered estate is an estate in land, the grant of a term of years absolute –

    (i) for a term of more than seven years from the date of the grant,

    (ii) to take effect in possession after the end of the period of three months beginning with the date of the grant,

    (iii) under which the right to possession is discontinuous,

    (iv) in pursuance of Part 5 of the Housing Act 1985 (the right to buy), or

    (v) in circumstances where section 171A of that Act applies (disposal by landlord which leads to a person no longer being a secure tenant),

(c) where the registered estate is a franchise or manor, the grant of a lease,

(d) the express grant or reservation of an interest of a kind falling within section 1(2)(a) of the Law of Property Act 1925, other than one which is capable of being registered under the Commons Registration Act 1965,

(e) the express grant or reservation of an interest of a kind falling within section 1(2)(b) or (e) of the Law of Property Act 1925, and

(f) the grant of a legal charge.

(3) In the case of a registered charge, the following are the dispositions which are required to be completed by registration –

(a) a transfer, and

(b) the grant of a sub-charge.

(4) Schedule 2 to this Act (which deals with the relevant registration requirements) has effect.

(5) This section applies to dispositions by operation of law as it applies to other dispositions, but with the exception of the following –

(a) a transfer on the death or bankruptcy of an individual proprietor,

(b) a transfer on the dissolution of a corporate proprietor, and

(c) the creation of a legal charge which is a local land charge.

(6) Rules may make provision about applications to the registrar for the purpose of meeting registration requirements under this section.

(7) In subsection (2)(d), the reference to express grant does not include grant as a result of the operation of section 62 of the Law of Property Act 1925.

Effect of dispositions on priority

28[1]   Basic rule

(1) Except as provided by sections 29 and 30, the priority of an interest affecting a registered estate or charge is not affected by a disposition of the estate or charge.

(2) It makes no difference for the purposes of this section whether the interest or disposition is registered.

29[2]   Effect of registered dispositions: estates

(1) If a registrable disposition of a registered estate is made for valuable consideration, completion of the disposition by registration has the effect of postponing to the interest under

[1] Commencement: 13 October 2003 (Land Registration Act 2002 (Commencement No 4) Order 2003, SI 2003/1725).

[2] Commencement: 13 October 2003 (Land Registration Act 2002 (Commencement No 4) Order 2003, SI 2003/1725).

the disposition any interest affecting the estate immediately before the disposition whose priority is not protected at the time of registration.

(2) For the purposes of subsection (1), the priority of an interest is protected –
    (a) in any case, if the interest –
        (i)   is a registered charge or the subject of a notice in the register,
        (ii)   falls within any of the paragraphs of Schedule 3, or
        (iii) appears from the register to be excepted from the effect of registration, and
    (b) in the case of a disposition of a leasehold estate, if the burden of the interest is incident to the estate.

(3) Subsection (2)(a)(ii) does not apply to an interest which has been the subject of a notice in the register at any time since the coming into force of this section.

(4) Where the grant of a leasehold estate in land out of a registered estate does not involve a registrable disposition, this section has effect as if –
    (a) the grant involved such a disposition, and
    (b) the disposition were registered at the time of the grant.

30[1]   Effect of registered dispositions: charges

(1) If a registrable disposition of a registered charge is made for valuable consideration, completion of the disposition by registration has the effect of postponing to the interest under the disposition any interest affecting the charge immediately before the disposition whose priority is not protected at the time of registration.

(2) For the purposes of subsection (1), the priority of an interest is protected –
    (a) in any case, if the interest –
        (i)   is a registered charge or the subject of a notice in the register,
        (ii)   falls within any of the paragraphs of Schedule 3, or
        (iii) appears from the register to be excepted from the effect of registration, and
    (b) in the case of a disposition of a charge which relates to a leasehold estate, if the burden of the interest is incident to the estate.

(3) Subsection (2)(a)(ii) does not apply to an interest which has been the subject of a notice in the register at any time since the coming into force of this section.

31[2]   Inland Revenue charges

The effect of a disposition of a registered estate or charge on a charge under section 237 of the Inheritance Tax Act 1984 (charge for unpaid tax) is to be determined, not in accordance with sections 28 to 30 above, but in accordance with sections 237(6) and 238 of that Act (under which a purchaser in good faith for money or money's worth takes free from the charge in the absence of registration).

---

[1]   Commencement: 13 October 2003 (Land Registration Act 2002 (Commencement No 4) Order 2003, SI 2003/1725).
[2]   Commencement: 13 October 2003 (Land Registration Act 2002 (Commencement No 4) Order 2003, SI 2003/1725).

PART 4
NOTICES AND RESTRICTIONS

Notices

32[1]   Nature and effect

(1) A notice is an entry in the register in respect of the burden of an interest affecting a registered estate or charge.

(2) The entry of a notice is to be made in relation to the registered estate or charge affected by the interest concerned.

(3) The fact that an interest is the subject of a notice does not necessarily mean that the interest is valid, but does mean that the priority of the interest, if valid, is protected for the purposes of sections 29 and 30.

33[2]   Excluded interests

No notice may be entered in the register in respect of any of the following –
- (a) an interest under –
    - (i)   a trust of land, or
    - (ii) a settlement under the Settled Land Act 1925,
- (b) a leasehold estate in land which –
    - (i)   is granted for a term of years of three years or less from the date of the grant, and
    - (ii) is not required to be registered,
- (c) a restrictive covenant made between a lessor and lessee, so far as relating to the demised premises,
- (d) an interest which is capable of being registered under the Commons Registration Act 1965, and
- (e) an interest in any coal or coal mine, the rights attached to any such interest and the rights of any person under section 38, 49 or 51 of the Coal Industry Act 1994.

34[3]   Entry on application

(1) A person who claims to be entitled to the benefit of an interest affecting a registered estate or charge may, if the interest is not excluded by section 33, apply to the registrar for the entry in the register of a notice in respect of the interest.

(2) Subject to rules, an application under this section may be for –
- (a) an agreed notice, or
- (b) a unilateral notice.

(3) The registrar may only approve an application for an agreed notice if –
- (a) the applicant is the relevant registered proprietor, or a person entitled to be registered as such proprietor,
- (b) the relevant registered proprietor, or a person entitled to be registered as such proprietor, consents to the entry of the notice, or
- (c) the registrar is satisfied as to the validity of the applicant's claim.

---

1   Commencement: 13 October 2003 (Land Registration Act 2002 (Commencement No 4) Order 2003, SI 2003/1725).
2   Commencement: 13 October 2003 (Land Registration Act 2002 (Commencement No 4) Order 2003, SI 2003/1725).
3   Commencement: 13 October 2003 (Land Registration Act 2002 (Commencement No 4) Order 2003, SI 2003/1725).

(4) In subsection (3), references to the relevant registered proprietor are to the proprietor of the registered estate or charge affected by the interest to which the application relates.

35[1] Unilateral notices

(1) If the registrar enters a notice in the register in pursuance of an application under section 34(2)(b) ('a unilateral notice'), he must give notice of the entry to –
  (a) the proprietor of the registered estate or charge to which it relates, and
  (b) such other persons as rules may provide.

(2) A unilateral notice must –
  (a) indicate that it is such a notice, and
  (b) identify who is the beneficiary of the notice.

(3) The person shown in the register as the beneficiary of a unilateral notice, or such other person as rules may provide, may apply to the registrar for the removal of the notice from the register.

36[2] Cancellation of unilateral notices

(1) A person may apply to the registrar for the cancellation of a unilateral notice if he is –
  (a) the registered proprietor of the estate or charge to which the notice relates, or
  (b) a person entitled to be registered as the proprietor of that estate or charge.

(2) Where an application is made under subsection (1), the registrar must give the beneficiary of the notice notice of the application and of the effect of subsection (3).

(3) If the beneficiary of the notice does not exercise his right to object to the application before the end of such period as rules may provide, the registrar must cancel the notice.

(4) In this section –
  'beneficiary', in relation to a unilateral notice, means the person shown in the register as the beneficiary of the notice, or such other person as rules may provide;
  'unilateral notice' means a notice entered in the register in pursuance of an application under section 34(2)(b).

37[3] Unregistered interests

(1) If it appears to the registrar that a registered estate is subject to an unregistered interest which –
  (a) falls within any of the paragraphs of Schedule 1, and
  (b) is not excluded by section 33,
he may enter a notice in the register in respect of the interest.

(2) The registrar must give notice of an entry under this section to such persons as rules may provide.

---

[1]   Commencement: 13 October 2003 (Land Registration Act 2002 (Commencement No 4) Order 2003, SI 2003/1725).
[2]   Commencement: 13 October 2003 (Land Registration Act 2002 (Commencement No 4) Order 2003, SI 2003/1725).
[3]   Commencement: 13 October 2003 (Land Registration Act 2002 (Commencement No 4) Order 2003, SI 2003/1725).

38¹   Registrable dispositions

Where a person is entered in the register as the proprietor of an interest under a disposition falling within section 27(2)(b) to (e), the registrar must also enter a notice in the register in respect of that interest.

39²   Supplementary

Rules may make provision about the form and content of notices in the register.

Restrictions

40³   Nature

(1) A restriction is an entry in the register regulating the circumstances in which a disposition of a registered estate or charge may be the subject of an entry in the register.

(2) A restriction may, in particular –
  (a) prohibit the making of an entry in respect of any disposition, or a disposition of a kind specified in the restriction;
  (b) prohibit the making of an entry –
    (i)   indefinitely,
    (ii)   for a period specified in the restriction, or
    (iii) until the occurrence of an event so specified.

(3) Without prejudice to the generality of subsection (2)(b)(iii), the events which may be specified include –
  (a) the giving of notice,
  (b) the obtaining of consent, and
  (c) the making of an order by the court or registrar.

(4) The entry of a restriction is to be made in relation to the registered estate or charge to which it relates.

41⁴   Effect

(1) Where a restriction is entered in the register, no entry in respect of a disposition to which the restriction applies may be made in the register otherwise than in accordance with the terms of the restriction, subject to any order under subsection (2).

(2) The registrar may by order –
  (a) disapply a restriction in relation to a disposition specified in the order or dispositions of a kind so specified, or
  (b) provide that a restriction has effect, in relation to a disposition specified in the order or dispositions of a kind so specified, with modifications so specified.

(3) The power under subsection (2) is exercisable only on the application of a person who appears to the registrar to have a sufficient interest in the restriction.

---

[1] Commencement: 13 October 2003 (Land Registration Act 2002 (Commencement No 4) Order 2003, SI 2003/1725).

[2] Commencement: 13 October 2003 (Land Registration Act 2002 (Commencement No 4) Order 2003, SI 2003/1725).

[3] Commencement: 13 October 2003 (Land Registration Act 2002 (Commencement No 4) Order 2003, SI 2003/1725).

[4] Commencement: 13 October 2003 (Land Registration Act 2002 (Commencement No 4) Order 2003, SI 2003/1725).

42¹   Power of registrar to enter

(1) The registrar may enter a restriction in the register if it appears to him that it is necessary or desirable to do so for the purpose of –

    (a) preventing invalidity or unlawfulness in relation to dispositions of a registered estate or charge,

    (b) securing that interests which are capable of being overreached on a disposition of a registered estate or charge are overreached, or

    (c) protecting a right or claim in relation to a registered estate or charge.

(2) No restriction may be entered under subsection (1)(c) for the purpose of protecting the priority of an interest which is, or could be, the subject of a notice.

(3) The registrar must give notice of any entry made under this section to the proprietor of the registered estate or charge concerned, except where the entry is made in pursuance of an application under section 43.

(4) For the purposes of subsection (1)(c), a person entitled to the benefit of a charging order relating to an interest under a trust shall be treated as having a right or claim in relation to the trust property.

43²   Applications

(1) A person may apply to the registrar for the entry of a restriction under section 42(1) if –

    (a) he is the relevant registered proprietor, or a person entitled to be registered as such proprietor,

    (b) the relevant registered proprietor, or a person entitled to be registered as such proprietor, consents to the application, or

    (c) he otherwise has a sufficient interest in the making of the entry.

(2) Rules may –

    (a) require the making of an application under subsection (1) in such circumstances, and by such person, as the rules may provide;

    (b) make provision about the form of consent for the purposes of subsection (1)(b);

    (c) provide for classes of person to be regarded as included in subsection (1)(c);

    (d) specify standard forms of restriction.

(3) If an application under subsection (1) is made for the entry of a restriction which is not in a form specified under subsection (2)(d), the registrar may only approve the application if it appears to him –

    (a) that the terms of the proposed restriction are reasonable, and

    (b) that applying the proposed restriction would –

        (i)   be straightforward, and

        (ii)   not place an unreasonable burden on him.

(4) In subsection (1), references to the relevant registered proprietor are to the proprietor of the registered estate or charge to which the application relates.

---

1 Commencement: 13 October 2003 (Land Registration Act 2002 (Commencement No 4) Order 2003, SI 2003/1725).

2 Commencement: 13 October 2003 (Land Registration Act 2002 (Commencement No 4) Order 2003, SI 2003/1725).

44[1]   Obligatory restrictions

(1) If the registrar enters two or more persons in the register as the proprietor of a registered estate in land, he must also enter in the register such restrictions as rules may provide for the purpose of securing that interests which are capable of being overreached on a disposition of the estate are overreached.

(2) Where under any enactment the registrar is required to enter a restriction without application, the form of the restriction shall be such as rules may provide.

45[2]   Notifiable applications

(1) Where an application under section 43(1) is notifiable, the registrar must give notice of the application, and of the right to object to it, to –
  (a) the proprietor of the registered estate or charge to which it relates, and
  (b) such other persons as rules may provide.

(2) The registrar may not determine an application to which subsection (1) applies before the end of such period as rules may provide, unless the person, or each of the persons, notified under that subsection has exercised his right to object to the application or given the registrar notice that he does not intend to do so.

(3) For the purposes of this section, an application under section 43(1) is notifiable unless it is –
  (a) made by or with the consent of the proprietor of the registered estate or charge to which the application relates, or a person entitled to be registered as such proprietor,
  (b) made in pursuance of rules under section 43(2)(a), or
  (c) an application for the entry of a restriction reflecting a limitation under an order of the court or registrar, or an undertaking given in place of such an order.

46[3]   Power of court to order entry

(1) If it appears to the court that it is necessary or desirable to do so for the purpose of protecting a right or claim in relation to a registered estate or charge, it may make an order requiring the registrar to enter a restriction in the register.

(2) No order under this section may be made for the purpose of protecting the priority of an interest which is, or could be, the subject of a notice.

(3) The court may include in an order under this section a direction that an entry made in pursuance of the order is to have overriding priority.

(4) If an order under this section includes a direction under subsection (3), the registrar must make such entry in the register as rules may provide.

(5) The court may make the exercise of its power under subsection (3) subject to such terms and conditions as it thinks fit.

---

[1]   Commencement: 13 October 2003 (Land Registration Act 2002 (Commencement No 4) Order 2003, SI 2003/1725).
[2]   Commencement: 13 October 2003 (Land Registration Act 2002 (Commencement No 4) Order 2003, SI 2003/1725).
[3]   Commencement: 13 October 2003 (Land Registration Act 2002 (Commencement No 4) Order 2003, SI 2003/1725).

47¹   Withdrawal

A person may apply to the registrar for the withdrawal of a restriction if –

    (a) the restriction was entered in such circumstances as rules may provide, and

    (b) he is of such a description as rules may provide.

PART 5

CHARGES

Relative priority

48²   Registered charges

(1) Registered charges on the same registered estate, or on the same registered charge, are to be taken to rank as between themselves in the order shown in the register.

(2) Rules may make provision about –

    (a) how the priority of registered charges as between themselves is to be shown in the register, and

    (b) applications for registration of the priority of registered charges as between themselves.

49³   Tacking and further advances

(1) The proprietor of a registered charge may make a further advance on the security of the charge ranking in priority to a subsequent charge if he has not received from the subsequent chargee notice of the creation of the subsequent charge.

(2) Notice given for the purposes of subsection (1) shall be treated as received at the time when, in accordance with rules, it ought to have been received.

(3) The proprietor of a registered charge may also make a further advance on the security of the charge ranking in priority to a subsequent charge if –

    (a) the advance is made in pursuance of an obligation, and

    (b) at the time of the creation of the subsequent charge the obligation was entered in the register in accordance with rules.

(4) The proprietor of a registered charge may also make a further advance on the security of the charge ranking in priority to a subsequent charge if –

    (a) the parties to the prior charge have agreed a maximum amount for which the charge is security, and

    (b) at the time of the creation of the subsequent charge the agreement was entered in the register in accordance with rules.

(5) Rules may –

    (a) disapply subsection (4) in relation to charges of a description specified in the rules, or

    (b) provide for the application of that subsection to be subject, in the case of charges of a description so specified, to compliance with such conditions as may be so specified.

---

[1]   Commencement: 13 October 2003 (Land Registration Act 2002 (Commencement No 4) Order 2003, SI 2003/1725).

[2]   Commencement: 13 October 2003 (Land Registration Act 2002 (Commencement No 4) Order 2003, SI 2003/1725).

[3]   Commencement: 13 October 2003 (Land Registration Act 2002 (Commencement No 4) Order 2003, SI 2003/1725).

(6) Except as provided by this section, tacking in relation to a charge over registered land is only possible with the agreement of the subsequent chargee.

50[1] Overriding statutory charges: duty of notification

If the registrar enters a person in the register as the proprietor of a charge which –

- (a) is created by or under an enactment, and
- (b) has effect to postpone a charge which at the time of registration of the statutory charge is –
    - (i) entered in the register, or
    - (ii) the basis for an entry in the register,

he must in accordance with rules give notice of the creation of the statutory charge to such person as rules may provide.

Powers as chargee

51[2] Effect of completion by registration

On completion of the relevant registration requirements, a charge created by means of a registrable disposition of a registered estate has effect, if it would not otherwise do so, as a charge by deed by way of legal mortgage.

52[3] Protection of disponees

(1) Subject to any entry in the register to the contrary, the proprietor of a registered charge is to be taken to have, in relation to the property subject to the charge, the powers of disposition conferred by law on the owner of a legal mortgage.

(2) Subsection (1) has effect only for the purpose of preventing the title of a disponee being questioned (and so does not affect the lawfulness of a disposition).

53[4] Powers as sub-chargee

The registered proprietor of a sub-charge has, in relation to the property subject to the principal charge or any intermediate charge, the same powers as the sub-chargor.

Realisation of security

54[5] Proceeds of sale: chargee's duty

For the purposes of section 105 of the Law of Property Act 1925 (mortgagee's duties in relation to application of proceeds of sale), in its application to the proceeds of sale of registered land, a person shall be taken to have notice of anything in the register immediately before the disposition on sale.

---

[1] Commencement: 13 October 2003 (Land Registration Act 2002 (Commencement No 4) Order 2003, SI 2003/1725).
[2] Commencement: 13 October 2003 (Land Registration Act 2002 (Commencement No 4) Order 2003, SI 2003/1725).
[3] Commencement: 13 October 2003 (Land Registration Act 2002 (Commencement No 4) Order 2003, SI 2003/1725).
[4] Commencement: 13 October 2003 (Land Registration Act 2002 (Commencement No 4) Order 2003, SI 2003/1725).
[5] Commencement: 13 October 2003 (Land Registration Act 2002 (Commencement No 4) Order 2003, SI 2003/1725).

55¹   Local land charges

A charge over registered land which is a local land charge may only be realised if the title to the charge is registered.

Miscellaneous

56²   Receipt in case of joint proprietors

Where a charge is registered in the name of two or more proprietors, a valid receipt for the money secured by the charge may be given by –

    (a) the registered proprietors,

    (b) the survivors or survivor of the registered proprietors, or

    (c) the personal representative of the last survivor of the registered proprietors.

57³   Entry of right of consolidation

Rules may make provision about entry in the register of a right of consolidation in relation to a registered charge.

PART 6
REGISTRATION: GENERAL

Registration as proprietor

58⁴   Conclusiveness

(1) If, on the entry of a person in the register as the proprietor of a legal estate, the legal estate would not otherwise be vested in him, it shall be deemed to be vested in him as a result of the registration.

(2) Subsection (1) does not apply where the entry is made in pursuance of a registrable disposition in relation to which some other registration requirement remains to be met.

59⁵   Dependent estates

(1) The entry of a person in the register as the proprietor of a legal estate which subsists for the benefit of a registered estate must be made in relation to the registered estate.

(2) The entry of a person in the register as the proprietor of a charge on a registered estate must be made in relation to that estate.

(3) The entry of a person in the register as the proprietor of a sub-charge on a registered charge must be made in relation to that charge.

---

[1]   Commencement: 13 October 2003 (Land Registration Act 2002 (Commencement No 4) Order 2003, SI 2003/1725).

[2]   Commencement: 13 October 2003 (Land Registration Act 2002 (Commencement No 4) Order 2003, SI 2003/1725).

[3]   Commencement: 13 October 2003 (Land Registration Act 2002 (Commencement No 4) Order 2003, SI 2003/1725).

[4]   Commencement: 13 October 2003 (Land Registration Act 2002 (Commencement No 4) Order 2003, SI 2003/1725).

[5]   Commencement: 13 October 2003 (Land Registration Act 2002 (Commencement No 4) Order 2003, SI 2003/1725).

60[1]   Boundaries

(1) The boundary of a registered estate as shown for the purposes of the register is a general boundary, unless shown as determined under this section.

(2) A general boundary does not determine the exact line of the boundary.

(3) Rules may make provision enabling or requiring the exact line of the boundary of a registered estate to be determined and may, in particular, make provision about –
- (a) the circumstances in which the exact line of a boundary may or must be determined,
- (b) how the exact line of a boundary may be determined,
- (c) procedure in relation to applications for determination, and
- (d) the recording of the fact of determination in the register or the index maintained under section 68.

(4) Rules under this section must provide for applications for determination to be made to the registrar.

61[2]   Accretion and diluvion

(1) The fact that a registered estate in land is shown in the register as having a particular boundary does not affect the operation of accretion or diluvion.

(2) An agreement about the operation of accretion or diluvion in relation to a registered estate in land has effect only if registered in accordance with rules.

Quality of title

62[3]   Power to upgrade title

(1) Where the title to a freehold estate is entered in the register as possessory or qualified, the registrar may enter it as absolute if he is satisfied as to the title to the estate.

(2) Where the title to a leasehold estate is entered in the register as good leasehold, the registrar may enter it as absolute if he is satisfied as to the superior title.

(3) Where the title to a leasehold estate is entered in the register as possessory or qualified the registrar may –
- (a) enter it as good leasehold if he is satisfied as to the title to the estate, and
- (b) enter it as absolute if he is satisfied both as to the title to the estate and as to the superior title.

(4) Where the title to a freehold estate in land has been entered in the register as possessory for at least twelve years, the registrar may enter it as absolute if he is satisfied that the proprietor is in possession of the land.

(5) Where the title to a leasehold estate in land has been entered in the register as possessory

---

[1]   Commencement: 13 October 2003 (Land Registration Act 2002 (Commencement No 4) Order 2003, SI 2003/1725).

[2]   Commencement: 13 October 2003 (Land Registration Act 2002 (Commencement No 4) Order 2003, SI 2003/1725).

[3]   Commencement: 13 October 2003 (Land Registration Act 2002 (Commencement No 4) Order 2003, SI 2003/1725).

for at least twelve years, the registrar may enter it as good leasehold if he is satisfied that the proprietor is in possession of the land.

(6) None of the powers under subsections (1) to (5) is exercisable if there is outstanding any claim adverse to the title of the registered proprietor which is made by virtue of an estate, right or interest whose enforceability is preserved by virtue of the existing entry about the class of title.

(7) The only persons who may apply to the registrar for the exercise of any of the powers under subsections (1) to (5) are –
    (a) the proprietor of the estate to which the application relates,
    (b) a person entitled to be registered as the proprietor of that estate,
    (c) the proprietor of a registered charge affecting that estate, and
    (d) a person interested in a registered estate which derives from that estate.

(8) In determining for the purposes of this section whether he is satisfied as to any title, the registrar is to apply the same standards as those which apply under section 9 or 10 to first registration of title.

(9) The Lord Chancellor may by order amend subsection (4) or (5) by substituting for the number of years for the time being specified in that subsection such number of years as the order may provide.

63[1]   Effect of upgrading title
(1) On the title to a registered freehold or leasehold estate being entered under section 62 as absolute, the proprietor ceases to hold the estate subject to any estate, right or interest whose enforceability was preserved by virtue of the previous entry about the class of title.

(2) Subsection (1) also applies on the title to a registered leasehold estate being entered under section 62 as good leasehold, except that the entry does not affect or prejudice the enforcement of any estate, right or interest affecting, or in derogation of, the title of the lessor to grant the lease.

64[2]   Use of register to record defects in title
(1) If it appears to the registrar that a right to determine a registered estate in land is exercisable, he may enter the fact in the register.

(2) Rules may make provision about entries under subsection (1) and may, in particular, make provision about –
    (a) the circumstances in which there is a duty to exercise the power conferred by that subsection,
    (b) how entries under that subsection are to be made, and
    (c) the removal of such entries.

---

[1]   Commencement: 13 October 2003 (Land Registration Act 2002 (Commencement No 4) Order 2003, SI 2003/1725).
[2]   Commencement: 13 October 2003 (Land Registration Act 2002 (Commencement No 4) Order 2003, SI 2003/1725).

Alteration of register

65[1]   Alteration of register

Schedule 4 (which makes provision about alteration of the register) has effect.

Information etc

66[2]   Inspection of the registers etc

(1) Any person may inspect and make copies of, or of any part of –
  (a) the register of title,
  (b) any document kept by the registrar which is referred to in the register of title,
  (c) any other document kept by the registrar which relates to an application to him, or
  (d) the register of cautions against first registration.

(2) The right under subsection (1) is subject to rules which may, in particular –
  (a) provide for exceptions to the right, and
  (b) impose conditions on its exercise, including conditions requiring the payment of fees.

67[3]   Official copies of the registers etc

(1) An official copy of, or of a part of –
  (a) the register of title,
  (b) any document which is referred to in the register of title and kept by the registrar,
  (c) any other document kept by the registrar which relates to an application to him, or
  (d) the register of cautions against first registration,
is admissible in evidence to the same extent as the original.

(2) A person who relies on an official copy in which there is a mistake is not liable for loss suffered by another by reason of the mistake.

(3) Rules may make provision for the issue of official copies and may, in particular, make provision about –
  (a) the form of official copies,
  (b) who may issue official copies,
  (c) applications for official copies, and
  (d) the conditions to be met by applicants for official copies, including conditions requiring the payment of fees.

68[4]   Index

(1) The registrar must keep an index for the purpose of enabling the following matters to be ascertained in relation to any parcel of land –
  (a) whether any registered estate relates to the land,
  (b) how any registered estate which relates to the land is identified for the purposes of the register,

---

[1]   Commencement: 13 October 2003 (Land Registration Act 2002 (Commencement No 4) Order 2003, SI 2003/1725).
[2]   Commencement: 13 October 2003 (Land Registration Act 2002 (Commencement No 4) Order 2003, SI 2003/1725).
[3]   Commencement: 13 October 2003 (Land Registration Act 2002 (Commencement No 4) Order 2003, SI 2003/1725).
[4]   Commencement: 13 October 2003 (Land Registration Act 2002 (Commencement No 4) Order 2003, SI 2003/1725).

(c) whether the land is affected by any, and, if so what, caution against first registration, and

(d) such other matters as rules may provide.

(2) Rules may –
    (a) make provision about how the index is to be kept and may, in particular, make provision about –
        (i) the information to be included in the index,
        (ii) the form in which information included in the index is to be kept, and
        (iii) the arrangement of that information;
    (b) make provision about official searches of the index.

69[1]   Historical information

(1) The registrar may on application provide information about the history of a registered title.

(2) Rules may make provision about applications for the exercise of the power conferred by subsection (1).

(3) The registrar may –
    (a) arrange for the provision of information about the history of registered titles, and
    (b) authorise anyone who has the function of providing information under paragraph (a) to have access on such terms as the registrar thinks fit to any relevant information kept by him.

70[2]   Official searches

Rules may make provision for official searches of the register, including searches of pending applications for first registration, and may, in particular, make provision about –
    (a) the form of applications for searches,
    (b) the manner in which such applications may be made,
    (c) the form of official search certificates, and
    (d) the manner in which such certificates may be issued.

Applications

71[3]   Duty to disclose unregistered interests

Where rules so provide –
    (a) a person applying for registration under Chapter 1 of Part 2 must provide to the registrar such information as the rules may provide about any interest affecting the estate to which the application relates which –
        (i) falls within any of the paragraphs of Schedule 1, and
        (ii) is of a description specified by the rules;
    (b) a person applying to register a registrable disposition of a registered estate must provide to the registrar such information as the rules may provide about any unregistered interest affecting the estate which –
        (i) falls within any of the paragraphs of Schedule 3, and
        (ii) is of description specified by the rules.

---

[1] Commencement: 13 October 2003 (Land Registration Act 2002 (Commencement No 4) Order 2003, SI 2003/1725).

[2] Commencement: 13 October 2003 (Land Registration Act 2002 (Commencement No 4) Order 2003, SI 2003/1725).

[3] Commencement: 13 October 2003 (Land Registration Act 2002 (Commencement No 4) Order 2003, SI 2003/1725).

72[1]   Priority protection

(1) For the purposes of this section, an application for an entry in the register is protected if –

    (a) it is one to which a priority period relates, and

    (b) it is made before the end of that period.

(2) Where an application for an entry in the register is protected, any entry made in the register during the priority period relating to the application is postponed to any entry made in pursuance of it.

(3) Subsection (2) does not apply if –

    (a) the earlier entry was made in pursuance of a protected application, and

    (b) the priority period relating to that application ranks ahead of the one relating to the application for the other entry.

(4) Subsection (2) does not apply if the earlier entry is one to which a direction under section 46(3) applies.

(5) The registrar may defer dealing with an application for an entry in the register if it appears to him that subsection (2) might apply to the entry were he to make it.

(6) Rules may –

    (a) make provision for priority periods in connection with –

        (i) official searches of the register, including searches of pending applications for first registration, or

        (ii) the noting in the register of a contract for the making of a registrable disposition of a registered estate or charge;

    (b) make provision for the keeping of records in relation to priority periods and the inspection of such records.

(7) Rules under subsection (6)(a) may, in particular, make provision about –

    (a) the commencement and length of a priority period,

    (b) the applications for registration to which such a period relates,

    (c) the order in which competing priority periods rank, and

    (d) the application of subsections (2) and (3) in cases where more than one priority period relates to the same application.

73[2]   Objections

(1) Subject to subsections (2) and (3), anyone may object to an application to the registrar.

(2) In the case of an application under section 18, only the person who lodged the caution to which the application relates, or such other person as rules may provide, may object.

(3) In the case of an application under section 36, only the person shown in the register as the beneficiary of the notice to which the application relates, or such other person as rules may provide, may object.

(4) The right to object under this section is subject to rules.

---

[1]   Commencement: 13 October 2003 (Land Registration Act 2002 (Commencement No 4) Order 2003, SI 2003/1725).

[2]   Commencement: 13 October 2003 (Land Registration Act 2002 (Commencement No 4) Order 2003, SI 2003/1725).

(5) Where an objection is made under this section, the registrar –
  (a) must give notice of the objection to the applicant, and
  (b) may not determine the application until the objection has been disposed of.

(6) Subsection (5) does not apply if the objection is one which the registrar is satisfied is groundless.

(7) If it is not possible to dispose by agreement of an objection to which subsection (5) applies, the registrar must refer the matter to the adjudicator.

(8) Rules may make provision about references under subsection (7).

74[1]   Effective date of registration

An entry made in the register in pursuance of –
  (a) an application for registration of an unregistered legal estate, or
  (b) an application for registration in relation to a disposition required to be completed by registration,
has effect from the time of the making of the application.

Proceedings before the registrar

75[2]   Production of documents

(1) The registrar may require a person to produce a document for the purposes of proceedings before him.

(2) The power under subsection (1) is subject to rules.

(3) A requirement under subsection (1) shall be enforceable as an order of the court.

(4) A person aggrieved by a requirement under subsection (1) may appeal to a county court, which may make any order which appears appropriate.

76[3]   Costs

(1) The registrar may make orders about costs in relation to proceedings before him.

(2) The power under subsection (1) is subject to rules which may, in particular, make provision about –
  (a) who may be required to pay costs,
  (b) whose costs a person may be required to pay,
  (c) the kind of costs which a person may be required to pay, and
  (d) the assessment of costs.

(3) Without prejudice to the generality of subsection (2), rules under that subsection may include provision about –
  (a) costs of the registrar, and

---

[1]   Commencement: 13 October 2003 (Land Registration Act 2002 (Commencement No 4) Order 2003, SI 2003/1725).
[2]   Commencement: 13 October 2003 (Land Registration Act 2002 (Commencement No 4) Order 2003, SI 2003/1725).
[3]   Commencement: 13 October 2003 (Land Registration Act 2002 (Commencement No 4) Order 2003, SI 2003/1725).

(b) liability for costs thrown away as the result of neglect or delay by a legal representative of a party to proceedings.

(4) An order under subsection (1) shall be enforceable as an order of the court.

(5) A person aggrieved by an order under subsection (1) may appeal to a county court, which may make any order which appears appropriate.

Miscellaneous

77¹   Duty to act reasonably
(1) A person must not exercise any of the following rights without reasonable cause –
    (a) the right to lodge a caution under section 15,
    (b) the right to apply for the entry of a notice or restriction, and
    (c) the right to object to an application to the registrar.

(2) The duty under this section is owed to any person who suffers damage in consequence of its breach.

78²   Notice of trust not to affect registrar
The registrar shall not be affected with notice of a trust.

PART 7
SPECIAL CASES

The Crown

79³   Voluntary registration of demesne land
(1) Her Majesty may grant an estate in fee simple absolute in possession out of demesne land to Herself.

(2) The grant of an estate under subsection (1) is to be regarded as not having been made unless an application under section 3 is made in respect of the estate before the end of the period for registration.

(3) The period for registration is two months beginning with the date of the grant, or such longer period as the registrar may provide under subsection (4).

(4) If on the application of Her Majesty the registrar is satisfied that there is a good reason for doing so, he may by order provide that the period for registration ends on such later date as he may specify in the order.

(5) If an order under subsection (4) is made in a case where subsection (2) has already applied, that application of the subsection is to be treated as not having occurred.

---

[1]   Commencement: 13 October 2003 (Land Registration Act 2002 (Commencement No 4) Order 2003, SI 2003/1725).

[2]   Commencement: 13 October 2003 (Land Registration Act 2002 (Commencement No 4) Order 2003, SI 2003/1725).

[3]   Commencement: 13 October 2003 (Land Registration Act 2002 (Commencement No 4) Order 2003, SI 2003/1725).

80[1]   Compulsory registration of grants out of demesne land

(1) Section 4(1) shall apply as if the following were included among the events listed –

   (a) the grant by Her Majesty out of demesne land of an estate in fee simple absolute in possession, otherwise than under section 79;

   (b) the grant by Her Majesty out of demesne land of an estate in land –

      (i) for a term of years absolute of more than seven years from the date of the grant, and

      (ii) for valuable or other consideration, by way of gift or in pursuance of an order of any court.

(2) In subsection (1)(b)(ii), the reference to grant by way of gift includes grant for the purpose of constituting a trust under which Her Majesty does not retain the whole of the beneficial interest.

(3) Subsection (1) does not apply to the grant of an estate in mines and minerals held apart from the surface.

(4) The Lord Chancellor may by order –

   (a) amend this section so as to add to the events in subsection (1) such events relating to demesne land as he may specify in the order, and

   (b) make such consequential amendments of any provision of, or having effect under, any Act as he thinks appropriate.

(5) In its application by virtue of subsection (1), section 7 has effect with the substitution for subsection (2) of –

'(2) On the application of subsection (1), the grant has effect as a contract made for valuable consideration to grant the legal estate concerned'.

81[2]   Demesne land: cautions against first registration

(1) Section 15 shall apply as if demesne land were held by Her Majesty for an unregistered estate in fee simple absolute in possession.

(2) The provisions of this Act relating to cautions against first registration shall, in relation to cautions lodged by virtue of subsection (1), have effect subject to such modifications as rules may provide.

82[3]   Escheat etc

(1) Rules may make provision about –

   (a) the determination of a registered freehold estate in land, and

   (b) the registration of an unregistered freehold legal estate in land in respect of land to which a former registered freehold estate in land related.

(2) Rules under this section may, in particular –

   (a) make provision for determination to be dependent on the meeting of such registration requirements as the rules may specify;

---

[1] Commencement: 13 October 2003 (Land Registration Act 2002 (Commencement No 4) Order 2003, SI 2003/1725).

[2] Commencement: 13 October 2003 (Land Registration Act 2002 (Commencement No 4) Order 2003, SI 2003/1725).

[3] Commencement: 13 October 2003 (Land Registration Act 2002 (Commencement No 4) Order 2003, SI 2003/1725).

(b) make provision for entries relating to a freehold estate in land to continue in the register, notwithstanding determination, for such time as the rules may provide;

(c) make provision for the making in the register in relation to a former freehold estate in land of such entries as the rules may provide;

(d) make provision imposing requirements to be met in connection with an application for the registration of such an unregistered estate as is mentioned in subsection (1)(b).

83[1]   Crown and Duchy land: representation

(1) With respect to a Crown or Duchy interest, the appropriate authority –

(a) may represent the owner of the interest for all purposes of this Act,

(b) is entitled to receive such notice as that person is entitled to receive under this Act, and

(c) may make such applications and do such other acts as that person is entitled to make or do under this Act.

(2) In this section –

'the appropriate authority' means –

(a) in relation to an interest belonging to Her Majesty in right of the Crown and forming part of the Crown Estate, the Crown Estate Commissioners;

(b) in relation to any other interest belonging to Her Majesty in right of the Crown, the government department having the management of the interest or, if there is no such department, such person as Her Majesty may appoint in writing under the Royal Sign Manual;

(c) in relation to an interest belonging to Her Majesty in right of the Duchy of Lancaster, the Chancellor of the Duchy;

(d) in relation to an interest belonging to the Duchy of Cornwall, such person as the Duke of Cornwall, or the possessor for the time being of the Duchy of Cornwall, appoints;

(e) in relation to an interest belonging to a government department, or held in trust for Her Majesty for the purposes of a government department, that department;

'Crown interest' means an interest belonging to Her Majesty in right of the Crown, or belonging to a government department, or held in trust for Her Majesty for the purposes of a government department;

'Duchy interest' means an interest belonging to Her Majesty in right of the Duchy of Lancaster, or belonging to the Duchy of Cornwall;

'interest' means any estate, interest or charge in or over land and any right or claim in relation to land.

84[2]   Disapplication of requirements relating to Duchy land

Nothing in any enactment relating to the Duchy of Lancaster or the Duchy of Cornwall shall have effect to impose any requirement with respect to formalities or enrolment in relation to a disposition by a registered proprietor.

85[3]   Bona vacantia

Rules may make provision about how the passing of a registered estate or charge as bona vacantia is to be dealt with for the purposes of this Act.

---

[1] Commencement: 13 October 2003 (Land Registration Act 2002 (Commencement No 4) Order 2003, SI 2003/1725).

[2] Commencement: 13 October 2003 (Land Registration Act 2002 (Commencement No 4) Order 2003, SI 2003/1725).

[3] Commencement: 13 October 2003 (Land Registration Act 2002 (Commencement No 4) Order 2003, SI 2003/1725).

Pending actions etc

86¹ Bankruptcy

(1) In this Act, references to an interest affecting an estate or charge do not include a petition in bankruptcy or bankruptcy order.

(2) As soon as practicable after registration of a petition in bankruptcy as a pending action under the Land Charges Act 1972, the registrar must enter in the register in relation to any registered estate or charge which appears to him to be affected a notice in respect of the pending action.

(3) Unless cancelled by the registrar in such manner as rules may provide, a notice entered under subsection (2) continues in force until –
  (a) a restriction is entered in the register under subsection (4), or
  (b) the trustee in bankruptcy is registered as proprietor.

(4) As soon as practicable after registration of a bankruptcy order under the Land Charges Act 1972, the registrar must, in relation to any registered estate or charge which appears to him to be affected by the order, enter in the register a restriction reflecting the effect of the Insolvency Act 1986.

(5) Where the proprietor of a registered estate or charge is adjudged bankrupt, the title of his trustee in bankruptcy is void as against a person to whom a registrable disposition of the estate or charge is made if –
  (a) the disposition is made for valuable consideration,
  (b) the person to whom the disposition is made acts in good faith, and
  (c) at the time of the disposition –
      (i)   no notice or restriction is entered under this section in relation to the registered estate or charge, and
      (ii) the person to whom the disposition is made has no notice of the bankruptcy petition or the adjudication.

(6) Subsection (5) only applies if the relevant registration requirements are met in relation to the disposition, but, when they are met, has effect as from the date of the disposition.

(7) Nothing in this section requires a person to whom a registrable disposition is made to make any search under the Land Charges Act 1972.

87² Pending land actions, writs, orders and deeds of arrangement

(1) Subject to the following provisions, references in this Act to an interest affecting an estate or charge include –
  (a) a pending land action within the meaning of the Land Charges Act 1972,
  (b) a writ or order of the kind mentioned in section 6(1)(a) of that Act (writ or order affecting land issued or made by any court for the purposes of enforcing a judgment or recognisance),
  (c) an order appointing a receiver or sequestrator, and
  (d) a deed of arrangement.

---

¹ Commencement: 13 October 2003 (Land Registration Act 2002 (Commencement No 4) Order 2003, SI 2003/1725).
² Commencement: 13 October 2003 (Land Registration Act 2002 (Commencement No 4) Order 2003, SI 2003/1725).

(2) No notice may be entered in the register in respect of –
  (a) an order appointing a receiver or sequestrator, or
  (b) a deed of arrangement.

(3) None of the matters mentioned in subsection (1) shall be capable of falling within paragraph 2 of Schedule 1 or 3.

(4) In its application to any of the matters mentioned in subsection (1), this Act shall have effect subject to such modifications as rules may provide.

(5) In this section, 'deed of arrangement' has the same meaning as in the Deeds of Arrangement Act 1914.

Miscellaneous

88[1]   Incorporeal hereditaments
In its application to –
  (a) rentcharges,
  (b) franchises,
  (c) profits a prendre in gross, or
  (d) manors,
this Act shall have effect subject to such modification as rules may provide.

89[2]   Settlements
(1) Rules may make provision for the purposes of this Act in relation to the application to registered land of the enactments relating to settlements under the Settled Land Act 1925.

(2) Rules under this section may include provision modifying any of those enactments in its application to registered land.

(3) In this section, 'registered land' means an interest the title to which is, or is required to be, registered.

90[3]   PPP leases relating to transport in London
(1) No application for registration under section 3 may be made in respect of a leasehold estate in land under a PPP lease.

(2) The requirement of registration does not apply on the grant or transfer of a leasehold estate in land under a PPP lease.

(3) For the purposes of section 27, the following are not dispositions requiring to be completed by registration –
  (a) the grant of a term of years absolute under a PPP lease;
  (b) the express grant of an interest falling within section 1(2) of the Law of Property Act 1925, where the interest is created for the benefit of a leasehold estate in land under a PPP lease.

---

[1] Commencement: 13 October 2003 (Land Registration Act 2002 (Commencement No 4) Order 2003, SI 2003/1725).
[2] Commencement: 13 October 2003 (Land Registration Act 2002 (Commencement No 4) Order 2003, SI 2003/1725).
[3] Commencement: 13 October 2003 (Land Registration Act 2002 (Commencement No 4) Order 2003, SI 2003/1725).

(4) No notice may be entered in the register in respect of an interest under a PPP lease.

(5) Schedules 1 and 3 have effect as if they included a paragraph referring to a PPP lease.

(6) In this section, 'PPP lease' has the meaning given by section 218 of the Greater London Authority Act 1999 (which makes provision about leases created for public-private partnerships relating to transport in London).

PART 8
ELECTRONIC CONVEYANCING

91[1] Electronic dispositions: formalities

(1) This section applies to a document in electronic form where –
  (a) the document purports to effect a disposition which falls within subsection (2), and
  (b) the conditions in subsection (3) are met.

(2) A disposition falls within this subsection if it is –
  (a) a disposition of a registered estate or charge,
  (b) a disposition of an interest which is the subject of a notice in the register, or
  (c) a disposition which triggers the requirement of registration,
    which is of a kind specified by rules.

(3) The conditions referred to above are that –
  (a) the document makes provision for the time and date when it takes effect,
  (b) the document has the electronic signature of each person by whom it purports to be authenticated,
  (c) each electronic signature is certified, and
  (d) such other conditions as rules may provide are met.

(4) A document to which this section applies is to be regarded as –
  (a) in writing, and
  (b) signed by each individual, and sealed by each corporation, whose electronic signature it has.

(5) A document to which this section applies is to be regarded for the purposes of any enactment as a deed.

(6) If a document to which this section applies is authenticated by a person as agent, it is to be regarded for the purposes of any enactment as authenticated by him under the written authority of his principal.

(7) If notice of an assignment made by means of a document to which this section applies is given in electronic form in accordance with rules, it is to be regarded for the purposes of any enactment as given in writing.

(8) The right conferred by section 75 of the Law of Property Act 1925 (purchaser's right to have the execution of a conveyance attested) does not apply to a document to which this section applies.

(9) If subsection (4) of section 36A of the Companies Act 1985 (execution of documents)

---

1   Commencement: 13 October 2003 (Land Registration Act 2002 (Commencement No 4) Order 2003, SI 2003/1725).

applies to a document because of subsection (4) above, subsection (6) of that section (presumption of due execution) shall have effect in relation to the document with the substitution of 'authenticated' for 'signed'.

[(9A) If subsection (3) of section 29C of the Industrial and Provident Societies Act 1965 (execution of documents) applies to a document because of subsection (4) above, subsection (5) of that section (presumption of due execution) shall have effect in relation to the document with the substitution of 'authenticated' for 'signed'.][1]

(10) In this section, references to an electronic signature and to the certification of such a signature are to be read in accordance with section 7(2) and (3) of the Electronic Communications Act 2000.

92[2]   Land registry network
(1) The registrar may provide, or arrange for the provision of, an electronic communications network for use for such purposes as he thinks fit relating to registration or the carrying on of transactions which –
  (a) involve registration, and
  (b) are capable of being effected electronically.

(2) Schedule 5 (which makes provision in connection with a network provided under subsection (1) and transactions carried on by means of such a network) has effect.

93[3]   Power to require simultaneous registration
(1) This section applies to a disposition of –
  (a) a registered estate or charge, or
  (b) an interest which is the subject of a notice in the register,
where the disposition is of a description specified by rules.

(2) A disposition to which this section applies, or a contract to make such a disposition, only has effect if it is made by means of a document in electronic form and if, when the document purports to take effect –
  (a) it is electronically communicated to the registrar, and
  (b) the relevant registration requirements are met.

(3) For the purposes of subsection (2)(b), the relevant registration requirements are –
  (a) in the case of a registrable disposition, the requirements under Schedule 2, and
  (b) in the case of any other disposition, or a contract, such requirements as rules may provide.

(4) Section 27(1) does not apply to a disposition to which this section applies.

(5) Before making rules under this section the Lord Chancellor must consult such persons as he considers appropriate.

---

[1]   Amendment: Subsection inserted: Co-operatives and Community Benefit Societies Act 2003, s 5(8), with effect from 20 October 2003 (Co-operatives and Community Benefit Societies Act 2003 (Commencement No 1) Order 2003, SI 2003/2678).

[2]   Commencement: 13 October 2003 (Land Registration Act 2002 (Commencement No 4) Order 2003, SI 2003/1725).

[3]   Commencement: 13 October 2003 (Land Registration Act 2002 (Commencement No 4) Order 2003, SI 2003/1725).

(6) In this section, 'disposition', in relation to a registered charge, includes postponement.

94[1]   Electronic settlement

The registrar may take such steps as he thinks fit for the purpose of securing the provision of a system of electronic settlement in relation to transactions involving registration.

95[2]   Supplementary

Rules may –

(a) make provision about the communication of documents in electronic form to the registrar;

(b) make provision about the electronic storage of documents communicated to the registrar in electronic form.

PART 9

ADVERSE POSSESSION

96[3]   Disapplication of periods of limitation

(1) No period of limitation under section 15 of the Limitation Act 1980 (time limits in relation to recovery of land) shall run against any person, other than a chargee, in relation to an estate in land or rentcharge the title to which is registered.

(2) No period of limitation under section 16 of that Act (time limits in relation to redemption of land) shall run against any person in relation to such an estate in land or rentcharge.

(3) Accordingly, section 17 of that Act (extinction of title on expiry of time limit) does not operate to extinguish the title of any person where, by virtue of this section, a period of limitation does not run against him.

97[4]   Registration of adverse possessor

Schedule 6 (which makes provision about the registration of an adverse possessor of an estate in land or rentcharge) has effect.

98[5]   Defences

(1) A person has a defence to an action for possession of land if –

(a) on the day immediately preceding that on which the action was brought he was entitled to make an application under paragraph 1 of Schedule 6 to be registered as the proprietor of an estate in the land, and

(b) had he made such an application on that day, the condition in paragraph 5(4) of that Schedule would have been satisfied.[6]

(2) A judgment for possession of land ceases to be enforceable at the end of the period of two years beginning with the date of the judgment if the proceedings in which the judgment is given

---

[1]   Commencement: 13 October 2003 (Land Registration Act 2002 (Commencement No 4) Order 2003, SI 2003/1725).

[2]   Commencement: 13 October 2003 (Land Registration Act 2002 (Commencement No 4) Order 2003, SI 2003/1725).

[3]   Commencement: 13 October 2003 (Land Registration Act 2002 (Commencement No 4) Order 2003, SI 2003/1725).

[4]   Commencement: See Sch 6.

[5]   Commencement: 13 October 2003 (subss (2)–(7)); 13 October 2004 (sub (1)) (Land Registration Act 2002 (Commencement No 4) Order 2003, SI 2003/1725).

[6]   Subsection in italics not in force until 13 October 2004: Land Registration Act 2002 (Commencement No 4) Order 2003, SI 2003/1725, para 2(2)(a).

were commenced against a person who was at that time entitled to make an application under paragraph 1 of Schedule 6.

(3) A person has a defence to an action for possession of land if on the day immediately preceding that on which the action was brought he was entitled to make an application under paragraph 6 of Schedule 6 to be registered as the proprietor of an estate in the land.

(4) A judgment for possession of land ceases to be enforceable at the end of the period of two years beginning with the date of the judgment if, at the end of that period, the person against whom the judgment was given is entitled to make an application under paragraph 6 of Schedule 6 to be registered as the proprietor of an estate in the land.

(5) Where in any proceedings a court determines that –
    (a) a person is entitled to a defence under this section, or
    (b) a judgment for possession has ceased to be enforceable against a person by virtue of subsection (4),

the court must order the registrar to register him as the proprietor of the estate in relation to which he is entitled to make an application under Schedule 6.

(6) The defences under this section are additional to any other defences a person may have.

(7) Rules may make provision to prohibit the recovery of rent due under a rentcharge from a person who has been in adverse possession of the rentcharge.

PART 10
LAND REGISTRY

Administration

99[1]   The land registry
(1) There is to continue to be an office called Her Majesty's Land Registry which is to deal with the business of registration under this Act.

(2) The land registry is to consist of –
    (a) the Chief Land Registrar, who is its head, and
    (b) the staff appointed by him;
and references in this Act to a member of the land registry are to be read accordingly.

(3) The Lord Chancellor shall appoint a person to be the Chief Land Registrar.

(4) Schedule 7 (which makes further provision about the land registry) has effect.

100[2]   Conduct of business
(1) Any function of the registrar may be carried out by any member of the land registry who is authorised for the purpose by the registrar.

---

[1]   Commencement: 13 October 2003 (Land Registration Act 2002 (Commencement No 4) Order 2003, SI 2003/1725).

[2]   Commencement: 13 October 2003 (Land Registration Act 2002 (Commencement No 4) Order 2003, SI 2003/1725).

(2) The Lord Chancellor may by regulations make provision about the carrying out of functions during any vacancy in the office of registrar.

(3) The Lord Chancellor may by order designate a particular office of the land registry as the proper office for the receipt of applications or a specified description of application.

(4) The registrar may prepare and publish such forms and directions as he considers necessary or desirable for facilitating the conduct of the business of registration under this Act.

101[1] Annual report

(1) The registrar must make an annual report on the business of the land registry to the Lord Chancellor.

(2) The registrar must publish every report under this section and may do so in such manner as he thinks fit.

(3) The Lord Chancellor must lay copies of every report under this section before Parliament. Fees and indemnities

102[2] Fee orders

The Lord Chancellor may with the advice and assistance of the body referred to in section 127(2) (the Rule Committee), and the consent of the Treasury, by order –
  (a) prescribe fees to be paid in respect of dealings with the land registry, except under section 69(3)(b) or 105;
  (b) make provision about the payment of prescribed fees.

103[3] Indemnities

Schedule 8 (which makes provision for the payment of indemnities by the registrar) has effect.

Miscellaneous

104[4] General information about land

The registrar may publish information about land in England and Wales if it appears to him to be information in which there is legitimate public interest.

105[5] Consultancy and advisory services

(1) The registrar may provide, or arrange for the provision of, consultancy or advisory services about the registration of land in England and Wales or elsewhere.

(2) The terms on which services are provided under this section by the registrar, in particular terms as to payment, shall be such as he thinks fit.

---

[1] Commencement: 13 October 2003 (Land Registration Act 2002 (Commencement No 4) Order 2003, SI 2003/1725).
[2] Commencement: 27 June 2003 (Land Registration Act 2002 (Commencement No 3) Order 2003, SI 2003/1612).
[3] Commencement: 13 October 2003 (Land Registration Act 2002 (Commencement No 4) Order 2003, SI 2003/1725).
[4] Commencement: 13 October 2003 (Land Registration Act 2002 (Commencement No 4) Order 2003, SI 2003/1725).
[5] Commencement: 13 October 2003 (Land Registration Act 2002 (Commencement No 4) Order 2003, SI 2003/1725).

106[1]   Incidental powers: companies

(1) If the registrar considers it expedient to do so in connection with his functions under section 69(3)(a), 92(1), 94 or 105(1) or paragraph 10 of Schedule 5, he may –

    (a) form, or participate in the formation of, a company, or

    (b) purchase, or invest in, a company.

(2) In this section –

    'company' means a company within the meaning of the Companies Act 1985;

    'invest' means invest in any way (whether by acquiring assets, securities or rights or otherwise).

(3) This section is without prejudice to any powers of the registrar exercisable otherwise than by virtue of this section.

PART 11
ADJUDICATION

107[2]   The adjudicator

(1) The Lord Chancellor shall appoint a person to be the Adjudicator to Her Majesty's Land Registry.

(2) To be qualified for appointment under subsection (1), a person must have a 10 year general qualification (within the meaning of section 71 of the Courts and Legal Services Act 1990).

(3) Schedule 9 (which makes further provision about the adjudicator) has effect.

108[3]   Jurisdiction

(1) The adjudicator has the following functions –

    (a) determining matters referred to him under section 73(7), and

    (b) determining appeals under paragraph 4 of Schedule 5.

(2) Also, the adjudicator may, on application, make any order which the High Court could make for the rectification or setting aside of a document which –

    (a) effects a qualifying disposition of a registered estate or charge,

    (b) is a contract to make such a disposition, or

    (c) effects a transfer of an interest which is the subject of a notice in the register.

(3) For the purposes of subsection (2)(a), a qualifying disposition is –

    (a) a registrable disposition, or

    (b) a disposition which creates an interest which may be the subject of a notice in the register.

(4) The general law about the effect of an order of the High Court for the rectification or setting aside of a document shall apply to an order under this section.

---

[1]   Commencement: 13 October 2003 (Land Registration Act 2002 (Commencement No 4) Order 2003, SI 2003/1725).

[2]   Commencement: 28 April 2003 (subss (1), (2)) (Land Registration Act 2002 (Commencement No 2) Order 2003, SI 2003/1028); see Sch 9 (subs (3)).

[3]   Commencement: 13 October 2003 (Land Registration Act 2002 (Commencement No 4) Order 2003, SI 2003/1725).

109¹   Procedure

(1) Hearings before the adjudicator shall be held in public, except where he is satisfied that exclusion of the public is just and reasonable.

(2) Subject to that, rules may regulate the practice and procedure to be followed with respect to proceedings before the adjudicator and matters incidental to or consequential on such proceedings.

(3) Rules under subsection (2) may, in particular, make provision about –
  (a) when hearings are to be held,
  (b) requiring persons to attend hearings to give evidence or to produce documents,
  (c) the form in which any decision of the adjudicator is to be given,
  (d) payment of costs of a party to proceedings by another party to the proceedings, and
  (e) liability for costs thrown away as the result of neglect or delay by a legal representative of a party to proceedings.

110²   Functions in relation to disputes

(1) In proceedings on a reference under section 73(7), the adjudicator may, instead of deciding a matter himself, direct a party to the proceedings to commence proceedings within a specified time in the court for the purpose of obtaining the court's decision on the matter.

(2) Rules may make provision about the reference under subsection (1) of matters to the court and may, in particular, make provision about –
  (a) adjournment of the proceedings before the adjudicator pending the outcome of the proceedings before the court, and
  (b) the powers of the adjudicator in the event of failure to comply with a direction under subsection (1).

(3) Rules may make provision about the functions of the adjudicator in consequence of a decision on a reference under section 73(7) and may, in particular, make provision enabling the adjudicator to determine, or give directions about the determination of –
  (a) the application to which the reference relates, or
  (b) such other present or future application to the registrar as the rules may provide.

(4) If, in the case of a reference under section 73(7) relating to an application under paragraph 1 of Schedule 6, the adjudicator determines that it would be unconscionable because of an equity by estoppel for the registered proprietor to seek to dispossess the applicant, but that the circumstances are not such that the applicant ought to be registered as proprietor, the adjudicator –
  (a) must determine how the equity due to the applicant is to be satisfied, and
  (b) may for that purpose make any order that the High Court could make in the exercise of its equitable jurisdiction.

111³   Appeals

(1) Subject to subsection (2), a person aggrieved by a decision of the adjudicator may appeal to the High Court.

---

¹   Commencement: 13 October 2003 (Land Registration Act 2002 (Commencement No 4) Order 2003, SI 2003/1725).
²   Commencement: 13 October 2003 (Land Registration Act 2002 (Commencement No 4) Order 2003, SI 2003/1725).
³   Commencement: 13 October 2003 (Land Registration Act 2002 (Commencement No 4) Order 2003, SI 2003/1725).

(2) In the case of a decision on an appeal under paragraph 4 of Schedule 5, only appeal on a point of law is possible.

(3) If on an appeal under this section relating to an application under paragraph 1 of Schedule 6 the court determines that it would be unconscionable because of an equity by estoppel for the registered proprietor to seek to dispossess the applicant, but that the circumstances are not such that the applicant ought to be registered as proprietor, the court must determine how the equity due to the applicant is to be satisfied.

112[1]   Enforcement of orders etc
A requirement of the adjudicator shall be enforceable as an order of the court.

113[2]   Fees
The Lord Chancellor may by order –
    (a) prescribe fees to be paid in respect of proceedings before the adjudicator;
    (b) make provision about the payment of prescribed fees.

114[3]   Supplementary
Power to make rules under this Part is exercisable by the Lord Chancellor.

PART 12
MISCELLANEOUS AND GENERAL

Miscellaneous

115[4]   Rights of pre-emption
(1) A right of pre-emption in relation to registered land has effect from the time of creation as an interest capable of binding successors in title (subject to the rules about the effect of dispositions on priority).

(2) This section has effect in relation to rights of pre-emption created on or after the day on which this section comes into force.

116[5]   Proprietary estoppel and mere equities
It is hereby declared for the avoidance of doubt that, in relation to registered land, each of the following –
    (a) an equity by estoppel, and
    (b) a mere equity,
has effect from the time the equity arises as an interest capable of binding successors in title (subject to the rules about the effect of dispositions on priority).

---

[1] Commencement: 13 October 2003 (Land Registration Act 2002 (Commencement No 4) Order 2003, SI 2003/1725).

[2] Commencement: 13 October 2003 (Land Registration Act 2002 (Commencement No 4) Order 2003, SI 2003/1725).

[3] Commencement: 13 October 2003 (Land Registration Act 2002 (Commencement No 4) Order 2003, SI 2003/1725).

[4] Commencement: 13 October 2003 (Land Registration Act 2002 (Commencement No 4) Order 2003, SI 2003/1725).

[5] Commencement: 13 October 2003 (Land Registration Act 2002 (Commencement No 4) Order 2003, SI 2003/1725).

117[1] Reduction in unregistered interests with automatic protection

(1) Paragraphs 10 to 14 of Schedules 1 and 3 shall cease to have effect at the end of the period of ten years beginning with the day on which those Schedules come into force.

(2) If made before the end of the period mentioned in subsection (1), no fee may be charged for –
  (a) an application to lodge a caution against first registration by virtue of an interest falling within any of paragraphs 10 to 14 of Schedule 1, or
  (b) an application for the entry in the register of a notice in respect of an interest falling within any of paragraphs 10 to 14 of Schedule 3.

118[2] Power to reduce qualifying term

(1) The Lord Chancellor may by order substitute for the term specified in any of the following provisions –
  (a) section 3(3),
  (b) section 4(1)(c)(i) and (2)(b),
  (c) section 15(3)(a)(ii),
  (d) section 27(2)(b)(i),
  (e) section 80(1)(b)(i),
  (f) paragraph 1 of Schedule 1,
  (g) paragraphs 4(1), 5(1) and 6(1) of Schedule 2, and
  (h) paragraph 1 of Schedule 3,
such shorter term as he thinks fit.

(2) An order under this section may contain such transitional provision as the Lord Chancellor thinks fit.

(3) Before making an order under this section, the Lord Chancellor must consult such persons as he considers appropriate.

119[3] Power to deregister manors

On the application of the proprietor of a registered manor, the registrar may remove the title to the manor from the register.

120[4] Conclusiveness of filed copies etc

(1) This section applies where –
  (a) a disposition relates to land to which a registered estate relates, and
  (b) an entry in the register relating to the registered estate refers to a document kept by the registrar which is not an original.

(2) As between the parties to the disposition, the document kept by the registrar is to be taken –
  (a) to be correct, and
  (b) to contain all the material parts of the original document.

[1] Commencement: 13 October 2003 (Land Registration Act 2002 (Commencement No 4) Order 2003, SI 2003/1725).
[2] Commencement: 13 October 2003 (Land Registration Act 2002 (Commencement No 4) Order 2003, SI 2003/1725).
[3] Commencement: 13 October 2003 (Land Registration Act 2002 (Commencement No 4) Order 2003, SI 2003/1725).
[4] Commencement: 13 October 2003 (Land Registration Act 2002 (Commencement No 4) Order 2003, SI 2003/1725).

(3) No party to the disposition may require production of the original document.

(4) No party to the disposition is to be affected by any provision of the original document which is not contained in the document kept by the registrar.

121¹   Forwarding of applications to registrar of companies
The Lord Chancellor may by rules make provision about the transmission by the registrar to the registrar of companies (within the meaning of the Companies Act 1985) of applications under –
(a) Part 12 of that Act (registration of charges), or
(b) Chapter 3 of Part 23 of that Act (corresponding provision for oversea companies).

122²   Repeal of Land Registry Act 1862
(1) The Land Registry Act 1862 shall cease to have effect.

(2) The registrar shall have custody of records of title made under that Act.

(3) The registrar may discharge his duty under subsection (2) by keeping the relevant information in electronic form.

(4) The registrar may on application provide a copy of any information included in a record of title made under that Act.

(5) Rules may make provision about applications for the exercise of the power conferred by subsection (4).

Offences etc

123³   Suppression of information
(1) A person commits an offence if in the course of proceedings relating to registration under this Act he suppresses information with the intention of –
(a) concealing a person's right or claim, or
(b) substantiating a false claim.

(2) A person guilty of an offence under this section is liable –
(a) on conviction on indictment, to imprisonment for a term not exceeding two years or to a fine;
(b) on summary conviction, to imprisonment for a term not exceeding six months or to a fine not exceeding the statutory maximum, or to both.

124⁴   Improper alteration of the registers
(1) A person commits an offence if he dishonestly induces another –
(a) to change the register of title or cautions register, or
(b) to authorise the making of such a change.

---

1   Commencement: 13 October 2003 (Land Registration Act 2002 (Commencement No 4) Order 2003, SI 2003/1725).
2   Commencement: 13 October 2003 (Land Registration Act 2002 (Commencement No 4) Order 2003, SI 2003/1725).
3   Commencement: 13 October 2003 (Land Registration Act 2002 (Commencement No 4) Order 2003, SI 2003/1725).
4   Commencement: 13 October 2003 (Land Registration Act 2002 (Commencement No 4) Order 2003, SI 2003/1725).

(2) A person commits an offence if he intentionally or recklessly makes an unauthorised change in the register of title or cautions register.

(3) A person guilty of an offence under this section is liable –
    (a) on conviction on indictment, to imprisonment for a term not exceeding 2 years or to a fine;
    (b) on summary conviction, to imprisonment for a term not exceeding six months or to a fine not exceeding the statutory maximum, or to both.

(4) In this section, references to changing the register of title include changing a document referred to in it.

125[1] Privilege against self-incrimination

(1) The privilege against self-incrimination, so far as relating to offences under this Act, shall not entitle a person to refuse to answer any question or produce any document or thing in any legal proceedings other than criminal proceedings.

(2) No evidence obtained under subsection (1) shall be admissible in any criminal proceedings under this Act against the person from whom it was obtained or that person's spouse.

Land registration rules

126[2] Miscellaneous and general powers

Schedule 10 (which contains miscellaneous and general land registration rule-making powers) has effect.

127[3] Exercise of powers

(1) Power to make land registration rules is exercisable by the Lord Chancellor with the advice and assistance of the Rule Committee.

(2) The Rule Committee is a body consisting of –
    (a) a judge of the Chancery Division of the High Court nominated by the Lord Chancellor,
    (b) the registrar,
    (c) a person nominated by the General Council of the Bar,
    (d) a person nominated by the Council of the Law Society,
    (e) a person nominated by the Council of Mortgage Lenders,
    (f) a person nominated by the Council of Licensed Conveyancers,
    (g) a person nominated by the Royal Institution of Chartered Surveyors,
    (h) a person with experience in, and knowledge of, consumer affairs, and
    (i) any person nominated under subsection (3).

(3) The Lord Chancellor may nominate to be a member of the Rule Committee any person who appears to him to have qualifications or experience which would be of value to the committee in considering any matter with which it is concerned.

---

[1] Commencement: 13 October 2003 (Land Registration Act 2002 (Commencement No 4) Order 2003, SI 2003/1725).

[2] Commencement: 13 October 2003 (Land Registration Act 2002 (Commencement No 4) Order 2003, SI 2003/1725).

[3] Commencement: 13 October 2003 (Land Registration Act 2002 (Commencement No 4) Order 2003, SI 2003/1725).

Supplementary

128¹   Rules, regulations and orders

(1) Any power of the Lord Chancellor to make rules, regulations or orders under this Act includes power to make different provision for different cases.

(2) Any power of the Lord Chancellor to make rules, regulations or orders under this Act is exercisable by statutory instrument.

(3) A statutory instrument containing –
    (a) regulations under section 100(2), or
    (b) an order under section 100(3), 102 or 113,
is to be laid before Parliament after being made.

(4) A statutory instrument containing –
    (a) land registration rules,
    (b) rules under Part 11 or section 121,
    (c) regulations under paragraph 5 of Schedule 9, or
    (d) an order under section 5(1), 62(9), 80(4), 118(1) or 130,
is subject to annulment in pursuance of a resolution of either House of Parliament.

(5) Rules under section 93 or paragraph 1, 2 or 3 of Schedule 5 shall not be made unless a draft of the rules has been laid before and approved by resolution of each House of Parliament.

129²   Crown application

This Act binds the Crown.

130³   Application to internal waters

This Act applies to land covered by internal waters of the United Kingdom which are –
    (a) within England or Wales, or
    (b) adjacent to England or Wales and specified for the purposes of this section by order made by the Lord Chancellor.

131⁴   'Proprietor in possession'

(1) For the purposes of this Act, land is in the possession of the proprietor of a registered estate in land if it is physically in his possession, or in that of a person who is entitled to be registered as the proprietor of the registered estate.

(2) In the case of the following relationships, land which is (or is treated as being) in the possession of the second-mentioned person is to be treated for the purposes of subsection (1) as in the possession of the first-mentioned person –
    (a) landlord and tenant;
    (b) mortgagor and mortgagee;
    (c) licensor and licensee;

---

[1] Commencement: 4 April 2003 (Land Registration Act 2002 (Commencement No 1) Order 2003, SI 2003/935).

[2] Commencement: 4 April 2003 (Land Registration Act 2002 (Commencement No 1) Order 2003, SI 2003/935).

[3] Commencement: 4 April 2003 (Land Registration Act 2002 (Commencement No 1) Order 2003, SI 2003/935).

[4] Commencement: 4 April 2003 (Land Registration Act 2002 (Commencement No 1) Order 2003, SI 2003/935).

(d) trustee and beneficiary.

(3) In subsection (1), the reference to entitlement does not include entitlement under Schedule 6.

132[1] General interpretation

(1) In this Act –

'adjudicator' means the Adjudicator to Her Majesty's Land Registry;

'caution against first registration' means a caution lodged under section 15;

'cautions register' means the register kept under section 19(1);

'charge' means any mortgage, charge or lien for securing money or money's worth;

'demesne land' means land belonging to Her Majesty in right of the Crown which is not held for an estate in fee simple absolute in possession;

'land' includes –

(a) buildings and other structures,

(b) land covered with water, and

(c) mines and minerals, whether or not held with the surface;

'land registration rules' means any rules under this Act, other than rules under section 93, Part 11, section 121 or paragraph 1, 2 or 3 of Schedule 5;

'legal estate' has the same meaning as in the Law of Property Act 1925;

'legal mortgage' has the same meaning as in the Law of Property Act 1925;

'mines and minerals' includes any strata or seam of minerals or substances in or under any land, and powers of working and getting any such minerals or substances;

'registrar' means the Chief Land Registrar;

'register' means the register of title, except in the context of cautions against first registration;

'registered' means entered in the register;

'registered charge' means a charge the title to which is entered in the register;

'registered estate' means a legal estate the title to which is entered in the register, other than a registered charge;

'registered land' means a registered estate or registered charge;

'registrable disposition' means a disposition which is required to be completed by registration under section 27;

'requirement of registration' means the requirement of registration under section 4;

'sub-charge' means a charge under section 23(2)(b);

'term of years absolute' has the same meaning as in the Law of Property Act 1925;

'valuable consideration' does not include marriage consideration or a nominal consideration in money.

(2) In subsection (1), in the definition of 'demesne land', the reference to land belonging to Her Majesty does not include land in relation to which a freehold estate in land has determined, but in relation to which there has been no act of entry or management by the Crown.

(3) In this Act –

(a) references to the court are to the High Court or a county court,

(b) references to an interest affecting an estate or charge are to an adverse right affecting the title to the estate or charge, and

(c) references to the right to object to an application to the registrar are to the right under section 73.

---

1   Commencement: 4 April 2003 (Land Registration Act 2002 (Commencement No 1) Order 2003, SI 2003/935).

Final provisions

133[1]   Minor and consequential amendments

Schedule 11 (which makes minor and consequential amendments) has effect.

134[2]   Transition

(1) The Lord Chancellor may by order make such transitional provisions and savings as he thinks fit in connection with the coming into force of any of the provisions of this Act.

(2) Schedule 12 (which makes transitional provisions and savings) has effect.

(3) Nothing in Schedule 12 affects the power to make transitional provisions and savings under subsection (1); and an order under that subsection may modify any provision made by that Schedule.

135[3]   Repeals

The enactments specified in Schedule 13 (which include certain provisions which are already spent) are hereby repealed to the extent specified there.

136[4]   Short title, commencement and extent

(1) This Act may be cited as the Land Registration Act 2002.

(2) This Act shall come into force on such day as the Lord Chancellor may by order appoint, and different days may be so appointed for different purposes.

(3) Subject to subsection (4), this Act extends to England and Wales only.

(4) Any amendment or repeal by this Act of an existing enactment, other than –
    (a) section 37 of the Requisitioned Land and War Works Act 1945, and
    (b) Schedule 2A to the Building Societies Act 1986,
has the same extent as the enactment amended or repealed.

Schedules

Schedule 1[5]
Unregistered Interests Which Override First Registration

Sections 11 and 12

Leasehold estates in land
1   A leasehold estate in land granted for a term not exceeding seven years from the date of the grant, except for a lease the grant of which falls within section 4(1) (d), (e) or (f).

---

[1] Commencement: See Sch 11.
[2] Commencement: 4 April 2003 (subs (1)) (Land Registration Act 2002 (Commencement No 1) Order 2003, SI 2003/935); 13 October 2003 (subs (3)) (Land Registration Act 2002 (Commencement No 4) Order 2003, SI 2003/1725); See Sch 12 (subs (2)).
[3] Commencement: See Sch 13.
[4] Commencement: 4 April 2003 (Land Registration Act 2002 (Commencement No 1) Order 2003, SI 2003/935).
[5] Commencement: 13 October 2003 (Land Registration Act 2002 (Commencement No 4) Order 2003, SI 2003/1725).

Interests of persons in actual occupation

2   An interest belonging to a person in actual occupation, so far as relating to land of which he is in actual occupation, except for an interest under a settlement under the Settled Land Act 1925.

Easements and profits a prendre

3   A legal easement or profit a prendre.

Customary and public rights

4   A customary right.

5   A public right.

Local land charges

6   A local land charge.

Mines and minerals

7   An interest in any coal or coal mine, the rights attached to any such interest and the rights of any person under section 38, 49 or 51 of the Coal Industry Act 1994.

8   In the case of land to which title was registered before 1898, rights to mines and minerals (and incidental rights) created before 1898.

9   In the case of land to which title was registered between 1898 and 1925 inclusive, rights to mines and minerals (and incidental rights) created before the date of registration of the title.

Miscellaneous

10   A franchise.

11   A manorial right.

12   A right to rent which was reserved to the Crown on the granting of any freehold estate (whether or not the right is still vested in the Crown).

13   A non-statutory right in respect of an embankment or sea or river wall.

14   A right to payment in lieu of tithe. …[1]

[15 A right acquired under the Limitation Act 1980 before the coming into force of this Schedule.][2]

[16 A right in respect of the repair of a church chancel.][3]

---

[1]   Prospective amendment: Paragraphs in italics prospectively repealed by Land Registration Act 2002, s 117(1), with effect from 13 October 2013 (Land Registration Act 2002, s 117(1), Land Registration Act 2002 (Commencement No 4) Order 2003, SI 2003/1725).

[2]   Amendment: Paragraph inserted: Land Registration Act 2002, s 134(2), Sch 12, para 7, with effect from 13 October 2003 to 13 October 2006 (Land Registration Act 2002, s 134(2), Sch 12, para 7, Land Registration Act 2002 (Commencement No 4) Order 2003, SI 2003/1725).

[3]   Amendment: Paragraph inserted: Land Registration Act 2002 (Transitional Provisions) (No 2) Order 2003, SI 2003/2431, with effect from 13 October 2003 to 13 October 2013 (Land Registration Act 2002 (Commencement No 4) Order 2003, SI 2003/1725, Land Registration Act 2002 (Transitional Provisions) (No 2) Order 2003, SI 2003/2431).

Schedule 2[1]
Registrable Dispositions: Registration Requirements

Section 27

PART 1
REGISTERED ESTATES

Introductory

1   This Part deals with the registration requirements relating to those dispositions of registered estates which are required to be completed by registration.

Transfer

2—(1) In the case of a transfer of whole or part, the transferee, or his successor in title, must be entered in the register as the proprietor.

(2) In the case of a transfer of part, such details of the transfer as rules may provide must be entered in the register in relation to the registered estate out of which the transfer is made.

Lease of estate in land

3—(1) This paragraph applies to a disposition consisting of the grant out of an estate in land of a term of years absolute.

(2) In the case of a disposition to which this paragraph applies –
   (a) the grantee, or his successor in title, must be entered in the register as the proprietor of the lease, and
   (b) a notice in respect of the lease must be entered in the register.

Lease of franchise or manor

4—(1) This paragraph applies to a disposition consisting of the grant out of a franchise or manor of a lease for a term of more than seven years from the date of the grant.

(2) In the case of a disposition to which this paragraph applies –
   (a) the grantee, or his successor in title, must be entered in the register as the proprietor of the lease, and
   (b) a notice in respect of the lease must be entered in the register.

5—(1) This paragraph applies to a disposition consisting of the grant out of a franchise or manor of a lease for a term not exceeding seven years from the date of the grant.

(2) In the case of a disposition to which this paragraph applies, a notice in respect of the lease must be entered in the register.

Creation of independently registrable legal interest

6—(1) This paragraph applies to a disposition consisting of the creation of a legal rentcharge or profit a prendre in gross, other than one created for, or for an interest equivalent to, a term of years absolute not exceeding seven years from the date of creation.

(2) In the case of a disposition to which this paragraph applies –
   (a) the grantee, or his successor in title, must be entered in the register as the proprietor of the interest created, and

---

[1]   Commencement: 13 October 2003 (Land Registration Act 2002 (Commencement No 4) Order 2003, SI 2003/1725).

(b) a notice in respect of the interest created must be entered in the register.

(3) In sub-paragraph (1), the reference to a legal rentcharge or profit a prendre in gross is to one falling within section 1(2) of the Law of Property Act 1925.

Creation of other legal interest
7—(1) This paragraph applies to a disposition which –
  (a) consists of the creation of an interest of a kind falling within section 1(2)(a), (b) or (e) of the Law of Property Act 1925, and
  (b) is not a disposition to which paragraph 4, 5 or 6 applies.

(2) In the case of a disposition to which this paragraph applies –
  (a) a notice in respect of the interest created must be entered in the register, and
  (b) if the interest is created for the benefit of a registered estate, the proprietor of the registered estate must be entered in the register as its proprietor.

(3) Rules may provide for sub-paragraph (2) to have effect with modifications in relation to a right of entry over or in respect of a term of years absolute.

Creation of legal charge
8   In the case of the creation of a charge, the chargee, or his successor in title, must be entered in the register as the proprietor of the charge.

PART 2
REGISTERED CHARGES

Introductory
9   This Part deals with the registration requirements relating to those dispositions of registered charges which are required to be completed by registration.

Transfer
10   In the case of a transfer, the transferee, or his successor in title, must be entered in the register as the proprietor.

Creation of sub-charge
11   In the case of the creation of a sub-charge, the sub-chargee, or his successor in title, must be entered in the register as the proprietor of the sub-charge.

Schedule 3[1]
Unregistered Interests Which Override Registered Dispositions

Sections 29 and 30

Leasehold estates in land
1   A leasehold estate in land granted for a term not exceeding seven years from the date of the grant, except for –
  (a) a lease the grant of which falls within section 4(1)(d), (e) or (f);
  (b) a lease the grant of which constitutes a registrable disposition.

---

[1]   Commencement: 13 October 2003 (Land Registration Act 2002 (Commencement No 4) Order 2003, SI 2003/1725).

Interests of persons in actual occupation

2   An interest belonging at the time of the disposition to a person in actual occupation, so far as relating to land of which he is in actual occupation, except for –

(a)   an interest under a settlement under the Settled Land Act 1925;

(b)   an interest of a person of whom inquiry was made before the disposition and who failed to disclose the right when he could reasonably have been expected to do so;

(c)   an interest –

(i)   which belongs to a person whose occupation would not have been obvious on a reasonably careful inspection of the land at the time of the disposition, and

(ii)   of which the person to whom the disposition is made does not have actual knowledge at that time;

(d)   a leasehold estate in land granted to take effect in possession after the end of the period of three months beginning with the date of the grant and which has not taken effect in possession at the time of the disposition.

[2A—(1) An interest which, immediately before the coming into force of this Schedule, was an overriding interest under section 70(1)(g) of the Land Registration Act 1925 by virtue of a person's receipt of rents and profits, except for an interest of a person of whom inquiry was made before the disposition and who failed to disclose the right when he could reasonably have been expected to do so.

(2) Sub-paragraph (1) does not apply to an interest if at any time since the coming into force of this Schedule it has been an interest which, had the Land Registration Act 1925 (c 21) continued in force, would not have been an overriding interest under section 70(1)(g) of that Act by virtue of a person's receipt of rents and profits.][1]

Easements and profits a prendre

3—(1) A legal easement or profit a prendre, *except for an easement, or a profit a prendre which is not registered under the Commons Registration Act 1965 (c 64), which at the time of the disposition –*

(a)   is not within the actual knowledge of the person to whom the disposition is made, and

(b)   would not have been obvious on a reasonably careful inspection of the land over which the easement or profit is exercisable.

(2)   The exception in sub-paragraph (1) does not apply if the person entitled to the easement or profit proves that it has been exercised in the period of one year ending with the day of the disposition.[2]

Customary and public rights

4   A customary right.

5   A public right.

Local land charges

6   A local land charge.

Mines and minerals

7   An interest in any coal or coal mine, the rights attached to any such interest and the rights of any person under section 38, 49 or 51 of the Coal Industry Act 1994.

---

[1]   Amendment: Paragraph inserted: Land Registration Act 2002, s 134(2), Sch 12, para 8, with effect from 13 October 2003 (Land Registration Act 2002, Sch 12, para 8, Land Registration Act 2002 (Commencement No 4) Order 2003, SI 2003/1725).

[2]   Words in italics not in force until 13 October 2006: Land Registration Act 2002, s 134(2), Sch 12, para 10.

8   In the case of land to which title was registered before 1898, rights to mines and minerals (and incidental rights) created before 1898.

9   In the case of land to which title was registered between 1898 and 1925 inclusive, rights to mines and minerals (and incidental rights) created before the date of registration of the title.

Miscellaneous
10   *A franchise.*

11   *A manorial right.*

12   *A right to rent which was reserved to the Crown on the granting of any freehold estate (whether or not the right is still vested in the Crown).*

13   *A non-statutory right in respect of an embankment or sea or river wall.*

14   *A right to payment in lieu of tithe. ...*[1]

[15   A right under paragraph 18(1) of Schedule 12.][2]

[16   A right in respect of the repair of a church chancel.][3]

Schedule 4[4]
Alteration of the Register

Section 65

Introductory
1   In this Schedule, references to rectification, in relation to alteration of the register, are to alteration which –
  (a) involves the correction of a mistake, and
  (b) prejudicially affects the title of a registered proprietor.

Alteration pursuant to a court order
2— (1) The court may make an order for alteration of the register for the purpose of –
  (a) correcting a mistake,
  (b) bringing the register up to date, or
  (c) giving effect to any estate, right or interest excepted from the effect of registration.

(2) An order under this paragraph has effect when served on the registrar to impose a duty on him to give effect to it.

---

[1]   Prospective amendment: Paragraphs in italics prospectively repealed by Land Registration Act 2002, s 117(1), with effect from 13 October 2013 (Land Registration Act 2002, s 117(1), Land Registration Act 2002 (Commencement No 4) Order 2003, SI 2003/1725).

[2]   Amendment: Paragraph inserted: Land Registration Act 2002, 134(2), Sch 12, para 11, with effect from 13 October 2003 (Land Registration Act 2002, Sch 12, para 11, Land Registration Act 2002 (Commencement No 4) Order 2003, SI 2003/1725).

[3]   Amendment: Paragraph inserted: Land Registration Act 2002 (Transitional Provisions) (No 2) Order 2003, SI 2003/2431, with effect from 13 October 2003 to 13 October 2013 (Land Registration Act 2002 (Commencement No 4) Order 2003, SI 2003/1725, Land Registration Act 2002 (Transitional Provisions) (No 2) Order 2003, SI 2003/2431).

[4]   Commencement: 13 October 2003 (Land Registration Act 2002 (Commencement No 4) Order 2003, SI 2003/1725).

3—(1) This paragraph applies to the power under paragraph 2, so far as relating to rectification.

(2) If alteration affects the title of the proprietor of a registered estate in land, no order may be made under paragraph 2 without the proprietor's consent in relation to land in his possession unless –
- (a) he has by fraud or lack of proper care caused or substantially contributed to the mistake, or
- (b) it would for any other reason be unjust for the alteration not to be made.

(3) If in any proceedings the court has power to make an order under paragraph 2, it must do so, unless there are exceptional circumstances which justify its not doing so.

(4) In sub-paragraph (2), the reference to the title of the proprietor of a registered estate in land includes his title to any registered estate which subsists for the benefit of the estate in land.

4   Rules may –
- (a) make provision about the circumstances in which there is a duty to exercise the power under paragraph 2, so far as not relating to rectification;
- (b) make provision about the form of an order under paragraph 2;
- (c) make provision about service of such an order.

Alteration otherwise than pursuant to a court order
5   The registrar may alter the register for the purpose of –
- (a) correcting a mistake,
- (b) bringing the register up to date,
- (c) giving effect to any estate, right or interest excepted from the effect of registration, or
- (d) removing a superfluous entry.

6—(1) This paragraph applies to the power under paragraph 5, so far as relating to rectification.

(2) No alteration affecting the title of the proprietor of a registered estate in land may be made under paragraph 5 without the proprietor's consent in relation to land in his possession unless –
- (a) he has by fraud or lack of proper care caused or substantially contributed to the mistake, or
- (b) it would for any other reason be unjust for the alteration not to be made.

(3) If on an application for alteration under paragraph 5 the registrar has power to make the alteration, the application must be approved, unless there are exceptional circumstances which justify not making the alteration.

(4) In sub-paragraph (2), the reference to the title of the proprietor of a registered estate in land includes his title to any registered estate which subsists for the benefit of the estate in land.

7   Rules may –
- (a) make provision about the circumstances in which there is a duty to exercise the power under paragraph 5, so far as not relating to rectification;
- (b) make provision about how the register is to be altered in exercise of that power;
- (c) make provision about applications for alteration under that paragraph, including provision requiring the making of such applications;
- (d) make provision about procedure in relation to the exercise of that power, whether on application or otherwise.

Rectification and derivative interests

8   The powers under this Schedule to alter the register, so far as relating to rectification, extend to changing for the future the priority of any interest affecting the registered estate or charge concerned.

Costs in non-rectification cases

9—(1) If the register is altered under this Schedule in a case not involving rectification, the registrar may pay such amount as he thinks fit in respect of any costs or expenses reasonably incurred by a person in connection with the alteration which have been incurred with the consent of the registrar.

(2) The registrar may make a payment under sub-paragraph (1) notwithstanding the absence of consent if –

  (a) it appears to him –
    (i)   that the costs or expenses had to be incurred urgently, and
    (ii)   that it was not reasonably practicable to apply for his consent, or
  (b) he has subsequently approved the incurring of the costs or expenses.

Schedule 5[1]
Land Registry Network

Section 92

Access to network

1—(1) A person who is not a member of the land registry may only have access to a land registry network under authority conferred by means of an agreement with the registrar.

(2) An agreement for the purposes of sub-paragraph (1) ('network access agreement') may authorise access for –

  (a) the communication, posting or retrieval of information,
  (b) the making of changes to the register of title or cautions register,
  (c) the issue of official search certificates,
  (d) the issue of official copies, or
  (e) such other conveyancing purposes as the registrar thinks fit.

(3) Rules may regulate the use of network access agreements to confer authority to carry out functions of the registrar.

(4) The registrar must, on application, enter into a network access agreement with the applicant if the applicant meets such criteria as rules may provide.

Terms of access

2—(1) The terms on which access to a land registry network is authorised shall be such as the registrar thinks fit, subject to sub-paragraphs (3) and (4), and may, in particular, include charges for access.

(2) The power under sub-paragraph (1) may be used, not only for the purpose of regulating the use of the network, but also for –

  (a) securing that the person granted access uses the network to carry on such qualifying transactions as may be specified in, or under, the agreement,

---

[1]   Commencement: 13 October 2003 (Land Registration Act 2002 (Commencement No 4) Order 2003, SI 2003/1725).

(b) such other purpose relating to the carrying on of qualifying transactions as rules may provide, or

(c) enabling network transactions to be monitored.

(3) It shall be a condition of a network access agreement which enables the person granted access to use the network to carry on qualifying transactions that he must comply with any rules for the time being in force under paragraph 5.

(4) Rules may regulate the terms on which access to a land registry network is authorised.

Termination of access

3—(1) The person granted access by a network access agreement may terminate the agreement at any time by notice to the registrar.

(2) Rules may make provision about the termination of a network access agreement by the registrar and may, in particular, make provision about –

(a) the grounds of termination,

(b) the procedure to be followed in relation to termination, and

(c) the suspension of termination pending appeal.

(3) Without prejudice to the generality of sub-paragraph (2)(a), rules under that provision may authorise the registrar to terminate a network access agreement if the person granted access –

(a) fails to comply with the terms of the agreement,

(b) ceases to be a person with whom the registrar would be required to enter into a network access agreement conferring the authority which the agreement confers, or

(c) does not meet such conditions as the rules may provide.

Appeals

4—(1) A person who is aggrieved by a decision of the registrar with respect to entry into, or termination of, a network access agreement may appeal against the decision to the adjudicator.

(2) On determining an appeal under this paragraph, the adjudicator may give such directions as he considers appropriate to give effect to his determination.

(3) Rules may make provision about appeals under this paragraph.

Network transaction rules

5—(1) Rules may make provision about how to go about network transactions.

(2) Rules under sub-paragraph (1) may, in particular, make provision about dealings with the land registry, including provision about –

(a) the procedure to be followed, and

(b) the supply of information (including information about unregistered interests).

Overriding nature of network access obligations

6   To the extent that an obligation not owed under a network access agreement conflicts with an obligation owed under such an agreement by the person granted access, the obligation not owed under the agreement is discharged.

Do-it-yourself conveyancing

7—(1) If there is a land registry network, the registrar has a duty to provide such assistance as he thinks appropriate for the purpose of enabling persons engaged in qualifying transactions who wish to do their own conveyancing to do so by means of the network.

(2) The duty under sub-paragraph (1) does not extend to the provision of legal advice.

Presumption of authority

8   Where –
   (a) a person who is authorised under a network access agreement to do so uses the network for the making of a disposition or contract, and
   (b) the document which purports to effect the disposition or to be the contract –
      (i)   purports to be authenticated by him as agent, and
      (ii) contains a statement to the effect that he is acting under the authority of his principal,
he shall be deemed, in favour of any other party, to be so acting.

Management of network transactions

9—(1) The registrar may use monitoring information for the purpose of managing network transactions and may, in particular, disclose such information to persons authorised to use the network, and authorise the further disclosure of information so disclosed, if he considers it is necessary or desirable to do so.

(2) The registrar may delegate his functions under sub-paragraph (1), subject to such conditions as he thinks fit.

(3) In sub-paragraph (1), 'monitoring information' means information provided in pursuance of provision in a network access agreement included under paragraph 2(2)(c).

Supplementary

10   The registrar may provide, or arrange for the provision of, education and training in relation to the use of a land registry network.

11— (1) Power to make rules under paragraph 1, 2 or 3 is exercisable by the Lord Chancellor.

(2) Before making such rules, the Lord Chancellor must consult such persons as he considers appropriate.

(3) In making rules under paragraph 1 or 3(2)(a), the Lord Chancellor must have regard, in particular, to the need to secure –
   (a) the confidentiality of private information kept on the network,
   (b) competence in relation to the use of the network (in particular for the purpose of making changes), and
   (c) the adequate insurance of potential liabilities in connection with use of the network.

12   In this Schedule –
   'land registry network' means a network provided under section 92(1);
   'network access agreement' has the meaning given by paragraph 1(2);
   'network transaction' means a transaction carried on by means of a land registry network;
   'qualifying transaction' means a transaction which –
      (a) involves registration, and
      (b) is capable of being effected electronically.

Schedule 6[1]
Registration of Adverse Possessor

Section 97

Right to apply for registration

1—(1) A person may apply to the registrar to be registered as the proprietor of a registered estate in land if he has been in adverse possession of the estate for the period of ten years ending on the date of the application.

(2) A person may also apply to the registrar to be registered as the proprietor of a registered estate in land if –

    (a) he has in the period of six months ending on the date of the application ceased to be in adverse possession of the estate because of eviction by the registered proprietor, or a person claiming under the registered proprietor,

    (b) on the day before his eviction he was entitled to make an application under sub-paragraph (1), and

    (c) the eviction was not pursuant to a judgment for possession.

(3) However, a person may not make an application under this paragraph if –

    (a) he is a defendant in proceedings which involve asserting a right to possession of the land, or

    (b) judgment for possession of the land has been given against him in the last two years.

(4) For the purposes of sub-paragraph (1), the estate need not have been registered throughout the period of adverse possession.

Notification of application

2—(1) The registrar must give notice of an application under paragraph 1 to –

    (a) the proprietor of the estate to which the application relates,

    (b) the proprietor of any registered charge on the estate,

    (c) where the estate is leasehold, the proprietor of any superior registered estate,

    (d) any person who is registered in accordance with rules as a person to be notified under this paragraph, and

    (e) such other persons as rules may provide.

(2) Notice under this paragraph shall include notice of the effect of paragraph 4.

Treatment of application

3—(1) A person given notice under paragraph 2 may require that the application to which the notice relates be dealt with under paragraph 5.

(2) The right under this paragraph is exercisable by notice to the registrar given before the end of such period as rules may provide.

4   If an application under paragraph 1 is not required to be dealt with under paragraph 5, the applicant is entitled to be entered in the register as the new proprietor of the estate.

---

[1]   Commencement: 13 October 2003 (paras 1–4, 5(1)–(3), 6–15); 13 Oct 2004 (para 5(4), (5)) (Land Registration Act 2002 (Commencement No 4) Order 2003, SI 2003/1725).

5—(1) If an application under paragraph 1 is required to be dealt with under this paragraph, the applicant is only entitled to be registered as the new proprietor of the estate if any of the following conditions is met.

(2) The first condition is that –
   (a) it would be unconscionable because of an equity by estoppel for the registered proprietor to seek to dispossess the applicant, and
   (b) the circumstances are such that the applicant ought to be registered as the proprietor.

(3) The second condition is that the applicant is for some other reason entitled to be registered as the proprietor of the estate.

(4) The third condition is that –
   (a) the land to which the application relates is adjacent to land belonging to the applicant,
   (b) the exact line of the boundary between the two has not been determined under rules under section 60,
   (c) for at least ten years of the period of adverse possession ending on the date of the application, the applicant (or any predecessor in title) reasonably believed that the land to which the application relates belonged to him, and
   (d) the estate to which the application relates was registered more than one year prior to the date of the application.

(5) In relation to an application under paragraph 1(2), this paragraph has effect as if the reference in sub-paragraph (4)(c) to the date of the application were to the day before the date of the applicant's eviction.[1]

Right to make further application for registration
6—(1) Where a person's application under paragraph 1 is rejected, he may make a further application to be registered as the proprietor of the estate if he is in adverse possession of the estate from the date of the application until the last day of the period of two years beginning with the date of its rejection.

(2) However, a person may not make an application under this paragraph if –
   (a) he is a defendant in proceedings which involve asserting a right to possession of the land,
   (b) judgment for possession of the land has been given against him in the last two years, or
   (c) he has been evicted from the land pursuant to a judgment for possession.

7 If a person makes an application under paragraph 6, he is entitled to be entered in the register as the new proprietor of the estate.

Restriction on applications
8—(1) No one may apply under this Schedule to be registered as the proprietor of an estate in land during, or before the end of twelve months after the end of, any period in which the existing registered proprietor is for the purposes of the Limitation (Enemies and War Prisoners) Act 1945 (8 & 9 Geo. 6 c. 16) –
   (a) an enemy, or
   (b) detained in enemy territory.

(2) No-one may apply under this Schedule to be registered as the proprietor of an estate in land during any period in which the existing registered proprietor is –

---

[1] Subparagraphs in italics not in force until 13 October 2004: Land Registration Act 2002 (Commencement No 4) Order 2003, SI 2003/1725, para 2(2)(b).

(a) unable because of mental disability to make decisions about issues of the kind to which such an application would give rise, or

(b) unable to communicate such decisions because of mental disability or physical impairment.

(3) For the purposes of sub-paragraph (2), 'mental disability' means a disability or disorder of the mind or brain, whether permanent or temporary, which results in an impairment or disturbance of mental functioning.

(4) Where it appears to the registrar that sub-paragraph (1) or (2) applies in relation to an estate in land, he may include a note to that effect in the register.

Effect of registration

9—(1) Where a person is registered as the proprietor of an estate in land in pursuance of an application under this Schedule, the title by virtue of adverse possession which he had at the time of the application is extinguished.

(2) Subject to sub-paragraph (3), the registration of a person under this Schedule as the proprietor of an estate in land does not affect the priority of any interest affecting the estate.

(3) Subject to sub-paragraph (4), where a person is registered under this Schedule as the proprietor of an estate, the estate is vested in him free of any registered charge affecting the estate immediately before his registration.

(4) Sub-paragraph (3) does not apply where registration as proprietor is in pursuance of an application determined by reference to whether any of the conditions in paragraph 5 applies.

Apportionment and discharge of charges

10— (1) Where –

(a) a registered estate continues to be subject to a charge notwithstanding the registration of a person under this Schedule as the proprietor, and

(b) the charge affects property other than the estate,

the proprietor of the estate may require the chargee to apportion the amount secured by the charge at that time between the estate and the other property on the basis of their respective values.

(2) The person requiring the apportionment is entitled to a discharge of his estate from the charge on payment of –

(a) the amount apportioned to the estate, and

(b) the costs incurred by the chargee as a result of the apportionment.

(3) On a discharge under this paragraph, the liability of the chargor to the chargee is reduced by the amount apportioned to the estate.

(4) Rules may make provision about apportionment under this paragraph, in particular, provision about –

(a) procedure,

(b) valuation,

(c) calculation of costs payable under sub-paragraph (2)(b), and

(d) payment of the costs of the chargor.

Meaning of 'adverse possession'

11—(1) A person is in adverse possession of an estate in land for the purposes of this Schedule if, but for section 96, a period of limitation under section 15 of the Limitation Act 1980 would run in his favour in relation to the estate.

(2) A person is also to be regarded for those purposes as having been in adverse possession of an estate in land –

    (a) where he is the successor in title to an estate in the land, during any period of adverse possession by a predecessor in title to that estate, or

    (b) during any period of adverse possession by another person which comes between, and is continuous with, periods of adverse possession of his own.

(3) In determining whether for the purposes of this paragraph a period of limitation would run under section 15 of the Limitation Act 1980, there are to be disregarded –

    (a) the commencement of any legal proceedings, and

    (b) paragraph 6 of Schedule 1 to that Act.

Trusts

12   A person is not to be regarded as being in adverse possession of an estate for the purposes of this Schedule at any time when the estate is subject to a trust, unless the interest of each of the beneficiaries in the estate is an interest in possession.

Crown foreshore

13—(1) Where –

    (a) a person is in adverse possession of an estate in land,

    (b) the estate belongs to Her Majesty in right of the Crown or the Duchy of Lancaster or to the Duchy of Cornwall, and

    (c) the land consists of foreshore,

    paragraph 1(1) is to have effect as if the reference to ten years were to sixty years.

(2) For the purposes of sub-paragraph (1), land is to be treated as foreshore if it has been foreshore at any time in the previous ten years.

(3) In this paragraph, 'foreshore' means the shore and bed of the sea and of any tidal water, below the line of the medium high tide between the spring and neap tides.

Rentcharges

14   Rules must make provision to apply the preceding provisions of this Schedule to registered rentcharges, subject to such modifications and exceptions as the rules may provide.

Procedure

15   Rules may make provision about the procedure to be followed pursuant to an application under this Schedule.

Schedule 7[1]
The Land Registry

Section 99

Holding of office by Chief Land Registrar

1—(1) The registrar may at any time resign his office by written notice to the Lord Chancellor.

---

[1]   Commencement: 13 October 2003 (Land Registration Act 2002 (Commencement No 4) Order 2003, SI 2003/1725).

(2) The Lord Chancellor may remove the registrar from office if he is unable or unfit to discharge the functions of office.

(3) Subject to the above, a person appointed to be the registrar is to hold and vacate office in accordance with the terms of his appointment and, on ceasing to hold office, is eligible for reappointment.

Remuneration etc of Chief Land Registrar
2—(1) The Lord Chancellor shall pay the registrar such remuneration, and such travelling and other allowances, as the Lord Chancellor may determine.

(2) The Lord Chancellor shall –
- (a) pay such pension, allowances or gratuities as he may determine to or in respect of a person who is or has been the registrar, or
- (b) make such payments as he may determine towards provision for the payment of a pension, allowances or gratuities to or in respect of such a person.

(3) If, when a person ceases to be the registrar, the Lord Chancellor determines that there are special circumstances which make it right that the person should receive compensation, the Lord Chancellor may pay to the person by way of compensation a sum of such amount as he may determine.

Staff
3—(1) The registrar may appoint such staff as he thinks fit.

(2) The terms and conditions of appointments under this paragraph shall be such as the registrar, with the approval of the Minister for the Civil Service, thinks fit.

Indemnity for members
4   No member of the land registry is to be liable in damages for anything done or omitted in the discharge or purported discharge of any function relating to land registration, unless it is shown that the act or omission was in bad faith.

Seal
5   The land registry is to continue to have a seal and any document purporting to be sealed with it is to be admissible in evidence without any further or other proof.

Documentary evidence
6   The Documentary Evidence Act 1868 has effect as if –
- (a) the registrar were included in the first column of the Schedule to that Act,
- (b) the registrar and any person authorised to act on his behalf were mentioned in the second column of that Schedule, and
- (c) the regulations referred to in that Act included any form or direction issued by the registrar or by any such person.

Parliamentary disqualification
7   In Part 3 of Schedule 1 to the House of Commons Disqualification Act 1975 (other disqualifying offices), there is inserted at the appropriate place –
'Chief Land Registrar.';
and a corresponding amendment is made in Part 3 of Schedule 1 to the Northern Ireland Assembly Disqualification Act 1975.

Schedule 8[1]

Indemnities

Section 103

Entitlement

1—(1) A person is entitled to be indemnified by the registrar if he suffers loss by reason of –

(a) rectification of the register,

(b) a mistake whose correction would involve rectification of the register,

(c) a mistake in an official search,

(d) a mistake in an official copy,

(e) a mistake in a document kept by the registrar which is not an original and is referred to in the register,

(f) the loss or destruction of a document lodged at the registry for inspection or safe custody,

(g) a mistake in the cautions register, or

(h) failure by the registrar to perform his duty under section 50.

(2) For the purposes of sub-paragraph (1)(a) –

(a) any person who suffers loss by reason of the change of title under section 62 is to be regarded as having suffered loss by reason of rectification of the register, and

(b) the proprietor of a registered estate or charge claiming in good faith under a forged disposition is, where the register is rectified, to be regarded as having suffered loss by reason of such rectification as if the disposition had not been forged.

(3) No indemnity under sub-paragraph (1)(b) is payable until a decision has been made about whether to alter the register for the purpose of correcting the mistake; and the loss suffered by reason of the mistake is to be determined in the light of that decision.

Mines and minerals

2 No indemnity is payable under this Schedule on account of –

(a) any mines or minerals, or

(b) the existence of any right to work or get mines or minerals,

unless it is noted in the register that the title to the registered estate concerned includes the mines or minerals.

Costs

3—(1) In respect of loss consisting of costs or expenses incurred by the claimant in relation to the matter, an indemnity under this Schedule is payable only on account of costs or expenses reasonably incurred by the claimant with the consent of the registrar.

(2) The requirement of consent does not apply where –

(a) the costs or expenses must be incurred by the claimant urgently, and

(b) it is not reasonably practicable to apply for the registrar's consent.

(3) If the registrar approves the incurring of costs or expenses after they have been incurred, they shall be treated for the purposes of this paragraph as having been incurred with his consent.

---

[1]   Commencement: 13 October 2003 (Land Registration Act 2002 (Commencement No 4) Order 2003, SI 2003/1725).

4—(1) If no indemnity is payable to a claimant under this Schedule, the registrar may pay such amount as he thinks fit in respect of any costs or expenses reasonably incurred by the claimant in connection with the claim which have been incurred with the consent of the registrar.

(2) The registrar may make a payment under sub-paragraph (1) notwithstanding the absence of consent if –

(a) it appears to him –
   (i)   that the costs or expenses had to be incurred urgently, and
   (ii)   that it was not reasonably practicable to apply for his consent, or
(b) he has subsequently approved the incurring of the costs or expenses.

Claimant's fraud or lack of care
5—(1) No indemnity is payable under this Schedule on account of any loss suffered by a claimant –

(a)   wholly or partly as a result of his own fraud, or
(b)   wholly as a result of his own lack of proper care.

(2) Where any loss is suffered by a claimant partly as a result of his own lack of proper care, any indemnity payable to him is to be reduced to such extent as is fair having regard to his share in the responsibility for the loss.

(3) For the purposes of this paragraph any fraud or lack of care on the part of a person from whom the claimant derives title (otherwise than under a disposition for valuable consideration which is registered or protected by an entry in the register) is to be treated as if it were fraud or lack of care on the part of the claimant.

Valuation of estates etc
6   Where an indemnity is payable in respect of the loss of an estate, interest or charge, the value of the estate, interest or charge for the purposes of the indemnity is to be regarded as not exceeding –

(a) in the case of an indemnity under paragraph 1(1)(a), its value immediately before rectification of the register (but as if there were to be no rectification), and
(b) in the case of an indemnity under paragraph 1(1)(b), its value at the time when the mistake which caused the loss was made.

Determination of indemnity by court
7—(1) A person may apply to the court for the determination of any question as to –

(a) whether he is entitled to an indemnity under this Schedule, or
(b) the amount of such an indemnity.

(2) Paragraph 3(1) does not apply to the costs of an application to the court under this paragraph or of any legal proceedings arising out of such an application.

Time limits
8   For the purposes of the Limitation Act 1980 –

(a) a liability to pay an indemnity under this Schedule is a simple contract debt, and
(b) the cause of action arises at the time when the claimant knows, or but for his own default might have known, of the existence of his claim.

Interest
9   Rules may make provision about the payment of interest on an indemnity under this Schedule, including –

(a) the circumstances in which interest is payable, and

(b) the periods for and rates at which it is payable.

Recovery of indemnity by registrar

10—(1) Where an indemnity under this Schedule is paid to a claimant in respect of any loss, the registrar is entitled (without prejudice to any other rights he may have) –

(a) to recover the amount paid from any person who caused or substantially contributed to the loss by his fraud, or

(b) for the purpose of recovering the amount paid, to enforce the rights of action referred to in sub-paragraph (2).

(2) Those rights of action are –

(a) any right of action (of whatever nature and however arising) which the claimant would have been entitled to enforce had the indemnity not been paid, and

(b) where the register has been rectified, any right of action (of whatever nature and however arising) which the person in whose favour the register has been rectified would have been entitled to enforce had it not been rectified.

(3) References in this paragraph to an indemnity include interest paid on an indemnity under rules under paragraph 9.

Interpretation

11—(1) For the purposes of this Schedule, references to a mistake in something include anything mistakenly omitted from it as well as anything mistakenly included in it.

(2) In this Schedule, references to rectification of the register are to alteration of the register which –

(a) involves the correction of a mistake, and

(b) prejudicially affects the title of a registered proprietor.

Schedule 9[1]
The Adjudicator

Section 107

Holding of office

1—(1) The adjudicator may at any time resign his office by written notice to the Lord Chancellor.

(2) The Lord Chancellor may remove the adjudicator from office on the ground of incapacity or misbehaviour.

(3) Section 26 of the Judicial Pensions and Retirement Act 1993 (compulsory retirement at 70, subject to the possibility of annual extension up to 75) applies to the adjudicator.

(4) Subject to the above, a person appointed to be the adjudicator is to hold and vacate office in accordance with the terms of his appointment and, on ceasing to hold office, is eligible for reappointment.

---

[1] Commencement: 28 April 2003 (Land Registration Act 2002 (Commencement No 2) Order 2003, SI 2003/1028).

Remuneration
2—(1) The Lord Chancellor shall pay the adjudicator such remuneration, and such other allowances, as the Lord Chancellor may determine.

(2) The Lord Chancellor shall –
   (a) pay such pension, allowances or gratuities as he may determine to or in respect of a person who is or has been the adjudicator, or
   (b) make such payments as he may determine towards provision for the payment of a pension, allowances or gratuities to or in respect of such a person.

(3) Sub-paragraph (2) does not apply if the office of adjudicator is a qualifying judicial office within the meaning of the Judicial Pensions and Retirement Act 1993.

(4) If, when a person ceases to be the adjudicator, the Lord Chancellor determines that there are special circumstances which make it right that the person should receive compensation, the Lord Chancellor may pay to the person by way of compensation a sum of such amount as he may determine.

Staff
3—(1) The adjudicator may appoint such staff as he thinks fit.

(2) The terms and conditions of appointments under this paragraph shall be such as the adjudicator, with the approval of the Minister for the Civil Service, thinks fit.

Conduct of business
4—(1) Subject to sub-paragraph (2), any function of the adjudicator may be carried out by any member of his staff who is authorised by him for the purpose.

(2) In the case of functions which are not of an administrative character, sub-paragraph (1) only applies if the member of staff has a 10 year general qualification (within the meaning of section 71 of the Courts and Legal Services Act 1990).

5   The Lord Chancellor may by regulations make provision about the carrying out of functions during any vacancy in the office of adjudicator.

Finances
6   The Lord Chancellor shall be liable to reimburse expenditure incurred by the adjudicator in the discharge of his functions.

7   The Lord Chancellor may require the registrar to make payments towards expenses of the Lord Chancellor under this Schedule.

Application of Tribunals and Inquiries Act 1992
8   In Schedule 1 to the Tribunal and Inquiries Act 1992 (tribunals under the supervision of the Council on Tribunals), after paragraph 27 there is inserted –

'Land Registration   27B   The Adjudicator to Her Majesty's Land Registry.'

Parliamentary disqualification
9   In Part 1 of Schedule 1 to the House of Commons Disqualification Act 1975 (judicial offices), there is inserted at the end –

'Adjudicator to Her Majesty's Land Registry.';
and a corresponding amendment is made in Part 1 of Schedule 1 to the Northern Ireland
Assembly Disqualification Act 1975.

Schedule 10[1]
Miscellaneous and General Powers

Section 126

PART 1
MISCELLANEOUS

Dealings with estates subject to compulsory first registration
1—(1) Rules may make provision –
  (a) applying this Act to a pre-registration dealing with a registrable legal estate as if the
      dealing had taken place after the date of first registration of the estate, and
  (b) about the date on which registration of the dealing is effective.

(2) For the purposes of sub-paragraph (1) –
  (a) a legal estate is registrable if a person is subject to a duty under section 6 to make an
      application to be registered as the proprietor of it, and
  (b) a pre-registration dealing is one which takes place before the making of such an
      application.

Regulation of title matters between sellers and buyers
2—(1) Rules may make provision about the obligations with respect to –
  (a) proof of title, or
  (b) perfection of title,
      of the seller under a contract for the transfer, or other disposition, for valuable
      consideration of a registered estate or charge.

(2) Rules under this paragraph may be expressed to have effect notwithstanding any stipulation
to the contrary.

Implied covenants
3 Rules may –
  (a) make provision about the form of provisions extending or limiting any covenant
      implied by virtue of Part 1 of the Law of Property (Miscellaneous Provisions) Act 1994
      (implied covenants for title) on a registrable disposition;
  (b) make provision about the application of section 77 of the Law of Property Act 1925
      (implied covenants in conveyance subject to rents) to transfers of registered estates;
  (c) make provision about reference in the register to implied covenants, including
      provision for the state of the register to be conclusive in relation to whether covenants
      have been implied.

Land certificates
4 Rules may make provision about –
  (a) when a certificate of registration of title to a legal estate may be issued,
  (b) the form and content of such a certificate, and
  (c) when such a certificate must be produced or surrendered to the registrar.

---

1   Commencement: 13 October 2003 (Land Registration Act 2002 (Commencement No 4) Order 2003,
    SI 2003/1725).

PART 2

GENERAL

Notice

5—(1) Rules may make provision about the form, content and service of notice under this Act.

(2) Rules under this paragraph about the service of notice may, in particular –
- (a) make provision requiring the supply of an address for service and about the entry of addresses for service in the register;
- (b) make provision about –
  - (i) the time for service,
  - (ii) the mode of service, and
  - (iii) when service is to be regarded as having taken place.

Applications

6   Rules may –
- (a) make provision about the form and content of applications under this Act;
- (b) make provision requiring applications under this Act to be supported by such evidence as the rules may provide;
- (c) make provision about when an application under this Act is to be taken as made;
- (d) make provision about the order in which competing applications are to be taken to rank;
- (e) make provision for an alteration made by the registrar for the purpose of correcting a mistake in an application or accompanying document to have effect in such circumstances as the rules may provide as if made by the applicant or other interested party or parties.

Statutory statements

7   Rules may make provision about the form of any statement required under an enactment to be included in an instrument effecting a registrable disposition or a disposition which triggers the requirement of registration.

Residual power

8   Rules may make any other provision which it is expedient to make for the purposes of carrying this Act into effect, whether similar or not to any provision which may be made under the other powers to make land registration rules.

Schedule 11[1]

Minor and Consequential Amendments

Section 133

Settled Land Act 1925

1   Section 119(3) of the Settled Land Act 1925 ceases to have effect.

Law of Property Act 1925

2—(1) The Law of Property Act 1925 is amended as follows.

(2) In section 44, after subsection (4) there is inserted –

---

[1]   Commencement: 28 April 2003 (para 28) (Land Registration Act 2002 (Commencement No 2) Order 2003, SI 2003/1028); 13 October 2003 (paras 1–27, 29–40); (Land Registration Act 2002 (Commencement No 4) Order 2003, SI 2003/1725).

'(4A) Subsections (2) and (4) of this section do not apply to a contract to grant a term of years if the grant will be an event within section 4(1) of the Land Registration Act 2002 (events which trigger compulsory first registration of title).'

(3) In that section, in subsection (5), for 'the last three preceding subsections' there is substituted 'subsections (2) to (4) of this section'.

(4) In that section, at the end there is inserted –
'(12) Nothing in this section applies in relation to registered land or to a term of years to be derived out of registered land.'

(5) In section 84(8), the words from ', but' to the end are omitted.

(6) In section 85(3), for the words from the beginning to the second 'or' there is substituted 'Subsection (2) does not apply to registered land, but, subject to that, this section applies whether or not the land is registered land and whether or not'.

(7) In section 86(3), for the words from the beginning to the second 'or' there is substituted 'Subsection (2) does not apply to registered land, but, subject to that, this section applies whether or not the land is registered land and whether or not'.

(8) In section 87, at the end there is inserted –
'(4) Subsection (1) of this section shall not be taken to be affected by section 23(1)(a) of the Land Registration Act 2002 (under which owner's powers in relation to a registered estate do not include power to mortgage by demise or sub-demise).'

(9) In section 94(4), for the words from 'registered' to the end there is substituted 'on registered land'.

(10) In section 97, for 'Land Registration Act 1925' there is substituted 'Land Registration Act 2002'.

(11) In section 115(10), for the words from 'charge' to the end there is substituted 'registered charge (within the meaning of the Land Registration Act 2002)'.

(12) In section 125(2), for the words from '(not being' to '1925)' there is substituted '(not being registered land)'.

(13) In section 205(1)(xxii) –
   (a) for 'Land Registration Act 1925' there is substituted 'Land Registration Act 2002;', and
   (b) the words from ', and' to the end are omitted.

Administration of Estates Act 1925
3   In section 43(2) of the Administration of Estates Act 1925, for 'Land Registration Act 1925' there is substituted 'Land Registration Act 2002'.

Requisitioned Land and War Works Act 1945
4—(1) Section 37 of the Requisitioned Land and War Works Act 1945 is amended as follows.

(2) In subsection (2), for 'Land Registration Act 1925' there is substituted 'Land Registration Act 2002'.

(3) Subsection (3) ceases to have effect.

Law of Property (Joint Tenants) Act 1964
5   In section 3 of the Law of Property (Joint Tenants) Act 1964, for the words from 'any land' to the end there is substituted 'registered land'.

Gas Act 1965
6—(1) The Gas Act 1965 is amended as follows.

(2) In section 12(3), for 'Land Registration Act 1925' there is substituted 'Land Registration Act 2002'.

(3) In sections 12(4) and 13(6), for the words from 'be deemed' to the end there is substituted –
  '(a) for the purposes of the Land Charges Act 1925, be deemed to be a charge affecting land falling within Class D(iii), and
  (b) for the purposes of the Land Registration Act 2002, be deemed to be an equitable easement.'

Commons Registration Act 1965
7—(1) The Commons Registration Act 1965 is amended as follows.

(2) In sections 1(1), (2) and (3), 4(3) and 8(1), for 'under the Land Registration Acts 1925 and 1936' there is substituted 'in the register of title'.

(3) In section 9, for 'the Land Registration Acts 1925 and 1936' there is substituted 'in the register of title'.

(4) In section 12 (in both places), for 'under the Land Registration Acts 1925 and 1936' there is substituted 'in the register of title'.

(5) In section 22, in subsection (1), there is inserted at the appropriate place –
  ' "register of title" means the register kept under section 1 of the Land Registration Act 2002;'.

(6) In that section, in subsection (2), for 'under the Land Registration Acts 1925 and 1936' there is substituted 'in the register of title'.

Leasehold Reform Act 1967
8—(1) The Leasehold Reform Act 1967 is amended as follows.

(2) In section 5(5) –
  (a) for 'an overriding interest within the meaning of the Land Registration Act 1925' there is substituted 'regarded for the purposes of the Land Registration Act 2002 as an interest falling within any of the paragraphs of Schedule 1 or 3 to that Act', and
  (b) for 'or caution under the Land Registration Act 1925' there is substituted 'under the Land Registration Act 2002'.

(3) In Schedule 4, in paragraph 1(3) –
  (a) for paragraph (a) there is substituted –
    '(a)   the covenant may be the subject of a notice in the register of title kept under the Land Registration Act 2002, if apart from this subsection it would not be capable of being the subject of such a notice; and', and
  (b) in paragraph (b), for 'notice of the covenant has been so registered, the covenant' there is substituted 'a notice in respect of the covenant has been entered in that register, it'.

Law of Property Act 1969

9   In section 24(1) of the Law of Property Act 1969, for 'Land Registration Act 1925' there is substituted 'Land Registration Act 2002'.

Land Charges Act 1972

10—(1) The Land Charges Act 1972 is amended as follows.

(2) In section 14(1), for the words from 'Land Registration' to the end there is substituted 'Land Registration Act 2002'.

(3) In section 14(3) –
   (a) for the words from 'section 123A' to 'register)' there is substituted 'section 7 of the Land Registration Act 2002 (effect of failure to comply with requirement of registration)', and
   (b) for 'that section' there is substituted 'section 6 of that Act'.

(4) In section 17(1), in the definition of 'registered land', for 'Land Registration Act 1925' there is substituted 'Land Registration Act 2002'.

Consumer Credit Act 1974

11   In section 177(1) and (6) of the Consumer Credit Act 1974, for 'Land Registration Act 1925' there is substituted 'Land Registration Act 2002'.

Solicitors Act 1974

12— (1) The Solicitors Act 1974 is amended as follows.

(2) In sections 22(1) and 56(1)(f), for 'Land Registration Act 1925' there is substituted 'Land Registration Act 2002'.

(3) Section 75(b) ceases to have effect.

Local Land Charges Act 1975

13   In section 10(3)(b)(ii) of the Local Land Charges Act 1975, for 'under the Land Registration Act 1925' there is substituted 'in the register of title kept under the Land Registration Act 2002'.

Rent Act 1977

14   In section 136(b) of the Rent Act 1977, for the words from 'charge' to the end there is substituted 'registered charge (within the meaning of the Land Registration Act 2002)'.

Charging Orders Act 1979

15   In section 3(2) and (6) of the Charging Orders Act 1979, for 'Land Registration Act 1925' there is substituted 'Land Registration Act 2002'.

Highways Act 1980

16   Section 251(5) of the Highways Act 1980 ceases to have effect.

Inheritance Tax Act 1984

17   In section 238(3) of the Inheritance Tax Act 1984, for paragraph (a) there is substituted –
   '(a) in relation to registered land –
      (i) if the disposition is required to be completed by registration, the time of registration, and
      (ii) otherwise, the time of completion,'.

Housing Act 1985

18—(1) The Housing Act 1985 is amended as follows.

(2) In section 37(5), for the words from 'and' to the end there is substituted –
    '(5A) Where the Chief Land Registrar approves an application for registration of –
        (a)   a disposition of registered land, or
        (b)   the disponee's title under a disposition of unregistered land,
    and the instrument effecting the disposition contains a covenant of the kind mentioned in subsection (1), he must enter in the register a restriction reflecting the limitation imposed by the covenant'.

(3) In section 154(5), for 'Land Registration Acts 1925 to 1971' there is substituted 'Land Registration Act 2002'.

(4) In section 157(7), for the words from 'the appropriate' to the end there is substituted 'a restriction in the register of title reflecting the limitation'.

(5) In section 165(6), for 'section 83 of the Land Registration Act 1925' there is substituted 'Schedule 8 to the Land Registration Act 2002'.

(6) In Schedule 9A, in paragraph 2(2), for the words from the beginning to 'the disponor' there is substituted 'Where on a qualifying disposal the disponor's title to the dwelling-house is not registered, the disponor'.

(7) In that Schedule, for paragraph 4 there is substituted –
    '4—(1) This paragraph applies where the Chief Land Registrar approves an application for registration of –
        (a) a disposition of registered land, or
        (b) the disponee's title under a disposition of unregistered land,
    and the instrument effecting the disposition contains the statement required by paragraph 1.

    (2) The Chief Land Registrar must enter in the register –
        (a) a notice in respect of the rights of qualifying persons under this Part in relation to dwelling-houses comprised in the disposal, and
        (b) a restriction reflecting the limitation under section 171D(2) on subsequent disposal.'

(8) In that Schedule, for paragraph 5(2) there is substituted –
    '(2) If the landlord's title is registered, the landlord shall apply for the entry in the register of –
    (a) a notice in respect of the rights of the qualifying person or persons under the provisions of this Part, and
    (b) a restriction reflecting the limitation under section 171D(2) on subsequent disposal.'

(9) In that Schedule, paragraph 5(3) ceases to have effect.

(10) In that Schedule, in paragraph 6, for sub-paragraph (1) there is substituted –
    '(1) The rights of a qualifying person under this Part in relation to the qualifying dwelling house shall not be regarded as falling within Schedule 3 to the Land Registration Act 2002 (and so are liable to be postponed under section 29 of that Act, unless protected by means of a notice in the register).'

(11) In that Schedule, in paragraph 9(2), for 'Land Registration Acts 1925 to 1986' there is substituted 'Land Registration Act 2002'.

(12) In Schedule 17, in paragraph 2(2), for 'Land Registration Acts 1925 to 1971' there is substituted 'Land Registration Act 2002'.

(13) In Schedule 20, in paragraph 17(2), for 'Land Registration Acts 1925 to 1986' there is substituted 'Land Registration Act 2002'.

Building Societies Act 1986
19—(1) In Schedule 2A to the Building Societies Act 1986, paragraph 1 is amended as follows.

(2) In sub-paragraph (2), for 'charge or incumbrance registered under the Land Registration Act 1925' there is substituted 'registered charge (within the meaning of the Land Registration Act 2002)'.

(3) Sub-paragraph (4) ceases to have effect.

(4) In sub-paragraph (5), the definition of 'registered land' and the preceding 'and' cease to have effect.

Landlord and Tenant Act 1987
20   In sections 24(8) and (9), 28(5), 30(6) and 34(9) of the Landlord and Tenant Act 1987, for 'Land Registration Act 1925' there is substituted 'Land Registration Act 2002'.

Diplomatic and Consular Premises Act 1987
21—(1) The Diplomatic and Consular Premises Act 1987 is amended as follows.

(2) In section 5, after the definition of the expression 'diplomatic premises' there is inserted –
' "land" includes buildings and other structures, land covered with water and any estate, interest, easement, servitude or right in or over land,'.

(3) In Schedule 1, in paragraph 1 –
  (a)   before the definition of the expression 'the registrar' there is inserted –
         ' "registered land" has the same meaning as in the Land Registration Act 2002;', and
  (b)   the words from 'and expressions' to the end are omitted.

Criminal Justice Act 1988
22—(1) The Criminal Justice Act 1988 is amended as follows.

(2) In section 77(12) –
  (a) for 'Land Registration Act 1925' there is substituted 'Land Registration Act 2002', and
  (b) in paragraph (a), at the end there is inserted ', except that no notice may be entered in the register of title under the Land Registration Act 2002 in respect of such orders'.

(3) In section 79(1) and (4), for 'Land Registration Act 1925' there is substituted 'Land Registration Act 2002'. ...[1]

Housing Act 1988
23—(1) The Housing Act 1988 is amended as follows.

(2) In section 81, in subsection (9)(c), for 'Land Registration Acts 1925 to 1986' there is substituted 'Land Registration Act 2002'.

---

[1]   Prospective amendment: Paragraph in italics prospectively repealed by Proceeds of Crime Act 2002, s 457, Sch 12, from a date to be appointed (Proceeds of Crime Act 2002, s 458(1)).

(3) In that section, for subsection (10) there is substituted –

'(10) Where the Chief Land Registrar approves an application for registration of –

(a)   a disposition of registered land, or

(b)   the approved person's title under a disposition of unregistered land,

and the instrument effecting the disposition contains the statement required by subsection (1) above, he shall enter in the register a restriction reflecting the limitation under this section on subsequent disposal.'

(4) In section 90(4), for 'Land Registration Act 1925' there is substituted 'Land Registration Act 2002'.

(5) In section 133, in subsection (8) –

(a) for the words 'conveyance, grant or assignment' there is substituted 'transfer or grant',

(b) for the words 'section 123 of the Land Registration Act 1925' there is substituted 'section 4 of the Land Registration Act 2002', and

(c) in paragraph (c), for 'Land Registration Acts 1925 to 1986' there is substituted 'Land Registration Act 2002'.

(6) In that section, for subsection (9) there is substituted –

'(9) Where the Chief Land Registrar approves an application for registration of –

(a)   a disposition of registered land, or

(b)   a person's title under a disposition of unregistered land,

and the instrument effecting the original disposal contains the statement required by subsection (3)(d) above, he shall enter in the register a restriction reflecting the limitation under this section on subsequent disposal.'

Local Government and Housing Act 1989

24—(1) Section 173 of the Local Government and Housing Act 1989 is amended as follows.

(2) In subsection (8) –

(a) for the words 'conveyance, grant or assignment' there is substituted 'transfer or grant',

(b) for the words 'section 123 of the Land Registration Act 1925' there is substituted 'section 4 of the Land Registration Act 2002', and

(c) in paragraph (c), for 'Land Registration Acts 1925 to 1986' there is substituted 'Land Registration Act 2002'.

(3) For subsection (9) there is substituted –

'(9) Where the Chief Land Registrar approves an application for registration of –

(a) a disposition of registered land, or

(b) a person's title under a disposition of unregistered land,

and the instrument effecting the initial transfer contains the statement required by subsection (3) above, he shall enter in the register a restriction reflecting the limitation under this section on subsequent disposal.'

Water Resources Act 1991

25—(1) Section 158 of the Water Resources Act 1991 is amended as follows.

(2) In subsection (5) –

(a) for paragraphs (a) and (b) there is substituted –

'(a)   the agreement may be the subject of a notice in the register of title under the Land Registration Act 2002 as if it were an interest affecting the registered land;

    (b)   the provisions of sections 28 to 30 of that Act (effect of dispositions of registered land on priority of adverse interests) shall apply as if the agreement were such an interest;', and

(b) in paragraph (c), for 'where notice of the agreement has been so registered,' there is substituted 'subject to the provisions of those sections,'.

(3) In subsection (6), for 'Land Registration Act 1925' there is substituted 'Land Registration Act 2002'.

Access to Neighbouring Land Act 1992
26—(1) The Access to Neighbouring Land Act 1992 is amended as follows.

(2) In section 4(1), for 'Land Registration Act 1925' there is substituted 'Land Registration Act 2002'.

(3) In section 5, in subsection (4) –
  (a) in paragraph (b), for 'notice or caution under the Land Registration Act 1925' there is substituted 'notice under the Land Registration Act 2002', and
  (b) for 'entry, notice or caution' there is substituted 'entry or notice'.

(4) In that section, for subsection (5) there is substituted –
'(5) The rights conferred on a person by or under an access order shall not be capable of falling within paragraph 2 of Schedule 1 or 3 to the Land Registration Act 2002 (overriding status of interest of person in actual occupation).'

(5) In that section, in subsection (6), for 'Land Registration Act 1925' there is substituted 'Land Registration Act 2002'.

Further and Higher Education Act 1992
27—In Schedule 5 to the Further and Higher Education Act 1992, in paragraph 6(1) –
  (a) for 'Land Registration Acts 1925 to 1986' there is substituted 'Land Registration Act 2002', and
  (b) for 'those Acts' there is substituted 'that Act'.

Judicial Pensions and Retirement Act 1993
28 In Schedule 5 to the Judicial Pensions and Retirement Act 1993, there is inserted at the end –
'Adjudicator to Her Majesty's Land Registry'

Charities Act 1993
29— (1) The Charities Act 1993 is amended as follows.

(2) In section 37, for subsections (7) and (8) there is substituted –
  '(7) Where the disposition to be effected by any such instrument as is mentioned in subsection (1)(b) or (5)(b) above will be –
    (a)   a registrable disposition, or
    (b)   a disposition which triggers the requirement of registration,
    the statement which, by virtue of subsection (1) or (5) above, is to be contained in the instrument shall be in such form as may be prescribed by land registration rules.
  (8) Where the registrar approves an application for registration of –
    (a) a disposition of registered land, or
    (b) a person's title under a disposition of unregistered land,
    and the instrument effecting the disposition contains a statement complying with

subsections (5) and (7) above, he shall enter in the register a restriction reflecting the limitation under section 36 above on subsequent disposal.'

(3) In that section, in subsection (9) –
   (a) for 'the restriction to be withdrawn' there is substituted 'the removal of the entry', and
   (b) for 'withdraw the restriction' there is substituted 'remove the entry'.

(4) In that section, in subsection (11), for 'Land Registration Act 1925' there is substituted 'Land Registration Act 2002'.

(5) In section 39, in subsection (1), at the end there is inserted 'by land registration rules'.

(6) In that section, for subsections (1A) and (1B) there is substituted –
'(1A) Where any such mortgage will be one to which section 4(1)(g) of the Land Registration Act 2002 applies –
   (a) the statement required by subsection (1) above shall be in such form as may be prescribed by land registration rules; and
   (b) if the charity is not an exempt charity, the mortgage shall also contain a statement, in such form as may be prescribed by land registration rules, that the restrictions on disposition imposed by section 36 above apply to the land (subject to subsection (9) of that section).

(1B) Where –
   (a) the registrar approves an application for registration of a person's title to land in connection with such a mortgage as is mentioned in subsection (1A) above,
   (b) the mortgage contains statements complying with subsections (1) and (1A) above, and
   (c) the charity is not an exempt charity,
the registrar shall enter in the register a restriction reflecting the limitation under section 36 above on subsequent disposal.

(1C) Section 37(9) above shall apply in relation to any restriction entered under subsection (1B) as it applies in relation to any restriction entered under section 37(8).'

(7) In that section, in subsection (6), for the words from 'and subsections' to the end there is substituted 'and subsections (1) to (1B) above shall be construed as one with the Land Registration Act 2002'.

Leasehold Reform, Housing and Urban Development Act 1993
30—(1) The Leasehold Reform, Housing and Urban Development Act 1993 is amended as follows.

(2) In sections 34(10) and 57(11), for the words from 'rules' to the end there is substituted 'land registration rules under the Land Registration Act 2002'.

(3) In section 97, in subsection (1) –
   (a) for 'an overriding interest within the meaning of the Land Registration Act 1925' there is substituted 'capable of falling within paragraph 2 of Schedule 1 or 3 to the Land Registration Act 2002', and
   (b) for 'or caution under the Land Registration Act 1925' there is substituted 'under the Land Registration Act 2002'.

(4) In that section, in subsection (2), for 'Land Registration Act 1925' there is substituted 'Land Registration Act 2002'.

Law of Property (Miscellaneous Provisions) Act 1994

31—(1) The Law of Property (Miscellaneous Provisions) Act 1994 is amended as follows.

(2) In section 6 (cases in which there is no liability under covenants implied by virtue of Part 1 of that Act), at the end there is inserted –

'(4) Moreover, where the disposition is of an interest the title to which is registered under the Land Registration Act 2002, that person is not liable under any of those covenants for anything (not falling within subsection (1) or (2)) which at the time of the disposition was entered in relation to that interest in the register of title under that Act.'

(3) In section 17(3) –

(a) in paragraph (c), for the words from 'any' to the end there is substituted 'the Adjudicator to Her Majesty's Land Registry', and

(b) for 'section 144 of the Land Registration Act 1925' there is substituted 'the Land Registration Act 2002'.

Drug Trafficking Act 1994

32—(1) The Drug Trafficking Act 1994 is amended as follows.

(2) In section 26(12) –

(a) for 'Land Registration Act 1925' there is substituted 'Land Registration Act 2002', and

(b) in paragraph (a), at the end there is inserted ', except that no notice may be entered in the register of title under the Land Registration Act 2002 in respect of such orders'.

(3) In section 28(1) and (4), for 'Land Registration Act 1925' there is substituted 'Land Registration Act 2002'. ...[1]

Landlord and Tenant (Covenants) Act 1995

33—(1) The Landlord and Tenant (Covenants) Act 1995 is amended as follows.

(2) In sections 3(6) and 15(5)(b), for 'Land Registration Act 1925' there is substituted 'Land Registration Act 2002'.

(3) In section 20, in subsection (2), for the words from 'rules' to the end there is substituted 'land registration rules under the Land Registration Act 2002'.

(4) In that section, in subsection (6) –

(a) for 'an overriding interest within the meaning of the Land Registration Act 1925' there is substituted 'capable of falling within paragraph 2 of Schedule 1 or 3 to the Land Registration Act 2002', and

(b) for 'or caution under the Land Registration Act 1925' there is substituted 'under the Land Registration Act 2002'.

Family Law Act 1996

34— (1) The Family Law Act 1996 is amended as follows.

(2) In section 31(10) –

---

[1]   Prospective amendment: Paragraph in italics prospectively repealed by Proceeds of Crime Act 2002, s 457, Sch 12, from a date to be appointed (Proceeds of Crime Act 2002, s 458(1)).

(a) for 'Land Registration Act 1925' there is substituted 'Land Registration Act 2002', and
(b) for paragraph (b) there is substituted –
    '(b) a spouse's matrimonial home rights are not to be capable of falling within paragraph 2 of Schedule 1 or 3 to that Act.'

(3) In Schedule 4, in paragraph 4(6), for 'section 144 of the Land Registration Act 1925' there is substituted 'by land registration rules under the Land Registration Act 2002'.

Housing Act 1996

35 In section 13(5) of the Housing Act 1996, for the words from 'if' to the end there is substituted 'if the first disposal involves registration under the Land Registration Act 2002, the Chief Land Registrar shall enter in the register of title a restriction reflecting the limitation'.

Education Act 1996

36 In Schedule 7 to the Education Act 1996, in paragraph 11 –
(a) in sub-paragraph (a), for 'Land Registration Acts 1925 to 1986' there is substituted 'Land Registration Act 2002', and
(b) in sub-paragraphs (b) and (c), for 'those Acts' there is substituted 'that Act'.

School Standards and Framework Act 1998

37 In Schedule 22 to the School Standards and Framework Act 1998, in paragraph 9(1) –
(a) in paragraph (a), for 'Land Registration Acts 1925 to 1986' there is substituted 'Land Registration Act 2002', and
(b) in paragraphs (b) and (c), for 'those Acts' there is substituted 'that Act'.

Terrorism Act 2000

38 In Schedule 4 to the Terrorism Act 2000, in paragraph 8(1) –
(a) for 'Land Registration Act 1925' there is substituted 'Land Registration Act 2002', and
(b) in paragraph (a), at the end there is inserted ', except that no notice may be entered in the register of title under the Land Registration Act 2002 in respect of such orders'.

Finance Act 2000

39 In section 128 of the Finance Act 2000 –
(a) in subsection (2), for the words from 'rule' to the end there is substituted 'land registration rules under the Land Registration Act 2002', and
(b) in subsection (8)(a), for 'Land Registration Act 1925' there is substituted 'Land Registration Act 2002'.

International Criminal Court Act 2001

40 In Schedule 6 to the International Criminal Court Act 2001, in paragraph 7(1) –
(a) for 'Land Registration Act 1925' there is substituted 'Land Registration Act 2002', and
(b) in paragraph (a), at the end there is inserted ', except that no notice may be entered in the register of title under the Land Registration Act 2002 in respect of such orders'.

Schedule 12[1]
Transition

Section 134

Existing entries in the register

1   Nothing in the repeals made by this Act affects the validity of any entry in the register.

---

[1] Commencement: 13 October 2003 (Land Registration Act 2002 (Commencement No 4) Order 2003, SI 2003/1725).

2—(1) This Act applies to notices entered under the Land Registration Act 1925 as it applies to notices entered in pursuance of an application under section 34(2)(a).

(2) This Act applies to restrictions and inhibitions entered under the Land Registration Act 1925 as it applies to restrictions entered under this Act.

(3) Notwithstanding their repeal by this Act, sections 55 and 56 of the Land Registration Act 1925 shall continue to have effect so far as relating to cautions against dealings lodged under that Act.

(4) Rules may make provision about cautions against dealings entered under the Land Registration Act 1925.

(5) In this paragraph, references to the Land Registration Act 1925 include a reference to any enactment replaced (directly or indirectly) by that Act.

3   An entry in the register which, immediately before the repeal of section 144(1)(xi) of the Land Registration Act 1925, operated by virtue of rule 239 of the Land Registration Rules (S.I. 1925/1093) as a caution under section 54 of that Act shall continue to operate as such a caution.

Existing cautions against first registration
4   Notwithstanding the repeal of section 56(3) of the Land Registration Act 1925, that provision shall continue to have effect in relation to cautions against first registration lodged under that Act, or any enactment replaced (directly or indirectly) by that Act.

Pending applications
5   Notwithstanding the repeal of the Land Registration Act 1925, that Act shall continue to have effect in relation to an application for the entry in the register of a notice, restriction, inhibition or caution against dealings which is pending immediately before the repeal of the provision under which the application is made.

6   Notwithstanding the repeal of section 53 of the Land Registration Act 1925, subsections (1) and (2) of that section shall continue to have effect in relation to an application to lodge a caution against first registration which is pending immediately before the repeal of those provisions.

Former overriding interests
7   For the period of three years beginning with the day on which Schedule 1 comes into force, it has effect with the insertion after paragraph 14 of –
    '15   A right acquired under the Limitation Act 1980 before the coming into force of this Schedule.'

8   Schedule 3 has effect with the insertion after paragraph 2 of –
    '2A—(1) An interest which, immediately before the coming into force of this Schedule, was an overriding interest under section 70(1)(g) of the Land Registration Act 1925 by virtue of a person's receipt of rents and profits, except for an interest of a person of whom inquiry was made before the disposition and who failed to disclose the right when he could reasonably have been expected to do so.

(2) Sub-paragraph (1) does not apply to an interest if at any time since the coming into force of this Schedule it has been an interest which, had the Land Registration Act 1925 continued in force, would not have been an overriding interest under section 70(1)(g) of that Act by virtue of a person's receipt of rents and profits.'

9—(1) This paragraph applies to an easement or profit a prendre which was an overriding interest in relation to a registered estate immediately before the coming into force of Schedule 3, but which would not fall within paragraph 3 of that Schedule if created after the coming into force of that Schedule.

(2) In relation to an interest to which this paragraph applies, Schedule 3 has effect as if the interest were not excluded from paragraph 3.

10 For the period of three years beginning with the day on which Schedule 3 comes into force, paragraph 3 of the Schedule has effect with the omission of the exception.

11 For the period of three years beginning with the day on which Schedule 3 comes into force, it has effect with the insertion after paragraph 14 of –
     '15   A right under paragraph 18(1) of Schedule 12.'

12 Paragraph 1 of each of Schedules 1 and 3 shall be taken to include an interest which immediately before the coming into force of the Schedule was an overriding interest under section 70(1)(k) of the Land Registration Act 1925.

13 Paragraph 6 of each of Schedules 1 and 3 shall be taken to include an interest which immediately before the coming into force of the Schedule was an overriding interest under section 70(1)(i) of the Land Registration Act 1925 and whose status as such was preserved by section 19(3) of the Local Land Charges Act 1975 (transitional provision in relation to change in definition of 'local land charge').

Cautions against first registration
14—(1) For the period of two years beginning with the day on which section 15 comes into force, it has effect with the following omissions –
     (a) in subsection (1), the words 'Subject to subsection (3),', and
     (b) subsection (3).

(2) Any caution lodged by virtue of sub-paragraph (1) which is in force immediately before the end of the period mentioned in that sub-paragraph shall cease to have effect at the end of that period, except in relation to applications for registration made before the end of that period.

(3) This paragraph does not apply to section 15 as applied by section 81.

15—(1) As applied by section 81, section 15 has effect for the period of ten years beginning with the day on which it comes into force, or such longer period as rules may provide, with the omission of subsection (3)(a)(i).

(2) Any caution lodged by virtue of sub-paragraph (1) which is in force immediately before the end of the period mentioned in that sub-paragraph shall cease to have effect at the end of that period, except in relation to applications for registration made before the end of that period.

16 This Act shall apply as if the definition of 'caution against first registration' in section 132 included cautions lodged under section 53 of the Land Registration Act 1925.

Applications under section 34 or 43 by cautioners
17 Where a caution under section 54 of the Land Registration Act 1925 is lodged in respect of a person's estate, right, interest or claim, he may only make an application under section 34 or 43 above in respect of that estate, right, interest or claim if he also applies to the registrar for the withdrawal of the caution.

Adverse possession
18—(1) Where a registered estate in land is held in trust for a person by virtue of section 75(1) of the Land Registration Act 1925 immediately before the coming into force of section 97, he is entitled to be registered as the proprietor of the estate.

(2) A person has a defence to any action for the possession of land (in addition to any other defence he may have) if he is entitled under this paragraph to be registered as the proprietor of an estate in the land.

(3) Where in an action for possession of land a court determines that a person is entitled to a defence under this paragraph, the court must order the registrar to register him as the proprietor of the estate in relation to which he is entitled under this paragraph to be registered.

(4) Entitlement under this paragraph shall be disregarded for the purposes of section 131(1).

(5) Rules may make transitional provision for cases where a rentcharge is held in trust under section 75(1) of the Land Registration Act 1925 immediately before the coming into force of section 97.

Indemnities
19—(1) Schedule 8 applies in relation to claims made before the commencement of that Schedule which have not been settled by agreement or finally determined by that time (as well as to claims for indemnity made after the commencement of that Schedule).

(2) But paragraph 3(1) of that Schedule does not apply in relation to costs and expenses incurred in respect of proceedings, negotiations or other matters begun before 27 April 1997.

Implied indemnity covenants on transfers of pre-1996 leases
20—(1) On a disposition of a registered leasehold estate by way of transfer, the following covenants are implied in the instrument effecting the disposition, unless the contrary intention is expressed –
    (a) in the case of a transfer of the whole of the land comprised in the registered lease, the covenant in sub-paragraph (2), and
    (b) in the case of a transfer of part of the land comprised in the lease –
        (i) the covenant in sub-paragraph (3), and
        (ii) where the transferor continues to hold land under the lease, the covenant in sub-paragraph (4).

(2) The transferee covenants with the transferor that during the residue of the term granted by the registered lease the transferee and the persons deriving title under him will –
    (a) pay the rent reserved by the lease,
    (b) comply with the covenants and conditions contained in the lease, and
    (c) keep the transferor and the persons deriving title under him indemnified against all actions, expenses and claims on account of any failure to comply with paragraphs (a) and (b).

(3) The transferee covenants with the transferor that during the residue of the term granted by the registered lease the transferee and the persons deriving title under him will –

(a) where the rent reserved by the lease is apportioned, pay the rent apportioned to the part transferred,

(b) comply with the covenants and conditions contained in the lease so far as affecting the part transferred, and

(c) keep the transferor and the persons deriving title under him indemnified against all actions, expenses and claims on account of any failure to comply with paragraphs (a) and (b).

(4) The transferor covenants with the transferee that during the residue of the term granted by the registered lease the transferor and the persons deriving title under him will –

(a) where the rent reserved by the lease is apportioned, pay the rent apportioned to the part retained,

(b) comply with the covenants and conditions contained in the lease so far as affecting the part retained, and

(c) keep the transferee and the persons deriving title under him indemnified against all actions, expenses and claims on account of any failure to comply with paragraphs (a) and (b).

(5) This paragraph does not apply to a lease which is a new tenancy for the purposes of section 1 of the Landlord and Tenant (Covenants) Act 1995.

Schedule 13[1]
Repeals

Section 135

Short title and chapter	Extent of repeal
Land Registry Act 1862	The whole Act
Settled Land Act 1925	Section 119(3)
Law of Property Act 1925	In section 84(8), the words from ', but' to the end In section 205(1)(xxii), the words from ', and' to the end
Land Registration Act 1925	The whole Act
Law of Property (Amendment) Act 1926	Section 5
Land Registration Act 1936	The whole Act
Requisitioned Land and War Works Act 1945	Section 37(3)
Mental Health Act 1959	In Schedule 7, the entry relating to the Land Registration Act 1925
Charities Act 1960	In Schedule 6, the entry relating to the Land Registration Act 1925
Civil Evidence Act 1968	In the Schedule, the entry relating to the Land Registration Act 1925
Post Office Act 1969	In Schedule 4, paragraph 27
Law of Property Act 1969	Section 28(7)
Land Registration and Land Charges Act 1971	The whole Act

---

[1] Commencement: 13 October 2003 (Land Registration Act 2002 (Commencement No 4) Order 2003, SI 2003/1725).

Short title and chapter	Extent of repeal
Superannuation Act 1972	In Schedule 6, paragraph 16
Local Government Act 1972	In Schedule 29, paragraph 26
Solicitors Act 1974	Section 75(b)
Finance Act 1975	In Schedule 12, paragraph 5
Local Land Charges Act 1975	Section 19(3) In Schedule 1, the entry relating to the Land Registration Act 1925
Endowments and Glebe Measure 1976 (No 4)	In Schedule 5, paragraph 1
Administration of Justice Act 1977	Sections 24 and 26
Charging Orders Act 1979	Section 3(3) Section 7(4)
Limitation Act 1980	In section 17, paragraph (b) and the preceding 'and'
Highways Act 1980	Section 251(5)
Matrimonial Homes and Property Act 1981	Section 4
Administration of Justice Act 1982	Sections 66 and 67 and Schedule 5
Mental Health Act 1983	In Schedule 4, paragraph 6
Capital Transfer Tax Act 1984	In Schedule 8, paragraph 1
Administration of Justice Act 1985	In section 34, in subsection (1), paragraph (b) and the preceding 'and' and, in subsection (2), paragraph (b) In Schedule 2, paragraph 37(b)
Insolvency Act 1985	In Schedule 8, paragraph 5
Housing Act 1985	Section 36(3) Section 154(1), (6) and (7) Section 156(3) Section 168(5) In Schedule 9A, paragraphs 2(1), 3 and 5(3)
Land Registration Act 1986	Sections 1 to 4
Insolvency Act 1986	In Schedule 14, the entry relating to the Land Registration Act 1925
Building Societies Act 1986	In Schedule 2A, in paragraph 1, sub-paragraph (4) and, in sub-paragraph (5), the definition of 'registered land' and the preceding 'and' In Schedule 18, paragraph 2 In Schedule 21, paragraph 9(b)
Patronage (Benefices) Measure 1986 (No 3)	Section 6
Landlord and Tenant Act 1987	Section 28(6) In Schedule 4, paragraphs 1 and 2
Diplomatic and Consular Premises Act 1987	In Schedule 1, in paragraph 1, the words from 'and expressions' to the end
Land Registration Act 1988	The whole Act
Criminal Justice Act 1988	Section 77(13) In Schedule 15, paragraphs 6 and 7

Short title and chapter	Extent of repeal
Housing Act 1988	In Schedule 11, paragraph 2(3)
Finance Act 1989	Sections 178(2)(e) and 179(1)(a)(iv)
Courts and Legal Services Act 1990	In Schedule 10, paragraph 3 In Schedule 17, paragraph 2
Access to Neighbouring Land Act 1992	Section 5(2) and (3)
Leasehold Reform, Housing and Urban Development Act 1993	Section 97(3) In Schedule 21, paragraph 1
Coal Industry Act 1994	In Schedule 9, paragraph 1
Law of Property (Miscellaneous Provisions) Act 1994	In Schedule 1, paragraph 2
Drug Trafficking Act 1994	Section 26(13) In Schedule 1, paragraph 1
Family Law Act 1996	Section 31(11) In Schedule 8, paragraph 45
Trusts of Land and Appointment of Trustees Act 1996	In Schedule 3, paragraph 5
Housing Act 1996	Section 11(4)
Housing Grants, Construction and Regeneration Act 1996	Section 138(3)
Land Registration Act 1997	Sections 1 to 3 and 5(4) and (5) In Schedule 1, paragraphs 1 to 6
Greater London Authority Act 1999	Section 219
Terrorism Act 2000	In Schedule 4, paragraph 8(2) and (3)
Trustee Act 2000	In Schedule 2, paragraph 26
International Criminal Court Act 2001	In Schedule 6, paragraph 7(2)

LAND REGISTRATION RULES 2003, SI 2003/1417

PRELIMINARY

1[1] Citation and commencement

These rules may be cited as the Land Registration Rules 2003 and shall come into force on the day that section 1 of the Act comes into force.

PART 1
THE REGISTER OF TITLE

2[2] Form and arrangement of the register of title

(1) The register of title may be kept in electronic or paper form, or partly in one form and partly in the other.

(2) Subject to rule 3, the register of title must include an individual register for each registered estate which is –
(a) an estate in land, or
(b) a rentcharge, franchise, manor or profit a prendre in gross,
vested in a proprietor.

3[3] Individual registers and more than one registered estate, division and amalgamation

(1) The registrar may include more than one registered estate in an individual register if the estates are of the same kind and are vested in the same proprietor.

(2) On first registration of a registered estate, the registrar may open an individual register for each separate area of land affected by the proprietor's registered estate as he designates.

(3) Subsequently, the registrar may open an individual register for part of the registered estate in a registered title and retain the existing individual register for the remainder –
(a) on the application of the proprietor of the registered estate and of any registered charge over it, or
(b) if he considers it desirable for the keeping of the register of title, or
(c) on the registration of a charge of part of the registered estate comprised in the registered title.

(4) The registrar may amalgamate two or more registered titles, or add an estate which is being registered for the first time to an existing registered title, if the estates are of the same kind and are vested in the same proprietor –
(a) on the application of the proprietor of the registered estate and of any registered charge over it, or
(b) if he considers it desirable for the keeping of the register of title.

NOTE Schedules 1, 3 and 9 to these Rules have not been reproduced here but a selected number of Land Registry forms have been reproduced as Appendix 2 to this book.

[1] Commencement: 13 October 2003 (r 1; Land Registration Act 2002 (Commencement No 4) Order 2003, SI 2003/1725).

[2] Commencement: 13 October 2003 (r 1; Land Registration Act 2002 (Commencement No 4) Order 2003, SI 2003/1725).

[3] Commencement: 13 October 2003 (r 1; Land Registration Act 2002 (Commencement No 4) Order 2003, SI 2003/1725).

(5) Where the registrar has divided a registered title under paragraph (3)(b) or amalgamated registered titles or an estate on first registration with a registered title under paragraph (4)(b) he –

(a) must notify the proprietor of the registered estate and any registered charge, unless they have agreed to such action, and

(b) may make a new edition of any individual register or make entries on any individual register to reflect the division or amalgamation.

4[1] Arrangement of individual registers

(1) Each individual register must have a distinguishing number, or series of letters and numbers, known as the title number.

(2) Each individual register must consist of a property register, a proprietorship register and, where necessary, a charges register.

(3) An entry in an individual register may be made by reference to a plan or other document; in which case the registrar must keep the original or a copy of the document.

(4) Whenever the registrar considers it desirable, he may make a new edition of any individual register so that it contains only the subsisting entries, rearrange the entries in the register or alter its title number.

5[2] Contents of the property register

The property register of a registered estate must contain –

(a) a description of the registered estate which in the case of a registered estate in land, rentcharge or registered franchise which is an affecting franchise must refer to a plan based on the Ordnance Survey map and known as the title plan;

(b) where appropriate, details of –

    (i)   the inclusion or exclusion of mines and minerals in or from the registration under rule 32,

    (ii)   easements, rights, privileges, conditions and covenants benefiting the registered estate and other similar matters,

    (iii)   all exceptions arising on enfranchisement of formerly copyhold land, and

    (iv)   any other matter required to be entered in any other part of the register which the registrar considers may more conveniently be entered in the property register, and

(c) such other matters as are required to be entered in the property register by these rules.

6[3] Property register of a registered leasehold estate

(1) The property register of a registered leasehold estate must also contain sufficient particulars of the registered lease to enable that lease to be identified.

(2) If the lease contains a provision that prohibits or restricts dispositions of the leasehold estate, the registrar must make an entry in the property register stating that all estates, rights, interests, powers and remedies arising on or by reason of a disposition made in breach of that prohibition or restriction are excepted from the effect of registration.

---

[1]   Commencement: 13 October 2003 (r 1; Land Registration Act 2002 (Commencement No 4) Order 2003, SI 2003/1725).

[2]   Commencement: 13 October 2003 (r 1; Land Registration Act 2002 (Commencement No 4) Order 2003, SI 2003/1725).

[3]   Commencement: 13 October 2003 (r 1; Land Registration Act 2002 (Commencement No 4) Order 2003, SI 2003/1725).

7[1] Property register of a registered estate in a rentcharge, a franchise or a profit a prendre in gross

The property register of a registered estate in a rentcharge, franchise or a profit a prendre in gross must, if the estate was created by an instrument, also contain sufficient particulars of the instrument to enable it to be identified.

8[2] Contents of the proprietorship register

(1) The proprietorship register of a registered estate must contain, where appropriate –

  (a) the class of title,

  (b) the name of the proprietor of the registered estate including, where the proprietor is a company registered under the Companies Acts, or a limited liability partnership incorporated under the Limited Liability Partnerships Act 2000, its registered number,

  (c) an address for service of the proprietor of the registered estate in accordance with rule 198,

  (d) restrictions under section 40 of the Act, including one entered under section 86(4) of the Act, in relation to the registered estate,

  (e) notices under section 86(2) of the Act in relation to the registered estate,

  (f) positive covenants by a transferor or transferee and indemnity convenants by a transferee entered under rules 64 or 65,

  (g) details of any modification of the covenants implied by paragraphs 20(2) and (3) of Schedule 12 to the Act entered under rule 66,

  (h) details of any modification of the covenants implied under the Law of Property (Miscellaneous Provisions) Act 1994 entered under rule 67(6),

  (i) where the class of title is possessory, the name of the first proprietor of the registered estate and, where that proprietor is a company registered under the Companies Acts, or a limited liability partnership incorporated under the Limited Liability Partnerships Act 2000, its registered number, and

  (j) such other matters as are required to be entered in the proprietorship register by these rules.

(2) On first registration and on a subsequent change of proprietor, the registrar whenever practicable will enter in the proprietorship register the price paid or value declared and such entry will remain until there is a change of proprietor, or some other change in the register of title which the registrar considers would result in the entry being misleading.

9[3] Contents of the charges register

The charges register of a registered estate must contain, where appropriate –

  (a) details of leases, charges, and any other interests which adversely affect the registered estate subsisting at the time of first registration of the estate or created thereafter,

  (b) any dealings with the interests referred to in paragraph (a), or affecting their priority, which are capable of being noted on the register,

  (c) sufficient details to enable any registered charge to be identified,

  (d) the name of the proprietor of any registered charge including, where the proprietor is a company registered under the Companies Acts, or a limited liability partnership incorporated under the Limited Liability Partnerships Act 2000, its registered number,

  (e) an address for service of the proprietor of any registered charge in accordance with rule 198,

---

[1]   Commencement: 13 October 2003 (r 1; Land Registration Act 2002 (Commencement No 4) Order 2003, SI 2003/1725).

[2]   Commencement: 13 October 2003 (r 1; Land Registration Act 2002 (Commencement No 4) Order 2003, SI 2003/1725).

[3]   Commencement: 13 October 2003 (r 1; Land Registration Act 2002 (Commencement No 4) Order 2003, SI 2003/1725).

(f) restrictions under section 40 of the Act, including one entered under section 86(4) of the Act, in relation to a registered charge,

(g) notices under section 86(2) of the Act in relation to a registered charge, and

(h) such other matters affecting the registered estate or any registered charge as are required to be entered in the charges register by these rules.

PART 2
INDICES

10[1] Index to be kept under section 68 of the Act

(1) The index to be kept under section 68 of the Act must comprise –

(a) an index map from which it is possible to ascertain, in relation to a parcel of land, whether there is –

    (i) a pending application for first registration (other than of title to a relating franchise),

    (ii) a pending application for a caution against first registration (other than where the subject of the caution is a relating franchise),

    (iii) a registered estate in land,

    (iv) a registered rentcharge,

    (v) a registered profit a prendre in gross,

    (vi) a registered affecting franchise, or

    (vii) a caution against first registration (other than where the subject of the caution is a relating franchise),

and, if there is such a registered estate or caution, the title number, and

(b) an index of verbal descriptions of –

    (i) pending applications for first registration of title to relating franchises,

    (ii) pending applications for cautions against first registration where the subject of the caution is a relating franchise,

    (iii) registered franchises which are relating franchises,

    (iv) registered manors, and

    (v) cautions against first registration where the subject of the caution is a relating franchise,

and the title numbers of any such registered estates and cautions, arranged by administrative area.

(2) The information required to be shown in the index to be kept under section 68 is to be entered by the registrar in the index as soon as practicable.

11[2] Index of proprietors' names

(1) Subject to paragraph (2), the registrar must keep an index of proprietors' names, showing for each individual register the name of the proprietor of the registered estate and the proprietor of any registered charge together with the title number.

(2) Until every individual register is held in electronic form, the index need not contain the name of any corporate or joint proprietor of an estate or of a charge registered as proprietor prior to 1st May 1972.

(3) A person may apply in Form PN1 for a search to be made in the index in respect of either his own name or the name of some other person in whose property he can satisfy the registrar

---

[1] Commencement: 13 October 2003 (r 1; Land Registration Act 2002 (Commencement No 4) Order 2003, SI 2003/1725).

[2] Commencement: 13 October 2003 (r 1; Land Registration Act 2002 (Commencement No 4) Order 2003, SI 2003/1725).

that he is interested generally (for instance as trustee in bankruptcy or personal representative).

(4) On receipt of such an application the registrar must make the search and supply the applicant with details of every entry in the index relating to the particulars given in the application.

12[1] The day list

(1) The registrar must keep a record (known as the day list) showing the date and time at which every pending application under the Act or these rules was made and of every application for an official search with priority under rule 147.

(2) The entry of notice of an application for an official search with priority must remain on the day list until the priority period conferred by the entry has ceased to have effect.

(3) Where the registrar proposes to alter the register without having received an application he must enter his proposal on the day list and, when so entered, the proposal will have the same effect for the purposes of rules 15 and 20 as if it were an application to the registrar made at the date and time of its entry.

(4) In this rule the term 'pending application' does not include an application within Part 13, other than an application that the registrar designate a document an exempt information document under rule 136.

PART 3
APPLICATIONS: GENERAL PROVISIONS

13[2] Form AP1

(1) Any application made under the Act or these rules for which no other application form is prescribed must be made in Form AP1.

(2) Paragraph (1) does not apply to –
   (a) an application to remove from the register the name of a deceased joint registered proprietor,
   (b) applications made under rule 14, or
   (c) outline applications as defined in rule 54.

14[3] Electronic delivery of applications

Any application to which rule 15 applies (other than an outline application under rule 54) may during the currency of any notice given under Schedule 2, and subject to and in accordance with the limitations contained in that notice, be delivered by electronic means and the applicant shall provide, in such order as may be required by that notice, such of the particulars required for an application of that type as are appropriate in the circumstances and as are required by the notice.

15[4] Time at which applications are taken to be made

(1) An application received on a business day is to be taken as made at the earlier of –
   (a) the time of the day that notice of it is entered in the day list, or

1   Commencement: 13 October 2003 (r 1; Land Registration Act 2002 (Commencement No 4) Order 2003, SI 2003/1725).
2   Commencement: 13 October 2003 (r 1; Land Registration Act 2002 (Commencement No 4) Order 2003, SI 2003/1725).
3   Commencement: 13 October 2003 (r 1; Land Registration Act 2002 (Commencement No 4) Order 2003, SI 2003/1725).
4   Commencement: 13 October 2003 (r 1; Land Registration Act 2002 (Commencement No 4) Order 2003, SI 2003/1725).

(b)

    (i) midnight marking the end of the day it was received if the application was received before 12 noon, or

    (ii) midnight marking the end of the next business day after the day it was received if the application was received at or after 12 noon.

(2) An application received on a day which is not a business day is to be taken as made at the earlier of –

    (a) the time of a business day that notice of it is entered in the day list, or

    (b) midnight marking the end of the next business day after the day it was received.

(3) In this rule an application is received when it is delivered –

    (a) to the designated proper office in accordance with an order under section 100(3) of the Act, or

    (b) to the registrar in accordance with a written arrangement as to delivery made between the registrar and the applicant or between the registrar and the applicant's conveyancer, or

    (c) to the registrar under the provisions of any relevant notice given under Schedule 2.

(4) This rule does not apply to applications under Part 13, other than an application that the registrar designate a document an exempt information document under rule 136.

16[1] Applications not in order

(1) If an application is not in order the registrar may raise such requisitions as he considers necessary, specifying a period (being not less than twenty business days) within which the applicant must comply with the requisitions.

(2) If the applicant fails to comply with the requisitions within that period, the registrar may cancel the application or may extend the period when this appears to him to be reasonable in the circumstances.

(3) If an application appears to the registrar to be substantially defective, he may reject it on delivery or he may cancel it at any time thereafter.

(4) Where a fee for an application is paid by means of a cheque and the registrar becomes aware, before that application has been completed, that the cheque has not been honoured, the application may be cancelled.

17[2] Additional evidence and enquiries

If the registrar at any time considers that the production of any further documents or evidence or the giving of any notice is necessary or desirable, he may refuse to complete or proceed with an application, or to do any act or make any entry, until such documents, evidence or notices have been supplied or given.

18[3] Continuation of application on a transfer by operation of law

If, before an application has been completed, the whole of the applicant's interest is transferred by operation of law, the application may be continued by the person entitled to that interest in consequence of that transfer.

---

[1] Commencement: 13 October 2003 (r 1; Land Registration Act 2002 (Commencement No 4) Order 2003, SI 2003/1725).

[2] Commencement: 13 October 2003 (r 1; Land Registration Act 2002 (Commencement No 4) Order 2003, SI 2003/1725).

[3] Commencement: 13 October 2003 (r 1; Land Registration Act 2002 (Commencement No 4) Order 2003, SI 2003/1725).

19¹ Objections

(1) Subject to paragraph (5), an objection under section 73 of the Act to an application must be made by delivering to the registrar at the appropriate office a written statement signed by the objector or his conveyancer.

(2) The statement must –
- (a) state that the objector objects to the application,
- (b) state the grounds for the objection, and
- (c) give the full name of the objector and an address to which communications may be sent.

(3) Subject to paragraph (5), the written statement referred to in paragraph (1) must be delivered –
- (a) in paper form, or
- (b) to the electronic address, or
- (c) to the fax number.

(4) In paragraph (3) the reference to the electronic address and the fax number is to the electronic address or fax number for the appropriate office specified in a direction by the registrar under section 100(4) of the Act as that to be used for delivery of objections.

(5) Where a person is objecting to an application in response to a notice given by the registrar, he may alternatively do so in the manner and to the address stated in the notice as provided by rule 197(1)(c).

(6) In this rule the appropriate office is the same office as the proper office, designated under an order under section 100(3) of the Act, for the receipt of an application relating to the land in respect of which the objection is made, but on the assumption that if the order contains exceptions none of the exceptions apply to that application.

20² Completion of applications

(1) Any entry in, removal of an entry from or alteration of the register pursuant to an application under the Act or these rules has effect from the time of the making of the application.

(2) This rule does not apply to the applications mentioned in section 74 of the Act.

PART 4
FIRST REGISTRATION

21³ First registration - application by mortgagee

A mortgagee under a mortgage falling within section 4(1)(g) of the Act may make an application in the name of the mortgagor for the estate charged by the mortgage to be registered whether or not the mortgagor consents.

22⁴ Registration of a proprietor of a charge falling within section 4(1)(g) of the Act

(1) This rule applies to an application for first registration made –

---

1 Commencement: 13 October 2003 (r 1; Land Registration Act 2002 (Commencement No 4) Order 2003, SI 2003/1725).

2 Commencement: 13 October 2003 (r 1; Land Registration Act 2002 (Commencement No 4) Order 2003, SI 2003/1725).

3 Commencement: 13 October 2003 (r 1; Land Registration Act 2002 (Commencement No 4) Order 2003, SI 2003/1725).

4 Commencement: 13 October 2003 (r 1; Land Registration Act 2002 (Commencement No 4) Order 2003, SI 2003/1725).

(a) under rule 21, or

(b) by the owner of an estate that is subject to a legal charge falling within section 4(1)(g) of the Act.

(2) The registrar must enter the mortgagee of the legal charge falling within section 4(1)(g) of the Act as the proprietor of that charge if he is satisfied of that person's entitlement.

23[1] First registration - application form

(1) Subject to paragraph (2), an application for first registration must be made in Form FR1.

(2) Where Her Majesty applies for the first registration of an estate under section 79 of the Act, Form FR1 must be used with such modifications to it as are appropriate and have been approved by the registrar.

24[2] Documents to be delivered with a first registration application

(1) Unless the registrar otherwise directs, every application for first registration must be accompanied by –

(a) sufficient details, by plan or otherwise (subject to rules 25 and 26), so that the land can be identified clearly on the Ordnance Survey map,

(b) in the case of a leasehold estate, the lease, if in the control of the applicant, and a certified copy,

(c) all deeds and documents relating to the title that are in the control of the applicant,

(d) a list in duplicate in Form DL of all the documents delivered.

(2) On an application to register a rentcharge, franchise or profit a prendre in gross, the land to be identified under paragraph (1)(a) is the land affected by that estate or to which it relates.

25[3] First registration of mines and minerals

When applying for first registration of an estate in mines and minerals held apart from the surface, the applicant must provide –

(a) a plan of the surface under which the mines and minerals lie,

(b) any other sufficient details by plan or otherwise so that the mines and minerals can be identified clearly, and

(c) full details of rights incidental to the working of the mines and minerals.

26[4] First registration of cellars, flats, tunnels etc

(1) Subject to paragraph (2), unless all of the land above and below the surface is included in an application for first registration the applicant must provide a plan of the surface on under or over which the land to be registered lies, and sufficient information to define the vertical and horizontal extents of the land.

(2) This rule does not apply where only mines and minerals are excluded from the application.

---

[1] Commencement: 13 October 2003 (r 1; Land Registration Act 2002 (Commencement No 4) Order 2003, SI 2003/1725).

[2] Commencement: 13 October 2003 (r 1; Land Registration Act 2002 (Commencement No 4) Order 2003, SI 2003/1725).

[3] Commencement: 13 October 2003 (r 1; Land Registration Act 2002 (Commencement No 4) Order 2003, SI 2003/1725).

[4] Commencement: 13 October 2003 (r 1; Land Registration Act 2002 (Commencement No 4) Order 2003, SI 2003/1725).

27¹ First registration application where title documents are unavailable

An application for first registration by a person who is unable to produce a full documentary title must be supported by evidence –

(a) to satisfy the registrar that the applicant is entitled to apply under section 3(2) of the Act or required to apply under section 6(1) of the Act, and

(b) where appropriate, to account for the absence of documentary evidence of title.

28² Duty to disclose unregistered interests that override first registration

(1) Subject to paragraph (2), a person applying for first registration must provide information to the registrar about any of the interests that fall within Schedule 1 to the Act that –

(a) are within the actual knowledge of the applicant, and

(b) affect the estate to which the application relates,

in Form DI.

(2) The applicant is not required to provide information about –

(a) an interest that under section 33 or 90(4) of the Act cannot be protected by notice,

(b) an interest that is apparent from the deeds and documents of title accompanying the application under rule 24,

(c) a public right,

(d) a local land charge,

(e) a leasehold estate in land if –

(i) it is within paragraph 1 of Schedule 1 to the Act, and

(ii) at the time of the application, the term granted by the lease has one year or less to run.

(3) In this rule and in Form FR1, a 'disclosable overriding interest' is an interest that the applicant must provide information about under paragraph (1).

(4) Where the applicant provides information about a disclosable overriding interest under this rule, the registrar may enter a notice in the register in respect of that interest.

29³ First registration - examination of title

In examining the title shown by the documents accompanying an application for first registration the registrar may have regard to any examination of title by a conveyancer prior to the application and to the nature of the property.

30⁴ Searches and enquiries by the registrar

In examining title on an application for first registration the registrar may –

(a) make searches and enquiries and give notices to other persons,

(b) direct that searches and enquiries be made by the applicant,

(c) advertise the application.

---

1 Commencement: 13 October 2003 (r 1; Land Registration Act 2002 (Commencement No 4) Order 2003, SI 2003/1725).

2 Commencement: 13 October 2003 (r 1; Land Registration Act 2002 (Commencement No 4) Order 2003, SI 2003/1725).

3 Commencement: 13 October 2003 (r 1; Land Registration Act 2002 (Commencement No 4) Order 2003, SI 2003/1725).

4 Commencement: 13 October 2003 (r 1; Land Registration Act 2002 (Commencement No 4) Order 2003, SI 2003/1725).

31¹ First registration - foreshore

(1) Where it appears to the registrar that any land included in an application for first registration comprises foreshore, he must serve a notice of that application on –

    (a) the Crown Estate Commissioners in every case,

    (b) the Chancellor of the Duchy of Lancaster in the case of land in the county palatine of Lancaster,

    (c) the appropriate person in the case of land in the counties of Devon and Cornwall and in the Isles of Scilly and in the case of land within the jurisdiction of the Port of London Authority, and

    (d) the Port of London Authority in the case of land within its jurisdiction.

(2) A notice under paragraph (1) must provide a period ending at 12 noon on the twentieth business day after the date of issue of the notice in which to object to the application.

(3) A notice need not be served under paragraph (1) where, if it was served, it would result in it being served on the applicant for first registration.

(4) In this rule –

'the appropriate person' means such person as the Duke of Cornwall, or the possessor for the time being of the Duchy of Cornwall, appoints,

'foreshore' has the meaning given by paragraph 13(3) of Schedule 6 to the Act.

32² Mines and minerals - note as to inclusion or exclusion

Where, on first registration of an estate in land which comprises or includes the land beneath the surface, the registrar is satisfied that the mines and minerals are included in or excluded from the applicant's title he must make an appropriate note in the register.

33³ First registration - entry of beneficial rights

(1) The benefit of an appurtenant right may be entered in the register at the time of first registration if –

    (a) on examination of the title, or

    (b) on receipt of a written application providing details of the right and evidence of its existence,

the registrar is satisfied that the right subsists as a legal estate and benefits the registered estate.

(2) If the registrar is not satisfied that the right subsists as a legal interest benefiting the registered estate, he may enter details of the right claimed in the property register with such qualification as he considers appropriate.

34⁴ First registration - registration of a proprietor of a legal mortgage not within rule 22 or rule 38

(1) The registrar must enter the mortgagee of a legal mortgage to which this rule applies as the proprietor of that charge if on first registration of the legal estate charged by that charge he is satisfied of that person's entitlement.

(2) This rule applies to a legal mortgage –

    (a) which is either –

---

1   Commencement: 13 October 2003 (r 1; Land Registration Act 2002 (Commencement No 4) Order 2003, SI 2003/1725).

2   Commencement: 13 October 2003 (r 1; Land Registration Act 2002 (Commencement No 4) Order 2003, SI 2003/1725).

3   Commencement: 13 October 2003 (r 1; Land Registration Act 2002 (Commencement No 4) Order 2003, SI 2003/1725).

4   Commencement: 13 October 2003 (r 1; Land Registration Act 2002 (Commencement No 4) Order 2003, SI 2003/1725).

    (i) a charge on the legal estate that is being registered, or

    (ii) is a charge on such charge, and

  (b) which is not a charge falling within rule 22 or rule 38.

35[1] First registration - entry of burdens

(1) On first registration the registrar must enter a notice in the register of the burden of any interest which appears from his examination of the title to affect the registered estate.

(2) This rule does not apply to –

  (a) an interest that under section 33 or 90(4) of the Act cannot be protected by notice,

  (b) a public right,

  (c) a local land charge,

  (d) an interest which appears to the registrar to be of a trivial or obvious character, or the entry of a notice in respect of which would be likely to cause confusion or inconvenience.

36[2] First registration - note as to rights of light and air

On first registration, if it appears to the registrar that an agreement prevents the acquisition of rights of light or air for the benefit of the registered estate, he may make an entry in the property register of that estate.

37[3] First registration - notice of lease

(1) Subject to paragraph (2), before completing an application for registration of a leasehold estate with absolute title, the registrar must give notice of the application to the proprietor of the registered reversion.

(2) This rule only applies where –

  (a) at the time of the grant of the lease –

    (i) the reversion was not registered, or

    (ii) the reversion was registered but the grant of the lease was not required to be completed by registration,

  (b) the lease is not noted in the register of the registered reversion, and

  (c) it is not apparent from the application that the proprietor of the registered reversion consents to the registration.

(3) On completing registration of the leasehold estate, the registrar must enter notice of the lease in the register of the registered reversion.

(4) In this rule, 'the reversion' refers to the estate that is the immediate reversion to the lease that is the subject of the application referred to in paragraph (1) and 'registered reversion' refers to such estate when it is a registered estate.

38[4] Application of the Act to dealings prior to first registration

(1) If, while a person is subject to a duty under section 6 of the Act to make an application to be registered as proprietor of a legal estate, there is a dealing with that estate, then the Act

---

[1] Commencement: 13 October 2003 (r 1; Land Registration Act 2002 (Commencement No 4) Order 2003, SI 2003/1725).

[2] Commencement: 13 October 2003 (r 1; Land Registration Act 2002 (Commencement No 4) Order 2003, SI 2003/1725).

[3] Commencement: 13 October 2003 (r 1; Land Registration Act 2002 (Commencement No 4) Order 2003, SI 2003/1725).

[4] Commencement: 13 October 2003 (r 1; Land Registration Act 2002 (Commencement No 4) Order 2003, SI 2003/1725).

applies to that dealing as if the dealing had taken place after the date of first registration of that estate.

(2) The registration of any dealing falling within paragraph (1) that is delivered for registration with the application made pursuant to section 6 has effect from the time of the making of that application.

PART 5
CAUTIONS AGAINST FIRST REGISTRATION

39[1] Definitions
In this Part –

'cautioner' has the same meaning as in section 22 of the Act (read with rule 52),

'cautioner's register' is the register so named in rule 41(2) the contents of which are described in rule 41(5),

'relevant interest' means the interest claimed by the cautioner in the unregistered legal estate to which the caution against first registration relates.

40[2] Form and arrangement of the cautions register
(1) The cautions register may be kept in electronic or paper form, or partly in one form and partly in the other.

(2) Subject to paragraph (3), the cautions register will comprise an individual caution register for each caution against the registration of title to an unregistered estate.

(3) On registration of a caution, the registrar may open an individual caution register for each separate area of land affected by the caution as he designates.

41[3] Arrangement of individual caution registers
(1) Each individual caution register will have a distinguishing number, or series of letters and numbers, known as the caution title number.

(2) Each individual caution register will be in two parts called the caution property register and the cautioner's register.

(3) The caution property register will contain –
   (a) a description of the legal estate to which the caution relates, and
   (b) a description of the relevant interest.

(4) Where the legal estate to which the caution relates is an estate in land, a rentcharge, or an affecting franchise, the description will refer to a caution plan, which plan will be based on the Ordnance Survey map.

(5) The cautioner's register will contain –
   (a) the name of the cautioner including, where the cautioner is a company registered under the Companies Acts, or a limited liability partnership incorporated under the Limited Liability Partnerships Act 2000, its registered number,
   (b) an address for service in accordance with rule 198, and

---

[1]   Commencement: 13 October 2003 (r 1; Land Registration Act 2002 (Commencement No 4) Order 2003, SI 2003/1725).
[2]   Commencement: 13 October 2003 (r 1; Land Registration Act 2002 (Commencement No 4) Order 2003, SI 2003/1725).
[3]   Commencement: 13 October 2003 (r 1; Land Registration Act 2002 (Commencement No 4) Order 2003, SI 2003/1725).

(c) where appropriate, details of any person consenting to the lodging of the caution under rule 47.

42[1] Caution against first registration - application

An application for a caution against first registration must be made in Form CT1 and contain sufficient details, by plan or otherwise, so that the extent of the land to which the caution relates can be identified clearly on the Ordnance Survey map.

43[2] Withdrawal of a caution against first registration - application

An application to withdraw a caution against first registration must be made in Form WCT and, if the application is made in respect of part only of the land to which the individual caution register relates, it must contain sufficient details, by plan or otherwise, so that the extent of that part can be identified clearly on the Ordnance Survey map.

44[3] Cancellation of a caution against first registration - application

(1) Subject to paragraph (5), an application for the cancellation of a caution against first registration must be in Form CCT.

(2) Where the application is made in respect of part only of the land to which the individual caution register relates, it must contain sufficient details, by plan or otherwise, so that the extent of that part can be identified clearly on the Ordnance Survey map.

(3) Where a person applies under section 18(1)(a) of the Act or rule 45(a) or (b)(ii), evidence to satisfy the registrar that he is entitled to apply must accompany the application.

(4) Where the applicant, or a person from whom the applicant derives title to the legal estate by operation of law, has consented to the lodging of the caution, evidence of the facts referred to in rule 46 must accompany the application.

(5) Where an application is made for the cancellation of a caution against first registration by Her Majesty by virtue of rule 45(b)(i), Form CCT must be used with such modifications to it as are appropriate and have been approved by the registrar.

45[4] Other persons who may apply to cancel a caution against first registration

In addition to the owner of the legal estate to which the caution relates –
    (a) the owner of a legal estate derived out of that estate, and
    (b) where the land to which the caution relates is demesne land,
        (i) Her Majesty, or
        (ii) the owner of a legal estate affecting the demesne land,
may apply under section 18(1)(b) of the Act for cancellation of a caution against first registration.

---

[1] Commencement: 13 October 2003 (r 1; Land Registration Act 2002 (Commencement No 4) Order 2003, SI 2003/1725).

[2] Commencement: 13 October 2003 (r 1; Land Registration Act 2002 (Commencement No 4) Order 2003, SI 2003/1725).

[3] Commencement: 13 October 2003 (r 1; Land Registration Act 2002 (Commencement No 4) Order 2003, SI 2003/1725).

[4] Commencement: 13 October 2003 (r 1; Land Registration Act 2002 (Commencement No 4) Order 2003, SI 2003/1725).

46¹ Application for cancellation of a caution against first registration by a person who originally consented

A person to whom section 18(2) of the Act applies may make an application for cancellation of a caution against first registration only if –

    (a) the relevant interest has come to an end, or

    (b) the consent referred to in section 18(2) was induced by fraud, misrepresentation, mistake or undue influence or given under duress.

47² Consent to registration of a caution against first registration

For the purposes of section 18(2) of the Act a person consents to the lodging of a caution against first registration if before the caution is entered in the cautions register –

    (a) he has confirmed in writing that he consents to the lodging of the caution, and

    (b) that consent is produced to the registrar.

48³ Alteration of the cautions register by the court

(1) If in any proceedings the court decides that the cautioner does not own the relevant interest, or only owns part, or that such interest either wholly or in part did not exist or has come to an end, the court must make an order for alteration of the cautions register under section 20(1) of the Act.

(2) An order for alteration of the cautions register must state the caution title number of the individual caution register affected, describe the alteration that is to be made, and direct the registrar to make the alteration.

(3) For the purposes of section 20(2) of the Act an order for alteration of the cautions register may only be served on the registrar by making an application for him to give effect to the order.

49⁴ Alteration of the cautions register by the registrar

If the registrar is satisfied that the cautioner does not own the relevant interest, or only owns part, or that such interest did not exist or has come to an end wholly or in part, he must on application alter the cautions register under section 21(1) of the Act.

50⁵ Applications to the registrar to alter the cautions register and service of notice

(1) A person who wishes the registrar to alter the cautions register under section 21(1) of the Act must request the registrar to do so by an application, which must include –

    (a) written details of the alteration required and of the grounds on which the application is made, and

    (b) any supporting document.

(2) Before the registrar alters the cautions register under section 21(1) of the Act he must serve a notice on the cautioner giving details of the application, unless the registrar is satisfied that service of the notice is unnecessary.

---

1 Commencement: 13 October 2003 (r 1; Land Registration Act 2002 (Commencement No 4) Order 2003, SI 2003/1725).

2 Commencement: 13 October 2003 (r 1; Land Registration Act 2002 (Commencement No 4) Order 2003, SI 2003/1725).

3 Commencement: 13 October 2003 (r 1; Land Registration Act 2002 (Commencement No 4) Order 2003, SI 2003/1725).

4 Commencement: 13 October 2003 (r 1; Land Registration Act 2002 (Commencement No 4) Order 2003, SI 2003/1725).

5 Commencement: 13 October 2003 (r 1; Land Registration Act 2002 (Commencement No 4) Order 2003, SI 2003/1725).

51¹ Alteration of the cautions register - alteration of cautioner

(1) A person who claims that the whole of the relevant interest described in an individual caution register is vested in him by operation of law as successor to the cautioner may apply for the register to be altered under section 21(1) of the Act to show him as cautioner in the cautioner's register in place of the cautioner.

(2) If the registrar does not serve notice under rule 50(2) or if the cautioner does not object within the time specified in the notice, the registrar must give effect to the application.

52² Definition of 'the cautioner'

For the purpose of Chapter 2 of Part 2 and section 73(2) of the Act, the other person referred to in sections 22 and 73(2) of the Act shall be the person for the time being shown as cautioner in the cautioner's register, where that person is not the person who lodged the caution against first registration.

53³ The prescribed periods under section 16(2) and section 18(4) of the Act

(1) The period for the purpose of section 16(2) and section 18(4) of the Act is the period ending at 12 noon on the fifteenth business day after the date of issue of the notice under section 16(1) or section 18(3) of the Act, as the case may be, or such longer period as the registrar may allow following a request under paragraph (2), provided that the longer period never exceeds a period ending at 12 noon on the thirtieth business day after the date of issue of the notice.

(2) The request referred to in paragraph (1) is one by the cautioner to the registrar setting out why the longer period referred to in that paragraph should be allowed.

(3) If a request is received under paragraph (2), the registrar may, if he considers it appropriate, seek the views of the person who applied for registration or cancellation, as the case may be, and if, after considering any such views and all other relevant matters, he is satisfied that a longer period should be allowed he may allow such period (not exceeding a period ending at 12 noon on the thirtieth business day after the date of issue of the notice) as he considers appropriate, whether or not the period is the same as any period requested by the cautioner.

(4) A request under paragraph (2) must be made before the period ending at 12 noon on the fifteenth business day after the date of issue of the notice has expired.

PART 6
REGISTERED LAND: APPLICATIONS, DISPOSITIONS AND MISCELLANEOUS ENTRIES

Applications

54⁴ Outline applications

(1) An outline application is an application made in accordance with this rule.

(2) Subject to Schedule 2, any application may be made by outline application if it satisfies the following conditions –

---

[1]   Commencement: 13 October 2003 (r 1; Land Registration Act 2002 (Commencement No 4) Order 2003, SI 2003/1725).
[2]   Commencement: 13 October 2003 (r 1; Land Registration Act 2002 (Commencement No 4) Order 2003, SI 2003/1725).
[3]   Commencement: 13 October 2003 (r 1; Land Registration Act 2002 (Commencement No 4) Order 2003, SI 2003/1725).
[4]   Commencement: 13 October 2003 (r 1; Land Registration Act 2002 (Commencement No 4) Order 2003, SI 2003/1725).

    (a) the application must not be –
- (i) an application which can be protected by an official search with priority within the meaning of rule 147,
- (ii) an application for first registration,
- (iii) an application for a caution against first registration or in respect of the cautions register,
- (iv) an application dealing with part only of the land in a registered title, whether or not also involving any other registered title,
- (v) an application under Part 13, and

    (b) the right, interest or matter the subject of the application must exist at the time the application is made.

(3) During the currency of any notice given under Schedule 2, and subject to and in accordance with the limitations contained in that notice, an outline application may be made by –
- (a) an oral application,
- (b) telephone, or
- (c) electronic means.

(4) An outline application must contain the following particulars when made –
- (a) the title number(s) affected,
- (b) if there is only one proprietor or applicant for first registration and that person is an individual, his surname, otherwise the proprietor's or such applicant's full name or the full name of one of the proprietors or such applicants, as appropriate,
- (c) the nature of the application,
- (d) the name of the applicant,
- (e) the name and address of the person or firm lodging the application,
- (f) any other particulars specified in any notice made under Schedule 2.

(5) Every outline application must be allocated an official reference number and must be identified on the day list as such and must be marked with the date and time at which the application is taken as made and the registrar must acknowledge receipt of any outline application by notifying the applicant, as soon as practicable, of the official reference number allocated to it.

(6) Without prejudice to the power of the registrar to cancel an application under rule 16, the outline application must be cancelled by the registrar unless there is delivered at the appropriate office before the expiry of the reserved period the relevant application form prescribed by these rules, duly completed in respect of the outline application, quoting the official reference number of the outline application and accompanied by the appropriate documentation and the prescribed fee.

(7) If the outline application has been cancelled before the form required by paragraph (6) is delivered at the appropriate office, the registrar shall accept the form as an application in its own right.

(8) In this rule the 'appropriate office' is the same office as the proper office, designated under an order under section 100(3) of the Act, for the receipt of an application relating to the land in respect of which the outline application is made, but on the assumption that if the order contains exceptions none of the exceptions apply to the application.

(9) In this rule 'reserved period' means the period expiring at 12 noon on the fourth business day following the day that the outline application was taken as made.

55[1] Priority of applications

(1) Where two or more applications relating to the same registered title are under the provisions of rule 15 taken as having been made at the same time, the order in which, as between each other, they rank in priority shall be determined in the manner prescribed by this rule.

(2) Where the applications are made by the same applicant, they rank in such order as he may specify.

(3) Where the applications are not made by the same applicant, they rank in such order as the applicants may specify that they have agreed.

(4) Where the applications are not made by the same applicant, and the applicants have not specified the agreed order of priority, the registrar must notify the applicants that their applications are regarded as having been delivered at the same time and request them to agree, within a specified time (being not less than fifteen business days), their order of priority.

(5) Where the parties fail within the time specified by the registrar to indicate the order of priority of their applications the registrar must propose the order of priority and serve notice on the applicants of his proposal.

(6) Any notice served under paragraph (5) must draw attention to the right of any applicant who does not agree with the registrar's proposal to object to another applicant's application under the provisions of section 73 of the Act.

(7) Where one transaction is dependent upon another the registrar must assume (unless the contrary appears) that the applicants have specified that the applications will have priority so as to give effect to the sequence of the documents effecting the transactions.

56[2] Dispositions affecting two or more registered titles

(1) A disposition affecting two or more registered titles may, on the written request of the applicant, be registered as to some or only one of the registered titles.

(2) The applicant may later apply to have the disposition registered as to any of the other registered titles affected by it.

57[3] Duty to disclose unregistered interests that override registered dispositions

(1) Subject to paragraph (2), a person applying to register a registrable disposition of a registered estate must provide information to the registrar about any of the interests that fall within Schedule 3 to the Act that –
  (a) are within the actual knowledge of the applicant, and
  (b) affect the estate to which the application relates,
     in Form DI.

(2) The applicant is not required to provide information about –
  (a) an interest that under section 33 or 90(4) of the Act cannot be protected by notice,
  (b) a public right,
  (c) a local land charge, or
  (d) a leasehold estate in land if –

---

[1]   Commencement: 13 October 2003 (r 1; Land Registration Act 2002 (Commencement No 4) Order 2003, SI 2003/1725).

[2]   Commencement: 13 October 2003 (r 1; Land Registration Act 2002 (Commencement No 4) Order 2003, SI 2003/1725).

[3]   Commencement: 13 October 2003 (r 1; Land Registration Act 2002 (Commencement No 4) Order 2003, SI 2003/1725).

(i)   it is within paragraph 1 of Schedule 3 to the Act, and

(ii) at the time of the application, the term granted by the lease has one year or less to run.

(3) In this rule and in Form AP1, a 'disclosable overriding interest' is an interest that the applicant must provide information about under paragraph (1).

(4) The applicant must produce to the registrar any documentary evidence of the existence of a disclosable overriding interest that is under his control.

(5) Where the applicant provides information about a disclosable overriding interest under this rule, the registrar may enter a notice in the register in respect of that interest.

Registrable dispositions – Form

58[1]   Form of transfer of registered estates
A transfer of a registered estate must be in Form TP1, TP2, TP3, TR1, TR2, TR5, AS1 or AS3, as appropriate.

59[2]   Transfers by way of exchange
(1) Where any registered estate is transferred wholly or partly in consideration of a transfer of another estate, the transaction must be effected by a transfer in one of the forms prescribed by rule 58.

(2) A receipt for the equality money (if any) must be given in the receipt panel and the following provision must be included in the additional provisions panel –

'This transfer is in consideration of a transfer (or conveyance, or as appropriate,) of (brief description of property exchanged) dated today [if applicable, and of the sum stated above paid for equality of exchange].'.

60[3]   Transfer of leasehold land, the rent being apportioned or land exonerated
(1) A transfer of a registered leasehold estate in land which contains a legal apportionment of or exoneration from the rent reserved by the lease must include the following statement in the additional provisions panel, with any necessary alterations and additions –

'Liability for the payment of [*if applicable* the previously apportioned rent of (*amount*) being part of] the rent reserved by the registered lease is apportioned between the Transferor and the Transferee as follows –

(*amount*) shall be payable out of the Property and the balance shall be payable out of the land remaining in title number (*title number of retained land*) or

the whole of that rent shall be payable out of the Property and none of it shall be payable out of the land remaining in title number (*title number of retained land*) or

the whole of that rent shall be payable out of the land remaining in title number (*title number of retained land*) and none of it shall be payable out of the Property'.

(2) Where in a transfer of part of a registered leasehold estate which is held under an old tenancy that part is, without the consent of the lessor, expressed to be exonerated from the entire rent, and the covenants in paragraph 20(4) of Schedule 12 to the Act are included, that paragraph shall apply as if –

(a) the reference in paragraph 20(4)(a) to the rent apportioned to the part retained were to the entire rent, and

(b) the covenants in paragraphs 20(4)(b) and (c) extended to a covenant to pay the entire rent.

(3) Where in a transfer of part of a registered leasehold estate which is held under an old tenancy that part is, without the consent of the lessor, expressed to be subject to or charged with the entire rent, and the covenants in paragraph 20(3) of Schedule 12 to the Act are included, that paragraph shall apply as if –

(a) the reference in paragraph 20(3)(a) to the rent apportioned to the part transferred were to the entire rent, and

(b) the covenants in paragraphs 20(3)(b) and (c) extended to a covenant to pay the entire rent.

Execution by an attorney

61[1] Documents executed by attorney

(1) If any document executed by an attorney is delivered to the land registry, there must be produced to the registrar –

(a) the instrument creating the power, or

(b) a copy of the power by means of which its contents may be proved under section 3 of the Powers of Attorney Act 1971, or

(c) a document which under section 4 of the Evidence and Powers of Attorney Act 1940 or section 7(3) of the Enduring Powers of Attorney Act 1985 is sufficient evidence of the contents of the power, or

(d) a certificate by a conveyancer in Form 1.

(2) If an order under section 8 of the Enduring Powers of Attorney Act 1985 has been made with respect to a power or the donor of the power or the attorney appointed under it, the order must be produced to the registrar.

(3) In this rule, 'power' means the power of attorney.

62[2] Evidence of non-revocation of power more than 12 months old

(1) If any transaction between a donee of a power of attorney and the person dealing with him is not completed within 12 months of the date on which the power came into operation, the registrar may require the production of evidence to satisfy him that the power had not been revoked at the time of the transaction.

(2) The evidence that the registrar may require under paragraph (1) may consist of or include a statutory declaration by the person who dealt with the attorney or a certificate given by that person's conveyancer in Form 2.

63[3] Evidence in support of power delegating trustees' functions to a beneficiary

(1) If any document executed by an attorney to whom functions have been delegated under section 9 of the Trusts of Land and Appointment of Trustees Act 1996 is delivered to the registrar, the registrar may require the production of evidence to satisfy him that the person who dealt with the attorney –

---

[1] Commencement: 13 October 2003 (r 1; Land Registration Act 2002 (Commencement No 4) Order 2003, SI 2003/1725).

[2] Commencement: 13 October 2003 (r 1; Land Registration Act 2002 (Commencement No 4) Order 2003, SI 2003/1725).

[3] Commencement: 13 October 2003 (r 1; Land Registration Act 2002 (Commencement No 4) Order 2003, SI 2003/1725).

(a) did so in good faith, and

(b) had no knowledge at the time of the completion of the transaction that the attorney was not a person to whom the functions of the trustees in relation to the land to which the application relates could be delegated under that section.

(2) The evidence that the registrar may require under paragraph (1) may consist of or include a statutory declaration by the person who dealt with the attorney or a certificate given by that person's conveyancer either in Form 3 or, where evidence of non-revocation is also required pursuant to rule 62, in Form 2.

Covenants

64[1] Positive covenants

(1) The registrar may make an appropriate entry in the proprietorship register of any positive covenant that relates to a registered estate given by the proprietor or any previous proprietor of that estate.

(2) Any entry made under paragraph (1) must, where practicable, refer to the instrument that contains the covenant.

(3) If it appears to the registrar that a covenant referred to in an entry made under paragraph (1) does not bind the current proprietor of the registered estate, he must remove the entry.

65[2] Indemnity covenants

(1) The registrar may make an appropriate entry in the proprietorship register of an indemnity covenant given by the proprietor of a registered estate in respect of any restrictive covenant or other matter that affects that estate or in respect of a positive covenant that relates to that estate.

(2) Any entry made under paragraph (1) must, where practicable, refer to the instrument that contains the indemnity covenant.

(3) If it appears to the registrar that a covenant referred to in an entry made under paragraph (1) does not bind the current proprietor of the registered estate, he must remove the entry.

66[3] Modification of implied covenants in transfer of land held under an old tenancy

Where a transfer of a registered leasehold estate which is an old tenancy modifies or negatives any covenants implied by paragraphs 20(2) and (3) of Schedule 12 to the Act, an entry that the covenants have been so modified or negatived must be made in the register.

67[4] Covenants implied under Part I of the Law of Property (Miscellaneous Provisions) Act 1994 and under the Law of Property Act 1925

(1) Subject to paragraph (2), a registrable disposition may be expressed to be made either with full title guarantee or with limited title guarantee and, in the case of a disposition which is effected by an instrument in the Welsh language, the appropriate Welsh expression specified in section 8(4) of the 1994 Act may be used.

---

[1] Commencement: 13 October 2003 (r 1; Land Registration Act 2002 (Commencement No 4) Order 2003, SI 2003/1725).

[2] Commencement: 13 October 2003 (r 1; Land Registration Act 2002 (Commencement No 4) Order 2003, SI 2003/1725).

[3] Commencement: 13 October 2003 (r 1; Land Registration Act 2002 (Commencement No 4) Order 2003, SI 2003/1725).

[4] Commencement: 13 October 2003 (r 1; Land Registration Act 2002 (Commencement No 4) Order 2003, SI 2003/1725).

(2) In the case of a registrable disposition to which section 76 of the LPA 1925 applies by virtue of section 11(1) of the 1994 Act –

    (a) a person may be expressed to execute, transfer or charge as beneficial owner, settlor, trustee, mortgagee, or personal representative of a deceased person or under an order of the court, and the document effecting the disposition may be framed accordingly, and

    (b) any covenant implied by virtue of section 76 of the LPA 1925 in such a disposition will take effect as though the disposition was expressly made subject to –

        (i) all charges and other interests that are registered at the time of the execution of the disposition and affect the title of the covenantor,

        (ii) any of the matters falling within Schedule 3 to the Act of which the purchaser has notice and subject to which it would have taken effect, had the land been unregistered.

(3) The benefit of any covenant implied under sections 76 and 77 of the LPA 1925 or either of them will, on and after the registration of the disposition in which it is implied, be annexed and incident to and will go with the registered proprietorship of the interest for the benefit of which it is given and will be capable of being enforced by the proprietor for the time being of that interest.

(4) The provisions of paragraphs (2)(b) and (3) are in addition to and not in substitution for the other provisions relating to covenants contained in the LPA 1925.

(5) Except as provided in paragraph (6), no reference to any covenant implied by virtue of Part I of the 1994 Act, or by section 76 of the LPA 1925 as applied by section 11(1) of the 1994 Act, shall be made in the register.

(6) A reference may be made in the register where a registrable disposition of leasehold land limits or extends the covenant implied under section 4 of the 1994 Act.

(7) In this rule 'the LPA 1925' means the Law of Property Act 1925 and 'the 1994 Act' means the Law of Property (Miscellaneous Provisions) Act 1994.

68[1] Additional provisions as to implied covenants

(1) A document effecting a registrable disposition which contains a provision limiting or extending any covenant implied by virtue of Part I of the Law of Property (Miscellaneous Provisions) Act 1994 must include a statement referring to the section of that Act in which the covenant is set out.

(2) The statement required by paragraph (1) must be in one of the following forms –

    (a) 'The covenant set out in section (*number*) of the Law of Property (Miscellaneous Provisions) Act 1994 shall [not] extend to ....', or

    (b) 'The [transferor or lessor] shall not be liable under any of the covenants set out in section (*number*) of the Law of Property (Miscellaneous Provisions) Act 1994'.

69[2] Transfer of registered estate subject to a rentcharge

(1) Where the covenants set out in Part VII or Part VIII of Schedule 2 to the LPA 1925 are included in a transfer, the references to 'the grantees', 'the conveyance' and 'the conveying parties' shall be treated as references to the transferees, the transfer and the transferors respectively.

---

[1] Commencement: 13 October 2003 (r 1; Land Registration Act 2002 (Commencement No 4) Order 2003, SI 2003/1725).

[2] Commencement: 13 October 2003 (r 1; Land Registration Act 2002 (Commencement No 4) Order 2003, SI 2003/1725).

(2) Where in a transfer to which section 77(1)(B) of the LPA 1925 does not apply, part of a registered estate affected by a rentcharge is, without the consent of the owner of the rentcharge, expressed to be exonerated from the entire rent, and the covenants in paragraph (ii) of Part VIII of Schedule 2 to the LPA 1925 are included, that paragraph shall apply as if –

    (a) any reference to the balance of the rent were to the entire rent, and

    (b) the words ', other than the covenant to pay the entire rent,' were omitted.

(3) Where in a transfer to which section 77(1)(B) of the LPA 1925 does not apply, part of a registered estate affected by a rentcharge is, without the consent of the owner of the rentcharge, expressed to be subject to or charged with the entire rent, and the covenants in paragraph (i) of Part VIII of Schedule 2 to the LPA 1925 are included, that paragraph shall apply as if –

    (a) any reference to the apportioned rent were to the entire rent, and

    (b) the words '(other than the covenant to pay the entire rent)' were omitted.

(4) On a transfer of a registered estate subject to a rentcharge –

    (a) any covenant implied by section 77(1)(A) or (B) of the LPA 1925 may be modified or negatived, and

    (b) any covenant included in the transfer may be modified,

    by adding suitable words to the transfer.

(5) In this rule 'the LPA 1925' means the Law of Property Act 1925.

Mines or minerals

70[1] Description of land where mines or minerals situated

(1) This rule applies where –

    (a) a registered estate in land includes any mines or minerals but there is no note in the register that the title to the registered estate includes the mines or minerals, and

    (b) it is appropriate (for instance, because of a registrable disposition of part of the registered estate, or on a sub-division or amalgamation of a registered title) when describing the registered estate to do so by reference to the land where the mines or minerals are or may be situated.

(2) After the description required to be made in the property register under rule 5(a) the registrar may make an entry to the effect that the description is an entry made under that rule and is not a note that the registered estate includes the mines or minerals to which paragraph 2 of Schedule 8 to the Act refers.

71[2] Note as to inclusion of mines or minerals in the registered estate

(1) This rule applies where a registered estate includes any mines or minerals but there is no note in the register to that effect and the registered proprietor of the registered estate applies for a note to be entered that the registered estate includes the mines or minerals or specified mines or minerals.

(2) An application for the entry of the note must be accompanied by evidence to satisfy the registrar that the mines or minerals were vested in the applicant for first registration of the registered estate at the time of first registration and were so vested in the same capacity as the remainder of the estate in land then sought to be registered.

(3) If the registrar is satisfied that mines or minerals were so vested in that applicant he must enter the appropriate note.

---

[1]   Commencement: 13 October 2003 (r 1; Land Registration Act 2002 (Commencement No 4) Order 2003, SI 2003/1725).

[2]   Commencement: 13 October 2003 (r 1; Land Registration Act 2002 (Commencement No 4) Order 2003, SI 2003/1725).

Miscellaneous entries

72[1] Register entries arising from transfers and charges of part

(1) Subject to paragraphs (3) and (4), on a transfer or charge of part of the registered estate in a registered title the following entries must be made in the individual register of that registered title –

    (a) an entry in the property register referring to the removal of the estate comprised in the transfer or charge, and

    (b) entries relating to any rights, covenants, provisions, and other matters created by the transfer or charge which the registrar considers affect the retained or uncharged registered estate.

(2) Subject to paragraph (4), on a transfer or charge of part of the registered estate in a registered title entries will be made in the individual register of the registered title comprising the part transferred or charged relating to any rights, covenants, provisions, and other matters created by the transfer or charge which the registrar considers affect the transferred or charged part.

(3) The registrar may, instead of making the entry referred to in paragraph (1)(a), make a new edition of the registered title out of which the transfer or charge is made and, if the registrar considers it desirable, he may allot a new title number to that registered title.

(4) This rule only applies to a charge of part of a registered estate in a registered title if the registrar decides that the charged part will be comprised in a separate registered title from the uncharged part.

73[2] Application for register entries for express appurtenant rights over unregistered land

(1) A proprietor of a registered estate who claims the benefit of a legal easement or profit a prendre which has been expressly granted over an unregistered legal estate may apply for it to be registered as appurtenant to his estate.

(2) The application must be accompanied by the grant and evidence of the grantor's title to the unregistered estate.

(3) In paragraph (1) the reference to express grant does not include a grant as a result of the operation of section 62 of the Law of Property Act 1925.

74[3] Application for register entries for implied or prescriptive appurtenant rights

(1) A proprietor of a registered estate who claims the benefit of a legal easement or profit a prendre, which has been acquired otherwise than by express grant, may apply for it to be registered as appurtenant to his estate.

(2) The application must be accompanied by evidence to satisfy the registrar that the right subsists as a legal estate appurtenant to the applicant's registered estate.

(3) In paragraph (1) the reference to an acquisition otherwise than by express grant includes acquired as a result of the operation of section 62 of the Law of Property Act 1925.

---

[1]   Commencement: 13 October 2003 (r 1; Land Registration Act 2002 (Commencement No 4) Order 2003, SI 2003/1725).

[2]   Commencement: 13 October 2003 (r 1; Land Registration Act 2002 (Commencement No 4) Order 2003, SI 2003/1725).

[3]   Commencement: 13 October 2003 (r 1; Land Registration Act 2002 (Commencement No 4) Order 2003, SI 2003/1725).

75¹ Qualified register entries for appurtenant rights

(1) This rule applies where a proprietor of a registered estate makes an application under rule 73 or rule 74 and the registrar is not satisfied that the right claimed subsists as a legal estate appurtenant to the applicant's registered estate.

(2) The registrar may enter details of the right claimed in the property register with such qualification as he considers appropriate.

76² Note as to rights of light or air

If it appears to the registrar that an agreement prevents the acquisition of rights of light or air for the benefit of the registered estate, he may make an entry in the property register of that estate.

77³ No entry on reversionary title of a right of entry in lease

Where a right of re-entry is contained in a lease the registrar need not make any entry regarding such right in the registered title of the reversionary estate.

78⁴ Note of variation of lease etc on register

An application to register the variation of a lease or other disposition of a registered estate or a registered charge which has been completed by registration must be accompanied by the instrument (if any) effecting the variation and evidence to satisfy the registrar that the variation has effect at law.

79⁵ Determination of registered estates

(1) An application to record in the register the determination of a registered estate must be accompanied by evidence to satisfy the registrar that the estate has determined.

(2) Subject to paragraph (3), if the registrar is satisfied that the estate has determined, he must close the registered title to the estate and cancel any notice in any other registered title relating to it.

(3) Where an entry is made under rule 173 the registrar need not close the registered title to the estate until a freehold legal estate in land in respect of the land in which such former estate subsisted has been registered.

PART 7
NOTICES

80⁶ Certain interests to be protected by agreed notices

A person who applies for the entry of a notice in the register must apply for the entry of an agreed notice where the application is for –
    (a) a matrimonial home rights notice,

1 Commencement: 13 October 2003 (r 1; Land Registration Act 2002 (Commencement No 4) Order 2003, SI 2003/1725).
2 Commencement: 13 October 2003 (r 1; Land Registration Act 2002 (Commencement No 4) Order 2003, SI 2003/1725).
3 Commencement: 13 October 2003 (r 1; Land Registration Act 2002 (Commencement No 4) Order 2003, SI 2003/1725).
4 Commencement: 13 October 2003 (r 1; Land Registration Act 2002 (Commencement No 4) Order 2003, SI 2003/1725).
5 Commencement: 13 October 2003 (r 1; Land Registration Act 2002 (Commencement No 4) Order 2003, SI 2003/1725).
6 Commencement: 13 October 2003 (r 1; Land Registration Act 2002 (Commencement No 4) Order 2003, SI 2003/1725).

(b) an inheritance tax notice,

(c) a notice in respect of an order under the Access to Neighbouring Land Act 1992,

(d) a notice of any variation of a lease effected by or under an order under section 38 of the Landlord and Tenant Act 1987 (including any variation as modified by an order under section 39(4) of that Act),

(e) a notice in respect of a –

(i) public right, or

(ii) customary right.

81[1] Application for an agreed notice

(1) Subject to paragraph (2), an application for the entry in the register of an agreed notice (including an agreed notice in respect of any variation of an interest protected by a notice) must be –

(a) made in Form AN1,

(b) accompanied by the order or instrument (if any) giving rise to the interest claimed or, if there is no such order or instrument, such other details of the interest claimed as satisfy the registrar as to the nature of the applicant's claim, and

(c) accompanied, where appropriate, by –

(i) the consent referred to in section 34(3)(b) of the Act, and, where appropriate, evidence to satisfy the registrar that the person applying for, or consenting to the entry of, the notice is entitled to be registered as the proprietor of the registered estate or charge affected by the interest to which the application relates, or

(ii) evidence to satisfy the registrar as to the validity of the applicant's claim.

(2) Paragraph (1) does not apply to an application for the entry of a matrimonial home rights notice made under rule 82.

82[2] Application for a matrimonial home rights notice or its renewal

(1) An application under section 31(10)(a) or section 32 of, and paragraph 4(3)(b) of Schedule 4 to, the Family Law Act 1996 for the entry of an agreed notice in the register must be in Form MH1.

(2) An application to renew the registration of a matrimonial home rights notice or a matrimonial home rights caution under section 32 of, and paragraph 4(3)(a) of Schedule 4 to, the Family Law Act 1996 must be in Form MH2.

(3) An application in Form MH1, where the application is made under section 32 of, and paragraph 4(3)(b) of Schedule 4 to, the Family Law Act 1996, or in Form MH2 must be accompanied by –

(a) an office copy of the section 33(5) order, or

(b) a conveyancer's certificate that he holds an office copy of the section 33(5) order.

83[3] Application for entry of a unilateral notice

An application for the entry in the register of a unilateral notice must be in Form UN1.

---

[1] Commencement: 13 October 2003 (r 1; Land Registration Act 2002 (Commencement No 4) Order 2003, SI 2003/1725).

[2] Commencement: 13 October 2003 (r 1; Land Registration Act 2002 (Commencement No 4) Order 2003, SI 2003/1725).

[3] Commencement: 13 October 2003 (r 1; Land Registration Act 2002 (Commencement No 4) Order 2003, SI 2003/1725).

84¹ Entry of a notice in the register

(1) A notice under section 32 of the Act must be entered in the charges register of the registered title affected.

(2) The entry must identify the registered estate or registered charge affected and, where the interest protected by the notice only affects part of the registered estate in a registered title, it must contain sufficient details, by reference to a plan or otherwise, to identify clearly that part.

(3) In the case of a notice (other than a unilateral notice), the entry must give details of the interest protected.

(4) In the case of a notice (other than a unilateral notice) of a variation of an interest protected by a notice, the entry must give details of the variation.

(5) In the case of a unilateral notice, the entry must give such details of the interest protected as the registrar considers appropriate.

85² Removal of a unilateral notice

(1) An application for the removal of a unilateral notice from the register under section 35(3) of the Act must be in Form UN2.

(2) The personal representative or trustee in bankruptcy of the person shown in the register as the beneficiary of a unilateral notice may apply under section 35(3) of the Act; and if he does he must provide evidence to satisfy the registrar as to his appointment as personal representative or trustee in bankruptcy.

(3) If the registrar is satisfied that the application is in order he must remove the notice.

86³ Cancellation of a unilateral notice

(1) An application to cancel a unilateral notice under section 36 of the Act must be made in Form UN4.

(2) An application made under section 36(1)(b) of the Act must be accompanied by –
  (a) evidence to satisfy the registrar of the applicant's entitlement to be registered as the proprietor of the estate or charge to which the unilateral notice the subject of the application relates, or
  (b) a conveyancer's certificate that the conveyancer is satisfied that the applicant is entitled to be registered as the proprietor of the estate or charge to which the unilateral notice the subject of the application relates.

(3) The period referred to in section 36(3) of the Act is the period ending at 12 noon on the fifteenth business day after the date of issue of the notice or such longer period as the registrar may allow following a request under paragraph (4), provided that the longer period never exceeds a period ending at 12 noon on the thirtieth business day after the issue of the notice.

(4) The request referred to in paragraph (3) is one by the beneficiary to the registrar setting out why the longer period referred to in that paragraph should be allowed.

(5) If a request is received under paragraph (4) the registrar may, if he considers it appropriate, seek the views of the person who applied for cancellation and if after considering any such views and all other relevant matters he is satisfied that a longer period should be allowed he

¹   Commencement: 13 October 2003 (r 1; Land Registration Act 2002 (Commencement No 4) Order 2003, SI 2003/1725).
²   Commencement: 13 October 2003 (r 1; Land Registration Act 2002 (Commencement No 4) Order 2003, SI 2003/1725).
³   Commencement: 13 October 2003 (r 1; Land Registration Act 2002 (Commencement No 4) Order 2003, SI 2003/1725).

may allow such period (not exceeding a period ending at 12 noon on the thirtieth business day after the issue of the notice) as he considers appropriate, whether or not the period is the same as any period requested by the beneficiary.

(6) A request under paragraph (4) must be made before the period ending at 12 noon on the fifteenth business day after the date of issue of the notice under section 36(2) of the Act has expired.

(7) A person entitled to be registered as the beneficiary of a notice under rule 88 may object to an application under section 36(1) of the Act for cancellation of that notice and the reference to the beneficiary in section 36(3) includes such a person.

87[1] Cancellation of a notice (other than a unilateral notice or a matrimonial home rights notice)

(1) An application for the cancellation of a notice (other than a unilateral notice or a matrimonial home rights notice) must be in Form CN1 and be accompanied by evidence to satisfy the registrar of the determination of the interest.

(2) Where a person applies for cancellation of a notice in accordance with paragraph (1) and the registrar is satisfied that the interest protected by the notice has come to an end, he must cancel the notice or make an entry in the register that the interest so protected has come to an end.

(3) If the interest protected by the notice has only come to an end in part, the registrar must make an appropriate entry.

88[2] Registration of a new or additional beneficiary of a unilateral notice

(1) A person entitled to the benefit of an interest protected by a unilateral notice may apply to be entered in the register in place of, or in addition to, the registered beneficiary.

(2) An application under paragraph (1) must be –
   (a) in Form UN3, and
   (b) accompanied by evidence to satisfy the registrar of the applicant's title to the interest protected by the unilateral notice.

(3) Subject to paragraph (4), if an application is made in accordance with paragraph (2) and the registrar is satisfied that the interest protected by the unilateral notice is vested –
   (a) in the applicant, the registrar must enter the applicant in the register in place of the registered beneficiary, or
   (b) in the applicant and the registered beneficiary, the registrar must enter the applicant in addition to the registered beneficiary.

(4) Except where one of the circumstances specified in paragraph (5) applies, the registrar must serve notice of the application on the registered beneficiary before entering the applicant in the register.

(5) The registrar is not obliged to serve notice on the registered beneficiary if –
   (a) the registered beneficiary signs Form UN3 or otherwise consents to the application, or
   (b) the applicant is the registered beneficiary's personal representative and evidence of his title to act accompanies the application.

---

[1]   Commencement: 13 October 2003 (r 1; Land Registration Act 2002 (Commencement No 4) Order 2003, SI 2003/1725).
[2]   Commencement: 13 October 2003 (r 1; Land Registration Act 2002 (Commencement No 4) Order 2003, SI 2003/1725).

(6) In this rule, 'registered beneficiary' means the person shown in the register as the beneficiary of the notice at the time an application is made under paragraph (1).

89[1] Notice of unregistered interests

(1) If the registrar enters a notice of an unregistered interest under section 37(1) of the Act, he must give notice –

    (a) subject to paragraph (2), to the registered proprietor, and

    (b) subject to paragraph (3), to any person who appears to the registrar to be entitled to the interest protected by the notice or whom the registrar otherwise considers appropriate.

(2) The registrar is not obliged to give notice to a registered proprietor under paragraph (1)(a) who applies for entry of the notice or otherwise consents to an application to enter the notice.

(3) The registrar is not obliged to give notice to a person referred to in paragraph (1)(b) if –

    (a) that person applied for the entry of the notice or consented to the entry of the notice, or

    (b) that person's name and his address for service under rule 198 are not set out in the individual register in which the notice is entered.

90[2] Application for entry of a notice under paragraph 5(2) or, in certain cases, paragraph 7(2)(a) of Part 1 of Schedule 2 to the Act

An application to meet the registration requirements under –

    (a) paragraph 5(2) of Part 1 of Schedule 2 to the Act, or

    (b) paragraph 7(2)(a) of that Part, where the interest is created for the benefit of an unregistered estate,

must be made in Form AP1.

PART 8
RESTRICTIONS

91[3] Standard forms of restriction

(1) The forms of restriction set out in Schedule 4 are standard forms of restriction prescribed under section 43(2)(d) of the Act.

(2) The word 'conveyancer', where it appears in any of the standard forms of restriction, has the same meaning as in these rules.

(3) The word 'registered', where it appears in any of the standard forms of restriction in relation to a disposition, means completion of the registration of that disposition by meeting the relevant registration requirements under section 27 of the Act.

92[4] Application for a restriction and the prescribed period under section 45(2) of the Act

(1) Subject to paragraphs (5), (6), (7) and (8) an application for a restriction to be entered in the register must be made in Form RX1.

(2) The application must be accompanied by –

[1] Commencement: 13 October 2003 (r 1; Land Registration Act 2002 (Commencement No 4) Order 2003, SI 2003/1725).

[2] Commencement: 13 October 2003 (r 1; Land Registration Act 2002 (Commencement No 4) Order 2003, SI 2003/1725).

[3] Commencement: 13 October 2003 (r 1; Land Registration Act 2002 (Commencement No 4) Order 2003, SI 2003/1725).

[4] Commencement: 13 October 2003 (r 1; Land Registration Act 2002 (Commencement No 4) Order 2003, SI 2003/1725).

    (a) full details of the required restriction,

    (b) if the restriction –

        (i)   requires notice to be given to a person,

        (ii) requires a person's consent or certificate, or

        (iii) is a standard form of restriction that refers to a named person,

        that person's address for service,

    (c) if the application is made with the consent of the relevant registered proprietor, or a person entitled to be registered as such proprietor, and that consent is not given in Form RX1, the relevant consent,

    (d) if the application is made by or with the consent of a person entitled to be registered as the relevant registered proprietor, evidence to satisfy the registrar of his entitlement, and

    (e) if the application is made by a person who claims that he has a sufficient interest in the making of the entry, the statement referred to in paragraph (3) signed by the applicant or his conveyancer.

(3) The statement required under paragraph (2)(e) must either –

    (a) give details of the applicant's interest in the making of the entry of the required restriction, or

    (b) if the interest is one of those specified in rule 93, state which of them.

(4) If requested to do so, an applicant within paragraph (2)(e) must supply further evidence to satisfy the registrar that he has a sufficient interest.

(5) The registrar may accept a certificate given by a conveyancer that the conveyancer is satisfied that the person making or consenting to the application is entitled to be registered as the relevant proprietor, and that either –

    (a) the conveyancer holds the originals of the documents that contain evidence of that person's entitlement, or

    (b) an application for registration of that person as proprietor is pending at the land registry.

(6) If an application is made with the consent of the relevant registered proprietor, or a person entitled to be registered as such proprietor, the registrar may accept a certificate given by a conveyancer that the conveyancer holds the relevant consent.

(7) Paragraph (1) of this rule does not apply where –

    (a) a person applies for the entry of a standard form of restriction in the additional provisions panel of Form TP1, TP2, TP3, TR1, TR2, TR3, TR4, TR5, AS1, AS2 or AS3,

    (b) a person applies for the entry of a standard form of restriction in panel 7 of Form CH1, or

    (c) a person applies for the entry of a standard form of restriction in an approved charge.

(8) This rule does not apply to an application to the registrar to give effect to an order of the court made under section 46 of the Act.

(9) The period for the purpose of section 45(2) of the Act is the period ending at 12 noon on the fifteenth business day after the date of issue of the notice under section 45(1) or, if more than one such notice is issued, the date of issue of the latest notice.

(10) In this rule 'approved charge' means a charge, the form of which (including the application for the restriction) has first been approved by the registrar.

93[1] Persons regarded as having a sufficient interest to apply for a restriction

The following persons are to be regarded as included in section 43(1)(c) of the Act –

(a) any person who has an interest in a registered estate held under a trust of land where a sole proprietor or a survivor of joint proprietors (unless a trust corporation) will not be able to give a valid receipt for capital money, and who is applying for a restriction in Form A to be entered in the register of that registered estate,

(b) any person who has a sufficient interest in preventing a contravention of section 6(6) or section 6(8) of the Trusts of Land and Appointment of Trustees Act 1996 and who is applying for a restriction in order to prevent such a contravention,

(c) any person who has an interest in a registered estate held under a trust of land where the powers of the trustees are limited by section 8 of the Trusts of Land and Appointment of Trustees Act 1996, and who is applying for a restriction in Form B to be entered in the register of that registered estate,

(d) any person who has an interest in the due administration of the estate of a deceased person, where –
   (i) the personal representatives of the deceased hold a registered estate on a trust of land created by the deceased's will and the personal representatives' powers are limited by section 8 of the Trusts of Land and Appointment of Trustees Act 1996, and
   (ii) he is applying for a restriction in Form C to be entered in the register of that registered estate,

(e) the donee of a special power of appointment in relation to registered land affected by that power,

(f) the Charity Commissioners in relation to registered land held upon charitable trusts,

(g) the Church Commissioners, the Parsonages Board or the Diocesan Board of Finance if applying for a restriction –
   (i) to give effect to any arrangement which is made under any enactment or Measure administered by or relating to the Church Commissioners, the Parsonages Board or the Diocesan Board of Finance, or
   (ii) to protect any interest in registered land arising under any such arrangement or statute,

(h) any person with the benefit of a freezing order or an undertaking given in place of a freezing order, who is applying for a restriction in Form AA or BB,

(i) any person who has applied for a freezing order and who is applying for a restriction in Form CC or DD,

(j) a trustee in bankruptcy who has an interest in a beneficial interest in registered land held under a trust of land, and who is applying for a restriction in Form J to be entered in the register of that land,

(k) any person with the benefit of a charging order over a beneficial interest in registered land held under a trust of land who is applying for a restriction in Form K to be entered in the register of that land,

(l) a person who has obtained a restraint order under –
   (i) paragraph 5(1) or 5(2) of Schedule 4 to the Terrorism Act 2000, or
   (ii) section 41 of the Proceeds of Crime Act 2002,
   and who is applying for a restriction in Form EE or FF,

(m) a person who has applied for a restraint order under the provisions referred to in paragraph (1) and who is applying for a restriction in Form GG or HH,

(n) a person who has obtained an acquisition order under section 28 of the Landlord and Tenant Act 1987 and who is applying for a restriction in Form L or N,

---

[1] Commencement: 13 October 2003 (r 1; Land Registration Act 2002 (Commencement No 4) Order 2003, SI 2003/1725).

(o) a person who has applied for an acquisition order under section 28 of the Landlord and Tenant Act 1987 and who is applying for a restriction in Form N,

(p) a person who has obtained a vesting order under section 26(1) or 50(1) of the Leasehold Reform, Housing and Urban Development Act 1993 and who is applying for a restriction in Form L or N,

(q) a person who has applied for a vesting order under section 26(1) or 50(1) of the Leasehold Reform, Housing and Urban Development Act 1993 and who is applying for a restriction in Form N,

(r) the International Criminal Court where it applies for a restriction –
    (i) in Form AA or BB to give effect to a freezing order under Schedule 6 to the International Criminal Court Act 2001, or
    (ii) in Form CC or DD to protect an application for such a freezing order,

(s) a receiver or a sequestrator appointed by order who applies for a restriction in Form L or N,

(t) a trustee under a deed of arrangement who applies for a restriction in Form L or N,

(u) a person who has obtained an interim receiving order under section 246 of the Proceeds of Crime Act 2002 and who is applying for a restriction in Form EE or FF, and

(v) a person who has applied for an interim receiving order under section 246 of the Proceeds of Crime Act 2002 and who is applying for a restriction in Form GG or HH.

94[1] When an application for a restriction must be made

(1) A proprietor of a registered estate must apply for a restriction in Form A where –
    (a) the estate becomes subject to a trust of land, other than on a registrable disposition, and the proprietor or the survivor of joint proprietors will not be able to give a valid receipt for capital money, or
    (b) the estate is held on a trust of land and, as a result of a change in the trusts, the proprietor or the survivor of joint proprietors will not be able to give a valid receipt for capital money.

(2) A sole or last surviving trustee of land held on a trust of land must, when applying to register a disposition of a registered estate in his favour or to be registered as proprietor of an unregistered estate, at the same time apply for a restriction in Form A.

(3) Subject to paragraph (6), a personal representative of a deceased person who holds a registered estate on a trust of land created by the deceased's will, or on a trust of land arising under the laws of intestacy which is subsequently varied, and whose powers have been limited by section 8 of the Trusts of Land and Appointment of Trustees Act 1996, must apply for a restriction in Form C.

(4) Subject to paragraphs (6) and (7), a proprietor of a registered estate must apply for a restriction in Form B where –
    (a) a declaration of trust of that estate imposes limitations on the powers of the trustees under section 8 of the Trusts of Land and Appointment of Trustees Act 1996, or
    (b) a change in the trusts on which that estate is held imposes limitations or changes the limitations on the powers of the trustees under section 8 of the Trusts of Land and Appointment of Trustees Act 1996.

(5) Subject to paragraphs (6) and (7), an applicant for first registration of a legal estate held on a trust of land where the powers of the trustees are limited by section 8 of the Trusts of Land and Appointment of Trustees Act 1996 must at the same time apply for a restriction in Form B.

---

[1] Commencement: 13 October 2003 (r 1; Land Registration Act 2002 (Commencement No 4) Order 2003, SI 2003/1725).

(6) Paragraphs (3), (4) and (5) do not apply to legal estates held on charitable, ecclesiastical or public trusts.

(7) Paragraphs (4) and (5) apply not only where the legal estate is held by the trustees, but also where it is vested in the personal representatives of a sole or last surviving trustee.

(8) An application for a restriction must be made where required by paragraphs (2) or (3) of rule 176 or paragraph (2) of rule 178.

95[1] Form of obligatory restrictions

(1) The form of any restriction that the registrar is obliged to enter under any enactment shall be –
- (a) as specified in these rules,
- (b) as required by the relevant enactment, or
- (c) in other cases, such form as the registrar may direct having regard to the provisions of the relevant enactment.

(2) The form of the restriction required under –
- (a) section 44(1) of the Act is Form A,
- (b) section 37(5A) of the Housing Act 1985 is Form U,
- (c) section 157(7) of the Housing Act 1985 is Form V,
- (d) section 81(10) of the Housing Act 1988 is Form X,
- (e) section 133 of the Housing Act 1988 is Form X,
- (f) paragraph 4 of Schedule 9A to the Housing Act 1985 is Form W,
- (g) section 173(9) of the Local Government and Housing Act 1989 is Form X, and
- (h) section 13(5) of the Housing Act 1996 is Form Y.

96[2] Application for an order that a restriction be disapplied or modified

(1) An application to the registrar for an order under section 41(2) of the Act must be made in Form RX2.

(2) The application must –
- (a) state whether the application is to disapply or to modify the restriction and, if the latter, give details of the modification requested,
- (b) explain why the applicant has a sufficient interest in the restriction to make the application,
- (c) give details of the disposition or the kind of dispositions that will be affected by the order, and
- (d) state why the applicant considers that the registrar should make the order.

(3) If requested to do so, the applicant must supply further evidence to satisfy the registrar that he should make the order.

(4) The registrar may make such enquiries and serve such notices as he thinks fit in order to determine the application.

(5) A note of the terms of any order made by the registrar under section 41(2) of the Act must be entered in the register.

---

[1] Commencement: 13 October 2003 (r 1; Land Registration Act 2002 (Commencement No 4) Order 2003, SI 2003/1725).

[2] Commencement: 13 October 2003 (r 1; Land Registration Act 2002 (Commencement No 4) Order 2003, SI 2003/1725).

97[1] Application to cancel a restriction
(1) An application to cancel a restriction must be made in Form RX3.

(2) The application must be accompanied by evidence to satisfy the registrar that the restriction is no longer required.

(3) If the registrar is satisfied that the restriction is no longer required, he must cancel the restriction.

98[2] Application to withdraw a restriction from the register
(1) An application to withdraw a restriction must be made in Form RX4 and accompanied by the consents required under paragraphs (2) to (5).

(2) Subject to paragraphs (3), (4) and (5) an application to withdraw a restriction may only be made by or with the consent of all persons who appear to the registrar to have an interest in the restriction.

(3) An application to withdraw a restriction that requires the consent of a specified person may only be made by or with the consent of that person.

(4) An application to withdraw a restriction that requires notice to be given to a specified person may only be made by or with the consent of that person.

(5) An application to withdraw a restriction that requires a certificate to be given by a specified person may only be made by or with the consent of that person.

(6) No application may be made to withdraw a restriction –
   (a) that is entered under section 42(1)(a) of the Act and reflects some limitation on the registered proprietor's powers of disposition imposed by statute or the general law,
   (b) that is entered in the register following an application under rule 94,
   (c) that the registrar is under an obligation to enter in the register,
   (d) that reflects a limitation under an order of the court or registrar, or an undertaking given in place of such an order,
   (e) that is entered pursuant to a court order under section 46 of the Act.

(7) The registrar may accept a certificate given by a conveyancer that the conveyancer holds any consents required.

99[3] Cancellation of a restriction relating to a trust
When registering a disposition of a registered estate, the registrar must cancel a restriction entered for the purpose of protecting an interest, right or claim arising under a trust of land if he is satisfied that the registered estate is no longer subject to that trust of land.

100[4] Entry following a direction of the court regarding overriding priority in connection with a restriction
(1) Any entry in the register required under section 46(4) of the Act shall be in such form as the registrar may determine so as to ensure that the priority of the restriction ordered by the court is apparent from the register.

---

[1] Commencement: 13 October 2003 (r 1; Land Registration Act 2002 (Commencement No 4) Order 2003, SI 2003/1725).
[2] Commencement: 13 October 2003 (r 1; Land Registration Act 2002 (Commencement No 4) Order 2003, SI 2003/1725).
[3] Commencement: 13 October 2003 (r 1; Land Registration Act 2002 (Commencement No 4) Order 2003, SI 2003/1725).
[4] Commencement: 13 October 2003 (r 1; Land Registration Act 2002 (Commencement No 4) Order 2003, SI 2003/1725).

(2) Where the making of the entry is completed by the registrar during the priority period of an official search which was delivered before the making of the application for the entry, he must give notice of the entry to the person who applied for the official search or, if a conveyancer or other agent applied on behalf of that person, to that agent, unless he is satisfied that such notice is unnecessary.

PART 9
CHARGES

101[1] How ranking of registered charges as between themselves to be shown on register
Subject to any entry in the individual register to the contrary, for the purpose of section 48(1) of the Act the order in which registered charges are entered in an individual register shows the order in which the registered charges rank as between themselves.

102[2] Alteration of priority of registered charges
(1) An application to alter the priority of registered charges, as between themselves, must be made by or with the consent of the proprietor or a person entitled to be registered as the proprietor of any registered charge whose priority is adversely affected by the alteration, but no such consent is required from a person who has executed the instrument which alters the priority of the charges.

(2) The registrar may accept a conveyancer's certificate confirming that the conveyancer holds any necessary consents.

(3) The registrar must make an entry in the register in such terms as the registrar considers appropriate to give effect to the application.

103[3] Form of charge of registered estate
A legal charge of a registered estate may be made in Form CH1.

104[4] Application for registration of the title to a local land charge
An application to register the title to a charge over registered land which is a local land charge must be supported by evidence of the charge.

105[5] Overriding statutory charges
(1) An applicant for registration of a statutory charge that has the effect mentioned in section 50 of the Act must lodge Form SC with the application.

(2) If the applicant satisfies the registrar that the statutory charge has the priority specified in that Form SC, the registrar must make an entry showing that priority in the charges register of the affected registered title.

(3) If the applicant does not satisfy the registrar as mentioned in paragraph (2) but the registrar considers that the applicant has an arguable case, the registrar may make an entry in the charges

---

[1] Commencement: 13 October 2003 (r 1; Land Registration Act 2002 (Commencement No 4) Order 2003, SI 2003/1725).

[2] Commencement: 13 October 2003 (r 1; Land Registration Act 2002 (Commencement No 4) Order 2003, SI 2003/1725).

[3] Commencement: 13 October 2003 (r 1; Land Registration Act 2002 (Commencement No 4) Order 2003, SI 2003/1725).

[4] Commencement: 13 October 2003 (r 1; Land Registration Act 2002 (Commencement No 4) Order 2003, SI 2003/1725).

[5] Commencement: 13 October 2003 (r 1; Land Registration Act 2002 (Commencement No 4) Order 2003, SI 2003/1725).

register of the affected registered title that the applicant claims the priority specified in that Form SC.

(4) If the registrar makes an entry under paragraph (3) the registrar must give notice of the entry to the persons mentioned in rule 106(1) (subject to rule 106(2)).

(5) Where an entry has been made under paragraph (3) –
- (a) the proprietor of the statutory charge which gave rise to the entry, or
- (b) the proprietor of a charge entered in the charges register of the affected registered title which, subject to the effect of the entry, would rank in priority to or have equal priority with that statutory charge under rule 101,

may apply for the entry to be removed or to be replaced by an entry of the kind referred to in paragraph (2).

(6) Paragraph (5)(b) includes the proprietor of a statutory charge entered in the charges register of the affected registered title which has had an entry made in respect of it under paragraph (3) claiming priority over the statutory charge referred to in paragraph (5)(a).

(7) An applicant under paragraph (5) must provide evidence to satisfy the registrar that the registrar should take the action sought by the applicant under that paragraph.

(8) Before taking the action sought by the applicant under paragraph (5), the registrar must give notice of the application to any proprietors within that paragraph (other than the applicant).

106[1] Service of notice of overriding statutory charges

(1) The registrar shall give notice under section 50 of the Act to –
- (a) the registered proprietor of a registered charge, and
- (b) subject to paragraph (2), any person who appears to the registrar to be entitled to a charge protected by a notice,

entered in the charges register of the affected registered title at the time of registration of the statutory charge.

(2) The registrar shall not be obliged to give notice to a person referred to in paragraph (1)(b) if that person's name and his address for service under rule 198 are not set out in the individual register in which the notice is entered.

107[2] Further advances - notice of creation of subsequent charge

(1) A notice given for the purposes of section 49(1) of the Act by one of the methods mentioned in paragraph (2) ought to have been received at the time shown in the table in paragraph (4).

(2) The methods referred to in paragraph (1) are –
- (a) by post, to the postal address, whether or not in the United Kingdom, entered in the register as the prior chargee's address for service, or
- (b) by leaving the notice at that address, or
- (c) by sending to the box number at the relevant document exchange entered in the register as an additional address for service of the prior chargee, or
- (d) by electronic transmission to the electronic address entered in the register as an additional address for service of the prior chargee, or
- (e) where paragraph (3) applies, by post, document exchange, fax or electronic transmission to the address, box number or fax number provided.

---

[1] Commencement: 13 October 2003 (r 1; Land Registration Act 2002 (Commencement No 4) Order 2003, SI 2003/1725).

[2] Commencement: 13 October 2003 (r 1; Land Registration Act 2002 (Commencement No 4) Order 2003, SI 2003/1725).

(3) This paragraph applies where the prior chargee has provided to the subsequent chargee a postal address, document exchange box number, fax number, e-mail or other electronic address, and stated in writing to the subsequent chargee that notices to the prior chargee under section 49(1) of the Act may be sent to that address, box number or fax number.

(4) For the purposes of section 49(2) of the Act a notice sent in accordance with paragraph (2) or (3) ought to have been received at the time shown in the table below –

Method of delivery	*Time of receipt*
Post to an address in the United Kingdom	The second working day after posting
Leaving at a postal address	The working day after it was left
Post to an address outside the United Kingdom	The seventh working day after posting
Document exchange	On the second working day after it was left at the sender's document exchange
Fax	The working day after transmission
Electronic transmission to an electronic address entered in the register as an address for service or e-mail or other electronic means of delivery under paragraph (3)	The second working day after transmission

(5) A notice posted or transmitted after 1700 hours on a working day or posted or transmitted on a day which is not a working day is to be treated as having been posted or transmitted on the next working day.

(6) In this rule –

'post' means pre-paid delivery by a postal service which seeks to deliver documents within the United Kingdom no later than the next working day in all or the majority of cases, and to deliver outside the United Kingdom within such a period as is reasonable in all the circumstances,

'prior chargee' means the proprietor of a registered charge to whom notice is being given under section 49(1) of the Act,

'subsequent chargee' means the chargee giving notice under section 49(1) of the Act,

'working day' means any day from Monday to Friday (inclusive) which is not Christmas Day, Good Friday or any other day either specified or declared by proclamation under section 1 of the Banking and Financial Dealings Act 1971 or appointed by the Lord Chancellor.

108[1]   Obligations to make further advances

(1) The proprietor of a registered charge or a person applying to be so registered, who is under an obligation to make further advances on the security of that charge, may apply to the registrar for such obligation to be entered in the register for the purposes of section 49(3) of the Act.

(2) Except as provided in paragraph (3), the application must be made in Form CH2.

(3) Form CH2 need not be used if the application is contained in panel 7 of Form CH1, or in a charge received for registration where the form of that charge has been approved by the registrar.

(4) The registrar must make an entry in the register in such terms as he considers appropriate to give effect to an application under this rule.

---

[1]   Commencement: 13 October 2003 (r 1; Land Registration Act 2002 (Commencement No 4) Order 2003, SI 2003/1725).

109[1] Agreement of maximum amount of security

(1) Where the parties to a legal charge which is a registered charge or which is a registrable disposition have agreed a maximum amount for which the charge is security, the proprietor of the registered charge or a person applying to be registered as proprietor of the registrable disposition may apply to the registrar for such agreement to be entered in the register under section 49(4) of the Act.

(2) The application must be made in Form CH3.

(3) The registrar must make an entry in the register in such terms as he considers appropriate to give effect to an application under this rule.

110[2] Consolidation of registered charges

(1) A chargee who has a right of consolidation in relation to a registered charge may apply to the registrar for an entry to be made in respect of that right in the individual register in which the charge is registered.

(2) The application must be made in Form CC.

(3) The registrar must make an entry in the individual register in such terms as he considers appropriate to give effect to an application under this rule.

111[3] Certificate of registration of company charges

(1) When making an application for the registration of a charge created by a company registered under the Companies Acts, a limited liability partnership incorporated under the Limited Liability Partnerships Act 2000, or a Northern Ireland company, the applicant must produce to the registrar –

(a) a certificate issued under section 401 of the 1985 Act that the charge has been registered under section 395 of that Act, or

(b) (in the case of a charge created by a company registered in Scotland) a certificate issued under section 418 of the 1985 Act that the charge has been registered under section 410 of that Act, or

(c) (in the case of a charge created by a Northern Ireland company) a certificate issued under article 409 of the 1986 Order that the charge has been registered under article 403 of that Order.

(2) If the applicant does not produce the certificate required by paragraph (1) with the application for registration of the charge, the registrar must enter a note in the register that the charge is subject to the provisions of section 395 or section 410 of the 1985 Act, or article 403 of the 1986 Order (as appropriate).

(3) In this rule –

'the 1985 Act' means the Companies Act 1985,

'the 1986 Order' means the Companies (NI) Order 1986,

'Northern Ireland' company means a company formed and registered under the 1986 Order or a company formed and registered, or deemed to have been registered, in Northern Ireland under the former Northern Ireland Companies Acts,

---

[1] Commencement: 13 October 2003 (r 1; Land Registration Act 2002 (Commencement No 4) Order 2003, SI 2003/1725).

[2] Commencement: 13 October 2003 (r 1; Land Registration Act 2002 (Commencement No 4) Order 2003, SI 2003/1725).

[3] Commencement: 13 October 2003 (r 1; Land Registration Act 2002 (Commencement No 4) Order 2003, SI 2003/1725).

'former Northern Ireland Companies Acts' means the Joint Stock Companies Acts, the Companies Act 1862, the Companies (Consolidation) Act 1908, the Companies Act (Northern Ireland) 1932 and the Companies Acts (Northern Ireland) 1960 to 1983,

'Joint Stock Companies Acts' means the Joint Stock Companies Act 1856, the Joint Stock Companies Act 1857, the Joint Stock Banking Companies Act 1857 and the Act to enable Joint Stock Banking Companies to be formed on the principle of limited liability, or any one or more of those Acts (as the case may require), but does not include the Joint Stock Companies Act 1844.

112[1] Foreclosure - registration requirements

(1) Subject to paragraph (3), an application by a person who has obtained an order for foreclosure absolute to be entered in the register as proprietor of the registered estate in respect of which the charge is registered must be accompanied by the order.

(2) The registrar must –
- (a) cancel the registration of the charge in respect of which the order was made,
- (b) cancel all entries in respect of interests over which the charge has priority, and
- (c) enter the applicant as proprietor of the registered estate.

(3) The registrar may accept a conveyancer's certificate confirming that the conveyancer holds the order for foreclosure absolute or an office copy of it.

113[2] Variation of the terms of a registered charge

(1) An application to register an instrument varying the terms of a registered charge must be made –
- (a) by, or with the consent of, the proprietor of the registered charge and the proprietor of the estate charged, and
- (b) with the consent of the proprietor, or a person entitled to be registered as proprietor, of every other registered charge of equal or inferior priority that is prejudicially affected by the variation,

but no such consent is required from a person who has executed the instrument.

(2) The registrar may accept a conveyancer's certificate confirming that the conveyancer holds any necessary consents.

(3) If the registrar is satisfied that the proprietor of any other registered charge of equal or inferior priority to the varied charge that is prejudicially affected by the variation is bound by it, he shall make a note of the variation in the register.

(4) If the registrar is not so satisfied, he may make an entry in the register that an instrument which is expressed to vary the terms of the registered charge has been entered into.

114[3] Discharges and releases of registered charges

(1) Subject to rule 115, a discharge of a registered charge must be in Form DS1.

(2) Subject to rule 115, a release of part of the registered estate in a registered title from a registered charge must be in Form DS3.

---

[1]   Commencement: 13 October 2003 (r 1; Land Registration Act 2002 (Commencement No 4) Order 2003, SI 2003/1725).

[2]   Commencement: 13 October 2003 (r 1; Land Registration Act 2002 (Commencement No 4) Order 2003, SI 2003/1725).

[3]   Commencement: 13 October 2003 (r 1; Land Registration Act 2002 (Commencement No 4) Order 2003, SI 2003/1725).

(3) Any discharge or release in Form DS1 or DS3 must be executed as a deed or authenticated in such other manner as the registrar may approve.

(4) Notwithstanding paragraphs (1) and (2) and rule 115, the registrar is entitled to accept and act upon any other proof of satisfaction of a charge that he may regard as sufficient.

(5) An application to register a discharge in Form DS1 must be made in Form AP1 or DS2 and an application to register a release in Form DS3 must be made in Form AP1.

115[1] Discharges and releases of registered charges in electronic form
(1) During the currency of a notice given under Schedule 2 and subject to and in accordance with the limitations contained in such notice, notification of –
    (a) the discharge of, or
    (b) the release of part of a registered estate in a registered title from,
a registered charge may be delivered to the registrar in electronic form.

(2) Notification of discharge or release of part given in accordance with paragraph (1) shall be regarded as having the same effect as a discharge in Form DS1, or a release of part in Form DS3, as appropriate, executed in accordance with rule 114 by or on behalf the person who has delivered it to the registrar.

116[2] Transfer of a registered charge
A transfer of a registered charge must be in Form TR3, TR4 or AS2, as appropriate.

PART 10
BOUNDARIES

117[3] Definition
In this Part, except in rule 121, 'boundary' includes part only of a boundary.

118[4] Application for the determination of the exact line of a boundary
(1) A proprietor of a registered estate may apply to the registrar for the exact line of the boundary of that registered estate to be determined.

(2) An application under paragraph (1) must be made in Form DB and be accompanied by –
    (a) a plan, or a plan and a verbal description, identifying the exact line of the boundary claimed and showing sufficient surrounding physical features to allow the general position of the boundary to be drawn on the Ordnance Survey map, and
    (b) evidence to establish the exact line of the boundary.

119[5] Procedure on an application for the determination of the exact line of a boundary
(1) Where the registrar is satisfied that –
    (a) the plan, or plan and verbal description, supplied in accordance with rule 118(2)(a) identifies the exact line of the boundary claimed,

---

[1] Commencement: 13 October 2003 (r 1; Land Registration Act 2002 (Commencement No 4) Order 2003, SI 2003/1725).
[2] Commencement: 13 October 2003 (r 1; Land Registration Act 2002 (Commencement No 4) Order 2003, SI 2003/1725).
[3] Commencement: 13 October 2003 (r 1; Land Registration Act 2002 (Commencement No 4) Order 2003, SI 2003/1725).
[4] Commencement: 13 October 2003 (r 1; Land Registration Act 2002 (Commencement No 4) Order 2003, SI 2003/1725).
[5] Commencement: 13 October 2003 (r 1; Land Registration Act 2002 (Commencement No 4) Order 2003, SI 2003/1725).

(b) the applicant has shown an arguable case that the exact line of the boundary is in the position shown on the plan, or plan and verbal description, supplied in accordance with rule 118(2)(a), and

(c) he can identify all the owners of the land adjoining the boundary to be determined and has an address at which each owner may be given notice,

he must give the owners of the land adjoining the boundary to be determined (except the applicant) notice of the application to determine the exact line of the boundary and of the effect of paragraph (6).

(2) Where the evidence supplied in accordance with rule 118(2)(b) includes an agreement in writing as to the exact line of the boundary with an owner of the land adjoining the boundary, the registrar need not give notice of the application to that owner.

(3) Subject to paragraph (4), the time fixed by the notice to the owner of the land to object to the application shall be the period ending at 12 noon on the twentieth business day after the date of issue of the notice or such longer period as the registrar may decide before the issue of the notice.

(4) The period set for the notice under paragraph (3) may be extended for a particular recipient of the notice by the registrar following a request by that recipient, received by the registrar before that period has expired, setting out why an extension should be allowed.

(5) If a request is received under paragraph (4) the registrar may, if he considers it appropriate, seek the views of the applicant and if, after considering any such views and all other relevant matters, he is satisfied that a longer period should be allowed he may allow such period as he considers appropriate, whether or not the period is the same as any period requested by the recipient of the notice.

(6) Unless any recipient of the notice objects to the application to determine the exact line of the boundary within the time fixed by the notice (as extended under paragraph (5), if applicable), the registrar must complete the application.

(7) Where the registrar is not satisfied as to paragraph (1)(a), (b) and (c), he must cancel the application.

(8) In this rule, the 'owner of the land' means –

(a) a person entitled to apply to be registered as the proprietor of an unregistered legal estate in land under section 3 of the Act,

(b) the proprietor of any registered estate or charge affecting the land, and

(c) if the land is demesne land, Her Majesty.

120[1] Completion of application for the exact line of a boundary to be determined

(1) Where the registrar completes an application under rule 118, he must –

(a) make an entry in the individual register of the applicant's registered title and, if appropriate, in the individual register of any superior or inferior registered title, and any registered title affecting the other land adjoining the determined boundary, stating that the exact line of the boundary is determined under section 60 of the Act, and

(b) subject to paragraph (2), add to the title plan of the applicant's registered title and, if appropriate, to the title plan of any superior or inferior registered title, and any registered title affecting the other land adjoining the determined boundary, such particulars of the exact line of the boundary as he considers appropriate.

(2) Instead of, or as well as, adding particulars of the exact line of the boundary to the title plans mentioned in paragraph (1)(b), the registrar may make an entry in the individual registers

---

[1]   Commencement: 13 October 2003 (r 1; Land Registration Act 2002 (Commencement No 4) Order 2003, SI 2003/1725).

mentioned in paragraph (1)(a) referring to any other plan showing the exact line of the boundary.

121[1] Relationship between determined and undetermined parts of a boundary

Where the exact line of part of the boundary of a registered estate has been determined, the ends of that part of the boundary are not to be treated as determined for the purposes of adjoining parts of the boundary the exact line of which has not been determined.

122[2] Determination of the exact line of a boundary without application

(1) This rule applies where –
  (a)   there is –
    (i)   a transfer of part of a registered estate in land, or
    (ii)   the grant of a term of years absolute which is a registrable disposition of part of a registered estate in land,
  (b)   there is a common boundary, and
  (c)   there is sufficient information in the disposition to enable the registrar to determine the exact line of the common boundary.

(2) The registrar may determine the exact line of the common boundary and if he does he must –
  (a) make an entry in the individual registers of the affected registered titles stating that the exact line of the common boundary is determined under section 60 of the Act, and
  (b) subject to paragraph (3), add to the title plan of the disponor's affected registered title (whether or not the disponor is still the proprietor of that title, or still entitled to be registered as proprietor of that title) and to the title plan of the registered title under which the disposition is being registered, such particulars of the exact line of the common boundary as he considers appropriate.

(3) Instead of, or as well as, adding particulars of the exact line of the common boundary to the title plans mentioned in paragraph (2)(b), the registrar may make an entry in the individual registers of the affected registered titles referring to the description of the common boundary in the disposition.

(4) In this rule –
'common boundary' means any boundary of the land disposed of by a disposition which adjoins land in which the disponor at the date of the disposition had a registered estate in land or of which such disponor was entitled to be registered as proprietor, and
'disposition' means a transfer or grant mentioned in paragraph (1)(a).

123[3] Agreement about accretion or diluvion

(1) An application to register an agreement about the operation of accretion or diluvion in relation to a registered estate in land must be made by, or be accompanied by the consent of, the proprietor of the registered estate and of any registered charge, except that no such consent is required from a person who is party to the agreement.

(2) On registration of such an agreement the registrar must make a note in the property register that the agreement is registered for the purposes of section 61(2) of the Act.

---

[1]   Commencement: 13 October 2003 (r 1; Land Registration Act 2002 (Commencement No 4) Order 2003, SI 2003/1725).
[2]   Commencement: 13 October 2003 (r 1; Land Registration Act 2002 (Commencement No 4) Order 2003, SI 2003/1725).
[3]   Commencement: 13 October 2003 (r 1; Land Registration Act 2002 (Commencement No 4) Order 2003, SI 2003/1725).

PART 11
QUALITY OF TITLE

124¹ Application to upgrade title under section 62 of the Act

(1) An application for the registrar to upgrade title under section 62 of the Act must be made in Form UT1.

(2) An application referred to in paragraph (1) must, except where made under sections 62(2), (4) or (5) of the Act, be accompanied by such documents as will satisfy the registrar as to the title.

(3) An application under section 62(2) of the Act must be accompanied by –
   (a) such documents as will satisfy the registrar as to any superior title which is not registered,
   (b) where any superior title is registered with possessory, qualified or good leasehold title, such evidence as will satisfy the registrar that that title qualifies for upgrading to absolute title, and
   (c) evidence of any consent to the grant of the lease required from –
      (i) any chargee of any superior title, and
      (ii) any superior lessor.

(4) An application under section 62(3)(b) of the Act must, in addition to the documents referred to in paragraph (2), be accompanied by the documents listed at paragraph (3)(a) to (c).

(5) An application by a person entitled to be registered as the proprietor of the estate to which the application relates must be accompanied by evidence of that entitlement.

(6) An application by a person interested in a registered estate which derives from the estate to which the application relates must be accompanied by –
   (a) details of the interest, and
   (b) where the interest is not apparent from the register, evidence to satisfy the registrar of the applicant's interest.

125² Use of register to record defects in title

(1) An entry under section 64 of the Act that a right to determine a registered estate in land is exercisable shall be made in the property register.

(2) An application for such an entry must be supported by evidence to satisfy the registrar that the applicant has the right to determine the registered estate and that the right is exercisable.

(3) Subject to paragraph (4), the registrar must make the entry on receipt of an application which relates to a right to determine the registered estate on non-payment of a rentcharge.

(4) Before making an entry under this rule the registrar must give notice of the application to the proprietor of the registered estate to which the application relates and the proprietor of any registered charge on that estate.

(5) A person may apply to the registrar for removal of the entry if he is –
   (a) the person entitled to determine the registered estate,
   (b) the proprietor of the registered estate to which the entry relates,
   (c) a person entitled to be registered as proprietor of that estate, or

---

[1]   Commencement: 13 October 2003 (r 1; Land Registration Act 2002 (Commencement No 4) Order 2003, SI 2003/1725).

[2]   Commencement: 13 October 2003 (r 1; Land Registration Act 2002 (Commencement No 4) Order 2003, SI 2003/1725).

(d) any other person whom the registrar is satisfied has an interest in the removal of the entry.

(6) An application for removal of the entry must be supported by evidence to satisfy the registrar that the right to determine the registered estate is not exercisable.

PART 12
ALTERATIONS AND CORRECTIONS

126[1] Alteration under a court order - not rectification
(1) Subject to paragraphs (2) and (3), if in any proceedings the court decides that –
    (a) there is a mistake in the register,
    (b) the register is not up to date, or
    (c) there is an estate, right or interest excepted from the effect of registration that should be given effect to,
it must make an order for alteration of the register under the power given by paragraph 2(1) of Schedule 4 to the Act.

(2) The court is not obliged to make an order if there are exceptional circumstances that justify not doing so.

(3) This rule does not apply to an alteration of the register that amounts to rectification.

127[2] Court order for alteration of the register - form and service
(1) An order for alteration of the register must state the title number of the title affected and the alteration that is to be made, and must direct the registrar to make the alteration.

(2) Service on the registrar of an order for alteration of the register must be made by making an application for the registrar to give effect to the order, accompanied by the order.

128[3] Alteration otherwise than pursuant to a court order - notice and enquiries
(1) Subject to paragraph (5), this rule applies where an application for alteration of the register has been made, or where the registrar is considering altering the register without an application having been made.

(2) The registrar must give notice of the proposed alteration to –
    (a) the registered proprietor of any registered estate,
    (b) the registered proprietor of any registered charge, and
    (c) subject to paragraph (3), any person who appears to the registrar to be entitled to an interest protected by a notice,
where that estate, charge or interest would be affected by the proposed alteration, unless he is satisfied that such notice is unnecessary.

(3) The registrar is not obliged to give notice to a person referred to in paragraph (2)(c) if that person's name and his address for service under rule 198 are not set out in the individual register in which the notice is entered.

(4) The registrar may make such enquiries as he thinks fit.

---

[1] Commencement: 13 October 2003 (r 1; Land Registration Act 2002 (Commencement No 4) Order 2003, SI 2003/1725).

[2] Commencement: 13 October 2003 (r 1; Land Registration Act 2002 (Commencement No 4) Order 2003, SI 2003/1725).

[3] Commencement: 13 October 2003 (r 1; Land Registration Act 2002 (Commencement No 4) Order 2003, SI 2003/1725).

(5) This rule does not apply to alteration of the register in the specific circumstances covered by any other rule.

129[1] Alteration otherwise than under a court order - evidence

Unless otherwise provided in these rules, an application for alteration of the register (otherwise than under a court order) must be supported by evidence to justify the alteration.

130[2] Correction of mistakes in an application or accompanying document

(1) This rule applies to any alteration made by the registrar for the purpose of correcting a mistake in any application or accompanying document.

(2) The alteration will have effect as if made by the applicant or other interested party or parties –

    (a) in the case of a mistake of a clerical or like nature, in all circumstances,

    (b) in the case of any other mistake, only if the applicant and every other interested party has requested, or consented to, the alteration.

PART 13
INFORMATION ETC

Interpretation of this Part

131[3] Definitions

In this Part –

'commencement date' means the date of commencement of this Part,

'edited information document' means, where the registrar has designated a document an exempt information document, the edited copy of that document lodged under rule 136(2)(b),

'exempt information document' means the original and copies of a document so designated under rule 136(3),

'prejudicial information' means –

    (a)   information that relates to an individual who is the applicant under rule 136 and if disclosed to other persons (whether to the public generally or specific persons) would, or would be likely to, cause substantial unwarranted damage or substantial unwarranted distress to the applicant or another, or

    (b)   information that if disclosed to other persons (whether to the public generally or specific persons) would, or would be likely to, prejudice the commercial interests of the applicant under rule 136,

'priority period' means –

    (a)   where the application for an official search is entered on the day list before the date referred to in rule 216(3), the period beginning at the time when that application is entered on the day list and ending at midnight marking the end of the thirtieth business day thereafter, and

    (b)   where the application for an official search is entered on the day list on or after the date referred to in rule 216(3), the period beginning at the time when that application is entered on the day list and ending at midnight marking the end of the thirty sixth business day thereafter,

---

[1]   Commencement: 13 October 2003 (r 1; Land Registration Act 2002 (Commencement No 4) Order 2003, SI 2003/1725).

[2]   Commencement: 13 October 2003 (r 1; Land Registration Act 2002 (Commencement No 4) Order 2003, SI 2003/1725).

[3]   Commencement: 13 October 2003 (r 1; Land Registration Act 2002 (Commencement No 4) Order 2003, SI 2003/1725).

'protectable disposition' means a registrable disposition (including one by virtue of rule 38) of a registered estate or registered charge made for valuable consideration,

'purchaser' means a person who has entered into or intends to enter into a protectable disposition as disponee,

'registrable estate or charge' means the legal estate and any charge which is sought to be registered as a registered estate or registered charge in an application for first registration,

'search from date' means –

    (a)   the date stated on an official copy of the individual register of the relevant registered title, as the date on which the entries shown on that official copy were subsisting,

    (b)   the date stated at the time of an access by remote terminal, where provided for under these rules, to the individual register of the relevant registered title as the date on which the entries accessed were subsisting,

'transitional period' means the period of two years beginning with the commencement date,

'transitional period document' means –

    (a)   a lease or charge or a copy lease or charge kept by the registrar since before the commencement date, where an entry referring to the lease or charge was made in the register of title before the commencement date, or

    (b)   any other document kept by the registrar which is not referred to in the register of title but relates to an application to the registrar and was received by the registrar before the commencement date.

Delivery of applications and issuing of certificates

132[1] Delivery of applications and issuing of certificates by electronic and other means

(1) During the currency of a relevant notice given under Schedule 2, and subject to and in accordance with the limitations contained in that notice, any application under this Part may be made by delivering the application to the registrar by any means of communication other than post, document exchange or personal delivery, and the applicant must provide, in such order as may be required by that notice, such of the particulars required for an application of that type as are appropriate in the circumstances and as are required by the notice.

(2) During the currency of a relevant notice given under Schedule 2, and subject to and in accordance with the limitations contained in that notice, any certificates and other results of applications and searches under this Part may be issued by any means of communication other than post, document exchange or personal delivery.

(3) Except where otherwise provided in this Part, where information is issued under paragraph (2) it must be to like effect to that which would have been provided had the information been issued in paper form.

Inspection and copying

133[2] Inspection and copying

(1) This rule applies to the right to inspect and make copies of the registers and documents under section 66(1) of the Act.

(2) There is excepted from the right –

    (a) any exempt information document,

---

[1]   Commencement: 13 October 2003 (r 1; Land Registration Act 2002 (Commencement No 4) Order 2003, SI 2003/1725).

[2]   Commencement: 13 October 2003 (r 1; Land Registration Act 2002 (Commencement No 4) Order 2003, SI 2003/1725).

(b) any edited information document which has been replaced by another edited information document under rule 136(6),

(c) any Form EX1A,

(d) any Form CIT,

(e) any Form to which Form CIT has been attached under rule 140(3) or (4), and

(f) any document or copy of any document prepared by the registrar in connection with an application in a Form to which Form CIT has been attached under rule 140(3) or (4).

(3) Subject to rule 132(1), an application under section 66 of the Act must be in Form PIC.

(4) Where inspection and copying under this rule takes place at an office of the land registry it must be undertaken in the presence of a member of the land registry.

(5) In paragraph (2) the references to Form EX1A and Form CIT and Forms to which Form CIT has been attached include any equivalent information provided under rule 132 and the reference to an application in a Form to which Form CIT has been attached includes an equivalent application made by virtue of rule 132.

Official Copies

134[1] Application for official copies of a registered title, the cautions register or for a certificate of inspection of the title plan

(1) A person may apply for –

(a) an official copy of an individual register,

(b) an official copy of any title plan referred to in an individual register,

(c) an official copy of an individual caution register and any caution plan referred to in it, and

(d) a certificate of inspection of any title plan.

(2) Subject to rule 132(1), an application under paragraph (1) must be in Form OC1.

(3) A separate application must be made in respect of each registered title or individual caution register.

(4) Where, notwithstanding paragraph (3), an application is in respect of more than one registered title or individual caution register, but the applicant fails to provide a title number, or the title number provided does not relate to any part of the property in respect of which the application is made, the registrar may –

(a) deal with the application as if it referred only to one of the title numbers relating to the property,

(b) deal with the application as if it referred to all of the title numbers relating to the property, or

(c) cancel the application.

(5) In paragraph (4) the reference to title number includes in the case of an individual caution register a caution title number.

(6) Where the registrar deals with the application under paragraph (4)(b), the applicant is to be treated as having made a separate application in respect of each of the registered titles or each of the individual caution registers.

(7) An official copy of an individual caution register and any caution plan referred to in it must be issued disregarding any application or matter that may affect the subsistence of the caution.

---

[1]   Commencement: 13 October 2003 (r 1; Land Registration Act 2002 (Commencement No 4) Order 2003, SI 2003/1725).

135¹ Application for official copies of documents referred to in the register of title and other documents kept by the registrar

(1) Subject to paragraphs (2) and (3), a person may apply for an official copy of –

    (a)   any document referred to in the register of title and kept by the registrar,

    (b)   any other document kept by the registrar that relates to an application to him.

(2) There is excepted from paragraph (1) –

    (a) any exempt information document,

    (b) any edited information document which has been replaced by another edited information document under rule 136(6),

    (c) any Form EX1A,

    (d) any Form CIT,

    (e) any Form to which Form CIT has been attached under rule 140(3) or (4), and

    (f) any document or copy of any document prepared by the registrar in connection with an application in a Form to which Form CIT has been attached under rule 140(3) or (4).

(3) During the transitional period, paragraph (1) is also subject to rule 139.

(4) Subject to rule 132(1), an application under paragraph (1) must be made in Form OC2.

(5) In paragraph (2) the references to Form EX1A and Form CIT and Forms to which Form CIT has been attached include any equivalent information provided under rule 132 and the reference to an application in a Form to which Form CIT has been attached includes an equivalent application made by virtue of rule 132.

Exempt information documents

136² Application that the registrar designate a document an exempt information document

(1) A person may apply for the registrar to designate a relevant document an exempt information document if he claims that the document contains prejudicial information.

(2) Subject to rule 132(1), an application under paragraph (1) must –

    (a) be made in Form EX1 and EX1A, and

    (b) include a copy of the relevant document which excludes the prejudicial information and which is certified as being a true copy of the relevant document from which copy this information has been excluded.

(3) Subject to paragraph (4), provided that the registrar is satisfied that the applicant's claim is not groundless he must designate the relevant document an exempt information document.

(4) Where the registrar considers that designating the document an exempt information document could prejudice the keeping of the register, he may cancel the application.

(5) Where a document is an exempt information document, the registrar may make an appropriate entry in the individual register of any affected registered title.

(6) Where a document is an exempt information document and a further application is made under paragraph (1) which would, but for the existing designation, have resulted in its being so designated, the registrar must prepare another edited information document which excludes –

    (a) the information excluded from the existing edited information document, and

---

1   Commencement: 13 October 2003 (r 1; Land Registration Act 2002 (Commencement No 4) Order 2003, SI 2003/1725).

2   Commencement: 13 October 2003 (r 1; Land Registration Act 2002 (Commencement No 4) Order 2003, SI 2003/1725).

(b) any further information excluded from the edited information document lodged by the applicant.

(7) In this rule a 'relevant document' is a document –
(a) referred to in the register of title, or one that relates to an application to the registrar, the original or a copy of which is kept by the registrar, or
(b) that will be referred to in the register of title as a result of an application (the 'accompanying application') made at the same time as an application under this rule, or that relates to the accompanying application, the original or a copy of which will be or is for the time being kept by the registrar.

137[1] Application for an official copy of an exempt information document

(1) A person may apply for an official copy of an exempt information document.

(2) Subject to rule 132(1), application under paragraph (1) must be made in Form EX2.

(3) The registrar must give notice of an application under paragraph (1) to the person who made the relevant application under rule 136(1) unless he is satisfied that such notice is unnecessary or impracticable.

(4) If the registrar decides that –
(a) none of the information excluded from the edited information document is prejudicial information, or
(b) although all or some of the information excluded is prejudicial information, the public interest in providing an official copy of the exempt information document to the applicant outweighs the public interest in not doing so,
then he must provide an official copy of the exempt information document to the applicant.

(5) Where the registrar has decided an application under paragraph (1) on the basis that none of the information is prejudicial information, he must remove the designation of the document as an exempt information document and any entry made in respect of the document under rule 136(5).

138[2] Application for removal of the designation of a document as an exempt information document

(1) Where a document is an exempt information document, the person who applied for designation under rule 136(1) may apply for the designation to be removed.

(2) Subject to rule 132(1), an application made under paragraph (1) must be in Form EX3.

(3) Subject to paragraph (4), where the registrar is satisfied that the application is in order, he must remove the designation of the document as an exempt information document and remove any entry made in respect of the document under rule 136(5).

(4) Where –
(a) the document has been made an exempt information document under more than one application,
(b) an application under paragraph (1) is made by fewer than all of the applicants under rule 136(1), and
(c) the registrar is satisfied that the application is in order,
the registrar must replace the existing edited information document with one that excludes only the information excluded both from that edited information document

---

[1]   Commencement: 13 October 2003 (r 1; Land Registration Act 2002 (Commencement No 4) Order 2003, SI 2003/1725).
[2]   Commencement: 13 October 2003 (r 1; Land Registration Act 2002 (Commencement No 4) Order 2003, SI 2003/1725).

and the edited information documents lodged under rule 136(2)(b) by those applicants not applying under paragraph (1).

Transitional period documents

139[1] Inspection, copying and official copies of transitional period documents

(1) Subject to paragraph (2) and rule 140(2), during the transitional period a person may only inspect and make copies of, or of any part of, a transitional period document or obtain an official copy of a transitional period document at the registrar's discretion.

(2) Where a transitional period document is an exempt information document, paragraph (1) does not apply.

Inspection, official copies and searches of the index of proprietors' names in connection with court proceedings, insolvency and tax liability

140[2] Application in connection with court proceedings, insolvency and tax liability

(1) In this rule, a qualifying applicant is a person referred to in column 1 of Schedule 5 who gives the registrar the appropriate certificate referred to in column 2 of the Schedule or, where rule 132 applies, an equivalent certificate in accordance with a notice given under Schedule 2.

(2) A qualifying applicant may apply –
- (a) to inspect or make copies of any document (including a form) within rule 133(2) and, during the transitional period, any transitional period document,
- (b) for official copies of any document (including a form) within rule 135(2) and, during the transitional period, any transitional period document, and
- (c) for a search in the index of proprietors' names in respect of the name of a person specified in the application.

(3) Subject to rule 132(1), an application under paragraph (2) must be made in Form PIC, OC2 or PN1, as appropriate, with Form CIT attached.

(4) A qualifying applicant who applies –
- (a) to inspect and make copies of registers and documents not within paragraph (2)(a) under section 66 of the Act,
- (b) for official copies of registers and plans under rule 134(1) and of documents not within paragraph (2)(b) under rule 135,
- (c) for an historical edition of a registered title under rule 144,
- (d) for an official search of the index map under rule 145, or
- (e) for an official search of the index of relating franchises and manors under rule 146,

may attach Form CIT to the Form PIC, OC1, OC2, HC1, SIM or SIF, as appropriate, used in the application.

(5) In Form CIT and Schedule 5, references to tax are references to any of the taxes mentioned in the definition of tax in section 118(1) of the Taxes Management Act 1970.

Information about the day list, electronic discharges of registered charges and title plans

---

[1]   Commencement: 13 October 2003 (r 1; Land Registration Act 2002 (Commencement No 4) Order 2003, SI 2003/1725).

[2]   Commencement: 13 October 2003 (r 1; Land Registration Act 2002 (Commencement No 4) Order 2003, SI 2003/1725).

141[1] Day list information

(1) In this rule 'day list information' means information kept by the registrar under rule 12.

(2) A person may only apply for the day list information relating to a specified title number during the currency of a relevant notice given under Schedule 2, and subject to and in accordance with the limitations contained in the notice.

(3) The registrar must provide the day list information in the manner specified in the relevant notice.

(4) Unless otherwise stated by the registrar, the day list information provided must be based on the entries subsisting in the day list immediately before the information is provided.

(5) The registrar is not required to disclose under this rule details of an application under rule 136.

142[2] Enquiry as to discharge of a charge by electronic means

(1) A person may apply in respect of a specified registered title for confirmation of receipt by the registrar of notification of –

    (a) the discharge of a registered charge given by electronic means, or

    (b) the release of part of a registered estate from a registered charge given by electronic means.

(2) An application under paragraph (1) may only be made during the currency of a relevant notice given under Schedule 2, and subject to and in accordance with the limitations contained in the notice.

(3) The registrar is not required to disclose under this rule any information concerning a notification once the entries of the registered charge to which it relates have been cancelled from the relevant registered title, or the affected part of it.

143[3] Certificate of inspection of title plan

(1) Where a person has applied under rule 134 for a certificate of inspection of a title plan, on completion of the inspection the registrar must issue a certificate of inspection.

(2) Subject to rule 132(2), the certificate of inspection must be issued by the registrar in Form CI or to like effect.

Historical information

144[4] Application for an historical edition of a registered title kept by the registrar in electronic form

(1) A person may apply for a copy of –

    (a) the last edition for a specified day, or

    (b) every edition for a specified day,

of a registered title, and of a registered title that has been closed, kept by the registrar in electronic form.

---

[1]   Commencement: 13 October 2003 (r 1; Land Registration Act 2002 (Commencement No 4) Order 2003, SI 2003/1725).

[2]   Commencement: 13 October 2003 (r 1; Land Registration Act 2002 (Commencement No 4) Order 2003, SI 2003/1725).

[3]   Commencement: 13 October 2003 (r 1; Land Registration Act 2002 (Commencement No 4) Order 2003, SI 2003/1725).

[4]   Commencement: 13 October 2003 (r 1; Land Registration Act 2002 (Commencement No 4) Order 2003, SI 2003/1725).

(2) Subject to rule 132(1), an application under paragraph (1) must be made in Form HC1.

(3) Subject to paragraph (4), if an application under paragraph (1) is in order and the registrar is keeping in electronic form an edition of the registered title for the day specified in the application, he must issue –
   (a) if the application is under paragraph (1)(a), subject to rule 132(2), a paper copy of the edition of the registered title at the end of that day, or
   (b) if the application is under paragraph (1)(b), subject to rule 132(2), a paper copy of the edition of the registered title at the end of that day and any prior edition kept in electronic form of the registered title for that day.

(4) Where only part of the edition of the registered title requested is kept by the registrar in electronic form he must issue, subject to rule 132(2), a paper copy of that part.

Official searches of the index kept under section 68 of the Act

145[1] Searches of the index map
(1) Any person may apply for an official search of the index map.

(2) Subject to rule 132(1), an application under paragraph (1) must be made in Form SIM.

(3) If the registrar so requires, an applicant must provide a copy of an extract from the Ordnance Survey map on the largest scale published showing the land to which the application relates.

(4) If an application under paragraph (1) is in order, subject to rule 132(2), a paper certificate must be issued including such information specified in Part 1 of Schedule 6 as the case may require.

146[2] Searches of the index of relating franchises and manors
(1) Any person may apply for an official search of the index of relating franchises and manors.

(2) Subject to rule 132(1), an application under paragraph (1) must be made in Form SIF.

(3) If an application under paragraph (1) is in order, subject to rule 132(2), a paper certificate must be issued including such information specified in Part 2 of Schedule 6 as the case may require.

Official searches with priority

147[3] Application for official search with priority by purchaser
(1) A purchaser may apply for an official search with priority of the individual register of a registered title to which the protectable disposition relates.

(2) Where there is a pending application for first registration, the purchaser of a protectable disposition which relates to that pending application may apply for an official search with priority in relation to that pending application.

(3) Subject to rule 132(1), an application for an official search with priority must be made in Form OS1 or Form OS2, as appropriate.

---

[1] Commencement: 13 October 2003 (r 1; Land Registration Act 2002 (Commencement No 4) Order 2003, SI 2003/1725).
[2] Commencement: 13 October 2003 (r 1; Land Registration Act 2002 (Commencement No 4) Order 2003, SI 2003/1725).
[3] Commencement: 13 October 2003 (r 1; Land Registration Act 2002 (Commencement No 4) Order 2003, SI 2003/1725).

(4) Where the application is made in Form OS2 and an accompanying plan is required, unless the registrar allows otherwise, the plan must be delivered in duplicate.

148[1] Entry on day list of application for official search with priority

(1) An application for an official search with priority is to be taken as having been made on the date and at the time of the day notice of it is entered on the day list.

(2) Paragraph (3) has effect where –
- (a) an application for an official search is in order, and
- (b) the applicant has not withdrawn the official search.

(3) Subject to paragraph (4), the entry on the day list of notice of an application for an official search with priority confers a priority period on an application for an entry in the register in respect of the protectable disposition to which the official search relates.

(4) Paragraph (3) does not apply if the application for an official search with priority is cancelled subsequently because it is not in order.

149[2] Issue of official search certificate with priority

(1) If an application for an official search with priority is in order an official search certificate with priority must be issued giving the result of the search as at the date and time that the application was entered on the day list.

(2) An official search certificate with priority relating to a registered estate or to a pending application for first registration may, at the registrar's discretion, be issued in one or both of the following ways –
- (a) in paper form, or
- (b) under rule 132(2).

(3) Subject to paragraph (4), an official search certificate issued under paragraph (2) must include such information as specified in Part 3 or Part 4 of Schedule 6 as the case may require and may be issued by reference to an official copy of the individual register of the relevant registered title.

(4) If an official search certificate is to be, or has been, issued in paper form under paragraph (2)(a), another official search certificate issued under paragraph (2)(b) in respect of the same application need only include the information specified at A, F, G and H of Part 3 and A, H and I of Part 4 of Schedule 6, as the case may require.

150[3] Withdrawal of official search with priority

(1) Subject to paragraph (2), a person who has made an application for an official search with priority of a registered title or in relation to a pending first registration application, may withdraw that official search by application to the registrar.

(2) An application under paragraph (1) cannot be made if an application for an entry in the register in respect of the protectable disposition made pursuant to the official search has been made and completed.

(3) Once an official search has been withdrawn under paragraph (1) rule 148(3) shall cease to apply in relation to it.

---

[1] Commencement: 13 October 2003 (r 1; Land Registration Act 2002 (Commencement No 4) Order 2003, SI 2003/1725).

[2] Commencement: 13 October 2003 (r 1; Land Registration Act 2002 (Commencement No 4) Order 2003, SI 2003/1725).

[3] Commencement: 13 October 2003 (r 1; Land Registration Act 2002 (Commencement No 4) Order 2003, SI 2003/1725).

151¹ Protection of an application on which a protected application is dependent

(1) Subject to paragraph (4), paragraph (2) has effect where an application for an entry in the register is one on which an official search certificate confers a priority period and there is a prior registrable disposition affecting the same registered land, on which that application is dependent.

(2) An application for an entry in the register in relation to that prior registrable disposition is for the purpose of section 72(1)(a) of the Act an application to which a priority period relates.

(3) The priority period referred to in paragraph (2) is a period expiring at the same time as the priority period conferred by the official search referred to in paragraph (1).

(4) Paragraph (2) does not have effect unless both the application referred to in paragraph (1) and the application referred to in paragraph (2) are –
    (a) made before the end of that priority period, and
    (b) in due course completed by registration.

152² Protection of an application relating to a pending application for first registration on which a protected application is dependent

(1) Subject to paragraphs (4) and (5), paragraph (2) has effect where –
    (a) there is a pending application for first registration,
    (b) there is a pending application for an entry in the register on which an official search confers a priority period,
    (c) there is an application for registration of a prior registrable disposition affecting the same registrable estate or charge as the pending application referred to in sub-paragraph (b),
    (d) the pending application referred to in sub-paragraph (b) is dependent on the application referred to in sub-paragraph (c), and
    (e) the application referred to in sub-paragraph (c) is subject to the pending application for first registration referred to in sub-paragraph (a).

(2) An application for an entry in the register in relation to the prior registrable disposition referred to in paragraph (1)(c) is for the purpose of section 72(1)(a) of the Act an application to which a priority period relates.

(3) The priority period referred to in paragraph (2) is a period expiring at the same time as the priority period conferred by the official search referred to in paragraph (1)(b).

(4) Paragraph (2) does not have effect unless the pending application for first registration referred to in paragraph (1)(a) is in due course completed by registration of all or any part of the registrable estate.

(5) Paragraph (2) does not have effect unless both the pending application on which an official search confers priority referred to in paragraph (1)(b) and the application relating to the prior registrable disposition referred to in paragraph (1)(c) are –
    (a) made before the end of that priority period, and
    (b) in due course completed by registration.

---

¹   Commencement: 13 October 2003 (r 1; Land Registration Act 2002 (Commencement No 4) Order 2003, SI 2003/1725).

²   Commencement: 13 October 2003 (r 1; Land Registration Act 2002 (Commencement No 4) Order 2003, SI 2003/1725).

153¹ Priority of concurrent applications for official searches with priority and concurrent official search certificates with priority

(1) Where two or more official search certificates with priority relating to the same registrable estate or charge or to the same registered land have been issued and are in operation, the certificates take effect, as far as relates to the priority conferred, in the order of the times at which the applications for official search with priority were entered on the day list, unless the applicants agree otherwise.

(2) Where one transaction is dependent upon another the registrar must assume (unless the contrary appears) that the applicants for official search with priority have agreed that their applications have priority so as to give effect to the sequence of the documents effecting the transactions.

154² Applications lodged at the same time as the priority period expires

(1) Where an official search with priority has been made in respect of a registered title and an application relating to that title is taken as having been made at the same time as the expiry of the priority period relating to that search, the time of the making of that application is to be taken as within that priority period.

(2) Where an official search with priority has been made in respect of a pending application for first registration and a subsequent application relating to a registrable estate which is subject to that pending application for first registration, or was so subject before completion of the registration of that registrable estate, is taken as having been made at the same time as the expiry of the priority period relating to that search, the time of the making of that subsequent application is to be taken as within that priority period.

Official searches without priority

155³ Application for official search without priority

(1) A person may apply for an official search without priority of an individual register of a registered title.

(2) Subject to rule 132(1), an application for an official search without priority must be made in Form OS3.

(3) Where the application is in Form OS3 and an accompanying plan is required, unless the registrar allows otherwise, the plan must be delivered in duplicate.

156⁴ Issue of official search certificate without priority

(1) If an application for an official search without priority is in order, an official search certificate without priority must be issued.

(2) An official search certificate without priority may, at the registrar's discretion, be issued in one or both of the following ways –
   (a) in paper form, or
   (b) under rule 132(2).

1   Commencement: 13 October 2003 (r 1; Land Registration Act 2002 (Commencement No 4) Order 2003, SI 2003/1725).
2   Commencement: 13 October 2003 (r 1; Land Registration Act 2002 (Commencement No 4) Order 2003, SI 2003/1725).
3   Commencement: 13 October 2003 (r 1; Land Registration Act 2002 (Commencement No 4) Order 2003, SI 2003/1725).
4   Commencement: 13 October 2003 (r 1; Land Registration Act 2002 (Commencement No 4) Order 2003, SI 2003/1725).

(3) Subject to paragraph (4), an official search certificate without priority issued under paragraph (2) must include such information specified in Part 3 of Schedule 6 as the case may require and may be issued by reference to an official copy of the individual register of the relevant registered title.

(4) If an official certificate of search is to be, or has been, issued in paper form under paragraph (2)(a), another official search certificate issued under paragraph (2)(b) in respect of the same application need only include the information specified at A, F, G and H of Part 3 of Schedule 6, as the case may require.

Request for information

157[1] Information requested by telephone, oral or remote terminal application for an official search

(1) If an application under rule 147(3) or rule 155(2) has been made by telephone or orally by virtue of rule 132(1) in respect of a registered title, the registrar may, before or after the official search has been completed, at his discretion, inform the applicant, by telephone or orally, whether or not –

    (a) there have been any relevant adverse entries made in the individual register since the search from date given in the application, or

    (b) there is any relevant entry subsisting on the day list.

(2) If an application under rule 147(3) has been made by telephone or orally by virtue of rule 132(1) in respect of a legal estate subject to a pending application for first registration, the registrar may, before or after the official search has been completed, at his discretion, inform the applicant, by telephone or orally, whether or not there is any relevant entry subsisting on the day list.

(3) If an application under rule 147(3) or rule 155(2) has been made to the land registry computer system from a remote terminal by virtue of rule 132(1), the registrar may, before or after the official search has been completed, at his discretion, inform the applicant, by a transmission to the remote terminal, whether or not –

    (a) in the case of an official search of a registered title, there have been any relevant entries of the kind referred to in paragraph (1)(a) or (b), or

    (b) in the case of an official search of a legal estate subject to a pending application for first registration, there have been any relevant entries of the kind referred to in paragraph (2).

(4) Under this rule the registrar need not provide the applicant with details of any relevant entries.

Official searches for the purpose of the Family Law Act 1996 and information requests

158[2] Application for official search for the purpose of the Family Law Act 1996 by a mortgagee

(1) A mortgagee of land comprised in a registered title that consists of or includes all or part of a dwelling-house may apply for an official search certificate of the result of a search of the relevant individual register for the purpose of section 56(3) of the Family Law Act 1996.

(2) Subject to rule 132(1), an application under paragraph (1) must be made in Form MH3.

---

[1]   Commencement: 13 October 2003 (r 1; Land Registration Act 2002 (Commencement No 4) Order 2003, SI 2003/1725).

[2]   Commencement: 13 October 2003 (r 1; Land Registration Act 2002 (Commencement No 4) Order 2003, SI 2003/1725).

159¹ Issue of official search certificate result following an application made by a mortgagee for the purpose of section 56(3) of the Family Law Act 1996

(1) An official search certificate giving the result of a search in respect of an application made under rule 158 may, at the registrar's discretion, be issued in one or both of the following ways –

    (a) in paper form, or

    (b) under rule 132(2).

(2) Subject to paragraph (3), an official search certificate issued under paragraph (1) must include the information specified in Part 5 of Schedule 6.

(3) If an official search certificate is to be, or has been, issued under paragraph (1)(a), another official search certificate issued under rule 132(2) by virtue of paragraph (1)(b) in respect of the same application need only include the information specified at A, E and F of Part 5 of Schedule 6.

160² Information requested by an applicant for an official search for the purpose of the Family Law Act 1996

If an application has been made under rule 158 the registrar may, at his discretion, during the currency of a relevant notice given under Schedule 2, and in accordance with the limitations contained in that notice, before the official search has been completed, inform the applicant, by any means of communication, whether or not –

    (a) a matrimonial home rights notice or matrimonial home rights caution has been entered in the individual register of the relevant registered title, or

    (b) there is a pending application for the entry of a matrimonial home rights notice entered on the day list.

PART 14
MISCELLANEOUS AND SPECIAL CASES

Dispositions by operation of law within section 27(5) of the Act

161³ Applications to register dispositions by operation of law which are registrable dispositions

(1) Subject to paragraphs (2) and (3), an application to register a disposition by operation of law which is a registrable disposition must be accompanied by sufficient evidence of the disposition.

(2) Where a vesting order has been made, it must accompany the application.

(3) Where there is a vesting declaration to which section 40 of the Trustee Act 1925 applies, the application must be accompanied by the deed of appointment or retirement, and –

    (a) a certificate from the conveyancer acting for the persons making the appointment or effecting the retirement that they are entitled to do so, or

    (b) such other evidence to satisfy the registrar that the persons making the appointment or effecting the retirement are entitled to do so.

¹   Commencement: 13 October 2003 (r 1; Land Registration Act 2002 (Commencement No 4) Order 2003, SI 2003/1725).

²   Commencement: 13 October 2003 (r 1; Land Registration Act 2002 (Commencement No 4) Order 2003, SI 2003/1725).

³   Commencement: 13 October 2003 (r 1; Land Registration Act 2002 (Commencement No 4) Order 2003, SI 2003/1725).

Death of proprietor

162[1] Transfer by a personal representative

(1) An application to register a transfer by a personal representative, who is not already registered as proprietor, must be accompanied by the original grant of probate or letters of administration showing him as the personal representative.

(2) The registrar shall not be under a duty to investigate the reasons a transfer of registered land by a personal representative of a deceased sole proprietor or last surviving joint proprietor is made nor to consider the contents of the will and, provided the terms of any restriction on the register are complied with, he must assume, whether he knows of the terms of the will or not, that the personal representative is acting correctly and within his powers.

163[2] Registration of a personal representative

(1) An application by a personal representative to become registered as proprietor of a registered estate or registered charge –
  (a) in place of a deceased sole proprietor or the last surviving joint proprietor, or
  (b) jointly with another personal representative who is already so registered, or
  (c) in place of another personal representative who is already registered as proprietor,
must be accompanied by the evidence specified in paragraph (2).

(2) Subject to paragraph (3), the evidence that must accompany an application under paragraph (1) is –
  (a) the original grant of probate or letters of administration of the deceased proprietor showing the applicant as his personal representative, or
  (b) a court order appointing the applicant as the deceased's personal representative, or
  (c) (where a conveyancer is acting for the applicant) a certificate given by the conveyancer that he holds the original or an office copy of such grant of probate, letters of administration or court order.

(3) An application under paragraph (1)(c) must be accompanied by evidence to satisfy the registrar that the appointment of the personal representative whom the applicant is replacing has been terminated.

(4) When registering a personal representative of a deceased proprietor, the registrar must add the following after the personal representative's name –
  'executor or executrix (or administrator or administratrix) of [name] deceased'.

(5) Before registering another personal representative as a result of an application made under paragraph (1)(b) the registrar must serve notice upon the personal representative who is registered as proprietor.

164[3] Death of joint proprietor

An application for alteration of the register by the removal from the register of the name of a deceased joint proprietor of a registered estate or registered charge must be accompanied by evidence of his death.

---

1 Commencement: 13 October 2003 (r 1; Land Registration Act 2002 (Commencement No 4) Order 2003, SI 2003/1725).
2 Commencement: 13 October 2003 (r 1; Land Registration Act 2002 (Commencement No 4) Order 2003, SI 2003/1725).
3 Commencement: 13 October 2003 (r 1; Land Registration Act 2002 (Commencement No 4) Order 2003, SI 2003/1725).

Bankruptcy of proprietor

165[1] Bankruptcy notice

(1) The bankruptcy notice in relation to a registered estate must be entered in the proprietorship register and the bankruptcy notice in relation to a registered charge must be entered in the charges register in the following form –

'BANKRUPTCY NOTICE entered under section 86(2) of the Land Registration Act 2002 in respect of a pending action, as the title of the [proprietor of the registered estate] *or* [the proprietor of the charge dated .... referred to above] appears to be affected by a petition in bankruptcy against [*name of debtor*], presented in the [*name*] Court (Court Reference Number ....) (Land Charges Reference Number PA ....).'.

(2) The registrar must give notice of the entry of a bankruptcy notice to the proprietor of the registered estate or registered charge to which it relates.

(3) In this rule, 'bankruptcy notice' means the notice which the registrar must enter in the register under section 86(2) of the Act.

166[2] Bankruptcy restriction

(1) The bankruptcy restriction in relation to a registered estate must be entered in the proprietorship register and the bankruptcy restriction in relation to a registered charge must be entered in the charges register in the following form –

'BANKRUPTCY RESTRICTION entered under section 86(4) of the Land Registration Act 2002, as the title of [the proprietor of the registered estate] *or* [the proprietor of the charge dated .... referred to above] appears to be affected by a bankruptcy order made by the [*name*] Court (Court Reference Number ....) against [*name of debtor*] (Land Charges Reference Number WO ....).

[No disposition of the registered estate] *or* [No disposition of the charge] is to be registered until the trustee in bankruptcy of the property of the bankrupt is registered as proprietor of the [registered estate] *or* [charge].'.

(2) The registrar must give notice of the entry of a bankruptcy restriction to the proprietor of the registered estate or registered charge to which it relates.

(3) In this rule, 'bankruptcy restriction' means the restriction which the registrar must enter in the register under section 86(4) of the Act.

167[3] Action of the registrar in relation to bankruptcy entries

(1) Where the registrar is satisfied that –

   (a) the bankruptcy order has been annulled, or
   (b) the bankruptcy petition has been dismissed or withdrawn with the court's permission, or
   (c) the bankruptcy proceedings do not affect or have ceased to affect the registered estate or registered charge in relation to which a bankruptcy notice or bankruptcy restriction has been entered on the register,

he must as soon as practicable cancel any bankruptcy notice or bankruptcy restriction which

---

[1]   Commencement: 13 October 2003 (r 1; Land Registration Act 2002 (Commencement No 4) Order 2003, SI 2003/1725).

[2]   Commencement: 13 October 2003 (r 1; Land Registration Act 2002 (Commencement No 4) Order 2003, SI 2003/1725).

[3]   Commencement: 13 October 2003 (r 1; Land Registration Act 2002 (Commencement No 4) Order 2003, SI 2003/1725).

relates to that bankruptcy order, to that bankruptcy petition or to those proceedings from the register.

(2) Where it appears to the registrar that there is doubt as to whether the debtor or bankrupt is the same person as the proprietor of the registered estate or registered charge in relation to which a bankruptcy notice or bankruptcy restriction has been entered, he must as soon as practicable take such action as he considers necessary to resolve the doubt.

(3) In this rule –
'bankruptcy notice' means the notice which the registrar must enter in the register under section 86(2) of the Act, and
'bankruptcy restriction' means the restriction which the registrar must enter in the register under section 86(4) of the Act.

168[1] Registration of trustee in bankruptcy

(1) Where –
    (a) a proprietor has had a bankruptcy order made against him, or
    (b) an insolvency administration order has been made in respect of a deceased proprietor,
and the bankrupt's or deceased's registered estate or registered charge has vested in the trustee in bankruptcy, the trustee may apply for the alteration of the register by registering himself in place of the bankrupt or deceased proprietor.

(2) The application must be supported by, as appropriate –
    (a) the bankruptcy order relating to the bankrupt or the insolvency administration order relating to the deceased's estate, and
    (b) a certificate signed by the trustee that the registered estate or registered charge is comprised in the bankrupt's estate or deceased's estate, and
    (c) where the official receiver is the trustee, a certificate by him to that effect, and, where the trustee is another person, the evidence referred to in paragraph (3).

(3) The evidence referred to at paragraph (2)(c) is –
    (a) his certificate of appointment as trustee by the meeting of the bankrupt's or deceased debtor's creditors, or
    (b) his certificate of appointment as trustee by the Secretary of State, or
    (c) the order of the court appointing him trustee.

(4) In this rule, 'insolvency administration order' has the same meaning as in section 385(1) of the Insolvency Act 1986.

169[2] Trustee in bankruptcy vacating office

(1) This rule applies where –
    (a) a trustee in bankruptcy, who has been registered as proprietor, vacates his office, and
    (b) the official receiver or some other person has been appointed the trustee of the relevant bankrupt's estate, and
    (c) the official receiver or that person applies to be registered as proprietor in place of the former trustee.

(2) The application referred to in paragraph (1)(c) must be supported by the evidence required by rule 168(2)(c).

---

[1]   Commencement: 13 October 2003 (r 1; Land Registration Act 2002 (Commencement No 4) Order 2003, SI 2003/1725).
[2]   Commencement: 13 October 2003 (r 1; Land Registration Act 2002 (Commencement No 4) Order 2003, SI 2003/1725).

170[1] Description of trustee in register

Where the official receiver or another trustee in bankruptcy is registered as proprietor, the words 'Official Receiver and trustee in bankruptcy of [name]' or 'Trustee in bankruptcy of [name]' must be added to the register, as appropriate.

Overseas insolvency proceedings

171[2] Proceedings under the EC Regulation on insolvency proceedings

(1) A relevant person may apply for a note of a judgment opening insolvency proceedings to be entered in the register.

(2) An application under paragraph (1) must be accompanied by such evidence as the registrar may reasonably require.

(3) Following an application under paragraph (1) if the registrar is satisfied that the judgment opening insolvency proceedings has been made he may enter a note of the judgment in the register.

(4) In this rule –
'judgment opening insolvency proceedings' means a judgment opening proceedings within the meaning of article 3(1) of the Regulation,
'Regulation' means Council Regulation (EC) No 1346/2000,
'relevant person' means any person or body authorised under the provisions of article 22 of the Regulation to request or require an entry to be made in the register in respect of the judgment opening insolvency proceedings the subject of the application.

Pending land actions, writs and orders

172[3] Benefit of pending land actions, writs and orders

(1) For the purposes of section 34(1) of the Act, a relevant person shall be treated as having the benefit of the pending land action, writ or order, as appropriate.

(2) In determining whether a person has a sufficient interest in the making of an entry of a restriction under section 43(1)(c) of the Act, a relevant person shall be treated as having the benefit of the pending land action, writ or order, as appropriate.

(3) In this rule, 'a relevant person' means a person (or his assignee or chargee, if appropriate) who is taking any action or proceedings which are within section 87(1)(a) of the Act, or who has obtained a writ or order within section 87(1)(b) of the Act.

The Crown

173[4] Escheat etc

(1) Where a registered freehold estate in land has determined, the registrar may enter a note of that fact in the property register and in the property register of any inferior affected registered title.

---

[1]   Commencement: 13 October 2003 (r 1; Land Registration Act 2002 (Commencement No 4) Order 2003, SI 2003/1725).
[2]   Commencement: 13 October 2003 (r 1; Land Registration Act 2002 (Commencement No 4) Order 2003, SI 2003/1725).
[3]   Commencement: 13 October 2003 (r 1; Land Registration Act 2002 (Commencement No 4) Order 2003, SI 2003/1725).
[4]   Commencement: 13 October 2003 (r 1; Land Registration Act 2002 (Commencement No 4) Order 2003, SI 2003/1725).

(2) Where the registrar considers that there is doubt as to whether a registered freehold estate in land has determined, the entry under paragraph (1) must be modified by a statement to that effect.

Church of England

174[1] Entry of Incumbent on a transfer to the Church Commissioners
(1) Where by virtue of any Act or Measure a transfer to the Church Commissioners has the effect, subject only to being completed by registration, of vesting any registered land either immediately or at a subsequent time in an incumbent or any other ecclesiastical corporation sole, the registrar must register the incumbent or such other ecclesiastical corporation as proprietor upon receipt of –

    (a) an application,
    (b) the transfer to the Church Commissioners, and
    (c) a certificate by the Church Commissioners in Form 4.

(2) The certificate in Form 4 may be given either in the transfer or in a separate document.

(3) In this rule, 'Measure' means a Measure of the National Assembly of the Church of England or of the General Synod of the Church of England.

175[2] Entry of Church Commissioners etc as proprietor
(1) When any registered land is transferred to or (subject only to completion by registration) vested in the Church Commissioners, any ecclesiastical corporation, aggregate or sole, or any other person, by –
    (a) a scheme of the Church Commissioners, or
    (b) an instrument taking effect on publication in the London Gazette made pursuant to any Act or Measure relating to or administered by the Church Commissioners, or
    (c) any transfer authorised by any such Act or Measure,
the registrar must, on application, register the Church Commissioners, such ecclesiastical corporation or such other person as proprietor.

(2) The application must be accompanied by –
    (a) a certificate by the Church Commissioners in Form 5, and
    (b)
        (i) a copy of the London Gazette publishing the instrument, or
        (ii) the transfer (if any).

(3) The certificate in Form 5 may be given either in the transfer or in a separate document.

(4) In this rule, 'Measure' means a Measure of the National Assembly of the Church of England or of the General Synod of the Church of England.

Charities

176[3] Non-exempt charities – restrictions
(1) The restriction which the registrar is required by section 37(8) or section 39(1B) of the

1 Commencement: 13 October 2003 (r 1; Land Registration Act 2002 (Commencement No 4) Order 2003, SI 2003/1725).
2 Commencement: 13 October 2003 (r 1; Land Registration Act 2002 (Commencement No 4) Order 2003, SI 2003/1725).
3 Commencement: 13 October 2003 (r 1; Land Registration Act 2002 (Commencement No 4) Order 2003, SI 2003/1725).

Charities Act 1993 to enter in the register where one of those subsections applies must be the appropriate restriction.

(2) Any of the following applications must, if they relate to a registered or unregistered estate held by or in trust for a non-exempt charity, be accompanied by an application for entry of the appropriate restriction unless, in the case of a registered estate, that restriction is already in the register –

    (a) an application for first registration of an unregistered estate unless the disposition which triggers the requirement of registration is effected by an instrument containing the statement set out in rule 179(b) or rule 180(2)(b) or (c),

    (b) an application to register a transfer of a registered estate unless the disposition is effected by an instrument containing the statement set out in rule 179(b),

    (c) an application under rule 161 to register the vesting of a registered estate in a person other than the proprietor of that estate.

(3) Where a registered estate is held by or in trust for a corporation and the corporation becomes a non-exempt charity, the charity trustees must apply for entry of the appropriate restriction.

(4) In this rule 'the appropriate restriction' means a restriction in Form E.

177[1] Registration of trustees incorporated under Part VII of the Charities Act 1993
In any registrable disposition in favour of charity trustees incorporated under Part VII of the Charities Act 1993 they must be described as 'a body corporate under Part VII of the Charities Act 1993' and the application to register the disposition must be accompanied by the certificate granted by the Charity Commissioners under section 50 of that Act.

178[2] Registration of official custodian
(1) An application to register the official custodian as proprietor of a registered estate or a registered charge must be accompanied by –

    (a) an order of the court made under section 21(1) of the Charities Act 1993, or

    (b) an order of the Charity Commissioners made under sections 16 or 18 of the Charities Act 1993.

(2) Where the estate or charge is vested in the official custodian by virtue of an order under section 18 of the Charities Act 1993, an application to register him as proprietor (whether under Chapter 1 of Part 2 of the Act or following a registrable disposition) must be accompanied by an application for the entry of a restriction in Form F.

(3) Where the official custodian is registered as proprietor of a registered estate or a registered charge, except where the estate or charge is vested in him by virtue of an order under section 18 of the Charities Act 1993, the address of the charity trustees or, where the registered estate or registered charge is held on behalf of a charity which is a corporation, the address of the charity, must be entered in the register as his address for service under rule 198.

179[3] Statements to be contained in dispositions in favour of a charity
The statement required by section 37(5) of the Charities Act 1993 must, in an instrument to which section 37(7) of that Act applies, be in one of the following forms –

[1]   Commencement: 13 October 2003 (r 1; Land Registration Act 2002 (Commencement No 4) Order 2003, SI 2003/1725).
[2]   Commencement: 13 October 2003 (r 1; Land Registration Act 2002 (Commencement No 4) Order 2003, SI 2003/1725).
[3]   Commencement: 13 October 2003 (r 1; Land Registration Act 2002 (Commencement No 4) Order 2003, SI 2003/1725).

(a) 'The land transferred (or as the case may be) will, as a result of this transfer (or as the case may be) be held by (or in trust for) (charity), an exempt charity.'

(b) 'The land transferred (or as the case may be) will, as a result of this transfer (or as the case may be) be held by (or in trust for) (charity), a non-exempt charity, and the restrictions on disposition imposed by section 36 of the Charities Act 1993 will apply to the land (subject to section 36(9) of that Act).'.

180[1] Statements to be contained in dispositions by a charity

(1) The statement required by section 37(1) of the Charities Act 1993 must, in an instrument to which section 37(7) of that Act applies, be in one of the following forms –

(a) 'The land transferred (or as the case may be) is held by [(proprietors) in trust for] (charity), an exempt charity.'

(b) 'The land transferred (or as the case may be) is held by [(proprietors) in trust for] (charity), a non-exempt charity, but this transfer (or as the case may be) is one falling within paragraph ((a), (b) or (c) as the case may be) of section 36(9) of the Charities Act 1993.'

(c) 'The land transferred (or as the case may be) is held by [(proprietors) in trust for] (charity), a non-exempt charity, and this transfer (or as the case may be) is not one falling within paragraph (a), (b) or (c) of section 36(9) of the Charities Act 1993, so that the restrictions on disposition imposed by section 36 of that Act apply to the land.'.

(2) The statement required by section 39(1) of the Charities Act 1993 must, in a mortgage which is a registrable disposition or to which section 4(1)(g) of the Act applies, be in one of the following forms –

(a) 'The land charged is held by (or in trust for) (charity), an exempt charity.'

(b) 'The land charged is held by (or in trust for) (charity), a non-exempt charity, but this charge (or mortgage) is one falling within section 38(5) of the Charities Act 1993.'

(c) 'The land charged is held by (or in trust for) (charity), a non-exempt charity, and this charge (or mortgage) is not one falling within section 38(5) of the Charities Act 1993, so that the restrictions imposed by section 38 of that Act apply.'.

(3) The statement required by section 39(1A)(b) of the Charities Act 1993 must be in the following form –

'The restrictions on disposition imposed by section 36 of the Charities Act 1993 also apply to the land (subject to section 36(9) of that Act).'.

Companies and other corporations

181[2] Registration of companies and limited liability partnerships

(1) Where a company registered in England and Wales or Scotland under the Companies Acts applies to be registered as proprietor of a registered estate or of a registered charge, the application must state the company's registered number.

(2) If the company is a registered social landlord within the meaning of the Housing Act 1996, the application must also contain or be accompanied by a certificate to that effect.

(3) If the company is an unregistered housing association within the meaning of the Housing Associations Act 1985 and the application relates to grant-aided land as defined in Schedule 1 to that Act, the application must also contain or be accompanied by a certificate to that effect.

---

[1] Commencement: 13 October 2003 (r 1; Land Registration Act 2002 (Commencement No 4) Order 2003, SI 2003/1725).

[2] Commencement: 13 October 2003 (r 1; Land Registration Act 2002 (Commencement No 4) Order 2003, SI 2003/1725).

(4) Where a limited liability partnership incorporated under the Limited Liability Partnerships Act 2000 applies to be registered as proprietor of a registered estate or of a registered charge, the application must state the limited liability partnership's registered number.

182[1] Registration of trustees of charitable, ecclesiastical or public trust

(1) Subject to paragraph (4), where a corporation or body of trustees holding on charitable, ecclesiastical or public trusts applies to be registered as proprietor of a registered estate or registered charge, the application must be accompanied by the document creating the trust.

(2) If the registered estate or registered charge to which the application relates is held on trust for a registered social landlord within the meaning of the Housing Act 1996, the application must also contain or be accompanied by a certificate to that effect.

(3) If the registered estate or registered charge to which the application relates is held on trust for an unregistered housing association within the meaning of the Housing Associations Act 1985 and is grant-aided land as defined in Schedule 1 to that Act, the application must also contain or be accompanied by a certificate to that effect.

(4) Paragraph (1) of this rule does not apply in the case of a registered estate or a registered charge held by or in trust for a non-exempt charity.

183[2] Registration of other corporations

(1) Where a corporation aggregate, to which rules 181 and 182 do not apply, makes an application to be registered as proprietor of a registered estate or registered charge the application must also be accompanied by evidence of the extent of its powers to hold and sell, mortgage, lease and otherwise deal with land and, in the case of a charge, to lend money on mortgage.

(2) The evidence must include the charter, statute, rules, memorandum and articles of association or other documents constituting the corporation, together with such further evidence as the registrar may require.

(3) If the corporation is a registered social landlord within the meaning of the Housing Act 1996, the application must contain or be accompanied by a certificate to that effect.

(4) If the corporation is an unregistered housing association within the meaning of the Housing Associations Act 1985 and the application relates to grant-aided land as defined in Schedule 1 to that Act, the application must contain or be accompanied by a certificate to that effect.

184[3] Administration orders and liquidation of a company

(1) Paragraph (2) applies where a company which is the registered proprietor of a registered estate or registered charge [enters administration][4] under the Insolvency Act 1986.

(2) Upon the application of the company's administrator, supported by the order [or the notice of appointment][5], the registrar must make an entry in the individual register of the relevant

[1]   Commencement: 13 October 2003 (r 1; Land Registration Act 2002 (Commencement No 4) Order 2003, SI 2003/1725).
[2]   Commencement: 13 October 2003 (r 1; Land Registration Act 2002 (Commencement No 4) Order 2003, SI 2003/1725).
[3]   Commencement: 13 October 2003 (r 1; Land Registration Act 2002 (Commencement No 4) Order 2003, SI 2003/1725).
[4]   Amendment: Words substituted: Enterprise Act 2002 (Insolvency) Order 2003, SI 2003/2096, with effect from 15 September 2003, except in relation to any case where a petition for an administration order was presented before that date.
[5]   Amendment: Words inserted: Enterprise Act 2002 (Insolvency) Order 2003, SI 2003/2096, with effect from 15 September 2003, except in relation to any case where a petition for an administration order was presented before that date.

registered title as to the making of the order [or the notice of appointment]¹ and the appointment of the administrator.

(3) Paragraphs (4) and (5) apply where a company which is the registered proprietor of a registered estate or registered charge is in liquidation.

(4) Upon the application of the company's liquidator, the registrar must make an entry in the individual register of the relevant registered title as to the appointment of the liquidator.

(5) The application under paragraph (4) must be supported by the order, appointment by the Secretary of State or resolution under which the liquidator was appointed and such other evidence as the registrar may require.

185² Note of dissolution of a corporation

Where a corporation shown in an individual register as the proprietor of the registered estate or of a registered charge has been dissolved, the registrar may enter a note of that fact in the proprietorship register or in the charges register, as appropriate.

Settlements

186³ Settlements

Schedule 7 (which makes provision for the purposes of the Act in relation to the application to registered land of the enactments relating to settlements under the Settled Land Act 1925) has effect.

Adverse Possession

187⁴ Interpretation

Where the application is to be registered as proprietor of a registered rentcharge, the references in rules 188, 189, 190, 192 and 193 to Schedule 6 to the Act are to Schedule 6 as applied by rule 191.

188⁵ Applications for registration - procedure

(1) An application under paragraphs 1 or 6 of Schedule 6 to the Act must be in Form ADV1 and be accompanied by –

  (a) a statutory declaration made by the applicant not more than one month before the application is taken to have been made, together with any supporting statutory declarations, to provide evidence of adverse possession of the registered estate in land or rentcharge against which the application is made for a period which if it were to continue from the date of the applicant's statutory declaration to the date of the application would be –

---

¹ Amendment: Words inserted: Enterprise Act 2002 (Insolvency) Order 2003, SI 2003/2096, with effect from 15 September 2003, except in relation to any case where a petition for an administration order was presented before that date.

² Commencement: 13 October 2003 (r 1; Land Registration Act 2002 (Commencement No 4) Order 2003, SI 2003/1725).

³ Commencement: 13 October 2003 (r 1; Land Registration Act 2002 (Commencement No 4) Order 2003, SI 2003/1725).

⁴ Commencement: 13 October 2003 (r 1; Land Registration Act 2002 (Commencement No 4) Order 2003, SI 2003/1725).

⁵ Commencement: 13 October 2003 (r 1; Land Registration Act 2002 (Commencement No 4) Order 2003, SI 2003/1725).

(i)   where the application is under paragraph 1, of not less than ten years (or sixty years, if paragraph 13 of Schedule 6 to the Act applies) ending on the date of the application, or

(ii) where the application is under paragraph 6, of not less than two years beginning with the date of rejection of the original application under paragraph 1 and ending on the date of the application,

(b)   any additional evidence which the applicant considers necessary to support the claim.

(2) The statutory declaration by an applicant in support of an application under paragraph 1 of Schedule 6 to the Act must also –

(a)   exhibit a plan enabling the extent of the land to be identified on the Ordnance Survey map, unless the application is to be registered as proprietor of a registered rentcharge,

(b)   if reliance is placed on paragraph 1(2) of Schedule 6 to the Act, contain the facts relied upon with any appropriate exhibits,

(c)   contain confirmation that paragraph 1(3) of Schedule 6 to the Act does not apply,

(d)   where the application is to be registered as proprietor of a registered rentcharge, contain confirmation that the proprietor of the registered rentcharge has not re-entered the land out of which the rentcharge issues,

(e)   contain confirmation that to the best of his knowledge the restriction on applications in paragraph 8 of Schedule 6 to the Act does not apply,

(f)   contain confirmation that to the best of his knowledge the estate or rentcharge is not, and has not been during any of the period of alleged adverse possession, subject to a trust (other than one where the interest of each of the beneficiaries is an interest in possession),

(g)   if, should a person given notice under paragraph 2 of Schedule 6 to the Act require the application to be dealt with under paragraph 5 of that Schedule, it is intended to rely on one or more of the conditions set out in paragraph 5 of Schedule 6 to the Act, contain the facts supporting such reliance.

(3) The statutory declaration by an applicant in support of an application under paragraph 6 of Schedule 6 to the Act must also –

(a)   exhibit a plan enabling the extent of the land to be identified on the Ordnance Survey map, unless the application is to be registered as proprietor of a registered rentcharge or the extent is the same as in the previous rejected application,

(b)   contain full details of the previous rejected application,

(c)   contain confirmation that to the best of his knowledge the restriction on applications in paragraph 8 of Schedule 6 to the Act does not apply,

(d)   contain confirmation that to the best of his knowledge the estate or rentcharge is not, and has not been during any of the period of alleged adverse possession, subject to a trust (other than one where the interest of each of the beneficiaries is an interest in possession),

(e)   contain confirmation that paragraph 6(2) of Schedule 6 to the Act does not apply, and

(f)   where the application is to be registered as proprietor of a registered rentcharge, contain confirmation that the proprietor of the registered rentcharge has not re-entered the land out of which the rentcharge issues.

189[1]   Time limit for reply to a notice of an application

The period for the purpose of paragraph 3(2) of Schedule 6 to the Act is the period ending at 12 noon on the sixty-fifth business day after the date of issue of the notice.

---

[1]   Commencement: 13 October 2003 (r 1; Land Registration Act 2002 (Commencement No 4) Order 2003, SI 2003/1725).

190[1] Notice under paragraph 3(2) of Schedule 6 to the Act

(1) A notice to the registrar under paragraph 3(2) of Schedule 6 to the Act from a person given a registrar's notice must be –

(a) in Form NAP, and

(b) given to the registrar in the manner and at the address stated in the registrar's notice.

(2) Form NAP must accompany a registrar's notice.

(3) In this rule a 'registrar's notice' is a notice given by the registrar under paragraph 2 of Schedule 6 to the Act.

191[2] Adverse possession of rentcharges

Schedule 6 to the Act applies to the registration of an adverse possessor of a registered rentcharge in the modified form set out in Schedule 8.

192[3] Adverse possession of a rentcharge; non-payment of rent

(1) This rule applies where –

(a) a person is entitled to be registered as proprietor of a registered rentcharge under Schedule 6 to the Act, and

(b) if that person were so registered he would not be subject to a registered charge or registered lease or other interest protected in the register, and

(c) that person's adverse possession is based on non-payment of rent due under the registered rentcharge.

(2) Where paragraph (1) applies the registrar must –

(a) close the whole of the registered title of the registered rentcharge, or

(b) cancel the registered rentcharge, if the registered title to it also comprises other rentcharges.

193[4] Prohibition of recovery of rent after adverse possession of a rentcharge

(1) When –

(a) a person has been registered as proprietor of a rentcharge, or

(b) the registered title to a rentcharge has been closed, or

(c) a registered rentcharge has been cancelled, where the registered title also comprises other rentcharges,

following an application made under Schedule 6 to the Act, and, if appropriate, closure or cancellation under rule 192, no previous registered proprietor of the rentcharge may recover any rent due under the rentcharge from a person who has been in adverse possession of the rentcharge.

(2) Paragraph (1) applies whether the adverse possession arose either as a result of non-payment of the rent or by receipt of the rent from the person liable to pay it.

---

[1] Commencement: 13 October 2003 (r 1; Land Registration Act 2002 (Commencement No 4) Order 2003, SI 2003/1725).

[2] Commencement: 13 October 2003 (r 1; Land Registration Act 2002 (Commencement No 4) Order 2003, SI 2003/1725).

[3] Commencement: 13 October 2003 (r 1; Land Registration Act 2002 (Commencement No 4) Order 2003, SI 2003/1725).

[4] Commencement: 13 October 2003 (r 1; Land Registration Act 2002 (Commencement No 4) Order 2003, SI 2003/1725).

194¹ Registration as a person entitled to be notified of an application for adverse possession

(1) Any person who can satisfy the registrar that he has an interest in a registered estate in land or a registered rentcharge which would be prejudiced by the registration of any other person as proprietor of that estate under Schedule 6 to the Act or as proprietor of a registered rentcharge under that Schedule as applied by rule 191 may apply to be registered as a person to be notified under paragraph 2(1)(d) of Schedule 6.

(2) An application under paragraph (1) must be made in Form ADV2.

(3) The registrar must enter the name of the applicant in the proprietorship register as a person entitled to be notified under paragraph 2 of Schedule 6 to the Act.

Indemnity; interest on

195² Payment of interest on an indemnity

(1) Subject to paragraph (4), interest is payable on the amount of any indemnity paid under Schedule 8 to the Act for the period specified in paragraph (2) at the rate specified in paragraph (3).

(2) Interest is payable –
    (a) where paragraph 1(1)(a) of Schedule 8 applies, from the date of the rectification to the date of payment,
    (b) where any other sub-paragraph of paragraph 1(1) of Schedule 8 applies, from the date the loss is suffered by reason of the relevant mistake, loss, destruction or failure to the date of payment,

but excluding any period or periods where the registrar or the court is satisfied that the claimant has not taken reasonable steps to pursue with due diligence the claim for indemnity or, where relevant, the application for rectification.

(3) Interest is payable at the applicable rate or rates set for court judgment debts.

(4) Interest is payable in respect of an indemnity on account of costs or expenses within paragraph 3 of Schedule 8 from the date when the claimant pays them to the date of payment.

(5) A reference in this rule to a period from a date to the date of payment excludes the former date but includes the latter date.

Statements under the Leasehold Reform, Housing and Urban Development Act 1993

196³ Statements in transfers or conveyances and leases under the Leasehold Reform, Housing and Urban Development Act 1993

(1) The statement required by section 34(10) of the Leasehold Reform, Housing and Urban Development Act 1993 to be contained in a conveyance executed for the purposes of Chapter I of Part I of that Act must be in the following form:
    'This conveyance (or transfer) is executed for the purposes of Chapter I of Part I of the Leasehold Reform, Housing and Urban Development Act 1993.'.

(2) The statement required by section 57(11) of the Leasehold Reform, Housing and Urban

---

1   Commencement: 13 October 2003 (r 1; Land Registration Act 2002 (Commencement No 4) Order 2003, SI 2003/1725).
2   Commencement: 13 October 2003 (r 1; Land Registration Act 2002 (Commencement No 4) Order 2003, SI 2003/1725).
3   Commencement: 13 October 2003 (r 1; Land Registration Act 2002 (Commencement No 4) Order 2003, SI 2003/1725).

Development Act 1993 to be contained in any new lease granted under section 56 of that Act must be in the following form:

'This lease is granted under section 56 of the Leasehold Reform, Housing and Urban Development Act 1993.'.

PART 15
GENERAL PROVISIONS

Notices and Addresses for Service

197[1] Content of notice
(1) Every notice given by the registrar must –
   (a) fix the time within which the recipient is to take any action required by the notice,
   (b) state what the consequence will be of a failure to take such action as is required by the notice within the time fixed,
   (c) state the manner in which any reply to the notice must be given and the address to which it must be sent.

(2) Except where otherwise provided by these rules, the time fixed by the notice will be the period ending at 12 noon on the fifteenth business day after the date of issue of the notice.

198[2] Address for service of notice
(1) A person who is (or will as a result of an application be) a person within paragraph (2) must give the registrar an address for service to which all notices and other communications to him by the registrar may be sent, as provided by paragraph (3).

(2) The persons referred to in paragraph (1) are –
   (a) the registered proprietor of a registered estate or registered charge,
   (b) the registered beneficiary of a unilateral notice,
   (c) a cautioner named in an individual caution register,
   (d) a person whose name and address is required to be included in a standard restriction set out in Schedule 4 or whose consent or certificate is required, or upon whom notice is required to be served by the registrar or another person, under any other restriction,
   (e) a person entitled to be notified of an application for adverse possession under rule 194,
   (f) a person who objects to an application under section 73 of the Act,
   (g) a person who gives notice to the registrar under paragraph 3(2) of Schedule 6 to the Act, and
   (h) any person who while dealing with the registrar in connection with registered land or a caution against first registration is requested by the registrar to give an address for service.

(3) A person within paragraph (1) must give the registrar an address for service which is a postal address, whether or not in the United Kingdom.

(4) A person within paragraph (1) may give the registrar one or two additional addresses for service, provided that he may not have more than three addresses for service, and the address or addresses must be –
   (a) a postal address, whether or not in the United Kingdom, or
   (b) subject to paragraph (7), a box number at a United Kingdom document exchange, or
   (c) an electronic address.

---

[1] Commencement: 13 October 2003 (r 1; Land Registration Act 2002 (Commencement No 4) Order 2003, SI 2003/1725).
[2] Commencement: 13 October 2003 (r 1; Land Registration Act 2002 (Commencement No 4) Order 2003, SI 2003/1725).

(5) Subject to paragraphs (3) and (4) a person within paragraph (1) may give the registrar a replacement address for service.

(6) A cautioner who is entered in the register of title in respect of a caution against dealings under section 54 of the Land Registration Act 1925 may give the registrar a replacement or additional address for service provided that –
  (a) he may not have more than three addresses for service,
  (b) one of his addresses for service must be a postal address, whether or not in the United Kingdom, and
  (c) all of his addresses for service must be such addresses as are mentioned in paragraph (4).

(7) The box number referred to at paragraph (4)(b) must be at a United Kingdom document exchange to which delivery can be made on behalf of the land registry under arrangements already in existence between the land registry and a service provider at the time the box number details are provided to the registrar under this rule.

(8) In this rule an electronic address means –
  (a) an e-mail address, or
  (b) any other form of electronic address specified in a direction under paragraph (9).

(9) If the registrar is satisfied that a form of electronic address, other than an e-mail address, is a suitable form of address for service he may issue a direction to that effect.

(10) A direction under paragraph (9) may contain such conditions or limitations or both as the registrar considers appropriate.

(11) A person within paragraph (2)(d) shall be treated as having complied with any duty imposed on him under paragraph (1) where rule 92(2)(b) has been complied with.

199[1] Service of notice

(1) All notices which the registrar is required to give may be served –
  (a) by post, to any postal address in the United Kingdom entered in the register as an address for service,
  (b) by post, to any postal address outside the United Kingdom entered in the register as an address for service,
  (c) by leaving the notice at any postal address in the United Kingdom entered in the register as an address for service,
  (d) by directing the notice to the relevant box number at any document exchange entered in the register as an address for service,
  (e) by electronic transmission to the electronic address entered in the register as an address for service,
  (f) subject to paragraph (3), by fax, or
  (g) by any of the methods of service given in sub-paragraphs (a), (b), (c) and (d) to any other address where the registrar believes the addressee is likely to receive it.

(2) In paragraph (1) references to an address or box number 'entered in the register as an address for service' include an address for service given under rule 198(2)(h), whether or not it is entered in the register.

(3) The notice may be served by fax if the recipient has informed the registrar in writing –
  (a) that the recipient is willing to accept service of the notice by fax, and
  (b) of the fax number to which it should be sent.

---

[1]   Commencement: 13 October 2003 (r 1; Land Registration Act 2002 (Commencement No 4) Order 2003, SI 2003/1725).

(4) Service of a notice which is served in accordance with this rule shall be regarded as having taken place at the time shown in the table below –

Method of service	Time of service
Post to an address in the United Kingdom	The second working day after posting
Leaving at a postal address	The working day after it was left
Post to an address outside the United Kingdom	The seventh working day after posting
Document exchange	On the second working day after it was left at the registrar's document exchange
Fax	The working day after transmission
Electronic transmission to an electronic address	The second working day after transmission

(5) In this rule 'post' means pre-paid delivery by a postal service which seeks to deliver documents within the United Kingdom no later than the next working day in all or the majority of cases, and to deliver outside the United Kingdom within such a period as is reasonable in all the circumstances.

(6) In paragraphs (4) and (5), 'working day' means any day from Monday to Friday (inclusive) which is not Christmas Day, Good Friday or any other day either specified or declared by proclamation under section 1 of the Banking and Financial Dealings Act 1971 or appointed by the Lord Chancellor.

Specialist assistance

200[1] Use of specialist assistance by the registrar
(1) The registrar may refer to an appropriate specialist –
   (a) the examination of the whole or part of any title lodged with an application for first registration, or
   (b) any question or other matter which arises in the course of any proceedings before the registrar and which, in his opinion, requires the advice of an appropriate specialist.

(2) The registrar may act upon the advice or opinion of an appropriate specialist to whom he has referred a matter under paragraph (1).

(3) In this rule, 'appropriate specialist' means a person who the registrar considers has the appropriate knowledge, experience and expertise to advise on the matter referred to him.

Proceedings before the registrar

201[2] Production of documents
(1) The registrar may only exercise the power conferred on him by section 75(1) of the Act if he receives from a person who is a party to proceedings before him a request that he should require a document holder to produce a document for the purpose of those proceedings.

(2) The request must be made –
   (a) in paper form in Form PRD1 delivered to such office of the land registry as the registrar may direct, or

---

[1] Commencement: 13 October 2003 (r 1; Land Registration Act 2002 (Commencement No 4) Order 2003, SI 2003/1725).
[2] Commencement: 13 October 2003 (r 1; Land Registration Act 2002 (Commencement No 4) Order 2003, SI 2003/1725).

(b) during the currency of a relevant notice given under Schedule 2, and subject to and in accordance with the limitations contained in the notice, by delivering the request to the registrar, by any means of communication, other than as mentioned in sub-paragraph (a).

(3) The registrar must give notice of the request to the document holder.

(4) The address for the document holder provided in Form PRD1 is to be regarded for the purpose of rule 199 as an address for service given under rule 198(2)(h).

(5) The notice must give the document holder a period ending at 12 noon on the twentieth business day after the issue of the notice, or such other period as the registrar thinks appropriate, to deliver a written response to the registrar by the method and to the address stated in the notice.

(6) The response must –
    (a) state whether or not the document holder opposes the request,
    (b) if he does, state in full the grounds for that opposition,
    (c) give an address to which communications may be sent, and
    (d) be signed by the document holder or his conveyancer.

(7) The registrar must determine the matter on the basis of the request and any response submitted to him and, subject to paragraph (8), he may make the requirement by sending a notice in Form PRD2 to the document holder if he is satisfied that –
    (a) the document is in the control of the document holder, and
    (b) the document may be relevant to the proceedings, and
    (c) disclosure of the document is necessary in order to dispose fairly of the proceedings or to save costs,
and he is not aware of any valid ground entitling the document holder to withhold the document.

(8) The registrar may, as a condition of making the requirement, provide that the person who has made the request should pay the reasonable costs incurred in complying with the requirement by the document holder.

(9) In this rule, 'document holder' means the person who is alleged to have control of a document which is the subject of a request under paragraph (1).

202[1] Costs

(1) A person who has incurred costs in relation to proceedings before the registrar may request the registrar to make an order requiring a party to those proceedings to pay the whole or part of those costs.

(2) The registrar may only order a party to proceedings before him to pay costs where those costs have been occasioned by the unreasonable conduct of that party in relation to the proceedings.

(3) Subject to paragraph (5), a request for the payment of costs must be made by delivering to the registrar a written statement in paper form by 12 noon on the twentieth business day after the completion of the proceedings to which the request relates.

(4) The statement must –
    (a) identify the party against whom the order is sought and include an address where notice may be served on that party,

---

[1]   Commencement: 13 October 2003 (r 1; Land Registration Act 2002 (Commencement No 4) Order 2003, SI 2003/1725).

    (b) state in full the grounds for the request,

    (c) give an address to which communications may be sent, and

    (d) be signed by the person making the request or his conveyancer.

(5) During the currency of a relevant notice given under Schedule 2, and subject to and in accordance with the limitations contained in the notice, a request under this rule may also be made by delivering the written statement to the registrar, by any means of communication, other than as mentioned in paragraph (3).

(6) The registrar must give notice of the request to the party against whom the order is sought at the address provided under paragraph (4)(a) and if that party has an address for service in an individual register that relates to the proceedings, at that address.

(7) An address for a party provided under paragraph (4)(a) is to be regarded for the purpose of rule 199 as if it was an address for service given under rule 198(2)(h).

(8) The notice must give the recipient a period ending at 12 noon on the twentieth business day after the issue of the notice, or such other period as the registrar thinks appropriate, to deliver a written response to the registrar by the method and to the address stated in the notice.

(9) The response must –

    (a) state whether or not the recipient opposes the request,

    (b) if he does, state in full the grounds for that opposition,

    (c) give an address to which communications may be sent, and

    (d) be signed by the recipient or his conveyancer.

(10) The registrar must determine the matter on the basis of: the written request and any response submitted to him, all the circumstances including the conduct of the parties, and the result of any enquiries he considers it necessary to make.

(11) The registrar must send to all parties his written reasons for any order he makes under paragraph (1).

(12) An order under paragraph (1) may –

    (a) require a party against whom it is made to pay to the requesting party the whole or such part as the registrar thinks fit of the costs incurred in the proceedings by the requesting party,

    (b) specify the sum to be paid or require the costs to be assessed by the court (if not otherwise agreed), and specify the basis of the assessment to be used by the court.

Retention and return of documents

203[1] Retention of documents on completion of an application

(1) Subject to paragraphs (2) to (5), on completion of any application the registrar may retain all or any of the documents that accompanied the application and must return all other such documents to the applicant or as otherwise specified in the application.

(2) When making an application, an applicant or his conveyancer may request the return of all or any of the documents accompanying the application.

(3) Except on an application for first registration, a person making a request under paragraph (2) must deliver with the application certified copies of the documents which are the subject of the request.

(4) On an application for first registration, a person making a request under paragraph (2) for

---

[1]   Commencement: 13 October 2003 (r 1; Land Registration Act 2002 (Commencement No 4) Order 2003, SI 2003/1725).

the return of any statutory declaration, subsisting lease, subsisting charge or the latest document of title must deliver with the application certified copies of any such documents as are the subject of the request, but shall not be required to deliver copies of any other documents.

(5) Subject to the delivery of any certified copies required under paragraphs (3) or (4), the registrar must comply with any request made under paragraph (2).

(6) The registrar may destroy any document retained under paragraph (1) if he is satisfied that either –

(a) he has made and retained a sufficient copy of the document, or

(b) further retention of the document is unnecessary.

(7) If the registrar considers that he no longer requires delivery of certified copies of documents, or classes of documents, under this rule he may, in such manner as he thinks appropriate for informing persons who wish to make applications, give notice to that effect and on and after the date specified in such notice –

(a) the requirement under this rule to deliver certified copies of the documents covered by the notice no longer applies, and

(b) the registrar may amend any Schedule 1 form to reflect that fact.

(8) In paragraph (4) the 'latest document of title' means the document vesting the estate sought to be registered in the applicant or where the estate vested in the applicant by operation of law the most recent document that vested the estate in a predecessor of the applicant.

204[1] Request for the return of certain documents

(1) This rule applies to all documents on which any entry in the register of title is or was founded and which are kept by the registrar on the relevant date.

(2) During the period of 5 years beginning with the relevant date any person who delivered a document to the registrar may request the return of that document.

(3) Where at the time of the delivery of the document the person delivering the document was the registered proprietor, or was applying to become the registered proprietor, of any registered estate or registered charge in respect of which the entry referred to in paragraph (1) was made, a person who is at the date of the request the registered proprietor of any part of the same registered estate or registered charge may make a request under paragraph (2) for the document to be returned to him.

(4) Subject to paragraph (5), if, at the date of the request under paragraph (2), the document is kept by the registrar he must return it to the person making the request.

(5) If the registrar receives more than one request under paragraph (2) in respect of the same document, he may either retain the document or, in his discretion, return it to one of the persons making a request.

(6) At the end of the period mentioned in paragraph (2) if there is no outstanding request in relation to the document the registrar may destroy any document if he is satisfied that –

(a) he has retained a copy of the document, or

(b) further retention of the document is unnecessary.

(7) Where a request is made for the return of a document after the end of the period mentioned in paragraph (2), the registrar may treat the request as a request under paragraph (2).

(8) The 'relevant date' for the purpose of this rule is the date on which these rules come into force.

---

[1]   Commencement: 13 October 2003 (r 1; Land Registration Act 2002 (Commencement No 4) Order 2003, SI 2003/1725).

205[1] Release of documents kept by the registrar

The registrar may release any document retained under rule 203(1) or to which rule 204 applies upon such terms, if any, for its return as he considers appropriate.

Forms

206[2] Use of forms

(1) Subject to paragraph (4) and to rules 208 and 209, the Schedule 1 forms must be used where required by these rules and must be prepared in accordance with the requirements of rules 210 and 211.

(2) Subject to paragraph (4) and to rules 208 and 209, except where these rules require the use of a Schedule 1 form, the Schedule 3 forms must be used in all matters to which they refer, or are capable of being applied or adapted, with such alterations and additions as are desired and the registrar allows.

(3) Subject to rule 208(2), the forms of execution in Schedule 9 must be used in the execution of dispositions in the scheduled forms in the cases for which they are provided, or are capable of being applied or adapted, with such alterations and additions, if any, as the registrar may allow.

(4) A requirement in these rules to use a scheduled form is subject, where appropriate, to the provisions in these rules relating to the making of applications and issuing results of applications other than in paper form, during the currency of a notice given under Schedule 2.

207[3] Adaptation of certain Schedule 1 forms to provide for direct debit

(1) This rule applies where –
  (a) a Schedule 1 form has a payment of fee panel which does not provide for payment by direct debit, and
  (b) a fee order made under section 102 of the Act and sections 2 and 3 of the Public Offices Fees Act 1879 permits, where there is an agreement with the registrar, payment by direct debit of the fee for the matter in respect of which that form is prescribed, and
  (c) the registrar intends to enter into an agreement under the fee order which will enable a person to pay that fee by direct debit.

(2) Where paragraph (1) applies the registrar may amend the payment of fee panel of the affected form to include provision for payment by direct debit and make any consequential amendments to the form.

(3) Where a form has been amended under paragraph (2) a person not paying by direct debit may use the form as amended or as unamended.

208[4] Welsh language forms

(1) Where the registrar, in exercise of his powers under section 100(4) of the Act, publishes an instrument as the Welsh language version of a scheduled form, the instrument shall be regarded as being in the scheduled form.

---

1 Commencement: 13 October 2003 (r 1; Land Registration Act 2002 (Commencement No 4) Order 2003, SI 2003/1725).
2 Commencement: 13 October 2003 (r 1; Land Registration Act 2002 (Commencement No 4) Order 2003, SI 2003/1725).
3 Commencement: 13 October 2003 (r 1; Land Registration Act 2002 (Commencement No 4) Order 2003, SI 2003/1725).
4 Commencement: 13 October 2003 (r 1; Land Registration Act 2002 (Commencement No 4) Order 2003, SI 2003/1725).

(2) In place of the form of execution provided by Schedule 9, an instrument referred to in paragraph (1) may be executed using a form of execution approved by the registrar as the Welsh language version of the Schedule 9 form.

(3) An instrument containing a statement approved by the registrar as the Welsh language version of a statement prescribed by these rules shall be regarded as containing the prescribed statement.

(4) An instrument containing a provision approved by the registrar as the Welsh language version of a provision prescribed by these rules shall be regarded as containing the prescribed provision.

209[1] Use of non-prescribed forms
(1) This rule applies where –
  (a) an application should be accompanied by a scheduled form and a person wishes to make an application relying instead upon an alternative document that is not the relevant scheduled form, and
  (b) it is not possible for that person to obtain and lodge the relevant scheduled form (duly executed, if appropriate) at the land registry or it is only possible to do so at unreasonable expense.

(2) Such a person may make a request to the registrar, either before or at the time of making the application which should be accompanied by the relevant scheduled form, that he be permitted to rely upon the alternative document.

(3) The request must contain evidence to satisfy the registrar as mentioned in paragraph (1)(b) and include the original, or, if the request is made before the application, a copy, of the alternative document.

(4) If, after considering the request, the registrar is satisfied as mentioned at paragraph (1)(b) and that neither the rights of any person nor the keeping of the register are likely to be materially prejudiced by allowing the alternative document to be relied upon instead of the relevant scheduled form, he may permit such reliance.

(5) If the registrar allows the request it may be on condition that the person making the request provides other documents or evidence in support of the application.

(6) This rule is without prejudice to any of the registrar's powers under the Act.

210[2] Documents in a Schedule 1 form
(1) Subject to rule 211, any application or document in one of the Schedule 1 forms must –
  (a) be printed on durable A4 size paper,
  (b) be reproduced as set out in the Schedule as to its wording, layout, ruling, font and point size, and
  (c) contain all the information required in an easily legible form.

(2) Where on a Schedule 1 form (other than Form DL) any panel is insufficient in size to contain the required insertions, and the method of production of the form does not allow the depth of the panel to be increased, the information to be inserted in the panel must be continued on a continuation sheet in Form CS.

(3) When completing a Schedule 1 form containing an additional provisions panel, any

[1] Commencement: 13 October 2003 (r 1; Land Registration Act 2002 (Commencement No 4) Order 2003, SI 2003/1725).
[2] Commencement: 13 October 2003 (r 1; Land Registration Act 2002 (Commencement No 4) Order 2003, SI 2003/1725).

statement, certificate or application required or permitted by these rules to be included in the form for which the form does not otherwise provide and any additional provisions desired by the parties must be inserted in that panel or a continuation of it.

(4) Where the form consists of more than one sheet of paper, or refers to an attached plan or a continuation sheet, all the sheets and any plan must be securely fastened together.

211[1] Electronically produced forms

(1) Where the method of production of a Schedule 1 form permits –

(a) the depth of a panel may be increased or reduced to fit the material to be comprised in it, and a panel may be divided at a page break,

(b) instructions in italics may be omitted,

(c) inapplicable certificates and statements may be omitted,

(d) the plural may be used instead of the singular and the singular instead of the plural,

(e) panels which would contain only the panel number and the panel heading may be omitted, but such omission must not affect the numbering of subsequent panels,

(f) 'X' boxes may be omitted where all inapplicable statements and certificates have been omitted,

(g) the sub-headings in an additional provisions panel may be added to, amended, repositioned or omitted,

(h) 'Seller' may be substituted for 'Transferor' and 'Buyer' for 'Transferee' in a transfer on sale,

(i) the vertical lines which define the left and right boundaries of the panel may be omitted.

212[2] Documents where no form is prescribed

(1) Documents for which no form is prescribed must be in such form as the registrar may direct or allow.

(2) A document prepared under this rule must not bear the number of a Schedule 1 form.

(3) A document affecting a registered title must refer to the title number.

Documents accompanying applications

213[3] Identification of part of the registered title dealt with

(1) Subject to paragraphs (4) and (5) of this rule, a document lodged at the land registry dealing with part of the land in a registered title must have attached to it a plan identifying clearly the land dealt with.

(2) Where the document is a disposition, the disponor must sign the plan.

(3) Where the document is an application, the applicant must sign the plan.

(4) If the land dealt with is identified clearly on the title plan of the registered title, it may instead be described by reference to that title plan.

(5) Where a disposition complies with this rule, the application lodged in respect of it need not.

---

[1]   Commencement: 13 October 2003 (r 1; Land Registration Act 2002 (Commencement No 4) Order 2003, SI 2003/1725).

[2]   Commencement: 13 October 2003 (r 1; Land Registration Act 2002 (Commencement No 4) Order 2003, SI 2003/1725).

[3]   Commencement: 13 October 2003 (r 1; Land Registration Act 2002 (Commencement No 4) Order 2003, SI 2003/1725).

214[1] Lodging of copy instead of an original document

(1) Subject to paragraphs (2), (3) and (4), where a rule requires that an application be accompanied by an original document (for instance, a grant of representation) the applicant may, instead of lodging the original, lodge a certified or office copy of that document.

(2) This rule does not apply to –
  (a) any document required to be lodged under Part 4,
  (b) a scheduled form,
  (c) a document that is a registrable disposition.

(3) This rule does not apply also where the registrar considers that the circumstances are such that the original of a document should be lodged and the applicant has possession, or the right to possession, of that original document.

(4) Where this rule permits a certified or office copy of a document to be lodged the registrar may permit an uncertified copy of the document to be lodged instead.

215[2] Documents and other evidence in support of an application

(1) This rule applies where –
  (a) the lodging of a document (not being a scheduled form) or other evidence in support of an application is required by these rules, and
  (b) the document or other evidence is in the particular case unnecessary or the purpose of the lodging of the document or other evidence can be achieved by another document or other evidence.

(2) An applicant may request the registrar to be relieved of the requirement.

(3) The request must contain evidence to satisfy the registrar as mentioned in paragraph (1)(b).

(4) If, after considering the request, the registrar is satisfied as mentioned at paragraph (1)(b) and that neither the rights of any person nor the keeping of the register are likely to be materially prejudiced by relieving the applicant of the requirement, he may so relieve the applicant.

(5) If the registrar allows the request it may be on condition that the applicant provides other documents or evidence in support of the application.

(6) This rule is without prejudice to any of the registrar's powers under the Act.

Land Registry - when open to public

216[3] Days on which the Land Registry is open to the public

(1) Subject to paragraph (2), the land registry shall be open to the public daily except on Saturdays, Sundays, Christmas Day, Good Friday or any other day either specified or declared by proclamation under section 1 of the Banking and Financial Dealings Act 1971 or appointed by the Lord Chancellor.

(2) If the registrar is satisfied that adequate arrangements have been made or will be in place for opening the land registry to the public on Saturdays, he may, in such manner as he considers appropriate, give notice to that effect.

---

[1] Commencement: 13 October 2003 (r 1; Land Registration Act 2002 (Commencement No 4) Order 2003, SI 2003/1725).

[2] Commencement: 13 October 2003 (r 1; Land Registration Act 2002 (Commencement No 4) Order 2003, SI 2003/1725).

[3] Commencement: 13 October 2003 (r 1; Land Registration Act 2002 (Commencement No 4) Order 2003, SI 2003/1725).

(3) On and after the date specified in any notice given pursuant to paragraph (2), paragraph (1) shall have effect as though the word 'Saturdays' had been omitted.

(4) The date referred to in paragraph (3) must be at least eight weeks after the date of the notice.

(5) On and after the date specified in any notice given pursuant to paragraph (2), the periods in column 3 in the table below are substituted for the periods in column 2 in that table in the rules to which they relate.

(1) Rule	(2) Prescribed period before any notice given under rule 216(2) takes effect	(3) Prescribed period after any notice given under rule 216(2) takes effect
16(1)	Twenty business days	twenty-four business days
31(2)	the twentieth business day	the twenty-fourth business day
53(1)	the fifteenth business day	the eighteenth business day
53(1)	the thirtieth business day	the thirty-sixth business day
53(3)	the thirtieth business day	the thirty-sixth business day
53(4)	the fifteenth business day	the eighteenth business day
54(9)	the fourth business day	the fourth business day
55(4)	fifteen business days	Eighteen business days
86(3)	the fifteenth business day	the eighteenth business day
86(3)	the thirtieth business day	the thirty-sixth business day
86(5)	the thirtieth business day	the thirty-sixth business day
86(6)	the fifteenth business day	the eighteenth business day
92(9)	the fifteenth business day	the eighteenth business day
119(3)	the twentieth business day	the twenty-fourth business day
189	the sixty-fifth business day	the seventy-eighth business day
197(2)	the fifteenth business day	the eighteenth business day
201(5)	the twentieth business day	the twenty-fourth business day
202(3)	the twentieth business day	the twenty-fourth business day
202(8)	the twentieth business day	the twenty-fourth business day
218	the fifteenth business day	the eighteenth business day

Interpretation

217[1] General Interpretation

(1) In these rules –

'the Act' means the Land Registration Act 2002,

'affecting franchise' means a franchise which relates to a defined area of land and is an adverse right affecting, or capable of affecting, the title to an estate or charge,

'business day' means a day when the land registry is open to the public under rule 216,

'caution plan' has the meaning given by rule 41(4),

'caution title number' has the meaning given by rule 41(1),

---

[1] Commencement: 13 October 2003 (r 1; Land Registration Act 2002 (Commencement No 4) Order 2003, SI 2003/1725).

'certified copy' means a copy of a document which a conveyancer, or such other person as the registrar may permit, has certified on its face to be a true copy of the original and endorsed with his name and address, and the reference to a conveyancer includes where the document is one referred to in –

  (a)   rule 168(2)(a) or 168(3), the bankrupt's trustee in bankruptcy or the official receiver,
  (b)   rule 184(2), the company's administrator,
  (c)   rule 184(5), the company's liquidator,

'charges register' is the register so named in rule 4 the contents of which are described in rule 9,

'charity' and 'charity trustees' have the same meaning as in sections 96 and 97(1) of the Charities Act 1993 respectively,

'Companies Acts' means the Companies Act 1985, any Act amending or replacing that Act and any former enactment relating to companies,

'control' in relation to a document of which a person has control means physical possession, or the right to possession, or right to take copies of the document,

'conveyancer' means –

  (a)   a solicitor, or
  (b)   a licensed conveyancer within the meaning of section 11(2) of the Administration of Justice Act 1985, or
  (c)   a fellow of the Institute of Legal Executives,

  and a reference to a person's conveyancer is a reference to a solicitor, licensed conveyancer or fellow of the Institute of Legal Executives who is acting on that person's behalf,

'day list' has the same meaning given by rule 12,

'exempt charity' has the same meaning as in section 96 of the Charities Act 1993 and 'non-exempt charity' means a charity which is not an exempt charity,

'index map' has the meaning given by rule 10(1)(a),

'index of proprietors' names' has the meaning given by rule 11(1),

'index of relating franchises and manors' is the index described in rule 10(1)(b),

'individual caution register' is the register so named in rule 41(1) the arrangement of which is described in rule 41(2),

'individual register' is the register so named in rule 2 the contents and arrangement of which are described in rules 3 and 4,

'inheritance tax notice' means a notice in respect of an Inland Revenue charge arising under Part III of the Finance Act 1975 or section 237 of the Inheritance Tax Act 1984,

'matrimonial home rights caution' means a caution registered under the Matrimonial Homes Act 1967 before 14 February 1983,

'matrimonial home rights notice' means a notice registered under section 31(10)(a) or section 32 of, and paragraph 4(3)(a) or 4(3)(b) of Schedule 4 to, the Family Law Act 1996, or section 2(8) or section 5(3)(b) of the Matrimonial Homes Act 1983 or section 2(7) or section 5(3)(b) of the Matrimonial Homes Act 1967,

'official custodian' means the official custodian for charities,

'old tenancy' means a tenancy as defined in section 28 of the Landlord and Tenant (Covenants) Act 1995 which is not a new tenancy as defined in section 1 of that Act,

'overseas company' means a company incorporated outside Great Britain,

'property register' is the register so named in rule 4 the contents of which are described in rules 5, 6 and 7,

'proprietorship register' is the register so named in rule 4 the contents of which are described in rule 8,

'registered title' means an individual register and any title plan referred to in that register,

'relating franchise' means a franchise which is not an affecting franchise,

'Schedule 1 form' means a form in Schedule 1,

'Schedule 3 form' means a form in Schedule 3,

'scheduled form' means a Schedule 1 form or a Schedule 3 form,

'section 33(5) order' means an order made under section 33(5) of the Family Law Act 1996, 'statutory declaration' includes affidavit,

'title number' has the meaning given by rule 4,

'title plan' has the meaning given by rule 5,

'trust corporation' has the same meaning as in the Settled Land Act 1925,

'trusts' in relation to a charity has the same meaning as in section 97(1) of the Charities Act 1993,

'unregistered company' means a body corporate to which section 718(1) of the Companies Act 1985 applies.

(2) Subject to paragraph (3), a reference in these rules to a form by letter, or by number, or by a combination of both is to a scheduled form.

(3) A reference in these rules to Forms A to Y and Forms AA to HH (in each case inclusive) is to the standard form of restriction bearing that letter in Schedule 4.

PART 16
TRANSITIONAL

Cautions against dealings

218[1] Definitions
In this Part –

'the 1925 Act' means the Land Registration Act 1925,

'caution' means a caution entered in the register of title under section 54 of the 1925 Act,

'cautioner' includes his personal representative,

'the notice period' is the period ending at 12 noon on the fifteenth business day, or ending at 12 noon on such later business day as the registrar may allow, after the date of issue of the notice.

219[2] Consent under a caution
Any consent given under section 55 or 56 of the 1925 Act must be in writing signed by the person giving it or his conveyancer.

220[3] Notice under section 55(1) of the 1925 Act and under rule 223(3)
(1) Rule 199 applies to the method of service of a notice under section 55(1) of the 1925 Act and under rule 223(3).

(2) The notice period applies to a notice served under section 55(1) of the 1925 Act and to one served under rule 223(3).

221[4] Cautioner showing cause
(1) This rule applies where notice is served under section 55(1) of the 1925 Act or rule 223(3).

(2) At any time before expiry of the notice period, the cautioner may show cause why the registrar should not give effect to the application that resulted in the notice being served.

(3) To show cause, the cautioner must –

---

[1] Commencement: 13 October 2003 (r 1; Land Registration Act 2002 (Commencement No 4) Order 2003, SI 2003/1725).

[2] Commencement: 13 October 2003 (r 1; Land Registration Act 2002 (Commencement No 4) Order 2003, SI 2003/1725).

[3] Commencement: 13 October 2003 (r 1; Land Registration Act 2002 (Commencement No 4) Order 2003, SI 2003/1725).

[4] Commencement: 13 October 2003 (r 1; Land Registration Act 2002 (Commencement No 4) Order 2003, SI 2003/1725).

(a) deliver to the registrar, in the manner and to the address stated in the notice, a written statement signed by the cautioner or his conveyancer setting out the grounds relied upon, and

(b) show that he has a fairly arguable case for the registrar not to give effect to the application that resulted in the notice being served.

(4) If, after reading the written statement, and after making any enquiries he thinks necessary, the registrar is satisfied that cause has been shown, he must order that the caution is to continue until withdrawn or otherwise disposed of under these rules or the Act.

(5) Where the registrar makes an order under paragraph (4) –

(a) the registrar must give notice to the applicant and the cautioner that he has made the order and of the effect of sub-paragraph (b),

(b) the cautioner is to be treated as having objected under section 73 of the Act to the application that resulted in notice being served, and

(c) the notice given by the registrar under sub-paragraph (a) to the applicant is to be treated as notice given under section 73(5)(a) of the Act.

(6) If after service of the notice under section 55(1) of the 1925 Act or rule 223(3) the application that resulted in the notice being served is cancelled, withdrawn or otherwise does not proceed, the registrar must make an order that the caution will continue to have effect, unless he has already done so or the caution has been cancelled.

222[1] Withdrawal of a caution by the cautioner

(1) The cautioner may at any time apply to withdraw his caution in Form WCT.

(2) The form must be signed by the cautioner or his conveyancer.

223[2] Cancellation of a caution - application by the proprietor etc

(1) A person may apply to the registrar for the cancellation of a caution if he is –

(a) the proprietor of the registered estate or a registered charge to which the caution relates, or

(b) a person who, but for the existence of the caution, would be entitled to be registered as the proprietor of that estate or charge.

(2) An application for the cancellation of a caution must be in Form CCD.

(3) Where application is made under this rule, the registrar must give the cautioner notice of the application.

(4) Following the expiry of the notice period, unless the registrar makes an order under rule 221(4), the registrar must cancel the entry of the caution.

Rentcharges and adverse possession

224[3] Registered rentcharges held in trust under section 75(1) of the 1925 Act on commencement

Where a rentcharge is held in trust under section 75(1) of the Land Registration Act 1925

[1] Commencement: 13 October 2003 (r 1; Land Registration Act 2002 (Commencement No 4) Order 2003, SI 2003/1725).
[2] Commencement: 13 October 2003 (r 1; Land Registration Act 2002 (Commencement No 4) Order 2003, SI 2003/1725).
[3] Commencement: 13 October 2003 (r 1; Land Registration Act 2002 (Commencement No 4) Order 2003, SI 2003/1725).

immediately before the coming into force of section 97 of the Act, the beneficiary of the trust may apply –

    (a) to be registered as proprietor of the rentcharge, or

    (b) for the registration of the rentcharge to be cancelled.

Schedule 1
Schedule 1 Forms referred to in rules 206, 207 and 210

[Schedule 1 is not reproduced. However, some of the most commonly used Forms are reproduced at Appendix 2.]

Schedule 2[1]
Notices Publicising Arrangements for Electronic and Other Modes of Delivery of Applications and Other Matters

Rule 14

1

If the registrar is satisfied that adequate arrangements have been made or will be in place for dealing with the applications and other matters specified in paragraph 2 by means other than post, document exchange or personal delivery, he may, in such manner as he thinks appropriate, give notice publicising the arrangements.

2

The applications and other matters referred to in paragraph 1 are –

    (a) an application by electronic means under rule 14,

    (b) an outline application under rule 54,

    (c) a notification of discharge or release of a registered charge under rule 115,

    (d) an application and the result of an application or search under Part 13 to which rule 132 applies,

    (e) information requested by an applicant for an official search for the purpose of the Family Law Act 1996 under rule 160,

    (f) a request to the registrar that he require a person to produce documents under rule 201(2)(b),

    (g) a request for an order requiring a party to proceedings before the registrar to pay costs under rule 202(5).

3

Subject to paragraphs 4, 5 and 6, a notice given under paragraph 1 will be current from the time specified in the notice until the time, if any, specified in the notice or if no expiry date is specified in the notice, indefinitely.

4

A notice given under paragraph 1 may from time to time be varied, suspended, withdrawn, renewed or replaced by a further notice.

5

If and so long as owing the breakdown or other unavailability of facilities or data involved in giving effect to the arrangements made for dealing with applications covered by a notice given under paragraph 1, such arrangements cease, in whole or in part, to be effective, the notice shall cease, to the necessary extent, to be treated as current.

---

[1] Commencement: 13 October 2003 (r 1; Land Registration Act 2002 (Commencement No 4) Order 2003, SI 2003/1725).

6

Paragraph 5 will apply despite the absence of a variation, suspension or withdrawal of the notice under paragraph 4.

7

The provisions referred to in paragraph 2 will not prevent the registrar, at his discretion, from refusing to accept an application or request made, or to issue a result, under any of those provisions in an individual case.

Schedule 3
Schedule 3 Forms referred to in rule 206

Schedule 3 is not reproduced. It consists of:

Form 1 – Certificate as to execution of power of attorney (rule 61);
Form 2 – Statutory declaration/certificate as to non-revocation for powers more than 12 months old at the date of the disposition for which they are used (rule 62);
Form 3 – Statutory declaration/certificate in support of power delegating trustees' functions to a beneficiary (rule 63);
Form 4 – Certificate as to Vesting in an Incumbent or other Ecclesiastical Corporation (rule 174);
Form 5 – The Like Certificate under rule 175; and
Form 6 – Transfer where the Tenant for Life is already registered as proprietor (rule 186 and paragraph 5 of Schedule 7).

Schedule 4[1]
Standard Forms of Restriction

Rule 91

Form A (Restriction on dispositions by sole proprietor)
No disposition by a sole proprietor of the registered estate (except a trust corporation) under which capital money arises is to be registered unless authorised by an order of the court.

Form B (Dispositions by trustees - certificate required)
No disposition [*or specify details*] by the proprietors of the registered estate is to be registered unless they make a statutory declaration, or their conveyancer gives a certificate, that the disposition [*or specify details*] is in accordance with [*specify the disposition creating the trust*] or some variation thereof referred to in the declaration or certificate.

Form C (Dispositions by personal representatives - certificate required)
No disposition by [*name*], the [executor or administrator] of [*name*] deceased, other than a transfer as personal representative, is to be registered unless he makes a statutory declaration, or his conveyancer gives a certificate, that the disposition is in accordance with the terms [of the will of the deceased or the law relating to intestacy as varied by a deed dated *specify details of deed or specify appropriate details*] or [some variation or further variation] thereof referred to in the declaration or certificate, or is necessary for the purposes of administration.

Form D (Parsonage, church or churchyard land)
No disposition of the registered estate is to be registered unless made in accordance with [the Parsonages Measure 1938 (*in the case of parsonage land*) or the New Parishes Measure 1943 (*in the case of church or churchyard land*)] or some other Measure or authority.

---

[1]   Commencement: 13 October 2003 (r 1; Land Registration Act 2002 (Commencement No 4) Order 2003, SI 2003/1725).

Form E (Non-exempt charity - certificate required)

No disposition by the proprietor of the registered estate to which section 36 or section 38 of the Charities Act 1993 applies is to be registered unless the instrument contains a certificate complying with section 37(2) or section 39(2) of that Act as appropriate.

Form F (Land vested in official custodian on trust for non-exempt charity - authority required)

No disposition executed by the trustees of [*charity*] in the name and on behalf of the proprietor shall be registered unless the transaction is authorised by an order of the court or of the Charity Commissioners, as required by section 22(3) of the Charities Act 1993.

Form G (Tenant for life as registered proprietor of settled land, where there are trustees of the settlement)

No disposition is to be registered unless authorised by the Settled Land Act 1925, or by any extension of those statutory powers in the settlement, and no disposition under which capital money arises is to be registered unless the money is paid to (*name*) of (*address*) and (*name*) of (*address*), (the trustees of the settlement, who may be a sole trust corporation or, if individuals, must number at least two but not more than four) or into court.

Note - If applicable under the terms of the settlement, a further provision may be added that no transfer of the mansion house (shown on an attached plan or otherwise adequately described to enable it to be fully identified on the Ordnance Survey map or title plan) is to be registered without the consent of the named trustees or an order of the court.

Form H (Statutory owners as trustees of the settlement and registered proprietors of settled land)

No disposition is to be registered unless authorised by the Settled Land Act 1925, or by any extension of those statutory powers in the settlement, and, except where the sole proprietor is a trust corporation, no disposition under which capital money arises is to be registered unless the money is paid to at least two proprietors.

Note - This restriction does not apply where the statutory owners are not the trustees of the settlement.

Form I (Tenant for life as registered proprietor of settled land - no trustees of the settlement)

No disposition under which capital money arises, or which is not authorised by the Settled Land Act 1925 or by any extension of those statutory powers in the settlement, is to be registered.

Form J (Trustee in bankruptcy and beneficial interest - certificate required)

No disposition of the [registered estate or registered charge dated [*date*]] is to be registered without a certificate signed by the applicant for registration or his conveyancer that written notice of the disposition was given to [*name of trustee in bankruptcy*] (the trustee in bankruptcy of [*name of bankrupt person*]) at [*address for service*].

Form K (Charging order affecting beneficial interest - certificate required)

No disposition of the [registered estate or registered charge dated [*date*]] is to be registered without a certificate signed by the applicant for registration or his conveyancer that written notice of the disposition was given to [*name of person with the benefit of the charging order*] at [*address for service*], being the person with the benefit of [an interim] [a final] charging order on the beneficial interest of (*name of judgment debtor*) made by the (*name of court*) on (*date*) (*Court reference* ....).

Form L (Disposition by registered proprietor of a registered estate or proprietor of charge – certificate required)

No disposition [or specify details] of the registered estate [(other than a charge)] by the

proprietor of the registered estate [, or by the proprietor of any registered charge,] is to be registered without a certificate
[signed by [*name*] of [*address*] (or [his conveyancer] *or specify appropriate details*)]
or
[signed on behalf of [*name*] of [*address*] by [its secretary or conveyancer *or specify appropriate details*]]
that the provisions of [*specify clause, paragraph or other particulars*] of [*specify details*] have been complied with.

Form M (Disposition by registered proprietor of registered estate or proprietor of charge – certificate of registered proprietor of specified title number required)
No disposition [*or specify details*] of the registered estate [(other than a charge)] by the proprietor of the registered estate [or by the proprietor of any registered charge] is to be registered without a certificate signed by the proprietor for the time being of the estate registered under title number [*title number*] [(or his conveyancer *or specify appropriate details*)] or, if appropriate, signed on such proprietor's behalf by [its secretary or conveyancer *or specify appropriate details*], that the provisions of [*specify clause, paragraph or other particulars*] of [*specify details*] have been complied with.

Form N (Disposition by registered proprietor of registered estate or proprietor of charge - consent required)
No disposition [*or specify details*] of the registered estate [(other than a charge)] by the proprietor of the registered estate [or by the proprietor of any registered charge] is to be registered without a written consent
[signed by [*name*] of [*address*] (or [his conveyancer] *or specify appropriate details*)]
or
[signed on behalf of [*name*] of [*address*] by [its secretary or conveyancer *or specify appropriate details*]].

Form O (Disposition by registered proprietor of registered estate or proprietor of charge - consent of registered proprietor of specified title number required)
No disposition [*or specify details*] of the registered estate [(other than a charge)] by the proprietor of the registered estate [or by the proprietor of any registered charge] is to be registered without a written consent signed by the proprietor for the time being of the estate registered under title number [*title number*], [(or his conveyancer, *or specify appropriate details*)] or, if appropriate, signed on such proprietor's behalf by [its secretary or conveyancer *or specify appropriate details*].

Form P (Disposition by registered proprietor of registered estate or proprietor of charge - consent of proprietor of specified charge required)
No disposition [*or specify details*] of the registered estate [(other than a charge)] by the proprietor of the registered estate [or by the proprietor of any registered charge] is to be registered without a written consent signed by the proprietor for the time being of the charge dated [*date*] in favour of [*chargee*] referred to in the charges register [(or his conveyancer *or specify appropriate details*)] or, if appropriate, signed on such proprietor's behalf by [its secretary or conveyancer *or specify appropriate details*].

Form Q (Disposition by registered proprietor of registered estate or proprietor of charge - consent of personal representative required)
No disposition [*or specify details*] of [the registered estate or the registered charge dated [*date*] (referred to above)] by the proprietor [of the registered estate or of that registered charge] is to be registered after the death of [*name of the current proprietor(s) whose personal representative's consent will be required*] without the written consent of the personal representatives of the deceased.

Form R (Disposition by registered proprietor of registered estate or proprietor of charge - evidence of compliance with club rules required)

No disposition [*or specify details*] of the registered estate [(other than a charge)] by the proprietor of the registered estate [or by the proprietor of any registered charge] is to be registered unless authorised by the rules of the [*name of club*] of [*address*] as evidenced [by a resolution of its members or by a certificate signed by its secretary or conveyancer [*or specify appropriate details*]].

Form S (Disposition by proprietor of charge - certificate of compliance required)

No disposition [*or specify details*] by the proprietor of the registered charge dated [*date*] (referred to above) is to be registered without a certificate

[signed by [*name*] of [*address*] (or [his conveyancer] *or specify appropriate details*)]

or

[signed on behalf of [*name*] of [*address*] by [its secretary or conveyancer *or specify appropriate details*], that the provisions of [*specify clause, paragraph or other particulars*] of [*specify details*] have been complied with.

Form T (Disposition by proprietor of charge - consent required)

No disposition [*or specify details*] by the proprietor of the registered charge dated [*date*] (referred to above) is to be registered without a written consent

[signed by [*name*] of [*address*] (or [his conveyancer] *or specify appropriate details*)]

or

[signed on behalf of [*name*] of [*address*] by [its secretary or conveyancer *or specify appropriate details*].

Form U (Section 37 of the Housing Act 1985)

No transfer or lease by the proprietor of the registered estate or by the proprietor of any registered charge is to be registered unless a certificate by [*specify relevant local authority*] is given that the transfer or lease is made in accordance with section 37 of the Housing Act 1985.

Form V (Section 157 of the Housing Act 1985)

No transfer or lease by the proprietor of the registered estate or by the proprietor of any registered charge is to be registered unless a certificate by [*specify relevant local authority or housing association etc*] is given that the transfer or lease is made in accordance with section 157 of the Housing Act 1985.

Form W (Paragraph 4 of Schedule 9A to the Housing Act 1985)

No disposition (except a transfer) of a qualifying dwellinghouse (except to a qualifying person or persons) is to be registered without the consent of the Secretary of State given under section 171D(2) of the Housing Act 1985 as it applies by virtue of the Housing (Preservation of Right to Buy) Regulations 1993.

Form X (Section 81 or 133 of the Housing Act 1988 or section 173 of the Local Government and Housing Act 1989)

No disposition by the proprietor of the registered estate or in exercise of the power of sale or leasing in any registered charge (except an exempt disposal as defined by section 81(8) of the Housing Act 1988) is to be registered without the consent of the Secretary of State to that disposition under the provisions of (*as appropriate* [section 81 of that Act] *or* [section 133 of that Act] or [section 173 of the Local Government and Housing Act 1989]).

Form Y (Section 13 of the Housing Act 1996)

No transfer or lease by the proprietor of the registered estate or by the proprietor of any registered charge is to be registered unless a certificate by [*specify relevant registered social landlord*] is given that the transfer or lease is made in accordance with section 13 of the Housing Act 1996.

Form AA (freezing order on the registered estate)

Under an order of the (*name of court*) made on (*date*) (*claim no*) no disposition by the proprietor of the registered estate is to be registered except under a further order of the Court.

Form BB (freezing order on charge)

Under an order of the (*name of court*) made on (*date*) (*claim no*) no disposition by the proprietor of the charge is to be registered except under a further order of the Court.

Form CC (application for freezing order on the registered estate)

Pursuant to an application made on (*date*) to the (*name of court*) for a freezing order to be made under (*statutory provision*) no disposition by the proprietor of the registered estate is to be registered except with the consent of (*name of the person applying*) or under a further order of the Court.

Form DD (application for freezing order on charge)

Pursuant to an application made on (*date*) to the (*name of the court*) for a freezing order to be made under (*statutory provision*) no disposition by the proprietor of the registered charge dated (*date*) (referred to above) is to be registered except with the consent of (*name of the person applying*) or under a further order of the Court.

Form EE (restraint order or interim receiving order on the registered estate)

Under (*as appropriate* [a restraint order] *or* [an interim receiving order]) made under (*statutory provision*) on (*date*) (*claim no*) no disposition by the proprietor of the registered estate is to be registered without the consent of (*name of the prosecutor or other person who applied for the order*) or under a further order of the Court.

Form FF (restraint order or interim receiving order on charge)

Under (*as appropriate* [a restraint order] *or* [an interim receiving order]) made under (*statutory provision*) on (*date*) (*claim no*) no disposition by the proprietor of the registered charge dated (*date*) (referred to above) is to be registered without the consent of (*name of the prosecutor or other person who applied for the order*) or under a further order of the Court.

Form GG (application for restraint order or interim receiving order on the registered estate)

Pursuant to an application for (*as appropriate* [a restraint order] *or* [an interim receiving order]) to be made under (*statutory provision*) and under any order made as a result of that application, no disposition by the proprietor of the registered estate is to be registered without the consent of (*name of the prosecutor or other person applying*) or under a further order of the Court.

Form HH (application for restraint order or interim receiving order on charge)

Pursuant to an application for (*as appropriate* [a restraint order] *or* [an interim receiving order]) to be made under (*statutory provision*) and under any order made as a result of that application no disposition by the proprietor of the registered charge dated (*date*) (referred to above) is to be registered without the consent of (*name of the prosecutor or other person applying*) or under a further order of the Court.

Schedule 5[1]

Applications in Connection With Court Proceedings, Insolvency and Tax Liability - Qualifying
Applicants and Appropriate Certificates

Rule 140

Column 1	Column 2
Status of applicant	*Certificate in Form CIT*
An **Administrator** appointed for the purposes of the Insolvency Act 1986	Certificate K
An **Administrator** appointed under section 13 of the Criminal Justice (Scotland) Act 1987	Certificate J
A **Chief Officer of Police** or a police officer authorised to apply on behalf of	Certificate A
a Chief Officer	Certificate B Certificate C Certificate D Certificate E Certificate G
A person commissioned by the **Commissioners of Customs and Excise**	Certificate C Certificate D Certificate E Certificate H
A person authorised to apply by the **Commissioners of Inland Revenue**	Certificate E
A person authorised to apply by the **Commissioners of Inland Revenue** and having the consent of a General or Special Commissioner to make the application	Certificate L
A **constable**	Certificate H
The **Director of the Assets Recovery Agency** or a member of the Assets	Certificate H
Recovery Agency authorised to apply on behalf of the Director	Certificate I Certificate M
The **Director of Public Prosecutions** or a member of the Crown	Certificate A
Prosecution Service authorised to apply on behalf of the Director	Certificate B Certificate C Certificate D Certificate E
The **Director of the Serious Fraud Office** or a member of the Serious Fraud Office authorised to apply on behalf of the Director	Certificate A
	Certificate B Certificate E
The **Director-General of the Security Service** or a member of the Security Service authorised to apply on behalf of the Director-General	Certificate F

[1] Commencement: 13 October 2003 (r 1; Land Registration Act 2002 (Commencement No 4) Order 2003, SI 2003/1725).

Column 1	Column 2
A **Liquidator** appointed for the purposes of the Insolvency Act 1986	Certificate K
The **Lord Advocate** or a person conducting a prosecution in Scotland on behalf of the Lord Advocate	Certificate C Certificate D
The **Official Assignee** for bankruptcy for Northern Ireland or the **Official Assignee** for company liquidations for Northern Ireland	Certificate K
An Official Receiver for the purposes of the Insolvency Act 1986	Certificate K
A **Receiver** appointed under the Criminal Justice Act 1988, the Drug Trafficking Act 1994 or the Proceeds of Crime Act 2002	Certificate J
The **Scottish Ministers** or a person named by them	Certificate I
A person authorised by the **Secretary of State for the Department of Trade and Industry**	Certificate A Certificate B Certificate E
A person authorised by the **Secretary of State for Work and Pensions**	Certificate A Certificate B
A **trustee in bankruptcy**, being either a trustee in bankruptcy of a person adjudged bankrupt in England and Wales or Northern Ireland or a permanent or interim trustee in the sequestration of a debtor's estate in Scotland	Certificate K

Schedule 6[1]
Information to be Included in Certain Results of Official Searches

Rule 145

Part 1
INFORMATION TO BE INCLUDED IN THE RESULT OF AN OFFICIAL SEARCH OF THE INDEX MAP

A
The date and time of the official search certificate

B
A description of the land searched

C
The reference (if any) of the applicant or the person to whom the search is being sent: limited to 25 characters including spaces

---

[1]   Commencement: 13 October 2003 (r 1; Land Registration Act 2002 (Commencement No 4) Order 2003, SI 2003/1725).

D

Whether there is –

    (i) a pending application for first registration (other than of title to a relating franchise)

    (ii) a pending application for a caution against first registration (other than where the subject of the caution is a relating franchise)

    (iii) a registered estate in land

    (iv) a registered rentcharge

    (v) a registered profit a prendre in gross

    (vi) a registered affecting franchise, or

    (vii) a caution against first registration (other than where the subject of the caution is a relating franchise)

and, if there is such a registered estate or caution, the title number

Part 2

INFORMATION TO BE INCLUDED IN THE RESULT OF AN OFFICIAL SEARCH OF THE INDEX OF RELATING FRANCHISES AND MANORS

A

The date and time of the official search certificate

B

The administrative area(s) searched

C

The reference (if any) of the applicant or the person to whom the search is being sent: limited to 25 characters including spaces

D

Whether there is a verbal description of –

    (i) a pending application for first registration of title to a relating franchise

    (ii) a pending application for a caution against first registration where the subject of the caution is a relating franchise

    (iii) a registered franchise which is a relating franchise

    (iv) a registered manor, or

    (v) a caution against first registration where the subject of the caution is a relating franchise and the title numbers of any such registered estates and cautions arranged by administrative area

Part 3

INFORMATION TO BE INCLUDED IN THE RESULT OF AN OFFICIAL SEARCH OF AN INDIVIDUAL REGISTER OF A REGISTERED TITLE

A

The title number

B

The date and time of the official search certificate

C

If the official search certificate is part of a registered title, a short description of the property or plot number on the approved estate plan

D

The applicant's name

E

The applicant's, or his agent's, reference (if any): limited to 25 characters including spaces

F

Details of any relevant adverse entries made in the individual register since the end of the day specified in the application as the search from date

G

Notice of the entry of any relevant pending application affecting the registered title entered on the day list (other than an application to designate a document as an exempt information document under rule 136)

H

Notice of the entry of any relevant official search the priority period of which has not expired

I

If the official search is with priority, the date and time at which the priority expires

J

If the official search is without priority, a statement that the certificate will not confer on the applicant priority for any registrable disposition

Part 4
INFORMATION TO BE INCLUDED IN THE RESULT OF AN OFFICIAL SEARCH WITH PRIORITY IN RELATION TO A PENDING APPLICATION FOR FIRST REGISTRATION

A

The title number allotted to the pending application for first registration

B

The date and time of the official search certificate

C

If the official search is of part, a short description of the property

D

The applicant's name

E

The applicant's, or his agent's, reference (if any): limited to 25 characters including spaces

F

The full name of the person who has applied for first registration

G

The date and time at which the pending application for first registration was entered on the day list

H

Notice of the entry of any relevant pending application affecting the estate sought to be registered and entered on the day list subsequent to the date and time at which the pending application for first registration was entered on the day list (other than an application to designate a document as an exempt information document under rule 136)

I

Notice of the entry of any relevant official search the priority period of which has not expired affecting the pending application for first registration

J

The date and time at which priority expires

Part 5

INFORMATION TO BE INCLUDED IN THE RESULT OF AN OFFICIAL SEARCH BY A MORTGAGEE FOR THE PURPOSE OF SECTION 56(3) OF THE FAMILY LAW ACT 1996

A

The title number

B

The date and time of the official search certificate

C

The mortgagee's name

D

The mortgagee's, or his agent's, reference (if any): limited to 25 characters including spaces

E

Whether, at the date of the official search certificate, a matrimonial home rights notice or matrimonial home rights caution has been registered against the registered title searched and if so the date of registration and the name of the person in whose favour the notice or caution was registered

F

Whether there is a pending application for the entry of a matrimonial home rights notice entered on the day list

Schedule 7[1]
Settlements

Rule 186
General
1

Registered land which is settled land must be registered in the name of the tenant for life or the statutory owner.

---

[1] Commencement: 13 October 2003 (r 1; Land Registration Act 2002 (Commencement No 4) Order 2003, SI 2003/1725).

First registration – restriction required

2

An application for first registration of an unregistered legal estate which is settled land must be accompanied by an application for entry of a restriction in Form G, H, or I, as appropriate.

Standard forms of restriction applicable to settled land

3

(1) The restrictions in Forms G, H and I apply respectively to the various cases referred to in those forms, and may be modified as the registrar sees fit according to the circumstances.

(2) Where one of the restrictions referred to in sub-paragraph (1) should have been entered in the register and has not been, any person who has an interest in the settled land and who applies for such restriction shall be regarded as included in section 43(1)(c) of the Act.

(3) Subject to paragraphs 8 and 14, the restrictions referred to in sub-paragraph (1) are binding on the proprietor during his life, but do not affect a disposition by his personal representatives.

Transfer of land into settlement

4

(1) A transfer of registered land into settlement must include the following provisions, with any necessary alterations and additions –

'The Transferor and the Transferee declare that –

(a)   the property is vested in the Transferee upon the trusts declared in a trust deed dated (date) and made between (parties),

(b)   the trustees of the settlement are (names of trustees),

(c)   the power of appointment of new trustees is vested in (name),

(d)   the following powers relating to land are expressly conferred by the trust deed in addition to those conferred by the Settled Land Act 1925: (insert additional powers).

or if the tenant for life is a minor and the transferees are the statutory owner –

(a)   the property is vested in the Transferee as statutory owner under a trust deed dated (date) and made between (parties),

(b)   the tenant for life is (name), a minor, who was born on (date),

(c)   the trustees of the settlement are (names),

(d)   during the minority of the tenant for life the power of appointment of new trustees is vested in the Transferee,

(e)   the following powers relating to land are expressly conferred by the trust deed in addition to those conferred by the Settled Land Act 1925: (insert additional powers).'.

(2) An application for the registration of a transfer of registered land into settlement must be accompanied by an application for entry of a restriction in Form G, H or I, as appropriate.

(3) When the registrar receives the application he must register the transferee named in the transfer as the proprietor of the registered land and enter the appropriate restriction in the register.

Registered land brought into settlement

5

Where registered land has been settled and the existing registered proprietor is the tenant for life under the settlement, the registered proprietor must –

(a)   make a declaration in Form 6, and

(b)   apply for the entry of a restriction in Form G, modified if appropriate.

Registered land bought with capital money

6

(1) Where registered land is acquired with capital money the transfer must be in one of the forms prescribed by rule 206 and must include the following provisions, with any necessary alterations and additions –

'The Transferee declares that –

(a)   the consideration has been paid out of capital money,

(b)   the Property is vested in the Transferee upon the trusts declared in a trust deed dated (date) and made between (parties),

(c)   the trustees of the settlement are (names of trustees),

(d)   the power of appointment of new trustees is vested in (name),

(e)   the following powers relating to land are expressly conferred by the trust deed in addition to those conferred by the Settled Land Act 1925: (set out additional powers).'.

(2) An application for registration of the transfer must be accompanied by an application for entry of a restriction in Form G, H or I, as appropriate.

Duty to apply for restrictions when registered land is settled
7

(1) Where registered land is settled land the proprietor, or (if there is no proprietor) the personal representatives of a deceased proprietor, must apply to the registrar for the entry of such restrictions (in addition to a restriction in Form G, H or I) as may be appropriate to the case.

(2) The application must state that the restrictions applied for are required for the protection of the beneficial interests and powers under the settlement.

(3) Subject to section 43(3) of the Act, the registrar must enter such restrictions without inquiry as to the terms of the settlement.

(4) Nothing in this rule affects the rights and powers of personal representatives for purposes of administration.

Proprietor ceasing in his lifetime to be the tenant for life
8

Where a registered proprietor ceases in his lifetime to be a tenant for life and has not become absolutely entitled to the registered land –

(a)   he must transfer the land to his successor in tile, or, if the successor is a minor, to the statutory owner, and

(b)   on the registration of the successor in title or statutory owner as proprietor, the trustees of the settlement, if the settlement continues, must apply for such alteration in the restrictions as may be required for the protection of the beneficial interests and powers under the settlement.

Tenant for life or statutory owner entitled to have the settled land vested in him
9

Where a tenant for life or statutory owner who, if the registered land were not registered, would be entitled to have the settled land vested in him, is not the registered proprietor, the registered proprietor must at the cost of the trust estate execute such transfers as may be required for giving effect on the register to the rights of such tenant for life or statutory owner.

Registration of statutory owner during a minority otherwise than on death
10

(1) If a minor becomes entitled in possession (or will become entitled in possession on attaining full age) to registered land otherwise than on a death, the statutory owner during the minority is entitled to require the settled land to be transferred to him and to be registered as proprietor accordingly.

(2) The transfer to the statutory owner –

(a)   must be in Form TR1, and

(b)   must not refer to the settlement.

(3) An application to register the transfer must be accompanied by an application for entry of a restriction in Form H.

Registration of special personal representatives
11
(1) Where –
- (a) land was settled before the death of the sole or last surviving joint registered proprietor and not by his will, and
- (b) the settlement continues after his death,

the personal representatives in whom the registered land vests under the Administration of Estates Act 1925 may apply to be registered as proprietor in place of the deceased proprietor.

(2) The application must be accompanied by the grant of probate or letters of administration of the deceased proprietor limited to the settled land.

(3) The personal representatives must be registered in place of the deceased proprietor and the following added after his name –

'special executor or executrix (or administrator or administratrix) of [name], deceased.'.

Transfer on the death of the tenant for life
12
(1) Where the settlement continues after the death of the proprietor who was the tenant for life –
- (a) an application to register a transfer by the personal representatives to the person next entitled to the registered land which is settled land must be accompanied by –
  - (i) if the personal representatives are not already registered, the grant of probate or letters of administration of the deceased proprietor limited to the settled land,
  - (ii) a transfer in Form AS1 or AS2, as appropriate,
  - (iii) an application for entry of a restriction in Form G or H, as appropriate.
- (b) The transfer must contain the following provisions with any necessary alterations or additions –

  'The Personal Representatives and the Transferee declare that –
  - a   the Property is vested in the Transferee upon the trusts declared in [a trust deed dated (date) and made between (parties)] or [the will of (name of deceased) proved on (date)],
  - b   the trustees of the settlement are (names of trustees),
  - c   the power of appointment of new trustees is vested in (name),
  - d   the following powers relating to land are expressly conferred by the will in addition to those conferred by the Settled Land Act 1925: (set out additional powers).'.

(2) Where the settlement ends on the death of the proprietor, an application to register a transfer by the personal representatives to the person entitled must be accompanied by –
- (a) if the personal representatives are not already registered, the grant of probate or letters of administration of the deceased proprietor,
- (b) Form RX3 for cancellation of the restriction entered on the register relating to the settlement.

(3) The registrar shall not be under a duty to investigate the reasons any transfer is made by the personal representatives or consider the contents of the will and, provided the terms of any restriction on the register are complied with, he must assume, whether he knows of the terms of the will or not, that the personal representatives are acting correctly and within their powers.

Minority where settlement arises under a will or intestacy
13
(1) Where a settlement is created or arises under the will or intestacy of a person who died before 1st January 1997 –
- (a) The personal representatives under the will or intestacy under which the settlement is

created or arises must, during a minority, be registered as proprietors and will have all the powers conferred by the Settled Land Act 1925 on the tenant for life and on the trustees of the settlement.

(b) When a minor becomes beneficially entitled to an estate in fee simple or a term of years absolute in the registered land, or would, if he were of full age, be or have the powers of a tenant for life, the personal representatives must (unless they are themselves the statutory owner) during the minority give effect on the register to the directions of the statutory owner.

(c) In particular, the statutory owner shall, after administration is completed as respects the registered land, direct the personal representatives to apply for a restriction in Form H.

(2) The application for the restriction in form H must be made by the personal representatives.

(3) On an application by the personal representatives under sub-paragraph (2), the registrar shall be under no duty to consider or call for any information concerning –

(a) the reason the application is made, or

(b) the terms of the will or the devolution under the intestacy, or

(c) whether the direction by the statutory owner was actually given or not, or its terms,

and whether he has notice of those matters or not, he must assume that the personal representatives are acting according to the directions given and that the directions were given by the statutory owner and were correct.

(4) A disponee dealing with the personal representatives who complies with the restriction entered under sub-paragraph (2) is not concerned to see or enquire whether any directions have been given by the statutory owner with regard to the disposition to him.

(5) Where under subsection (3) of section 19 of the Settled Land Act 1925 there is a tenant for life of full age, he shall be entitled to be registered as proprietor during any minority referred to in that subsection, but subject to the restrictions in Forms G or I, as appropriate.

(6) Nothing in this paragraph shall affect the right of a statutory owner to be registered as proprietor.

Discharge of registered land from beneficial interests and powers under a settlement
14

Where the trustees of a settlement desire to discharge registered land from the beneficial interests and powers under the settlement they may do so by any document sufficient to discharge it.

Discharge from liability in respect of beneficial interests and powers under a settlement
15

Where a proprietor or the personal representatives of a deceased proprietor has or have, in good faith, complied with the requirements of this Schedule in executing a transfer of settled land or discharge of trustees and in applying for the appropriate restrictions that may be required for the protection of the beneficial interests and powers under a settlement –

(a) he is or they are absolutely discharged from all liability in respect of the equitable interests and powers taking effect under the settlement, and

(b) he is or they are entitled to be kept indemnified at the cost of the trust estate from all liabilities affecting the settled land.

Interpretation
16

(1) In this Schedule –

'capital' money has the same meaning as in the Settled Land Act 1925,

'personal representatives' includes the special personal representatives for the purposes of any settled land where they have been appointed in relation to that land,

'settled land' has the same meaning as in the Settled Land Act 1925,

'settlement' has the same meaning as in the Settled Land Act 1925, 'statutory owner' has the same meaning as in the Settled Land Act 1925,

'tenant for life' has the same meaning as in the Settled Land Act 1925,

'transfer' includes an assent and a vesting assent,

'trustees of the settlement' has the same meaning as in the Settled Land Act 1925,

'vesting assent' has the same meaning as in the Settled Land Act 1925.

(2) References in this Schedule to the 'tenant for life' shall, where the context admits, be read as referring to the tenant for life, statutory owner, or personal representatives who is or are entitled to be registered.

(3) Nothing in this Schedule modifies the provisions of section 2 of the Trusts of Land and Appointment of Trustees Act 1996 concerning settlements in relation to their application to registered land (as defined in section 89(3) of the Act).

Schedule 8[1]

Modified Form of Schedule 6 to the Act Applicable to Registered Rentcharges

Rule 191

Schedule 6

Registration of Adverse Possessor

Right to apply for registration

1

(1) A person may apply to the registrar to be registered as the proprietor of a registered rentcharge if he has been in adverse possession of the registered rentcharge for the period of ten years ending on the date of the application.

(2) However, a person may not make an application under this paragraph if –

  (a) he is a defendant in proceedings by the registered proprietor of the registered rentcharge for recovery of the rent or to enter into possession of the land out of which the registered rentcharge issues,

  (b) judgment in favour of the registered proprietor of the registered rentcharge in respect of proceedings of the nature mentioned in sub-paragraph (2)(a) has been given against him in the last two years, or

  (c) the registered proprietor of the registered rentcharge of which that person was in adverse possession has entered into possession of the land out of which the registered rentcharge issues.

(3) For the purposes of sub-paragraph (1), the registered rentcharge need not have been registered throughout the period of adverse possession.

Notification of application

2

(1) The registrar must give notice of an application under paragraph 1 to –

  (a) the proprietor of the registered rentcharge to which the application relates,

  (b) the proprietor of any registered charge on the registered rentcharge,

  (c) where the registered rentcharge is leasehold, the proprietor of any superior registered rentcharge,

  (d) any person who is registered in accordance with rules as a person to be notified under this paragraph, and

  (e) such other persons as rules may provide.

(2) Notice under this paragraph shall include notice of the effect of paragraph 4.

---

[1]   Commencement: 13 October 2003 (r 1; Land Registration Act 2002 (Commencement No 4) Order 2003, SI 2003/1725).

Treatment of application

3

(1) A person given notice under paragraph 2 may require that the application to which the notice relates be dealt with under paragraph 5.

(2) The right under this paragraph is exercisable by notice to the registrar given before the end of such period as rules may provide.

4

If an application under paragraph 1 is not required to be dealt with under paragraph 5, the applicant is entitled to be entered in the register as the new proprietor of the registered rentcharge.

5

(1) If an application under paragraph 1 is required to be dealt with under this paragraph, the applicant is only entitled to be registered as the new proprietor of the registered rentcharge if either of the following conditions is met.

(2) The first condition is that –

  (a) it would be unconscionable because of an equity by estoppel for the registered proprietor to seek to assert his title to the registered rentcharge against the applicant, and

  (b) the circumstances are such that the applicant ought to be registered as the proprietor.

(3) The second condition is that the applicant is for some other reason entitled to be registered as the proprietor of the registered rentcharge.

Right to make further application for registration

6

(1) Where a person's application under paragraph 1 is rejected, he may make a further application to be registered as the proprietor of the registered rentcharge if he is in adverse possession of the registered rentcharge from the date of the application until the last day of the period of two years beginning with the date of its rejection.

However, a person may not make an application under this paragraph if –

  (a) he is a defendant in proceedings by the registered proprietor of the registered rentcharge for recovery of the rent or to enter into possession of the land out of which the registered rentcharge issues,

  (b) judgment in favour of the registered proprietor of the registered rentcharge in respect of proceedings of the nature mentioned in sub-paragraph (2)(a) has been given against him in the last two years, or

  (c) the registered proprietor of the registered rentcharge of which that person was in adverse possession has entered into possession of the land out of which the registered rentcharge issues.

7

If a person makes an application under paragraph 6, he is entitled to be entered in the register as the new proprietor of the registered rentcharge.

Restriction on applications

8

(1) No one may apply under this Schedule to be registered as the proprietor of a registered rentcharge during, or before the end of twelve months after the end of, any period in which the existing registered proprietor is for the purposes of the Limitation (Enemies and War Prisoners) Act 1945 (8 & 9 Geo. 6 c. 16) –

  (a) an enemy, or

  (b) detained in enemy territory.

(2) No-one may apply under this Schedule to be registered as the proprietor of a registered rentcharge during any period in which the existing registered proprietor is –

    (a) unable because of mental disability to make decisions about issues of the kind to which such an application would give rise, or

    (b) unable to communicate such decisions because of mental disability or physical impairment.

(3) For the purposes of sub-paragraph (2), mental disability means a disability or disorder of the mind or brain, whether permanent or temporary, which results in an impairment or disturbance of mental functioning.

(4) Where it appears to the registrar that sub-paragraph (1) or (2) applies in relation to a registered rentcharge, he may include a note to that effect in the register.

Effect of registration

9

(1) Where a person is registered as the proprietor of a registered rentcharge in pursuance of an application under this Schedule, the title by virtue of adverse possession which he had at the time of the application is extinguished.

(2) Subject to sub-paragraph (3), the registration of a person under this Schedule as the proprietor of a registered rentcharge does not affect the priority of any interest affecting the registered rentcharge.

(3) Subject to sub-paragraph (4), where a person is registered under this Schedule as the proprietor of a registered rentcharge, the registered rentcharge is vested in him free of any registered charge affecting the registered rentcharge immediately before his registration.

(4) Sub-paragraph (3) does not apply where registration as proprietor is in pursuance of an application determined by reference to whether either of the conditions in paragraph 5 applies.

Apportionment and discharge of charges

10

(1) Where –

    (a) a registered rentcharge continues to be subject to a charge notwithstanding the registration of a person under this Schedule as the proprietor, and

    (b) the charge affects property other than the registered rentcharge,

the proprietor of the registered rentcharge may require the chargee to apportion the amount secured by the charge at that time between the registered rentcharge and the other property on the basis of their respective values.

(2) The person requiring the apportionment is entitled to a discharge of his registered rentcharge from the charge on payment of –

    (a) the amount apportioned to the registered rentcharge, and

    (b) the costs incurred by the chargee as a result of the apportionment.

(3) On a discharge under this paragraph, the liability of the chargor to the chargee is reduced by the amount apportioned to the registered rentcharge.

(4) Rules may make provision about apportionment under this paragraph, in particular, provision about –

    (a) procedure,

    (b) valuation,

    (c) calculation of costs payable under sub-paragraph (2)(b), and

    (d) payment of the costs of the chargor.

Meaning of 'adverse possession'

11

(1) A person is in adverse possession of a registered rentcharge for the purposes of this Schedule if, but for section 96, a period of limitation under section 15 of the Limitation Act 1980 would run in his favour in relation to the registered rentcharge.

(2) A person is also to be regarded for those purposes as having been in adverse possession of a registered rentcharge –

    (a) where he is the successor in title to the registered rentcharge, during any period of adverse possession by a predecessor in title to that registered rentcharge, or

    (b) during any period of adverse possession by another person which comes between, and is continuous with, periods of adverse possession of his own.

(3) In determining whether for the purposes of this paragraph a period of limitation would run under section 15 of the Limitation Act 1980, there are to be disregarded –

    (a)   the commencement of any legal proceedings, and

    (b)   paragraph 6 of Schedule 1 to that Act.

Trusts

12

A person is not to be regarded as being in adverse possession of a registered rentcharge for the purposes of this Schedule at any time when the registered rentcharge is subject to a trust, unless the interest of each of the beneficiaries in the registered rentcharge is an interest in possession.

Schedule 9
Forms of execution referred to in rule 206(3)

[Schedule 9 is not reproduced. It consists of the following forms of execution:

Form A – Where the instrument is to be executed personally by an individual;

Form B – Where the instrument is to be executed by an individual directing another to sign on his behalf;

Form C – Where the instrument is to be executed by a company registered under the Companies Acts, or an unregistered company, using its common seal;

Form D – Where the instrument is to be executed by a company registered under the Companies Acts, or an unregistered company, without using a common seal;

Form E – Where the instrument is to be executed on behalf of an overseas company without using a common seal; and

Form F – Where the instrument is to be executed by a limited liability partnership incorporated under the Limited Liability Partnerships Act 2000, without using a common seal.]

LAND REGISTRATION (REFERRAL TO THE ADJUDICATOR TO HM LAND REGISTRY) RULES 2003, SI 2003/2114

1 Citation and commencement

These rules may be cited as the Land Registration (Referral to the Adjudicator to HM Land Registry) Rules 2003 and shall come into force on 13 October 2003.

2 Interpretation

In these rules –

'the Act' means the Land Registration Act 2002;

'business day' means a day when the land registry is open to the public under rule 216 of the Land Registration Rules 2003;

'disputed application' means an application to the registrar under the Act to which an objection has been made;

'objection' means an objection made under section 73 of the Act;

'the parties' means the person who has made the disputed application and the person who has made an objection to that application.

3 Procedure for referral to the adjudicator

(1)   When the registrar is obliged to refer a matter to the adjudicator under section 73(7) of the Act, he must as soon as practicable –

    (a)   prepare a case summary containing the information set out in paragraph (2),

    (b)   send a copy of the case summary to the parties,

    (c)   give the parties an opportunity to make comments on the contents of the case summary in the manner, to the address, and within the time specified by him, and

    (d)   inform the parties in writing that the case summary together with copies of the documents listed in it will be sent to the adjudicator with the notice referred to in rule 5(2).

(2)   The case summary must contain the following information –

    (a)   the names of the parties,

    (b)   the addresses of the parties,

    (c)   details of their legal or other representatives (if any),

    (d)   a summary of the core facts,

    (e)   details of the disputed application,

    (f)   details of the objection to that application,

    (g)   a list of any documents that will be copied to the adjudicator, and

    (h)   anything else that the registrar may consider to be appropriate.

(3)   The registrar may amend the case summary as he considers appropriate having considered any written comments made to him by the parties under paragraph (1)(c).

4 Parties' addresses

(1)   If the address of a party set out in the case summary does not comply with paragraph (2), that party must provide the registrar with one that does.

(2)   An address complies with this paragraph if it –
- (a)   is a postal address in England and Wales, and
- (b)   is either that of the party or of his representative.

5   Notice of referral to the adjudicator

(1)   This rule applies –
- (a)   when the registrar has considered any written comments made by the parties under rule 3(1)(c), or
- (b)   if he has not received any comments from the parties within the time specified under rule 3(1)(c), on the expiry of that period, and
- (c)   when he has amended the case summary, if appropriate, under rule 3(3).

(2)   The registrar must as soon as practicable –
- (a)   send to the adjudicator a written notice, accompanied by the documents set out in paragraph (3), informing him that the matter is referred to him under section 73(7) of the Act,
- (b)   inform the parties in writing that the matter has been referred to the adjudicator, and
- (c)   send the parties a copy of the case summary prepared under rule 3 in the form sent to the adjudicator.

(3)   The notice sent to the adjudicator under paragraph (2)(a) must be accompanied by –
- (a)   the case summary prepared under rule 3 amended, if appropriate, by the registrar under rule 3(3), and
- (b)   copies of the documents listed in that case summary.

6   Specified time periods

(1)   For the purposes of rule 3(1)(c), the time specified by the registrar must not end before 12 noon on the fifteenth business day after the date on which the registrar sends the copy of the case summary to the relevant party under rule 3(1)(b) or such earlier time as the parties may agree.

(2)   On and after the date specified in any notice given pursuant to rule 216(2) of the Land Registration Rules 2003, paragraph (1) shall have effect with the substitution of the words 'eighteenth business day' for the words 'fifteenth business day'.

ADJUDICATOR TO HER MAJESTY'S LAND REGISTRY (PRACTICE AND PROCEDURE) RULES 2003, SI 2003/2171

1 Citation and Commencement

These Rules may be cited as the Adjudicator to Her Majesty's Land Registry (Practice and Procedure) Rules 2003 and shall come into force on 13th October 2003.

PART 1

INTRODUCTION

2 Interpretation

(1) In these Rules –

'applicant' means the party whom the adjudicator designates as such under rule 5 or under rule 24, or the party who makes a rectification application;

'hearing' means a sitting of the adjudicator for the purpose of enabling the adjudicator to reach or announce a substantive decision, but does not include a sitting of the adjudicator solely in the exercise of one or more of the following powers –

    (a) to consider an application, representation or objection made in the interim part of the proceedings;

    (b) to reach a substantive decision without an oral hearing; or

    (c) to consider whether to grant permission to appeal a decision or to stay the implementation of a decision pending the outcome of an appeal;

'matter' means the subject of either a reference or a rectification application;

'office copy' means an official copy of a document held or issued by a public authority;

'original application' means the application originally made to the registrar that resulted in a reference;

'proceedings' means, except in the expression 'court proceedings', the proceedings of the matter before the adjudicator but does not include any negotiations, communications or proceedings that occurred prior to the reference or rectification application;

'record of matters' means a record of references, rectification applications and certain other applications and decisions, kept in accordance with these Rules and in particular in accordance with rule 46;

'rectification application' means an application made to rectify or set aside a document under section 108(2) for determination of the matter by the adjudicator;

'reference' means a reference from the registrar to the adjudicator under section 73(7) for determination of the matter by the adjudicator;

'respondent' means the party or parties who the adjudicator designates as such under rule 5 or rule 24, or the party or parties making an objection to a rectification application;

'substantive decision' means a decision of the adjudicator on the matter or on any substantive issue that arises in it but does not include any direction in interim parts of the proceedings or any order as to costs or any order as to costs thrown away;

'substantive order' means an order or direction that records and gives effect to a substantive decision;

'the Act' means the Land Registration Act 2002 and a reference to a section by number alone is a reference to a section of the Act;

'witness statement' means a written statement signed by a witness containing the evidence that the witness intends to give; and

'working day' means any day other than a Saturday or Sunday, Christmas Day, Good Friday or any other bank holiday.

(2)   In these Rules a person has a document or other material in his possession or control if –

    (a)   it is in his physical possession;

    (b)   he has a right to possession of it; or

    (c)   he has a right to inspect or take copies of it.

3   The overriding objective

(1)   The overriding objective of these Rules is to enable the adjudicator to deal with matters justly.

(2)   Dealing with a matter justly includes, so far as is practicable –

    (a)   ensuring that the parties are on an equal footing;

    (b)   saving expense;

    (c)   dealing with the matter in ways that are proportionate -

        (i)   to the value of the land or other interests involved;

        (ii)   to the importance of the matter;

        (iii)   to the complexity of the issues in the matter; and

        (iv)   to the financial position of each party; and

    (d)   ensuring that the matter is dealt with expeditiously and fairly.

(3)   The adjudicator must seek to give effect to the overriding objective when he –

    (a)   exercises any power given to him by these Rules; or

    (b)   interprets these Rules.

(4)   The parties are required to help the adjudicator to further the overriding objective.

PART 2

REFERENCES TO THE ADJUDICATOR

4   Scope of this Part

The rules in this Part apply to references.

5   Notice of receipt by the adjudicator of a reference

Following receipt by the adjudicator of a reference, the adjudicator must –

    (a)   enter the particulars of the reference in the record of matters; and

    (b)   serve on the parties notice in writing of –

        (i)   the fact that the reference has been received by the adjudicator;

        (ii)   the date when the adjudicator received the reference;

        (iii)   the matter number allocated to the reference;

        (iv)   the name and any known address and address for service of the parties to the proceedings; and

        (v)   which party will be the applicant for the purposes of the proceedings and which party or parties will be the respondent.

6   Direction to commence court proceedings under section 110(1)

Where the adjudicator intends to direct a party to commence court proceedings under section 110(1), the parties may make representations or objections but any representations or objections must be concerned with one or more of the following –

(a)   whether the adjudicator should make such a direction;

(b)   which party should be directed to commence court proceedings;

(c)   the time within which court proceedings should commence; and

(d)   the questions the court should determine.

7   Notification to the adjudicator of court proceedings following a direction to commence court proceedings under section 110(1)

(1)   In this Part –

'the date that the matter before the court is finally disposed of' means the earliest date by which the court proceedings relating to the matter or on the relevant part (including any court proceedings on or in consequence of an appeal) have been determined and any time for appealing or further appealing has expired;

'the relevant part' means the part of the matter in relation to which the adjudicator has directed a party under section 110(1) to commence court proceedings; and

'the final court order' means the order made by the court that records the court's final determination (on appeal or otherwise).

(2)   A party who has been directed to commence court proceedings under section 110(1) must serve on the adjudicator –

(a)   within 14 days of the commencement of the court proceedings, a written notice stating –

(i)   that court proceedings have been issued in accordance with directions given by the adjudicator;

(ii)   the date of issue of the court proceedings;

(iii)   the names and any known addresses of the parties to the court proceedings;

(iv)   the name of the court at which the court proceedings will be heard; and

(v)   the case number allocated to the court proceedings;

(b)   within 14 days of the date of the court's decision on any application for an extension of time, a copy of that decision; and

(c)   within 14 days of the date that the matter before the court is finally disposed of, a copy of the final court order.

8   Adjournment of proceedings before the adjudicator following a direction to commence court proceedings on the whole of the matter under section 110(1)

(1)   This rule applies where the adjudicator has directed a party under section 110(1) to commence court proceedings for the court's decision on the whole of the matter.

(2)   Once he has received notice under rule 7(2)(a) that court proceedings have been issued, the adjudicator must adjourn all of the proceedings before him pending the outcome of the court proceedings.

(3)   Once he has received a copy of the final court order and unless the court directs otherwise, the adjudicator must close the proceedings before him without making a substantive decision.

9   Adjournment of proceedings before the adjudicator following a direction to commence court proceedings on part of the matter under section 110(1)

(1)   This rule applies where the adjudicator has directed a party under section 110(1) to commence court proceedings for the court's decision on the relevant part.

(2)   Once he has received notice under rule 7(2)(a) that court proceedings have been issued in relation to the relevant part, the adjudicator –

    (a)   must adjourn the proceedings before him in relation to the relevant part, pending the outcome of the court proceedings; and

    (b)   unless the court directs otherwise, must not make a substantive decision on the relevant part.

(3)   Once he has received a copy of the final court order on the relevant part and unless the court directs otherwise, the adjudicator must close the proceedings before him in relation to the relevant part without making a substantive decision on that relevant part.

(4)   The adjudicator may adjourn the proceedings in relation to any other part of the matter before him pending the outcome of the court proceedings.

(5)   While the court proceedings are still ongoing, the party directed to commence court proceedings must notify the court of any substantive decision made by the adjudicator within 14 days of service on that party of the substantive decision.

10   Notification where court proceedings are commenced otherwise than following a direction to commence court proceedings under section 110(1)

Where a party commences or has commenced court proceedings otherwise than following a direction under section 110(1) and those court proceedings concern or relate to the matter before the adjudicator, that party must serve –

    (a)   on the adjudicator within 14 days of the commencement of the court proceedings or, if later, within 7 days of service on that party of notification of the reference under rule 5(b), a written notice stating –

        (i)   that court proceedings have been issued;

        (ii)   the way and the extent to which the court proceedings concern or relate to the matter before the adjudicator;

        (iii)   the date of issue of the court proceedings;

        (iv)   the names and any known addresses of the parties to the court proceedings;

        (v)   the name of the court at which the court proceedings will be heard; and

        (vi)   the case number allocated to the court proceedings;

    (b)   on the adjudicator within 14 days of the date that the matter before the court is finally disposed of, a copy of the final court order; and

    (c)   on the court within 14 days of service on that party of such a decision, a copy of any substantive decision made by the adjudicator on the matter.

11   Adjournment of proceedings before the adjudicator where court proceedings are commenced otherwise than following a direction to commence court proceedings under section 110(1)

Where court proceedings are commenced otherwise than following a direction to commence court proceedings under section 110(1), the adjudicator may adjourn the whole or part of the proceedings before him pending the outcome of the court proceedings.

12   Applicant's statement of case and documents

Unless otherwise directed by the adjudicator, the applicant must serve on the adjudicator and each of the other parties within 28 days of service of the notification of the reference under rule 5(b) –

    (a)   his statement of case which must be in accordance with rule 14; and

    (b)   a copy of all of the documents listed in the list of documents contained in his statement of case in accordance with rule 47.

13   Respondent's statement of case and documents

The respondent must serve on the adjudicator and each of the other parties within 28 days of service of the applicant's statement of case –

(a)   his statement of case which must be in accordance with rule 14; and

(b)   a copy of all of the documents listed in the list of documents contained in his statement of case in accordance with rule 47.

14   Statement of case

(1)   Where under these Rules a party is required to provide a statement of case, that statement of case must be in writing and must include –

(a)   the name of the party and confirmation of the party's address for service;

(b)   the party's reasons for supporting or objecting to the original application;

(c)   the facts on which the party intends to rely in the proceedings;

(d)   a list of documents in accordance with rule 47 on which the party intends to rely in the proceedings; and

(e)   a list of witnesses that the party intends to call to give evidence in support of the party's case.

(2)   If in relation to part only of the matter –

(a)   a party has been directed to commence or has commenced court proceedings; or

(b)   the adjudicator has adjourned proceedings before him,

the adjudicator may direct that the statement of case should contain the information specified in paragraphs (1)(b) to (1)(e) inclusive only in relation to the part of the matter that is not before the court for the court's decision or has not been adjourned before the adjudicator.

PART 3

RECTIFICATION APPLICATION TO THE ADJUDICATOR TO
RECTIFY OR SET ASIDE DOCUMENTS

15   Scope of this Part

The rules in this Part apply to rectification applications.

16   Form and contents of a rectification application

(1)   A rectification application must –

(a)   be made in writing;

(b)   be dated and signed by the applicant or the applicant's duly authorised representative;

(c)   be addressed to the adjudicator;

(d)   include the following information –

(i)   the name and address of the person or persons against whom the order is sought;

(ii)   details of the remedy being sought;

(iii)   the grounds on which the rectification application is based;

(iv)   in accordance with rule 47 a list of documents on which the party intends to rely to support the rectification application;

(v)   a list of witnesses that the party intends to call to give evidence in support of the rectification application; and

(vi)   the applicant's name and address for service;

(e)   include the following copies –

(i)   a copy of each of the documents listed in the party's list of documents; and

       (ii)   a copy of the document to which the rectification application relates, or if a copy is not available, details of the document, which must include if available, its nature, its date, the parties to it and any version number or other similar identification number or code that it has; and

    (f)   be served on the adjudicator.

(2)   Following receipt by the adjudicator of a rectification application, the adjudicator must enter the particulars of the rectification application in the record of matters.

(3)   If, having considered the rectification application and made any enquiries he thinks necessary, the adjudicator is satisfied that it is groundless, he must reject the rectification application.

17   Notice of a rectification application

(1)   This rule does not apply where the adjudicator has rejected a rectification application under rule 16(3).

(2)   Where a rectification application has been received by the adjudicator, he must serve on the person against whom the order is sought and on any other person who, in the opinion of the adjudicator, should be a party to the proceedings –

    (a)   written notice of the rectification application; and

    (b)   a copy of the rectification application.

(3)   The adjudicator must specify in the notice under paragraph (2)(a) that if a party receiving the notice has any objection to the rectification application and that party wishes to lodge an objection, he must lodge his objection within 28 days of service of the notice under paragraph (2)(a).

18   Objection to a rectification application

A person lodges an objection under rule 17(3) if within 28 days of service of the notice under rule 17(2)(a) he serves –

    (a)   on the adjudicator –

        (i)   a written statement addressed to the adjudicator and dated and signed by the person lodging the objection or his duly authorised representative setting out the grounds for the objection;

        (ii)   in accordance with rule 47 a list of documents on which the party intends to rely to support his objection;

        (iii)   a copy of each of the documents listed in the list of documents;

        (iv)   a written list of witnesses that the party intends to call to give evidence in support of the objection; and

        (v)   written confirmation of his name and address for service; and

    (b)   on the other parties a copy of all the information and documents served on the adjudicator under sub-paragraph (a).

PART 4

PREPARATION FOR DETERMINATION OF REFERENCES AND RECTIFICATION APPLICATIONS

19   Scope of this Part

This Part sets out the procedure for the preparation for the determination of references and rectification applications.

20   Directions

The adjudicator may at any time, on the application of a party or otherwise, give directions, including (but not limited to) such as are provided for in these Rules, to enable the parties to prepare for the hearing or to assist the adjudicator to conduct the proceedings or to determine the whole or part of the matter or any question of dispute in the proceedings without a hearing.

21   Form of directions

(1)   Any direction made by the adjudicator must be –

  (a)   in writing;
  (b)   dated; and
  (c)   except in the case of requirement notices under rule 28, served by him on –
    (i)   every party to the proceedings;
    (ii)   where the person who made the application, representation or objection that resulted in the direction was not a party, that person; and
    (iii)   where the direction requires the registrar to take action, the registrar.

(2)   Directions containing a requirement must include a statement of the possible consequences of failure to comply with the requirement within any time limit specified by these Rules, or imposed by the adjudicator.

(3)   Directions requiring a party to provide or produce a document or any other material may require the party to provide or produce it to the adjudicator or to another party or both.

22   Consolidating proceedings

Where a reference or rectification application is related to another reference or rectification application and in the opinion of the adjudicator it is appropriate or practicable to do so, the adjudicator may direct that any or all of those related references or rectification applications be dealt with together.

23   Intention to appear

The adjudicator may give directions requiring a party to state whether that party intends to –

  (a)   attend or be represented at the hearing; and
  (b)   call witnesses.

24   Addition and substitution of parties

(1)   The adjudicator may give one or more of the following directions –

  (a)   that any person be added as a new party to the proceedings, if it appears to the adjudicator desirable for that person to be made a party;
  (b)   that any person cease to be a party to the proceedings, if it appears to the adjudicator that it is not desirable for that person to remain a party; and
  (c)   that a new party be substituted for an existing party, if –
    (i)   the existing party's interest or liability has passed to the new party; and
    (ii)   it appears to the adjudicator desirable to do this to enable him to resolve the whole or part of the matter or any question of dispute in the proceedings.

(2)   If the adjudicator directs that a new party is to be added to the proceedings, the adjudicator must specify –

  (a)   whether the new party is added as an applicant or a respondent; and
  (b)   how the new party is to be referred to.

(3) Each new party must be given a single identification that should be in accordance with the order in which they joined the proceedings, for example 'second applicant' or 'second respondent'.

(4) If the adjudicator directs that a new party is to be substituted for an existing party, the adjudicator must specify which party the new party is to substitute, for example 'respondent' or 'second applicant'.

(5) The adjudicator must serve on each new party a copy of each of the following –
- (a) the applicant's statement of case and copy documents served on the adjudicator under rule 12 or the applicant's rectification application served on the adjudicator under rule 16(1); and
- (b) the respondent's statement of case and copy documents served on the adjudicator under rule 13 or the documents and information served by the respondent on the adjudicator under rule 18(a).

(6) If the new party is added to or substituted for parties to proceedings on a reference, the new party must serve on the adjudicator and each of the other parties within 28 days of service on him of the documents specified in paragraph (5) –
- (a) his statement of case which must be in accordance with rule 14; and
- (b) copies of documents contained in his list of documents, which must be in accordance with rule 47.

(7) If the new party is added to or substituted for parties to proceedings on a rectification application, the new party must serve on the adjudicator and each of the other parties, within 28 days of service on him of the documents specified in paragraph (5) –
- (a) if the new party is added or substituted as an applicant, his rectification application which must be in accordance with rule 16(1); or
- (b) if the new party is added or substituted as a respondent, his objection to the rectification application which must be in accordance with rule 18(a).

(8) If a continuing party wishes to respond to the documents specified in paragraph (6) or (7), he may apply to the adjudicator for leave to do so.

(9) If the adjudicator grants the requested leave to respond, the adjudicator must require the party requesting leave to respond to serve a copy of his response on the adjudicator and all other parties.

(10) Following the addition or substitution of parties and if it is necessary to do so, the adjudicator may give consequential directions, including for –
- (a) the preparation and updating of a list of parties;
- (b) the delivery and service of documents; and
- (c) the waiver of the requirement to supply copies of documents listed in the new party's list of documents where copies have already been served on the adjudicator in the course of the proceedings.

25   Further information, supplementary statements and further responses to statements of case

The adjudicator may give directions requiring a party to provide one or more of the following –
- (a) a statement of the facts in dispute or issues to be decided;
- (b) a statement of the facts on which that party intends to rely and the allegations he intends to make;
- (c) a summary of the arguments on which that party intends to rely; and

(d)   such further information, responses to statements of case or supplementary statements as may reasonably be required for the determination of the whole or part of the matter or any question in dispute in the proceedings.

26   Witness statements

The adjudicator may give directions requiring a party to provide a witness statement made by any witness on whose evidence that party intends to rely in the proceedings.

27   Disclosure and inspection of documents

(1)   Any document or other material supplied to the adjudicator or to a party under this rule or under rule 28 may only be used for the purpose of the proceedings in which it was disclosed.

(2)   The adjudicator may give directions requiring a party who has a document or other material in his possession or control –

(a)   to deliver to the adjudicator the original or a copy of that document or other material and, if the adjudicator thinks necessary, to supply copies of that document or material to another party; or

(b)   to permit another party to inspect and take copies of that document or other material and specifying the time and place for disclosure and inspection of that document or other material.

28   Requirement notices

(1)   The adjudicator may, at any time, require the attendance of any person to give evidence or to produce any document or other material specified by the adjudicator which is in that person's possession or control.

(2)   The adjudicator must make any such requirement in a requirement notice.

(3)   The requirement notice must be in the form specified by the adjudicator provided that the requirement notice –

(a)   is in writing;
(b)   identifies the person who must comply with the requirement;
(c)   identifies the matter to which the requirement relates;
(d)   states the nature of the requirement being imposed by the adjudicator;
(e)   specifies the time and place at which the adjudicator requires the person to attend and, if appropriate, produce any document or other material; and
(f)   includes a statement of the possible consequences of failure to comply with the requirement notice.

(4)   The party on whose behalf it is issued must serve the requirement notice.

(5)   Subject to paragraph (6) a requirement notice will be binding only if, not less than 7 working days before the time that the person is required to attend –

(a)   the requirement notice is served on that person; and
(b)   except in the case where that person is a party to the proceedings, the necessary expenses of his attendance are offered and (unless he has refused the offer of payment of his expenses) paid to him.

(6)   At any time before the time that the person is required to attend, that person and the party on whose behalf the requirement notice is issued may substitute a shorter period for the period of 7 working days specified in paragraph (5) by –

(a)   agreeing in writing such shorter period; and

(b)   before the time that the person is required to attend, serving a copy of that agreement on the adjudicator.

(7)   Where a requirement has been imposed on a person under paragraph (1), that person may apply to the adjudicator for the requirement to be varied or set aside.

(8)   Any application made under paragraph (7) must be made to the adjudicator before the time when the person is to comply with the requirement to which the application under paragraph (7) relates.

29   Estimate of length of hearing
The adjudicator may require the parties to provide an estimate of the length of the hearing.

30   Site inspections
(1)   In this rule –

'the appropriate party' is the party who is in occupation or has ownership or control of the property;
'the property' is the land or premises that the adjudicator wishes to inspect for the purposes of determining the whole or part of the matter; and
'a request for entry' is a written request from the adjudicator to the appropriate party, requesting permission for the adjudicator to enter onto and inspect the property and such a request may include a request to be accompanied by one or more of –
(a)   another party;
(b)   such number of the adjudicator's officers or staff as he considers necessary; and
(c)   if a member of the Council on Tribunals informs the adjudicator that he wishes to attend the inspection, that member.

(2)   The adjudicator, at any time for the purpose of determining the whole or part of the matter, may serve a request for entry on an appropriate party.

(3)   The request for entry must specify a time for the entry that, unless otherwise agreed in writing by the appropriate party, must be not earlier than 7 days after the date of service of the request for entry.

(4)   The adjudicator must serve a copy of the request for entry on any party (other than the appropriate party) and any member of the Council on Tribunals named in the request for entry and, if reasonably practicable to do so in the circumstances, must notify them of any change in the time specified.

(5)   If the adjudicator makes a request for entry and the appropriate party withholds or refuses his consent to the whole or part of the request without reasonable excuse, the adjudicator may take such refusal into account when making his substantive decision.

(6)   If a request for entry includes a request for a member of the Council on Tribunals to accompany the adjudicator and the appropriate party consents to the presence of that member, then that member shall be entitled to attend the site inspection but must not take an active part in the inspection.

31   Preliminary issues
(1)   At any time and on the application of a party or of his own motion, the adjudicator may dispose of any matter or matters that are in dispute as a preliminary issue.

(2)   If in the opinion of the adjudicator the decision on the preliminary issue will dispose of the whole of the matter then the decision on the preliminary issue must be –

    (a)   made in accordance with the provisions in these Rules on substantive decisions; and

    (b)   treated as a substantive decision.

PART 5

HEARINGS AND SUBSTANTIVE DECISIONS

32   Scope of this Part

This Part sets out the procedure for determination of references and rectification applications, the format of substantive decisions and substantive orders and rules on costs.

33   Substantive decision without a hearing

(1)   There is a presumption that a substantive decision is made following a hearing.

(2)   Subject to paragraph (1), the adjudicator may make a substantive decision without a hearing if –

    (a)   he is satisfied that there is no important public interest consideration that requires a hearing in public; and

    (b)   unless paragraph (3) applies, he has served written notice on the parties in accordance with these Rules that he intends to make a substantive decision without a hearing or that he has received an application requesting that the substantive decision be made without a hearing and –

        (i)   the parties agree to the substantive decision being made without a hearing; or

        (ii)   the parties fail to object within the specified period for objection to the substantive decision being made without a hearing.

(3)   The adjudicator is not required to serve notice under paragraph (2)(b) if all parties have requested the adjudicator to make the substantive decision without a hearing.

34   Notice of hearing

(1)   Where the adjudicator is to hold a hearing, he must serve written notice of his intention to hear on such parties as he considers necessary.

(2)   The adjudicator must specify in the notice under paragraph (1), the date, time and location of the hearing.

(3)   The adjudicator must serve the notice under paragraph (1) –

    (a)   no later than 28 days before the hearing; or

    (b)   before the expiry of such shorter notice period as agreed by all the parties on whom he intends to serve notice under paragraph (1).

35   Representation at the hearing

(1)   At the hearing a party may conduct his case himself or, subject to paragraph (2), be represented or assisted by any person, whether or not legally qualified.

(2) If, in any particular case, the adjudicator is satisfied that there is sufficient reason for doing so, he may refuse to permit a particular person to represent or assist a party at the hearing.

36   Publication of hearings
The adjudicator must publish details of all listed hearings at the office of the adjudicator and, if different, the venue at which the hearing is to take place.

37   Attendance at hearings by members of the Council on Tribunals
A member of the Council on Tribunals shall be entitled to attend any hearing of the adjudicator whether or not it is in private, but shall take no part in the hearing or in the deliberations on the matter.

38   Absence of parties
(1)   If any party does not attend and is not represented at any hearing of which notice has been served on him in accordance with these Rules, the adjudicator –

    (a)   may proceed with the hearing and reach a substantive decision in
        that party's absence if –
        (i)   the adjudicator is not satisfied that any reasons given for
            the absence are justified;
        (ii)   the absent party consents; or
        (iii) it would be unjust to adjourn the hearing; or
    (b)   must otherwise adjourn the hearing.

(2)   Following a decision by the adjudicator under paragraph (1) to proceed with or adjourn the hearing, the adjudicator may make such consequential directions as he sees fit.

39   Substantive decision of the adjudicator
(1)   Where there is a hearing, the substantive decision of the adjudicator may be given orally at the end of the hearing or reserved.

(2)   A substantive decision of the adjudicator, whether made at a hearing or without a hearing, must be recorded in a substantive order.

(3)   The adjudicator may not vary or set aside a substantive decision.

40   Substantive orders and written reasons
(1)   A substantive order must –
    (a)   be in writing;
    (b)   be dated;
    (c)   be signed by the adjudicator;
    (d)   state the substantive decision that has been reached;
    (e)   state any steps that must be taken to give effect to that substantive decision; and
    (f)   state the possible consequences of a party's failure to comply with the substantive
        order within any specified time limits.

(2)   The substantive order must be served by the adjudicator on –
    (a)   every party to the proceedings; and
    (b)   where the substantive order requires the registrar to take action, the registrar.

(3)   A substantive order requiring a party to provide or produce a document or any other material may require the party to provide or produce it to any or all of the adjudicator, the registrar or another party.

(4)   Unless the adjudicator directs otherwise, the substantive order must be publicly available.

(5)   Where the substantive order is publicly available, the adjudicator may provide copies of it to the public on request.

(6)   The adjudicator must give in writing to all parties his reasons for –
    (a)   his substantive decision; and
    (b)   any steps that must be taken to give effect to that substantive decision.

(7)   The adjudicator's reasons referred to in paragraph (6) need not be given in the substantive order.

41   Substantive orders on a reference that include requirements on the registrar

(1)   Where the adjudicator has made a substantive decision on a reference, the substantive order giving effect to that substantive decision may include a requirement on the registrar to –
    (a)   give effect to the original application in whole or in part as if the objection to that original application had not been made; or
    (b)   cancel the original application in whole or in part.

(2)   A requirement on the registrar under this rule may include –
    (a)   a condition that a specified entry be made on the register of any title affected; or
    (b)   a requirement to reject any future application of a specified kind by a named party to the proceedings –
        (i)   unconditionally; or
        (ii)   unless that party satisfies specified conditions.

42   Costs

(1)   In this rule –
    (a)   'all the circumstances' are all the circumstances of the proceedings and include –
        (i)   the conduct of the parties during (but not prior to) the proceedings;
        (ii)   whether a party has succeeded on part of his case, even if he has not been wholly successful; and
        (iii)   any representations made to the adjudicator by the parties; and
    (b)   the conduct of the parties during the proceedings includes –
        (i)   whether it was reasonable for a party to raise, pursue or contest a particular allegation or issue;
        (ii)   the manner in which a party has pursued or defended his case or a particular allegation or issue; and
        (iii)   whether a party who has succeeded in his case in whole or in part exaggerated his case.

(2)   The adjudicator may, on the application of a party or of his own motion, make an order as to costs.

(3)   In deciding what order as to costs (if any) to make, the adjudicator must have regard to all the circumstances.

(4)   An order as to costs may –
    (a)   require a party to pay the whole or such part of the costs of another party and –
        (i)   specify a fixed sum or proportion to be paid; or
        (ii)   specify that the costs are to be assessed by the adjudicator if not agreed; and
    (b)   specify the time within which the costs are to be paid.

(5)   An order as to costs must be recorded in a costs order.

(6) A costs order must –
   (a) be in writing;
   (b) be dated;
   (c) be signed by the adjudicator;
   (d) state the order as to costs; and
   (e) be served by the adjudicator on the parties.

(7) Where the costs are to be assessed by the adjudicator, he may assess the costs –
   (a) on the standard basis; or
   (b) on the indemnity basis,
but in either case the adjudicator will not allow costs that have been unreasonably incurred or are unreasonable in amount.

(8) The adjudicator must inform the parties of the basis on which he will be assessing the costs.

(9) Where the amount of the costs are to be assessed on the standard basis, the adjudicator must –
   (a) only allow costs which are proportionate to the matters in issue; and
   (b) resolve any doubt that he may have as to whether costs were reasonably incurred or reasonable and proportionate in favour of the paying party.

(10) In deciding whether costs assessed on the standard basis were either proportionately and reasonably incurred or proportionate and reasonable in amount, the adjudicator must have regard to all the circumstances.

(11) Where the amount of the costs are to be assessed on the indemnity basis, the adjudicator must resolve any doubt that he may have as to whether costs were reasonably incurred or were reasonable in amount in favour of the paying party.

(12) In deciding whether costs assessed on the indemnity basis were either reasonably incurred or reasonable in amount, the adjudicator must have regard to all the circumstances.

(13) Once the adjudicator has assessed the costs, he must serve on the parties written notice –
   (a) of the amount which must be paid;
   (b) by whom and to whom the amount must be paid; and
   (c) if appropriate, the time by when the amount must be paid.

43   Costs thrown away
(1) In this rule –

'costs thrown away' means costs of the proceedings resulting from any neglect or delay of the legal representative during (but not prior to) the proceedings and which –
   (a) have been incurred by a party; or
   (b) have been –
      (i) paid by a party to another party; or
      (ii) awarded to a party,
      under an order made under rule 42;
'an order as to costs thrown away' means an order requiring the legal representative concerned to meet the whole or part of the costs thrown away; and
'the legal representative' means the legally qualified representative of a party.

(2)   The adjudicator may, on the application of a party or otherwise, make an order as to costs thrown away provided the adjudicator is satisfied that –

    (a)   a party has incurred costs of the proceedings unnecessarily as a result of the neglect or delay of the legal representative; and

    (b)   it is just in all the circumstances for the legal representative to compensate the party who has incurred or paid the costs thrown away, for the whole or part of those costs.

(3)   If the adjudicator has received an application for or proposes to make an order as to costs thrown away, he may give directions to the parties and the legal representative about the procedure to be followed to ensure that the issues are dealt with in a way that is fair and as simple and summary as the circumstances permit.

(4)   An order as to costs thrown away may –

    (a)   specify the amount of costs to be paid by the legal representative; and

    (b)   if the adjudicator considers it appropriate, specify the time within which the costs are to be paid.

(5)   An order as to costs thrown away must be recorded in a costs thrown away order.

(6)   A costs thrown away order must –

    (a)   be in writing;

    (b)   be dated;

    (c)   be signed by the adjudicator;

    (d)   state the order as to costs thrown away; and

    (e)   be served by the adjudicator on the parties and the legal representative.

PART 6

APPEALS FROM ADJUDICATOR

44   Scope of this Part

This Part contains provisions in relation to appeals to the High Court of decisions by the adjudicator and includes provisions about the adjudicator staying implementation of his decision pending the outcome of an appeal.

45   Appeals to the High Court

(1)   Where a party is granted permission to appeal, the adjudicator may, of his own motion or on the application of a party, stay the implementation of the whole or part of his decision pending the outcome of the appeal.

(2)   A party who wishes to apply to the adjudicator to stay the implementation of the whole or part of a decision pending the outcome of the appeal must make such an application to the adjudicator at the same time that he applies to the adjudicator for permission to appeal.

(3)   Where a party applies under paragraph (2) to the adjudicator to stay implementation of the whole or part of a decision, that party must at the same time provide reasons for the application.

(4)   Before reaching a decision as to whether to grant permission to appeal a decision or to stay implementation of a decision, the adjudicator must allow the parties the opportunity to make representations or objections.

(5)   The adjudicator must serve written notice on the parties of any decision that he makes as to whether to grant permission to appeal or to stay the implementation of the whole or part of his decision pending the outcome of the appeal.

(6)   Where the adjudicator's decision to grant permission to appeal or to stay implementation of a decision relates to a decision contained in a substantive order, the adjudicator must serve on the registrar a copy of the notice under paragraph (5).

(7)   The notice under paragraph (5) must –
- (a)   be in writing;
- (b)   be dated;
- (c)   specify the decision made by the adjudicator;
- (d)   include the adjudicator's reasons for his decision; and
- (e)   be signed by the adjudicator.

PART 7

GENERAL

46   Record of matters
(1)   The adjudicator must keep at his principal office a record of matters that records the particulars of all –
- (a)   references;
- (b)   rectification applications;
- (c)   substantive decisions; and
- (d)   all applications and decisions made under rule 45.

(2)   Subject to paragraph (3), the record of matters must be open to the inspection of any person without charge at all reasonable hours on working days.

(3) Where the adjudicator is satisfied that it is just and reasonable to do so, the adjudicator may exclude from inspection any information contained in the record of matters.

(4)   Depending on all the circumstances, it may be just and reasonable for the adjudicator to exclude from inspection any information contained in the record of matters if it is in the interest of morals, public order, national security, juveniles or the protection of the private lives of the parties to the proceedings, or where the adjudicator considers that publicity would prejudice the interests of justice.

47   List of documents and documents
(1)   For the purposes of these Rules, a list of documents must be in writing and must contain the following information where available in relation to each document –
- (a)   a brief description of the nature of the document;
- (b)   whether the document is in the possession or control of the party;
- (c)   whether the document is an original, a copy certified to be a true copy of the original, an office copy or another type of copy;
- (d)   the date of the document;
- (e)   the document parties or the original author and recipient of the document; and
- (f)   the version number or similar identification number or code of the document.

(2) Unless the adjudicator otherwise permits, where a document provided for the purposes of the proceedings is or contains a coloured map, plan or drawing, any copy provided of that map, plan or drawing must be in the same colours as the map, plan or drawing of which it is a copy (so for example, where a plan shows the boundary of a property in red, a copy of the plan must also show the boundary in red).

48   Evidence

(1)   The adjudicator may require any witness to give evidence on oath or affirmation and for that purpose there may be administered an oath or affirmation in due form.

(2)   No person may be compelled to give any evidence or produce any document or other material that that person could not be compelled to give or produce on a trial of an action in a court of law in England and Wales.

49   Expert evidence

No party may call an expert, or submit an expert's report as evidence, without the adjudicator's permission.

50   Service of documents

(1)   A party's address for service must be a postal address in England and Wales.

(2)   The address for service in paragraph (1) must be either that of the party or of the party's representative who has been appointed as his representative for the purposes of the proceedings.

(3)   A party's address for service remains that party's address for service for the purposes of these Rules unless and until he serves on the adjudicator and the other parties notice of a different address for service.

(4)   Any document to be served on or delivered to any person (other than the adjudicator) under these Rules may only be served –
  (a)   by first class post to his postal address given as his address for service;
  (b)   by leaving it at his address for service;
  (c)   subject to paragraph (5), by document exchange;
  (d)   subject to paragraph (6), by fax;
  (e)   subject to paragraph (7), by email; or
  (f)   where no address for service has been given, by post to or leaving it at his registered office, principal place of business, head or main office or last known address, as appropriate.

(5)   A document may be served on any person other than the adjudicator by document exchange in England and Wales if, in advance, the recipient has informed the adjudicator and all parties in writing –
  (a)   that the recipient is willing to accept service by document exchange; and
  (b)   of the box number at the document exchange to which the documents should be addressed.

(6)   A document may be served by fax on any person other than the adjudicator, to a fax number at the address for service for that person if, in advance, the recipient has informed the adjudicator and all parties in writing –
  (a)   that the recipient is willing to accept service by fax; and
  (b)   of the fax number to which the documents should be sent.

(7)   A document may be served by email on any person other than the adjudicator, if, in advance, the recipient has informed the adjudicator and all parties in writing –

(a)   that the recipient is willing to accept service by email;

(b)   of the email address to which documents should be sent, which shall be deemed to be at the recipient's address for service; and

(c)   if the recipient wishes to so specify, the format in which documents must be sent.

(8)   Any document addressed to the adjudicator must be sent –

(a)   by first class post to an address specified by the adjudicator; or

(b)   by such other method as the adjudicator may specify, including document exchange, fax or email.

(9)   Where under paragraph (8)(b) the adjudicator specifies another method of service, the adjudicator may –

(a)   specify that that method may be used generally or only in relation to a certain document or documents;

(b)   specify that the specified method is no longer available or substitute that specified method with another specified method; and

(c)   make such directions in relation to the use of the specified method as he deems appropriate.

(10)   Any document served on an unincorporated body may be sent to its secretary, manager or similar officer duly authorised to accept such service.

(11)   Any document which is served in accordance with this rule shall be regarded as having been served on the day shown in the table below –

Method of service	*Day of service*
First class post to a postal address within England and Wales	The second working day after it was posted.
Leaving it at a postal address within England and Wales	The working day after it was left.
Document exchange within England and Wales	The second working day after it was left at the document exchange.
Fax	The working day after it was transmitted.
Email	The working day after it was transmitted.

(12)   The adjudicator may direct that service under these Rules of any document may be dispensed with and in those circumstances may make such consequential directions as he deems appropriate.

51   Applications, actions by the adjudicator of his own motion, notification, representations and objections

(1)   This rule does not apply to Part 3 and rule 45.

(2)   An application to the adjudicator must –

(a)   be in writing;

(b)   state the name of the person applying or on whose behalf the application is made;

(c)   be addressed to the adjudicator;

(d)   state the nature of the application;

(e)   state the reason or reasons for the application; and

(f)   if any of the parties or persons who would be affected by the application consent to it, either –
   (i)   be signed by all the parties or persons who consent or their duly authorised representatives; or
   (ii)   have attached to it a copy of their written consent.

(3)   The adjudicator may dispense with any or all of the requirements under paragraph (2) –
   (a)   in relation to an application made to the adjudicator at a time when all persons who would be affected by the application are present before the adjudicator; or
   (b)   if the adjudicator otherwise considers it appropriate or practicable to do so.

(4)   For the purposes of paragraph (2)(f), the written consent referred to in that paragraph may be in the form of a letter, fax or email.

(5)   If an application is not consented to by all persons who will be affected by the application then, subject to paragraph (10), the adjudicator must serve written notice on persons who have not consented to the application but who would be affected by it.

(6)   In the notice under paragraph (5) the adjudicator must state –
   (a)   that the application has been made;
   (b)   details of the application;
   (c)   that the person has a right to make written objections to or representations about the application; and
   (d)   the period within which such objections or representations must be lodged with the adjudicator.

(7)   If the adjudicator intends to act of his own motion under these Rules then, subject to paragraph (10), he must serve written notice of his intention on all persons who will be affected by the action.

(8)   In the notice under paragraph (7) the adjudicator must state –
   (a)   that the adjudicator intends to take action of his own motion;
   (b)   the action the adjudicator intends to take;
   (c)   that a person has a right to make written objections or representations to the action that the adjudicator intends to take; and
   (d)   the period within which such objections or representations must be lodged with the adjudicator.

(9)   A person lodges an objection or representation if within the specified period he serves –
   (a)   on the adjudicator a written statement setting out the grounds for his objection or representation; and
   (b)   on all the other persons who will be affected by the action a copy of the written statement served on the adjudicator under sub-paragraph (a).

(10)   The adjudicator shall not be required to serve notice under paragraphs (5) and (7) if, in the circumstances, he does not consider it appropriate or practicable to do so.

(11)   Paragraph (10) does not apply to notices required to be served by rule 33.

52   Consideration by the adjudicator of applications (including applications for directions), representations and objections

(1)   In relation to any application, representation or objection made to the adjudicator, unless –

(a)   the adjudicator is satisfied that it is frivolous or vexatious; or

(b)   it is received by the adjudicator after the expiry of any time limit specified for making that application, representation or objection,

the adjudicator must consider all applications, representations or objections made to him.

(2)   If an application, representation or objection is received by the adjudicator after the expiry of any time limit specified for making it, the adjudicator may consider the application, representation or objection, but he is not bound to do so.

(3)   In considering any application, representation or objection, the adjudicator must make all enquiries he thinks necessary and must, if required by these Rules or if he considers it necessary, give the person making the application, representation or objection and the parties or other persns who will be affected by it the opportunity to
appear before him or to submit written representations.

(4)   The adjudicator may decide to accept or reject an application, representation or objection in whole or in part.

(5)   Following his consideration of any applications, representations or objections that are made to him, the adjudicator must notify the person who made the application, representation or objection and the parties and any other persons who will be affected by it, of his decision in accordance with these Rules.

53   Adjournment
In addition to the powers and obligations to adjourn proceedings contained in Part 2 and rule 38, the adjudicator may adjourn the whole or part of the proceedings when and to the extent that he feels it reasonable to do so.

54   Power to vary or set aside directions
Subject to these Rules, the adjudicator may at any time, on the application of a party or otherwise, vary or set aside directions made under these Rules.

55   Failure to comply with a direction
(1) Where a party has failed to comply with a direction given by the adjudicator (including a direction to commence court
proceedings under section 110(1)) the adjudicator may impose a sanction on the defaulting party –

(a)   on the application of any other party; or

(b)   of his own motion.

(2)   Where the defaulting party was the person who made (or has been substituted for or added to the party who made) the original application, the sanction may include requiring the registrar to cancel the original application in whole or in part.

(3)   Where the defaulting party was a person who objected to (or has been substituted for or added to the party who objected to) the original application, the sanction may include requiring the registar to give effect to the original application in whole or in part as if the objection had not been made.

(4)   A sanction that includes either of the requirements on the registrar under paragraph (2) or (3) shall be treated as the substantive decision on that matter.

(5)   If the sanction does not include either of the requirements on the registrar under

paragraph (2) or (3), the adjudicator must serve written notice on the parties of his decision as to what if any sanctions are imposed, and he may make consequential directions.

56   Errors of procedure

Where, before the adjudicator has made his final substantive order in relation to a matter, there has been an error of procedure such as a failure to comply with a rule –

(a)   the error does not invalidate any step taken in the proceedings, unless the adjudicator so orders; and

(b)   the adjudicator may make an order or take any other step that he considers appropriate to remedy the error.

57   Accidental slips or omissions

The adjudicator may at any time amend an order or direction to correct a clerical error or other accidental slip or omission.

58   Time and place

If the adjudicator deems it appropriate to do so, he may alter –

(a)   any time limit specified in these Rules;

(b)   any time limit set by the adjudicator; or

(c)   the date, time or location appointed for a hearing or for any other appearance of the parties before him.

59   Calculation of time

(1)   Where a period of time for doing an act is specified by these Rules or by a direction of the adjudicator, that period is to be calculated –

(a)   excluding the day on which the period begins; and

(b)   unless otherwise specified, by reference to calendar days.

(2)   Where the time specified by these Rules or by a direction of the adjudicator for doing an act ends on a day which is not a working day, that act is done in time if it is done on the next working day.

60   Representation of parties

(1)   If a party who was previously unrepresented appoints a representative or, having been represented, appoints a replacement representative, that party must, as soon as reasonably practicable following the appointment, notify the adjudicator and the other parties in writing –

(a)   of the fact that he has appointed a representative or replacement representative;

(b)   the name and contact details of the representative or replacement representative;

(c)   whether the representative or replacement representative has been authorised by the party to accept service of documents; and

(d)   if the representative or replacement representative has been authorised to accept service, the address for service.

(2)   If a party who was previously represented ceases to be represented, that party must, as soon as reasonably practicable following the ending of his representation, notify the adjudicator and the other parties in writing –

(a)   of the fact that he is no longer represented; and

(b)   where the party's address for service had previously been the address of the representative, the party's new address for service.

61 Independence of adjudicator's staff

When undertaking a non-administrative function of the adjudicator on the adjudicator's authorisation, a member of the adjudicator's staff is not subject to the direction of the Lord Chancellor or any other person or body.

LAND REGISTRATION ACT 2002 (TRANSITIONAL PROVISIONS) ORDER 2003, SI 2003/1953

Preliminary

1 Citation, commencement and interpretation

(1)   This Order may be cited as the Land Registration Act 2002 (Transitional Provisions) Order 2003 and shall come into force on the day that section 1 of the Act comes into force.

(2)   In this Order –

'the 1925 Act' means the Land Registration Act 1925,
'the 1925 Rules' means the Land Registration Rules 1925,
'the 1972 Rules' means the Land Registration (Souvenir Land) Rules 1972,
'the 1991 Rules' means the Land Registration (Open Register) Rules 1991,
'the 1993 Rules' means the Land Registration (Official Searches) Rules 1993,
'the 2003 Rules' means the Land Registration Rules 2003,
'the Act' means the Land Registration Act 2002,
'commencement' means the day when section 1 of the Act comes into force,
'the Regulations' means the Land Registration (Conduct of Business) Regulations 2000.

General and administrative

2 Chief Land Registrar

The person holding the office of Chief Land Registrar immediately before commencement shall continue to be the Chief Land Registrar notwithstanding that he has not been appointed under section 99(3) of the Act.

3 Extension of effect of statutory provisions - first registration, dealings, etc.

(1)   Notwithstanding the repeal of the 1925 Act, that Act shall continue to have effect in relation to any application referred to in paragraph (2) that is pending immediately before commencement.

(2)   Paragraph (1) applies to –
      (a)   an application for the first registration of land,
      (b)   any other application (whether or not being one within paragraphs 5 or 6 of Schedule 12 to the Act) that, if completed, would result in a change to the register.

(3)   Paragraph (1) is subject to articles 5, 7 and 24.

4 Extension of effect of statutory provisions for the purpose of the Order

Notwithstanding the repeal of the 1925 Act, that Act shall continue in force to the extent necessary to enable the remaining provisions of this Order to have effect.

5 Notices

(1)   The 2003 Rules apply to the giving of –
      (a)   any notice under this Order, and

(b)   any notice under the 1925 Act, as continued under Schedule 12 to the Act or article 3, other than a notice to which paragraph (3) applies.

(2)   Section 79 of the 1925 Act does not apply to any notice to which paragraph (1)(b) applies.

(3)   Subject to the modification referred to in paragraph (4), sub-sections (1) and (2) of section 30 of the 1925 Act apply to any notice required to be given under sub-section (1) of that section, as continued under article 3.

(4)   The modification referred to in paragraph (3) is the omission of the words 'by registered post' from section 30(1) of the 1925 Act.

Disputes, objections, appeals and proceedings

6   Hearing of existing disputes

(1)   This article applies to any pending application in relation to which there is, immediately before commencement, a dispute to which rule 299(1) of the 1925 Rules applies that has not been finally disposed of.

(2)   For the purposes of paragraph (1) there is a dispute to which rule 299(1) of the 1925 Rules applies where –

    (a)   in relation to a caution lodged under section 54 of the 1925 Act or rule 215(2) of the 1925 Rules, an application has been lodged that has resulted in the notice referred to in rule 218 of the 1925 Rules being issued before commencement, provided that (whether before or after commencement) the registrar is satisfied that cause has been shown under rule 219(3) of the 1925 Rules, and

    (b)   in the case of any other pending application, a person has, before commencement, objected to the application under rule 298(1) of the 1925 Rules, provided that the registrar is satisfied subsequently that the objection cannot be treated as groundless under rule 298(4) of the 1925 Rules.

(3)   Neither the objection that has led to the dispute, nor any subsequent objection to the same application, shall constitute an objection for the purpose of section 73 of the Act.

(4)   The registrar must deal with or continue to deal with the existing dispute and any dispute resulting from any subsequent objection to the same application, in accordance with rule 299 of the 1925 Rules and, where appropriate, the Land Registration (Hearings Procedure) Rules 2000 until the dispute has been finally disposed of.

(5)   Subject to the modifications referred to in paragraph (6), the Regulations shall continue to apply in relation to any dispute referred to in paragraph (1) to enable relevant acts of the registrar to which those regulations relate to be done or continue to be done by a person nominated by the registrar under the Regulations.

(6)   The modifications referred to in paragraph (5) are –

    (a)   substitution of the following sub-paragraph for regulation 2(d) of the Regulations -

        '(d)   "qualified officer" means a member of staff of the land registry who holds a 10 year general qualification within the meaning of section 71 of the Courts and Legal Services Act 1990; and',

    (b)   substitution of the words 'qualified officer' for the words 'qualified registrar' where they occur in regulations 3(1), 5(1) and 6(1) of the Regulations,

(c)   substitution of the word 'person' for the word 'registrar' where it occurs in regulations 3(2), 5(2) and 6(2) of the Regulations, and

(d)   substitution of the words 'qualified officer' for the word 'registrar' where it occurs in regulations 5(3) and 6(3) of the Regulations.

7   Objection after commencement

(1)   This article applies to any application that is pending immediately before commencement in relation to which an objection is made after commencement that is not an objection to which article 6(3) applies.

(2)   Notwithstanding paragraph 5 of Schedule 12 to the Act, the objection shall constitute an objection to which section 73 of the Act applies.

8   Appeals

Rule 300 of the 1925 Rules (Appeal to the court) shall continue to have effect in relation to –

(a)   any decision by the registrar under rule 298(4) of the 1925 Rules that an objection is groundless (whether the decision is made before commencement, or after commencement in relation to an application that is pending immediately before commencement), and

(b)   any decision or order by the registrar under rule 299 of the 1925 Rules (whether made before commencement, or after commencement in relation to a dispute to which article 6 applies).

9   Legal Proceedings

(1)   This article applies to any proceedings which were instituted before commencement but which have not been concluded immediately before commencement.

(2)   Any proceedings to which paragraph (1) applies may be continued until concluded, whether by final determination by the court or otherwise, as if the 2002 Act had not been passed.

(3)   Where in any proceedings the court gives judgment or makes an order, or has already done so before commencement, and the effect of the judgment or order is to require an entry or cancellation to be made in the register or the register to be rectified or altered, then the proceedings shall not be treated as concluded for the purpose of paragraphs (1) and (2) until the entry or cancellation has been made, or the register rectified or altered, as required by the court.

(4)   Paragraphs (2) and (3) have effect without prejudice to the need for any order of the court or alteration of the register made after commencement to comply with rule 127 of the 2003 Rules.

(5)   In this article –

'court' has the same meaning as in the 1925 Act, and 'proceedings' means any proceedings within the jurisdiction of the court by virtue of a provision of the 1925 Act.

Souvenir land

10   Souvenir land - application of articles and definitions

(1)   Articles 11, 12 and 13 apply where –

(a)   there is in force in relation to registered land immediately before commencement a declaration by the registrar under rule 3 of the 1972 Rules, and

(b)   particulars of the declaration have been entered in the register under rule 6 of those rules.

(2)   In articles 11, 12 and 13 –

'declaration' means the declaration by the registrar under rule 3 of the 1972 Rules,
'proprietor' in relation to souvenir land means the registered proprietor or, where the registered
    proprietor has died, been made bankrupt or, being a corporate body, has been dissolved,
    the person who would be entitled to be registered as proprietor in his place but for any
    unregistered transaction effected after the declaration was made,
'souvenir land' means the registered land subject to a declaration,
'third party' means a person other than the proprietor.

11   Souvenir land – restriction on dispositions

(1)   Where any unregistered transaction with souvenir land has been effected after the
declaration was made and has resulted in one or more third parties becoming entitled to apply
to be registered as proprietor of any part or parts of the land, the proprietor must not dispose
of that land otherwise than in a manner that gives effect in the register to the interests of the
third parties.

(2)   The particulars of a declaration entered in the individual register of any souvenir land
shall take effect after commencement as if there were a restriction in the proprietorship register
in the following terms –

    'No disposition is to be registered without the consent of the person or persons (if any)
    entitled to apply to be registered as proprietor of the land disposed of, or any part of it, as
    the result of any unregistered transaction effected since [date] being the date when a
    declaration made under rule 3 of the Land Registration (Souvenir Land) Rules 1972 was
    noted in the register.'

(3)   The registrar may amend the registered title to any souvenir land so as to substitute for
the particulars of the declaration a restriction in the terms set out in paragraph (2).

12   Application to cancel entries relating to souvenir land

(1)   A proprietor who claims that there has been no unregistered transaction with the
souvenir land, or a particular part of the land, after the declaration was made, so that no third
party has become entitled to be registered as proprietor of it, may apply in Form RX3 in
Schedule 1 to the 2003 Rules in relation to that land to cancel in the register the particulars of
the declaration or, where the registrar has registered a restriction in substitution for those
particulars under article 11(3), that restriction.

(2)   If the registrar is satisfied that there has been no such transaction as is referred to in
paragraph (1), he must –
    (a)   where the application relates to the whole of the land in a registered title, cancel the
           relevant entry in the register,
    (b)   where the application relates to part only of the land in a registered title, give effect
           to the application in the register in such manner as he thinks appropriate.

13   Application for registration by a third party

(1)   This article applies where, in relation to any souvenir land, a third party is able to satisfy
the registrar that one or more unregistered transactions have been effected since the declaration
was made and that, as a result of them and any other events that have taken place –
    (a)   the registered estate is now vested in him, or
    (b)   a legal estate derived (whether directly or indirectly) out of the land is vested in him,
           or

(c)   a legal estate such as is referred to in sub-paragraph (a) or (b) has been transferred to him (either directly or indirectly) by the person in whom it has become vested.

(2)   The third party may apply to be registered as the proprietor of a legal estate if that estate is one to which section 3 of the Act would apply if the estate were an unregistered estate within that section.

(3)   Before determining an application under paragraph (2), the registrar must give notice of it to the person named in the proprietorship register as proprietor unless that person has consented to the application.

Cautions

14   Cautions against first registration

(1)   In relation to a caution against first registration lodged for registration before commencement, Part 5 of the 2003 Rules applies with the modifications set out in paragraph (2).

(2)   The modifications referred to in paragraph (1) are –
(a)   paragraphs (2) to (5) of rule 41 do not apply,
(b)   in rule 51(1) of the 2003 Rules, the omission of the word 'cautioner's'.

15   Cautions against conversion

(1)   This article applies where, immediately before commencement, there is an entry in respect of a caution lodged under rule 215(2) of the 1925 Rules in the register of any title.

(2)   In the event of an application to upgrade the title under any of subsections (1) to (5) of section 62 of the Act, the registrar shall, before determining the application, give notice of it to the person named in the entry referred to in paragraph (1).

(3)   Where the person to whom notice is given, or any person deriving title under that person, responds to the notice by claiming any estate, right or interest in the land in the title, then, to the extent that the estate, right or interest subsists and is otherwise enforceable against the land, the claim is to be treated for the purpose of section 62(6) of the Act as one for an estate right or interest whose enforceability is preserved by virtue of the existing entry about the class of title.

16   Mortgage cautions

(1)   Subject to this article, mortgage cautions and sub-mortgage cautions entered in the register shall continue to have the same effect after commencement as they had immediately before commencement.

(2)   Subject to paragraphs (3) and (4), the registrar must cancel a mortgage caution or a sub-mortgage caution where –
(a)   the cautioner, or some other person who can satisfy the registrar that he is entitled to the benefit of the protected mortgage or protected sub-mortgage, makes an application to withdraw it in Form WCT in Schedule 1 to the 2003 Rules, or
(b)   evidence is produced that satisfies the registrar, that the protected mortgage or protected sub-mortgage has been discharged, or
(c)   an application is made to register the protected mortgage, and any protected sub-mortgage, under section 27 of the Act and the registrar approves the application.

(3)   Where there is a sub-mortgage caution entered in the register and application is made to cancel the relevant mortgage caution under sub-paragraph (a) or (b) of paragraph (2), the registrar must give notice of the application to the sub-mortgage cautioner.

(4)   An application to register a protected mortgage under section 27(2)(f) of the Act must comply with the 2003 Rules and be accompanied by –

(a)   the original deed creating the protected mortgage, and

(b)   where title to the protected mortgage is vested in someone other than the cautioner, the documents proving devolution of title to the applicant.

(5)   When registering a protected mortgage, the registrar must make an entry showing that it has priority in relation to other entries in the register from the date that the mortgage caution was entered in the register.

(6)   Where application is made to register a disposition of the registered estate or registered charge affected by a mortgage caution or sub-mortgage caution, the registrar must –

(a)   give notice of the application to the cautioner,

(b)   retain the mortgage caution or sub-mortgage caution in the register unless it is to be cancelled in accordance with paragraph (2).

(7)   In this article –

'cautioner' means the person named in a mortgage caution or sub-mortgage caution,

'mortgage caution' means a caution entered in the register in a specially prescribed form under section 106 of the 1925 Act as originally enacted,

'protected mortgage' means the mortgage that is protected by a mortgage caution,

'protected sub-mortgage' means the sub-mortgage that is protected by a sub-mortgage caution,

'sub-mortgage caution' means a sub-mortgage caution to which rule 228 of the 1925 Rules applied before commencement.

17   Modification of paragraph 2(3) of Schedule 12 to the Act

Paragraph 2(3) of Schedule 12 to the Act shall have the effect as if there were inserted at the end ', but with the substitution for the words in section 55(1) from "prescribed" to "served" of the words "period prescribed under paragraph 2(4) of Schedule 12 to the Land Registration Act 2002".'

18   Non-standard restrictions in approved instruments

(1)   This article applies where a person applies in an approved instrument to enter a restriction in the register and the registrar considers that there is a standard form of restriction which is to like or similar effect to the restriction applied for (or would be but for the fact that it does not purport to restrict the entry of a notice).

(2)   Where this article applies –

(a)   the registrar must enter in the register the standard form of restriction referred to in paragraph (1) instead of the restriction applied for,

(b)   the application is to be treated as though it was an application for entry in the register of a standard form of restriction, and

(c)   rule 92(1) of the 2003 rules does not apply to the application.

(3)   In this article –

'approved instrument' means a charge, or transfer –

(a)   which contains the application for the restriction applied for (whether in the body of the instrument or, in the case of a charge, in an incorporated document within the meaning of rule 139 of the 1925 Rules),

(b)   the form of which (including the application for the restriction) has been approved by the registrar before commencement as capable of being accepted for registration, and

(c)   in relation to which the approval referred to in sub-paragraph (b) has not been withdrawn, and

'standard form of restriction' means one referred to in rule 91 of the 2003 Rules.

Outline applications

19   Outline applications

(1)   This article applies where, immediately before commencement –

   (a)   there is in force a notice given under rule 83A(9) of the 1925 Rules that allows an outline application to be delivered in respect of any category of application (including, for the avoidance of doubt, a caution to which rule 215 of those rules applies),

   (b)   an outline application has been validly delivered in relation to such an application,

   (c)   the reserved period referred to in rule 83A(8) of the 1925 Rules has not expired, and

   (d)   the form required by rule 83A(6) of the 1925 Rules has not been lodged.

(2)   Notwithstanding the repeal of the 1925 Act, the registrar must give effect to the application in the register as of the time at which the outline application was delivered, provided the applicant lodges the appropriate form required by rule 83A(6) of the 1925 Rules at the appropriate office before expiry of the reserved period referred to in rule 83A(8) of those rules and the application otherwise complies with those rules.

(3)   In paragraph (2), 'appropriate office' means the office of the land registry that, immediately before commencement, would have been the proper office within the meaning of rule 1(5A) of the 1925 Rules.

Matrimonial home rights cautions

20   Matrimonial home rights cautions

(1)   The registrar shall not be required, on the application of the proprietor of the registered estate affected, to serve the notice referred to in rule 223 of the 2003 Rules in relation to a matrimonial caution except upon production of –

   (a)   a release in writing of the matrimonial home rights protected by the matrimonial caution, or

   (b)   a statutory declaration that, as to the whole or any part of the land to which the matrimonial caution relates, no charge under section 2 of the Matrimonial Homes Act 1967, section 2 of the Matrimonial Homes Act 1983 or section 31 of the Family Law Act 1996 has ever arisen or, if such a charge has arisen, it is no longer subsisting.

(2)   In this article 'matrimonial caution' means a caution registered under section 2(7) of the Matrimonial Homes Act 1967 before 14th February 1983 which remains in the register after commencement.

Index of relating franchises and manors

21   Index of relating franchises and manors

(1)   As soon as practicable after commencement, the registrar must take such steps as he considers appropriate to create the index of relating franchises and manors from the material parts of the index map maintained by the registrar under rule 8 of the 1925 Rules and other relevant information under his control in such a form that it complies with rule 10(1)(b).

(2)   Rule 10(1)(b) shall not have effect until the index of relating franchises and manors has been created so as to comply with it.

(3)   Until the index of relating franchises and manors has been created so as to comply with rule 10(1)(b), the registrar must ensure that official certificates of the result of searches of the index of relating franchises and manors issued in accordance with rule 146(3) of the 2003 Rules contain the same information as if the index of relating franchises and manors had been so created.

(4)   In this article –

'index of relating franchises and manors' means the index to be kept under rule 10(1)(b), and 'rule 10(1)(b)' means rule 10(1)(b) of the 2003 Rules.

Compulsory first registration

22   Dispositions void under section 123A of the 1925 Act

(1) After commencement, a void disposition is to be treated for all purposes as an event to which the requirement of registration applied and as a transfer, grant or creation that has become void as a result of the application of section 7(1) of the Act.

(2) In this article 'void disposition' means a disposition of unregistered land that, before commencement, has become void as a result of the application of section 123A(5) of the 1925 Act.

23   Other dispositions affected by section 123A of the 1925 Act

(1)   Subject to paragraph (2), a relevant disposition is to be treated for all purposes after commencement as an event to which the requirement of registration applies.

(2)   For the purposes of section 6(4) of the Act, the period for registration is the period that expires at the end of the applicable period referred to in section 123A(3) of the 1925 Act, or such longer period as the registrar may provide under section 6(5) of the Act.

(3)   In this article 'relevant disposition' means a disposition of unregistered land where –
    (a)   before commencement section 123A of the 1925 Act applied to it,
    (b)   no application to register the relevant legal estate in accordance with section 123A(2) of the 1925 Act had been made before commencement, and
    (c)   immediately before commencement the applicable period referred to in section 123A(3) of the 1925 Act had not expired.

Land and charge certificates

24   Abolition of land and charge certificates

(1)   Notwithstanding paragraph 5 of Schedule 12 to the Act, Part V of the 1925 Act shall cease to apply in relation to any application that is pending immediately before commencement.

(2)   Rules 203 and 204 of the 2003 Rules do not apply to –
    (a)   any land certificate or charge certificate held by the registrar immediately before commencement, or
    (b)   any land certificate or charge certificate lodged in connection with any application, including any application that is pending immediately before commencement, or
    (c)   any document incorporated in any land certificate or charge certificate.

(3)   The registrar may destroy –
   (a)   any land certificate or charge certificate held by him or which comes into his possession,
   (b)   any document incorporated in such a land certificate or charge certificate.

(4)   Paragraph (3) applies notwithstanding an entry in the register to which paragraph 3 of Schedule 12 to the Act applies but without prejudice to the continuing effect of such an entry.

Obligation to make further advances

25   Obligation to make further advances
Where, immediately before commencement, an obligation to make a further advance is noted in the register under section 30(3) of the 1925 Act, the obligation is to be treated after commencement as entered in the register according to rules for the purpose of section 49(3)(b) of the Act.

Forms

26   Period of grace for use of old forms
(1) Subject to paragraph (3), an applicant may use in place of any new form the relevant old form –

   (a)   for the period of 3 months following commencement, and
   (b)   thereafter, where use of the relevant old form is expressly required by law or under the terms of a valid contract entered into before commencement.

(2)   Where the relevant old form is used in accordance with paragraph (1) the 2003 Rules apply to the use of that form as they would apply to the use of the new form.

(3) Where there is an entry in Column 3 in the Schedule, paragraph (1) only applies to the use of the relevant old form –
   (a)   where the entry limits use of the relevant old form to particular cases, in those cases specified in the entry, and
   (b)   where the entry places an additional requirement on the applicant, if the applicant complies with that requirement.

(4) In this article –

'new form' means a form prescribed by the 2003 Rules that is referred to in Column 1 in the Schedule, and
'relevant old form' in relation to any particular new form means the form prescribed by the 1925 Rules, the 1991 Rules, the 1993 Rules or the Land Registration (Matrimonial Home Rights) Rules 1997 (as the case may be) that is shown against the new form in Column 2 in the Schedule.

27   Exclusion of Forms 112A, 112B and 112C from inspection or copying
Rules 133(2) and 135(2) of the 2003 Rules apply to any Form 112A, Form 112B or Form 112C, as lodged under the 1991 Rules or article 26, as they apply to any Form CIT.

Official searches and official copies

28 Priority of unexpired official searches

(1) This article applies to an official search with priority made before commencement under the 1993 Rules whose priority period has not expired at commencement.

(2) Section 72 of the Act and rules 151 to 154 of the 2003 Rules (as appropriate) shall apply to the official search as if it had been made under Part 13 of the 2003 Rules but with the priority period being that which applied to it under the 1993 Rules.

29 Office copies issued before commencement

Office copies of and extracts from the register and of and from documents, to which section 113 of the 1925 Act applied before commencement, are to be treated for all purposes after commencement as official copies to which section 67 of the Act applies.

Schedule

Article 26

Column 1	Column 2	Column 3
New form	*Relevant old form*	*Requirements or limitations*
AP1	AP1	***Requirements –*** (1) Where a fee is payable then the applicant must lodge with the form a cheque or postal order for the requisite fee or a request in writing for the fee to be paid by Direct Debit under an authorised agreement with the land registry. (2) The full name of the person applying to change the register must be inserted in the form. (3) Where the application is to register a registrable disposition, but there are no disclosable overriding interests, the form must include a statement to that effect, or be accompanied by such a statement in writing signed by the applicant.
AS1	AS1	
AS2	AS2	
AS3	AS3	
CH1	113	***Requirement –*** Where a fee is payable then the applicant must lodge with the form a cheque or postal order for the requisite fee or a request in writing for the fee to be paid by Direct Debit under an authorised agreement with the land registry.
CI	102	
CIT	112A, or 112B, or 112C	***Limitation –*** The relevant old form may only be used where it is signed by a qualifying applicant (within the meaning of rule 140 of the 2003 Rules) who is able to complete one or more of the certificates contained in the particular form.
CN1	CT1	***Limitation –*** The relevant old form may only be used where application is made to cancel notice of an unregistered lease or rentcharge.

		Requirement – Where a fee is payable then the applicant must lodge with the form a cheque or postal order for the requisite fee or a request in writing for the fee to be paid by Direct Debit under an authorised agreement with the land registry.

CT1	CT1	**Limitation –**
		The relevant old form may not be used
		    (a) Where the estate affected by the caution is a rentcharge, a franchise or a profit a prendre in gross, or
		    (b) Where the applicant wishes to provide a certificate by a conveyancer as to the cautioner's interest in place of a statutory declaration.
		
		Requirements –
		(1) The applicant must lodge with the form a cheque or postal order for the fee payable or a request in writing for the fee to be paid by Direct Debit under an authorised agreement with the land registry.
		(2) Where the estate affected by the caution is a lease, the applicant must add a note as to whether or not the lease is discontinuous.

DL	DL	**Requirement –** The applicant must leave panels 2 and 3 of the relevant old form blank and use the accompanying application form to provide the relevant information.
DS1	DS1	
DS2	DS2	**Requirement –** The full name of the applicant must be inserted in the form.
DS3	DS3	
FR1	FR1	**Requirements –** (1) The applicant must lodge with the form a cheque or postal order for the fee payable or a request in writing for the fee to be paid by Direct Debit under an authorised agreement with the land registry. (2) The full name of the applicant must be inserted in the form. (3) Where there are no disclosable overriding interests, the form must include a statement to that effect, or be accompanied by such a statement in writing signed by the applicant.
MH1	MH1	**Limitation –** The relevant old form may not be used where the applicant wishes to provide a certificate by a conveyancer as to the existence of an order made under section 33(5) of the Family Law Act 1996.
MH2	MH2	**Limitation –** The relevant old form may not be used where the applicant wishes an order made under section 33(5) of the Family Law Act 1996.
MH3	MH3	

OC1	109	**Requirements –** (1) Where a title number is not quoted and the application relates to a caution against first registration, a rentcharge, a franchise, a profit a prendre in gross or a manor, panel 6 of the relevant old form must be amended accordingly. (2) Where the applicant wishes to apply for a certificate of inspection of a title plan, the words 'Form 102' in panel 3 of the relevant old form must be amended to read 'Form CI'.
OC2	110	**Limitation –** The relevant old form may not be used to apply for an official copy of any document that is not referred to in the register.
OS1	94A	
OS2	94B	
OS3	94C	
PIC	111	**Limitation –** The relevant old form may not be used to apply for personal inspection of any document that is not referred to in the register.
PN1	104	
SIM	96	
TP1	TP1	
TP2	TP2	
TP3	TP3	
TR1	TR1	
TR2	TR2	
TR3	TR3	
TR4	TR4	
WCT	WCT	

LAND REGISTRATION (PROPER OFFICE) ORDER 2003, SI 2003/2040

1   Citation and commencement

This Order may be cited as the Land Registration (Proper Office) Order 2003 and shall come into force on 13th October 2003.

2   Applications to which this Order applies

(1)   This Order applies to any application to the registrar except an application delivered to the registrar –

      (a)   in accordance with a written arrangement as to delivery made between the registrar and the applicant or between the registrar and the applicant's conveyancer, or

      (b)   under the provisions of any relevant notice given under Schedule 2 to the Land Registration Rules 2003.

(2)   In this article 'conveyancer' means –

      (a)   a solicitor, or

      (b)   a licensed conveyancer within the meaning of section 11(2) of the Administration of Justice Act 1985, or

      (c)   a fellow of the Institute of Legal Executives.

3   Designation of the proper office

The proper office for the receipt of an application to which this Order applies is any office of the land registry specified in column 1 of the Schedule which is opposite an administrative area shown in column 2 of the Schedule in which the land to which that application relates is wholly or partly situated.

SCHEDULE

Article 3

Column 1	Column 2
Office of the land registry	Administrative Area
Land Registry, Birkenhead (Old Market) Office	Merseyside Staffordshire Stoke-on-Trent
Land Registry, Birkenhead (Rosebrae) Office	Cheshire Halton Hammersmith and Fulham Kensington and Chelsea Warrington
Land Registry, Coventry Office	West Midlands Worcestershire
Land Registry, Croydon Office	Bexley Bromley Croydon

	Kingston upon Thames Merton Sutton
Land Registry, Durham (Boldon) Office	Cumbria Surrey
Land Registry, Durham (Southfield) Office	Darlington Durham Hartlepool Middlesbrough Northumberland Redcar and Cleveland Stockton-on-Tees Tyne and Wear
Land Registry, Gloucester Office	Bracknell Forest Bristol Gloucestershire Oxfordshire Reading Slough South Gloucestershire Warwickshire West Berkshire Windsor and Maidenhead Wokingham
Land Registry, Harrow Office	Brent Camden City of Westminster The City of London Harrow Islington The Inner Temple and the Middle Temple
Land Registry, Kingston Upon Hull Office	Kingston upon Hull Lincolnshire Norfolk North East Lincolnshire North Lincolnshire Suffolk
Land Registry, Lancashire	Blackburn with Darwen Blackpool Lancashire
Land Registry, Leicester Office	Buckinghamshire Leicester Leicestershire Milton Keynes Northamptonshire Rutland
Land Registry, Lytham Office	Greater Manchester
Land Registry, Nottingham (East) Office	Nottingham Nottinghamshire South Yorkshire

Land Registry, Nottingham (West) Office	Derby Derbyshire West Yorkshire
Land Registry, Peterborough Office	Bedfordshire Cambridgeshire Essex Luton Peterborough Southend-on-Sea Thurrock

Land Registry, Plymouth Office	Bath and North East Somerset
	Cornwall
	Devon
	Isles of Scilly
	North Somerset
	Plymouth
	Somerset:
	    Sedgemoor
	    Taunton Deane
	    West Somerset
	Torbay

Land Registry, Portsmouth Office	Brighton and Hove
	East Sussex
	Hampshire:
	    East Hampshire
	    Havant
	Isle of Wight
	Portsmouth
	West Sussex

Land Registry, Stevenage Office	Barking and Dagenham Hackney Havering Hertfordshire Newham Redbridge Tower Hamlets Waltham Forest
Land Registry, Swansea Office Cofrestrfa Tir Swyddfa Abertawe	Barnet Ealing Enfield Harringey Hillingdon Hounslow

Land Registry, Telford Office	Greenwich Herefordshire Lambeth Lewisham Richmond upon Thames Shropshire Southwark The Wrekin Wandsworth
Land Registry, Tunbridge Wells Office	Kent Medway
Land Registry, Wales Office Cofrestrfa Tir Swyddfa Cymru	All counties and county boroughs in Wales

Land Registry, Weymouth Office	Bournemouth
	Dorset
	Hampshire:
	    Basingstoke & Deane
	    Eastleigh
	    Fareham
	    Gosport
	    Hart
	    New Forest
	    Rushmoor
	    Test Valley
	    Winchester
	Poole
	Somerset:
	    Mendip
	    South Somerset
	Southampton
	Swindon
	Wiltshire

Land Registry, York Office	East Riding of Yorkshire North Yorkshire York

LAND REGISTRATION FEE ORDER 2003, SI 2003/2092

1   Citation, commencement and interpretation

(1)   This Order may be cited as the Land Registration Fee Order 2003 and shall come into force on the day that section 1 of the Act comes into force.

(2)   In this Order unless the context otherwise requires –

'account holder' means a person or firm holding a credit account;

'the Act' means the Land Registration Act 2002;

'charge' includes a sub-charge;

'credit account' means an account authorised by the registrar under article 15(1);

'large area application' is as defined in article 6(1);

'large scale application' is as defined in article 6(1);

'premium' means the amount or value of any monetary consideration given by the lessee as part of the same transaction in which a lease is granted by way of fine, premium or otherwise, but, where a registered leasehold estate of substantially the same land is surrendered on the grant of a new lease, the premium for the new lease shall not include the value of the surrendered lease;

'profit' means a profit a prendre in gross;

'monetary consideration' means a consideration in money or money's worth (other than a nominal consideration or a consideration consisting solely of a covenant to pay money owing under a mortgage);

'the rules' means the Land Registration Rules 2003 and a rule referred to by number means the rule so numbered in the rules;

'rent' means the largest amount of annual rent the lease reserves within the first five years of its term that can be quantified at the time an application to register the lease is made;

'Scale 1' means Scale 1 in Schedule 1;

'Scale 2' means Scale 2 in Schedule 2;

'scale fee' means a fee payable in accordance with a scale set out in Schedule 1 or 2 whether or not reduced in accordance with article 2(6);

'scale fee application' means an application which attracts a scale fee, or which would attract such a fee but for the operation of article 6;

'Schedule' means a Schedule to this Order;

'share', in relation to land, means an interest in that land under a trust of land;

'surrender' includes a surrender not made by deed;

'voluntary application' means an application for first registration (other than for the registration of title to a rentcharge, a franchise or a profit) which is not made wholly or in part pursuant to section 4 of the Act (when title must be registered).

(3)   Expressions used in this Order have, unless the contrary intention appears, the meaning which they bear in the rules.

PART 2

Scale fees

2   Applications for first registration and applications for registration of a lease by an original lessee

(1)   The fee for an application for first registration is payable under Scale 1 on the value of the estate in land comprised in the application assessed under article 7 unless the application is —

(a)   for the registration of title to a lease by the original lessee or his personal representative, where paragraph (2) applies;

(b)   for the first registration of a rentcharge, where paragraph (4) applies;

(c)   for the first registration of a franchise or a profit, where paragraph (5) applies;

(d)   a voluntary application, where paragraph (6) applies; or

(e)   a large scale application or a large area application, where article 6 applies.

(2)   The fee for an application for the registration of title to a lease (whether or not it is a registrable disposition) by the original lessee or his personal representative is payable under Scale 1 —

(a)   on an amount equal to the sum of the premium and the rent; or

(b)   where

(i)   there is no premium; and

(ii)   either there is no rent or the rent cannot be quantified at the time the application is made,on the value of the lease assessed under article 7 subject to a minimum fee of £40, unless either of the circumstances in paragraph (3) applies.

(3)   Paragraph (2) shall not apply if the application is —

(a)   a voluntary application, where paragraph (6) applies; or

(b)   large scale application or a large area application, where article 6 applies.

(4)   The fee for an application for the first registration of a rentcharge is £40.

(5)   The fee for an application for the first registration of a franchise or a profit is payable under Scale 1 on the value of the franchise or the profit assessed under article 7.

(6)   The fee for a voluntary application is the fee which would otherwise be payable under paragraphs (1) and (2) for applications to which those paragraphs apply reduced by 25 per cent and, where the reduced fee would be a figure which includes pence, the fee must be adjusted to the nearest £10.

3   Transfers of registered estates for monetary consideration, etc.

(1)   Subject to paragraphs (2), (3) and (4), the fee for an application for the registration of —

(a)   a transfer of a registered estate for monetary consideration;

(b)   a transfer for the purpose of giving effect to a disposition for monetary consideration of a share in a registered estate;

(c)   a surrender of a registered leasehold estate for monetary consideration, other than a surrender to which paragraph (3) of Schedule 4 applies,

is payable under Scale 1 on the amount or value of the consideration.

(2)   Paragraph (1) shall not apply if the application is —

(a)   a large scale application, where article 6 applies; or

(b)   for the registration of a transfer of a matrimonial home made pursuant to an order of the court, where article 4(1)(h) applies.

(3)   Where a sale and sub-sale of a registered estate are made by separate deeds of transfer, a separate fee is payable for each deed of transfer.

(4)   Where a single deed of transfer gives effect to a sale and a sub-sale of the same registered estate a single fee is assessed upon the greater of the monetary consideration given by the purchaser and the monetary consideration given by the sub-purchaser.

(5)   The fee for an application to cancel an entry in the register of notice of an unregistered lease which has determined is payable under Scale 1 on the value of the lease immediately before its determination.

4   Transfers otherwise than for monetary consideration, etc.

(1)   Unless the application is a large scale application (where article 6 applies), the fee for an application for the registration of –

(a)   a transfer of a registered estate otherwise than for monetary consideration (unless paragraph (2) applies);

(b)   a surrender of a registered leasehold estate otherwise than for monetary consideration;

(c)   a transmission of a registered estate on death or bankruptcy;

(d)   an assent of a registered estate (including a vesting assent);

(e)   an appropriation of a registered estate;

(f)   a vesting order or declaration to which section 27(5) of the Act applies;

(g)   an alteration of the register (unless paragraph (3) applies); or

(h)   a transfer of a matrimonial home (being a registered estate) made pursuant to an order of the Court,

is payable under Scale 2 on the value of the registered estate which is the subject of the application, assessed under article 7, but after deducting from it the amount secured on the registered estate by any charge subject to which the registration takes effect.

(2)   Where a transfer of a registered estate otherwise than for monetary consideration is for the purpose of giving effect to the disposition of a share in a registered estate the fee for an application for its registration is payable under Scale 2 on the value of that share.

(3)   In any application for alteration of the register –

(a)   if it appears to the registrar that the fee is excessive, he may reduce it; and

(b)   if it appears to him unreasonable that the applicant should pay a fee, he may waive it.

5   Charges of registered estates

(1)   The fee for an application for the registration of a charge is payable under Scale 2 on the amount of the charge assessed under article 8 unless it is an application to which paragraphs (2), (3) or (4) apply.

(2)   No fee is payable for an application to register a charge lodged with or before the completion of a scale fee application ('the primary application') that will result in the chargor being registered as proprietor of the registered land included in the charge unless –

(a)   the charge includes a registered estate which is not included in the primary application, where paragraph (4) applies; or

(b)   the primary application is a voluntary application, in which case this paragraph shall apply only if the application to register the charge accompanies the primary application.

(3)   No fee is to be paid for an application to register a charge made by a predecessor in title of the applicant that is lodged with or before completion of an application for first registration of the estate included in the charge.

(4)   Where a charge also includes a registered estate which is not included in the primary application any fee payable under Scale 2 is to be assessed on an amount calculated as follows:

$$\frac{\text{Value of the additional property}}{\text{Value of all the property included in the charge}} \times \text{Amount secured by charge}$$

(5)   The fee for an application for the registration of –
    (a)   the transfer of a registered charge for monetary consideration; or
    (b)   a transfer for the purpose of giving effect to the disposition for monetary consideration of a share in a registered charge,
is payable under Scale 2 on the amount or value of the consideration.

(6)   The fee for an application for the registration of the transfer of a registered charge otherwise than for monetary consideration is payable under Scale 2 on –
    (a)   the amount secured by the registered charge at the time of the transfer; or
    (b)   where the transfer relates to more than one charge, the aggregate of the amounts secured by the registered charges at the time of the transfer.

(7)   The fee for an application for the registration of a transfer for the purpose of giving effect to a disposition otherwise than for monetary consideration of a share in a registered charge is payable under Scale 2 on –
    (a)   the proportionate part of the amount secured by the registered charge at the time of the transfer; or
    (b)   where the transfer relates to more than one charge, the proportionate part of the aggregate of the amounts secured by the registered charges at the time of the transfer.

(8)   This article takes effect subject to article 6 (large scale applications).

6   Large scale applications, etc.
(1) In this article –
    (a)   'large area application' means an application for first registration which relates to land having a total area exceeding 100 hectares;
    (b)   'large scale application' means a scale fee application which relates to 20 or more land units, other than –
        (i)   a large area application; or
        (ii)   a low value application,
    (c)   'low value application' means a scale fee application, other than an application for first registration, where the value of the land or the amount of the charge to which it relates (as the case may be) does not exceed £30,000;

(d)   'land unit' means –
  (i)   the land registered under a single title number; or
  (ii)   on a first registration application, a separate area of land not adjoining any other unregistered land affected by the same application.

(2)   Unless the application is one in respect of a charge lodged with another application and falls within article 5(2), the fee for a large scale application is the greater of –
  (a)   the scale fee; and
  (b)   a fee calculated on the following basis –
      (i)   where the application relates to not more than 500 land units, £10 for each land unit; or
      (ii)   where the application relates to more than 500 land units, £5,000 plus £5 for each land unit in excess of 500, up to a maximum of £40,000.

(3)   The fee for a large area application is the Scale 1 fee and if the registrar considers that the cost of the work involved in dealing with the application would substantially exceed the scale fee otherwise payable, he may direct that an additional fee be paid but the fee is not to exceed the cost of the work involved.

(4)   If a large area application or a large scale application is a voluntary application, the fee payable under this article is reduced in accordance with article 2(6).

PART 3

Valuation

7   Valuation (first registration and registered estates)
(1)   For the purposes of this Order, the value of the estate in land, franchise, profit or share is the maximum amount for which, in the registrar's opinion, it could be sold in the open market free from any charge –
  (a)   in the case of a surrender, at the date immediately before the surrender;
  (b)   in any other case, at the date of the application.

(2)   As evidence of the amount referred to in paragraph (1), the registrar may require a written statement signed by the applicant or his conveyancer or by any other person who, in the registrar's opinion, is competent to make the statement.

(3)   Where an application for first registration is made on –
  (a)   the purchase of a leasehold estate by the reversioner;
  (b)   the purchase of a reversion by the leaseholder; or
  (c)   any other like occasion,
and an unregistered interest is determined, the value of the land is the combined value of the reversionary and determined interests assessed in accordance with paragraphs (1) and (2).

8   Valuation (charges)
On an application for registration of a charge, the amount of the charge is –
  (a)   where the charge secures a fixed amount, that amount;
  (b)   where the charge secures further advances and the maximum amount that can be advanced or owed at any one time is limited, that amount;
  (c)   where the charge secures further advances and the total amount that can be advanced or owed at any one time is not limited, the value of the property charged;

(d)   where the charge is by way of additional or substituted security or by way of guarantee, an amount equal to the lesser of –
    (i)   the amount secured or guaranteed; and
    (ii)   the value of the property charged.

(e)   where the charge secures an obligation or liability which is contingent upon the happening of a future event ('the obligation'), and is not a charge to which sub-paragraph (d) applies, an amount equal to –
    (i)   the maximum amount or value of the obligation; or
    (ii)   if that maximum amount is greater than the value of the property charged, or is not limited by the charge, or cannot be calculated at the time of the application, the value of the property charged.

(2)   Where a charge of a kind referred to in paragraph (1)(a) or (1)(b) is secured on unregistered land or other property as well as on a registered estate or registered charge, the fee is payable on an amount calculated as follows –

$$\frac{\text{Value of the registered estate or registered charge}}{\text{Value of all the property charged}} \times \text{Amount of the charge}$$

(3)   Where one deed contains two or more charges made by the same chargor to secure the same debt, the deed is to be treated as a single charge, and the fee for registration of the charge is to be paid on the lesser of –
    (a)   the amount of the whole debt; and
    (b)   an amount equal to the value of the property charged.

(4)   Where one deed contains two or more charges to secure the same debt not made by the same chargor, the deed is to be treated as a separate single charge by each of the chargors and a separate fee is to be paid for registration of the charge by each chargor on the lesser of –
    (a)   the amount of the whole debt; and
    (b)   an amount equal to the value of the property charged by that chargor.

(5)   In this article 'value of the property charged' means the value of the registered estate or the amount of the registered charge or charges affected by the application to register the charge, less the amount secured by any prior registered charges.

PART 4

Fixed Fees and Exemptions

9   Fixed fees

(1)   Subject to paragraphs (2), (3) and (4), the fees for the applications and services specified in Schedule 3 shall be those set out in that Schedule.

(2)   The fee for an application under rule 140 shall be the aggregate of the fees payable for the services provided, save that the maximum fee for any one application shall be £200.

(3)   The registrar may, if he thinks fit, waive any fee or part of a fee or any category of fee payable under this article.

(4) If –

    (a)   having regard to the extent of the land to which an application for a search of the index map relates; or

    (b)   in an application for the determination of the exact line of a boundary under rule 118, the registrar considers that the cost of the work involved in dealing with that application would substantially exceed any fee otherwise payable under this Order, such additional fee shall be payable as the registrar shall direct as appropriate to cover the excess cost of the work involved.

(5)   Notification of the additional fee under paragraph (4) shall be given to the applicant and, if he then elects to withdraw his application, no fee shall be payable.

10   Exemptions

No fee is payable in respect of any of the applications and services specified in Schedule 4.

PART 5

General and Administrative Provisions

11   Refund of fees

(1)   Where an amount exceeding the fee payable under this Order has been paid, there shall be refunded any excess remaining after the deduction, if the registrar so directs, of an amount not exceeding £10 in respect of the cost of repayment.

(2)   Where the person or firm lodging the application is an account holder, any amount to be refunded under paragraph (1) may at the discretion of the registrar be repaid to the account holder by crediting the amount to the account holder's credit account.

(3)   If any application is cancelled or withdrawn no part of the fee shall be refunded unless –

    (a)   the registrar so directs; or

    (b)   article 9(5) applies.

12   Cost of surveys, advertisements and special enquiries

Unless the registrar directs otherwise, the applicant is to meet the costs of any survey, advertisement or other special enquiry that the registrar requires to be made or published in dealing with an application.

13   Applications not otherwise referred to

Upon an application for which no other fee is payable under this Order and which is not exempt from payment, there shall be paid such fee (if any) not exceeding a fee in accordance with Scale 1 on the value of the registered estate or on the amount of the charge as the registrar shall direct having regard to the work involved.

14   Method of payment

(1)   Fees payable under this Order shall be collected in money.

(2)   Except where the registrar otherwise permits, every fee shall be paid by means of a cheque or postal order crossed and made payable to the Land Registry.

(3)   Where there is an agreement with the applicant, a fee may be paid by direct debit to such bank account of the Land Registry as the registrar may from time to time direct.

(4)   Where the amount of the fee payable on an application is immediately quantifiable, the fee shall be payable on delivery of the application.

(5)   Where the amount of the fee payable on an application is not immediately quantifiable, the applicant shall pay the sum of £40 towards the fee when the application is made and shall lodge at the same time an undertaking to pay on demand the balance of the fee due, if any.

(6)   Where an outline application is made, the fee payable shall be the fee payable under paragraph (9) of Part 1 of Schedule 3 in addition to the fee otherwise payable under this Order.

15   Credit accounts

(1)   Any person or firm may, if authorised by the registrar, use a credit account in accordance with this article for the payment of fees for applications and services of such kind as the registrar shall from time to time direct.

(2)   To enable the registrar to consider whether or not a person or firm applying to use a credit account may be so authorised, that person or firm shall supply the registrar with such information and evidence as the registrar may require to satisfy him of the person or firm's fitness to hold a credit account and the ability of the person or firm to pay any amounts which may become due from time to time under a credit account.

(3)   To enable the registrar to consider from time to time whether or not an account holder may continue to be authorised to use a credit account, the account holder shall supply the registrar, when requested to do so, with such information and evidence as the registrar may require to satisfy him of the account holder's continuing fitness to hold a credit account and the continuing ability of the account holder to pay any amounts which may become due from time to time under the account holder's credit account.

(4)   Where an account holder makes an application where credit facilities are available to him, he may make a request, in such manner as the registrar directs, for the appropriate fee to be debited to the account holder's credit account, but the registrar shall not be required to accept such a request where the amount due on the account exceeds the credit limit applicable to the credit account, or would exceed it if the request were to be accepted.

(5)   Where an account holder makes an application where credit facilities are available to him, and the application is accompanied neither by a fee nor a request for the fee to be debited to his account, the registrar may debit the fee to his account.

(6)   A statement of account shall be sent by the registrar to each account holder at the end of each calendar month or such other interval as the registrar shall direct.

(7)   The account holder must pay any sums due on his credit account before the date and in the manner specified by the registrar.

(8)   The registrar may at any time and without giving reasons terminate or suspend any or all authorisations given under paragraph (1).

(9)   In this article 'credit limit' in relation to a credit account authorised for use under paragraph (1) means the maximum amount (if any) which is to be due on the account at any time, as notified by the registrar to the account holder from time to time, by means of such communication as the registrar considers appropriate.

SCHEDULE 1

Articles 2, 3, 13 & 14

SCALE 1

NOTE 1: Where the amount or value is a figure which includes pence, it may be rounded down to the nearest £1.

NOTE 2: The third column, which sets out the reduced fee payable where article 2(6) (voluntary registration: reduced fees) applies, is not part of the scale.

Amount or value £	Fee £	Reduced fee where article 2(6) (voluntary registration: reduced fees) applies £
0–50,000	40	30
50,001–80,000	60	45
80,001–100,000	100	75
100,001–200,000	150	110
200,001–500,000	250	190
500,001–1,000,000	450	340
1,000,001 and over	750	560

SCHEDULE 2

Articles 4, 5 & 14

SCALE 2

NOTE: Where the amount or value is a figure which includes pence, it may be rounded down to the nearest £1.

Amount or value £	Fee £
0–100,000	40
100,001–200,000	50
200,001–500,000	70
500,001–1,000,000	100
1,000,001 and over	200

SCHEDULE 3

Articles 9 & 14

PART 1

FIXED FEE APPLICATIONS

	Fee
(1) To register:	
(a) a standard form of restriction contained in Schedule 4 of the rules, or	
(b) a notice (other than a notice to which section 117(2)(b) of the Act applies), or	
(c) a new or additional beneficiary of a unilateral notice, or	
(d) an entry for which no other provision is made by this Order and for which the registrar considers a fee should be paid:	

– total fee for up to three registered titles	£40
– additional fee for each subsequent registered title	£20
Provided that no such fee is payable if, in relation to each registered title affected, the application is accompanied by a scale fee application or another application which attracts a fee under this paragraph.	
(2) To register a restriction in a form not contained in Schedule 4 of the rules – for each registered title	£80
(3) To register a caution against first registration (other than a caution to which section 117(2)(a) of the Act applies)	£40
(4) To alter a cautions register – for each individual cautions register	£40
(5) To close or partly close a registered leasehold or a registered rentcharge title other than on surrender – for each registered title closed or partly closed	
Provided that no such fee is payable if the application is accompanied by a scale fee application.	
(6) To upgrade from one class of registered title to another	£40
Provided that no such fee is payable if the application for upgrading is accompanied by a scale fee application.	
(7) To cancel an entry in the register of notice of an unregistered rentcharge which has determined – for each registered title affected	£40
Provided that no such fee is payable if the application is accompanied by a scale fee application.	
(8) To enter or remove a record of a defect in title pursuant to section 64(1) of the Act	£40
Provided that no such fee is payable if the application is accompanied by a scale fee application.	
(9) An outline application to secure priority for a dealing with registered land which cannot be protected by an official search with priority of the register:	
(a) where delivered directly to the registrar's computer system by means of a remote terminal	£2
(b) where delivered by any other means	£4
Such fee is payable in addition to any other fee which is payable in respect of the application.	
(10) For an order in respect of a restriction under section 41(2) of the Act – for each registered title affected	£40
(11) To register a person in adverse possession of a registered estate - for each registered title affected	£100
(12) For registration as a person entitled to be notified of an application for adverse possession – for each registered title affected	£40
(13) Subject to article 9(4), for the determination of the exact line of a boundary under rule 118 - for each registered title	£80

PART 2

SERVICES – INSPECTION AND COPYING

(1) Inspection of the following, including in each case the making of a copy, on any one occasion when a person gains access to the registrar's computer system by means of a remote terminal under rule 132:	
(a) for each individual register	£2
(b) for each title plan	£2
(c) for any or all of the documents referred to in an individual register (other than the documents referred to in paragraph (7) below)	£2
(d) for each individual caution register	£2
(e) for each caution plan	£2
(f) for any other document kept by the registrar which relates to an application to him – per document	£2
(2) Inspection (otherwise than under paragraph (1) above):	
(a) for each individual register	£4
(b) for each title plan	£4
(c) for any or all of the documents referred to in an individual register (other than the documents referred to in paragraph (7) below ....)	£4
(d) for each individual caution register	£4
(e) for each caution plan	£4
(f) for any other document kept by the registrar which relates to an application to him – per document	£4
(3) Official copy in respect of a registered title:	
(a) for each individual register	
(i) where requested from a remote terminal	£2
(ii) where requested by any other permitted means	£4
(b) for each title plan	
(i) where requested from a remote terminal	£2
(ii) where requested by any other permitted means	£4
(4) Official copy in respect of a cautions register	
(a) for each individual caution register	
(i) where requested from a remote terminal	£2
(ii) where requested by any other permitted means	£4
(b) for each caution plan	
(i) where requested from a remote terminal	£2
(ii) where requested by any other permitted means	£4
(5) Official copy of any or all of the documents referred to in an individual register (other than documents referred to in paragraph (7) below) – for each registered title	
(a) where requested from a remote terminal	£2
(b) Where requested by any other permitted means	£4
(6) Official copy of any other document kept by the registrar which relates to an application to him – for each document	

(a) where requested from a remote terminal	£2
(b) where requested by any other permitted means	£4
(7) Where permitted (being unavailable as of right) inspection or official copy (or both) of a transitional period document – for each document	£8
(8) Copy of an historical edition of an individual register – for each title	£8
(9) Application to the registrar to ascertain the title number or numbers (if any) under which the estate is registered where the applicant seeks to inspect or to be supplied with an official copy of an individual register or of a title plan and the applicant has not supplied a title number, or the title number supplied does not relate to any part of the land described by the applicant	£4

PART 3

SERVICES – SEARCHES

(1) An official search of an individual register or of a pending first registration application made to the registrar by means of a remote terminal communicating with the registrar's computer system – for each title	£2
(2) An official search of an individual register by a mortgagee for the purpose of section 56(3) of the Family Law Act 1996 made to the registrar by means of a remote terminal communicating with the registrar's computer system – for each title	£2
(3) An official search of an individual register or of a pending first registration application other than as described in paragraphs (1) and (2) – for each title	£4
(4) The issue of a certificate of inspection of a title plan – for each registered title affected	£4
(5) Subject to article 9(4), an official search of the index map:	
(a) where any part of the land to which the search relates is registered – for each registered title in respect of which a result is given	£4
(b) where no part of the land to which the search relates is registered – for each application	£4
(6) Search of the index of proprietors' names – for each name	£10
(7) Official search of the index of relating franchises and manors – for each administrative area:	
(a) where requested from a remote terminal	£2
(b) where requested by any other permitted means	£4

PART 4

SERVICES – OTHER INFORMATION

(1) Application to be supplied with the name and address of the registered proprietor of a registered title identified by its postal address – for each application	£4
(2) Application for return of a document under rule 204	£8
(3) Application for day list information on any one occasion when a person gains access to the registrar's computer system by means of a remote terminal – for each title	£1

(4) Application that the registrar designate a document an exempt information document	£20
(5) Application for an official copy of an exempt information document under rule 137	£40

SCHEDULE 4

Article 10

EXEMPTIONS

No fee is payable in respect of:

(1)   reflecting a change in the name, address or description of a registered proprietor or other person referred to in the register, or in the cautions register, or changing the description of a property;

(2)   giving effect in the register to a change of proprietor where the registered estate or the registered charge, as the case may be, has become vested without further assurance (other than on the death or bankruptcy of a proprietor) in some person by the operation of any statute (other than the Act), statutory instrument or scheme taking effect under any statute or statutory instrument;

(3)   registering the surrender of a registered leasehold estate where the surrender is consideration or part consideration for the grant of a new lease to the registered proprietor of substantially the same premises as were comprised in the surrendered lease and where a scale fee is paid for the registration of the new lease;

(4)   registering a discharge of a registered charge;

(5)   registering a matrimonial home rights notice, or renewal of such a notice, or renewal of a matrimonial home rights caution under the Family Law Act 1996;

(6)   entering in the register the death of a joint proprietor;

(7)   cancelling the registration of a notice, (other than a notice in respect of an unregistered lease or unregistered rentcharge), caution against first registration, caution against dealings, including a withdrawal of a deposit or intended deposit, inhibition, restriction, or note;

(8)   the removal of the designation of a document as an exempt information document;

(9)   approving an estate layout plan or any draft document with or without a plan;

(10)   an order by the registrar (other than an order under section 41(2) of the Act);

(11)   deregistering a manor;

(12)   an entry in the register of a note of the dissolution of a corporation;

(13)   registering a restriction in form A in Schedule 4 to the rules.

LAND REGISTRATION (ACTING CHIEF LAND REGISTRAR) REGULATIONS 2003, SI 2003/2281

1   Citation and commencement

These Regulations may be cited as the Land Registration (Acting Chief Land Registrar) Regulations 2003 and shall come into force on 13th October 2003.

2   Appointment

(1)   The Lord Chancellor may appoint a person to carry out the functions of the registrar during any vacancy in that office.

(2)   The person appointed under paragraph (1) must, at the time of appointment, be a member of the land registry and also a member of the Senior Civil Service.

(3)   Subject to paragraph (4), the person appointed shall carry out the functions of the registrar during any vacancy.

(4)   An appointment under paragraph (1) shall cease if the person appointed –
   (a)   ceases to be a member of the land registry, or
   (b)   resigns his appointment under paragraph (1) by giving notice in writing to the Lord Chancellor, or
   (c)   has his appointment revoked by the Lord Chancellor on the grounds of being unable or unfit to discharge the functions of the registrar.

(5)   For the purpose of paragraph (2), a person is to be treated as a member of the Senior Civil Service if, at the time of his appointment, he holds a Civil Service grade which is, or is equivalent to, a grade at any time covered by the Senior Civil Service.

LAND REGISTRATION (ACTING ADJUDICATOR) REGULATIONS 2003, SI 2003/2342

1 Citation and commencement
These Regulations may be cited as the Land Registration (Acting Adjudicator) Regulations 2003 and shall come into force on 13th October 2003.

2 Appointment
(1) The Lord Chancellor may, in order to facilitate the disposal of the business of the adjudicator, appoint a person to carry out the functions of the adjudicator during any vacancy in that office.

(2) To be qualified for appointment under paragraph (1), a person must hold the office of district judge (as defined in section 74(1) of the Courts and Legal Services Act 1990).

(3) The person appointed shall carry out the functions of the adjudicator during the vacancy, unless within that period, he –
    (a)   dies; or
    (b)   resigns by giving notice in writing to the Lord Chancellor; or
    (c)   is removed by the Lord Chancellor on the grounds of incapacity or misbehaviour.

3 Functions
Every person appointed, whilst acting under these Regulations, shall have all the jurisdiction and powers of the person appointed to the office of adjudicator pursuant to section 107 of the Land Registration Act 2002.

APPENDIX 2

STATUTORY FORMS

The following Land Registry forms have been reproduced as Appendix 2 to this book:[1]

Form ADV1	657
Form AN1	659
Form AP1	662
Form AS1	664
Form CH1	666
Form CT1	668
Form EX1	672
Form EX2	674
Form FR1	677
Form NAP	680
Form OC2	682
Form RX1	684
Form SIM	687
Form TP1	689
Form TR1	693
Form UN1	695

---

[1] These Forms are reproduced with the kind permission of the Land Registry.

Application for registration of a person in adverse possession under Schedule 6 to the Land Registration Act 2002	Land Registry 

If you need more room than is provided for in a panel, use continuation sheet CS and attach to this form.

1. Administrative area and postcode if known

2. Title number(s)

3. If you have already made this application by **outline application,** insert reference number:

4. Property *Insert address, including postcode, or other description of the property affected by the application.*

This application affects *Place "X" in the appropriate box.*

☐ the whole of the registered estate in land in the above title number(s)

☐ part of the registered estate in land in the above title number(s)

☐ the registered rentcharge in the above title number(s)

Unless the application affects only a registered rentcharge, or the application is made under paragraph 6(1) of Schedule 6 to the Land Registration Act 2002 and the extent is the same as that in the paragraph 1 application, ensure that a plan enabling the land to be identified on the Ordnance Survey map is incorporated in the statutory declaration.

5. Application and fee *A fee calculator for all types of applications can be found on Land Registry's website at www.landregistry.gov.uk/fees* **Registration of a person in adverse possession** Fee paid £ **Fee payment method:** *Place "X" in the appropriate box.* I wish to pay the appropriate fee payable under the current Land Registration Fee Order: ☐ by cheque or postal order, amount £ ———————— made payable to "Land Registry". ☐ by Direct Debit under an authorised agreement with Land Registry.	FOR OFFICIAL USE ONLY Record of fee paid ————————————— Particulars of under/over payment ————————————— Fees debited £ Reference number

6. Documents lodged with this form *Number the documents in sequence; copies should also be numbered and listed as separate documents. If you supply the original document and a certified copy, we shall assume that you request the return of the original; if a certified copy is not supplied, we may retain the original document and it may be destroyed.*

1. Statutory Declaration

7. The application has been lodged by: Land Registry Key No. (if appropriate) Name (if different from the applicant) Address/DX No. Reference E-mail	FOR OFFICIAL USE ONLY Codes Dealing Status
Telephone No.	Fax No.	

8. Where you would like us to deal with someone else *We shall deal only with the applicant, or the person lodging the application if different, unless you place "X" against one or more of the statements below and give the necessary details.*

☐ Send title information document to the person shown below

☐ Raise any requisitions or queries with the person shown below

☐ Return original documents lodged with this form (see note in panel 6) to the person shown below
If this applies only to certain documents, please specify.

Name
Address/DX No.

Reference
E-mail

Telephone No.	Fax No.

9. Applicant **for entry on the register** *Give full name(s) of the applicant(s), not that of any conveyancer acting. For a company include company's registered number, if any. For Scottish companies use an SC prefix and for limited liability partnerships use an OC prefix before the registered number, if any. For foreign companies give territory in which incorporated.*

Unless otherwise arranged with Land Registry headquarters, a certified copy of the constitution in English or Welsh will be required if the above named is a body corporate but is not a company registered in England or Wales or Scotland under the Companies Acts.

10. Address(es) for service of the applicant. The address(es) will be entered in the register and used for correspondence and the service of notice *You may give up to three addresses for service one of which must be a postal address but does not have to be within the UK. The other addresses can be any combination of either a postal address, a box number at a UK document exchange or an electronic address.*

11. This application is made under *Place "X" in the appropriate box.*

☐ Schedule 6, paragraph 1, to the Land Registration Act 2002

☐ Schedule 6, paragraph 6(1), to the Land Registration Act 2002

12. If applying under Schedule 6, Paragraph 1, to the Land Registration Act 2002 please confirm which, if any, of the following conditions you intend to rely on: *Place "X" in the appropriate box.*

☐ Schedule 6, paragraph 5(2)

☐ Schedule 6, paragraph 5(3)

☐ Schedule 6, paragraph 5(4)

13. I confirm that the enclosed statutory declaration dated _____ complies with rule 188 of the Land Registration Rules 2003 and that, to the best of my knowledge and belief, the facts stated in the declaration have not changed

Complete by inserting date of the statutory declaration prepared for this application.

**14. Signature of applicant
or their conveyancer** _____ **Date** _____

Application to enter an agreed notice	**Land Registry**	

Form MH1 must be used for registration of a matrimonial home rights notice.
If you need more room than is provided for in a panel, use continuation sheet CS and attach to this form.

1.	**Administrative area and postcode** if known

2.	**Title number(s)**

3.	If you have already made this application by **outline application**, insert reference number:	

4. **Property** *Insert address, including postcode, or other description.*

The interest to be protected by the agreed notice affects *Place "X" in the appropriate box.*

☐ the whole of the registered estate

☐ the part of the registered estate defined on the attached plan and shown
State reference e.g. "edged red".

☐ the registered charge dated   in favour of
         referred to in the Charges Register

5.	**Application and fee** *A fee calculator for all types of applications can be found on Land Registry's website at www.landregistry.gov.uk/fees*	FOR OFFICIAL USE ONLY Record of fee paid
	Agreed notice Fee paid £	
	Fee payment method: *Place "X" in the appropriate box.* I wish to pay the appropriate fee payable under the current Land Registration Fee Order:	Particulars of under/over payment
	☐ by cheque or postal order, amount £ _____ made payable to "Land Registry".	Fees debited £
	☐ by Direct Debit under an authorised agreement with Land Registry.	Reference number

6. **Documents lodged with this form** *If this application is accompanied by either Form AP1 or FR1 please only complete the corresponding panel on Form AP1 or DL. Number the documents in sequence; copies should also be numbered and listed as separate documents. Alternatively, you may prefer to use Form DL. If you supply the original document and a certified copy, we shall assume that you request the return of the original; if a certified copy is not supplied, we may retain the original document and it may be destroyed.*

7.	**The applicant is:** *Please provide the full name(s) of the person(s) applying for the notice.*	FOR OFFICIAL USE ONLY
	The application has been lodged by: Land Registry Key No (if appropriate) Name (if different from the applicant) Address/DX No.	Codes Dealing
	Reference E-mail	Status
	Telephone No. Fax No.	

8. **Where you would like us to deal with someone else** *We shall deal only with the applicant, or the person lodging the application if different, unless you place "X" against one or more of the statements below and give the necessary details.*	

☐ Send title information document to the person shown below

☐ Raise any requisitions or queries with the person shown below

☐ Return original documents lodged with this form (see note in panel 6) to the person shown below
If this applies only to certain documents, please specify.

Name
Address/DX No.

Reference
E-mail

Telephone No.	Fax No.

9. **The applicant applies to enter an agreed notice protecting the following interest:** *Please state below the interest to be noted.*

The above interest is set out in [paragraph   page   of] the document [numbered   ] in [panel 6][Form AP1][Form DL].

If this is a variation of an interest which is already protected on the register by a notice, please identify the notice: *For example, specify the date of registration of the existing entry.*

10. *Place "X" in the appropriate box.*

☐ The applicant is the registered proprietor of the registered [estate][charge] affected by the interest.

☐ The applicant is the person **entitled** to be registered as the proprietor of the registered [estate][charge] affected. **Complete panel 12 below.**

☐ The consent of the registered proprietor of the registered [estate][charge] accompanies this application. **Complete panel 11 below.**

☐ The consent of the person entitled to be registered as proprietor of the registered [estate][charge] accompanies this application. **Complete panel 11 and 12 below.**

☐ None of the above statements apply but evidence to establish the validity of the applicant's claim accompanies this application.

11. **Evidence of consent** *Place "X" in the appropriate box if instructed to do so in panel 10.*

☐ The [registered proprietor of][person entitled to be registered as proprietor of] the registered [estate][charge] consents to the entry of the notice and panel 14 has been completed.

☐ The consent referred to in panel 10 is contained on page____ of the document numbered_____ referred to in [panel 6][Form AP1][Form DL].

12. **Evidence of entitlement to be registered as proprietor** *Please complete if instructed to do so in panel 10.*

Evidence that the [applicant][person consenting to this application] is entitled to be registered as proprietor of the registered [estate][charge] is contained in the document numbered _____ referred to in [panel 6][Form AP1][Form DL].

13. **Signature of applicant or their conveyancer**_____ Date_____

14. Declaration of consent *Please complete if instructed to do so in panel 11.*

I/We *Give full name(s).* consent to the entry of a notice in the register of the title(s) specified in panel 2 to protect the interest details of which are given in panel 9 affecting the [part of the] registered estate described in panel 4.

Signature _____   Date_____

Signature _____   Date_____

Signature _____   Date_____

Signature _____   Date_____

© Crown copyright (ref: LR/HQ/CD-ROM) 6/03

Application to   **Land Registry**
change the register

If you need more room than is provided for in a panel, use continuation sheet CS and attach to this form.

1.	**Administrative area and postcode** if known
2.	**Title number(s)**

3. If you have already made this application by **outline application**, insert reference number:

4. **This application affects** *Place "X" in the appropriate box.*

☐ the **whole** of the title(s) *Go to panel 5.*

☐ **part** of the title(s) *Give a brief description of the property affected.*

5. **Application, priority and fees** *A fee calculator for all types of applications can be found on Land Registry's website at www.landregistry.gov.uk/fees*

Nature of applications numbered   Value £   Fees paid £
in priority order
1.
2.
3.
TOTAL £

Fee payment method: *Place "X" in the appropriate box.*
I wish to pay the appropriate fee payable under the current Land
Registration Fee Order:

☐ by cheque or postal order, amount £   made
payable to "Land Registry".

☐ by Direct Debit under an authorised agreement with Land
Registry.

FOR OFFICIAL USE ONLY
Record of fees paid

Particulars of under/over payments

Fees debited £

Reference number

6. **Documents lodged with this form** *Number the documents in sequence; copies should also be numbered and listed as separate documents. Alternatively you may prefer to use Form DL. If you supply the original document and a certified copy, we shall assume that you request the return of the original; if a certified copy is not supplied, we may retain the original document and it may be destroyed.*

7. **The applicant is:** *Please provide the full name(s) of the person(s) applying to change the register.*

The application has been lodged by:
Land Registry Key No. (if appropriate)
Name (if different from the applicant)
Address/DX No.

Reference
E-mail
Telephone No.   Fax No.

FOR
OFFICIAL
USE ONLY
Codes
Dealing

Status

8.	**Where you would like us to deal with someone else** *We shall deal only with the applicant, or the person lodging the application if different, unless you place "X" against one or more of the statements below and give the necessary details.*

☐ Send title information document to the person shown below

☐ Raise any requisitions or queries with the person shown below

☐ Return original documents lodged with this form (see note in panel 6) to the person shown below
If this applies only to certain documents, please specify.

Name
Address/DX No.

Reference
E-mail

Telephone No.	Fax No.

9.	**Address(es) for service of the proprietor(s) of the registered estate(s). The address(es) will be entered in the register and used for correspondence and the service of notice.** *Place "X" in the appropriate box(es). You may give up to three addresses for service **one** of which **must** be a postal address but does not have to be within the UK. The other addresses can be any combination of a postal address, a box number at a UK document exchange or an electronic address.*

☐ Enter the address(es) from the transfer/assent/lease

☐ Enter the address(es), including postcode, as follows:

☐ Retain the address(es) currently in the register for the title(s)

10.	**Disclosable overriding interests** *Place "X" in the appropriate box.*

☐ This is not an application to register a registrable disposition or it is but no disclosable overriding interests affect the registered estate(s) *Section 27 of the Land Registration Act 2002 lists the registrable dispositions. Rule 57 of the Land Registration Rules 2003 sets out the disclosable overriding interests. Use Form DI to tell us about any disclosable overriding interests that affect the registered estate(s) identified in panel 2.*

☐ Form DI accompanies this application

The registrar may enter a notice of a disclosed interest in the register of title.

11.	**Information in respect of any new charge** *Do not give this information if a Land Registry MD reference is printed on the charge, unless the charge has been transferred.*

Full name and address (including postcode) for service of notices and correspondence of the person to be registered as proprietor of each charge. *You may give up to three addresses for service **one** of which **must** be a postal address but does not have to be within the UK. The other addresses can be any combination of a postal address, a box number at a UK document exchange or an electronic address. For a company include company's registered number, if any. For Scottish companies use an SC prefix and for limited liability partnerships use an OC prefix before the registered number, if any. For foreign companies give territory in which incorporated.*

Unless otherwise arranged with Land Registry headquarters, we require a certified copy of the chargee's constitution (in English or Welsh) if it is a body corporate but is not a company registered in England and Wales or Scotland under the Companies Acts.

12.	**Signature of applicant or their conveyancer**	Date

Assent of whole
of registered title(s)

Land Registry

If you need more room than is provided for in a panel, use continuation sheet CS and attach to this form.

1.	Title number(s) of the Property *Leave blank if not yet registered.*

2.	Property

3.	Date

4.	Name of deceased proprietor *Give full name.*

5.	Personal Representative of deceased proprietor *Give full name(s) and company's registered number, if any.*

6.	Transferee **for entry on the register** *Give full name(s) and company's registered number, if any. For Scottish companies use an SC prefix and for limited liability partnerships use an OC prefix before the registered number, if any. For foreign companies give territory in which incorporated.*

Unless otherwise arranged with Land Registry headquarters, a certified copy of the Transferee's constitution (in English or Welsh) will be required if it is a body corporate but is not a company registered in England and Wales or Scotland under the Companies Acts.

7.	Transferee's intended **address(es) for service (including postcode) for entry on the register** *You may give up to three addresses for service **one** of which **must** be a postal address but does not have to be within the UK. The other addresses can be any combination of a postal address, a box number at a UK document exchange or an electronic address.*

8.	**The Personal Representative transfers the Property to the Transferee**

9. The Personal Representative transfers with *Place "X" in the box that applies and add any modification.*

☐ full title guarantee   ☐ limited title guarantee

10. Declaration of trust *Where there is more than one Transferee, place "X" in the appropriate box.*

☐ The Transferees are to hold the Property on trust for themselves as joint tenants

☐ The Transferees are to hold the Property on trust for themselves as tenants in common in equal shares

☐ The Transferees are to hold the Property *Complete as necessary.*

11. Additional provisions *Insert here any required or permitted statement, certificate or application and any agreed covenants, declarations, etc.*

12. Execution *The Personal Representative must sign this assent in the presence of a witness or execute it as a deed using the space below. If there is more than one Personal Representative, all must sign or execute. Forms of execution are given in Schedule 9 to the Land Registration Rules 2003. If the assent contains Transferee's covenants or declarations or contains an application by the Transferee (e.g. for a restriction), it must also be signed by the Transferee in the presence of a witness or executed as a deed by the Transferee (signed or executed by all of the Transferees, if there is more than one).*

© Crown copyright (ref: LR/HQ/CD-ROM) 6/03

**Legal charge of a
registered estate**

Land Registry

This form should be accompanied by Form AP1 or Form FR1.
If you need more room than is provided for in a panel, use continuation sheet CS and attach to this form.

1. Title number(s) of the Property *Leave blank if not yet registered.*

2. Property

3. Date

4. Lender *Give full name(s) and company's registered number, if any.*

5. Borrower **for entry on the register** *Give full name(s) and company's registered number, if any. For Scottish companies use an SC prefix and for limited liability partnerships use an OC prefix before the registered number, if any. For foreign companies give territory in which incorporated.*

6. **The Borrower with** *(Delete as appropriate)* **[full title guarantee][limited title guarantee] charges the Property by way of legal mortgage as security for the payment of the sums detailed in panel 8**

7. *Place "X" in the appropriate box(es).*

☐ The Lender is under an obligation to make further advances and applies for the obligation to be entered in the register

☐ The Borrower applies to enter the following restriction in the proprietorship register of the registered estate

8. Additional provisions *Insert here details of the sums to be paid (amounts and dates), etc.*

9. Execution *The Borrower must execute this charge as a deed using the space below. If there is more than one Borrower, all must execute. Forms of execution are given in Schedule 9 to the Land Registration Rules 2003. If a note of an obligation to make further advances has been applied for in panel 7 this document must be signed by the Lender or its conveyancer.*

Caution against first registration	Land Registry	**CT1**

If you need more room than is provided for in a panel, use continuation sheet CS and attach to this form.

1. Administrative area and postcode if known

2. Address or description of the property affected by the caution

3. Application and fee *A fee calculator for all types of applications can be found on Land Registry's website at www.landregistry.gov.uk/fees*

Caution against first registration   Fee paid £

Fee payment method: *Place "X" in the appropriate box.*
I wish to pay the appropriate fee payable under the current Land Registration Fee Order:

☐ by cheque or postal order, amount £ _____ made payable to "Land Registry".

☐ by Direct Debit under an authorised agreement with Land Registry.

FOR OFFICIAL USE ONLY
Record of fee paid

Particulars of under/over payment

Fees debited £

Reference number

4. The cautioner is: *Please provide the full name of the person applying for the caution.*

The application has been lodged by:
Land Registry Key No. (if appropriate)
Name (if different from the cautioner)
Address/DX No.

Reference
E-mail
Telephone No.   Fax No.

FOR OFFICIAL USE ONLY
Status codes

RED

5. The estate to which the caution relates is *Place "X" in the appropriate box(es) and complete as necessary. In the case of a leasehold, rentcharge, franchise or profit a prendre in gross, please provide full details below of the particular leasehold, rentcharge, franchise or profit affected. Include the date, nature and parties of the instrument by which the estate was created, if known; the amount of the rentcharge; the nature of the franchise or profit; and length of the term, if leasehold.*

☐ the freehold

☐ a lease dated _____ for a term of _____ from _____
made between

Is the lease discontinuous? ☐ Yes   ☐ No
If Yes, please include full particulars of the discontinuous term, e.g. affected days, weeks, months etc.

☐ a rentcharge   ☐ a franchise   ☐ a profit a prendre in gross

6. Extent of land to which the caution relates *Place "X" in the appropriate box.*

☐ The property is clearly identified on the attached plan and shown _____ *Enter reference e.g. "edged red".*

☐ The description in panel 2 is sufficient to enable the property to be clearly identified on the Ordnance Survey map

7. Address(es) for service of the cautioner. The address(es) will be entered in the cautions register and used for correspondence and the service of notice *You may give up to three addresses for service **one** of which **must** be a postal address but does not have to be within the UK. The other addresses can be any combination of a postal address, a box number at a UK document exchange or an electronic address. Where the cautioner is a company, include the company's registered number (if any). For Scottish Companies use an SC prefix and for limited liability partnerships use an OC prefix before the registered number, if any.*

8. *Place "X" in the appropriate box and give the full name of the person making the declaration, or giving the certificate. You must make the declaration in panel 9 unless you are a conveyancer acting on behalf of the cautioner, in which case you can give a certificate in panel 10.*

☐ The declarant is (one of) the cautioner(s) or a person authorised by the cautioner to make the declaration in panel 9.
The declarant's full name is

☐ The certificate in panel 10 has been completed by a conveyancer on behalf of the cautioner.
The full name of the individual giving the certificate is

9. The declarant solemnly and sincerely declares that the cautioner is interested in the estate referred to in panel 5 as
This panel must set out the nature of the cautioner's interest. Do not exhibit any documents.

and I make this solemn declaration conscientiously believing the same to be true by virtue of the Statutory Declarations Act 1835.

Signature of Declarant

Declared at

this   day of   before me,

Name
(BLOCK CAPITALS)

Address

Qualification
This declaration must be made in the presence of a person empowered to administer oaths, such as a commissioner for oaths or a practising solicitor.

10. I certify that the cautioner is interested in the estate described in panel 5 as
This panel must set out the nature of the cautioner's interest. Do not exhibit any documents.

Signature _____

Name_____
(BLOCK CAPITALS)

Address _____

_____

_____

**11. Signature of applicant
or their conveyancer** _____ Date _____

12. Consent to the lodging of this caution is given by

Name(s) *BLOCK CAPITALS*

Signature(s)

1. _____

1. _____

2. _____

2. _____

3. _____

3. _____

Caution applications do not require any consents. However, a person may consent to the lodging of a caution in accordance with rule 47 of the Land Registration Rules 2003. By so consenting that person may only apply to cancel the caution under section 18(1) of the Land Registration Act 2002 if one of the exceptions under rule 46 of the Land Registration Rules 2003 applies.

Application for the registrar to designate a document as an exempt information document

Land Registry

You must also complete Form EX1A

If you need more room than is provided for in a panel, use continuation sheet CS and attach to this form.

1.	Administrative area and postcode if known

2.	Title number(s) of the registered estate(s) to which the document relates

3.	Property description(s) of the registered estate(s) to which the document relates

4.	Title number or file reference under which this document is held

5.	Application and fee *A fee calculator for all types of applications can be found on Land Registry's website at www.landregistry.gov.uk/fees* **Designation of a document** Fee paid £ **as an exempt information** **document** **Fee payment method:** *Place "X" in the appropriate box.* I wish to pay the appropriate fee payable under the current Land Registration Fee Order: ☐ by cheque or postal order, amount £_____ made payable to "Land Registry". ☐ by Direct Debit under an authorised agreement with Land Registry.	FOR OFFICIAL USE ONLY Record of fee paid Particulars of under/over payment Fees debited £ Reference number

6.	**The application has been lodged by:** Land Registry Key No. (if appropriate) Name Address DX/No. Reference E-mail	FOR OFFICIAL USE ONLY Codes Dealing **EX1** Status **RED**
	Telephone No. Fax No.	

7.	If this application is being made on behalf of someone else please state their details: Name: Address: *If we serve notice of an application for an official copy of the document, we shall serve it on the person whose details appear in this panel; if this panel is not completed, we shall serve it on the person identified in panel 6.*

8.	Please provide details of the document which contains prejudicial information *Include date, parties and nature of document.*

9. **I enclose** a copy of the document referred to in panel 8 which excludes the prejudicial information

This copy is **certified** as being a true copy of the original from which copy the prejudicial information has been excluded
Please note that the document referred to in panel 8 must still be sent with any application accompanying this application.

I apply for the registrar to designate the document referred to in panel 8 as an exempt information document

10. Signature of applicant
or their conveyancer _____ **Date** _____

**Application for official copy of
an exempt information
document**

Land Registry

Land Registry _____ Office

Use one form per document. If you need more room than is provided for in a panel, use continuation sheet CS and attach to this form.

1.	**Administrative area and postcode** if known

2.	**Title number(s) of the registered estate(s) to which the document relates** *If the document relates to many titles, you only need to quote one.*

3.	**Property description(s) of the registered estate(s) to which the document relates** *If the document relates to many properties, you only need to quote the property relating to the title number shown in panel 2.*

4.	**Title number or file reference under which this document is held**

5. Payment of fee *Place "X" in the appropriate box.*

☐ The Land Registry fee of £ [   ] accompanies this
application.

☐ Debit the Credit Account mentioned in panel 6 with the
appropriate fee payable under the current Land Registration
Fee Order.

For official use only
Impression of fees

6. The applicant is: *Please provide the full name of the person applying for the official copy.*

The application has been lodged by:
Land Registry Key No. (if appropriate)
Name (if different from the applicant)
Address/DX No.

Reference
E-mail

Telephone No. | Fax No.

7. If the official copy is to be sent to anyone other than the applicant in panel 6, please supply the name and address of the person to whom it should be sent.

    Reference

8. **I apply for an official copy of the following document which has been designated an exempt information document**
    Include date, parties and nature of document.

9. **Please state the reason(s) why you consider an official copy of the edited information document is not sufficient for your purposes**

10. Please state why you consider that none of the information omitted from the edited information document is prejudicial information

OR

If you accept that some or all of the information is prejudicial information, please give details and state why you consider that the public interest in providing an official copy of the exempt information document outweighs the public interest in not doing so

11. Signature of applicant or their conveyancer _____ Date _____

First registration application	Land Registry

If you need more room than is provided for in a panel, use continuation sheet CS and attach to this form.

1.	**Administrative area and postcode** if known

2.	**Address or other description of the estate to be registered**

On registering a rentcharge, profit a prendre in gross, or franchise, show the address as follows:- "Rentcharge, franchise etc, over 2 The Grove, Anytown, Northshire NE2 9OO".

3. **Extent to be registered** *Place "X" in the appropriate box and complete as necessary.*

☐ The land is clearly identified on the plan to the _____
Enter nature and date of deed.

☐ The land is clearly identified on the attached plan and shown _____
Enter reference e.g. "edged red".

☐ The description in panel 2 is sufficient to enable the land to be clearly identified on the Ordnance Survey map
When registering a rentcharge, profit a prendre in gross or franchise, the land to be identified is the land affected by that estate, or to which it relates.

4. **Application, priority and fees** *A fee calculator for all types of applications can be found on Land Registry's website at www.landregistry.gov.uk/fees*

Nature of applications
in priority order   Value/premium £   Fees paid £

1. **First registration of the estate**
2.
3.
4.
                                                  TOTAL £

Fee payment method: *Place "X" in the appropriate box.*
I wish to pay the appropriate fee payable under the current Land Registration Fee Order:

☐ by cheque or postal order, amount £ _____ made payable to "Land Registry".

☐ by Direct Debit under an authorised agreement with Land Registry.

FOR OFFICIAL USE ONLY
Record of fees paid

Particulars of under/over payments

Fees debited £

Reference number

5. **The title applied for is** *Place "X" in the appropriate box.*

☐ absolute freehold   ☐ absolute leasehold   ☐ good leasehold   ☐ possessory freehold
☐ possessory leasehold

6. **Documents lodged with this form** *List the documents on Form DL. We shall assume that you request the return of these documents. But we shall only assume that you request the return of a statutory declaration, subsisting lease, subsisting charge or the latest document of title (for example, any conveyance to the applicant) if you supply a certified copy of the document. If certified copies of such documents are not supplied, we may retain the originals of such documents and they may be destroyed.*

7. **The applicant is:** *Please provide the full name of the person applying to be registered as the proprietor.*

Application lodged by:
Land Registry Key No.(if appropriate)
Name (if different from the applicant)
Address/DX No.

Reference
E-mail

Telephone No.	Fax No.

FOR OFFICIAL USE ONLY Status codes

8.	**Where you would like us to deal with someone else** *We shall deal only with the applicant, or the person lodging the application if different, unless you place "X" against one or more of the statements below and give the necessary details.*

☐ Send title information document to the person shown below

☐ Raise any requisitions or queries with the person shown below

☐ Return original documents lodged with this form (see note in panel 6) to the person shown below
If this applies only to certain documents, please specify.

Name
Address/DX No.

Reference
E-mail

Telephone No.	Fax No.

9. **Address(es) for service of every owner of the estate. The address(es) will be entered in the register and used for correspondence and the service of notice.** *In this and panel 10, you may give up to three addresses for service one of which must be a postal address but does not have to be within the UK. The other addresses can be any combination of a postal address, a box number at a UK document exchange or an electronic address. For a company include the company's registered number, if any. For Scottish companies, use an SC prefix, and for limited liability partnerships, use an OC prefix before the registered number if any. For foreign companies give territory in which incorporated.*

Unless otherwise arranged with Land Registry headquarters, we require a certified copy of the owner's constitution (in English or Welsh) if it is a body corporate but is not a company registered in England or Wales or Scotland under the Companies Acts.

10. **Information in respect of a chargee or mortgagee** *Do not give this information if a Land Registry MD reference is printed on the charge, unless the charge has been transferred.*
Full name and address (including postcode) for service of notices and correspondence of the person entitled to be registered as proprietor of each charge. *You may give up to three addresses for service; see panel 9 as to the details you should include.*

Unless otherwise arranged with Land Registry headquarters, we require a certified copy of the chargee's constitution (in English or Welsh) if it is a body corporate but is not a company registered in England and Wales or Scotland under the Companies Acts.

11. **Where the applicants are joint proprietors** *Place "X" in the appropriate box*

☐ The applicants are holding the property on trust for themselves as joint tenants

☐ The applicants are holding the property on trust for themselves as tenants in common in equal shares

☐ The applicants are holding the property *(complete as necessary)*

12. **Disclosable overriding interests** *Place "X" in the appropriate box.*

☐ No disclosable overriding interests affect the estate

☐ Form DI accompanies this application

Rule 28 of the Land Registration Rules 2003 sets out the disclosable overriding interests that you must tell us about. You must use Form DI to tell us about any disclosable overriding interests that affect the estate.

The registrar may enter a notice of a disclosed interest in the register of title.

13. The title is based on the title documents listed in Form DL which are all those that are in the possession or control of the applicant.

Place "X" in the appropriate box. If applicable complete the second statement; include any interests disclosed only by searches other than local land charges. Any interests disclosed by searches which do not affect the estate being registered should be certified.

☐ All rights, interests and claims affecting the estate known to the applicant are disclosed in the title documents and Form DI if accompanying this application. There is no-one in adverse possession of the property or any part of it.

☐ In addition to the rights, interests and claims affecting the estate disclosed in the title documents or Form DI if accompanying this application, the applicant only knows of the following:

14. *Place "X" in this box if you are NOT able to give this certificate.* ☐

We have fully examined the applicant's title to the estate, including any appurtenant rights, or are satisfied that it has been fully examined by a conveyancer in the usual way prior to this application.

15. We have authority to lodge this application and request the registrar to complete the registration.

16. Signature of applicant or their conveyancer _____ **Date** _____

Note: Failure to complete the form with proper care may deprive the applicant of protection under the Land Registration Act if, as a result, a mistake is made in the register.

© Crown copyright (ref: LR/HQ/CD-ROM) 6/03

Notice to the registrar in respect of an adverse possession application

Land Registry

If you need more room than is provided for in a panel, use continuation sheet CS and attach to this form.

1. **Title number(s)** of the property affected by the application

2. **Property** *Insert address, including postcode, or other description of the property affected by the application.*

3. **Name(s) of applicant(s)** *i.e. the person(s) making the application for registration based on adverse possession.*

4. **Your name and address** *Conveyancers should give their client's name(s), followed by their own name and address for service.*

5. *Place "X" in the appropriate box(es).*

☐ **I consent to the registration of the applicant(s)**

☐ **I require the registrar to deal with the application under Schedule 6, paragraph 5, to the Land Registration Act 2002**

☐ **I object to the registration on the grounds stated in panel 6**

6. Please give details of the grounds of your objection:

7. **Signature of person named in panel 4 above (the conveyancer if the panel gives their details as well)** _____ **Date** _____

Application for official copies of documents only

Land Registry

OC2

Land Registry _____ Office

The correct title number must be quoted. Use one form per title. If you need more room than is provided for in a panel, use continuation sheet CS and attach to this form.

1. Administrative area and postcode if known	

2. Title number	

3. Property description *Please give a full property description.*	

4. Payment of fee *Place "X" in the appropriate box.*

☐ The Land Registry fee of £ [   ] accompanies this application.

☐ Debit the Credit Account mentioned in panel 5 with the appropriate fee payable under the current Land Registration Fee Order.

For official use only

Impression of fees

5. The application has been lodged by:
Land Registry Key No. (if appropriate)
Name
Address/DX No.

Reference
E-mail

Telephone No.	Fax No.

6. If the official copies are to be sent to anyone other than the applicant in panel 5, please supply the name and address of the person to whom they should be sent.

Reference

7. I apply for official copies of the documents listed below

Documents which are referred to in the register of the above title
Applications specifying "All", "Any", etc., will be rejected.

Nature of document	Date of document	Title number under which it is filed	No. of copies

Documents which are not referred to in the register
Please supply as much detail as possible.

Nature of document	Date of document, if known	No. of copies

8. Signature of applicant _____ **Date** _____

**Application to enter
a restriction**

Land Registry

RX1

If you need more room than is provided for in a panel, use continuation sheet CS and attach to this form.

1.   Administrative area and postcode if known

2.   Title number(s)

3. If you have already made this application by **outline application**, insert reference number:

4.   Property *Insert address or other description.*

The restriction applied for is to affect *Place "X" in the appropriate box and complete as necessary.*

☐ the whole of each registered estate

☐ the part(s) of the registered estate(s) shown on the attached plan by *State reference e.g. "edged red".*

☐ the registered charge(s) dated _____ in favour of _____ referred to in the Charges Register

5.   Application and fee *A fee calculator for all types of applications can be found on Land Registry's website at www.landregistry.gov.uk/fees*

Restriction   Fee paid £ _____

Fee payment method: *Place "X" in the appropriate box.*

I wish to pay the appropriate fee payable under the current Land Registration Fee Order:

☐ by cheque or postal order, amount £ _____ made payable to "Land Registry".

☐ by Direct Debit under an authorised agreement with Land Registry.

FOR OFFICIAL USE ONLY
Record of fee paid
Particulars of under/over payment
Fees debited £
Reference number

6.   Documents lodged with this application *If this application is accompanied by either Form AP1 or FR1 please only complete the corresponding panel on Form AP1 or DL. Number the documents in sequence; copies should also be numbered and listed as separate documents, alternatively you may prefer to use Form DL. If you supply the original document and a certified copy, we shall assume that you request the return of the original; if a certified copy is not supplied, we may retain the original document and it may be destroyed.*

7.   The applicant is: *Please provide the full name of the person applying for the restriction.*

The application has been lodged by:
Land Registry Key No. (if appropriate)
Name (if different from the applicant)
Address/DX No.

Reference
E-mail

Telephone No.   Fax No.

FOR OFFICIAL USE ONLY
Codes
Dealing
Status

8. Where you would like us to deal with someone else *We shall deal only with the applicant, or the person lodging the application if different, unless you place "X" against one or more of the statements below and give the necessary details.*

☐ Send title information document to the person shown below

☐ Raise any requisitions or queries with the person shown below

☐ Return original documents lodged with this form (see note in panel 6) to the person shown below
 If this applies only to certain documents, please specify.

Name
Address/DX No.

Reference
E-mail

Telephone No.	Fax No.

9. Entitlement to apply for a restriction *Place "X" in the appropriate box.*

☐ The applicant is the registered proprietor of the registered estate/charge referred to in panel 4.

☐ The applicant is the person **entitled** to be registered as proprietor of the registered estate/charge referred to in panel 4. **Complete panel 12.**

☐ The consent of the registered proprietor of the registered estate/charge referred to in panel 4 accompanies this application or the applicant's conveyancer certifies that he holds this consent. **Complete panel 11.**

☐ The consent of the person **entitled** to be registered as proprietor of the registered estate/charge referred to in panel 4 accompanies this application or the applicant's conveyancer certifies that he holds this consent. **Complete panels 11 and 12.**

☐ Evidence that the applicant has sufficient interest in the making of the entry of the restriction applied for in panel 10 accompanies this application. **Complete panel 13.**

10. The applicant applies to enter the following restriction against the registered estate/charge referred to in panel 4: *Please set out the form of restriction required. Schedule 4 to the Land Registration Rules 2003 contains standard forms of restrictions. Use this form to apply for a standard form of restriction (as set out in Schedule 4 to the Land Registration Rules 2003) or, where appropriate, a restriction in another form. If the restriction is not a standard form of restriction, the registrar must be satisfied that the terms of the proposed restriction are reasonable and that applying the proposed restriction would be straightforward and not place an unreasonable burden on him. If the restriction requires notice to be given to a person, requires a person's consent or certificate or is a standard form restriction that refers to a named person, **include that person's address for service**.*

11. Evidence of consent *Please complete this panel if instructed to do so in panel 9. Place "X" in the appropriate box.*

☐ The [registered proprietor of][person entitled to be registered as the proprietor of] the registered estate/charge referred to in panel 4 consents to the entry of the restriction and that person or their conveyancer has completed panel 15.

☐ I am the applicant's conveyancer and certify that I hold the consent referred to in panel 9.

☐ The consent referred to in panel 9 is contained on page___of the document numbered ___ referred to in [panel 6][Form AP1][Form DL].

12. Evidence of entitlement to be registered as proprietor *Please complete this panel if instructed to do so in panel 9. Place "X" in the appropriate box.*

☐ I am the applicant's conveyancer and certify that I am satisfied that the applicant/person consenting to this application is entitled to be registered as proprietor and that I hold the originals of the documents that contain evidence of that person's entitlement, or an application for registration of that person as proprietor is pending at Land Registry.

☐ Evidence that the applicant/person consenting to this application is entitled to be registered as proprietor is contained in the document(s) numbered ____ referred to in [panel 6][Form AP1][Form DL].

13. Evidence that the applicant has sufficient interest *Please complete this panel if instructed to do so in panel 9.*

State brief details of the applicant's interest in the making of the entry of the restriction applied for in panel 10.

Evidence of this interest is contained in the document(s) numbered referred to in [panel 6] [Form AP1][Form DL].

14. Signature of applicant
   or their conveyancer _____ **Date** _____

15. Consent
Consent to the entry of the restriction specified in panel 10 is given by:

Names BLOCK LETTERS	Signatures
1.	1.
2.	2.
3.	3.

**Application for an
official search
of the index map**

Land Registry

SIM

Land Registry_____Office

If you need more room than is provided for in a panel, use continuation sheet CS and attach to this form.

1. Administrative area

2. Property to be searched
Postal number or description

Name of road

Name of locality

Town

Postcode

Ordnance Survey map reference (if known)

Known title number(s)

3. Payment of fee *Place "X" in the appropriate box.*

☐ The Land Registry fee of £ [   ] accompanies this application.

☐ Debit the Credit Account mentioned in panel 4 with the appropriate fee payable under the current Land Registration Fee Order.

For official use only
Impression of fees

4. The application has been lodged by:
Land Registry Key No. (if appropriate)
Name
Address/DX No.

Reference
E-mail

Telephone No.   Fax No.

5.	If the result of search is to be sent to anyone other than the applicant in panel 4, please supply the name and address of the person to whom it should be sent.

Reference

6. I apply for an official search of the index map in respect of the land referred to in panel 2 above and shown _____ **on the attached plan.**

Any attached plan must contain sufficient details of the surrounding roads and other features to enable the land to be identified satisfactorily on the Ordnance Survey map. A plan may be unnecessary if the land can be identified by postal description.

7.   Signature of applicant _____ **Date** _____

Explanatory notes

1.   The purpose and scope of Official Searches of the Index Map are described in Practice Guide 10 'Official searches of the Index Map' obtainable from any Land Registry office. It can also be viewed online at www.landregistry.gov.uk.

2.   Please send this application to the appropriate Land Registry office. This information is contained in Practice Guide 51 'Areas served by Land Registry offices'.

3.   Please ensure that the appropriate fee payable under the current Land Registration Fee Order accompanies your application. If paying fees by cheque or postal order, these should be crossed and payable to "Land Registry". Where you have requested that the fee be paid by Credit Account, receipt of the certificate of result is confirmation that the appropriate fee has been debited.

**Transfer of part
of registered title(s)**

Land Registry

If you need more room than is provided for in a panel, use continuation sheet CS and attach to this form.

1. Stamp Duty

Place "X" in the appropriate box or boxes and complete the appropriate certificate.

☐ It is certified that this instrument falls within category ☐ in the Schedule to the Stamp Duty (Exempt Instruments) Regulations 1987

☐ It is certified that the transaction effected does not form part of a larger transaction or of a series of transactions in respect of which the amount or value or the aggregate amount or value of the consideration exceeds the sum of

£ [   ]

☐ It is certified that this is an instrument on which stamp duty is not chargeable by virtue of the provisions of section 92 of the Finance Act 2001

2. Title number(s) out of which the Property is transferred *Leave blank if not yet registered.*

3. Other title number(s) against which matters contained in this transfer are to be registered, if any

4. Property transferred *Insert address, including postcode, or other description of the property transferred. Any physical exclusions, e.g. mines and minerals, should be defined. Any attached plan must be signed by the transferor.*

The Property is defined: *Place "X" in the appropriate box.*

☐ on the attached plan and shown *State reference e.g. "edged red".*

☐ on the Transferor's title plan and shown *State reference e.g. "edged and numbered 1 in blue".*

5. Date

6. Transferor *Give full name(s) and company's registered number, if any.*

7. Transferee **for entry on the register** *Give full name(s) and company's registered number, if any. For Scottish companies use an SC prefix and for limited liability partnerships use an OC prefix before the registered number, if any. For foreign companies give territory in which incorporated.*

Unless otherwise arranged with Land Registry headquarters, a certified copy of the Transferee's constitution (in English or Welsh) will be required if it is a body corporate but is not a company registered in England and Wales or Scotland under the Companies Acts.

8. Transferee's intended **address(es) for service (including postcode) for entry on the register** *You may give up to three addresses for service **one** of which **must** be a postal address but does not have to be within the UK. The other addresses can be any combination of a postal address, a box number at a UK document exchange or an electronic address.*

9. **The Transferor transfers the Property to the Transferee**

10. Consideration *Place "X" in the appropriate box. State clearly the currency unit if other than sterling. If none of the boxes applies, insert an appropriate memorandum in the additional provisions panel.*

☐ The Transferor has received from the Transferee for the Property the sum of *In words and figures.*

☐ *Insert other receipt as appropriate.*

☐ The transfer is not for money or anything which has a monetary value

11. The Transferor transfers with *Place "X" in the appropriate box and add any modifications.*

☐ full title guarantee ☐ limited title guarantee

12. Declaration of trust *Where there is more than one Transferee, place "X" in the appropriate box.*

☐ The Transferees are to hold the Property on trust for themselves as joint tenants

☐ The Transferees are to hold the Property on trust for themselves as tenants in common in equal shares

☐ The Transferees are to hold the Property *Complete as necessary.*

13. Additional provisions
Use this panel for:
- *definitions of terms not defined above*
- *rights granted or reserved*
- *restrictive covenants*
- *other covenants*
- *agreements and declarations*
- *other agreed provisions.*

The prescribed subheadings may be added to, amended, repositioned or omitted.

Definitions

Rights granted for the benefit of the Property

Rights reserved for the benefit of other land *The land having the benefit should be defined, if necessary by reference to a plan.*

Restrictive covenants by the Transferee *Include words of covenant.*

Restrictive covenants by the Transferor *Include words of covenant.*

14. Execution *The Transferor must execute this transfer as a deed using the space below. If there is more than one Transferor, all must execute. Forms of execution are given in Schedule 9 to the Land Registration Rules 2003. If the transfer contains Transferee's covenants or declarations or contains an application by the Transferee (e.g. for a restriction), it must also be executed by the Transferee (all of them, if there is more than one).*

Transfer of whole of registered title(s)	Land Registry

If you need more room than is provided for in a panel, use continuation sheet CS and attach to this form.

1. Stamp Duty

Place "X" in the appropriate box or boxes and complete the appropriate certificate.

☐ It is certified that this instrument falls within category ☐ in the Schedule to the Stamp Duty (Exempt Instruments) Regulations 1987

☐ It is certified that the transaction effected does not form part of a larger transaction or of a series of transactions in respect of which the amount or value or the aggregate amount or value of the consideration exceeds the sum of ☐ £

☐ It is certified that this is an instrument on which stamp duty is not chargeable by virtue of the provisions of section 92 of the Finance Act 2001

2. Title Number(s) of the Property *Leave blank if not yet registered.*

3. Property

4. Date

5. Transferor *Give full names and company's registered number if any.*

6. Transferee for entry on the register *Give full name(s) and company's registered number, if any. For Scottish companies use an SC prefix and for limited liability partnerships use an OC prefix before the registered number, if any. For foreign companies give territory in which incorporated.*

Unless otherwise arranged with Land Registry headquarters, a certified copy of the Transferee's constitution (in English or Welsh) will be required if it is a body corporate but is not a company registered in England and Wales or Scotland under the Companies Acts.

7. Transferee's intended address(es) for service (including postcode) for entry on the register *You may give up to three addresses for service one of which **must** be a postal address but does not have to be within the UK. The other addresses can be any combination of a postal address, a box number at a UK document exchange or an electronic address.*

8. The Transferor transfers the Property to the Transferee

9. Consideration *Place "X" in the appropriate box. State clearly the currency unit if other than sterling. If none of the boxes applies, insert an appropriate memorandum in the additional provisions panel.*

☐ The Transferor has received from the Transferee for the Property the sum of *In words and figures.*

☐ *Insert other receipt as appropriate.*

☐ The transfer is not for money or anything which has a monetary value

10. The Transferor transfers with *Place "X" in the appropriate box and add any modifications.*

☐ full title guarantee   ☐ limited title guarantee

11. Declaration of trust *Where there is more than one Transferee, place "X" in the appropriate box.*

☐ The Transferees are to hold the Property on trust for themselves as joint tenants

☐ The Transferees are to hold the Property on trust for themselves as tenants in common in equal shares

☐ The Transferees are to hold the Property *Complete as necessary.*

12. Additional provisions *Insert here any required or permitted statements, certificates or applications and any agreed covenants, declarations, etc.*

13. Execution *The Transferor must execute this transfer as a deed using the space below. If there is more than one Transferor, all must execute. Forms of execution are given in Schedule 9 to the Land Registration Rules 2003. If the transfer contains Transferee's covenants or declarations or contains an application by the Transferee (e.g. for a restriction), it must also be executed by the Transferee (all of them, if there is more than one).*

Application to enter **a unilateral notice**	**Land Registry**
	# UN1

To enter an agreed notice use Form AN1. To enter a notice to protect matrimonial home rights use Form MH1.
If you need more room than is provided for in a panel, use continuation sheet CS and attach to this form.

1.	**Administrative area and postcode** if known
2.	**Title number(s)**
3.	If you have already made this application by **outline application,** insert reference number:
4.	**Property** **The interest to be protected by the unilateral notice affects** *Place "X" in the appropriate box and complete as necessary.* ☐ the whole of the registered estate ☐ the part of the registered estate shown on the attached plan *State reference e.g. "edged red".* ☐ the registered charge dated ⸻ in favour of ⸻ referred to in the charges register

5.	**Application and fee** *A fee calculator for all types of applications can be found on Land Registry's website at www.landregistry.gov.uk/fees*	**FOR OFFICIAL USE ONLY** Record of fee paid
	Unilateral notice Fee paid £	
	Fee payment method: *Place "X" in the appropriate box.* I wish to pay the appropriate fee payable under the current Land Registration Fee Order:	Particulars of under/over payment
	☐ by cheque or postal order, amount £⸻ made payable to "Land Registry".	Fees debited £
	☐ by Direct Debit under an authorised agreement with Land Registry.	Reference number

6.	**Documents lodged with this form (if any)** *If this application is accompanied by either Form AP1 or FR1 please only complete the corresponding panel on Form AP1 or DL. Number the documents in sequence; copies should also be numbered and listed as separate documents. If you supply the original document and a certified copy, we shall assume that you request the return of the original; if a certified copy is not supplied, we may retain the original document and it may be destroyed.*

7.	**The applicant applies for the entry of a unilateral notice against the title(s) referred to in panel 2**

8.	**The applicant is:** *Please provide the full name of the person applying for the notice.*	**FOR OFFICIAL USE ONLY**
	The application has been lodged by: Land Registry Key No. (if appropriate) Name (if different from the applicant) Address/DX No.	Codes Dealing
	Reference E-mail	Status **RED**
	Telephone No. Fax No.	

9.   Address(es) for service of the beneficiary. The address(es) will be entered in the register and used for correspondence and the service of notice. *List the full name and address of each person to be entered in the register as beneficiary of the notice. You may give up to three addresses for service* ***one*** *of which* ***must*** *be a postal address but does not have to be within the UK. The other addresses can be any combination of a postal address, a box number at a UK document exchange or an electronic address. For a company include company's registered number if any. For Scottish companies use an SC prefix and for limited liability partnerships use an OC prefix before the registered number, if any. For foreign companies give territory in which incorporated.*

10. *Complete this panel and* ***either*** *panel 11* ***or*** *panel 12. Place "X" in the appropriate box.*

☐ The declarant is the beneficiary or a person authorised by the beneficiary to make the declaration in panel 11.
The declarant's full name is

☐ The certificate in panel 12 has been completed by a conveyancer on behalf of the beneficiary.
The conveyancer's full name is

Firm name (if any)

Address

11. The declarant solemnly and sincerely declares that the beneficiary is interested in the property described in panel 4 as
This panel must set out the nature of the beneficiary's interest.

The interest described above is not a public right or a customary right.

And I make this solemn declaration conscientiously believing the same to be true by virtue of the Statutory Declarations Act 1835.

Signature of declarant

Declared at

this   day of   before me,

Signature

Name
(BLOCK CAPITALS)

Address

Qualification
This declaration must be made in the presence of a person empowered to administer oaths, such as a commissioner for oaths or a practising solicitor.

12. I certify that the beneficiary is interested in the property described in panel 4 as
This panel must set out the nature of the beneficiary's interest.

I certify that the interest described above is not a public right or a customary right.

Signature

Name
(BLOCK CAPITALS)

Address

13. Signature of applicant
 or their conveyancer _____ **Date** _____

Index

References are to paragraph numbers

Absolute title, *see* Freehold; Leasehold
  (title)
Access to information   18.1 *et seq,*
  see also Inspection of register;
    Official copies; Search, official
Access order
  neighbouring land, notice
    registration   10.17(c)
Accretion and diluvion   14.7(f),
           16.9–16.11
  boundary of registered estate in
    land   16.10, 16.11
    agreement by landowners,
      registration requirement   16.11
    provision on   16.10
Address
  electronic   20.43
  proprietor, in proprietorship
    register   14.10(c)
  proprietor of charge, charges
    register   14.12(e)
  service, for   20.42, 20.43
    cautioner, by   20.44
  tacking, for notice   12.66
Adjudicator   34.1 *et seq*
  appeal from   34.21
    appeal to, refusal/termination
      of network access   27.21,
           34.12(2)
  appointment, removal and
    qualifications   34.10
  document rectification   34.13, 34.14
  enforcement of requirement by   34.15
  functions   34.1, 34.12
  information suppression,
    offence   35.2
  jurisdiction   34.12, 34.13
  reference to   20.30, 34.3, 34.12(1),
           34.15 *et seq*
  adverse possession registration
    application   30.30, 30.36,
           30.40, 34.20
    appeal to court   30.40, 34.23
    duty on registrar   34.4, 34.12(1)
    hearing   34.15

indemnity issue   23.20
paper determination   34.15
procedure   34.15–34.20
reference to court   34.17, 34.18
ruling or general directions   34.19
statement of case preparation   34.15
timetable   34.15
whole application or
  specific issues   34.12(1), 34.19
staff and delegation to   34.11
supervision of   34.2
Administration order
  administrator   13.26
  information, etc, applicant   18.35
  register entry applicant   13.26
  Practice Guide   13.24
Adverse possession, *see* Squatter
Agent
  electronic document
    authentication of , deeming
      provision   26.17
    corporation, execution for   26.19,
           26.20
Air, right of   2.41, 14.7(b), (e), 8.52
Alteration of register   14.23, 22.1 *et seq*
  cautions register, *see* Caution
    against first registration
  circumstances for   22.1, 22.3
  costs   22.21
  court order, by   22.5, 22.6–22.15
    contents of order   22.6
    discretion of court   22.8
    duty on court   22.7
    limitations   22.8
    purposes   22.6, 22.7
    service on registrar/form   22.6
  dealings, to reflect (electronic
    system), *see* Electronic system
  estate or right excepted from
    registration, to give effect
      to   22.6, 22.16
  improper, offence   35.3, 35.4, 35.6
  indemnity, *see* Indemnity
  mistakes   22.1, 22.3, 22.6, 22.7, 22.16

Alteration of register – *cont*
  network access agreement,
    under   22.20
  Practice Guide   22.2
  prospective effect only   22.4
  'rectification'   22.3
    indemnity   23.3, 23.4
    proprietor not in possession,
      fraud etc   22.11, 22.15
    protection of proprietor
      in possession   22.10–2.14, 22.17
      'proprietor in possession' 22.12,
         22.13
  registrar, by   22.5, 22.16–22.24
    application for, and form 22.18
    circumstances   22.16
    limitations   22.17
    notice   22.18
    objection   22.19
    without application   22.18
  spent entry, removal of   22.5, 22.16,
      22.20
  unauthorised, offence   35.5, 35.6
  updating   22.1, 22.6, 22.7, 22.16
    notice entry   10.13(d)
    notice and restriction
      cancellation   10.28, 10.99
Appeals, *see* Adjudicator
Applications   20.16–20.36
  circumstances for, list   20.16
  completion   20.33–20.36
    document retention or return 20.34
  defective, cancellation   20.19
  electronic   20.4, 20.18
  evidence   20.17(b), 20.22–20.25
    further, power   20.22
    registrar's powers   20.22
    requirement for   20.22
  failure to apply for titles other
    affected, rules for   20.20
  form of   20.5(a), 20.18
  mistake, alteration by registrar 22.23,
    22.24
  objection to, *see* Objection to
    application
  office or certified copy,
    circumstances for   20.25
  plan   20.24
  prescribed form   20.17(a)
  requisitions by registrar   20.19
  rule-making powers   20.17
  time effective   20.33

  time made and priority   20.17(c),
    20.26–20.28
    rules setting out time of
      application   20.26, 20.27
    two or more at same time,
      priority   20.28
    transfer by operation of law
      before completed   20.21
Appurtenant rights   2.34, 8.46–8.52
  agreement preventing acquisition
    of rights   2.41, 8.52
  entry in register on first
    registration   2.34, 14.7(a)
    application for   2.34
    claimed right, details of   14.7(a)
  prescription, implied grant or
    reservation, claim on basis
    of   8.48–8.50
    application and evidence   8.49
    notice on servient owner   8.50
    objection by servient owner   8.50
    register entries   8.50
  registered land, application for
    entry of notice after
    registration   8.51, 8.52
  unregistered land, over, by
    proprietor of registered
    land   8.47
    claimed right, details of   8.47
    form for application   8.47
    objection by servient owner   8.47
Arrangement, deed of
  restriction, protection by
    10.102(d), 10.103, 10.104
Assent/vesting assent
  transfer by   2.10, 20.37, 8.27
    charge, of, *see* Charge
Assignment
  notice of, electronic   26.18
Attorney, *see* Power of attorney

Bankruptcy   13.9–13.18
  see also Operation of law
  disposition after, protection of
    purchaser   9.13, 13.15
  notice on register   13.10, 13.11,
    14.10(e), 14.12(g)
    duration   13.12
    terms   13.11
  notice to proprietor   13.12, 13.14
  order, registration of   13.13
  petition, registration of   13.10

Bankruptcy – *cont*
  restriction   13.14, 14.10(d),14.12(f),
                       10.64(b)
    duration   13.14
    terms   13.14
    transfer on, registration exception   8.6
Beneficiary
  adverse possession by   33.12
  adverse possession claim, protection
    from   33.11
  charging order over interest, *see*
    Charging order
  delegation of functions to, evidence
    as to status   20.12
  interest binding registered
    proprietor   4.7, 15.5
  restriction entry protection interest
        10.7, 10.56(c), 10.68(a), 10.105
  transfer to   2.10, 2.11
  unilateral notice, of   10.30,
                            20.29, 20.42(b),
  see also Notice (on register)
Boundary   16.1 *et seq*
  accretion and diluvion, *see* Accretion and
    diluvion
  fixing exact line   16.2–16.8
    application for determination   16.5
      applicant   16.5
      disputed, procedure for   16.6, 20.30
      form and documents with   16.5
      notice to adjoining owners and
        objection right   16.6
      procedural steps   16.6
      record of determination   16.7
    background to rules   16.2–16.4
    determination without
      application   16.8
      power of registrar   16.8
      record of   16.8
    plans   16.5, 16.8
  general rule   16.1
  mistake as to, adverse possession
    claim   30.42–30.48, 32.2
    general boundary, must be   30.47
    requirements to be met   30.42,
                            30.45–30.48
    transitional provision   33.17
  see also Squatter
Building society
  discharge of charge, execution
    as deed   12.92
Business lease   2.15

Caution against dealings
  prospective abolition   5.1, 7.6, 10.1,
                                       10.3
  transitional   10.106–10.110
    cancellation application   10.110
    notice on cautioner, procedure
      after   10.107, 10.108
    withdrawal application   10.109
Caution against first registration   5.1 *et seq*
  adverse possession claim,
    transitional provision for   33.18
  applicant   5.4
    limitation on   5.5
  application   5.6
    form   5.6
    informing landowner of   5.6
    objection power   5.16
    pending   14.17
  background   5.2
  cancellation application   5.17–5.20
    applicants   5.17
    application form   5.18
    limitation on right   5.20
    objection to   20.29
  'cautioner'   5.7
  consent to lodging of   5.20
  Crown land   6.3
  index, details in   14.14, 14.17
  lodging procedure   5.4 *et seq*
  notice to cautioner
    cancellation application   5.19
    first registration application   5.14
  objection rights of cautioner
    cancellation, to   5.19
    first registration, to   5.14
    period for, and extension   5.13, 5.19
  plan   5.3, 5.6
  Practice Guide   5.1
  protection conferred by   5.13, 5.14
  purpose of   5.1
  'reasonable cause' requirement   5.21
  register   5.2, 5.3
    alteration to   5.9–5.11, 22.1, 22.22
      court order   5.10
      improper, offence   35.3, 35.4, 35.6
      network access agreement,
        under   22.20
      purposes   5.9
      registrar, by   5.11
    inspection right   18.3
    mistake   5.9, 22.1
      indemnification for   5.12, 23.9
    official copies   18.11

Caution against first registration – *cont*
  register – *cont*
    parts of   5.3
    updating   5.9
    removal   5.15, 5.17–5.20
    time-limit   5.5, 6.3
    transitional   5.22
    vacation, High Court jurisdiction   5.21
    withdrawal right   5.8
    form   5.8
Certificate
  charge certificate, abolition of,
  see Charge land certificate, abolition
  of, *see* Land certificate official search,
  see Search, official
Challenge or objection
  application, to, provision for, *see*
    Objection to application
Charge   12.1 *et seq*
  adverse possession registration,
    effect on   31.6–31.9
  application to register   12.22, 12.23
    form   12.22
  cancellation, *see* 'discharge and
    release' *below*
  certificate, abolition   21.1, 21.3
    alternative documents   21.5
    destruction power   21.4(c)
    existing certificates, treatment of 21.4
  company   12.28
    discharge, execution of   12.91
    registration   20.36
  consolidation   12.38–12.41
    entry for right of   12.39–12.41
    form   12.39, 12.40
  creation   12.9, 12.10
  deed, by   12.2, 12.12
  definition   12.1
  details in charges register   14.12
  discharge and release   12.86–12.107
    documentary discharge   12.87–12.97
      application forms   12.87, 12.89
      execution of form by
        lender bodies   12.90–12.96
      release of part forms   12.88, 12.89
      special arrangement for
        significant number 12.95, 12.96
      unregistered land, charge
        secured on   12.97
    electronic notification   12.86,
             12.103–12.107, 26.1
  forms of   12.86

  notice, charges protected by,
    see Notice (on register)
    restriction relating to charge   12.107
  disposition of   12.6–12.8
    disponee only protected   12.6, 12.7
    form and content   12.9
    powers of proprietor   12.6, 12.7
    registrable   8.23
    sub-charge   12.8
    ultra vires   12.6, 12.7
  effect of registered   4.3, 9.8
  equitable   9.14–9.16, 12.5, 12.59
    discharge, *see* Notice (on register)
  first registration, register entry on   2.35
  floating, discharge of   12.101
  foreclosure   12.84, 12.85
    entry in register as proprietor
      of estate   12.84, 12.85
  form   12.10 *et seq*
    approved form   12.14–12.21
      advantages   12.15
      amendment after approval   12.20
      application for   12.16, 12.17
      contents criteria   12.18
      deeds of variation,
        priority   12.34–12.36
      reference number   12.19
      time taken for approval   12.19
    CH1   12.10–12.13
    standard form likely   12.13
  formalities   7.5, 12.9
  further advance, *see* Tacking
  grant of legal   8.22
  inspection   18.4
    transitional   18.32, 18.33
  local land charge, *see* Local
    land charge
  official copy of register entries   12.29
  official search by chargee protects
    disposition   19.18
  overriding, *see* Statutory charge
  owner's power to make   7.2–7.5
  part of estate, on   14.7
  priority of competing
    charges   12.48–12.59
    alteration of priority 12.49, 12.72
      application form   12.49
      consent   12.49
      e-conveyancing disposition   28.2
      entry on register   12.49
    deed of priority/postponement,
      approval   12.21

Charge – *cont*
  priority of competing charges – *cont*
    equitable charge, *see* 'equitable'
      above
    registered charges, general rule   12.48
      exceptions   12.48
    statutory charges   12.51–12.58
      application to register   12.52
      dispute referral   12.58
      entry on register   12.53, 12.54
      form   12.52
      notice duty on registrar   12.51,
        12.55, 12.58
      overriding nature of   12.51
      removal or replacement of
        entry   12.56, 12.57
  proprietor
    charges register details   14.12(d), (e)
    entry on register   8.22, 8.23
    powers of   12.6–12.8
      limitations on, restriction
        entry for   12.7
    transferee   8.23
  realisation of security   12.79–12.83
    joint proprietors, receipt by   12.83
    registration of local land
      charge for   12.80, 12.81
    surplus after sale, provision
      for   12.82, 19.21
  registrable disposition of   8.23, 12.6
  registration co-ordination with
    registrar of companies   20.36
  restriction entry   12.7, 12.11, 14.12(f)
    application for   12.24
    cancellation or withdrawal   12.107
    consent of proprietor, form of   12.24
    forms   10.67(c), 12.24–12.26
    order of court, on   12.27
    standard restriction   12.24
  sub-charge   2.35, 7.4, 12.6–12.8
    creation
      method   12.3, 12.4
      power   12.6
    essence of   7.4, 12.8
    proprietor's powers   12.8
    tacking, *see* Tacking
    registered proprietor   8.23
  transfer   12.42–12.47
    assent of charge (AS2)   12.42
      contents   12.46
      signature   12.47
    contents of form (TR3)   12.43
    deed, as   12.44, 12.47

    execution of   12.44, 12.45, 12.47
    forms for   12.42
    portfolio of charges (TR4) 12.42, 12.45
    registrable disposition   8.23
  variation
    application   12.30–12.37
      consents required   12.30, 12.31,
        12.33, 12.34
      form   12.34, 12.35
    deed
      approval   12.21
      execution of   12.32, 12.34
      registration application   12.34–12.37
      retention by Registry   12.37
    note on register   12.36
Charges register, *see* Register of title
Charging order
  interest in trust, over, protection
    by restriction   10.7, 10.59–10.61
    applicants   10.68(h)
    form of restriction   10.60
    notice of intended disposition   10.61
Charity   13.22, 13.38–13.41
  disposition by, statement
    in instrument   13.40
  disposition to   13.39, 13.41
    non-exempt charity, restriction   13.39
    statement in instrument   13.39
  official custodian, registration as
    proprietor   13.41
  restriction application   10.68(c), 10.79
Charity Commission
  restriction, applicant for   10.68(c)
Church chancel repair right   4.14(9),
    4.18, 11.2
Church Commissioners
  land acquired by/transferred to, etc
    registration of transferee   20.14
    vesting in incumbent,
      registration of   20.13
    restriction, applicant for   10.68(d)
Coal/coal mine
  notice protection not available   10.11
  overriding interest, rights as   4.14(7),
    11.2(d)
  search system   4.14(7)
Common, right of   11.14, 11.15
  grant, registration exception   8.12
  notice protection not available   10.10
Company
  charge   12.28, 20.36
    discharge   12.91, 12.95, 12.96
      foreign company   12.93

Company – *cont*
  charge – *cont*
    registration co-ordination with
      registrar of companies   20.36
  dissolution, *see* Dissolution of
    company
  execution by electronic
    document   26.15,
      26.19–26.21
    forms   20.38
    seal   26.19
  insolvency, *see* Insolvency
  Land Registry powers to
    form/invest in   36.8, 36.9
  registration provisions   13.20, 13.21
Compulsory first registration   2.8–2.24
  applicant   2.21
  application for, *see* First registration
  dealings pending registration,
    treatment of   2.24
  exclusions   2.8
  new triggers   2.8, 2.9
    power to add 'events'   2.20
  non-compliance   2.22
    retransfer where void for
      non-registration   2.23
  procedure, *see* First registration
  'qualifying estate'   2.8, 2.9
    transfers to be registered   2.10, 2.11
  registrable dispositions   2.10–2.19
    exclusions   2.11
    gift   2.10, 2.28
    lease grant   2.8, 2.13–2.16
    mortgage, legal   2.19, 2.21, 2.35
    reversionary estate transfer/
      lease of reversion   2.12, 2.18
    reversionary lease   2.16
    right to buy a lease, grant of   2.17
    valuable/other consideration,
      transfer for   2.10
  requirement of registration   2.21–2.23
  time-limit   2.22
Confidentiality, *see* Exempt
  information document
Consent
  caution against first registration   5.20
  charge
    priority alteration, to   12.49
    restriction entry, form   12.24
    variation   12.30, 12.31, 12.33,
      12.34
  home information pack in electronic
    form   27.4

    notice on register   10.15(b), 10.21, 10.22
      dispensing with, power   10.53, 10.100
    restriction   10.66
      dispensing with, power   10.53, 10.100
      withdrawal   10.95, 10.96
    squatter's application for
      registration, to   30.28, 30.29, 30.31
Contract for sale
  electronic form   26.6, 27.5, 27.6
    automatic validation   27.5
    notice on register   19.5, 27.7
    release, instead of
      'exchange'   26.6, 27.7
    time of effect   26.10, 27.7
Conveyancer
  electronic network, use of,
    see Network access agreement
Copies
  see also Official copies
  filed, *see* Filed copies
  right to make, *see* Inspection of register
Copyhold
  property register entry   14.6
Corn rent   4.14(13), 4.18
Corporate body
  see also Company
  dissolution   8.7, 13.33
  entry on register for   14.11(b), 14.12(h)
  execution of electronic
    document   26.15, 26.19–26.21
  execution of form of discharge
    of charge   12.94
    significant number at once,
      arrangement for   12.95, 12.96
  insolvency, *see* Insolvency
  registration   13.23
Costs
  alteration of register, of   22.21
  recoverable loss, indemnity
    payment   23.14, 23.15
County court
  proceedings in, direction
    for   34.17, 34.18
Court order
  transfer by, registration of   2.10
Court proceedings
  see also County court
  applications in connection with
      18.34–18.37
    'qualifying applicants'   18.35
Covenant
  implied
    lease pre-1996, in transfer of   25.6

Covenant – *cont*
  implied – *cont*
    rentcharge, estate subject to,
      see Rentcharge
    title, as to, *see* Covenants for title
    indemnity, *see* Indemnity
      covenant
    positive   25.1, 25.4
      indemnity covenant for   25.5
      property register entry   14.6
      proprietorship register
        entry   14.10(f)–(h), 25.4
      removal   25.4
    restrictive, *see* Restrictive covenant
    title, for, *see* Covenants for title
Covenants for title   25.2, 25.3
  full or limited title guarantee   25.3(a)
  implied   25.1, 25.3(b)
  LRA 2002 provisions   25.2
  limiting or extending, statement
    on   25.3(c)
  old law, may still arise   25.3(d)
  rules   25.3
Crown land   6.1–6.3, 13.2–13.6
  bona vacantia, registration as   13.33
  demesne land, first registration
    application   6.1, 33.13
    caution against   6.3
    compulsory   6.2
    incentive for   13.2
    voluntary nature   6.1
  escheat to, see Escheated land
  foreshore vested in, *see* Foreshore
Crown rent
  overriding interest
    first registration   4.14(11), 4.18
    registered disposition   11.2
Customary right   4.14(4), 10.17(e),
    11.2

DIY conveyancing   27.26
Date, *see* Effective date
Day list   14.22, 14.23
  alteration to register of title
    by registrar, note of proposal   14.23
  contents   14.22
  entry on, date of official search   19.11,
    19.27
  requirement for   14.22, 19.6
Dealings
  see also Disposition
  caution against, *see* Caution against
    dealings

dematerialised form, *see* Electronic
    system
first registration, pending, *see*
    Compulsory first registration
Death of registered proprietor   8.5, 13.7,
    see also Personal representative
Deed
  charge, relating to, *see* Charge
  electronic document taking
    effect as   26.7, 26.10, 26.14, 26.16
    no attestation or
      statement that a deed   26.16
  execution as   8.27, 20.37
    guidance   20.37
  variation by   8.40
Deeds (title)
  lost   2.27
Defect in title   17.1–17.6
  determination right   17.1, 17.2
  entry for   17.3–17.5
    application for   17.4
    notice requirement and
      objection right   17.4
    registrar's power   17.4
    removal application   17.6
    applicants   17.6
Delegated powers, *see* Rules
  and Orders
Demesne land   6.1, 33.13
Dependent estates
  registration   15.9
Determination
  record of   8.53, 8.54, 13.5
    application for   8.54, 13.6
    escheated land   13.6
    modified statement   13.5
    right   17.1–17.6,
      see also Defect in title
Devolution on death,
  see Operation of law
Diluvion, *see* Accretion and diluvion
Discontinuous lease, *see* Lease
Disposition   7.1 *et seq*, 8.1 *et seq*
  electronic   26.8, 28.2, 28.3
  formalities   7.5
  forms   20.5(b)
  invalid transfer, *see* Void
    conveyance
  legal estate, effect as   8.1
  limitations on power to make   7.1, 7.6
    no entry on register for
      limitation, effect   7.6
      example   7.7, 7.8

Disposition – *cont*
  limitations on power to make – *cont*
    liability   7.8
    power to make   7.2–7.5
    principles adopted by LRA 2002   7.2
    priorities   9.2 *et seq*,
      see also Priority of interests
    protection of disponee
      caution, prospective repeal,
        see Caution against dealings
      restriction, *see* Restriction
      registration requirements,
        see Registrable disposition
    unregistered interest overriding,
      see Overriding interest
Dispute procedure, *see* Adjudicator
Dissolution of company   8.7, 13.33
  bona vacantia, property
    passing   13.33
  entry on register for   14.11(b), 14.12(h)
    application for   13.33
Divestment, statutory   17.1
Document
  alteration, offence   35.4, 35.6
  destruction power   20.34, 20.35
  dispensation power   20.34
  electronic, *see* Electronic system
  execution, *see* Execution of documents
  filed copies, *see* Filed copies
  loss or destruction while at
    Registry   23.8
  mistake
    alteration power   22.23, 22.24
    indemnity   18.41, 23.7
  office copy, acceptability   20.25
  production   20.5(e), 34.7, 35.7
    costs   34.7, 34.8
    determination of objection   34.7
  rectification of conveyancing
    document   34.13, 34.14
  retention or return by registrar,
    provisions   20.34
    certified copies, supply of   20.34
    land and charge certificates   21.4(b)
    request for return, transitional   20.35
    time received, rules for   20.26
Document exchange   20.45
Drainage rights   11.15
Duchy of Lancaster or Cornwall
  bona vacantia, registration as   13.33

Easement
  see also Appurtenant rights

    equitable   4.14(3)
  grant/reservation
    exception from registration   8.12
    form not prescribed   20.6
    notice on register   4.3, 10.13
    registration requirement   8.12–8.16,
      see also Registrable disposition
  legal, as overriding interest,
    see Overriding interest
  prescription, etc
    agreement precluding
      acquisition on basis of   2.41, 8.52
    claim on basis of   8.48–8.50
    property register entry   14.6, 14.7
    registered proprietor's application
      to register   8.51
E-conveyancing, *see* Electronic system
Effective date
  registration, of   15.10, 20.33
Electronic system   26.1 *et seq*
  access regulation, *see* Network
    access agreement
  address for service   20.43, 20.45
  application form   20.4, 20.18
  background   26.1–26.4
  closed titles, information
    on   18.44, 18.45
  compulsory nature   28.1–28.5
    definition   28.3
    reason for   28.1
  contract for sale, *see* Contract for sale
  discharge of charge
    notification   12.86, 12.103–12.106
    form END1   12.103
    informing borrower   12.105
    new system (ED), piloting of   12.106
    procedure (ENDs)   12.104
  dispositions by   26.8, 28.2, 28.3
    pre-conditions   26.9–26.13
  do-it-yourself conveyancing   27.26
  document   26.5, 26.6 *et seq*
    assignment, notice of   26.18
    authentication, *see* 'signature'
      below
    deed, regarded as   26.7, 26.10, 26.14,
                                               26.16
    effect of statutory compliance   26.7,
                                        26.14–26.18
    purchaser's rights   26.22
    requirements for   26.8–26.13
    time and date takes effect 26.10, 27.7
    writing, deeming provision   26.15
  formal requirements   26.5–26.22

Electronic system – *cont*
free-standing transaction,
  example 27.3–27.10
  completion 27.9, 27.10
  draft contract 27.5, 27.6
  enquiries 27.4, 27.6
  home information pack 27.4
  'notional register', building
    up of 27.5, 27.8
funds transfer 27.9, 28.5
introduction of 1.3, 1.20, 2.14
Land Registry Direct,
  delivery by 20.26
linked transactions, *see* Linked
  transactions
loss of document 23.8
network, electronic
  communications 27.12, 36.8
access agreement, *see* Network access
  agreement
'chain management' and
  monitoring 27.25
do-it-yourself conveyancing 27.26
education and training on use 36.8
rule-making powers 27.12
use 27.12
out of hours service 27.10
overriding interests, effect on 11.1
proposal for 1.6, 1.7
protection of register,
  mechanisms 27.1 *et seq*
  security conditions 26.12, 26.13
  see also Network access agreement
service 20.45
settlement 28.5, 36.8
signature 26.11
  agent authenticating 26.17, 26.20
  certification 26.12
  company/corporation 26.15,
    26.19–26.21
    presumption 26.21
  conveyancers, by 27.8, 27.23, 27.24
  deeming provision 26.15
  forms 26.11
    requirement for 26.11
  time document received 20.26
Embankment rights 4.14(12), 4.18, 11.2
Entry right
grant of legal right 8.17, 8.19, 8.20,
    10.13(c)
Equity/equitable interest
e-conveyancing disposition 28.2
easement 4.14(3)

estoppel, equity arising by 4.7, 9.16
fixed equitable charge,
  discharge 12.86, 12.98 *et seq,*
  see also Notice (on register)
'mere equity' 9.17
registration requirements not
  met, result 15.2, 15.8
void conveyance or transfer,
  whether vests, *see* Void
  conveyance
Escheated land 6.1, 13.3–13.6, 14.7(h)
circumstances for escheat 13.3
entry of escheat on register 8.53, 13.4
incumbrances, carrying over of 13.6
title remaining open 13.6
Estate contract
noting on register 19.5, 27.7
Estate in land
first registration, compulsory 2.9,
  see also Compulsory first
  registration
first registration, voluntary 2.1, 2.3, 2.4,
  see also First registration
registered, *see* Registered estate
Estoppel, equity arising by
see also Equity/equitable interest
squatter's registration as
  proprietor, enabling 30.37–30.40,
    32.7
    Adjudicator, reference to 30.40, 34.20
    appeal to High Court 30.40, 34.23
    lesser relief 30.39, 30.40, 34.20
Evidence
see also Applications
admissibility
  certified copy 20.25
  criminal proceedings 35.7
  official copy 18.6
adverse possession, of, *see* Squatter
upgrade of title, for 3.18
Excepted from effect of
  registration, estate etc is 2.37–2.40,
    22.6, 22.16,
  see also Overriding interest
Execution of documents 20.37–20.39
attorney, by, *see* Power of attorney
deed, as, *see* Deed
electronic, *see* Electronic system:
  document
foreign company 20.38, 20.39
forms, prescribed 20.38
joint owners, transfer to 8.36

Exempt information
    document   18.13–18.27
    agreed notice, instrument
        subject of   10.24(a)
    application form   18.18
    cancellation for prejudicing
        register   18.19–18.23
        guidance on   18.20–18.23
    designation duty   18.19
    'edited information
        document' (EDID)   18.18, 18.25
    entry on register to reflect
        EID   18.24
        removal on de-designation   18.30
    lease, use for   18.26, 18.27
    meaning of EID   18.13
    official copy, application
        for   18.28–18.30
        dispute procedure   18.29
        form   18.28
        notice and representation right   18.29
        public interest   18.28, 18.30
    personal nature of   18.27
    'prejudicial information'   18.15, 18.16
    price   18.22
    'relevant document'   18.14, 18.16
    removal of designation   18.27, 18.30,
            18.31
    transitional period   18.32, 18.33

Family charge
    rentcharge giving effect to   25.12
Fax   20.45
Fee simple absolute in possession   8.2
    see also Freehold
    first registration, voluntary   2.3
Fees
    exemptions   36.11
    first registration application   2.25
    fixed   36.11
    Orders   1.15, 1.19, 36.10, 36.11
    prescribing power   36.10
    scale fees   36.11
Filed copies   18.38–18.41
    indemnification right   18.41, 23.7
    no investigation of originals   18.41
    presumption as to conclusiveness   18.38
        documents   18.38, 18.39
        non-original documents   18.38, 18.40
First registration   2.1 *et seq*
    application   2.25–2.41
        documents with   2.25, 2.26, 20.25

    evidence in default of full
        documentary title   2.27
    examination of title by registrar   2.28,
            2.29
        powers of registrar   2.28
    fee   2.25
    form   2.25
    pending   14.17
        official search in relation to   19.5,
            19.15
    appurtenant rights, entry
        for   2.34, 14.7(a)
    agreement preventing
        acquisition   2.41, 8.52
    burdens, record of   2.35–2.41
        charges/mortgages   2.35
        exceptions (no record
            required)   2.37–2.40
            local land charge   2.39
            public right   2.38
            trivial interests   2.40
            unprotectable interests   2.37,
            10.6–10.12
    notice entry   10.13(a)
    other   2.36
    right of light or air   2.41, 14.7
    caution against, *see* Caution against
        first registration
    classes of title, *see* Title
    compulsory, *see* Compulsory first
        registration
    Crown land, *see* Crown land
    effect of   4.1 *et seq*, 15.5
        priorities, on   4.1, 4.13
    foreshore   2.31, 2.32
        Crown objection right   2.31, 2.32
    franchise   14.18
    invalid transfer, *see* Void conveyance
    mines and minerals, *see* Mines/mineral
        rights
    overriding unregistered interests,
        see Overriding interest
    voluntary   2.1–2.7
        applicants   2.2
        interests subject of   2.1, 2.3–2.7
Floating charge
    discharge of   12.101
Foreign corporation,
    see Overseas company
Foreshore
    see also Accretion and diluvion
    adverse possession   33.13–33.16
        evidence   33.16

Foreshore – *cont*
  adverse possession – *cont*
    limitation period for recovery   33.14
    treatment of land as foreshore
      for   33.15
    demesne land, held as   33.13
    escheated land   6.1
    first registration   2.31, 2.32
      Crown objection right   2.31, 2.32
    meaning   33.15
Forged transfer   15.1, 23.3,
  see also Void conveyance
Forms   20.2–20.15, 20.38
  application, for, *see* Applications
  change to register, for   20.6
  execution of documents   20.38
  non-prescribed, acceptance of 20.4, 20.8
  none prescribed   20.6, 20.39
  old forms, use of   20.3
  restriction
    other application form,
      panel on   10.67
    separate application   10.66
  Schedule 1, prescribed by   20.3–20.7
    categories   20.5
    electronically produced   20.7
    use of   20.4
    versions   20.7
  Schedule 3, prescribed by   20.8–20.15
    attorney, execution by,
      see Power of attorney
    Church land   20.13, 20.14
    Sch 1 form, use in preference   20.8
    tenant for life declaration   20.15
  transfer of registered estate   8.29–8.36
Franchise
  'affecting franchise'   2.26(a), 14.5, 14.16
    index entry   14.17
  caution against, discovering   14.18
  first registration, voluntary   2.1, 2.5, 2.6
    form   2.25
    pending application   14.18
  how arise   4.14.(8)
  index, details in   14.16, 14.18
    search of   14.19
  lease of
    notice   10.13(c)
    registration of   8.11
  legal estate   8.2
  overriding interest
    first registration   4.14(8), 4.18
    registered disposition   11.2
  property register details   14.5, 14.9

  registration in own right   2.5, 2.6, 8.2,
      14.2, 14.16
  'relating franchise'   2.26(a), 14.16, 14.18
Fraud
  electronic signature   27.24
  indemnity claim
    failure for   23.16, 23.18
    recourse of registrar for   23.25
  mistake in register   22.11, 22.15
Freehold
  absolute, registration with
    beneficial/equitable interests,
      subject to   4.7
    effect of   4.2
    first registration   3.3
    interests of which proprietor
      has notice (squatters)   4.5, 4.6
    registered interests to which
      estate subject   4.3
    unregistered interests to which
      estate subject   4.4, 4.12 *et seq*,
      see also Overriding interest
  possessory, registration with   4.8
    first registration   3.5
    proprietorship register entry   14.10(i)
  qualified, registration with   4.8
    first registration   3.4
  titles   3.2–3.5
  upgrade of title, *see* Title
Freezing order
  restriction application   10.68(e), (f)

Gift   2.10, 2.28

HM Land Registry, *see* Land Registry
High Court
  appeal to, from Adjudicator's
    decision   34.21–34.24
  proceedings in, direction
    for   34.17, 34.18
Home information pack   27.4
  consent to electronic form   27.4
Housing Act transfer   2.12
Housing association,
  unregistered   13.21–13.23

Incorporeal rights
  first registration, voluntary   2.1, 2.5–2.7
Indemnity   23.1 *et seq*
  background   23.1
  claim   23.19–23.23
    Adjudicator, from reference to   23.20

Indemnity – *cont*
  claim – *cont*
    application to registrar,
      contents   23.23
    court determination of   23.22
    decision of registrar challenge 23.21
    procedure   23.23
    contributory negligence   23.17
    entitlement   23.19
    failure of claim, circumstances
      for fraud/lack of proper
      care   23.16–23.18
      persons deriving title,
        effect on   23.18
    lapse of time   23.16
    grounds   23.2–23.10
    judicial review of decision on   23.21
    loss or destruction of document
      while at Registry   23.8
      electronic   23.8
    mines and minerals   23.11
    mistake
      cautions register   5.12, 23.9
      filed copies   18.41, 23.7
      official copy, in   23.6
      official search, in   23.5
      register, in   22.1, 23.3, 23.4, 27.14
    overriding charge, registrar's
      failure of duty as to   12.51, 23.10
    Practice Guide   23.23
    recourse rights of registrar 23.24–23.29
      enforcement of rights of
        action   23.26–23.29
      fraud, where   23.25
    recoverable losses   23.12–23.15
      consequential losses 23.12, 23.13
      costs   23.14, 23.15
      detailing in application   23.23
      interest   23.13
      loss of estate, interest or
        charge   23.13, 23.23
      surveyor, costs of   23.23
    rectification of register 23.3, 23.4, 23.13
    upgrade of title, payable on 3.20, 23.3
    valuation by District Valuer   23.23
Indemnity covenant
  covenant   25.1, 25.5
    circumstances for   25.5
    proprietorship register
      entry   14.10(f), (g), 25.5
Index   14.13, 14.14-14.19
  cautions   14.14
  details in   14.14–14.18

    form of   14.15
    franchises and manors   14.16, 14.18
    index map   14.16, 14.17
      electronic map format   14.17
    matters to be found from 14.14, 14.17
    search, official   14.15, 14.19
    'verbal description', of   14.16, 14.18
  Index of proprietor's names 14.20, 14.21
    contents   14.20
    requirement for   14.20
    search   14.21
      applicants   14.21
      'qualifying applicants',
        application by   18.34–18.37
Information
  see also Inspection of register;
    Filed copies; Official copies;
    Search, official
  historical   18.42–18.45, 36.8
    electronic   18.44, 18.45
  'home information pack'   27.4
  registrar, publication by   36.6
  suppression, offence   35.2
Inheritance tax notice   10.17(b)
Inland Revenue charge 9.2, 9.12–9.17
  special priority rule   9.12
  notice of disponee of charge   9.13
Insolvency
  applications in connection with   18.35
  corporate   13.19, 13.24–13.37
    application by liquidator   13.27
    compulsory   13.30, 13.31
    creditors' voluntary
      winding-up   13.29
    disposition by liquidator   13.32
    dissolution, *see* Dissolution of
      company
    entry on register   13.31
    evidence required   13.28–13.30
    members' voluntary
      winding-up   13.28
    Practice Guide   13.24
    restriction   13.31
  overseas proceedings, see Overseas
    company
  personal, *see* Bankruptcy
Inspection
  interest revealable by 9.13, 11.8, 11.14
Inspection of register   18.3–18.12
  see also Official copies
  application   18.10
    form   18.10
  copies, right to make   18.3, 18.4

Inspection of register – *cont*
exceptions   18.5, 18.10
'qualifying applicants',
application by   18.34–18.37
exempt document application etc,
see Exempt information document
scope   18.3–18.5, 18.9, 18.10
charges   18.4
leases   18.4
title plan, certificate of (form)   20.5(d)
Interest
indemnity payment, on   23.13
Interest affecting registered estate or
charge
protection of, *see* Notice (on register)
Internet
downloading register copies
and plans   24.3
e-conveyancing, *see* Electronic
system
searches   26.3
Interpretation   1.20–1.22

Joint proprietors
charge, of, receipt on discharge   12.83
death of one   8.5
declaration of trust   8.36
restriction entry   10.64(a)
Judicial review   23.21, 34.9, 34.12

Lake, *see* Accretion and diluvion
Land certificate   21.1, 21.2
abolition   21.1, 21.3
alternative documents   21.5
destruction power   21.4(c)
existing certificates, treatment of   21.4
lost or stolen   21.4(d)
Land registration rules   1.15, 27.17
Land Registry   36.1–36.11
see also Register of title
advisory or consultancy
services   36.7, 36.8
Chief Land Registrar, *see* Registrar
continuance   36.1
district   36.3
fees, *see* Fees
indemnity from, *see* Indemnity
joint ventures with   36.8, 36.9
opening hours   36.5
Practice Guides and Bulletins   1.23
Landlord
protection of rights, property
register   14.8

Lease
assignment, sub-let etc limitation   14.8
business lease   2.15
change in law under
LRA 2002   2.4, 2.13–2.15
charges register, details in   14.12(a), (b)
compulsory first registration   2.8, 2.13
lease and copy, submission of   2.26
minimum length for   2.9, 2.13–2.15
mortgage of lease   2.19
reversionary lease   2.16
right to buy lease, grant of   2.17
contract to grant   3.9
covenants, obligations and
liabilities   4.9, 8.15, 8.16
restrictive covenants   9.8, 10.9
deed, grant by (more than
3 years)   2.14
discontinuous   2.3, 8.8, 8.9
entry right, grant of   8.17, 8.20, 10.13(c)
exempt information document
application, *see* Exempt
information document
first registration, grant
requiring   24.6,
see also Leasehold (title)
form not prescribed   8.39, 20.6
franchise, of   8.11
freehold title inspection   24.6
grant, as transfer, *see* Registrable
disposition
inspection   18.4
transitional   18.32, 18.33
manor, of   8.11
mistake, alteration by registrar   22.23
more than 7-year term   2.9, 8.8
not registrable, grant of, priority
rule   9.10
notice on superior title   8.10, 10.13(c)
PPP lease   2.3, 2.11
registrable disposition, grant as, *see*
Registrable disposition
reversion, of   2.18, 8.8
reversionary
grant   8.8
proprietary rights of reversioner
in lease, effect of   4.9
registration of, notice
requirement   3.8
unregistered, overriding
interest   11.12
short
easement for benefit of   8.14, 8.15

Lease – *cont*
  short – *cont*
    notice protection not available   10.8
    overriding interest, as   4.14(1), 4.17,
                       11.3, 11.4
  transfer, pre-1996 lease, covenants
    implied   25.6
  validity of, implied covenant   25.3(b)
  variation   8.40, 8.41, 10.17(d)
  voluntary first registration   2.3, 2.4, 2.13
    minimum unexpired period   2.3
Leasehold (title)
  absolute, registration with   4.9
    first registration   3.7–3.9
    matters to which
      subject   4.9, 4.12 *et seq*
  good leasehold, registration with   4.10
    first registration   3.10
    matters to which
      subject   4.10, 4.12 *et seq*
  possessory, registration with   4.11
    first registration   3.12
    matters to which
      subject   4.11, 4.12 *et seq*
    proprietorship register entry   14.10(i)
  qualified, registration with   4.11
    first registration   3.11
    matters to which
      subject   4.11, 4.12 *et seq*
  titles   3.6–3.12
    absolute, circumstances for
      notice requirement   3.8
  transfer (pre-1996 lease), implied
    covenants   25.6
Legal estate
  registered, *see* Registered estate
  transfer/transfer of part   8.3,
    see also Registrable disposition
  vesting of, on registration   15.1, 15.5,
                        15.8
Legal Services Commission
  statutory charge   12.51
Legislative background   1.1 *et seq*
  LRA 1925   1.2 *et seq*
    effect and interpretation of   1.20–1.22
    Rules under, *see* Rules and Orders
  LRA 2002   1.3 *et seq*
    introduction of Bill   1.10
    reports behind   1.4–1.9
Lessor
  deduction of title   24.6
    contract to grant lease   3.9

Lien
  unpaid vendor's   9.7
Light, right of   2.41, 14.7(b), (e), 8.52
Limited liability partnership
  charge   12.28
  execution of document   20.38
  registration   13.20, 13.21
Limitation Act
  adverse possession, defeat of,
    see Squatter
  indemnity claim, period for   23.16
  interests acquired under   4.5, 9.13, 15.5
Linked transactions
  compulsory e-conveyancing
    required   28.1
  electronic management   27.2, 27.11,
               27.16(4), 27.25
  monitoring   24.25
Liquidator   13.27, 13.31, 13.32, 18.35
Local land charge   2.39, 12.80
  overriding interest, as   8.22, 12.80
    first registration   4.14.(6)
    registered disposition   11.2
  registration, circumstances for   12.80
    application   12.81
  registers, regime for   4.14.(6)

Manor
  index, details in   14.16, 14.18
    search of   14.19
  lease of
    notice   10.13(c)
    registration of   8.11
  legal estate   8.2
  manorial right as overriding
    interest
    first registration   4.14(10), 4.18
    registered disposition   11.2
  provisions as to   2.7, 2.8
Map, index
  electronic, under LRA 2002,
    see Index
  old, under LRA 1925   14.14
Marriage consideration   9.6
Matrimonial home rights
  protection by caution or notice 10.17(a),
                10.19, 19.23
    agreed notice   10.26, 10.27
      form of application   10.27
    search   19.22, 19.23
      certificate   19.23
Mines/mineral rights   2.8, 2.33

Mines/mineral rights – *cont*
disposition of, apart from
  surface 8.45
no express note 8.45
note on title 2.33, 8.44
  application for 8.44
indemnity, precondition
  for 23.11, 8.44
overriding interest
  first registration 4.14(7)
  registered disposition 11.2
property register entry 14.6
Minor interest 9.1, 9.2
Mistake
caution register, in 5.9, 22.1, 5.12
document in, *see* Document
indemnity for, *see* Indemnity
register, in, *see* Alteration of register;
  Indemnity
Mortgage
charge definition, within 12.1,
  see also Charge
compulsory first registration 2.19,
  2.21, 2.35
consolidation 12.38–12.41
  entry for right of 12.39–12.41
  meaning 12.38
demise or sub-demise, by 2.2, 7.3,
  12.2, 12.4
deposit of land certificate
  with lender obsolete 12.5, 12.86
entry on register, circumstances 2.35
first registration limitation 2.2
further advance obligation 12.11, 12.35
limitation period for possession
  or foreclosure rights 29.6
official search
  matrimonial home rights
    search 19.22, 19.23
'relevant time' for notification
  of person with rights 19.22
with priority, effect of 19.18
without priority 19.21
registration procedure,
  see Charge
sub-mortgage 2.35, 7.4, 12.3
variation, *see* Charge

Name, *see* Index of proprietors'
  names; Proprietor, registered
National Land Registration
  Service 4.14(6), 4.14(7), 26.3
Network access agreement 27.13–27.24

access regulation 27.18
alteration to register,
  authorisation 22.20
authority conferred by 27.13, 27.16
charges 27.15
entry into 27.13
  application for 20.16
  criteria for applicant 27.14
    ceasing to meet 27.19
  refusal 27.21, 34.12(2)
execution of documents 27.8, 27.23,
  27.24
  client's authority 27.24
  presumption of authority 27.24
failure to comply 27.19
linked transactions, *see* Linked
  transactions
prevailing nature of obligations
  under 27.22
purposes of access 27.13
'qualifying transactions' 27.16(2)
rules, compliance obligation 27.17
termination 27.19–27.21
  registrar, by 27.19, 27.20
  appeal 27.21, 34.12(2)
terms 17.2, 27.15–27.18
Notice by registrar
content 20.40–20.45
objection in response to,
  procedure 20.31
service 20.40
  address for, provision of 20.42, 20.43
  cautioner, address for 20.44
  means of 20.45
  time of 20.45
time for action by recipient 20.46
Notice (on register) 10.1 *et seq*
agreed 10.14, 10.15–10.28
application
  additional notice 10.49
  documents with 10.20–10.23
  form 10.19
  new notice 10.48
approval, circumstances for 10.15
cancellation 10.28, 10.48
confidentiality, methods for 10.24
consensual 10.15(b), 10.21, 10.22
duty to apply for entry 10.17, 10.18
matrimonial home rights, relating
  to, see
non-consensual 10.15(c), 10.16,
  10.23, 10.25
record on register 10.24, 10.45

Notice (on register) – *cont*
  agreed – *cont*
    example entry   10.45
    variation   10.48, 10.49
    application for entry   10.14 *et seq*
    applicant   10.14, 10.15(a)
  bankruptcy petition, of,
    see Bankruptcy
  charge protected by,
    discharge of   12.86, 12.98–12.102
    application, other
      than unilateral notice
                     12.99–12.101
    floating charge, evidence   12.101
    forms/acceptable
      documents   12.100
    application, unilateral notice 12.102
    cancellation   20.29
  circumstances for entry   10.13
  contract of sale, of   27.7
  easement   4.3
  effect of   9.8, 10.5, 20.24
  form and content   10.44–10.46
  interests protectable   10.5
    excepted interests   10.6–10.12
  meaning   10.5
  rules   10.2
  unilateral   10.14, 10.24(b), 10.29 *et seq*
    address for service   20.42(b)
    application   10.30
      additional notice   10.49
      form   10.30
      new notice   10.48
    beneficiary change, register
      update on   10.42, 10.43
      form and procedure   10.43
    cancellation   10.35–10.38
      evidence   10.35
      notification duty of registrar   10.36
      objection to application and
        adjudication 10.37, 10.38, 20.29
    example   10.46
    meaning and purpose   10.29
    notification of entry of   10.31, 10.34
    'reasonable cause' requirement
                     10.39, 10.40
    record on register   10.46
    removal   10.32, 10.48
      form   10.32
    safeguards   10.33–10.41
    unregistered overriding interest 4.21,
                     11.19, 11.22
    variation   10.48

    withdrawal order   10.40
      High Court jurisdiction   10.41
    validity of interest , and   10.5
    variation of interest, protection
      on   10.47–10.49
Notice (or knowledge)   4.5, 9.13, 11.19,
                     15.5

Notification
  objection to application, of   20.30, 34.4
  person prejudiced by squatter's
    registration, *see* Squatter

Objection to adverse possession
  claim, *see* Squatter
Objection to application   20.29–20.32
  Adjudicator, reference to   20.30
  exceptions to right   20.29
  general right   20.29
  methods   20.31
  notice by registrar, in response
    to   20.31
  notice to applicant   20.30, 34.4
  procedure   20.30, 20.31
  'reasonable cause' requirement   20.32
Occupation, person in, *see* Overriding
  interest
Offences   35.1 *et seq*
  improper or unauthorised
    alteration of register   34.3–35.6
    document referred to, change to 35.4
  penalties   35.2, 35.6
  self-incrimination privilege   35.7
  suppression of information   35.2
Office/certified copy
  see also Official copies
  acceptability as evidence   20.25
Official copies   18.6–18.9, 21.5
  application (register/title
    plan/caution register)   18.11
    form   18.11
  application (document referred
    to in register)   18.12
  evidence, admissible in   18.6
  exceptions   18.10, 18.12
  'qualifying applicants',
    application by   18.34–18.37
  exempt information document,
    of, *see* Exempt information
    document
  mistake in   23.6
  parties obtaining   27.13
  priority protection, pre-requisite
    for   19.7

Official Receiver 13.18, 18.35

Official search, *see* Search, official

Operation of law 2.11
  transfer by, registration of 8.4, 13.7
    application for registration
      already started prior to 20.21
    exceptions to registration
      requirement 8.4–8.7, 13.7
     bankruptcy of sole
      proprietor 8.6, 13.16
     death of sole proprietor 8.5, 13.7
     dissolution of corporate
      proprietor 8.7

Overreaching check LRA 2002
  s 42(1)(b) in Tables
  restriction to ensure 10.57, 10.64(a)

Overriding interest
  approach of LRA 2002
    to 4.15 *et seq*, 11.1
  church chancel repair right 4.14(9),
    4.18, 11.2(k)
  corn rent 4.14(13), 4.18, 11.2
  creation of 11.2
  Crown rent 4.14(11), 4.18, 11.2(g)
  customary right 4.14(4), 11.2(a)
  disclosure duty 4.19, 4.20, 8.26, 27.17
  easement, legal 4.14(3), 4.17,
    11.13–11.17
    conditions for overriding
      effect 11.14
    long dormant and
      unregistered 11.16
    property register entry for claim 14.7
    transitional 11.17
  e-conveyancing, effect on 11.1
  embankment/river or sea
    wall rights 4.14(12), 4.18, 11.2(h)
  first registration, overriding 4.13, 4.14
    duty on registration applicant
      to disclose 4.19, 4.20
    effect of 4.4, 4.12–4.21, 9.8
    list 4.14
    removal of status, *see* Squatter
  franchise 4.14(8), 4.18, 11.2(e)
  lease for 7 years or less 4.14(1), 4.17,
    11.3, 11.4
  local land charge 4.14.(6), 11.2(c)
  manorial rights 4.14(10), 4.18, 11.2(f)
  mineral rights 4.14(7), 11.2(d)
  notice by registrar 4.21
  notice on register 4.21, 10.13(b)

occupation, interest of person
  in 41.4(2), 4.17, 11.3, 11.5–11.12
  exceptions to rule 11.6–11.12
    interest not disclosed on
      inquiry 11.7
    interest under settlement 11.6
    not discoverable on
      inspection and not
      known of 11.8–11.11
    general rule 11.5
    narrowing of protection 11.5
    old law compared 11.5
    rent and profits, receipt of 11.5

PPP lease 4.14(14), 11.2(j)

phasing out 4.18, 11.2
  caution lodging power 4.18

Practice Guide 4.12

profit à prendre,
  see Profit à prendre

public right 4.14(5), 11.2(b)

register alteration 22.6(c), 22.7

registrable disposition,
  overriding 4.13, 9.8, 11.1 *et seq*
  background 11.1
  list 11.2
  removal of status 11.2
  reversionary lease 11.12
  scope and effect of 1.20, 11.1
  tithe, payment in lieu of 11.2(i)
  transitional 11.17

Overriding statutory charges 12.51–12.58

Overseas company
  execution by 20.38, 20.39
  insolvency proceedings 13.34–13.37
    disposition, application
      for registration 13.35
    judgment opening, under
      EC Regulation, note of 13.37
    winding up as unregistered
      company 13.36

Owner's powers 7.2–7.5
  charge of registered estate,
    see Charge
  disposition of registered estate,
    see Disposition

Parcel of land
  division or amalgamation,
    see Register of title
  information about, *see* Index

Part of registered estate
  transfer of 8.29, 8.33(d), 8.37

Penalties, *see* Offences

Pending action
  bankruptcy   13.10
  land action, notice and/or
    restriction protecting   10.23(c),
       10.102–10.105
Pending application
  index, on   14.17
Personal representative
  assent by, *see* Assent
  assent of charge,
    see Charge: transfer
  disposition by   13.8
  registration as proprietor   8.5, 13.7
    evidence with application   8.5
  search by   14.21
  transfer continued by   20.21
  trust, land in, restriction
    application   10.75–10.78
Plan
  boundary line determination,
    for   16.5, 16.8
  first registration application,
    with   2.26(a)
  internet copy   24.3
  official copy   18.11
  official search of part, for   19.9(b)
  part of land, for application
    dealing with   20.24
  register of title, in   14.4
  title plan   20.24, 21.5(b)
Possession proceedings,
  see Squatter
Possessory title, *see* Freehold;
  Leasehold title
Power of attorney   20.8
  evidence of validity   20.10
  execution by attorney   20.9–20.12
  revocation
    evidence that not revoked   20.11
    treatment as valid after   20.11
  trustees of land delegation
    of functions by   20.12
Practice Guides and Bulletins   1.23
Pre-emption right   9.15
  created on or after
    13 October 2003, effect   9.15
  restriction protecting   10.57(b)
  status of   9.15
Prescription/implied grant   11.16, 11.17
  appurtenant right claim based on   8.48
Price   14.11(a), 18.22
Priority of applications   20.17(c)
Priority of interests   9.1 *et seq*

  basic rule, first in time   9.2, 9.3
  charges, *see* Charge
  estoppel, equity arising by   9.14, 9.16
  exceptions to basic rule   9.2, 9.3 *et seq*
    Inland Revenue charge,
      see Inland Revenue charge
  registrable disposition for value, on
    registration of, *see* Registrable
    disposition
  lease grant which is not registrable
    disposition   9.10
  mere equity   9.14, 9.17
  notice to protect   10.5, 10.45, 10.62
    variation, protection on   10.47
  pre-emption rights   9.14, 9.15
  registered charges, *see* Charge
  registration requirement   9.3
  restriction ordered by court,
    effect   10.82
  unregistered   9.2, 9.13,
    see also Unregistered interest
Priority protection, *see* Search, official
Privilege or right, *see* Easement;
  Profit à prendre
Profit à prendre
  see also Appurtenant rights
  entry in register on first
    registration   2.34, 14.7(a)
    claimed right, details of   14.7(a)
  first registration, voluntary   2.1, 2.5, 2.6
  form   2.25
  grant or reservation
    exception from registration   8.12
    registration requirement   8.12–8.16,
      see also Registrable disposition
  in gross   8.2, 8.13
  index entry   14.17
  legal, as overriding interest
    first registration   4.14(3)
    property register details   14.7
    registered disposition   11.3, 11.13–11.17
    conditions for overriding effect   11.14
    transitional   11.17
  legal estate   8.2
  prescription, etc, claim on
    basis of   8.48–8.50
  property register details   14.9
  proprietor of   8.13
  registration in own right   2.5, 2.6, 14.2
Proof of title   24.1–24.6
  commencement of title   24.6
  LRA 1925, under   24.1, 24.2
  no rules made   24.5

Proof of title – *cont*
  rule-making power 24.4
  Standard Conditions 24.5
Property register, *see* Register of title
Proprietor, registered
  address in register 14.10(c)
  consent, *see* Consent
  first, *see* First registration
  'in possession' 22.12
  index of names, *see* Index
    of proprietors' names
  interests binding 4.5–4.7, 4.9, 15.5, 15.6
  joint, *see* Joint properietors
  limitation on powers 10.56(a)
  name in register 14.10(b)
  notification by registrar
    restriction entry, of 10.88, 10.89
    objection 10.90, 10.91
    unilateral notice entry, of 10.31, 10.34
    objection 10.37, 10.38, 10.91
  possessory title 14.10(i)
  seller not 24.2, 24.4
  vesting of legal estate in, *see* Registration
    of title
Proprietorship register,
  see Register of title
Public-private partnership lease 2.3, 2.11
  notice protection not available 10.12
  overriding interest
    first registration 2.3, 4.14(14)
    registered disposition 11.2
Public register 18.2, 24.3
Public right 2.38, 2.39
  notice in respect of 10.17(e)
  overriding interest, as
    first registration 4.14(5)
    registered disposition 11.2
Purchaser
  definition for search with
    priority 19.7

Qualified title, *see* Freehold;
  Leasehold title

Receiver
  appointment, restriction
    requirement 10.102, 10.104
    applicant, receiver as 10.68(i)
Rectification of conveyancing
  document 34.13, 34.14
Rectification of register,
  see Alteration of register;
  Indemnity

Register of title 14.1–14.12
  alteration, *see* Alteration of
    register
  amalgamation of titles 14.3
  charges register 14.4, 14.12
    contents 14.12
    leases 14.12(a), (b)
    proprietor of charge,
      details of 14.12(d), (e)
  closing 8.54
  contents 14.4 *et seq*
  copies, *see* Inspection of
    register; Official copies
  dependent estates, how entered
    on 15.9
  division of parcel of land 14.3
  form of 14.2, 14.3
    electronic or paper 14.2
  information, accessing 18.1 *et seq*,
    see also Information
  inspection right, *see* Inspection
    of register
  internet access 24.3
  mistakes, *see* Alteration of register
  number, *see* Title number
  on-line access 24.3
  plan 14.4, 14.5
  property register 14.4, 14.5–14.9
    boundary agreement (accretion
      and diluvion) 16.11
    contents 14.5–14.7
    defect in title 17.4
    leases 14.8
  proprietorship register 14.4, 14.10,
               14.11
    contents 14.10, 14.11, 25.4,
      30.20(d), 30.21–30.24
  protection of proprietor in
    possession, principle 22.9–22.12
  provision for 14.1
  public document 18.2, 24.3
  rectification, *see* Alteration of register
  registered estates, *see* Registered
    estate
  registrar's flexibility and
    functions 14.3, 14.4
  restrictions, *see* Restriction
  search of 14.1, 14.19, 24.3
    application form 14.19
    certificate of 14.19
    see also Search, official
  updating, *see* Alteration of register

Registered disposition, *see* Disposition;
  Registrable disposition
  unregistered interest overriding,
    see Overriding interest
Registered estate
  determination
    application for record on
      register   8.54
    closing of register   8.54
    methods   8.53
    right   17.1, 17.2
  index, details in   14.14, 14.17
  meaning   8.2
  register of title, in   14.2
    description   14.5
    determination right   14.7(g)
  registrable disposition of,
    see Registrable disposition
Registered proprietor, *see* Proprietor,
  registered
Registrable disposition   8.1–8.43
  application for registration,
    rules   8.24–8.42
    generally applicable   8.25–8.28
  deed required   8.27
  discontinuous lease   8.8, 8.9
  effect of non-registration   8.2, 15.2
  effect of registration   8.1
  effective date of registration   15.10
  form and content formalities   7.5
  grant of lease   8.8-8.10, 8.39–8.41
    application form   8.39
    notice on register   8.21
    registered proprietor   8.10
    types registrable   8.8, 8.9
  grant of legal charge   8.22
  grant of legal easement,
    right or privilege   8.12–8.16, 8.42
    covenant in lease not
      registrable   8.15, 8.16
    duration immaterial   8.14
    easement for benefit of
      short lease   8.14, 8.15
    exceptions from registration
      requirement   8.12
    notice on affected title   8.13, 8.21,
      10.13(c)
    registration requirement   8.12, 8.13
  grant or reservation of
    rentcharge or legal right
    of entry   8.17–8.21, 8.42
    entry right   8.17, 8.19, 8.20
    express grant   8.17

register entries   8.18, 8.21, 10.13(c)
interests overriding, *see* Overriding
  interest
lease of franchise or manor   8.11, 8.21,
overriding interest, disclosure
  duty   8.26
priority
  basic rule   9.2
  exceptions, *see* 'valuable
    consideration for, registration
    of *below*
registered charge, of   8.23, 12.42–12.47
  transfer/grant of sub-charge   8.23
registered estate, of   8.3–8.22, 8.29–8.37
  consideration   8.31, 8.32
  exceptions to registration
    requirement   8.4–8.7
  exchange etc, separate forms   8.35
  forms   8.29–8.36
  joint proprietors, declaration
    of trust   8.36
  mixed titles etc, single form
    for   8.34
  part, transfer of   8.29, 8.33(d), 8.37
  portfolio of titles   8.33(c), (e)
  unregistered title, completed
    by registration   8.33(a)
  'registration requirements'   8.2
  transfer   8.3–8.7
valuable consideration, for,
  registration of   9.2, 9.4–9.9
  basic priority rule,
    relationship with   9.9
    example   9.9
  interests postponed   9.7
  interests protected   9.8, 11.1 *et seq*,
    see also Overriding interest
  leasehold estate   9.8
  'registrable disposition of
    registered estate'   9.5
  special priority rule for   9.4
  'valuable consideration'   9.6
Registrar
  challenge to decision, *see*
    Judicial review
  challenge to application to,
    see Objection to application
  Chief Land
    annual report   36.4
    appointment   36.1
    functions   36.2–36.5
    district   36.3

Registrar – *cont*
dispute, reference to Adjudicator,
  see Adjudicator
powers   34.4–34.9, 36.6
  determinations, for   34.4, 34.5
  information publication   36.6
  specific   34.6–34.9
    document production   20.5(e), 34.7,
                       34.8
'Registration gap'   9.7, 26.2, 28.3
Registration of title   15.1 *et seq*
  conclusive register   1.8, 7.1, 26.2
  date, effective   15.10
  dependent estates   15.9
  effect   15.1 *et seq*
  first registration, *see* First registration
  fundamental change in
    nature of   1.20, 26.2
    proposals   1.3, 1.8
  vesting of legal estate on   15.1, 15.5, 15.8
    exception   15.2
    'legal estate'   15.1
  void conveyance or transfer, effect
    of, *see* Void conveyance
Registration requirements   8.2, 15.2,
  see also Registrable disposition
Rent and profits
  'occupation' through, end of
    protection for   11.5
Rentcharge
  adverse possession claim   29.5, 30.16(d),
                  30.57(f), 33.1-33.10
    circumstances for   33.1–33.3
    non-payment   33.1–33.3, 33.9
    payment to third party   33.1–33.3,
                       33.9
    principle for   33.4
    registered estate claim
      compared   33.5–33.8,
      see also Squatter
    registration as proprietor,
      effect   33.10
  entry right, grant of   8.17, 8.19, 10.13(c)
  failure by freeholder to pay   17.1, 17.5
  first registration, voluntary   2.1, 2.5, 2.6
  form   2.25
  grant or reservation, express
    notice entry   10.13(c)
    registration   8.17–8.21,
      see also Registrable disposition
  implied covenants, transfer of
    registered estate subject
      to   25.7–25.12

    family charge, covenants
      applying   25.12
    part only transferred   25.9–25.11
    entire rent, extends to   25.10, 25.11
    whole estate transferred   25.8
  index entry   14.17
  legal estate   8.2
  non-payment/payment to
    third party, *see* 'adverse
    possession claim' *above*
  property register details   14.5, 14.9
Rents and profits, receipt of   11.5
Reports
  joint Law Commission/
    HM Land Registry   1.4–1.9
  conclusive register, proposal
    for   1.7, 1.8
Restriction   4.3, 7.6, 10.50 *et seq*
  application for   10.65–10.79
    applicants   10.65, 10.68
    sufficient interest, person
      with   10.65, 10.68, 10.69
    consent   10.53, 10.66
    discretionary   10.65–10.71
    form and information with   10.66,
                       10.67
    mandatory   10.72–10.79
    charity land   10.79
    land becoming subject to
      trust/change in trust   10.73
    limitations on trustees' powers
      under trust   10.77, 10 78
    personal representative holding
      land in trust   10.75–10.78
    sole trustee   10.74, 10.77, 10.78
  notification of registered
    proprietor   10.88, 10.89
  objection   10.90, 10.91
  procedure   10.66
  background   10.1–10.3
  bankruptcy, *see* Bankruptcy
  cancellation   10.97–10.99
    no longer required   10.97
    objection   10.97
    spent or superfluous   10.99
    examples   10.99
    trust of land, end of   10.98
  charge, relating to   14.12(f),
    see also Charge
  charging order over interest
    in trust, *see* Charging order
  charity, relating to   13.39

Restriction – *cont*
  constructive trust or similar
    claim, for   10.58
  court order for   10.80–10.85
    application procedure   10.85
    power   10.80
    priority, issues of   10.82–10.84
      notice duty   10.84
    standard forms   10.81
  disapplication or modification   10.52,
                  10.53, 10.100, 10.101
    applicant   10.52
    form   10.100
    procedure   10.100, 10.101
  entry of   10.54–10.85
    application, on, *see* 'application
      for' *above*
    court order, on, *see* 'court order
      for' *above*
    duty on registrar   10.64
    notice of   10.63
    powers of registrar   10.55–10.63
      challenge by proprietor   10.63
    form   10.54, 10.70, 10 81, 10.85
  freezing register   10.51(a), 10.81, 10.82
  invalidity or unlawfulness,
    to prevent   10.56
  joint proprietors   10.64(a)
  meaning and effect   10.50–10.53
  non-standard, approval
    conditions   10.71
  notice on register, interaction
    with   10.62, 10.82
  overreaching, for   10.57
  pending land action   10.102–10.105
  proprietorship register   14.10(d)
  'reasonable cause' requirement   10.87
  receiver/sequestrator,
    appointment of   10.102–10.104
  rules   10.2
  safeguards   10.86–10.91
  specified dispositions   10.51(b)
  standard   10.70
  statutory requirement for   10.64(c)
  trust of land, relating to, *see* Trust
  withdrawal   10.93–10.96
    applicant   10.93
    application   10.94
    consent to   10.95, 10.96
    excepted restrictions   10.94
    part of estate, relating to   10.96
  writs and orders   10.102–10.105

Restrictive covenant   25.13, 25.14
  creation not registrable
    disposition   25.13, 25.14
  enforcement, circumstances
    for   25.13
  indemnity covenant for   25.5
  lessor and lessee, between   9.8
    notice protection not available 10.9
  presumption of benefit and
    rebuttal of   25.13
Right to buy   2.12
  lease, grant of   2.17, 8.8
River
  bank, *see* Accretion and
    diluvion
  wall   4.14(12), 4.18, 11.2
Rules and Orders   1.11, 1.12–1.19
  LRA 1925, under   1.13
  LRA 2002, under   1.14, 1.15
    fees   1.15, 1.19
    general rule-making powers   1.17
    land registration rules
      distinguished   1.15, 27.17
    miscellaneous Rules and
      Orders   1.19
    principal Rules (2003)   1.18
    rule-making powers   1.14, 1.17
Rules Committee   1.16

Sale, legal chargee's power
  surplus after, provision for 12.82, 19.21
Sea
  see also Accretion and diluvion;
    Foreshore
  bed   13.2
  wall   4.14(12), 4.18, 11.2
Seal, company   26.19
Search (non-Land Registry),
  see National Land Registration
  Service
Search, official
  application
    day list, in   14.22
    form of   19.1
  certificate, with priority   19.13–19.16
    information in   19.14, 19.15
    issue methods   19.16
    more than one, priority of   19.19
  certificate, without priority   19.20
  index, of, *see* Index
  index of proprietor's names, of,
    see Index of proprietor's names

Search, official – *cont*

matrimonial home rights

    search 19.23, 19.24

    certificate 19.23

    form for and methods 19.23

    notification of person with

      rights 19.22

mistake in 23.6

outline application 19.8, 19.24–19.29

    circumstances for 19.24, 19.25

      examples 19.25

    form of application 19.26

    reference number 19.27

    reserved period 19.28

      registration application

        made after expiry of 19.29

part of land in title/pending

    application 19.9, 19.20

parties making 27.13

principles of LRA 1925

    continued 19.3

priority protection 19.4 *et seq*

    applicants 19.8

      chargee, by, purchaser

        protected 19.8, 19.18

    application 19.8–19.12

      methods 19.9

    certificate issue 19.13

    circumstances for 19.5

    date of 19.11

    defined terms 19.7

    estate contract, new provision

      for 19.5

    exceptions to 19.4

    first registration, pending

      application for 19.5, 19.9, 19.15, 19.16

    forms 19.9, 19.10

    more than one transaction, for 19.18

    official copy pre-requisite 19.7

    period of 19.7, 19.11, 19.17

    'protectable disposition' 19.7

    'purchaser' 19.7

    records, *see* Day list

    registered title, of 19.9, 19.16

    restriction ordered by court,

      conflict 10.82–10.84

    withdrawal 19.12

without priority 19.20, 19.21

    applicants 19.20

    certificate issue 19.20

    form 19.20

    methods for application 19.20

    reasons for 19.21

Self-incrimination privilege 35.7

Sequestrator

    appointment, restriction for 10.102, 10.104

    applicant, sequestrator as 10.68(i)

Service

see also Address; Notice by

    registrar

table of methods and time of 20.45

Settlement (funds)

    electronic 27.9, 28.5

      registrar's powers 28.5, 36.8

Settlement, interest under 13.42, 13.43

    disposition of land 10.7

    restriction to protect 11.6

      notice not available 10.7

    rules, provisions in 13.43

    tenant for life

      declaration by 20.15

      registration of 13.43

Signature

    electronic, *see* Electronic system

Social landlord 13.21–13.23

Solicitor

    electronic network, use of,

      see Network access agreement

    mistake 23.26, 23.28, 23.29

Special power of appointment

    restriction, donee applicant for 10.68(b)

Squatter 4.5, 4.6

    adverse possession 29.1 *et seq*

      approach of LRA 2002 29.1–29.3

      meaning 30.3, 30.8

      overriding status removal 4.16(1), 11.5, 11.8–11.11

      period of 30.1, 30.7

      when binds first proprietor 4.6, 15.5

      previous law 4.5

      transitional provision 4.6, 4.14(15)

    application to be registered

      as proprietor 20.16, 30.1 *et seq*

    circumstances for no

      valid application 30.11–30.14

    eviction, right may outlast 30.10, 30.16(b)

    evidence 30.15–30.18

    application to be registered

      as proprietor

      form 30.15

      further application 30.49–30.60, 30.61

Squatter – *cont*
application to be registered as
    proprietor – *cont*
  defence to possession
    proceedings   32.3
  evidence   30.56–30.58
  form   30.56
  no right, situations where   30.54
  notice   30.59, 30.60
  right   30.49, 30.50
  statutory declaration   30.56, 30.57
  general rule   30.1, 30.2
  mental or physical disability
    of registered proprietor   30.11(4),
        30.12–30.14
    indemnity for loss if mistake   30.14
  notice of, *see* 'notification
    procedure' *below*
  objection to   30.21, 30.28–30.30,
        30.60
    reference to Adjudicator   30.30
  procedure   30.15–30.18
  registrar's actions on receipt
        30.19 *et seq*
  rejection of application   30.49
    possession proceedings
      by proprietor after   30.51–30.53
  second squatter after eviction
    of first squatter   30.5
  statutory declaration   30.15–30.18
    contents   30.16, 30.18
  successful application,
    see 'registration as
    proprietor' *below*
  successors in title   30.3, 30.4-30.6
  written acknowledgement
    of title   30.9
  inspection and report by
    surveyor   30.19
  limitation period for recovery
    of estate
  circumstances for   29.5
  disapplication   29.4, 29.5, 29.7, 30.8,
        30.9, 32.1
    legal proceedings, effect of   30.8
    mortgagee, position of   29.6
    in possession   29.7
    scope of disapplication   29.5
  notification procedure   30.19–30.27
    address for service   30.23, 30.25
    consent to application   30.28, 30.29,
        30.31
    content of notice   30.26

counter-notice   30.21, 30.26–30.28,
        30.31–30.48
  conditions to met by squatter
    to prevail, *see* 'registration
    as proprietor' *below*
  effect of   30.33, 30.49
  form   30.32
  none served, effect   30.34, 30.61
  time-limit for service   30.32
  further application, of   30.59, 30.60
  persons entitled   30.20, 30.21, 30.52
  proprietorship register
    entry for person
      entitled   14.11(c), 30.20(d),
        30.21–30.24
  application for entry on
    register   30.23
  responses possible   30.28
possession proceedings against   30.11,
    30.51–30.55, 32.1 *et seq*
  defences to   32.2–32.7, 33.18
    effect of   30.61, 32.1
    equitable   32.7
    statutory   32.2–32.6
  general rule   32.1
  judgement for possession ceasing
    to be enforceable   32.4–32.6
registration as proprietor   30.33–30.35,
    31.1 *et seq*, 32.1 *et seq*
  charge, registered, whether
    binds   31.6–31.9
    apportionment process   31.9
  circumstances   30.61
  conditions following counter-
    notice, on satisfaction of   30.33,
    30.35–30.48, 30.61, 31.6
  Adjudicator, reference to   30.36,
        30.40, 34.20
  boundary, reasonable
    mistake as to   30.42–30.48,
        32.2, 33.17
  estoppel   30.37–30.40, 34.20, 34.23
  other right to land   30.41
  registered charge remains
    binding   31.7–31.9
  effect of   31.1 *et seq*
  entitlement on re-application   30.55,
        30.61
  former proprietor's position   31.4
  leasehold   31.2, 31.3
  status of right   30.61, 30.62
  title and rights   31.1–31.5
  transitional provisions   33.17, 33.18

Squatter – *cont*
  transitional provisions – *cont*
    caution, right to register   33.18
    trust land, *see* Trust
Standard Conditions of Sale   24.5
Statutory charge   12.51–12.58
  duty on registrar   12.51, 23.10
Statutory duty
  breach   5.21, 10.39, 10.40, 10.87
Statutory instrument, *see* Rules
  and Orders

Tacking   12.60–12.78
  agreement of subsequent
    chargee   12.72
  existing practice   12.61
  notice   12.63–12.66
    address for entry on
      register   12.66
    service methods   12.63–12.65
    statutory effect given to   12.62
  further advance obligation   12.35,
      12.67–12.71
    entry on register   12.67–12.71
      application form CH1   12.11, 12.69
      application form CH2   12.69, 12.70
      charge submission, by   12.69
      duty on registrar   12.71
  maximum amount, agreement
    of   12.73–12.78
    entry on register of agreement   12.73,
      12.75
      amendment application   12.77
      application form CH3   12.76
      duty on registrar   12.76
      example   12.74
      safeguards, provision for   12.75
  methods   12.60 *et seq*
Tax
  applications in connection with   18.35
  inheritance tax notice   10.17(b)
  unpaid, charge for, *see* Inland
    Revenue charge
Tenant
  see also Lease; Leasehold (title)
  upgrade of reversionary title,
    applicant for   3.16, 3.18
Third party
  rentcharge, adverse possession
    claim, payment to   33.1–33.3, 33.9
  variation binding, registration of   8.41

Time
  see also Effective date; Limitation
    Act; Priority
  application, of, *see* Applications
  day list entry, *see* Day list
  electronic document   26.10
  official search, *see* Official search
Tithe
  right to payment in lieu   11.2
Title
  classes of, first registration   3.1 *et seq*
  commencement   24.6, 29.2
  covenants, *see* Covenants for title
  default in documents/chain
    incomplete, evidence
    requirement   2.27
  defects, *see* Defect in title
  examination on first
    registration   2.28, 2.29
  freehold   3.2–3.5
    absolute   3.3
    possessory   3.5
    qualified   3.4
    registration issues, *see* Freehold
  guarantee, *see* Covenants for title
  historical information on   18.42–18.45
  leasehold   3.6–3.12
    absolute   3.7–3.9
    good   3.10
    possessory   3.12
    qualified   3.11
    registration issues, *see*
      Leasehold (title)
  not absolute, priorities on
    disposition of   9.8
  number, *see* Title number
  proof, *see* Proof of title
  proprietorship register, class in   14.10(a)
  register of, *see* Register of title
  registration as basis for   29.1
  State guarantee   22.1
  upgrade   3.13–3.20
    applicants   3.16
      evidence of entitlement   3.18
      expanded categories   3.16
    application   3.17
    effect   3.19
    forms   3.17
    indemnity by registrar,
      provision for   3.20, 23.3
    registrar's power   3.13, 3.14
      restrictions on   3.15
  Title Information Document   21.5(c)

Title number   14.14, 14.17, 14.20
  reference to on forms   20.6
Title plan   20.24, 21.5(b)
Transfer
  forged or invalid   15.2,
    see also Void conveyance
  operation of law, by,
    see Operation of law
  part of estate   14.7
  registered estate, of, *see* Registrable
    disposition
Transitional period documents   18.32,
    18.33
  discretionary documents   18.32
  EID designation applications   18.33
  leases and charges   18.32
  'qualifying applicants',
    application by   18.34–18.37
  return by registrar   20.35
Trust
  see also Beneficiary; Charity;
    Settlement, interest in
  adverse possession   33.11
    bare trust claimed by squatter   32.7
    land held in trust   33.11, 33.12
  body holding on, registration   13.22
  charging order over interest,
    see Charging order
  constructive   10.58
  disposition of land held in   10.7
  registered proprietor subject to   4.7, 15.5
  restriction
    circumstances for   10.73–10.78
    cancellation circumstances   10.98
    see also Beneficiary
Trustee in bankruptcy   14.21
  disposition by, when void   13.15
  information, application for   18.35
  registration as proprietor   13.16–13.18
    circumstances for   13.17
    Official Receiver or another
      in place of   13.18
  restriction applicant   10.68(g)
  transfer continued by   20.21
Trustees
  delegation by trustees of land,
    procedure   20.12
  disposition by, restriction for   10.57
  transfer to   2.10, 2.11

Unilateral notice   12.102, 20.29

Unregistered interest
  adverse possession, *see* Squatter
  discoverable   9.13, 11.8, 11.14
  effective date of registration   15.10
  knowledge or notice of   4.5, 9.13, 11.19
  notice on register   4.21, 10.13(b), 11.22
  overriding first registration, *see*
    Overriding interest
  overriding registered disposition,
    see Overriding interest
  proof of title   24.4
  registration of, disclosure for   4.19, 4.20,
    11.18–11.22
    form for   4.19, 11.19
    no disclosure required   11.20
Unregistered land
  charge secured on, discharge of   12.97
  disappearance of/of concepts
    related to   1.22
  first registration of   1.9, 2.1 *et seq*,
    see also First registration
  proof of title   24.6, 29.2
Upgrading title, *see* Title

Valuable consideration, *see* Registrable
  disposition
Value declared
  proprietorship register, in   14.11(a)
Variation
  charge, of, *see* Charge
  lease/other registered
    disposition   8.40, 8.41
    non-registration sanction   8.41
    notice registration   10.17(d)
    registrable disposition, of   8.40
Void conveyance   15.3–15.8
  first registration, relating to   15.4–15.6
    equitable interests   15.5, 15.6
  indemnity   23.3
  registered disposition, relating
    to   15.7, 15.8
    equitable interests   15.8
Voluntary first registration, *see* First
  registration

Welsh language forms   20.4, 20.8
Winding up
  England and Wales, company
    registered in, *see* Insolvency
  foreign company, *see* Overseas
    company
Writ or order affecting land
    10.102–10.105